The UDF

The UDF

A History of the
United Democratic Front
in South Africa, 1983–1991

JEREMY SEEKINGS

DAVID PHILIP   *Cape Town*

JAMES CURREY   *Oxford*

OHIO UNIVERSITY PRESS   *Athens*

First published in 2000:

in Africa by David Philip Publishers (Pty) Ltd, 208 Werdmuller Centre, Claremont, 7708 South Africa

in the United Kingdom by James Currey Publishers, 73 Botley Road, Oxford, OX2 0BS,

and in North America by Ohio University Press, Scott Quadrangle, Athens, Ohio 45701, United States.

ISBN 0-86486-403-5 (David Philip)
ISBN 0-85255-842-2 (James Currey)
ISBN 0-8214-1336-8 (Ohio University Press)

British Library Cataloguing in Publication Data:

Seekings, Jeremy
    The UDF : a history of the United Democratic Front in South Africa, 1983–1991
    1. United Democratic Front – History 2. Apartheid – South Africa 3. South Africa – Politics and government – 1989–1994
    I. Title
    322.420968

US CIP data available upon request.

Printed in South Africa by Rustica Press, Old Mill Road, Ndabeni, Cape Town.

Contents

....

Foreword

by Popo Molefe

The democratic breakthrough in South Africa and the accession to power in 1994 of the democratic forces led by the ANC have been hailed as the world's greatest miracle in the history of transitions to democracy. The relatively peaceful attainment of freedom in our country has been the result of enormous sacrifices, pain and suffering. Many individuals and organisations contributed to achieving democracy. Much has been written about this. But the story of South Africa's transition would be incomplete without an account of the United Democratic Front, or UDF. It would also be a great injustice to the many courageous men and women who tirelessly built the UDF.

The UDF played a critical role in the transition by advancing the mass pillar of our 'national democratic revolution'. It intensified the mobilisation of the masses of South Africans by providing them with a common focal point of struggle and uniting them through their grassroots organisations. It provided a basis for united action by hundreds of organisations and thousands of activists who yearned for freedom. It shifted decisively the balance of power against the P.W. Botha regime. The regime lost the initiative to the liberation movement: its reform strategy lay in ruins, it had run out of ideas and its brutal repression provoked defiance not compliance.

I was privileged to have been part of this movement, and to have had the opportunity to rub shoulders with heroic leaders from earlier periods of the struggle for democracy. Leaders such as Comrade Albertina Sisulu, Oscar Mpetha, Archie Gumede, Billy Nair, Curnick Ndlovu, Henry Fazzie, Edgar Ngoyi, Steve Tshwete and Peter Nchabaleng were stalwarts of the ANC. Their presence in the UDF ensured that it carried forward the tradition of the Congress Alliance.

This history of the UDF by Jeremy Seekings is a remarkable account of a coalition of grassroots organisations that made such an important contribution to the struggle for democracy. It is a comprehensible, comprehensive, fascinating and seminal work. It analyses and records the activities of the UDF in a manner that is rare and amazing. It is a fitting tribute to those comrades who gave their lives, including Matthew Goniwe, Victoria Mxenge and Peter Nchabaleng.

Politicians, students and indeed all South Africans must not miss reading Jeremy

Seekings's history of the UDF. It is essential that future generations should know of the role that the UDF played in that exciting and dramatic period in the struggle for freedom. This book provides an important link between what has become known as 'the roaring eighties' and the current process of transformation of our country.

In addition, this book is timely even though it comes almost ten years after the dissolution of the UDF. There are several remarkable lessons we can learn and have learned. First, there was the resilience and dedication to the struggle in the face of extreme repression and brutality by the regime. Layer after layer of activists rose to the challenge to carry on resistance, even at times when almost every leader was either on trial or in detention. The success of the UDF was due in part to the nurturing of successive tiers of leadership. Among the leaders who came to the fore through the UDF were some remarkable women, including Joyce Mabudhafasi, Cheryl Carolus and Noma-India Mfeketo.

Secondly, the amazing way in which the UDF united under its aegis hundreds of organisations that had never worked together before suggests unique skills and organisational ability by the many activists of the UDF. Perhaps this is something that South Africa needs in her pursuit of nation-building and the consolidation of her multi-cultural and multi-lingual society.

Thirdly, the remarkable manner in which the UDF managed the internal strains and stresses which often threatened to blow it apart is rare in front organisations. That we managed to remain united after the bruising debate of December 1983 on the referendum suggests a high and almost incredible degree of mutual tolerance amongst UDF leaders and activists. This is an important legacy that remains with South Africans.

The structures for decision-making within the UDF may have often seemed tedious, but they taught us the importance of consensus politics and participatory democracy. These were to be critical in the creation of the new government of a free South Africa. Without such practices, state repression would have produced intolerance at the local level. In addition the regular debate within the UDF on democracy and accountability, the insistence that unaccountable leaders be recalled and the importance attached to criticism and self-criticism served to weaken any potential autocratic tendencies in the 'new' South Africa.

Jeremy Seekings's book assists South Africans to nurture and take forward the values of democracy, open debate, criticism and self-criticism, patience and mutual tolerance. Above all, it serves as an inspiration to those who carry the mandate to build a democratic South Africa. I am delighted that the story of the UDF is finally being told.

Popo Molefe, Premier of the North-West Province,
former General Secretary of the UDF

Preface

This book was conceived in discussions between the final leadership of the UDF and Glenn Moss, then of Ravan Press, in 1991. The project took much longer to complete than they expected and I am indebted to them for their patience. This book could not have been written without the considerable assistance of many former UDF officials, but Popo Molefe and Azhar Cachalia should be singled out for their help. At Ravan, Glenn, his colleagues and successors were ever understanding. At a later stage David Philip Publishers in Cape Town assumed the role of publishers of this book and I am grateful for their keen involvement in the project. At the outset of the project some funding was provided by the International Centre of the Swedish Labour Movement, for which I am grateful. Further financial support was provided by the Research Committee of the University of Cape Town.

Institutional support was provided by the Departments of Political Studies and Sociology at the University of Cape Town, and by the South African Research Program at Yale University. Howard Barrell facilitated my initial involvement in the project. Jenny Marot doggedly transcribed tape-recorded interviews. Archivists and librarians at the Historical Papers collection at the University of the Witwatersrand (especially Michelle Pickover), the South African Historical Archives Trust, the Mayibuye Centre at the University of the Western Cape, the African Studies Library at the University of Cape Town, and the Stirling Memorial Library at Yale, all helped enormously, as have many of the lawyers who defended anti-apartheid activists in political trials in the 1980s. Rory Riordan and Howard Barrell generously allowed me to look at interviews they had conducted.

Parts of this book were presented at seminars and conferences in Pietermaritzburg, Cape Town, Oxford, New Haven (Yale), Durham (Duke), London and Montreal; I am grateful to Graeme Bloch, Ciraj Rasool, Dan O'Meara, Courtney Jung, Ian Shapiro, Dan Johns, Shula Marks and Yunus Carrim for organising the seminars or providing valued criticisms. I have benefited from enjoyable discussions with Howard Barrell, Matthew Chaskalson, Janet Cherry, Mike Tetelman, Ineke van Kessel, Nicoli Nattrass and Martin Wittenberg. Janet Cherry and Nicoli Nattrass commented on the entire manuscript.

My greatest debt is to the many former UDF activists who agreed to be interviewed (often more than once), provided documents and helped me to contact other activists. I am sure that many will find fault with my interpretations of events, and may even consider my account too negative in that it pays close attention to differences and divisions within the Front. I do not intend my account to be read as a denigration of the achievements of the people involved. My purpose in examining differences within the Front has been to shed light on the strategic and tactical choices made by its leaders, primarily through identifying the pressures and constraints within which these choices were made. No one is above criticism – and the UDF's leaders themselves were among their own strongest critics – but I hope that readers of this book will be persuaded that the UDF leaders should be credited with a remarkable achievement. With little or no prior experience, they played a central role in building a countrywide and broadly encompassing movement which exerted severe pressure on the state, foreclosed alternatives to democratisation, and brought the African National Congress back from the semi-periphery to the centre of South African politics. I feel privileged to have been one of the historians of the UDF.

Abbreviations

AAC	Anti-Apartheid Conference
AIC	International Centre of the Swedish Labour Movement
ANC	African National Congress
AYCO	Alexandra Youth Congress
AZAPO	Azanian People's Organisation
AZASO	Azanian Student's Organisation
BC	Black Consciousness
BLA	Black Local Authority
CAHAC	Cape Areas Housing Action Committee
CAL	Cape Action League
CAST	Civic Association of the Southern Transvaal
CAYCO	Cape Youth Congress
CDF	Conference for a Democratic Future
CEI	Community Education and Information (project)
CONTRALESA	Congress of Traditional Leaders of South Africa
COSAS	Congress of South African Students
COSATU	Congress of South African Trade Unions
CUSA	Council of Unions of South Africa
CWIU	Chemical Workers Industrial Union
DHAC	Durban Housing Action Committee
ECCO	Eastern Cape Civic Organisation
ECDAFF	Eastern Cape Development and Funding Forum
EPG	Eminent Persons Group
FEDSAW	Federation of South African Trade Unions
GAWU	General and Allied Workers Union
IYY	International Youth Year
JODAC	Johannesburg Democratic Action Committee
JORAC	Joint Rent Action Committee
JWC	Joint Working Committee

MACUSA	Motor Assembly and Components Workers Union of South Africa
MALAYO	Masibosane Lamontville Youth Organisation
MAWU	Metal and Allied Workers Union
MDM	Mass Democratic Movement
MK	Umkhonto weSizwe
MSC	Million Signature Campaign
MWSA	Media Workers Association of South Africa
NACTU	National Council of Trade Unions
NAFCOC	National African Federated Chamber of Commerce
NDF	National Democratic Front
NEC	National Executive Committee
NECC	National Education Crisis Committee
NGC	National General Council
NIC	Natal Indian Congress
NOTPECO	Northern Transvaal People's Congress
NOW	Natal Organisation of Women
NUM	National Union of Mineworkers
NUMSA	National Union of Metalworkers of South Africa
NUSAS	National Union of South African Students
NWC	National Working Committee
PAC	Pan Africanist Congress
PC	President's Council
PE	Port Elizabeth
PEBCO	Port Elizabeth Black Civic Organisation
PEYCO	Port Elizabeth Youth Congress
PFP	Progressive Federal Party
PWV	Pretoria–Witwatersrand–Vereeniging region (now Gauteng)
REC	Regional Executive Committee
RGC	Regional General Council
RMC	Release Mandela Committee
SAAWU	South African Allied Workers Union
SACBC	Southern African Catholic Bishops Conference
SACC	South African Council of Churches
SACP	South African Communist Party
SAIC	South African Indian Council
SANCO	South African National Civic Organisation
SASO	South African Student Organisation
SAYCO	South African Youth Congress
SCA	Soweto Civic Association
SOYCO	Soweto Youth Congress
SPCC	Soweto Parents Crisis Committee
SPD	Soweto People's Delegation
SRC	students representative council
TASC	Transvaal Anti-SAIC Committee

TIC	Transvaal Indian Committee
UBCO	Uitenhage Black Civic Organisation
UDF	United Democratic Front
UNISA	University of South Africa
UWC	University of the Western Cape
UWO	United Women's Organisation
UYCO	Uitenhage Youth Congress
WCCA	Western Cape Civic Association

Frances Baard at the national launch of the UDF in Cape Town, August 1983.

Paul Weinberg (South Photographs)

Women and child dancing at a UDF meeting. UDF rallies were often fun as well as having a serious purpose.

Jimi Matthews

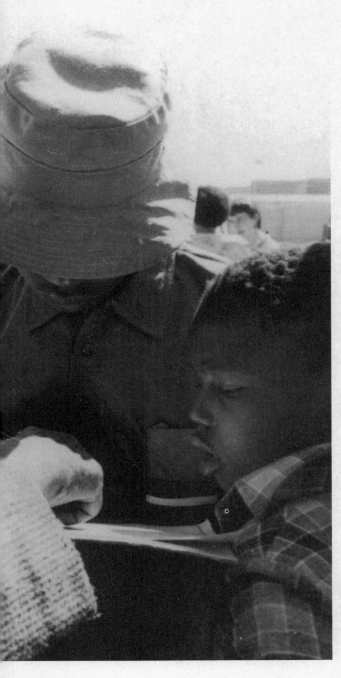

*Million Signatures
Campaign, 1984:
Helen Joseph collecting
signatures.*

Paul Weinberg
(South Photographs)

Protest against the proposed Tricameral Parliament in Durban. The UDF had strong support in Indian areas in 1983–4, although later there was a decline in active support.

Omar Badsha

Mourners at a funeral in the Northern Transvaal, 1986. Sekhukhuneland was one of the few rural areas where the UDF built strong support. At this funeral, mourners in UDF T-shirts stand in front of a Communist Party flag, whilst the coffin in front of them is draped with an ANC flag.

Paul Weinberg (South Photographs)

Young man with T-shirt proclaiming 'Freedom first education later'. In 1985–6 the UDF was opposed to slogans such as this, and sought to promote a more sustainable challenge to apartheid through the framework of 'people's power'.

Omar Badsha

Desmond Tutu and other religious leaders addressing a public meeting in 1989.

Eric Miller (iAfrika Photos)

Students at the University of the Witwatersrand protest against the banning of the UDF, February 1988.

Eric Miller (iAfrika Photos)

In many small towns such as Oudtshoorn, huge numbers of people joined in mass demonstrations against apartheid and in support of the UDF and ANC in late 1989.

Eric Miller (iAfrika Photos)

Trevor Manuel being arrested in Cape Town. Between 1986 and 1989 the UDF was hit hard by detentions.

Mike Hutchings

From right to left: 'Terror' Lekota (UDF publicity secretary), Valli Moosa (former acting general secretary) and, on the far left, Peter Mokaba (former UDF Northern Transvaal executive member, and president of the South African Youth Congress) toyi-toyi together.

Mike Hutchings

Hanover Park, Cape Town. In the face of repression, urban walls provided valuable space for political graffiti and other messages, such as these calls to boycott elections to racially segregated institutions.

Mike Hutchings

Protest took place against beach apartheid in Cape Town, 1989, as part of the UDF's defiance campaign.

Mike Hutchings

Popo Molefe, UDF general secretary, on his release from jail in 1989 after his conviction in the Delmas Treason Trial was overturned on appeal.

Mike Hutchings (iAfrika Photos)

Chapter One

The United Democratic Front, Freedom and Democracy in South Africa

On the afternoon of 20 August 1983 the United Democratic Front (UDF) was launched in a community hall in Cape Town. Ten thousand people attended – too many to fit into the hall, even though some resorted to sitting on the rafters (to the consternation of the organisers). Those who could not get into the hall were urged into a marquee, put up to circumvent state restrictions on open-air meetings. Here loudspeakers and a large video screen relayed the proceedings from inside the hall. But the mood of the crowd was not dampened by these conditions, for there was a widespread belief that this was a pivotal event in the history of the struggle for freedom and democracy in South Africa.

The first major speaker was the Rev. Frank Chikane, a 32-year-old church minister from Soweto who was active in the underground structures of the banned African National Congress (ANC) and who had played an important role in the preparations for the UDF. Speaking above the roar of the crowd, Chikane proclaimed: 'Comrades and friends, this day today is … going to go into the records of history as an important event bolstering the tide of the struggle, speeding up that day when the people shall live together as brothers and sisters, without … exploitation and oppression.' '*Amandla* [power],' shouted Chikane and other speakers; '*Awethu* [is ours],' responded the crowd.[1]

The significance of the event lay in the number and range of people and organisations brought together for the launch of the UDF. The keynote speaker was another churchman, the master orator Allan Boesak from the Western Cape. In a rousing speech, Boesak told the crowd:

We have arrived at a historic moment. We have brought together under the aegis of the United Democratic Front the broadest and most significant coalition of groups and organisations struggling against apartheid, racism and injustice since the early 1950s. We have been able to create a unity among freedom-loving people this country has not seen for many years … Indeed, I believe we are standing at the birth of what could become the greatest and most significant people's movement in more than a quarter of a century.[2]

Moreover, the UDF was bringing together people who demanded immediate changes. As Boesak put it: 'We want all of our rights, we want them here, and we want them now ... Now is the time!'

The public launch was preceded by a launch conference attended by 1500 delegates and observers from three recently formed regional UDF structures, several embryonic regional structures, and over five hundred anti-apartheid organisations across the country. Many other people from all over South Africa were there, as well as a large number from Cape Town itself. Both the conference and the public launch may have been the largest of their kind in the history of anti-apartheid politics in South Africa.

Over the following months resistance to apartheid was to escalate even faster than the ever-hopeful Boesak had envisaged, impelling a political transformation sooner than even Chikane might have dared to hope. Merely six years later the National Party government committed itself to the democratisation of South Africa, and just four years after that, in April 1994, South Africans voted in the country's first nationwide non-racial democratic elections. In just over a decade anti-apartheid politics shifted from protest to confrontation, to negotiation and finally to government.

When it was formed in 1983 the UDF had a specific and limited objective: to co-ordinate opposition to the National Party government's reforms, and in particular to the introduction of the 'Tricameral Parliament', which provided racially segregated representation in central government for coloured and Indian as well as white South Africans. The proposed parliament excluded the African majority altogether though African people were granted greater representation in segregated local government institutions. The UDF led opposition to the Tricameral Parliament, campaigned for a boycott of the first elections to the new coloured and Indian houses of parliament in August 1984, and denounced the new provisions for African representation in local government. But the UDF did not fade away once the new parliament and system of local government were up and running.

It was the government itself that was soon on the defensive as a popular revolt swelled up in African townships, swept through schools, and drew in the emerging independent labour movement. Just days after the parliamentary elections, civic and student protests in the Vaal Triangle and East Rand (to the south and east of Johannesburg) escalated into violent confrontation. The 'Vaal Uprising' dramatically marked the start of a two-year-long township revolt. In early 1985 direct action and confrontation spread across the Witwatersrand and into the northern Orange Free State and Eastern Cape. In the second half of 1985 it engulfed the Western Cape, Eastern Transvaal and, in a somewhat different form, Natal.

Most of the organisations at the forefront of the township revolt considered themselves affiliates of the UDF, devoured UDF-produced media, and sent delegates to the meetings of UDF structures. Protests took place under the banner of the UDF, whilst protesters identified themselves with the Front and even considered themselves members of it. The UDF provided a broad organisational framework and a symbolic coherence to resistance.

By mid-1986 it seemed that the authority of the state had been rendered precarious and that revolution was 'around the corner'. Anti-apartheid activists had rendered many townships 'ungovernable', and there were moves towards establishing localised 'people's power' in opposition to state power. Notwithstanding this, some of the necessary conditions for revolution did not exist.[3] This became apparent when, in June 1986, the state imposed a nationwide State of Emergency, detaining tens of thousands of opponents, suppressing most political opposition, and embarking on a counter-revolutionary programme of selective (and belated) investment in urban development.

Conditions may not have favoured a revolution, but they were pushing the state towards what has been called a democratic 'transplacement', where democratic change occurs as a result of a ruling group responding to persistent pressure from opposition groups.[4] Neither repression nor development succeeded in ending resistance or destroying the UDF. Indeed, mass detentions and the disruption of the opposition served to increase the importance of the UDF as a symbol and as a mechanism of nationwide co-ordination. Effectively banned in 1988, the UDF continued under the guise of the Mass Democratic Movement (in association with independent trade unions). At the end of 1989, amidst a general revival of overt defiance and protest, the UDF unilaterally declared itself 'unbanned' and resumed public activity. In February 1990, just six and a half years after the UDF was formed, and faced with resurgent popular defiance, the National Party government unbanned the ANC and other proscribed organisations, released Nelson Mandela, and shortly afterwards entered into formal talks over transforming South African into a non-racial democracy.

The UDF played a central role in this transformation of South African politics from its launch in 1983 until its disbanding on its eighth anniversary in August 1991. The UDF inspired and mobilised people across South Africa to resist the state's institutions and policies; it helped to build an unprecedented organisational structure from the local to the national levels; it co-ordinated diverse protests and campaigns; it promoted the profile and underground structures of the ANC; and it nurtured a political culture that emphasised democratic rights and claims indivisible by race. Speaking in 1991, the ANC's Walter Sisulu paid generous tribute to the UDF:

> The formation of the UDF decisively turned the tide against the advances being made by the [National Party] regime ... The formation of the UDF captured the imagination of the masses, and structures of the UDF literally mushroomed all over the country ... The UDF struck great success in rendering the structures of apartheid unworkable. Moreover, it succeeded in placing the central question of political power on the agenda ... Its achievements and its role must occupy a prominent place in the annals of our heroic history.[5]

Such praise was surely deserved. Varied critics have charged that the UDF was neither united, nor democratic, nor a front; the UDF is said to have set itself the wrong goals, had the wrong structures, or employed the wrong strategies and tactics. But few have disputed the importance of the UDF itself.

Of course, the UDF alone cannot be credited with South Africa's political transformation. It was central to escalating opposition to apartheid, but never embraced that opposition in its entirety. At the national level, important roles were also played by the UDF's close ally, the Congress of South African Trade Unions (COSATU), by the ANC itself, and to a lesser extent by rival anti-apartheid groupings. At the local level, many of the individuals and organisations at the forefront of the struggle had a tenuous relationship with the UDF. As we shall see, the UDF should not be regarded as synonymous with the entire extra-parliamentary movement against apartheid.

The UDF was also heir to a long history of resistance. As speaker after speaker made clear at its launch in 1983, it had deep roots in the struggles for freedom and democracy in South Africa. Speakers repeatedly invoked the ANC, its leadership and the Freedom Charter (drafted by the ANC and its allies at the Congress of the People in 1955), whilst the crowd sang a series of freedom songs praising Mandela, ANC president Oliver Tambo and other leaders, and the ANC's armed wing, Umkhonto weSizwe (MK).[6]

The prominence attached to the ANC at the UDF's launch reflected in part the strong links between the ANC in exile, its underground structures inside the country, and the nascent UDF. But it also reflected more broadly the centrality of the ANC to the struggles for freedom and democracy in twentieth-century South Africa. Although dwarfed in terms of support by a series of other movements in the first half of the century, and banned and brutally suppressed for much of the second half, the ANC succeeded in surviving each setback. Its longevity increasingly underpinned its political pre-eminence.

The ANC was formed in 1912 (although initially known as the South African Native National Congress), two years after British colonies and Boer republics were joined together into the Union of South Africa. The early ANC was dominated by a mission-educated, Anglophile, professional African elite whose goal was neither to resist colonisation nor to transform it, but rather to achieve full political and economic assimilation into colonial society. Instead of making progress towards a common non-racial society, however, the ANC spent its first three decades in unsuccessful opposition to the extension of racial segregation and discrimination. Moreover, with brief and localised exceptions, it failed to build broad support in either urban or rural areas. The mass movements of the early twentieth century were far removed from the elitist ANC: millenarian movements in rural areas, propagating a more Africanist message holding out the prospect of liberation from white settler rule.

It was not until the 1950s that the ANC itself was radicalised and transformed into a mass-based movement. This radicalisation was driven by new leaders who brought with them new political ideas. Some of these came through the Communist Party, adopting a Marxist vision of social change that went far beyond the political and economic inclusion of an African elite in a non-racial capitalist democracy. Others came through the ANC Youth League, formed in 1944 to advance Africanist anti-colonial ideas within the ANC. The ANC adopted these new ideas just as rapid industrialisation, proletarianisation and urbanisation created whole new industrial and urban constituencies and led to burgeoning industrial conflict and urban struggles.

In the aftermath of a nationwide Defiance Campaign in 1952, the ANC's membership reached 100 000. It was unable to continue this level of mobilisation through the 1950s, but did maintain its position as the mass-based movement in the forefront of the struggle against apartheid. In 1955, together with its allies among Indian, coloured and white South Africans, the ANC organised the Congress of the People where the Freedom Charter was ratified. Its pre-eminence was briefly challenged when its most fervently Africanist wing split away to form the Pan Africanist Congress (PAC), which took the lead in the protests in 1960 that culminated in the Sharpeville massacre. Amid the ensuing disorder the government banned the ANC and PAC, both of which chose then to turn to armed struggle.

By the mid-1960s overt political activity inside the country had been entirely and brutally suppressed. ANC (and PAC) leaders were either in jail or in exile and the armed struggle had petered to a halt. The liberation movements were reduced to obscure passivity. It was in this repressive context that new movements emerged in the 1970s, movements that eschewed formal political activity. The Black Consciousness Movement brought together the growing educated black elite – where 'black' explicitly comprised Indian, coloured and African – into a movement that challenged notions of white superiority and black inferiority. Meanwhile, the black working class provided the basis for the emergence and growth of an independent trade union movement.

There were few links between the Black Consciousness and independent trade union movements, nor was there much contact between either of them and the exiled liberation movements. But as people inside the country began to think once again about formal political activity, they were drawn toward the liberation movements, and especially the ANC. In the mid-1970s the ANC began to rebuild its underground structures inside the country, and forged links with some of the school students at the forefront of the 1976 student-led uprising in Soweto and elsewhere. By the early 1980s the ANC had re-emerged as a central, albeit banned, player on the South African political stage.

The seventy-odd years between the 1910s and the early 1980s may have formed a period of heroic and persistent struggles, but they were marked by few successes and many defeats. A series of constitutional and legislative reforms whittled away almost all the meagre rights in a common society enjoyed by black South Africans. At the turn of the century African (and coloured) elites in the Cape were covered by the Cape's non-racial franchise, albeit one qualified in terms of income and property. Not only was this non-racial franchise not extended to the other provinces in 1910, but was later severely diluted by discriminatory franchise 'reforms' in the early 1930s, and then emasculated by the removal of African voters in 1936, before being finally destroyed with the removal of coloured voters in 1956. Segregation proceeded in many other areas in the first half of the century, before being systematically implemented as apartheid by National Party governments after 1948. Each of these extensions to racial discrimination and segregation involved a defeat for the ANC and other opponents.

Notwithstanding these defeats, the South African polity retained a curious duality that posed chronic strategic dilemmas for the varied movements struggling for freedom and democracy. On the one hand, the polity was broadly democratic with respect to certain categories of 'insider' South Africans: the government was accountable to representatives elected in regular and competitive elections, and was subject to a nominally independent judiciary, whilst the principles of the rule of law and of equality before the law were upheld – again nominally – throughout the sordid history of segregation and apartheid. Many disfranchised South Africans aspired to inclusion in this political system. For them, the struggle was to defend the vestiges of their democratic and civil rights, and to demand their extension.

But the polity did not simply exclude the majority of South Africans; it also ensured their subjugation in brutal ways. Many colonised African people thus aspired to liberation from white rule. The struggle was for self-determination, or for national liberation. At the extreme end of the spectrum, they aspired to the physical expulsion of the white 'settlers'. The struggle was one for liberation and independence *from* authoritarian white rule rather than inclusion *in* liberal democratic framework.

Most major organisations and movements combined elements of both democratic and liberation struggles. Their ideologues engaged in long-winded debates over how to characterise this combination, tying themselves into intellectual knots in bizarre arguments over 'internal colonialism', 'colonialism of a special type', 'racial capitalism', and so on. Scholars, too, have struggled to characterise the approaches of movements struggling for political change. Many of them have referred uneasily to 'African nationalism', in apparent symmetry with its supposed rival, 'Afrikaner nationalism', and in parallel to anti-colonial movements in the rest of Africa. But the nationalist label ill fits the whole of the phenomenon in question. One response has been to distinguish between two versions of 'African nationalism': an exclusive 'Africanism' and an inclusive 'South Africanism', the former making its priority the liberation of the African 'nation', the latter aspiring rather to the achievement of democratic rights for all members of a supra-racial South African 'nation'. The ANC generally advocated the second approach; it was, in the words of Gail Gerhart, 'less an African nationalist movement in the strict sense of the term than a movement to win democratic rights for Africans'.[7]

Different conceptions of the nature of the struggle informed organisations' choice of strategies and tactics. Indeed, the key debates within anti-apartheid politics concerned strategy as much as ideology.[8] The debate focused on a choice between broadening the struggle through drawing more groups into an anti-apartheid alliance, or intensifying it through the escalation of direct confrontation with the South African state. The former strategy generally involved building alliances among social groups and classes that were directly involved in the political and economic system so as to isolate proponents of segregation or apartheid. The importance of such groups and classes lay in their integration into the social, economic or political system. But their very integration meant that they had something to lose, and therefore generally preferred gradualist change and were wary of direct confrontation. The latter strategy, in contrast, generally involved mobilising social groups and classes not directly involved in the political and economic system that were prepared to challenge that system directly and fully. In their different ways, both strategies acknowledged the strengths and the weaknesses of the apartheid state.

The 'gradualists' employed strategies, tactics and discourses corresponding more closely to a civil rights struggle than to a national or anti-colonial liberation struggle. The roots of this position lay in the assimilationist elites that dominated the early ANC (and corresponding movements among coloured and Indian South Africans). These groups publicised their grievances through the burgeoning press, used the courts, petitioned the authorities in Cape Town and London, and canvassed for sympathetic candidates in parliamentary elections. In short, they sought to turn 'white' opinion against segregation.[9] But without significant support bases in the country as a whole, the assimilationist elite was easily run over by the steamroller of segregation and apartheid.

A continuing, albeit diluted, concern with civil or democratic rights continued into the 1950s, even after more radical ANC Youth Leaguers gained control of the ANC, and in the face of apartheid. The Freedom Charter, for example, incorporated a discourse of rights alongside a discourse of liberation. The persistence of this rights discourse within the Charterist movement – the ANC-led movement that endorsed the Freedom Charter – reflected its lingering influence in the African areas of the Cape, reinforced by the intensified struggles of Indian and coloured South Africans and legitimised by the Communist Party's 'two-stage' theory of revolution, which held that a first stage of bourgeois or liberal democracy was a necessary prerequisite for any second stage of socialism.

The interaction between political movements based among South Africa's different racial groups is often overlooked in scholarly studies that focus on one or other of these movements. Politics in Indian and coloured areas continued to focus on rights long after the assimilationist project had collapsed in African areas. The key issues in coloured and Indian politics in the 1950s concerned the defence of their rights to live and trade in non-racial areas, and above all of the right of coloured South Africans in the Cape to vote on a non-racial franchise. Furthermore, racially defined nationalism made little sense to minority groups even when their former rights were being removed. Former ANC Youth Leaguers faced a situation where alliances with coloured and Indian South Africans required strategies and discourses that retained much less appeal among African South Africans at that time.

The ideas and strategies that found support among the overwhelming majority of African South Africans in the first half of the century were relatively confrontational and separatist, and less gradualist. This 'Africanist' approach had its roots in rural

areas where people were inclined to resist the disruptions brought by the mod-
ernising state rather than to embrace modernity (as did the mission-educated elite in
the early ANC). Even up to the 1950s and 1960s, rural politics revolved around
defensive popular resistance against state policies such as land registration, livestock
dipping, and reforms of chiefly authority. Many rural areas became strongholds of
independent Christian churches (independent, that is, of the white-dominated mission churches), and of millenarian movements promising not a common society but
the very opposite, the expulsion of white people from southern Africa. Protests took
the form of boycotts, of non-collaboration, and of intermittent revolt. In the early
part of the century Africanist movements dwarfed the ANC in terms of membership.[10]

The ANC's transformation into a mass movement in the 1950s was based on its
engagement with popular politics in rural and urban areas at a time when both rural
and urban politics were being radicalised through the massive movement of people
from rural to urban areas.[11] The strength of the Charterist movement as a whole,
however, was based on the ANC's engagement with popular African politics combined at the same time with its forging of alliances with movements among
coloured, Indian and even white South Africans. The Charterist movement thus
straddled both the more Africanist and the more gradualist approaches. This was
facilitated by the form of the Charterist movement, which brought together the
ANC, the South African Indian Congress, the South African Coloured People's
Organisation and the (white) Congress of Democrats as the Congress Alliance. The
ANC could thus serve as the vehicle for a more Africanist political project, whilst the
overall Congress Alliance could accommodate a more gradualist project.

The circumstances of the armed struggle and exile in the 1960s and 1970s encouraged a confrontationist rhetoric, focused on power rather than rights, and emphasising 'national liberation' rather than democratisation. The ANC incorporated
Africanist ideas into a Marxist discourse, asserting that the white pro-capitalist classes subjected the black working-class population to national oppression and class
exploitation. The victory of the latter over the former was rendered inevitable by the
laws of history. But for all this revolutionary bombast, key ANC leaders saw the
armed struggle more in terms of 'armed propaganda' – shifting the consciousness of
black and white South Africans – than an actual campaign for the armed seizure of
state power. Meanwhile, inside the country, social and economic change was forging
new constituencies for both gradualist and confrontationist strategies.

NEW PLAYERS ON THE POLITICAL STAGE

The UDF carried forward struggles that had ebbed and flowed for decades. But the
struggles of the 1980s, unlike those of the 1910s or the 1930s or the 1950s, were to
culminate in South Africa's negotiated transition to representative democracy. Why
were the struggles of the 1980s so much more successful than those of earlier
decades? And why did the UDF play a leading role in them after its initial concerns
had passed by?

The UDF's publicly stated objectives were initially limited to the co-ordination of opposition to the National Party government's 'constitutional reforms', and particularly the proposed Tricameral Parliament. The UDF certainly succeeded in mobilising widespread and concerted opposition to these reforms. But protests and defiance did not prevent the Tricameral Parliament or new local government institutions from being established. The government presumably hoped that the young UDF would follow the path trodden by anti-segregation protesters earlier in the century, when protest organisations had collapsed or declined into ineffective passivity in the aftermath of defeat.

Instead, the UDF grew in strength, following the enactment of the institutional reforms which it had been founded to resist. Although it struggled to redefine its role, and cracks appeared in its fragile unity, it came to achieve a prominence and influence greater even than the ANC and Congress Alliance had in the 1950s. To some extent this was the result of the lessons which its leaders learnt from the experience of opposition in preceding decades. In particular, leaders recognised the importance of mass action (as Anthony Marx has shown)[12] and of appropriate organisation (as we shall see). To some extent it was the result of the nature of the reforms themselves. The Tricameral Parliament was unlike previous major constitutional reforms in that it extended rather than whittled away the parliamentary representation of non-white South Africans. If the reforms had the intention and potential of 'co-opting' coloured and Indian voters into the defence of apartheid, they also thereby opened spaces for resistance which had not previously existed. Continued resistance could delegitimise the new institutions and at the same time maintain pressure on the government to offer greater concessions.

More fundamentally important than any of these factors was the transformed character of South African society. The South Africa of the 1980s was very different from the South Africa of the 1940s or 1950s. Social and economic change resulted in the growth of powerful new political constituencies, providing the UDF with a stage on which to construct and take part in an altogether new political drama. In short, sustained growth in manufacturing and service sector employment, urbanisation and greatly expanded schooling had produced educated, settled and increasingly skilled urban black working classes, and an embryonic black middle class.

The urban African population grew steadily through the post-war decades. From about 2.2 million in 1951, it increased to 3.4 million in 1960, 4.4 million in 1970 and 5.6 million by 1980.[13] This fast-growing urban population was far more important politically than the much larger rural African population, because the latter remained unable to mount any sustained challenge to the apartheid state. Scattered rural revolts in the 1940s and 1950s were easily isolated and crushed.[14] The countryside did not provide favourable terrain for a guerrilla struggle – as the exiled liberation movements discovered – and anyway, struggles in the countryside hardly affected the urban and industrial core of the South African economy and society.

Growth was accompanied by social change as the character of the urban African population was fundamentally transformed. As the historian Philip Bonner and others have shown, the urban African population in the 1940s and early 1950s was a population undergoing urbanisation, rather than a fully urbanised one; most urban men and women were born and raised in rural areas, only later migrating to the towns. Such first-generation immigrants did not begin to think of themselves as settled urban residents rather than migrants for some time. This was especially the case on the Reef, which accounted for well over half the urban African population.[15]

This transformation was driven primarily by the growth of manufacturing and service sector employment. Newly urbanised workers invaded land and established squatter settlements, to which the government responded by setting up site and service schemes and building tens of thousands of matchbox houses in new townships like Soweto. Men brought their wives from rural areas to the towns, or formed relationships with women already in the towns; either way, the ties between these first-generation urban immigrants and their rural kin weakened. Bonner detects the emergence, in the new townships in the late 1950s, of 'a new sense of common identity ... which overrode many of the ethnic and social divisions which had characterised the previous two decades'. This 'gradual process of coalescence' was made manifest 'in the political ferment of 1959–61', before being 'masked by the blanket of repression that was thrown over South Africa in the following decade'.[16]

During the 1960s and 1970s these first-generation immigrants put down deeper and deeper roots in the urban areas. The core of this increasingly settled urban population held the coveted Section 10 (1) (a), (b) and (c) rights defined by the 1945 Blacks (Urban Areas) Consolidation Act (and subsequent amendments). African people qualified for these rights by being born in urban areas, by working there for a specified length of time, or by being the dependent spouse or child of a qualified urban worker. African people without these rights in their pass books were not permitted to remain in urban areas for longer than seventy-two hours. The whole system of influx control served to keep such unauthorised people out of the urban areas – but at the same time it allowed an ever-growing number of people to abide there legally. Curiously, there are no aggregate official data on the precise number of African people with Section 10 rights.[17] One estimate put the number of qualified adult urban workers at 1.5 million in 1970, with most of the 1.8 million urban youngsters under the age of 20 and an unknown number of spouses and unemployed also qualifying.[18]

The key new urban constituency was the fast-growing number of second generation urban residents, born or socialised in urban areas. There do not seem to be any data on the number of urban-born residents, but official census data provide a breakdown according to age, and hence date of birth. What these data suggest is that the growth of the urban population between 1960 and 1980 was almost entirely the result of natural increase – with the number of births far exceeding the declining number of people in the oldest age cohorts. The proportion of the African population born after 1950 and living in households (excluding hostels) in metropolitan areas grew from one-third in 1960, to half in 1970, and two-thirds in 1980. By 1980 there were over half a million people aged between 10 and 20 and a slightly lower number aged between 20 and 30 in metropolitan households.[19] It is likely that most of these people were born in urban areas, and grew up in the urban environment. They comprised

South Africa's first substantial fully urbanised generation of African people.

These second-generation urban residents had very different experiences of child-hood and adolescence from those of their parents. It is this social group that provided most of the national and provincial leadership of anti-apartheid political movements in the 1980s. Frank Chikane, for example, was born in 1951 and grew up in the newly built township of Tladi in western Soweto. He went to secondary school locally, and on to the famous Orlando High School in 1970–1 to compete his schooling, and then went on to the University of the North. Popo Molefe, later general secretary of the UDF, was born a year after Chikane, and grew up not far from where Chikane lived. His schooling career was slowed down by family poverty, but he finally achieved Standard 10 in 1976. Murphy Morobe, who was to become the UDF's publicity secretary, was born slightly later. He was also in Standard 10 in 1976, at the prestigious Morris Isaacson High School in Soweto.

Chikane, Molefe and Morobe were among the urban African adolescents to experience a massive expansion in primary and, later, secondary schooling. In urban areas this expansion occurred in two distinct periods. Firstly, from the mid-1950s, there was a huge increase in the provision of primary schooling for African children. Secondly, from 1972, there was a massive expansion of secondary schooling in urban areas. By 1980 senior secondary education was transformed from 'the prerogative of an elite' into 'a mass phenomenon'.[20] In greater Soweto, for example, there were just eight secondary schools up to 1972; by 1976 there were twenty secondary schools, with three times as many students as in 1972. By the end of 1984 there were fifty-five secondary schools.[21] A growing proportion of urban youth were in secondary school, and spent longer and longer there. Not only did they grow up in a very different environment from that of their parents, but they were educated to a formal level far beyond any previous generation.

The result of all this was the emergence of an urban school-based culture and consciousness. As the historian Clive Glaser shows, secondary schooling provided the space for the development of an entirely new set of radical, urban political identities very different from the rural-orientated and generally more ethnic identities of the previous generation.

> By the mid-1970s, high school students were uniquely placed to assume political leadership in Soweto. Secondary schools, which cut across narrow, street-level identities, had a unifying influence. They drew together literate youths, with similar experiences and grievances, on a large scale. High schools, with their core of intellectually inquisitive students and their ready-made network of extra-mural associations, were receptive to the Black Consciousness ideology ... School students, with energy and independence, and brimming with a self-belief inspired by Black Consciousness, occupied the political vacuum left by the outlawed Congress movements.[22]

The 1976–7 student-led revolts demonstrated the importance of this new educated urban generation.

There was also a marked expansion of tertiary education. In 1960 there were fewer than 800 African students at universities (excluding the University of South Africa, Unisa, which offered correspondence courses). By 1983 there were about 20 000 African students at universities, with a further 12 700 enrolled in Unisa. Most of this expansion occurred during the 1970s.[23] The political importance of African university students bore no relation to their meagre numbers: it was university campuses that provided the main recruiting ground for Black Consciousness, and it was university graduates who took radical ideas back into schools and townships, as teachers, as doctors, and through drama groups.[24]

The expansion of urban schooling was accompanied by the transformation of urban employment, and this had a profound impact on the character of urban society. The 1960s and 1970s were years of steady growth in employment: in the industrial heartland of the Pretoria–Witwatersrand–Vaal (PWV) region, the number of African employees in manufacturing grew from 160 000 to 375 000 between 1960 and 1980. Employment in services grew to 634 000. During the 1970s there were also changes in the occupational breakdown of employment as the occupational colour bar was relaxed. Unskilled African employment declined, whilst semi-skilled, skilled, clerical and administrative, and professional employment rose. In 1960 almost all African workers were unskilled, but by 1980 unskilled labour accounted for less than half of African employment in the Johannesburg area, and between half and two-thirds in other areas of the PWV. The decline in unskilled employment accelerated in the recessionary 1980s.[25]

Just as significantly, wages rose in real terms (that is to say, taking inflation into account). A steady rise in manufacturing wages in the 1960s was followed by a sharp increase in the early 1970s such that average manufacturing wages doubled in value in real terms over the two decades. The bulk of this increase reflected the rapid upward occupational mobility already discussed: as African workers moved into more skilled jobs, average wages rose. Most of the children who were born in the 1950s and went through secondary school in the late 1960s or 1970s thus entered the labour market at a time of marked upward occupational mobility and rising real wages.

This period saw the growth of a fully urbanised, settled African working class, most of whom enjoyed a rising standard of living and were confident that improved schooling would lead to further material improvement in future. But this upwardly mobile working class was confined to overcrowded and inadequate living conditions. Little housing had been built since the early 1960s, and municipal infrastructure and services were appalling. Few townships were electrified, and many continued to use a bucket system for sewerage. Such neglect was based on the government's strategy of concentrating development in the bantustans. In the mid-1970s state officials came to recognise the folly of this strategy, especially in the light of the 1976–7 uprisings in Soweto and elsewhere. The state began to allow the private sector to build new urban housing and local government to develop urban infrastructure in 'white' South Africa. But most such improvements had to be financed through revenue raised in the townships themselves. Urban development, itself slow and uneven, therefore meant increases in the rents and service charges which served as local government taxation, or in substantial mortgage bond payments to banks.[26]

Discontent with rising municipal rents and service charges was exacerbated when the economy slid into recession from mid-1981. In most urban areas unemployment rose and a rising proportion of the urban population was pushed into poverty (although, at the same time, a large proportion of urban African households continued to enjoy rising real incomes owing to continuing upward occupational mobility and hence rising wages). The recession hit some areas especially hard. Worst hit were areas that depended on heavy manufacturing; these included the Vaal Triangle, the East Rand and Port Elizabeth–Uitenhage, where a majority of households suffered declining real incomes. The recession left a growing number of young men and women (or 'youth') out of school and out of work – and available for forms of direct action at which other people might have balked.

Upwardly mobile educated youngsters lived with their unskilled or semi-skilled parents; rich and poor households lived alongside each other; the employed and well-paid were neighbours to the unemployed and poor. This provided fertile ground for the growth of civic organisations, which took action over material grievances such as rent increases and inadequate infrastructure or services, and over overtly political grievances concerning democracy and freedom. Secondary schools provided similarly fertile ground for school-based organisations such as the Charterist Congress of South African Students (COSAS), whilst secondary school graduates moved into leading roles in trade unions and in township-based 'youth congresses'. At the same time, the growing ranks of the unemployed and poor produced many further recruits for any revolutionary movement.

Just as urban politics in the 1940s and 1950s bore the imprint of the first-generation urban residents' rural roots and experiences of urbanisation, so urban politics in the 1970s and 1980s was fundamentally shaped by second-generation urban residents' experiences of growing up in as well as being confined to apartheid townships. The changing character of urban society provided the bases for both gradualist and confrontational politics – to return to the strategic typologies used earlier in this chapter. On the one hand, a growing number of urban African people became enmeshed in a web of social, economic and legal relationships which involved aspects of inclusion: they saw themselves as having rights to and claims on some kind of common society, and favoured tactics such as strikes and boycotts that drew on the strength they derived from their integration into the modern economy and state system. At the same time, a substantial section of the urban population was economically marginalised as well as politically subordinated, and continuted to be drawn to forms of action that undermined or challenged the political, social and economic system.

The urban African population was not alone in undergoing important changes in the 1960s and 1970s. The urban coloured and Indian populations also underwent considerable change, although these changes did not unambiguously favour opponents of the apartheid state. During the 1960s and 1970s the urban coloured and Indian working class became fully settled, or – more accurately – resettled, since huge numbers of people were forcibly removed under the 1950 Group Areas Act. Although employed in more skilled and better-paid jobs than their African counterparts, many coloured and Indian working-class families lived in run-down and crime-ridden areas. This provided conditions in which radical civic organisations emerged and briefly flourished in the late 1970s and early 1980s. But reformist National Party leaders recognised from the mid-1970s that the support of coloured and Indian South Africans was crucial to any successful counter-revolutionary project. The government therefore sought to encourage a nascent process of embourgeoisement of the coloured and Indian working class, investing heavily in housing, infrastructural development, health facilities and schooling, as well as promising a degree of inclusion within the framework of representative democracy. As a result, in the 1980s neither the coloured or Indian working class nor the middle class was a consistent supporter of the UDF and the anti-apartheid movement in general.[27]

One section of the coloured and Indian urban population was to provide important support for the UDF: secondary school and university students. The 1960s and 1970s saw an expansion of secondary and tertiary education for coloured and Indian people, although not on the same scale as among Africans. In 1960 there were less than 40 000 coloured and Indian students in the final five years of school. This number grew sixfold by 1983, when it stood at almost 235 000. The number of coloured and Indian students at residential universities rose from under 2000 in 1960 to over 14 000 in 1983. Radicalised school and university students provided a small but important core of support for political movements in coloured and Indian areas.[28]

The growth of the social and economic bases for mass-based resistance – especially among urban African people – was matched by the return to prominence of radical political ideas. The Black Consciousness Movement had resuscitated political debate, the independent trade unions promoted a resurgence of socialist thought, universities openly taught Marxism, the churches discovered a new interest in prophetic Christianity and liberation theology, and an 'alternative' media blossomed. The state's reforms pushed the issues of rights and representation to the centre of public debate. The success of 'liberation' struggles in Vietnam, Nicaragua and the frontline states encouraged thinking towards the seizure of power, while the resurgence of the ANC and its armed wing (MK) provided further impetus.

The possibilities for political organisation in the 1980s were underwritten by new technologies and resources. Telephones and private cars were no longer the preserve of an elite, as in the 1950s. Air transport further facilitated inter-regional contact and co-ordination. The photocopier and new printing technologies made the production of newsletters, posters and pamphlets easier. T-shirts provided a new medium for publicity. South Africa was newsworthy internationally, and changes in the broadcasting media allowed township riots, police brutality and press conferences to reach television screens across the world the same day. Later in the decade the personal computer and the fax machine would further transform communication within the UDF, the Front's own media production, and its contact with local and international media. The 1980s also saw political organisations enjoy access to unprecedented financial resources, mostly from abroad; this paid for full-time employees, extensive media production and transport.

WHAT WAS THE UDF?

This book provides a critical history of the UDF during the tumultuous years between 1983 and 1991. But what was 'it', this UDF? Was it an organisation or a movement? What kind of an organisation, or what kind of a movement, was it? What was it a front for or of?

The formal organisational contours of the UDF are easily delineated: at the national level it comprised a federation of regional UDF bodies, each of which was a front or umbrella structure for highly diverse affiliated organisations. The affiliates ranged from student groups to civic associations, overtly political organisations to sports clubs. They existed independently of, and remained formally autonomous from, the UDF. Indeed, the UDF's structures were formally accountable to the affiliates. The UDF was not a party, did not have branches, and never allowed for individual or personal membership. But it had its own discrete structures at national, regional and sub-regional levels. These structures organised events and campaigns, produced media, helped to build affiliates at both the local level and in the different 'sectors' (such as students, 'youth', women and civic associations), and channelled funds, as well as playing a general co-ordinating role for the UDF's affiliates.

How these different parts fitted together in practice was much less clear. At the core of this uncertainty lay the relationship between the Front and its affiliates. State officials accused the UDF of being a tight-knit organisation, directing the activities of its affiliates across the country in order to advance the revolutionary objectives of the ANC and South African Communist Party. On the other hand, many of the UDF's own affiliates sought to retain decision-making autonomy from the UDF, seeing it as a vehicle for co-ordination rather than complete integration. Indeed, a number of Charterist organisations sought to build alternative co-ordinating structures at different times in the 1980s. Whilst state officials were clearly wrong to see affiliates as mere branches, it was also true that the UDF's own structures intruded into the activities of its affiliates in many ways. Tom Lodge therefore advises that 'Any analysis of the UDF should not be limited to the bureaucratic boundaries of its often patchy organisation, for the UDF functions more in the fashion of a social movement than a deliberately contrived political machine.'[29]

The relationship between the Front and its affiliates was shaped by three aspects of its structure. Firstly, the Front was organised primarily as a federation of regionally based fronts. The character of the UDF in different regions therefore varied in part according to the composition of its affiliates in each region. In the Eastern Cape and Border, for example, the UDF operated as a more integrated organisation of affiliates, almost all of which were based in African areas, whereas in the Western Cape and Natal the UDF's affiliates were relatively heterogeneous, and this led to the Front operating in more of a co-ordinating role.

Secondly, its structures and objectives were only loosely specified. It never had a constitution, but instead adopted a vaguely worded Declaration and Working Principles. This meant that the Front could be almost whatever its leaders wanted it to be. This was in general a source of strength, enabling it to build and encompass unprecedented nationwide political networks and alliances. Having the form of a front facilitated effective activity over agreed, specific and discrete issues, whilst preserving the formal autonomy of affiliates. Organisations could affiliate even though they disagreed with other affiliates over broad ideals or even over the strategies they used in their individual activities. This loose form represented a choice on the part of the UDF's founders, an acknowledgement of the fragmentation, vulnerability and diversity of South Africa's extra-state opposition. But it also ensured tension, as issues of strategy, accountability, direction and character were addressed through ongoing debate and conflict, and could never be resolved conclusively.

A key goal of the UDF was to broaden itself through incorporating new affiliates, whether through building or consolidating organisations in new social constituencies or geographical areas, or forming alliances with existing organisations outside the Front and drawing them into it. The strategic logic of contesting what was termed the political 'middle ground', with organisation building and alliance building in more cautious and conservative constituencies, sometimes brought the UDF's structures into conflict with its more militant and confrontational affiliates, which favoured the intensification of resistance and denounced the wooing of the 'middle ground' as a reformist compromise.

Thirdly, the Front was seen by most of its leaders and affiliates as having specific, if unspecified, roles that differed from those of its individual affiliates. In other words, the UDF was to perform roles beyond those already played by affiliates in their particular sectors or areas. This meant that there were continued pressures on the UDF to develop its own structures, separate from its affiliates, to execute its roles. As these structures grew, so their supposed relationship of accountability to the affiliates was transformed.

These three features of the UDF ensured that the degree of autonomy of the UDF's national and regional structures from the affiliates, and indeed vice versa, was an unstable product of informal bargaining. 'What is the UDF?' was a question repeatedly debated within the Front itself – but it was a question that could never be resolved in the abstract, and could only be resolved in practice within a particular region or sub-region and for a finite period of time. In a sense, there was no single UDF, but rather many different UDFs, varying according to time, place and the vantage point of the observer. Overall, however, there were some broad shifts over time. It is to these that we must now turn if we are to understand more fully what the UDF was, and was not.

THE CHANGING FORM AND ACTIVITIES OF THE UDF

When the UDF was formed in August 1983 its founders had only a vague sense of what they were setting up. They were even unsure as to whether the posts of general secretary and publicity secretary should be paid full-time posts, or not. Because the immediate impetus to the formation of the UDF was the state's strategy of building support among Indian and coloured South Africans through the introduction of the Tricameral Parliament, the priority for the UDF was to build as broad an alliance as possible in Indian and coloured areas, to reject the state's reforms. A loosely constituted front with the specific goal of opposing government reforms could more easily accommodate groups that were wary of formal politics – as well as groups with contrasting views on political ideology and strategy.

The perceived need for flexibility led the founders of the UDF to put forward Working Principles rather than a rigid constitution at its launch in 1983. The Working Principles structured the Front as a federation of regional UDF structures (each of which adopted its own Working Principles, closely resembling the national ones). The national UDF was controlled by the regions. Its supreme decision-making body was the National General Council (NGC), which was supposed to meet at least annually and consisted of regional delegations. The UDF's National Executive Committee (NEC) comprised a handful of office-holders elected by the NGC and a battery of representatives sent directly by each region. Organisations affiliated at the regional level, sending representatives to meetings of the Regional General Council (RGC) and electing a Regional Executive Committee (REC).[30]

Regional variations within the extra-parliamentary political opposition meant that the UDF itself differed from region to region. The most important distinction occurred between those regions with prominent affiliates based in coloured and Indian areas, and those where UDF affiliates were based in African areas only. Regional UDF structures were formed first in the regions in the first category – Transvaal, Western Cape and Natal. RECs in these regions were large, with members representing all the major affiliates, and RGCs met regularly. In short, the UDF was constituted as a front and closely controlled by affiliates. RECs in the Eastern Cape and Border were much smaller, and RGC meetings less frequent; the UDF operated more as a regional party leadership for township-based activists, and was more closely linked into operational underground ANC structures.

The base of the UDF was its diverse affiliates whose autonomy was fundamental to the early UDF. Its leaders emphasised that the UDF was 'a front, an alliance of organisations that have come together on the basis of a minimum programme, namely the opposition to the "new deal"' – meaning the state's constitutional and policy reforms. The alliance was described as 'tactical', with organisations uniting 'under the banner of the UDF' on the basis of agreement over 'as little as five per cent' of their views or activities. The little they had in common was more important than their considerable differences. The UDF took this form so as 'to unite a broadest possible spectrum of people across class and colour lines ... to bring together a maximum number of organisations of the people.'[31]

Such catch-all formulations provided little guidance as to how the UDF should operate, what structures to set up, and what kinds of strategy it should adopt. By the end of 1983 acute disagreements had arisen over strategy, reflecting different visions of what the UDF was for, and hence what it was. The crucial strategic choice facing the UDF was the old choice between intensifying and broadening resistance. During

1983–4 the UDF's national leadership argued that the UDF should serve as the vehicle for forging the broadest possible unity against the proposed Tricameral Parliament. They saw mass action as the most effective way of radicalising popular consciousness, and hence building a mass movement, but believed that excessive militancy might alienate important allies and constituencies, especially – but not only – in coloured and Indian areas. Some UDF leaders and affiliates dissented from this view, believing that conditions were propitious for more militant actions and strategies in African townships and arguing that a gradualist approach played into the state's hands. Debates over strategy led to a near split in December 1983 and January 1984. The UDF's first major campaign, the Million Signatures Campaign of early 1984, was designed in part to rebuild unity within the Front.

The strategic debate was reopened in the second half of 1984, when the Tricameral Parliament was elected and the UDF's initial mission fell away. It was already clear that the relationship between UDF structures and affiliates differed in practice from the strict accountability envisaged at the outset. Specialist structures often proved more effective than affiliates, especially when events required a rapid reaction or decision. Thus, as one REC assessed, whilst 'the working principles describe the UDF as a *front* comprised of affiliated organisations ... we have often been forced to operate as an *organisation*'.[32] From their regional or national vantage point many UDF leaders began to see affiliates as being accountable to the UDF, rather than vice versa.

This situation was exacerbated by further factors. The UDF leadership was committed to building organisation, and in some areas did so through forming UDF structures rather than autonomous affiliated organisations. More broadly, even independent affiliates formed through the involvement of UDF leaders had a more dependent relationship on the Front than affiliates formed independently or prior to its establishment. Secondly, most funds from foreign donors (and clandestinely from the ANC) were channelled through the UDF rather than directly to affiliates. Thirdly, some affiliates were weakened as key leaders were drawn into the UDF.

The Front's shift towards ever greater autonomy from its affiliates was accelerated by the changing external context of escalating protest in African townships. The state accused the UDF of direct responsibility for these protests, but the UDF's own general secretary complained at the time that the Front was 'trailing behind the masses'. The UDF's contribution to the revolt was more indirect than direct: its formation and initial campaigns inspired and informed local political mobilisation, and its structures facilitated contact between activists from different areas, but it rarely provided direct co-ordination or instigation.

In the face of revolt and consequent state persecution, UDF leaders decided to transform the Front so as to provide more effective political leadership. In April 1985 the Front held its first National General Council meeting. The Working Principles were amended, with the UDF's stated goals reformulated to encompass opposition to apartheid in general. Larger goals required a broader role for the UDF's structures. The initially unwieldy NEC was massively slimmed down to turn it into a more effective decision-making structure – but one which was also more independent of regional structures and affiliates.

The UDF also shifted its strategic emphasis from broadening the anti-apartheid alliance to intensifying the revolt. This was based on a diagnosis that the state was in deep crisis. For the first time the UDF leadership explicitly disregarded organisational weaknesses as well as the conservatism of some supporters and the so-called political 'middle ground':

> It is often said that we have tried to march too far ahead of our organisations and that we have not done sufficient ground work. Yet we remember that our people will not wait until we believe we have adequately prepared the ground. The anger that is exploding all over the country bears testimony to our people's readiness for mass action, and we must be committed to taking this forward.[33]

The transformation of the UDF into a more vanguardist, party-like organisation, responsive to the most militant sections of the 'people', did not mean that its structures immediately assumed the role of co-ordinating struggles at the township level. Until 1986 most direct co-ordination was provided by individual affiliates or by forums separate from the UDF's own structures. There were a variety of reasons for this, but they had in common an underlying perception that the UDF was removed or separate from local politics in African townships. Most township organisations considered themselves affiliates of the UDF, paraded under its banner, and distributed its publications. Indeed, in many parts of the country, individual people referred to themselves as 'members' of the UDF. But the UDF was seen as a component within – rather than an overall organisational framework for – the Charterist movement; it was somehow 'out there'.

At the national level, and in some regions, the UDF operated in an increasingly party-like way yet with tenuous accountability to its locally based affiliates. Its roles were organisation building and the provision of ideological direction through its media. As general campaigns gave way to repeated episodes of localised confrontation, the UDF shifted further towards becoming what was referred to as a national 'political and ideological centre'. The UDF began to employ full-time organisers, convened (or assisted with) national conferences to improve liaison between otherwise localised struggles, and expanded its media to include a theoretical journal.

The UDF's role can be illustrated with respect to the question of 'people's power' in late 1985 and the first half of 1986. The concept and strategy of 'people's power' was formulated by national UDF ideologues in response to organisational developments on the ground, especially in the Eastern Cape and Border. The proliferation of street committees, and the assumption by civics of administrative and judicial roles in townships where local government structures had largely collapsed, provided the basis for this strategy of 'people's power'. It emphasised the exercise of democratic control by civic organisations over semi-liberated townships. The UDF's role in this was primarily in formulating and publicising a strategy which made sense of existing local developments in regions at the forefront of the revolt, and could subsequently be applied elsewhere.

The form of the UDF during 1985–6 gave rise to two contrasting criticisms. On the one hand, the UDF was criticised for behaving more like a party and less like a front. It was accused of intervening in the affairs of its affiliates, and making decisions on its own which should have been made by its affiliates. On the other hand, it was said that the UDF was not providing enough leadership, and that a more integrated or party-like organisational framework was needed! Within the Charterist movement there were attempts to set up alternative and more militant national co-ordinating forums.

Conditions were dramatically changed, however, with the declaration of a nation-wide State of Emergency in June 1986. Thousands of leaders in the extra-parliamentary opposition were detained, and most of the rest were forced into hiding or exile. Public meetings were virtually prohibited, and media coverage severely restricted. The UDF itself, together with major affiliates, was effectively banned in February 1988.

Remarkably, the UDF continued to operate throughout this period, albeit in ways transformed by repression. At the national level, the UDF held regular meetings and even conferences, but covertly. At the regional level, however, UDF structures were devastated. The national leadership was thus cut off from the UDF's affiliates. The existing gap between the UDF at the national level and its most militant locally based affiliates grew into a chasm.

The UDF became increasingly centralised at the national level and in those regions where its structures maintained a presence. Leadership sought to direct affiliates, but with almost no accountability to them. More and more funds flowed through the national leadership; much of this was used to employ UDF organisers at the sub-regional level. These circumstances fuelled accusations that the UDF was run by an undemocratic 'cabal' that monopolised resources and decision making, and stifled democratic debate. Its most virulent critics accused the 'cabal' of building the UDF into a substitute for, rather than a complement to, the banned ANC. Nationally, and in Natal and the Western Cape, criticism of the 'cabal' took on a racial dimension, with activists in African areas critical of the disproportionate influence wielded by Indian and coloured activists in UDF leadership.

Partly in response to the growing criticisms of the UDF, discussion began over the prospect of a broader 'united front' encompassing the UDF and other Charterist groupings outside the fold of the UDF, in unions, townships and elsewhere. In 1989 this idea of a 'united front' was given expression in the amorphous Mass Democratic Movement.

In addition, the UDF reassessed political conditions and recognised its own limitations, prompting it to retreat from the insurrectionary perspective or rhetoric of 1985–7. The UDF rediscovered the dictum that had guided it in its first years: 'We should remember that the pace of a column is not determined by the fittest and fastest soldier but by the slowest and weakest.'[34] The UDF revived its concern with the 'middle ground'. The task of broadening the alliance (beyond even the ranks of the Mass Democratic Movement) revolved increasingly around the idea of an anti-apartheid conference, eventually held as the Conference for a Democratic Future in December 1989.

By the beginning of 1990, when the UDF's NEC met publicly for the first time in four years, the UDF looked in some respects as it had in 1983–4. Its leadership was much the same, as were its strategies and discourses. But the UDF had changed. It was no longer a regionally based and affiliate-controlled front co-ordinating campaigns, but had become a nationally driven centre providing strategic and ideological direction. More importantly, most local-level organisations at the start of 1990 saw themselves as separate from, albeit supportive of, the UDF, in fundamentally different ways from the affiliates of 1983–4. And a growing number of Charterist activists were hostile to the UDF leadership and, indeed, to the UDF itself.

The revival of the UDF was interrupted, however, by the unexpected unbanning of the ANC in February 1990. Some of the UDF's leaders and affiliates called on the UDF to disband immediately. But most of the UDF's national leadership, supported by the ANC's senior leadership, argued that the UDF should continue to play a curtailed role. Whilst the ANC would assume 'national political leadership', especially in negotiations with the government, the UDF should continue to co-ordinate socio-economic struggles, help to build the ANC, and pull the political 'middle ground' into support for the ANC.

At the regional level, however, few UDF structures were revived. In March 1991, when the NGC of the UDF met for the first time since 1985, the Front was said to be 'at its weakest in the entire history of its existence'.[35] The weakness of its regional structures, combined with opposition from many affiliates, led to the decision to disband the Front. An altogether new national umbrella body would be formed to co-ordinate civic or developmental struggles. The tide of struggle had changed, and the UDF could claim credit for playing a central part in this. But the tide carried away the UDF itself.

THE SYMBOLIC ROLES OF THE UDF

Between 1983 and 1991 the UDF underwent considerable change in terms of what it did, how its structures operated, and indeed what structures it had. It grew from being just a front for the co-ordination of joint campaigns by its affiliates, into a more party-like set of structures with many employees and activities independent of its supposed affiliates. Throughout its life, however, a distinction can be drawn between the UDF and its affiliates. The UDF was an organisation which played important roles in the struggles waged by its affiliates. But it was not itself a movement, and should not be considered as encompassing its affiliates as if they were mere branches.

Most township-based organisations in particular maintained their independence of the UDF, which they saw as a component within the overall struggle against the apartheid state rather than the all-encompassing umbrella body. Affiliates may have identified with the UDF, used its resources, and sent representatives to its meetings to exchange information and to co-ordinate with each other. But they retained their own individual and diverse primary concerns, and remained somehow apart from the Front. Indeed, the UDF's slogan proclaimed 'UDF Unites, Apartheid Divides', but this unity was fragile and limited at best, and lapsed into fragmentation and dissent at times.

This book therefore focuses on the UDF as a set of national, regional and sub-regional structures, and does not examine the histories of the UDF's affiliates. This is a history of a political organisation rather than a social movement; it is organisational rather than social history. But, as Lodge advised, an analysis of the UDF bounded by the UDF's organisational limits would be incomplete. A history of the UDF must identify those limits, but also go beyond them to grapple with the Front's symbolic dimension: its ability to inspire, to mobilise and to educate politically large numbers of people into a broadly coherent struggle against apartheid. If the ANC's armed struggle should be viewed as 'armed propaganda', then one part of the UDF's own work may be described as 'unarmed propaganda'.

In South Africa the UDF played a significant role in forging a sense of unity and coherence in the struggle, despite the organisational limits of its co-ordination and the otherwise often fragmented character of localised township and rural protest.[36] The UDF's existence alone was inspirational. The UDF showed that there was space for resistance; it instilled hope; and it injected defiance. According to the UDF's own assessment: 'When the UDF came into being in 1983, it took the message of hope and freedom to every corner of our country, to remote and isolated villages, and through door to door work, to every house in our townships.'[37] As the ANC's Walter Sisulu said, the UDF 'succeeded in placing the central question of political power on the agenda'.[38]

At an ideological and strategic level, UDF-produced media and the discussions at UDF meetings shaped the development of popular protest far beyond any direct co-ordination that the UDF did provide or could have provided. More broadly still, the UDF helped to transform people's understanding of the issues and their roles in them. They shaped and reshaped the collective identities of followers and participants, helping to construct what has been called 'a sense of "we."'[39] In these different ways the UDF helped to forge disparate struggles into a nationwide and explicitly political movement. Many township organisations identified themselves with the UDF even though they did not see it as 'their' front. Indeed, affiliation itself came to be understood less in formal terms, that is, according to prescribed procedures, and more in terms of the 'relations of co-operation, ideological identification and mutual support that exist between hundreds of organisations and the Front'.[40] Hence neither the organisation (the UDF) nor the broader political movement can be understood except in relation to the other.[41]

There were two periods when the UDF's symbolic role was particularly important. During 1983–4, the imagery of defiance, the emphasis on unity and non-racialism, and the prominence of discourses of rights provided important foundations not only for opposition to the state's constitutional reforms but for subsequent township-based protests as well. In early 1986 the UDF's articulation of 'people's power' facilitated a reintegration of different strands in resistance. At other times, however, the UDF's symbolic role was much less important. Just as it is important to distinguish between the UDF and the broader movement of resistance (in which UDF affiliates played leading roles), it is also important to note that the UDF was by no means the only or even the most important source of 'meaning' in the 1980s.

As social movement theorists and historians alike have pointed out, episodes of collective action and especially confrontation rapidly recast political cultures and collective identities. One scholar writes of the French Revolution:

> In the heat of debate and political conflict, the very notion of 'the political' expanded and changed shape. The structure of the polity changed under the impact of increasing political participation and popular mobilisation; political language, political ritual and political organisation all took on new forms and meanings ... By the end of the decade of revolution, French people (and Westerners more generally) had learned a new political repertoire.[42]

In South Africa, the township revolt was accompanied by the growth of vibrant new revolutionary political cultures in these townships. The 1980s were the decade of the toyi-toyi and the necklace, the comrade and the collaborator, of ungovernability and people's power.

The imagery and discourses of the UDF were conspicuously muted in the symbolism or rhetoric of most protesters at the local level. Popular protest drew on the political traditions of the past – but not, for the most part, on the same traditions as the UDF nor from the UDF itself. The symbolism of resistance was that of the exiled ANC; the UDF was sometimes incorporated as a symbol in this, but as a subordinate symbol. Thus songs exhorted the ANC, not the UDF; chants praised the armed struggle, not non-violent strategies; and the flags draped over the coffins at political rallies were in the colours of the ANC, not the UDF. Indeed, on the street few people identified themselves as, first and foremost, UDF supporters or members. This was in part the choice of the UDF itself. The UDF never saw its role as challenging the ANC. At a symbolic level, the UDF sought to provide the space for the proliferation of ANC imagery and discourses, for the strengthening of loyalties to the ANC rather than the UDF. In this sense, the UDF was indeed a 'front' for the ANC.

There were two important exceptions to this marginalisation of the UDF's own symbols. Firstly, the imagery and discourses of the UDF had a particular resonance in some coloured and Indian areas, where discourses of rights were more appealing than the liberatory discourses associated with the exiled ANC. Secondly, the 'UDF' was prominent in political rhetoric and the identities of participants in situations of intra-African conflict. This was clearly the case in Natal, where it was common to refer to 'UDF forces', 'UDF supporters' and 'UDF areas' in contrast to those identified with the more conservative Inkatha movement. People killed and were killed according to whether they wore UDF T-shirts or not.[43] Similarly, identification with the UDF was central to violent clashes between supporters of the UDF and those of the non-Charterist Azanian People's Organisation (AZAPO) in Port Elizabeth, Uitenhage and elsewhere in 1985–6. But these remained exceptions to a general picture in which the symbolism of the ANC was paramount.

The study of the UDF's symbolic impact within the broader movement of resistance has been made difficult by the limited extent of the literature on political cultures and identities at the local level. The sub-disciplines of urban anthropology and urban sociology are among the academic victims of apartheid. In this book I rely largely on analysis of UDF statements, pamphlets and newsletters, its leaders' speeches, and independent press coverage, rather than of the perceptions of people outside the UDF. Through examining its practices and especially the political discourses its leaders employed, we can begin to discern the outline of the kinds of collective identity which the UDF helped to forge. But there remains a clear need for further research into the political perceptions of people on the ground.

COMMOM PURPOSE VERSUS DIFFERENCE IN ANTI-APARTHEID POLITICS

One of the key themes running through this book is the attempt to overcome chronic differences and divisions among the opponents of apartheid so as to build up a broad, united and effective movement. At the risk of some repetition, it may help to spell out the major actors involved in this drama.

On the one side was the National Party government, under P.W. Botha (as Prime Minister until 1984, and then as State President under the new constitution). The National Party sought to reform apartheid by allowing coloured and Indian South Africans representation in parliament but *de facto* on a subordinate basis to white South Africans. The government also sought to defuse discontent among the urban African population by allowing representation in racially segregated local government, and continued with its policy of granting 'independence' to the bantustans.

One set of opponents of apartheid sought to take advantage of these openings. The business-backed, liberal Progressive Federal Party mobilised among white voters so as to oppose the National Party in parliament. Some coloured and Indian politicians – especially in the coloured Labour Party – sought to use the proposed coloured and Indian chambers of parliament to oppose apartheid. Inkatha, led by Chief Mangosuthu Buthelezi, used the KwaZulu bantustan state structures to push for political change in the country as a whole. Buthelezi, the Chief Minister of KwaZulu, refused to accept independence for the bantustan, and was strongly opposed to the extension of parliamentary representation to coloured and Indian but not African people.

A second set of opponents of apartheid was strongly critical of such entrist tactics. But they remained deeply divided over how to do so. Three general groupings can be identified. First, some of the fast-growing independent trade unions promoted a broadly socialist vision in which racial factors were downplayed. Secondly, a wide range of Charterist activists were united by their allegiance to the banned ANC and its allies in the Congress Alliance. For them, the Freedom Charter served as the manifesto of the national democratic vision – hence the term 'Charterist'. The third group of anti-apartheid activists was increasingly defined by a shared criticism of the Charterist movement, which they judged to be insufficiently radical. They accused the Charterist movement of perpetuating racial differences through multi-racialism, and of being under-committed to the economic empowerment of African people.

Some of these activists were adherents of Black Consciousness (most notably in the Azanian People's Organisation, AZAPO), whilst others came out of the old Unity Movement tradition in the Cape.

To complicate the picture still further, the Charterist movement was itself far from monolithic. The strength of the movement was based on its being a 'broad church', attracting diverse adherents, but this diversity inevitably entailed division too. Whilst united around basic tenets – an allegiance to the ANC, the Freedom Charter, and an acceptance of white democrats and the need for a broad alliance against apartheid under African leadership – there remained deep differences over strategies, tactics and even principles. One wing of the movement was more 'Africanist', committed primarily to the 'liberation' of the African population and critical of the influence of non-African activists. The other wing was focused more on democratisation, and was prepared to consider even entrist tactics of participation in processes initiated by the state. The former wing was inclined to insurrectionary tactics, the latter to gradualist tactics based on building alliances in the 'middle ground' of South African politics so as to isolate the apartheid regime. Some activists combined elements of both wings. The result was that the UDF was constantly buffeted by gales that confused even senior insiders. The UDF never encompassed the entire Charterist movement. Over time, many of the more militant Charterist groups chose to operate outside it.

SOURCES ON THE UDF

There are surprisingly few existing studies of the UDF, the 1980s or the period of transition starting in 1989–90. The UDF was the subject of a handful of articles written in the 1980s and it figures in overview accounts of the period such as Robert Price's excellent *The Apartheid State in Crisis* and Lodge's essays in *All, Here and Now: Black Politics in South Africa in the 1980s*.[44] But such studies barely examine the UDF as an organisation, and tend to be based on a narrow range of secondary sources (especially press reports). The only existing study that makes extensive use of a wider range of primary material is Ineke van Kessel's 1995 doctoral thesis.[45] Van Kessel's thesis and this study cover some of the same ground, use some of the same sources, and were researched over much the same period. But each of our studies has a somewhat different focus. Whereas my book focuses on the UDF primarily in terms of its national and regional structures, Van Kessel's thesis incorporates some discussion of the UDF as an organisation into a much broader discussion of resistance against apartheid in the 1980s. The core of her thesis comprises case studies of a UDF-affiliated community newspaper and civic organisation, and of the Charterist youth movement that was in the Northern Transvaal.

There are a number of important secondary studies on related topics, however. Howard Barrell's published and unpublished work identifies the strengths and weaknesses of the ANC.[46] Anthony Marx's *Lessons of Struggle* assesses the ideological and strategic shifts among anti-apartheid movements.[47] There are surveys of the trade union movement,[48] the general development of student and youth organisation,[49] of civic movements,[50] and of local politics in a variety of areas.[51] Steven Mufson's

Fighting Years provides an evocative account of the political culture of the time.[52] The process of transition has been partly documented.[53] But there remain huge gaps. There are few regional studies of opposition politics, no overviews of political movements and political change in coloured and Indian areas, no detailed case studies yet of nationwide student organisations (especially COSAS), of the South African Youth Congress (SAYCO), or of education crisis groups such as the National Education Crisis Committee (NECC). There is almost nothing on the ANC (and Communist Party) underground inside the country.

Any history of the UDF must therefore be based almost entirely on primary material. Fortunately there is no shortage of source material on the UDF; this includes its own documentation, trial records, and reports in the commercial and 'alternative' media. In addition, there are many participants who can be interviewed.

The UDF, like earlier organisations opposed to segregation and apartheid in twentieth-century South Africa, produced a remarkable volume of documents. Some of this documentation was produced for immediate public consumption – for example, press statements, newsletters and ephemera. Other documents were widely distributed within the UDF and its affiliates – for example, the quasi-published reports of national conferences (even those held under the Emergency). The vast majority, however, were intended for internal use only. These include the minutes of meetings of key structures such as the NEC and National Secretariat, RECs (in some regions), and even Area Committees (in a few cases). In addition, there are many internal reports to national and regional conferences, together with other notes, memoranda and correspondence.

The documentation that has survived does not provide an even coverage of the UDF. Much that was said and done was not recorded. Few records of meetings were kept during the Emergency years of 1985–6 to 1989. The range and volume of documents is greatest for the period 1989–91, not just because the UDF operated openly out of public offices, but also because this was the era of big budgets, the personal computer and the fax machine. More (and longer) documents were produced, the originals of letters were kept, and more thorough attempts were made to account for the organisation's growing finances. Furthermore, some regions – especially the Eastern Cape and Border – produced very little documentation. Coverage was also uneven within regions. In the Western Cape, for example, Area Committees based in coloured or white areas kept more extensive records than the Townships Area Committee. Documents therefore reveal some of the UDF's features more than others.

Trial records provide a very useful source on the early UDF. In the so-called Delmas Treason Trial, UDF general secretary Popo Molefe and publicity secretary 'Terror' Lekota stood accused of treason and other crimes.[54] Almost 300 witnesses gave evidence, with the court transcript weighing in at over 27 000 pages (and this excludes most of the technical and summary legal argument). In addition, over 1500 documents were submitted as exhibits. But trial evidence needs to be treated with caution: the prosecution was shown to have falsified evidence, and no doubt suppressed evidence that undermined its case, whilst the defence was similarly selective, and the accused themselves were not above lying if necessary to avoid conviction or mitigate sentence. More generally, trial evidence is organised for a particular purpose – to prove or disprove the guilt of the accused – and according to particular conventions. Trials are theatre, albeit elaborate theatre; they are not clear windows into the past. Social scientists therefore have to use trial evidence very carefully, reading it with one eye on the structure of the legal process and another on the needs of the different participants.[55]

Edward Feit, who used trial evidence in his studies of resistance politics in the 1950s and early 1960s, decided to ignore most of the evidence of either the accused or the accusers (the police). Most of the evidence he used was from other witnesses, if and when he was satisfied 'beyond reasonable doubt that *in its essential details* the story told is true, that it has a hard core of evidence which no questioning or challenge by counsel can chip away'.[56] My approach was not dissimilar, although I paid more attention to the evidence given by police or accused under cross-examination, and to evidence they gave which was not contradicted by their opponents. Like Feit, I disregarded evidence which was too clearly self-serving, although much of it might have been accurate.

The records of the Delmas Treason Trial and other large collections of UDF documents are held at the University of the Witwatersrand (Wits), whilst further documents are stored at the Mayibuye Centre of the University of the Western Cape. The Wits collection also includes a number of invaluable documents prepared by the trial's defence lawyers, including notes on consultations with the accused. Many of the important UDF documents will be reproduced in a forthcoming volume of the documentary series *From Protest to Challenge*, by Gail Gerhart and Thomas Karis.[57]

The gaps in the documentary and trial records meant that much of this study is based on interviews. Appendix A provides a complete list of interviews used in this study. Interviews have been particularly important in regions such as the Eastern Cape and Border where little was written down and less still has survived. But oral testimony is not without problems. Most fundamentally, an interview involves a relationship between interviewer and interviewee. The relationship comprises elements of both co-operation and conflict: co-operation in the unveiling of an otherwise hidden past; conflict, in that interviewer and interviewee inevitably both seek to steer the discussion in particular directions. The interviewer is thus integrally involved in the production of the interview, and not just in its interpretation.[58] On the interviewee's side, recollections of the past are inevitably coloured by reflection and hindsight, whether consciously or not. Recollection is often selective in that people remember most clearly or focus on the events and thoughts that somehow led to the present rather than those which led to historical dead-ends. Finally, there is always a danger that interviewers spend most of their time interviewing people with whom they establish a good relationship, and about topics on which they are in broad agreement – to the neglect of other points of view and other topics.

This book includes a number of long quotations from interviews. I hope that oral testimony enriches the text, but I do not claim to have enabled interviewees to 'speak for themselves'. It is I, the author, who have selected who to quote, on what, and where; I, not the interviewees, have framed the quotations and shaped the ways in which they are likely to be read and understood. And it is I who have rendered other voices silent. I am particularly aware of two groups of people whom I have not interviewed. First, I have spoken to few critics or opponents of the UDF (although I draw on what such people have written about it). Secondly, I have spoken to few ordinary people, people on the ground who were at most peripherally involved in the activities of the Front. Unfortunately there are few existing South African studies of popular culture and consciousness, and especially of their more political dimensions. Without secondary sources to assist, and short of time, I have left these stones unturned.

The fact that the project was initiated by the NEC of the UDF seems to have encouraged most former UDF office-holders to agree to be interviewed and to help track down documents. Two groups of people involved in the UDF were, however, uncooperative. The first group comprised some of the stronger Charterist critics of the 'cabal' that allegedly ran the UDF; some of them were former UDF office-holders, whilst others just held office in affiliates. For them, the fact that the project was initiated by UDF leaders associated with the 'cabal' seems to have been sufficient reason to have nothing to do with me; I assume that the project was seen as propaganda for the 'cabal', that it was too much of an 'inside' account. The second group comprised mostly white Communist Party-linked activists. Their principal objection seems to have been that the history of the UDF should have been written by an 'insider', someone with a track record of involvement in the UDF. Bizarrely, the project was too much of an inside one for some, too much of an outside one for others.

This book is subtitled 'A History of the United Democratic Front' because it is just that. There will no doubt be other histories, with different focuses or interpretations. I hope that this book points to the need for further research. There are unused sources which might become available in future (including accounts of the UDF by police informants or by ANC underground informants, as well as fuller financial records), and there is no limit to the number of interviews that could be conducted on the topic. The different regions warrant more focused studies, and individuals there could usefully be interviewed. I have not made use of the records of the Truth and Reconciliation Commission, which include many accounts of police and military brutality against UDF officials and activists. I have no doubt that fresh studies will point out errors as well as gaps in this book, and will challenge my interpretations. I look forward to them with interest.

Chapter Two
....

The Origins of the UDF, 1976–1982

On 23 January 1983 at a conference in Johannesburg, Allan Boesak called for the formation of a 'united front' of 'churches, civic associations, trade unions, student organisations, and sports bodies' to oppose the state's constitutional reforms. The call for a united front had not been part of his prepared speech. 'I had made this statement as an aside', he later admitted, 'and was surprised to see what it developed into'.[1] What it developed into, just eight months later, was the UDF.

While the immediate spur to the formation of the UDF was the prospective Tricameral Parliament, the UDF represented the culmination of six years of fundamental transformation in extra-parliamentary politics in South Africa. Changing social, economic and political conditions at the local level gave rise to a newly militant political culture and to the formation of a host of new civic, student, youth, worker and other organisations. Ideologically, the period was marked by the dramatic resurgence of Charterism: the ideology of inclusive nationalism and non-racialism associated with the Freedom Charter and the ANC. Strategically, the period saw a shift from the intellectual-led transformation of consciousness that had characterised the Black Consciousness (BC) movement in the 1970s to the focus on mass organisation and collective action which was to characterise the following decade.

POLITICAL OPPOSITION AFTER THE SOWETO UPRISING, 1977–9

This period of transformation was initiated by the student-led uprising of 1976–7. The uprising brought to an end fifteen years of relative quiescence. Although it did not seriously challenge the apartheid state, and many of the leading participants soon fled the country, it defined a new terrain of struggle. Crucially, as we saw in Chapter 1, the revolt marked the emergence of a fully urbanised African working class aspiring to full inclusion in the country's economic and political system. This was recognised by the National Party government, which developed a counter-revolutionary strategy – the so-called Total Strategy – that encompassed urban policy reforms to pacify the urban African working class, and constitutional reforms to expand the government's support base through the inclusion of coloured and Indian people in a new constitutional arrangement.

Opponents of apartheid, inside and outside the country, responded by seeking strategies that could build on urban militancy and frustrate the government's ambitions. The uprising deepened a nascent crisis of direction within the BC movement, which had dominated extra-parliamentary politics through the first half of the 1970s. Black Consciousness had been born amidst the demoralisation of the late 1960s, and in response prioritised struggles around culture and identity. The movement was particularly successful among university-educated metropolitan professionals, who comprised the backbone of the South African Students Organisation (SASO) and Black People's Convention. Its weakness was its neglect of broad organisation building and collective action. This was evident in 1976–7, when the young protesters employed the angry rhetoric of BC but turned instead to the ANC for a framework for challenging apartheid state power.[2] Although the ANC still had little in the way of an underground inside the country, it offered a long history of struggle, revolutionary ambitions, organisation and funding abroad, and, perhaps above all, an active armed wing, Umkhonto weSizwe (MK).

The uprising indicated the potency of collective action and exposed the limits of existing organisation inside the country, prompting a variety of organisation-building and alliance-building initiatives. SASO leaders urged the broader BC movement to link up with the exile-based liberation movements. Steve Biko, who was the key figure in the BC movement although restricted to King William's Town in the Border region, proposed some kind of a united front, based in exile and encompassing the ANC, PAC, BC and other smaller anti-apartheid groupings. But, at the same time, the creation of exile-based BC structures brought the BC movement into direct competition with the ANC, impeding any alliance.[3] At the local level, in several areas, civic, church and BC leaders came together to deal with some of the practical problems produced by the revolt – in at least one case, self-consciously adopting the form of a 'united front'.[4]

These initiatives were soon stifled. In September 1977 Biko was killed in police custody, and the following month the state banned leading BC and other opposition organisations and detained hundreds of activists. Many senior student leaders were already in jail, on trial or awaiting trial. Perversely, this repression had the unintended effect of facilitating changes in opposition politics by opening space for the ANC to expand its influence rapidly. Invigorated by the 1976–7 uprising and eager to carry the momentum of resistance forward, activists across the country entered into intense discussions. What kind of organisations should be formed, and how should they relate to the banned ANC? This was a period of intellectual curiosity and strategic ferment, with activists avidly devouring literature from the liberation movements or on revolutionary struggles elsewhere in the world. Student 'graduates' of 1976, ex-SASO university students and veteran ANC leaders from the 1950s came together in formal or informal study groups, which served as centres for both thinking and experimenting with new forms of organisation.

A key group was located in Soweto, initially based around a veteran Charterist leader, Joe Gqabi. Gqabi, born in 1929, had been one of MK's first trained cadres, and spent over a decade on Robben Island. In 1976 he had forged strong links with student leaders, who described him as being 'more on the youth side, more accessible, more open to discussion' than some of the other ANC veterans living in Soweto.[5] Together with student leaders, Gqabi had brought together an informal group where tactics, ideology and the ANC were discussed. In December 1976 he was arrested, and charged with terrorism, together with a young MK cadre called Tokyo Sexwale and others. Gqabi himself was acquitted in early 1978, and immediately set about reviving and expanding the Soweto study group. In June he left the country, although he stayed in close contact from Botswana during 1978–9. He was assassinated in Harare in 1981.

The Soweto student activists in the study group played central roles in the rise of an above-ground Charterist movement.[6] The group's initial core comprised former student leaders, most of whom had followed Gqabi into exile by 1981. Among those who remained was Jabu Ngwenya, one of a number of people whose importance behind the scenes in the early 1980s was disguised by the fact that he never filled a prominent public leadership position. Another was Popo Molefe, a matric student in 1976. The membership of the group subsequently changed, and the boundaries between it and broader ANC-supporting networks blurred as the latter grew. Among the new members who were drawn in were Oupa Monareng, who had just started teaching when he joined the group in 1980; Zwelakhe Sisulu, a journalist and son of jailed ANC leader Walter Sisulu; and Vincent Mogane, another behind-the-scenes figure. They were later joined by several former Soweto students who had spent time on Robben Island – including Eric Molobi, Amos Masondo and Murphy Morobe. The group also became less 'cell'-like, working closely with other, older ANC supporters such as Samson Ndou and Curtis Nkondo.

The group was guided by Gqabi's approach, which emphasised careful organisation building, the importance of broad unity, the need for collective action, and effective if clandestine co-ordination. This contrasted starkly with the former BC approach described as 'all talk and no action'.[7] Under Gqabi's influence, 'the study group was like an activating group, a core, where almost everything [was] being discussed and decided'. The group would analyse the situation, study ANC literature and the experiences of foreign liberation struggles, and formulate 'what we used to call the progressive ideology'. Above all, it 'would strategise', mandating individuals to build or work within organisations in different sectors – clandestinely, for the most part. Molefe and Mogane worked in BC organisations, for example, whilst Ngwenya raised funds from the churches, and others worked with students, cultural groups and trade unions.[8]

Study groups were also formed in Cape Town. According to Johnny Issel, a banned former SASO activist from the University of the Western Cape:

There was a political lull in the entire country ... [There was] a lot of introspection going on, a lot of thinking, a lot of discussion groups, little corners critiquing the Black Consciousness movement. People were reading *What Is to Be Done?* by Lenin. Others were reading Trotsky, *1905*, trying to find answers, trying to find out where do we go from here? What do we do?

Issel and others in Cape Town's coloured areas formed a reading group. The group was ideologically mixed, although most of its members were shifting towards the ANC. Like Gqabi's followers, they reached out into other circles:

> Our discussion group was very small. But we tried to broaden out, to work with other groups. If you have a vicious enemy and you're small, one of the best ways to defend yourself is to broaden, to enlarge yourself. We got involved with youth groups, particularly church youth groups. We got involved with teachers. We tried to get involved with just practically everybody.

They were also concerned 'to do something'. Guided by literature from the Philippines and elsewhere, they began to organise in the 'community'.[9]

A similar process was taking place in Durban, although there it was emphatically Charterist. Even before 1976 some BC leaders in Durban had forged close ties with the ANC. More importantly, a group of young Indian activists had been immersed in SACP literature whilst university students in the early 1970s, and steered clear of BC. The key figure in this group was Pravin Gordhan, a pharmacist by profession and political strategist by inclination. Gordhan, the lawyer Yunus Mahomed and other former students from the University of Durban–Westville were dissatisfied with the elite politics of the older NIC leadership, and sought instead to promote what they called 'mass politics' through strategies that would harness the supposed ability of the 'masses' to 'make history'. Faced with the pervasive social conservatism and wariness of politics in Indian areas, they began to formulate what was to become a specifically 'civic' strategy of organising around civic issues whilst publicly eschewing overt politics. They were in very close contact throughout with the ANC and SACP in exile, particularly through former Robben Islander Mac Maharaj. Barrell describes this group as one of the ANC's 'more important underground units'.[10]

In other towns across the country young activists were also searching for an ideological framework to help them understand conditions and guide them strategically. For most of them it was a confusing period. As Port Elizabeth student activist Monde Mditshwa recalls:

> We would get some ANC literature, we had to interpret it ourselves, and sometimes it would confuse us. Sometimes we would meet with the elderly comrades, but most of the time we were on our own. It was a matter of us consulting with them, from time to time, going to their house very quietly because they didn't want to be known to be ANC. It was hot, I mean ANC those days was hot, no one wanted to be known.[11]

People surreptitiously read ANC literature, tuned into the ANC's Radio Freedom, and sought out ANC veterans. But most of them were cut off from and unsure of the changing patterns of politics in the major centres.

Until late 1979 these groups had little or no contact with each other, but had several features in common. They were either firmly within the Charterist fold or were gravitating towards it. At the same time, all the groups recognised that the armed struggle alone would not bring about political change; what was needed was political organisation, above ground, inside the country. Moreover, building strong organisation would entail working together with non-Charterists in broad-based movements. Thus Charterists involved themselves in ostensibly non-partisan civic organising in residential areas.

Less obviously, Charterists participated as well in a series of organisations which appeared to fall fully within the BC tradition. These included the Azanian People's Organisation (AZAPO), launched in April 1978, as well as BC-orientated trade unions.[12] Gqabi supported ANC participation in ostensibly BC structures on the grounds that ideological differences should not inhibit broader anti-apartheid unity. Molefe, who was strongly influenced by Gqabi, participated in AZAPO 'on the understanding that what was required was to unite the masses of our people regardless of ideological inclination and harness them in the struggle for national democracy and freedom'. Molefe and Mogane helped to build an AZAPO branch in Soweto, which was formally launched in early 1979 with Molefe as chairman. In 1980 Molefe unsuccessfully proposed the formation of a Soweto-wide front, to include organisations such as AZAPO, COSAS, trade unions, and so on. He remained in AZAPO until it became clear that it was unable to transcend the limits of BC:

> We saw [BC's] strategic approach as parochial and hemming the expansion of the anti-apartheid movement ... We had to posit a kind of alternative [to apartheid and racism] capable of uniting the largest section of South Africans committed to a peaceful and just future – an alternative that could lay the foundation for racial reconciliation.

Through the early 1980s Molefe sought to broaden and unite resistance against apartheid.[13]

On the ground the lines were not sharply drawn, and Charterists were all too aware of their own weaknesses. Many Charterist activists sought to strengthen anti-apartheid forces whilst building the Charterist presence within them. This approach was broadly shared by key figures in the ANC in exile, who until 1979–80 remained open-minded even about opposing apartheid from within state structures such as the South African Indian Council and Coloured Representative Council. The ANC also maintained a working relationship with the bantustan-based Inkatha and other groups until late 1979.

The period 1977–9 was also one of strategic ferment for the ANC in exile. ANC leaders began to reassess their assumption that armed incursions alone would ignite a mass revolutionary movement. In 1977 the ANC established a department of Internal Reconstruction and Development to oversee building internal underground structures, and soon after appointed Mac Maharaj as the department's secretary. Maharaj, in contact with Gordhan, argued strongly that 'political reconstruction inside South Africa by political means' needed to receive priority over military incursions. Top ANC leaders were converted to this view when, visiting Vietnam in 1978, they were told about the successful Vietnamese emphasis on building a mass political base from which the armed struggle could operate.[14]

In January 1979 the ANC's National Executive appointed a six-man Politico-Military Strategy Commission to examine the ANC's strategy and operational structures. The Commission included key ANC, SACP and MK leaders – and Gqabi. In March it presented its recommendations to the National Executive, which finally accepted most of them in August. The gist of the new approach was that:

> The ANC ... had to take one step back in the conduct of armed operations if it was eventually to be able to mount a sustained armed struggle. Its strategic emphasis should temporarily fall on organising by political means inside South Africa. This would enable it to create an organised domestic political base with two components: one, a front of popular organisations operating in the legal and semi-legal spheres; the other an underground organisation operating clandestinely but relating to, recruiting within and maintaining a presence inside public bodies ... The ANC hoped that the political base so created would serve as the foundation for a sustained armed struggle (interspersed with popular insurrectionary activity) for the seizure of power.[15]

The ANC's rethinking mirrored the state's Total Strategy in that both recognised the importance of contesting the political domain and the subordinate role of the military (at least in the short and medium term).

The Commission suggested that the primary task of the ANC underground should be to build what Barrell terms 'a broad front comprising popular organisations inside South Africa operating legally and semi-legally'. 'Membership of the front should be based on an organisation's commitment to the struggle for political freedoms. It should express the broadest possible working together of all organisations, groups and individuals genuinely opposed to racist autocracy.' The Commission was emphatic about the need to work with non-Charterists. The ANC should not, in the Commission's words, 'shun any organisation' engaging in active opposition to apartheid on the grounds that 'it did not embrace [the ANC's] long-term revolutionary aims or criticised part of [the ANC's] strategy' or that there might 'in the long term ... be a parting of the ways' between it and the ANC. Furthermore, legal and semi-legal organisations should beware of inviting state repression through too overt an espousal of Charterism.[16] In all, the Commission effectively endorsed the approaches that Gqabi and Maharaj had promoted, including, in Gqabi's case, those towards AZAPO.

This view of front politics, advocated by Gqabi and endorsed in the ANC's Strategic Review, was to be reflected in repeated efforts over the following three years, culminating in the formation of the UDF. But many, perhaps most, Charterist activists inside the country adopted an approach to political work that was overtly Charterist and sectarian. This was to be particularly evident during 1979–80, when an overtly Charterist movement was reconstituted for the first time since the 1960s. Where Gqabi's and Gordhan's approaches were cautious, this new approach was assertive and confrontational. In some ways they were complementary, but there were also obvious tensions and it proved difficult to maintain a balance.

CHARTERISM RESURGENT, 1978–80

Ideology and strategy were also furiously debated in prison, where activists of different political persuasions were thrown together. Whereas outside prison most activists had sought to maintain broad-based unity against the state, in prison people polarised into harshly antagonistic groups, either supportive of or hostile to the ANC, and with corresponding views on forming a new national organisation independent of and perhaps a rival to the ANC.

Modder B Prison on the East Rand provided one such venue for fierce debate among African activists detained in October 1977. To some extent the disputes were, as Tom Manthata put it, 'more personal than ideological'. But they also involved broad strategic differences. On the one side was a group who argued that the BC movement needed only to amend its existing ideological and strategic positions, and form a new organisation independent of the ANC. Prominent in this group was Tom Manthata from Soweto. On the other side was a growing number of detainees who shared ideological and strategic views with the ANC. These included former SASO president Diliza Mji from Natal, Curtis Nkondo and, from mid-1978, several former student leaders from Soweto. They argued against the launch of any organisation that was not under Charterist control lest it turn into what Nkondo called 'a third force'; if Charterists and others were to work together it should be within a loose alliance or structure. According to Nkondo, 'If you want to know the preparations for the formation of the UDF, [it was] at Modder B [that] we began to plan.'[17]

A similarly polarised debate occurred on Robben Island. Veteran ANC leaders struggled with BC activists jailed in the mid-1970s for the loyalties of the students who arrived in or after 1976. The students were steeped in BC rhetoric, but were not hostile to the ANC. After one of the older SASO leaders, 'Terror' Lekota, was recruited to Charterism, many of the younger students followed. Anthony Marx calculates that, of thirty-one student prisoners from Port Elizabeth, twenty-five converted to Charterism, one to the PAC, and only five remained within the BC fold.[18]

Once released, the participants in the polarised debates in prison sought to build more assertive and overtly Charterist organisations. In June 1979 former Modder B detainees took the lead in forming an explicitly Charterist Congress of South African Students (COSAS). Gqabi was furious when members of the new COSAS executive, who were subject to his direction in the ANC underground, reported to him in Botswana. The word 'Congress', he argued, linked the organisation to the ANC.

He was very cross with us having pushed for 'Congress of South African

Students' [as the] name, because he said it was very unnecessary. It was not the time for publicity. It was not the time for being identified with the Movement, and we had spoiled the whole thing, because he doesn't think [that COSAS would] go any further because it is just clearly ANC.[19]

COSAS was indeed soon the target of state repression, as Gqabi had feared. Its twenty-odd senior activists were detained at the end of 1979. As a result of the detentions, combined with COSAS's weak support outside the Transvaal, it proved somewhat out of touch with the student protests which spread around the country in early 1980.

The formation of COSAS was soon overshadowed by the relaunch of AZAPO. The release of the last detainees from Modder B and elsewhere provided fresh impetus to AZAPO, which elected a new leadership in September 1979. Curtis Nkondo was elected president, in the mistaken belief that he was either PAC-inclined or would unite different groups. In fact, Nkondo used his position to strengthen a Charterist network outside AZAPO and reduce the chances of its becoming a 'third force' to rival the ANC. He worked very closely with COSAS, with Charterist university students within the newly formed Azanian Students Organisation (AZASO), and with Thozamile Botha and other Charterist leaders of the likewise newly formed Port Elizabeth Black Civic Organisation (PEBCO). Not surprisingly, Nkondo's unsubtle advocacy of Charterism antagonised anti-Charterists in the AZAPO leadership, and they secured his expulsion in early 1980.[20]

In part through these developments in AZAPO and COSAS, a Charterist movement began to cohere inside the country. The ANC's underground was highly fragmented, but semi-public national networks began to emerge. Nkondo had helped build personal links, and a series of events raised the public profile of the ANC. The *Sunday Post* newspaper ran a Free Mandela petition campaign and published the Freedom Charter, which COSAS and other organisations publicly adopted. MK launched a series of spectacular attacks, including one against the Sasolburg oil refinery. Trials and funerals provided further impetus and opportunity for the public demonstration of Charterist symbols.

The young Indian activists grouped around Gordhan in Durban linked up with coloured civic activists in Cape Town and with older ANC leaders in Johannesburg such as Samson Ndou. New alternative newsletters, starting with the student-produced *SASPU National* and the community-based *Grassroots* in Cape Town, reinforced networks through coverage of developments in different parts of the country. These networks also began to involve white democrats, adding a new dimension to non-racialism. White churchmen helped with financial resources, and white student activists helped with media. School boycotts in 1980 provided new recruits to Charterist politics.

At the same time, Charterists were making important gains through more broadly based and less overtly political struggles on the ground. Civic organisations proliferated in Durban's Indian areas and Cape Town's coloured areas, as well as in Soweto and Port Elizabeth. The Durban activists sought to keep their local-level civic work separate from high-profile politics. In 1980, when it seemed appropriate to take up the latter (in part to counter Inkatha, now antagonistic to the ANC), they formed a Release Mandela Committee (RMC). Veteran ANC leader Archie Gumede was elected chairperson, with other office-holders including Griffiths Mxenge, a lawyer and leading member of the ANC underground, and Paul David, a young Indian lawyer working closely with Gordhan.[21]

PLANTING FLAGS: THE DELINEATION OF THE CHARTERIST MOVEMENT IN 1981

The open advocacy of Charterism in 1979–80 intensified ideological and organisational rivalries within extra-parliamentary politics. During 1980 tensions simmered, before ideological divisions were clearly delineated the following year. The year 1981 was one of 'flag-planting', as a Western Cape activist put it.[22] By the end of the year Charterists had planted their flag at the head of resistance politics. An essential ingredient in their success was the development of new ways of maintaining the uneasy balance between overt Charterist evangelism and building more broadly based resistance.

The first site of partisan conflict in 1980–1 was AZAPO, whose anti-Charterist national leaders stoutly defended the organisation and also steadily marginalised AZAPO's few Charterists. In January 1981 the top AZAPO leadership opposed the Soweto branch's proposal to hold a commemoration service for the victims of a South African Defence Force raid on an alleged ANC base in Mozambique. Marginalised at AZAPO's national congress and at a follow-up workshop soon after, Charterists abandoned the organisation. This was the one battle they lost that year.[23]

In April a similar showdown occurred in the Western Cape. Until then organisations in Cape Town, including study groups, civics and *Grassroots*, had generally bridged ideological or partisan differences. This unity ended with the funeral of an old Charterist, Hennie Ferrus, in Worcester. Ferrus himself had personified Charterist flexibility, energetically participating in the Labour Party and even segregated state structures. Charterists seized control over the funeral, supplanting both the non-Charterist activists with whom they had previously worked and the Labour Party leadership. As divisions deepened during the year, old friendships, study groups and civics split – or 'exploded', as the activist Marcus Solomon put it. Charterists, now organised into what was dubbed the 'High Command', secured the leading position, including control of *Grassroots*.[24]

At about the same time, the assertion of Charterist leadership at the national level was marked by a high-profile campaign against the twentieth anniversary of South Africa's becoming a Republic. Prompted by the ANC in exile, Molefe and other Charterist activists in Soweto put together a campaign which took speakers to meetings across the country. Simultaneously, MK attacked a range of targets. The campaign invigorated the Charterist movement. According to Molefe:

We (I think for the first time) were able to arrive at the conclusion that the Charterist movement was beginning to be firmly established inside the country. In our view the campaign had been quite a successful one, it had generated a lot of excitement. It had also reactivated our people, they were really ready now for a range of other activities. But also crucial in its impact, it had been used to lay the basis for building organisations. Structures we had set [up] had enabled activists to meet regularly [and] reflect on how to take the gains that they had made forward.[25]

The inclusion for the first time of white speakers on platforms promoted the practice of non-racialism which distinguished Charterism from AZAPO.

Spurred on by the setback in AZAPO and the success of the Anti-Republic campaign, Charterist activists aggressively contested control over other important organisations and events. After careful preparations, Charterist student leaders gained control of AZASO at its national conference in June, publicly associated it with the Congress movement, and launched a stinging critique of BC. Control of AZASO opened up access to university campuses, which in turn facilitated recruitment into Charterist politics. In the assessment of Oupa Monareng, 'the fate of the Black Consciousness movement was decided at that conference'.[26] Charterist activists also took control of the 16 June commemoration service in Soweto, using the opportunity for another denunciation of BC.

This competition extended into Indian politics, which from mid-1981 became focused on the prospect of direct elections to the South African Indian Council (SAIC). In Johannesburg, BC activists set up a broad-based *ad hoc* Anti-SAIC Committee, but this was soon taken over by their Charterist rivals, who thereafter dominated the struggle against the SAIC.[27] The younger Indian activists in Johannesburg, led by Valli Moosa and Ismail Momoniat, had close connections to Gordhan's group in Durban. In October 1981 they jointly organised a conference in Durban. Attended by many African as well as Indian activists, this conference was the largest Charterist gathering since 1961. The Anti-Republic and Anti-SAIC campaigns, together with a campaign supporting striking workers at the Wilson-Rowntree factory in East London organised by the Charterist South African Allied Workers' Union (SAAWU), had brought fresh coherence to the newly delineated Charterist movement.

The Charterist resurgence came at a price, however. In late 1981 the police swooped on leading Charterist activists across the country. The detainees included Gordhan and Mahomed in Durban, and Issel in Cape Town. In Johannesburg, the detainees included Monareng, Chikane, Ndou, Sisulu, Momoniat, and a dozen or so white student and trade union activists. SAAWU leaders Sisa Njikelana and Thozamile Gqweta were detained in East London, and SAAWU experienced particularly severe repression as a result of its opposition to Ciskei's 'independence'. By January over a hundred people were in detention. In Durban, Griffiths Mxenge was killed in a covert security operation disguised as a criminal attack.

· THE STRATEGIC LESSONS OF 1981

The campaigns of 1981 were not important solely because they dramatically raised the public profile of the ANC, but also because they provided important strategic lessons. Crucially, Charterists gained experience in the difficult task of balancing an advocacy of Charterism with the broadening of overall resistance. In contrast to the Charterist initiatives of 1979, the campaigns of 1981 were publicly organised by single-issue committees which boosted but did not compromise organisation building on the ground.

In organising the Anti-Republic campaign Molefe and other former members of the Gqabi group sought to forge a broad alliance, albeit under Charterist control. The campaign was directed by an Ad Hoc Anti-Republic Commemoration Committee structured as a broad front comprising individuals from a variety of backgrounds and organisations. AZAPO and other organisations were invited to participate, but declined because the campaign embraced white democrats (or perhaps they smelt a Charterist rat). In practice, the real work was done by what Molefe calls a 'small committee', comprising mostly members of the Soweto study group. This core ran 'the day to day affairs of the organisation, arranging meetings, planning for pamphlets to be printed and distributed, sending task forces to other areas', and so on. Committee members organised and addressed meetings in other parts of the country. Molefe, for example, went to the Orange Free State, Mogane to the Northern and Eastern Transvaal, and Ngwenya to the Eastern Cape and Natal.[28]

The campaign provided several clear strategic lessons. Firstly, it suggested the need for a new division of responsibility within the underground. Whereas the Soweto-based study group had divided responsibilities by sector, it had now become important to distinguish between high-profile or overtly political roles, and lower-profile organisational roles. According to Molefe, 'we were beginning to define different roles for ourselves. We were beginning to realise that some people were more important as leadership figureheads and others were more important as activists who would do the real work on the ground on a daily basis.'[29]

Secondly, political campaigns should be organised through front-type structures. This not only avoided the risk of co-ordinating structures becoming an independent 'third force', but also exposed fewer activists and organisations to possible state repression. Front-type structures also enabled the Charterist movement to address the specific needs of different constituencies, as became much clearer later in the year.

The success of the Anti-Republic campaign persuaded some of the more strident Charterists of the merits of the more patient approach favoured by Gqabi, Molefe and Gordhan. Molefe recalls:

The way in which the Anti-Republic Campaign Committee was structured, the fact that it included a range of organisations who had been independent but joined together by common commitment, by this common programme of action, and the strategic objective of frustrating the celebration of the Republic, would have necessarily given rise to the idea of broader alliance politics beyond Soweto. We were beginning to talk about this idea of a united front.

The idea of unity against apartheid was continually being raised in literature from the ANC. Ismael Mohamed, a veteran activist in Johannesburg, recalls that the ANC in exile was pushing internal activists to form a 'national democratic front', based on the Anti-Republic Committee. 'So', Molefe adds, 'there was really [a] convergence of views around this issue of the united front, both from outside and inside the country.' Some people moved in this direction 'as a result of theoretical studies', he says; in other cases it arose 'directly out of the experience of the people struggling on the ground'.[30]

Molefe explicitly called for the formation of a broad front in an address to the annual conference of the South African Council of Churches. The sectarianism of AZAPO made it 'imperative' to form a new, apparently supra-partisan 'united front'.

> The broad front envisaged here … can be pursued in the following manner: By formulating initially an *ad hoc* committee consisting of all social, political, religious and cultural organisations from all sections of the oppressed masses. It must be noted that we are thinking of political bodies, sports bodies, churches, teachers' organisations, workers, nurses' associations, etc. … The purpose of the *ad hoc* committee would be to consult in order to formulate similar stances on national issues like commemorations, boycotts, etc. It would serve to create a dynamic system of co-ordination and communication between the organisations and the masses and amongst the organisations themselves …[31]

The call followed extensive discussion, encompassing even Maharaj in exile. But, as Barrell emphasises, 'at no stage on this (or on any other) issues did the external mission issue an instruction to underground members'. It was left to internal activists to take and formulate such initiatives.[32] The Anti-SAIC campaign also pointed to the need for organisation that could encompass Indian democrats. As Molefe recalls,

> In Johannesburg a series of meetings were held after the Anti-SAIC campaign, and in other parts of the country, to say: 'We have now mobilised so many Indian people around this issue of the South African Indian Council. We have managed to gain tremendous acceptance among our people for the Freedom Charter and our non-racial principles, the idea of a unitary, non-racial, democratic South Africa, the rejection of the schemes of the regime. What now do we do with these people?' It's a highly politicised mass of the people, you cannot simply say that they can participate in the civic associations. You need something much higher. What do you do? So the debate began to develop then.[33]

The lessons of the Anti-SAIC campaign could only be fully digested when the activists detained in late 1981 were released in mid-1982. By then the context had shifted. On the one hand, the state had tabled revised proposals for constitutional reforms. On the other, the formation of an essentially Africanist national organisation had been proposed. Both factors hastened the need for some kind of non-racial or multiracial front, under Charterist leadership.

MALUTI

During this period of discussion about continued and broadened co-ordination in late 1981 and early 1982, a new proposal arose which served to sharpen the debate. This was the so-called 'Maluti' initiative, which was clouded in confusion and controversy. It was never discussed publicly, and few leading Charterists felt that they had a good grasp of what was going on. More than ten years later people still provide varying accounts.[34]

The proposal was to form an organisation or movement to be called Maluti. This would be a broad Africanist front, based on the ANC but also encompassing the PAC. The proposal seems to have been formulated by M.K. Malefane – a little-known character linked to Nelson Mandela's wife Winnie during her banishment to Brandfort in the Orange Free State. Malefane, 'a young stylish Rastafarian artist', lived with Winnie Mandela; later he was described as her 'agent', representing her at meetings which she could not attend because of her banning order.[35] Malefane told Archie Gumede in Durban that it would unite anti-apartheid groups in the form of a front. Curtis Nkondo was told that it was 'a kind of compromise with the PAC, a merger, bringing the organisations together again'. Samson Ndou was under the impression that it also included some former ANC members, Africanists who had been expelled from the ANC in 1975. One young Cape Town activist thought that Maluti's proponents 'wanted to reformulate the Freedom Charter', and the idea came from ANC cadres 'in Swaziland'. Some people understood that Maluti would be structured like a front, whilst others believed that it would be a unitary organisation. Whatever the details, it was clearly associated with the Africanist wing of the ANC, and made advocates of non-racialism very uneasy. It may indeed have even been in part a reaction to the growing role of Indian and white activists in opposition politics during 1981.

The initiative appealed to some of the younger Charterist activists in COSAS and AZASO, but it clearly needed broader support. Malefane therefore visited Gumede, the most senior 1950s ANC leader still inside the country. He told Gumede that the project had Winnie Mandela's backing, implying that it had been sanctioned by the ANC. Gumede thought it was a good idea, believing that 'something had to be done' – although the NIC was not supportive. African ANC supporters in Cape Town were also approached, but were concerned about what they saw as an attack on the Freedom Charter. They sought 'clarification' from the exiled ANC, but before they heard anything, Johannesburg-based activists had dealt with the issue.

Senior ANC underground activists in Johannesburg first heard about Maluti indirectly, and this aroused their suspicions. Molefe recalls that 'we were worried, we thought that it was an attempt to set up a movement to rival the African National Congress'. They arranged a rare and risky meeting of underground leaders in Durban and Johannesburg. Gumede, Mxenge and others flew to Johannesburg but, realising that they were being tailed by the police, decided not to go to the meeting place and instead returned to Durban. Eventually the proponents of Maluti convened a national meeting in Cape Town. Molefe was sent from Johannesburg with the explicit mission to squash the proposal, which he did.

Molefe subsequently visited Winnie Mandela after the Cape Town meeting, under the impression that 'Winnie was behind' the whole initiative. Like many others, Molefe believed she had been 'misled'. Molefe relates: 'I explained to her that there was no way in which such an organisation could get off the ground if people who mattered were not consulted on the issue, and that there was no clarity as to what this organisation was all about, what was its objective, how it would relate to existing liberation movements, and so on.' Winnie Mandela told Molefe that the 'idea [had been] sanctioned by the ANC outside', and Malefane claimed that 'our representatives in Swaziland, Lesotho, Botswana and Lusaka had given the go-ahead'. Molefe was sceptical, since 'the people who should have known about it' knew nothing. Whatever the position, the proposal was killed. Malefane later tried to revive the idea, packaging it as a 'cultural movement', but without any success.

Maluti had some impact on the debates around forming a united front. Samson Ndou goes so far as to suggest that the whole idea of a front was a reaction to the Maluti proposal, and Curtis Nkondo describes discussions of a united front as being 'counter to the Maluti'. Molefe suggests that it served to sharpen thinking around the issues, especially the merits of fronts over unitary organisation. 'We were jealously guarding the unity of our people under the leadership of the African National Congress at that stage. Once we were unable to play a role in the Black Consciousness movement, we couldn't understand ourselves forming another unitary political structure in the country.' As Molefe saw it, any unitary structure that adopted ANC principles and symbols risked repression: 'the heavy hand of the regime would have descended upon it and crushed it'. Conversely, any unitary structure which did not clearly align itself with the ANC risked becoming a divisive 'third force'.

Maluti also exposed the fragility of non-racialism. After the Anti-SAIC and other campaigns in 1981, key Charterist activists inside the country were concerned to find ways of ensuring the continued involvement of Indian and white South Africans in the Charterist movement. Maluti threatened this project. The NIC in Durban, as Gumede relates, were hostile to the proposal from the start, and must have been spurred on by the spectre of Africanism within the Charterist movement. Throughout 1982 Indian activists in Johannesburg and Durban played a central role in the moves towards forming a united front.

'ALMOST BY ACCIDENT': TOWARDS A FRONT, 1982–3

During mid- and late 1982 several processes came together to strengthen moves towards forming a united front. On the one hand, there was a clear need not only to sustain the 1981 Anti-SAIC campaign, but to broaden it to oppose the government's proposed constitutional reforms. At the same time, organisations in Indian areas needed to be linked up with those elsewhere, not least to safeguard non-racialism and to prevent the recurrence of an Africanist tendency within the Charterist movement. Non-Charterist challenges also needed to be headed off, and organisation in

African areas had to be further strengthened. On the other hand, there was widespread agreement about the need to separate overt and covert political activity, with tactical fronts playing the leading public role in the former.

The detention of activists from late 1981 into early 1982 and the trial in 1982 of the ANC operative Barbara Hogan reinforced the importance of a more careful demarcation between overt and covert political roles. Hogan was sentenced to ten years in jail for providing the ANC with information – a heavy sentence, which emphasised the cost of being caught doing ANC work. Moreover, the Hogan episode pointed to worrying lapses of security on the part of ANC units in Botswana. It therefore made sense to keep some activists out of direct ANC work. Indeed, on several occasions senior activists inside the country found that junior activists had been recruited for underground work by ANC units in Botswana, and responded by putting pressure on them to break off those links – much to the chagrin of the ANC units there.[36]

Furthermore, the hazards of overt politics deterred many people from participation in organisation and protest. Activists like Gordhan and Molefe had recognised the importance of this before, and based their organisational work around it. Many other activists reached the same conclusions in 1981–2. This was most clearly the case with respect to COSAS. Ostensibly an organisation for school students, it had in fact prioritised overtly political issues and most of its leadership had left school. In early 1982 COSAS's leaders decided that it must build stronger support and organisation in schools. At its annual conference in Cape Town in May 1982, it restricted its membership to school students, and initiated moves to form separate youth organisations for ex-students. Similarly, a growing number of African civic leaders (especially in the PWV and Eastern Cape) recognised the need to focus more closely on civic issues and downplay overtly political causes, whilst other Charterist activists immersed themselves in trade union work.

These lessons were conceptualised in terms of a strategic framework which distinguished between 'first-level' and 'second-level' organisations. A first-level organisation would be, in Molefe's words, a grassroots organisation 'which concerns itself primarily with immediate problems of particular groups', such as civics concerned with socio-economic grievances in the townships. Second-level organisations would take up overtly political issues, channelling 'mass mobilisation of the oppressed masses around issues which affect them as a whole'. Given the threat of repression and the need to broaden resistance to the state, the preferred structure for second-level organisations was that of the 'tactical front': a front of organisations united over opposition to specific issues such as Republic Day or the SAIC elections.[37] Given the proliferation of first-level organisations, however, there was pressure to form some kind of national political co-ordination which went beyond specific issues. When the UDF was formed, therefore, it was broader than merely the 'tactical front' that some of its leaders said it was.

Local organisation building preoccupied many Charterist leaders. The 1981 campaigns had revealed the weakness of local level organisation in African areas. The ANC, through its underground channels and propaganda 'had a very consistent theme, which was that of organise, organise, organise',[38] and in late 1981 had encouraged an abortive attempt to form a national body for civic organisations.[39] In 1982 activists worked at building a trilogy of organisations in African townships: a civic organisation for adults or parents, a COSAS branch for school students, and a youth organisation. In Soweto, for example, Molefe, Masondo and Mogane rebuilt the moribund Soweto Civic Association. They also formed an Anti-Community Councils Committee, described by Molefe as 'in effect a mini-front to oppose community council elections'. It included representatives of different organisations in Soweto (initially including AZAPO). Younger activists began to work towards the formation of what was to become the Soweto Youth Congress.[40]

In mid-1982 several factors combined to inject fresh impetus into attempts to formalise national networks into some kind of organisation. Firstly, most of the activists detained in late 1981 were released between March and July, although banning orders were slapped on some of them (including Gordhan) as well as on some activists who had not been detained. Secondly, political activity and networks were extending into hitherto weakly organised parts of the country. Molefe and Mogane, for example, established contact with activists in parts of the Northern Cape, Orange Free State and Eastern Transvaal.[41]

But the most important factor was the state's publication of revised constitutional proposals in May, and of further proposals in November. Those Indian and coloured activists committed to non-racialism feared that the state's reforms might drive a massive wedge between coloured and Indian South Africans on one hand and the excluded African majority on the other. 'We thought it would be disastrous, and that it was absolutely a political necessity to oppose that.'[42] The 1981 campaigns in Indian and coloured areas would need to be carried forward.

In addition, non-Charterists in several parts of the country were at least as vocal in condemnation of the state's reforms as the Charterists, and the latter feared being sidelined. In Cape Town, anti-Charterists from a range of backgrounds had joined Charterists in a Disorderly Bills Action Committee, so named in response to one of the Koornhof Bills. In Johannesburg, AZAPO supporters convened a meeting in September to discuss the government's proposals, inviting the Transvaal Anti-SAIC Committee and various civic organisations. Non-Charterists made several calls for a 'united front' in 1981 and early 1982, and the call was taken up at an AZAPO meeting in Soweto in October. Moves also began in Port Elizabeth and East London over the formation of broad-based, non-Charterist local fronts. AZAPO was very adept at using the press, conveying an impression of great industry that belied its weaknesses on the ground. Probably in response to such events (and perhaps concerned about Maluti) the ANC in exile sent messages into South Africa in late 1982, urging its underground units to form some kind of a co-ordinating structure to rival AZAPO. In addition, dissident members of the coloured Labour Party (including its Natal leader and former national deputy leader, Norman Middleton) approached leaders in civic and welfare organisations about opposing the reforms, which the Labour Party seemed about to embrace.[43]

These factors prompted sustained discussion within Charterist circles in Johannesburg over ways of opposing the constitutional reforms whilst ensuring Charterist hegemony. Three proposals circulated. The first was to revive the old Transvaal Indian Congress (TIC), which had been dormant for decades but had never been banned. The second idea was to form an ostensibly non-racial organisation targeted at coloureds and Indians; the name 'Transvaal People's Congress' was mentioned. But as some Soweto-based activists pointed out, 'a joint body for coloureds and Indians wasn't on, given the different level of organisation'. The third idea was to form an all-embracing front. The problem with this was that the role of a front was to bring together different organisations and bridge political differences, but in the Transvaal there were still no mass-based organisations in coloured and Indian areas to bring into a front. Most Charterist activists in Johannesburg's Indian and coloured areas therefore felt that the idea of a front was premature. Indian activists in the Transvaal Anti-SAIC Committee (TASC) resolved therefore to revive the TIC, and agreed to announce this publicly at a TASC congress already scheduled for the end of January 1983.[44]

One of the leading advocates of a united front at the time was Molefe, who saw a front as a way of accommodating political differences.

> The idea of a united front made simple political sense. The real difficulty was how to overcome obstacles to that unity. It seemed to me that there were a number of organisations which shared the common goal of ridding South Africa of apartheid. Although they differed in political outlook, they nevertheless shared their common goal. The bringing together of these organisations under the umbrella of a front with a common goal offered a way of overcoming obstacles to unity.[45]

But Molefe had little influence among the younger TASC activists. Another advocate of a front was Cas Saloojee, a middle-aged Indian activist who had led struggles against the Group Areas Act in Johannesburg in the 1970s. Like Molefe, Saloojee envisaged a front that could bring together Charterist and non-Charterist activists. He himself had spoken to Labour Party dissidents.

Viewed from Johannesburg's Indian areas, the idea of a front had clear weaknesses. Viewed from other parts of the country, however, it seemed more appealing, given the growing number of Charterist organisations in Durban, Cape Town and elsewhere. Pravin Gordhan and the younger NIC activists in Durban concurred on the need for a broad front, which they saw as a shell, suited to organising regionally diverse organisations under repressive conditions. A clear image could be projected on the shell's surface, they said, but its contents would be left intact if the shell were cracked through state repression. A front would also facilitate the necessary emergence of African leadership, whilst being neither a competitor to the ANC nor simply a front for it.[46]

These open questions became more pressing in the first week of January when the Labour Party met for its annual congress in Eshowe in Natal. After a vote on 4 January, it announced that it would participate in the proposed Tricameral Parliament. Norman Middleton and several other prominent Labour Party dissidents immediately resigned in protest. On 7 January the *Cape Times* published on its front page an interview with Allan Boesak, a minister in the Nederduitse Gereformeerde Sendingkerk, chaplain of students at the University of the Western Cape, and newly elected president of the World Alliance of Reformed Churches. Boesak agreed with his interviewer that the formation of a 'united front' was likely, in order to oppose what he called the 'disgusting' and 'opportunistic' decision of the Labour Party.[47]

On 8 January Oliver Tambo delivered the ANC's annual anniversary statement, in which he 'condemned without reservation' the Labour Party's decision. He declared 1983 to be the 'year of united action'. In the middle of his speech he made the following exhortation: 'We must organise the people into strong mass democratic organisation; we must organise all revolutionaries into underground units of the ANC; we must organise all combatants into units of Umkhonto weSizwe; we must organise all democratic forces into one front for national liberation.'[48] Barrell suggests that the specific contents of Tambo's address were probably slow to circulate inside South Africa, and probably did not inform the discussion later in January.[49]

It was Boesak's call rather than Tambo's which catalysed a flurry of interest in establishing a broad front against the government's reforms. Boesak himself was regarded with some wariness by Charterists – especially in Cape Town, but also in Johannesburg – who were alarmed by his BC background. As Momoniat puts it, 'he wasn't really accepted within the progressive fold'. But Boesak's call pushed him into prominence just as the TASC leaders in Johannesburg reached agreement that their congress on 23–24 January should be a national rather than just a Transvaal event.[50] The TASC leaders agreed that 'the Anti-SAIC congress must be a broad-based congress, a nice forum to get people from all over the country'. For this, however, they needed an effective guest speaker. In 1981 they had used 'all the Tutus and the Motlanas and the Beyers Naudés and we had gone through the whole lot of them,' says Saloojee, 'and by that time I personally felt that we must introduce some new people to attract people to come to our meetings.'[51] Coloured Charterists from the Johannesburg area met and agreed to form an Ad Hoc Anti-PC Committee to oppose the constitutional proposals put forward by the President's Council (PC), and the stand taken by the Labour Party.[52] But no coloured leader in the Charterist movement had anywhere near the stature and public profile of Boesak. He was therefore invited to speak at the congress.

Saloojee further argued that the TASC congress should be used for a call for the formation of a broad front, and not just for the revival of the TIC. Other TASC leaders were undecided. On the one hand, 'Boesak's call opened up the possibility of launching some kind of a national front to fight the tricameral parliament. Because obviously the tricameral thing didn't just affect Indians. I mean the coloured community was involved, and people were looking at black local authorities.'[53] On the other hand it was still unclear whether sufficient Charterist organisation existed to provide the basis for a front. No decision was made, even when TASC and NIC activists met for a planning meeting in mid-January or during 'furious consultations' over the following days. Even on the very eve of the congress – on the evening of Friday 22 January – there was no agreement as to what precisely should be called for. The younger TASC activists, including Momoniat and Moosa, were opposed to Saloojee's suggestion. It was only late in the evening that NIC activists arrived from Durban and swung the argument in Saloojee's favour. They had already held discussions on the issue in Durban, including some with coloured Charterists from Cape Town, and had a better sense of the national picture. Furthermore, they agreed that Boesak should be invited to make the appeal, since he was seen as more attractive to 'moderates' than other possible speakers, such as SAAWU's Gqweta, and was unrivalled as an orator. 'Finally the younger ones within the Anti-SAIC Committee said: "all right, we will agree to this provided you go and pick him up at the airport ...', and you must provide him with lunch and you must tell him that one of the things that he must say or do is to call for a front against this thing."'[54] The following morning, Saloojee collected Boesak from the airport.

> On the way, we are talking about what the Labour Party did and all that. I did not want to sound like a commissar coming from some place and [saying]: 'Now you must toe the political line for us', and all that. And Allan actually said: 'You know, the Labour Party's doing this; we can't be indifferent to it ... This is not just a thing for the coloured people.' ... He saw the political issues very clearly. Then I just told him – you know, I was trying to be a little subtle – I said: 'We also met for the Anti-SAIC and thought it's a damned good idea, you know, if we try and call for a front of organisations and people against the tricameral system and all that.' He said: 'I'm going to be making a plea for that in my speech.' ... I took him home for lunch ..., and I saw that he had reasonably clear ideas about what should be done.[55]

Saloojee had good contacts in the South African and foreign media, and organised a strong press contingent to hear Boesak call that afternoon for the formation of a 'united front'.

Boesak's call for a united front may have been an unscheduled 'aside', as he later put it, or at least included almost at the last minute, but the enthusiastic response was not surprising. His call fell on ground that was not just fertile but already prepared. Support for a broad front had grown from frail beginnings in the aftermath of 1976–7, through steadily integrating networks and through setbacks and advances in organisation building, before burgeoning after the successful campaigns of 1981. Although Charterist leaders in different parts of the country may not have agreed over what such a body entailed, or precisely when it should be formed, by the end of 1982 most of them supported the idea of a nationwide front.

The South African government later attributed the idea of the UDF to the ANC, and the judge in the Delmas Treason Trial concluded without any direct evidence that 'the UDF was conceived in the councils of the ANC'.[56] Leading officials within the ANC had certainly been supportive of the idea of a Charterist-led front of anti-apartheid organisations inside the country since 1979, but the exiled ANC leadership's role was one of encouragement rather than direct instigation. Publicly, the ANC's Mac Maharaj said that 'The UDF is not a creation of the African National

Congress'[57] – but, a sceptic might respond, he would say that, wouldn't he? Privately, Maharaj was apparently taken by surprise when he heard that a front had been proposed at the TASC congress.[58]

While members of the ANC underground were central to the idea of a front, the relationship between them and the ANC in exile was not simply one of subordination. It was instead, in Pravin Gordhan's words, 'more a question of reporting than receiving'.[59] The decision to call for a front at the TASC congress was only taken after three weeks of intense debate on the very eve of the congress. In the end, the proposal to launch a front 'was done almost by accident', as Momoniat puts it.[60]

·······························

Chapter Three

'The Freedom Breeze': The Formation of the UDF, January–August 1983

THE TRANSVAAL ANTI-SAIC CONFERENCE

Allan Boesak addressed the Transvaal Anti-SAIC Committee congress in January 1983 with his usual eloquence and passion. 'He made a truly remarkable speech …, he moved people in a deep way,' commented Cas Saloojee; 'he just created one helluva sensation'.[1] In his speech Boesak discussed the government's constitutional proposals, concluding that 'now, all of a sudden, the government's problems have become our problems. Apartheid's crisis has become our crisis.' He urged people to say 'no' to apartheid: 'This is the politics of refusal, and it is the only dignified response black people can give in this situation.' He continued: 'In order to do this we need a united front…'.[2] It was a brief reference in the middle of his speech, but it was enough.

TASC leaders proposed that a commission should be formed to look into the feasibility of such a front. It would report back to the conference the next day. About 25 selected activists, mostly from coloured or Indian areas, took part in this commission. It began its meeting at about 9 o'clock that evening. Discussion was not always calm, with Cape Town activists complaining that they had not been informed about the proposal beforehand. But eventually, in the small hours of the morning, agreement was reached on two key issues: the general form of the front, and the process of actually forming it.[3]

The front would be loosely constituted as a broad front. It would not be for political organisations only, but would seek to involve other organisations as long as they accepted a non-racial, non-collaborationist approach. It would not commit itself to the Freedom Charter (so as to avoid too explicit an association with the ANC). The front would be organised on a regional and essentially federal basis. The choice of a primarily regional rather than racial basis reflected a shift in thinking since the 1950s, in part because racially organised opposition would be falling into the government's trap; as one speaker put it, 'rather, let's change the rules of the game'.[4] It also reflected the existing pattern of regionally based organisation in the country, and members of the commission thought that it would enable the front to 'reach out to people on the ground' more effectively.

The commission issued a statement, drafted overnight by Saloojee (who chaired the meeting) and lawyer Zac Yacoob of the Natal Indian Congress (NIC).[5] The 'broad principles' on which the new front would be constituted were:

- A belief in democracy.
- An unshakeable belief in the creation of a non-racial, unitary state in South Africa undiluted by racial or ethnic considerations as formulated in the bantustan policy.
- An adherence to the need for unity in struggle through which all democrats, regardless of race, religion or colour, shall take part.
- A recognition of the necessity to work in consultation with, and reflect accurately the demands of, democratic people wherever they may be in progressive worker, community and student organisations.[6]

The statement did not present a vision of the future comparable to that in the Freedom Charter but simply set out a very general critique of the state's reforms and some similarly general principles which participants in the front should subscribe to. But the statement did contain principles which would drive away some sections of the extra-parliamentary opposition. The explicit commitment to a non-racialism that accommodated white democrats would deter groups within the BC tradition, and the absence of any explicitly anti-capitalist principle would offend socialist, anti-nationalist groups.

A steering committee was formed to take the process further. It comprised representatives from organisations that could immediately commit themselves to the front: the TASC itself, the NIC and the Release Mandela Committee. This ensured that the Natal and Transvaal were represented. The Western Cape was represented by 'contact persons', because the organisations present felt that they had no mandate to commit themselves. The Eastern Cape and Border regions were not represented. Most of the steering committee's initial members were older Charterist leaders, although the actual organisational work was done by younger activists, who became *de facto* members of the committee. They included Valli Moosa from Johannesburg, Saleem Badat and Trevor Manuel from Cape Town, and Yunus Mahomed from Durban. Moosa became a *de facto* full-time organiser.

One outstanding question remained: what was the front to be called? Some participants in the commission had proposed the name National Democratic Front (NDF), which was the name of a communist-led front against dictatorship in the Philippines.[7] Activists also identified with fronts in Nicaragua and elsewhere which called themselves 'national' fronts. But Western Cape activists opposed this suggestion because of the ideological significance of the name. A national front implied a national struggle, whereas the idea of the united front drew on a tradition which saw the struggle in terms of class as well. Cape Town activists were wary of any initiative that smacked of populism or nationalism.

The debate was resolved almost accidentally. Saloojee thought that the commis-sion had chosen the name NDF for the time being, and the typed draft of the state-ment referred to the 'national democratic front' and NDF – although some of the references to the NDF were scratched out, and UDF written in by hand instead! When Saloojee addressed the meeting the next day, he used, he says, 'the words "united democratic front" to describe the movement – united and hopefully very democratic'. The press reported the call as being for a United Democratic Front, and the name stuck. A retyped version of the commission's statement refers to the UDF only.[8] 'In the confusion, the name "united" instead of "national" took hold'.[9]

CONSULTATION AND PREPARATION

The brief of the steering committee was to maintain inter-regional co-ordination whilst, in the separate regions, organisations and individuals were canvassed and regional UDF structures formed. But little progress was made during February and early March. At the root of the problem was the close relationship between the unit-ed front initiative and the revival of the Transvaal Indian Congress (TIC). Both ini-tiatives had been called for at the January conference, and there was a large overlap between the personnel associated with them. Opposition was strongest in Cape Town, where the proposed front was denounced variously as a 'liberal' or 'Indian' initiative. But it was not only the socialist intellectuals of the Western Cape who were critical or wary. Many Charterists elsewhere shared their concern over 'ethnic' organisation, whilst many African activists saw the initiatives as primarily or solely a matter for Indian organisations.

The purpose of reviving the TIC was to recreate an overt Charterist movement in Indian areas. It would be, as Molefe later said, 'an organisation that the Indian com-munity would find it easy to associate with, something they could call their own', at the same time as providing links to the African-based mainstream of the Charterist movement.[10] But any approach that involved a recognition of some specific 'Indian-ness' risked legitimising apartheid-style distinctions. Terror Lekota later stated that 'you cannot just declare non-racialism; you must build it'.[11] But could non-racialism be built through a multiracial approach?[12]

Criticism of the TIC as 'ethnic' and 'retrogressive', and a suspicion that the UDF would be 'a conglomerate of ethnically-orientated groups' led to AZAPO and Unity Movement-inspired groups in the Western Cape opposing both initiatives. Their arguments made many waverers wary. As the front initiative seemed to flag, the steering committee decided to send Moosa around the country to allay suspicions about the TIC and UDF. Moosa's first stop was Durban, where he found the NIC still enthusiastic about the proposed front. In East London he had a meeting with Sisa Njikelana of the trade union SAAWU, who also seemed keen. Moosa then flew to Cape Town where the real challenge lay. He later recalled: 'The Cape Town people wanted to hear nothing ... absolutely nothing about the UDF.' Moosa, joined by Yunus Mahomed from Durban, finally persuaded a group of Cape Town activists to participate – provided the front was called the UDF and the national launch was held in Cape Town.[13]

The trip laid to rest many fears about the TIC and UDF, finally resolved the question of the prospective front's name, and thus revived the whole initiative. In the Transvaal, Natal and Western Cape, committees were established to consult with organisations in the region, prepare for a regional conference, and draft a constitution. In May the Natal UDF region was launched and a Regional Executive Committee elected in Durban. The Transvaal region followed in June, although the regional leadership was formally elected later. The Western Cape was finally launched in late July.

The formation of regional UDF structures resulted in the national steering committee evolving into an 'Interim National Committee'. Whereas the old committee comprised representatives of the few organisations committed from the outset, the new committee consisted of delegates from the UDF regions. The new members included Transvaal activists Molefe and Chikane, and the Western Cape activist Andrew Boraine, a former president of the predominantly white National Union of South African Students (NUSAS). The new committee thus comprised a wider range of activists – including more African activists and a white activist – than the old steering committee.[14]

The Interim National Committee held a crucial two-day planning meeting in Johannesburg at the end of July. They were joined by two veteran ANC leaders – Albertina Sisulu, wife of the jailed Walter Sisulu, and Mewa Ramgobin from Durban – both of whom had been banned by the state until the end of June, and by former Robben Islander Steve Tshwete from the Border region. The key question facing the committee was when to launch the UDF nationally. The committee worried that they were not yet ready, with only three regions formed (including the Transvaal, which still had no elected leadership). But the government was expected to introduce the new constitutional legislation into parliament in August. Not only was nationally co-ordinated opposition deemed to be urgent but an August launch would register timely defiance. Furthermore, AZAPO and other anti-Charterist groups had just formed a co-ordinating body, the National Forum, challenging the Charterists for the leading role in extra-parliamentary politics. The committee therefore decided to launch the UDF nationally on 20 August.[15]

As this launch date was just three weeks away a whole set of other issues needed to be resolved. After much debate, the committee agreed on the slogan 'UDF Unites, Apartheid Divides', the logo of a procession of people against an outline map of South Africa, and the colours yellow, red and black – different colours from the ANC's green, black and gold.

The July meeting discussed what kind of document the UDF would adopt. The regions had followed the example set at the January conference of adopting Declarations which just stated basic principles and a commitment to collective opposition to the state's reforms. The national UDF, it was felt, should adopt a Declaration pulled together out of the regional ones. But the meeting recognised that such general Declarations did not adequately specify the criteria for affiliation. The UDF may have been seen as promoting unity against apartheid but there were limits as to how far unity should stretch. Acceptance of the Declaration was not sufficient. The meeting agreed that three categories of organisation would be excluded: those that participated in bantustan state structures because, it was argued, the UDF was committed to a unitary South Africa; those that participated in central or local government because such institutions were not based on the will of the people; and those that wilfully broke the sports or cultural boycotts because these boycotts were aimed at promoting a non-racial South Africa. There was unqualified acceptance of the inclusion of 'white democrats', though the Progressive Federal Party would not be allowed to affiliate because it participated in parliament. Inkatha posed the most difficult problem. After long discussion it was agreed that Inkatha would not be invited, and the matter would be reconsidered if it applied to affiliate. On the other hand, the Zion Christian Church, the Federation of South African Trade Unions (FOSATU) and non-racial sports bodies would all be approached.[16]

The committee also had to discuss who would be elected into leadership positions. The choices were governed by one overriding concern, that the UDF's national officials be predominantly African. This was deemed desirable both in principle and to counter the widespread perception that the front was dominated by Indian and coloured organisations.[17] Finding willing candidates was far from easy, however; as Mahomed recalls, 'you had to spend a lot of time convincing people they should do it, not like today with big fights for [official leadership] positions.'[18]

There was broad support for Popo Molefe being appointed as general secretary, although Molefe himself later said that he had been reluctant: 'I felt I did not have the necessary experience to handle that kind of job … it was just too big a job for me.'[19] The post of publicity secretary was less readily filled. Lekota's name was put forward but opposed by Natal.[20] Lekota had kept a low profile since returning from Robben Island in 1982, and not everyone was aware of his conversion from BC to the ANC. There were, however, no other obvious candidates. The most controversial post was the presidency. The Natal and Transvaal regions nominated Albertina Sisulu. But the Western Cape objected, apparently because of tensions between Charterist women's organisations in the Cape and Transvaal. They instead proposed ANC veteran Oscar Mpetha. The issue was not resolved, and debate continued over the following weeks. 'We used to say it was like the Currie Cup,' recalls Momoniat, comparing the debate to South Africa's premier inter-provincial sporting competition.[21]

Zac Yacoob was appointed interim publicity secretary, to co-ordinate the production of posters, stickers and pamphlets issued under the title of *UDF News*. Two weeks later Yacoob claimed that over 400 000 copies of *UDF News* had been distributed countrywide, reaching over one million readers! He added that over 15 000 stickers and over 5000 posters had been distributed.[22] This media blitz was made possible by fund-raising led by Mewa Ramgobin and Saloojee. Ramgobin recalls that about R100 000 was raised for the national launch, mostly in small contributions from Indian businessmen and professionals in Natal.[23]

The embryonic UDF leadership had to move fast to organise the national launch for 20 August. The launch was to involve two elements: first a conference of delegates, and second a public rally. The first stages of logistical planning were undertaken by Western Cape activists.[24] Then in mid-August Transvaal and Natal activists arrived in Cape Town to form, with some of the Western Cape leaders, an Advanced Planning Committee. The committee included already prominent participants such as Yacoob, Molefe, Moosa, Lekota and Gumede, together with Manuel and other Cape Town activists, and the recently unbanned Ramgobin and Gordhan. They were assisted by 'a few other people who were not standing in the limelight',[25] such as a former Soweto student who had recently returned from a spell on Robben Island, Khehla Shubane.

One set of preparations concerned the logistics of the conference and the rally. A venue was organised: the Rocklands Community Centre in Mitchell's Plain, a coloured settlement on the Cape Flats. Mitchell's Plain was chosen to emphasise the UDF's appeal for the support of coloured South Africans. Accommodation and catering were arranged for the delegates to the conference – increasingly difficult tasks as the estimated number of delegates and observers rose from just 250 to 2000. People would sleep in halls, churches and mosques, and hundreds of mattresses were hired. The rally was publicised through the distribution of copies of *UDF News* and announcements in churches and mosques. Buses were hired, and 160 marshals were organised. Banners were painted by a group of students at the NUSAS head office.[26]

This was all done amidst growing police harassment though not outright repression. The police seized, but later released, 40 000 copies of *UDF News* at a roadblock in Paarl. They patrolled the area around the NUSAS office, stopping and searching students. And they printed bogus pamphlets announcing that the launch had been cancelled. Fearing that delegates would be stopped and harassed on the road to Cape Town, the launch organisers set up a head office in a house in Mitchell's Plain under the general supervison of the banned Cape Town activist Johnny Issel. Delegates would phone the office when they left their home towns, and at points on their journey, so that their movements and any delays could be monitored.

A second set of preparations concerned sorting out the various issues left outstanding after the July meeting. The Advanced Planning Committee finalised a Declaration and Working Principles (in place of a constitution), and reached agreement on a set of national officials. These would be formally agreed to at the conference on the Saturday morning, but the leadership held a caucus meeting beforehand so as to reach agreement and not expose disagreements in public.

The Declaration proclaimed a common opposition to the Tricameral Parliament and Koornhof Bills. Otherwise, as Molefe later wrote, it 'goes no further than committing members to a non-racial, democratic and unitary South Africa, the particulars of which they are free to fill in for themselves'.[27] It was not a statement of either lofty ideals or far-reaching demands, as was the Freedom Charter, but a statement of common purpose:

We commit ourselves to uniting all our people wherever they may be, in the cities and countryside, the factories and mines, schools, colleges and universities, houses and sports fields, churches, mosques and temples, to fight for our freedom ... We pledge to stand together in this United Democratic Front and fight side by side against the government's constitutional proposals and the Koornhof Bills.[28]

The Working Principles made it quite clear that affiliates were to remain autonomous: 'All regional formations and member organisations shall have complete independence within the umbrella of the United Democratic Front, provided that actions and policies of members are not inconsistent with the policy of the UDF.'[29] The 'policy of the UDF' was later clarified to mean common opposition to the state's reforms. The autonomy of affiliates meant that a wide range of organisations could participate without fear of losing their separate identities, aims and tactics. As one observer wrote, 'If this was not the case, the front would collapse within a very short time because many organisations ... would not tolerate interference in their internal affairs.'[30]

The Working Principles structured the UDF as a federation of regional UDF structures – as had been agreed since the start of the year. The national UDF was controlled by the regions. The UDF's supreme decision-making body was its National General Council (NGC), which was supposed to meet at least annually and comprised regional delegations. The UDF's National Executive Committee (NEC) consisted of a handful of office-holders elected by the NGC and a battery of representatives sent directly by each region. Although these structures were clearly specified, the initial Working Principles were confusing in other respects. They referred, for example, not to affiliation but to 'membership', and to the UDF forming 'local branches'. This reflected the uncertainty among the UDF's founders themselves as to precisely what it was that they were forming, notwithstanding their avid consumption of literature from the ANC and elsewhere on different forms of organisation.[31]

The most controversial issue facing the Advanced Planning Committee was who should be elected as president of the front. Molefe recalls:

There was quite a heated debate on that issue. It was threatening to divide us even before we launched the United Front. And I think largely it was because we had not worked together nationally. We did not really know one another that much. And people were very sentimental about leadership coming from their own region.[32]

The Western Cape region would not accept Sisulu as sole president. 'We didn't want to put it to the vote,' Molefe says, 'because it was clear that it might have left gaping wounds.' Each region then put forward a nominee: Sisulu from the Transvaal, Mpetha from the Western Cape, and Gumede from Natal.

So we saw therefore the 'troika', the presidency of three, as necessary to allow for a process of unity and mutual trust to develop. That is why the UDF ended up with three presidents – Albertina Sisulu, Oscar Mpetha and Archie Gumede. This was a serious division on which unanimity could not be reached. Thus, the election of three presidents was ultimately a compromise.[33]

Molefe and Lekota would be the national general secretary and publicity secretary respectively, and Saloojee and Ramgobin would serve as joint national treasurers. Each of the three constituted regions nominated two national vice-presidents and two further NEC members.

This composition reflected a conscious concern to project a leadership which was both non-racial and acknowledged the 'primacy of African leadership' (as Molefe put it). The three presidents and both secretaries were all African. The NEC as a whole consisted of twelve African, five coloured, seven Indian and one white South African. The national and regional secretaries were 1970s activists, most of whom had come through Black Consciousness; most of the other NEC members (including the three presidents) were older Charterists from the 1950s or 1960s. Every member of the NEC, with one possible exception, was a formal or informal member of the ANC political underground.[34] The association with the ANC was underscored by the Planning Committee's choice of veteran Charterist leaders from the 1950s as patrons for the front.

On the morning of Saturday 20 August about 1000 delegates and 500 observers, from over 500 organisations, gathered in the Rocklands Community Centre in Mitchell's Plain for the UDF's founding conference. The conference opened with Frank Chikane explaining why a broad front was needed. The UDF Declaration was approved, as were the Working Principles with one amendment. A delegation from the Border region, who had not been present in the pre-conference discussions, demanded the addition of what became known as the 'Border clause', or paragraph 3.4 of the Working Principles. This stipulated that 'The Front shall not purport to replace the accredited liberation movements of the people.' The choice of national leadership was approved, as were the suggested patrons – with the addition of Nelson Mandela and other jailed Charterist leaders. A message of support from Mandela was delivered to the conference by a delegate from the Free State, M.K. Malefane, the initiator of Maluti.[35]

The UDF's founding leadership also raised a concrete set of tasks. The list comprised, in full:

- To establish the United Democratic Front as the only representative front representing all sections of our people
- To popularise the UDF within and outside the country.
- Mobilise all organisations and communities into the UDF.
- Establish UDF branches throughout the country.
- Implement door-to-door campaigns throughout the country.
- Encourage the strengthening of all grassroots democratic organisations.
- Promote meaningful co-operation and united action across all communities and other barriers.

- Ensure democratic participation and consultation in all aspects of the campaign.

This was apparently what the Working Principles referred to as the Programme of Action, although it soon became clear that it did not serve this purpose, and a conference was held later in the year to draft a Programme of Action. But the list was telling in its emphasis on organisation building, on forging broad unity, and on its ambitions as being – or becoming – the only body representing all sections of the population. The official launch report, widely circulated within the country after the conference, repeated these general points, emphasising organisation building – to 'build and strengthen non-racial, democratic organisations as an alternative to apartheid itself' – and calling for campaigns around 'any aspect of apartheid that affects people's daily lives'.

Late on the Saturday afternoon the conference was forced to come to a close, and the doors of the community centre were opened to allow people in for the public rally. Four or five thousand people had been expected; later estimates of how many people actually attended varied from six to fifteen thousand, with the UDF itself claiming twelve thousand. The rally was formally opened by a veteran ANC activist, Frances Baard. She reminded the audience of a speech made in Cape Town, over twenty years before, by the British Prime Minister Harold Macmillan, about the wind of change sweeping across Africa. In 1983, Frances Baard continued, you could smell the 'freedom air' sweeping through South Africa. 'The freedom breeze is going throughout the whole of South Africa and we are going to be free.'

Successive speeches at the rally celebrated the Charterist tradition and drew on Charterist symbolism. Frank Chikane and veteran white activist Helen Joseph both compared the occasion to the 1955 Congress of the People. Baard called for the release of 'our leaders' Mandela and the other prisoners on the Island. NIC president George Sewpersadh proclaimed: 'The ideals of the Freedom Charter will be pursued by the United Democratic Front ... We will continue with the struggle until our leaders like Nelson Mandela are free to govern this country.' Joseph quoted from the Freedom Charter: 'Shoulder to shoulder, sparing nothing of our strength and courage until we have won our liberty.'

But, key speakers insisted, the UDF was not a Charterist front. Gumede said that the UDF was

> composed of different organisations which do not agree in all respects with each other's points of view, but we are all agreed that apartheid must be banished from the face of South Africa. It is a front at this stage which is established with the sole purpose of struggling against the constitutional bills and the Koornhof Act [*sic*] which are intended to entrench apartheid in our society. The individual organisations of this front retain their identity *in toto* but they are determined to co-operate one with another in the specific issue of fighting and struggling against the Constitutional Bills and the Koornhof Bill.

The UDF's immediate concerns with the state's reforms were clearly linked to the longer and broader struggle, as Chikane recognised:

> We reject the constitutional proposals and the Koornhof Bills because these will only serve to entrench the apartheid system, [to] concretize the deprivation of African people of their birthright, [and to co-opt] the so-called coloureds and Indians as junior partners in perpetrating the evils of apartheid … And I want to call upon all peace-loving people in South Africa to put [their] hands together, to walk side by side, to fight against the implementation of these reform proposals, so that we can destroy the system and put up a government by the people, where [the] people shall govern according to their will.

A similar point was made in the final speech of the day, by Allan Boesak: 'We are here to say that what we are working for is one, undivided South Africa that shall belong to all of its people, an open democracy from which no single South African shall be excluded, a society in which the human dignity of all its people shall be respected.' This vision of a democratic society was, of course, a far cry from the government's proposed new constitutional dispensation.

Boesak provided the main speech at the UDF launch. Born in 1946, Boesak had grown up in poverty before becoming a church minister. In the early 1970s he studied abroad, returning in 1976 to the post of student chaplain at the highly politicised University of the Western Cape. His political profile rose fast, fuelled by his massive output of politically engaged sermons and writings and his attempts to unite the black Reformed churches. His election as president of the international World Alliance of Reformed Churches in August 1982 confirmed his stature.

But Boesak's appeal was not due to any office he held, or organisation he led, but was instead the direct result of his immensely powerful oratory. According to one press report:

> As an orator, Dr Boesak plays on his audience like a violin virtuoso on a Stradivarius. He can raise his audience to heights of outrage with carefully phrased and beautifully articulated passion. Then he can coarsen his accent and introduce humour so the audience can chuckle and relax awhile before Dr Boesak gathers momentum to sweep them up into another crescendo of high oratory.[36]

In terms of both style and content, Boesak closely resembled the American civil rights leader, Martin Luther King. Both King and Boesak based their speeches upon the theme of rights. At the UDF launch, Boesak spoke of the 'God-given rights' of all South Africans, 'rights which are neither conferred by nor derived from the state'. The struggle was a struggle for these rights, for justice and peace.

The rally enthused people. But, as Archie Gumede had said, there must be more than just sloganeering. There would have to be 'sweat, labour and careful thought and careful action. You must be aware that the system has many ways of provoking people into rash actions and that is one of the things that all of you must guard against ... We must avoid adventurism, and we must act conscientiously and with determination until we overcome.' The day after the national launch, the new national leadership met to evaluate the launch. They felt that it was still not quite clear what the UDF was to do, and indeed that 'there was no clear understanding of the concept of a front'. The Declaration and Working Principles needed to be discussed more fully, and more time had to be spent on formulating a programme of action.

AFFILIATES AND ABSENTEES

The launch was attended by delegates of 565 organisations, 400 of which were already affiliates at the regional level, whilst almost all the others were to affiliate thereafter. These organisations comprised an astonishingly diverse group in geographical and social terms. What united them was more than their common opposition to the state's reforms: with a few exceptions, all were led by activists who considered themselves supporters or even members of the ANC.

The largest number of participating organisations came from the Western Cape, although this was somewhat misleading as 235 of them were in fact branches of Inter-Church Youth. Leaving these aside, there were almost the same number of organisations from each of the three constituted UDF regions – Transvaal, Natal and Western Cape. There were also a handful of organisations from the Eastern Cape, Orange Free State, the Cape's West Coast, and Southern Cape, together with a delegation from the Border region.

The UDF itself distinguished its affiliates in terms of 'sectors': students, youth, civics, women, religious, political and other. The student organisations consisted of 16 branches of AZASO, five of NUSAS, and 2 others in higher educational institutions, and 24 branches of COSAS, including a surprising 18 in the Western Cape. The youth organisations included recently formed youth congresses in places like Soweto, Atteridgeville and Alexandra in the PWV, together with 35 branches of the Cape Youth Congress. The worker sector comprised a disappointingly small number of trade unions, including SAAWU, the General and Allied Workers' Union (GAWU) and the smaller Charterist unions, the BC-orientated Council of Unions of South Africa (CUSA) and the Commercial, Catering and Allied Workers' Union.

The civic sector was made up of 82 civic organisations. Of these 29 were in the Transvaal. From Cape Town there were 21 affiliates of the Cape Areas Housing Action Committee (CAHAC) in coloured areas, and 6 zones of the Western Cape Civic Association in African townships. There were 24 civic organisations from Natal, and 2 from Port Elizabeth. There were 19 branches of the United Women's Organisation, as well as the rival Women's Front, from the Western Cape, and a further 12 women's organisations from other regions. The 'political' sector comprised organisations like the TIC, NIC and RMC as well as sub-regional UDF structures in different parts of the Western Cape and Natal. The remaining organisations, lumped into the 'other' sector, included the newspaper *Grassroots* and other alternative media organisations, detainee action groups and health-related groups.

Overall, there were more organisations from coloured and Indian areas, or with predominantly coloured and Indian members, than predominantly African organisations (although some of the African organisations had much larger membership). Well over half the youth organisations – excluding Inter-Church Youth – were based in coloured and Indian areas, as were two-thirds of the civic organisations. A small number of organisations operated in primarily white constituencies, such as NUSAS among white students. The range of organisations present at the UDF's launch thus broadly reflected the Front's concern, first and foremost, with the prospective Tricameral Parliament and the threatened co-option of coloured and Indian South Africans into support for apartheid.

The participation of white democrats had ceased to be a major issue within Charterist politics between 1981 and 1983, although it continued to mark a divide between the Charterist and BC movements.[37] The UDF's launch was addressed by Helen Joseph, who was appointed as a patron of the Front along with Beyers Naudé of the South African Council of Churches, and the jailed Congress activist Denis Goldberg. Boesak directly addressed 'the question of whites and blacks working together' in his speech at the launch. He referred to critics who said that 'white people cannot play a meaningful role in the struggle for justice in this country because they are always, by definition, the oppressor'. Boesak said that he understood why people felt this way.

> But it is not true that apartheid has the support of all white people. There are those who have struggled with us, who have gone to jail, who have been tortured and banned. There are those who have died in the struggle for justice. And we must not allow our anger for apartheid to become the basis for blind hatred for *all* white people. Let us not build our struggle upon hatred, bitterness and a desire for revenge. Let us even now seek to lay the foundation for reconciliation between white and black in this country by working together, praying together, struggling together for justice. No, the nature and quality of our struggle for liberation cannot be determined by the colour of one's skin, but rather by the quality of one's commitment to justice, peace and human liberation.[38]

Boesak echoed the Freedom Charter, declaring that 'South Africa belongs to all its people'. This was a clear statement of an 'inclusive South African nationalism', of a struggle for democratic rights.

Almost all the organisations came from the metropolitan areas of the PWV, Durban and Cape Town, with a smattering of organisations from Bloemfontein, Port Elizabeth and Pietermaritzburg. Fewer than 50 – or one in ten – of the organisations came from outside the metropolitan areas, with 16 of these from three Boland towns. In all, there were bodies present from fewer than 20 of the 400 or so non-metropolitan towns around the country, and none based primarily in rural areas.

It is difficult to categorise these organisations in terms of social class. Some – like the trade unions, and many of the civic organisations – organised among unambiguously working-class groups. But a high proportion of the bodies present at the launch organised among a relatively educated elite. This was most clearly the case with AZASO or NUSAS branches at universities. Many AZASO members may have come from working-class families, but university education was a passport to rapid upward social mobility. Similarly, it seems that most leading members of organisations based in coloured and Indian areas had some higher education. While further research is needed into the social bases of different organisations at that time, it seems that the UDF's affiliates in 1983 can be understood best as organisations dominated by a relatively highly educated, upwardly mobile, petty bourgeoisie – with striking exceptions. The social basis of many UDF affiliates was to broaden during the 1980s, and many organisations were formed in poorer parts of the country.

The organisations varied considerably in size. The unions, whilst small in comparison with some of the absent independent unions, had by far the largest membership. A handful of organisations – mostly student organisations – had extensive memberships. But most were little more than groups of activists. Most of the youth groups, for example, had between ten and a hundred members. Some of them, especially the civics, were able to mobilise large numbers of people around particular issues and enjoyed considerable popular support but had few regular formal members.

The UDF had therefore a long way to go before it could achieve its ambition, stated in its Declaration, of 'uniting all our people wherever they may be, in the cities and countryside ...' But in drawing together a large number of organisations it had made a strong beginning. The absence of bodies from many parts of the country was primarily the result of the character of organisation in these areas at the time. In most towns, let alone rural areas, there were no civic, student or youth groups. The only organisations were linked to churches, to sport, or to social and cultural activity; in almost all cases these eschewed politics altogether and the UDF aspired but failed to unite their members. The bodies that attended the launch were all concerned with politics, indirectly if not directly. There were very few political or quasi-political organisations that chose not to affiliate – except for those that aligned with non-Charterist movements or sought to remain emphatically non-aligned.

Three major political movements stood outside the UDF: the independent trade union movement, AZAPO and its allies in the National Forum, and Inkatha. The first and last of these were mass-based, whilst the other had an influence far beyond its meagre size. These movements warrant individual examination.

TRADE UNIONS

The emergence of the independent trade union movement was one of the important political developments of the 1970s. From small beginnings, and despite intermittent state repression, the movement had grown rapidly. The major grouping of independent trade unions, the Federation of South African Trade Unions (FOSATU), had under 17 000 members in 1980. This grew to 120 000 members in 1984, concentrated in southern Natal and the PWV. These unions' membership was still a small percentage of the workforce but they represented by far the largest organised section of the African working class. The working class was not just important in terms of numbers, but also symbolically, since most anti-apartheid activists inside the country professed an anti-capitalist ideology.

The independent trade union movement comprised three groups of unions: industrial unions affiliated to FOSATU; the much weaker industrial unions affiliated to the BC-orientated CUSA; and a heterogeneous group of mostly general unions with strong historical or current links to the ANC. This last group included the Western Province General Workers' Union (GWU) and Food and Canning Workers' Union, the East London-based SAAWU and the Johannesburg-based GAWU. In the early 1980s these groupings held a series of unsuccessful unity talks. One of the stumbling blocks was the difference in their views on political alliances.

Some of the unions in the third group (SAAWU, GAWU) were integrally involved in the emerging Charterist networks of the early 1980s, and their affiliation to the UDF was never in doubt. Indeed, many national and Transvaal UDF leaders had worked for GAWU at one time or another. On the other hand, CUSA affiliated nominally to both the UDF and the rival National Forum. The key question was the UDF's relationship with FOSATU and the Western Cape-based unions in the third group – the General Workers' Union and the Food and Canning Workers' Union.

The UDF's approach to the unions varied between regions. In Natal the NIC-dominated UDF leadership largely overlooked the African working class. In the Transvaal, the TASC–TIC leadership's influence was tempered by African activists based primarily in Soweto, but most of the latter emphasised the need to organise the African working class through the 'community' rather than the workplace. In the two regions where FOSATU unions were strongest, therefore, the UDF initially made little effort to woo them. This attitude was informed by Charterists' assessment of the ideological and political position of the FOSATU unions as being 'workerist'.

Workerism involved an insistence on working-class leadership, the advocacy of socialist ideals and opposition to nationalist or national democratic struggles, and a wariness of participation in struggles outside the workplace. For many unionists this reflected a strategic assessment of the practical risks of taking on overtly political struggles against the state, or of the organisational problems with a membership which included supporters of Inkatha in Natal and the coloured Labour Party in the Eastern Cape. For other unionists workerism was derived from an ideological hostility to nationalism and hence the ANC, or to the perceived Stalinism of SACP activists with influence in the ANC. Some held the syndicalist view that the socialist struggle needed to be led by workplace-based organisation.

It was only in the Western Cape that the nascent UDF leadership actively sought the unions' support in early 1983. They were encouraged by the historically close links between the locally based General Workers' Union and the Food and Canning Workers' Union and the ANC. More importantly, these unions offered unique access to the coloured and African working class, which was especially important in the Cape. Access to coloured workers was needed in order to contest the Labour Party's appeal in the struggle over the Tricameral Parliament. Access to African workers was needed to demonstrate the UDF's non-racial and socialist credentials. After wavering, the independent unions decided against affiliating to the new front.

The unions put forward three major arguments against affiliation. Firstly, given that there were strong critics of Charterism within the unions, affiliation might lead to splits within unions and a breakdown in the unions' unity talks. Secondly, some unionists were unhappy with the decision-making structures of the Front, which gave equal weight to organisations comprising activists only and those which, like the trade unions, were mass-based. Thirdly, many unionists argued that the multi-class character of the Front and many of its affiliates would lead to the diminution of workers' influence on decisions, whatever the rhetoric of 'working-class leadership'.[39] These last two arguments were certainly valid, but it was not clear whether they constituted objections to affiliation. The working class had an interest in a multi-class alliance against disfranchisement, and affiliation to the UDF did not mean a loss of autonomy, even with regard to the Front's struggles against specific state reforms.

It would seem that the primary objection to affiliation among the leaders of these Western Cape unions and FOSATU was political. The unionists were committed to socialist goals and suspicious of nationalist politics. Their priority was to build up specifically working-class organisation, advance the class struggle, and thereby nurture a specifically working-class consciousness that would underpin a socialist movement in society as a whole. The ANC was seen as opposed to this project, and the UDF was guilty by association. The unions might co-operate with the UDF, but should preserve themselves as unblemished vessels of the socialist project.

The consequence of all this was that when the UDF's National Interim Committee met at the end of July, none of the three constituted regions had any major union affiliates. The Committee recognised, somewhat belatedly, that they needed to explain the UDF to the unions. Lekota was delegated to approach FOSATU, as well as to ensure that the East London-based SAAWU sent Gqweta and other prominent leaders to the UDF's national launch; Gqweta was to be given the role of the workers' speaker at the launch rally.[40]

Unfortunately, conflict in the Ciskei prevented Gqweta and the SAAWU leaders from attending the UDF launch, and GAWU's Samson Ndou had to fill in. Changing society, he said, was the responsibility of workers. 'The struggle of the working class will have to go beyond the factory gates,' he exhorted, emphasising that workers go home at the end of the day and face problems of housing and transport, whilst their children suffer inadequate and racist education. Workers, he concluded, must join with other people to overthrow exploitation and oppression. One of the conference resolutions also focused on 'workers', concluding with commitments

to work for a South Africa in which the oppression and exploitation of workers will cease to exist, to encourage the building of democratic trade unions, to oppose the migrant labour system ..., [and] to strengthen the unity between genuine democratic trade unions and all patriotic and freedom-loving people in the struggle for political rights for all'.[41]

In September UDF leaders held meetings with FOSATU, as well as with some of the smaller unions. Although FOSATU had already decided to run its own separate educational campaign against the constitutional reforms, the UDF and FOSATU agreed to co-operate. This co-operation was soon manifest when some FOSATU and other unions joined with the UDF and UDF affiliates in an *ad hoc* committee to co-ordinate protests against the banning of SAAWU, a UDF-affiliated union, in the Ciskei. In October FOSATU held an internal seminar on the issue of affiliation to the UDF, which formally recommended against affiliation 'because of the different class interests'. FOSATU's central committee confirmed this decision the next day. But the discussion over affiliation was said to have been 'very thought provoking', and there clearly needed to be further thinking about the unions' relationship with political organisations, especially at the local level.[42]

The non-affiliation of the major independent unions cost the UDF access to a large and organised constituency. In June one UDF meeting was told that 'a lot of workers have very little knowledge of [the] UDF and are scared because of it'. The UDF national leadership continued to seek better relationships with the unions. It set up a Labour Unit, comprising the former trade unionists and Robben Island prisoners Billy Nair and Curnick Ndlovu, who were to play an important role in improving relationships between the UDF and the unions.[43]

INKATHA

The UDF faced a very different problem with respect to Inkatha, the other mass-based black political movement in South Africa. Inkatha was emphatically opposed to the constitutional reforms but at the same time participated in bantustan state structures and from 1979 was hostile to the ANC in exile. To complicate matters still further, Inkatha had support in some Natal townships, where its advocacy of 'tradition', its African (and later Zulu) nationalism, and its use of anti-Indian rhetoric exacerbated the UDF's difficulties in expanding its own support base.[44]

The UDF's attitude to Inkatha was ambiguous. On the one hand, the UDF brought together different groups committed to a strategy of boycotting state institutions: apart from the NIC and their counterparts in the Transvaal, these included former BC activists in the Transvaal, activists influenced by the Unity Movement tradition in the Western Cape, and uncompromising participants in the liberation struggle from the Border and Eastern Cape. In July 1983 the UDF's pre-launch leadership drafted a policy on affiliation which seemed to preclude organisations from operating in bantustan structures because, it argued, the UDF was committed to a unitary South Africa. And Chikane said at the UDF's national launch that the UDF would 'exclude those who work within the system'.[45]

At the same time, however, some UDF leaders sought to avoid any confrontation with Inkatha, and discouraged direct verbal attacks on it. The July 1983 meeting did not rule out Inkatha's affiliation but deferred the issue, hoping that Inkatha would not apply! There was no explicit criticism of Inkatha at the UDF's national launch, and a resolution on the bantustans stopped short of an outright rejection of working within bantustan structures. Molefe later explained that, at least until the end of October 1983, the UDF refrained from public attacks on Inkatha so as not to 'antagonise the thousands of honest Inkatha supporters who genuinely wanted change' and to avoid being distracted from its primary task of opposing the state's reforms.[46]

In turn Inkatha's attitude to the UDF was also ambiguous. Mangosuthu Buthelezi, Inkatha's president and the KwaZulu Chief Minister, was very hostile to the NIC leaders, whom he blamed for the breakdown of his relationship with the ANC in exile in 1979, and whose anti-SAIC campaigns he saw as a challenge to his preferred entryist approach to opposition politics. But it was also clear that there was more to the UDF than just the NIC. Furthermore, Inkatha's political position was in flux as a result of the Labour Party's decision to participate in the new constitutional dispensation. Previously Inkatha and the Labour Party had been allies in the South African Black Alliance, but Inkatha firmly rejected the constitutional reforms and the Labour Party's decision, and the Alliance collapsed.[47]

In January 1983, smarting from what he took as a personal rejection by the Labour Party, Buthelezi welcomed the proposal to form a united front, claiming he had 'always stood for black unity in spite of minor differences between us'. By August he was more ambivalent, wary of the UDF's allegiance to the ANC. He criticised the UDF for cold-shouldering him but seemed to offer the prospect of coming to some kind of an agreement. In September he repeated a cautious welcome for the UDF.[48] From Inkatha's point of view, an agreement with the UDF would have legitimised Inkatha's position of opposing the constitutional reforms – including, albeit inconsistently, the Black Local Authorities – whilst participating in the bantustan state structures, and would have strengthened Inkatha's bargaining position *vis-à-vis* the state and limited the scope for its being undermined from a more 'radical' position within its home region of Natal–KwaZulu.

Events in Natal undermined, however, the prospect of any such agreement. In August the South African government announced that several Durban townships would be incorporated into the KwaZulu bantustan, provoking strong opposition from local civic leaders. In October supporters of Inkatha and incorporation attacked and killed four opponents in Lamontville. Days later, Inkatha supporters killed five students and injured over a hundred at the University of Zululand at Ngoye, where the UDF's affiliate AZASO had strong support.[49]

The UDF's NEC had briefly discussed the incorporation issue in September; overwhelmed by more pressing issues, it did nothing. But the Ngoye massacre was different. Together with AZASO and AZAPO, the UDF held a joint press conference in Johannesburg. The massacre was strongly condemned, Inkatha was denounced for siding with 'the oppressor', and Buthelezi was described as a 'traitor' and 'collaborator'. Buthelezi, a speaker warned, would be 'destroyed' with the rest of the bantustan system. The Transvaal UDF Media Committee issued a pamphlet which accused Inkatha of collaboration with the apartheid system.[50]

Soon after this Buthelezi wrote to UDF co-president Archie Gumede, the first in a long exchange of letters between the two senior Zulu-speaking leaders that would continue through the 1980s. Buthelezi invited the UDF leadership to address the

KwaZulu Legislative Assembly, 'to explore with us the extent to which the goals we have in common demand a synchronising of Black strategies and tactics'. Denouncing the proposed constitutional reforms, Buthelezi emphasised the importance of 'African brotherhood' and the need 'to establish a united Black response'. Echoing the UDF's own approach, Buthelezi proposed 'burying some of our differences and co-operating in the substantial area of common cause between us' to build 'unity in the struggle'. Although the press misleadingly reported that the invitation immediately came to naught, Gumede in fact referred it to the UDF's NEC for discussion.[51]

Before the NEC met there was further communication between Gumede and Buthelezi. Gumede complained to Buthelezi of continuing attacks on members of UDF affiliates which seemed to be intimidatory. Buthelezi ominously replied: 'You know very well ... that if I unleashed violence through my organisation or through the Zulu people ... all that has happened so far would be like a Sunday school children's picnic.' In December Buthelezi wrote again, denouncing the pamphlet produced by the Transvaal UDF Media Committee. In each of these communications, however, Buthelezi distinguished between the reasonable and destructive elements within the UDF.[52] Meanwhile, Gumede shared a platform at a meeting in northern Natal with the chairperson of the Inkatha Women's Brigade.

At its next meeting in January 1984 the UDF's NEC discussed what it called the 'controversial question' of meeting Buthelezi. The NEC was divided: there was strong opposition from some UDF regions and affiliates to any meeting, but other individuals, including Gumede, and Cape Town's Joe Marks, were willing to compromise. Eventually the NEC decided against any contact in the light of Inkatha's violence against UDF supporters. Molefe later suggested that the NEC did not rule out a meeting with Inkatha some time in the future, and 'under different circumstances the UDF was prepared to meet Chief Buthelezi as the leader of Inkatha, not as Chief Minister of KwaZulu and at a venue outside the homeland'. Gumede communicated the decision to Buthelezi. He told Buthelezi that the UDF agreed on the importance of unity but was opposed to bantustan state structures, including the KwaZulu Legislative Assembly, which the UDF had been invited to address. Gumede also complained about violent attacks by Inkatha supporters and the exclusion of UDF-affiliated student organisations from KwaZulu schools and colleges.[53]

The relationship between Inkatha and the UDF continued to deteriorate. Inkatha supporters disrupted a UDF meeting in Esikhawini, Gumede was knocked unconscious and two other UDF speakers were assaulted. In further correspondence, Buthelezi continued to hold out an olive branch to Gumede personally but was clearly and increasingly opposed to the UDF as a whole, accusing it of a 'calculated political vendetta' against him and Inkatha. Buthelezi also claimed that there had been plots to assassinate him. In August Inkatha's information officer described the UDF as 'a reactionary political band'. In response, Lekota wrote a savage criticism of bantustan politicians – who 'thrive and batten on the sufferings of our people' in the service of their paymasters in Pretoria – although he avoided a direct attack on Inkatha or Buthelezi.[54]

Could the UDF have pursued an alternative approach to Inkatha? Maré and Hamilton consider that 'a clash between the two was inevitable following the political history of the 1970s and the changes that had occurred in resistance to apartheid'. The tide had swung decisively against resistance from within state structures to resistance against all state structures.[55] In broad terms Maré and Hamilton are surely right. The UDF's rejection of Buthelezi's invitation reflected the dogmatic hostility to bantustan state structures and insistence on boycott tactics that characterised most of the Charterist movement. And it was Inkatha's participation in local state structures that led to much of the confrontation in 1983–4 and later years.

But this general verdict needs to be qualified. Firstly, an entryist tradition was strong in African areas in Natal, and NIC leaders saw the boycott as a tactic rather than a principle. Secondly, Inkatha need not have been equated with the KwaZulu bantustan state. And lastly, in the later 1980s both the UDF and ANC forged a close working relationship with KaNgwane's chief minister, Enos Mabuza. The UDF did have the option of meeting Buthelezi as president of Inkatha outside Ulundi, at the same time expressing their reservations about his participation in the KwaZulu state. The fact of violence on the ground was as good a reason to meet as not to do so.

The UDF's rejection of the option of meeting Buthelezi reflected the character of the UDF and of Charterist politics in Natal as much as Inkatha's own attitudes and practices. AZASO and COSAS were hostile to Inkatha on the grounds of its conservatism as well as its participation in the KwaZulu state. Their members, as well as other UDF supporters, undoubtedly provoked Inkatha on the ground. The NIC was also ambivalent, at best, about Inkatha because of the latter's Africanist and anti-Indian views. These UDF affiliates overrode the more conciliatory views of African leaders such as Gumede and the weak civic movement in townships. The conciliatory option was further undermined by the divisive incorporation issue cunningly introduced by the South African state. Above all, the newly formed UDF's overriding concern at the end of 1983 was to preserve the fragile unity built to oppose the Tricameral Parliament; this meant heeding the more dogmatic views of affiliates such as AZASO and COSAS and disregarding the conciliatory views of individual leaders.

THE NATIONAL FORUM AND AZAPO

Concern over the challenge for political leadership by non-Charterists was an important factor in the Charterists' initiative to form a united front. As we saw in Chapter 2, AZAPO in the Transvaal and Unity Movement-inspired groups in the Cape had themselves called for the formation of a united front during 1981–2. This process was revived with the release from Robben Island of prisoners who had remained committed to BC. Less than two weeks after Boesak called for a united front at the TASC conference, AZAPO made a similar call at its own national congress. In June AZAPO and its Cape allies formed a loose co-ordinating body, the National Forum. Although AZAPO and other participants in the National Forum fulfilled the criteria set down for affiliation and had no fundamental disagreements with the UDF's

Declaration, they declined to affiliate to the Front.

AZAPO and its allies objected to the multiracial approach of key UDF affiliates, the participation of white South Africans, and the controlling role of underground ANC activists. AZAPO's initial response to the proposed UDF was shaped by its perception, shared by many African Charterists, that the UDF initiative was closely bound up with the proposed revival of the TIC. AZAPO leaders described the TIC proposal as a 'retrogressive step', and worried that the UDF would be a 'conglomerate of ethnically orientated groups'. At its national congress in early February a senior leader declared that 'as long as people still recognise ethnicity in the liberation struggle the goal of a free and united Azania shall remain a pipe dream'. Another warned against 'opportunist elements, both inside and outside the [liberation] movement' whose concern with short-term gains had led them to become 'easy victims for adventurism and drama'. AZAPO leaders rebuffed informal approaches by Charterist leaders to participate in the formation of the Front.[56]

More strident criticisms were made by a group of Cape Town-based socialists who were strongly influenced by the Unity Movement. Led by the intellectual Neville Alexander, they opposed any form of multiracial organisation, which, they said, could easily become 'thinly disguised reactionary racism'. They also dismissed UDF leaders' distinction between apartheid and capitalism as 'liberal', and condemned the participation of organisations representing white students (NUSAS), white women (the Black Sash) and black traders (the Western Cape Traders' Association). 'There can be no place in our struggle for our class enemies, collaborationist elements, and representatives of the aspiring black middle class.'[57]

The launch of the National Forum in mid-June was attended by over 800 people, reportedly from 164 organisations – including observers from a handful of Charterist organisations. Alexander provided a savage critique of '"ethnic" or "national" group approaches'. He demanded that advocates of 'non-racialism' be separated into those who were really 'multiracialists' and the genuine 'anti-racialists'. Only the latter should be accommodated within the liberation movement. The Forum adopted a starkly socialist Manifesto of the Azanian People, which ruled out the Charterist position. The rivalry between the two broad political movements intensified immediately. The more sectarian Charterists issued statements criticising the National Forum and Azanian Manifesto. AZASO students reportedly beat up BC students in Durban, and prevented AZAPO leaders from delivering speeches. In mid-July the AZAPO-linked Azanian Students Movement was revived to compete with COSAS in schools. The Cape Town groups associated with the National Forum reconstituted themselves as the Cape Action League (CAL). The prospective UDF was denounced as 'a massive fraud', 'yet another betrayal of the interests of the exploited and oppressed, yet another setback in their struggle'.[58]

In its reaction the pre-launch national UDF leadership was more open-minded than many of the more fervent advocates of Charterism. The UDF's National Interim Committee noted in July that the National Forum was a very loosely structured alliance, which was not even due to meet for another nine months, and resolved that 'the UDF should therefore not be caught up in bickering with proponents of the

National Forum'. The UDF leadership also agreed that BC organisations were welcome to affiliate to the UDF if they accepted the UDF Declaration and, rather ominously, were 'prepared to subject themselves to the overall UDF discipline'.[59] There
were no takers, and the divisive exchange in the press continued.

The UDF leadership decided to try and improve the relationship. This led to a
meeting in mid-November between a Transvaal UDF delegation, cosisting of Moss
Chikane, Cas Saloojee and Eric Molobi, and AZAPO's Sadek Variava, Phambile
Ntlokoa and Haroon Patel. The meeting was not successful. To begin with, the UDF
delegates were disgruntled at meeting with what they saw as a junior AZAPO delegation. According to Chikane:

> We could hear voices of persons like Saths Cooper and Muntu Myeza in the
> adjacent room ... I was very dissatisfied about that, because I felt that this issue
> of what I call press war had to be resolved at a senior level and I felt that they
> should have involved much more senior people from their organisation,
> because in our delegation, for instance, we had the national treasurer and
> myself, of course, I was the local secretary. Eric Molobi was Transvaal treasurer
> as well.[60]

Chikane is rather harsh in his criticism. Cooper and Myeza were the national leaders
of AZAPO, more senior in their organisation than any of the UDF delegation were in
theirs. Furthermore, Chikane and Molobi were probably no more senior than
Haroon Patel, for instance, who was very influential in AZAPO even if he did not
hold a senior office. It is difficult to avoid the impression that the UDF's leadership's
efforts in 1983–4 were half-hearted. Their competitive concern to marginalise anti-
Charterist groups weighed heavily against their concern to build broad unity against
the state.

Whatever the problems of the composition of the delegation, the meeting quickly
became unpleasant. According to Chikane's version:

> The atmosphere was very unsettling. The AZAPO delegation started by
> launching an attack on us. They attacked the UDF before we even started talks,
> saying that we are busy organising the daughters and sons of the bosses instead
> of organising the black people. It was making us feel very uncomfortable. They
> went further to say, talking amongst themselves, that in fact the idea to form
> the United Democratic Front was taken in Lower Houghton [an affluent white
> suburb of Johannesburg].[61]

On the substantial issue of co-operation between the organisations, the AZAPO delegation said that they would work with the UDF as far as possible without compro-
mising their policy or principles. Chikane understood this as meaning that AZAPO
would not work with the UDF whilst the latter included whites. When Chikane
reported back to the Transvaal UDF, it was decided that there should be no further
meetings with AZAPO.

In January 1984 at AZAPO's national congress, its president Lybon Mabasa strongly attacked the TIC and UDF. Mabasa's criticisms of the UDF are worth quoting at some length because, ironically, they strike at the heart of the UDF's very success.

> The United Democratic Front (UDF) unlike the National Forum has first constituted itself into an organisation structure with symbolic leadership and has coerced support from across the political spectrum. They have not had a firm commitment as to who is included and excluded. Radical and liberal groups, Church and secular groups work side by side as political partners. Even organisations such as the Black Sash who have a close and cordial relationship with ruling-class parties exist within the UDF. Organisations which have a chameleon-like attitude to the issue of participation in government-created platforms also function within the UDF.[62]

Mabasa continued with remarks on the transience of any organisation based on *ad hoc* committees concerned with different issues. 'As things change *ad hoc* committees dissolve and structures crumble and the UDF will be faced with the problem of leaders without followership [*sic*]. Unity is good but not at all cost.'[63] In fact, it was AZAPO and CAL which were to experience this problem: their leadership included impressive intellectuals and made good use of the media but few of their affiliated groups organised on the ground.

Relations grew steadily worse during 1984. In March the Transvaal UDF declined an invitation from AZAPO to join in a meeting to commemorate the 1960 Sharpeville massacre – because, Moss Chikane argued, 'of the treatment we got when we attempted to get AZAPO to affiliate to the UDF'. The UDF later decided that it 'must not get involved in issues that have been organised or originated from AZAPO'. In June it took the intervention of Soweto church ministers to secure an agreement between the UDF and AZAPO over arrangements for meetings in Soweto's Regina Mundi Cathedral to celebrate 'Soweto Day', the anniversary of the student march and massacre of 16 June 1976.[64] There was little subsequent co-operation between AZAPO or the Forum and the UDF, and AZAPO and the National Forum faded into obscurity. Too insistent on ideological purity and neglectful of mass organisation and action, they could not compete with the UDF's flamboyant and all-embracing approach.

Chapter Four
....

'Siyaya':
Forming the UDF
in the Regions

Prior to 1983, extra-parliamentary resistance inside South Africa had been fragile and fragmented. In Molefe's assessment: 'People were divided and what little unity existed was threatened by the constitutional proposals. It seemed to me that the exclusion of Africans had the potential to alienate Africans from coloureds and Indians, who were being offered a form of token representation in the proposed parliamentary structure.'[1] In its formation the UDF represented open defiance of the government's attempts to divide and segregate South Africans. 'UDF Unites, Apartheid Divides' proclaimed the UDF's slogan. Indeed, almost six hundred organisations attended its national launch, bringing together coloured, Indian, African and even white activists – notwithstanding the absence of the major non-Charterist movements. The occasion was invigorating. '*Siyaya, siyaya noba, kunzima,*' sang the crowd at the launch: 'We are going, we are going, even if it is difficult.'

At the national level, however, the UDF was a federation of regional structures. The NEC itself was primarily a committee of notables. It was at the regional level that the nascent UDF was based. The formation of regional structures was no easy task, as regional activists had to confront the deep social divisions fostered by decades of apartheid. In every region the character of the UDF was profoundly shaped by the political differences based in racial segregation.

In 1983 organisation and networks were generally stronger in coloured and Indian areas than in African areas. During the 1970s a new generation of coloured and Indian activists emerged, many through the BC movement, and hence more likely to describe themselves as 'South African' or 'black' than in terms of apartheid racial categories. They had begun to build civic and youth organisation on the ground, and linked up with veterans of the 1950s in campaigns around Republic Day, the South African Indian Council and so on. By 1983 there were extensive networks across the coloured and Indian areas of Cape Town, Johannesburg and Durban.

Most of the younger coloured and Indian activists were university graduates in professional occupations including law. They were generally comfortably off, and could raise funds for their organisations from the coloured and Indian professional and business classes. Some of them could and did travel extensively within South Africa, and even abroad to meet exiled ANC officials. They had easy access to the media, homes large enough to hold meetings, and their own private transport. They played leading roles in the founding and production of the 'alternative' press and in 'service' organisations.

Political organisation was generally weak outside the coloured and Indian areas in the metropolitan centres. There were exceptions – and these were given extensive and celebratory coverage in *SASPU National*, *Grassroots* and other alternative media. But even such exceptions were often transitory, with organisation cohering around a specific issue and then declining into passivity. In early 1983 a number of activists – including Lekota and Moss Chikane – were worried that organisation in African townships was still too weak to warrant the formation of the UDF. These sceptics were persuaded that a front should be formed on the grounds that it would stimulate organisation building.[2]

This is not to say that there was no organisation in African townships across the country. Rather, the most common form of organisation was very locally based and led by conservative civic leaders, often dissident members of the racially segregated township councils. Such 'popular conservatives' organised around material concerns such as evictions, rent increases and shack clearances ordered by the township council. They were generally as little interested in the brashly political UDF as the UDF's educated activists were in them. In many townships radical political activists had begun to organise around civic issues, and were to supplant more conservative civic leaders at the forefront of civic protest. But during 1983 the majority of such activists were isolated from the metropolitan-based networks which underpinned the UDF, felt themselves too vulnerable, or were not interested in what they saw as an essentially Indian initiative.[3] The UDF, therefore, was at first poorly grounded in most African townships.

Most of the groups which affiliated to the UDF organised in racially segregated constituencies. The UDF, as a front, therefore took on a *de facto* multiracial form, although with non-racial leadership at every level. This meant that the particular combination of organisations which affiliated in any region shaped the character of the Front in that region. At the same time, given the fact that the UDF was initially concerned with the threatened co-option of Indians and coloureds, Indian and coloured activists – with all their advantages – came to play major roles in the Front. This posed difficulties within the Front's non-racial co-ordinating structures.

THE TRANSVAAL

Much of the discussion in late 1982 about forming a nationwide front took place in Johannesburg, as we saw in Chapter 2. The TASC congress's appeal for a united front was thus promptly taken up by the Charterist activists based in TASC and Soweto. This core convened a series of clandestine meetings to canvass support for the proposed front. Momoniat recalls:

There were dozens of meetings ... Depending on how secret the meetings were, they would be held either at my house, or I would find venues in Lenz [Lenasia] or all over ... I think we were very, very careful about not showing the cops too much. We just showed them our public face, ... very consciously not exposing other people unnecessarily. And so many of the meetings would not have been arranged on the phone.[4]

If the proposed front was to avoid being seen as a mere adjunct of the TIC and NIC, then it was essential to draw in African activists. 'From the start', Momoniat continues, 'we were very clear [about] the whole notion of African leadership.' Momoniat himself invited the Pretoria activist Moss Chikane, for example, to one important meeting. Three interim secretaries were elected to co-ordinate the process: Jabu Ngwenya and Monde Mditshwa (both members of the Soweto study group) and Chikane himself – all three African. Moosa also served as a interim secretary but worked on the national as much as on the provincial level.[5]

Chikane had reservations about the front on account of the weakness of radical political organisation in African townships.[6] He accordingly raised his concerns at a regional planning meeting in April, and they were discussed at some length at a large meeting in Johannesburg's Khotso House at the beginning of May. But the general feeling within the newly constituted regional consultative committee was that the formation of the front should not be delayed. The Transvaal UDF was formally constituted at a further meeting at Khotso House on 21 May, attended by about eighty people. A draft declaration was discussed, amended and adopted. No elections were held, so the consultative committee would continue as a steering committee.[7]

One reason why the regional leadership went ahead with forming the UDF was that it comprised activists from those areas around Johannesburg where there was a strong Charterist presence. Almost all the members of the consultative committee came from Indian and coloured areas (including Momoniat, Prema Naidoo, Dr Essop Jassat, Moosa, Firoz Cachalia and Ismael Mahomed) or from Soweto (Frank Chikane, Molobi, Masondo, Ndou, Molefe, Ngwenya). In Indian and coloured areas there were not only TASC (and later the TIC) and the newly formed Anti-President's Council Ad Hoc Committee but also civic, student and youth groups. In Soweto Molefe and Masondo had spearheaded a revival of the Civic Association, rebuilding its branches in the different townships within Soweto, and co-ordinating these through an inter-branch committee (this served as a prototype for the general councils and area committees set up later by the UDF). There was also an active COSAS branch, AZASO members and workers belonging to the General and Allied Workers' Union (GAWU). In these areas, therefore, there were enough organisations to warrant some overarching co-ordinating structure.

The regional leaders were aware of the existence of a few organisations elsewhere in the region, and of clusters of activists who were in the process of setting up new organisations. The members of the consultative committee, and other members of the ANC underground, were allocated the task of contacting activists in other areas. Molefe, for example, liaised with activists in the Vaal Triangle, where there was no formal organisation. Neverthelesss, there were compelling reasons for proceeding speedily with the formation of the UDF – the national political situation, and the need to make Charterist-led opposition to the constitutional reforms as visible as possible – regardless of the level of organisation on the ground.

The geographical pattern of involvement in the UDF was evident in the composition of the Transvaal REC, finally elected in early August. All but 6 of the 25 REC members came from Indian and coloured residential areas to the west of Johannesburg (Lenz/Lenasia, Eldorado Park, Bosmont) or Soweto. The exceptions were Moss Chikane from Pretoria, the elderly Hans Hlalethwa from Winterveld (a sprawling shack settlement north of Pretoria in the bantustan of Bophuthatswana), George du Plessis (a former coloured Labour Party member from Reiger Park on the East Rand), SAAWU unionist Herbert Barnabas, and Frances Baard. None of the REC members lived in the African townships of the East Rand, the Vaal Triangle or the West Rand beyond Soweto.

The UDF's leadership and affiliates were highly concentrated even within the metropolitan area of the PWV. Coloured and Indian areas comprised just 5 per cent of the total PWV population, and Soweto accounted for perhaps 15 per cent. The rest of the PWV's black population lived in areas where the UDF had little organised presence: on the East Rand, around Pretoria, in the Vaal Triangle, on the mines, and in white employers' servants' quarters. Moreover, the African industrial working class was concentrated on the East Rand and Vaal Triangle – areas where radical civic and student organisation was weak. The most powerful organisations in both areas were FOSATU-affiliated trade unions, whose leaders avoided involvement in extraworkplace struggles and were especially wary of the apparently middle-class, nationalist leadership of the UDF. The UDF's affiliates were thus socially as well as geographically concentrated.

With uneven support within the metropolitan PWV, the Transvaal UDF had hardly any affiliates further afield. Only one REC member came from outside the PWV: civic leader Hoffman Galeng from the township of Huhudi outside Vryburg in the Northern Cape! There was very little formal organisation beyond the PWV, apart from pockets in Pietersburg, at the nearby University of the North (Turfloop), in Potchefstroom in the Western Transvaal, and in parts of Sekhukhuneland. The TIC also had links into some small towns.

The regional UDF leaders were right to think that the formation of the UDF would coincide with, if not prompt, broader organisational development. At the same time as the Transvaal UDF was coming together, Charterist activists formed a number of other overtly political and in most cases stridently Charterist organisations. The TIC and the Anti-President's Council Committee provided homes for opponents of the government's constitutional reforms in Indian and coloured areas respectively. Youth congresses were established at mid-year in Soweto, Alexandra, and the Pretoria townships of Mamelodi and Atteridgeville to provide a political home for young activists who had left school but were too junior to play leading roles in civic organisations. In August a Release Mandela Campaign committee was formed (known by the same initials as the existing Durban-based Release Mandela

Committee). Discussions about forming an organisation in white areas led to the launch, towards the end of the year, of the Johannesburg Democratic Action Committee (JODAC). Meanwhile COSAS was extending its organisation across a number of townships.

Not all of these new bodies fitted neatly into the newly formed UDF. The Transvaal RMC, in particular, became a base for Charterists who were critical of the UDF's moderation, its reticence about openly championing the Charterist cause, and the prominent role of TIC and NIC activists. Its leading members included Aubrey Mokoena, a former BC leader whose banning order expired at the end of June, and Jabu Ngwenya, who had briefly served as co-secretary of the initial regional leadership. Curtis Nkondo became the chairperson. The RMC was intended as a more Africanist counterweight to the TIC within both the broader Charterist movement and the UDF. Marginalised within the UDF, the RMC later sought to provide a rival focus for the Charterist movement as a whole.[8]

During mid-1983, however, the key tension within Charterist politics in Johannesburg did not involve the TIC and RMC, but was instead focused on Freeway House – a building in Johannesburg which housed a number of support or service organisations. Leftist white ex-NUSAS students joined together with Indian and African activists in organisations producing alternative media, especially *SASPU National*, and providing political education and research facilities for the Charterist movement. From early 1982 tensions had grown around personal and strategic differences, and these slowly crystallised into distinct camps. In mid-1983 the 'Freeway House' camp proposed Auret van Heerden for the post of regional UDF publicity secretary. Van Heerden had played a pivotal role in building a Charterist movement in white student politics, and in forging inter-regional networks in the early 1980s. But he was disliked and mistrusted, especially by some of the TASC activists, who effectively vetoed his election. Marginalised, this charismatic organiser and strategist subsequently played little part in overt Charterist politics.[9]

NATAL

Charterist politics in Natal were superficially similar to those in the Transvaal because of the similar roles played by the NIC and TASC–TIC. But Natal, or at least the Durban metropolitan area, had a very different demographic and social character from that of the PWV. One reason for this was the much larger Indian population. Whereas in the PWV there were at least twelve times as many African as Indian and coloured people, in Durban there were only twice as many – a million Africans compared to half a million Indians.[10] Secondly, the African population of Durban was overwhelmingly Zulu-speaking, and retained much closer links to rural areas than did their counterparts in the PWV. The settled second-generation urban African population was much smaller in Durban than in the PWV.

These factors help to explain the extraordinary role that NIC activists played in Natal as well as nationally. In the 1970s the NIC had 'kept the Charterist flag flying'[11] whilst most other Charterist activity was underground. In the late 1970s it was revitalised by Gordhan and other younger activists, who also built civic organisations under the umbrella of the Durban Housing Areas Action Committee (DHAC), nurtured student organisation and protest, and set up the *Ukusa* community newsletter and the civic-orientated Community Research Unit. Young coloured and Indian activists followed Gordhan's lead in Pietermaritzburg.[12]

Gordhan and his colleagues built up a strong network of young Charterist activists, but the areas that they worked in remained socially and politically conservative. There was a general 'lack of common cause and identification', as Moodley puts it, between Indian and African South Africans. This was underpinned by different living conditions and positions in the occupational hierarchy, notwithstanding the existence of poverty and poor living conditions in Indian areas such as Chatsworth or the size of the urban Indian working class. Society in Indian areas was culturally distinct and isolationist, and there was widespread wariness of Zulus.[13]

At the national level the prominence of the NIC and TASC–TIC was balanced by other Charterist groups based in African areas, especially Soweto. This was not the case in Durban, where Charterist politics had a more markedly lopsided character. There was little formal Charterist organisation in Durban's African townships in the early 1980s, with the exception of Lamontville, an old location situated close to the middle of Durban. The shallow urban roots of the urban African population were reflected in the virtual absence of student protest in 1976, the muted impact of the Black Consciousness movement, and the small number of young radicalised African activists in the early 1980s. The Molefes, Chikanes and Morobes of the Transvaal had almost no counterparts in Natal. COSAS was weak, and AZASO's influence was limited to university campuses. The only major exception was the Masibosane Lamontville Youth Organisation (Malayo) in Lamontville. In Pietermaritzburg there were pockets of youth organisation in Sobantu and Edendale.[14]

The larger townships around Durban – Umlazi, KwaMashu and large parts of Inanda – fell within KwaZulu. Through a combination of patronage, repression and an ambiguous mix of African nationalist and Zulu ethnic ideology, Inkatha maintained some support – particularly among older and poorer people holding on to what Sitas refers to as resilient 'countryside traditions'[15] – and deterred competition. Although FOSATU unions had members in these townships, with some workers being members both of a union and of Inkatha, there was little contact between them and Durban's Charterists. In so far as there was a Charterist movement in African areas, it was concentrated in the older townships outside the boundaries of KwaZulu. Its leading members were men like Gumede, from Clermont, older and more conservative than the Soweto-based leaders, and often willing to oppose apartheid from within state structures. One of Lamontville's elected township councillors was an ANC veteran and former Robben Islander, Harrison Msizi Dube.

Politics in Durban's African townships was beginning to change, however, just as the UDF was being formed. In 1982 Pietermaritzburg's Sobantu township was riven by struggles against rent increases, and bus fare increases in Durban sparked an unsuccessful bus boycott and the first inter-township organisation. In early 1983, rent increases in Durban's townships provoked considerable opposition, especially in

Lamontville where the younger Malayo activists joined up with Dube, who took the lead in forming first a local Rent Action Committee and then the Joint Rent Action Committee (JORAC) to co-ordinate civic resistance across Durban and up the coast. Several other township councillors besides Dube were involved in JORAC, including Ian Mkhize and Richard Gumede from Hambanathi outside Tongaat. In April 1983, just as the UDF was being put together, Dube was assassinated. This precipitated several months of riots and brutal policing; it removed a figure who would have played a major role in the UDF in Natal.[16]

The Charterist movement in Natal thus had a dual character, divided in large part along racial lines. DHAC brought together civic groups in coloured and Indian areas, whilst JORAC linked civic groups in African townships. There was no non-racial youth organisation. AZASO and the Release Mandela Committee were both non-racial, but AZASO was confined to university campuses and the RMC was barely active after 1981. All the same informal networks did cross racial boundaries. Activists from Malayo, in particular, participated in the NIC-led *ad hoc* campaign committees such as the Anti-Republic Day Committee. Some of the younger African activists participated in *Ukusa*, and the NIC ran workshops for and channelled resources into organisations in African areas. Lamontville's Rev. Mcebisi Xundu attended the TASC congress in Johannesburg. But by and large there was a significant gap between the different sides of the Charterist movement. Gordhan never met Dube, for example.[17]

Preparations for the formation of the UDF in Natal were therefore dominated by NIC activists. Together with a few coloured activists in DHAC – including Virgil Bonhomme – they organised a series of planning meetings. 'Committees of Concern' were formed in several coloured areas where there was no other vehicle for people concerned about the state's reforms.[18] The Natal UDF was formally launched in Natal on 14 May 1983 – the first in the country.

Almost half the Natal REC members were from the NIC or DHAC, including the medical professor Jerry Coovadia (of the NIC) as chairperson, the artisan Bonhomme as vice-chairperson, and lawyer Yunus Mahomed (of the NIC) as co-secretary. Some prominent NIC leaders were still banned, and could not participate formally. These included Mewa Ramgobin, Gordhan, M.J. Naidoo and George Sewpersadh in Durban and A.S. Chetty in Pietermaritzburg. The African members of the REC were headed by Archie Gumede, who was elected as president. Victoria Mxenge, a lawyer and the widow of Griffiths Mxenge, became co-treasurer, and AZASO leader Joe Phaahla co-secretary. The Rev. M. Xundu and Malayo's Lechesa Tsenoli served on the REC, along with several other little-known African activists. Three white activists from the Black Sash and the church organisation Diakonia were also members.[19]

Although the gap between Indian, coloured and African activists diminished somewhat during 1983, the Natal UDF was still constrained by the lack of prominent African leaders. Moreover, several of the leading African Charterists were not Zulu – including Mxenge, Xundu, Tsenoli and the former SASO activist Diliza Mji – providing Inkatha with ammunition to throw at the UDF. In December 1982 Lekota returned from Robben Island. But he was slow to re-enter regional politics and did not attend the Natal UDF launch. Moreover, he was another non-Zulu. Many of the younger African ANC supporters were suspicious of the UDF, seeing it as an NIC initiative, and sought instead to be involved in the ANC's military underground. It was not until the return of 1950s veteran Curnick Ndlovu from jail in September 1983 that these suspicions and differences were addressed directly.[20]

A wider range of organisations affiliated to the UDF than the composition of the leadership might suggest. There were even a number of supposed sports clubs, including the Northern Natal Darts and Table Tennis Unions. Almost all the affiliates, however, were from the Durban metropolitan area, as was the entire REC. In Pietermaritzburg, as in Durban, organisation in African areas was very weak, and activists in Indian and coloured areas were wary of assuming a high-profile political role too rapidly, so they formed a Committee of Concern rather than an explicitly UDF structure.[21]

In the hands of the NIC–DHAC activists, the Natal UDF quickly became 'an efficient political machine', in administrative terms.[22] But it was soon faced with a problem that it was ill equipped to handle when Inkatha shifted from an ambiguous position to outright hostility in late 1983 and early 1984. The threat of incorporation into KwaZulu polarised local politics in many townships. On the one side were those councillors who welcomed incorporation, most of whom were Inkatha leaders, and some of whom were prepared to use considerable force to get their way. On the other side were the many opponents of incorporation – including JORAC members Mkhize and R. Gumede who resigned from the Hambanathi Council in protest.[23] But the UDF was slow to fill this political vacuum.

After leading trade unionists heavily criticised Buthelezi and Inkatha at the launch of COSATU in Durban in December 1985, Sitas suggested that they had missed the opportunity to mobilise around Zulu-ness, challenging Inkatha's claim to represent all Zulus.[24] COSATU could have seized much of the middle ground of politics in Natal. A similar criticism can be levelled against the UDF: the character, activities and concerns of the UDF in Natal meant that opportunities were not seized, spaces were not filled; this might have pre-empted much of the subsequent violence. Archie Gumede later expressed regret that 'the UDF divided Zulus'. His implication was that this was not inevitable: the UDF should have shown that it was not anti-Zulu, and contested Inkatha's claim to represent all Zulu-speakers.[25]

THE WESTERN CAPE

In Cape Town, as in Durban, the social boundaries fostered by apartheid proved hard to transcend. But whereas Indian activists in Natal drove the process of forming a regional UDF structure to a speedy conclusion, the process proved difficult in Cape Town's peculiar political conditions. Here coloured Charterists had to pay much closer attention to their non-racial credentials than their Indian counterparts in Durban. The fact that Cape Town's coloured population was twice the size of its African population made it perversely more, rather than less, difficult to build a mass-based political movement that straddled racial divisions. It was not until late July that the UDF was formed in the Western Cape.

The core of the Charterist movement in Cape Town comprised younger coloured activists. Many came from working-class backgrounds, but their families' standard of living had steadily improved in the 1970s whilst they themselves had studied at the universities of the Western Cape (UWC) or Cape Town. They resembled the second-generation urban African activists in the PWV: thoroughly urban, well educated, upwardly mobile, and politicised through the BC movement or the churches. They provided the driving force in the civic movement brought together under the umbrella Cape Areas Housing Action Committee (CAHAC), in the community-based newspaper *Grassroots*, in the Cape Youth Congress (CAYCO), and in the church-based Inter-Church Youth. The more prominent figures among them were Trevor Manuel of CAHAC, Cheryl Carolus of the United Women's Organisation (UWO) and Johnny de Vries of AZASO. Casting a shadow over them was the older but banned activist Johnny Issel.

These young Charterists competed for the leading position in coloured opposition politics with an array of broadly socialist activists influenced to varying extents by the Unity Movement. Towering over the latter was the remarkable socialist and anti-racist intellectual, Neville Alexander. Alexander and the other critics of Charterism were intellectually combative but organisationally weak. Their crucial weakness was their lack of any mass base in African areas. In contrast the coloured Charterists' great strength was their alliance with townships activists, which lent some credence to their claimed commitment to non-racialism and working-class leadership of the struggle.

The leading figures in Cape Town's African townships were Charterist veterans of the ANC campaigns of the 1950s and, in some cases, of MK activities in the early 1960s. These included Oscar Mpetha, Christmas Tinto, Zoli Malindi and Wilson Sidina. In the late 1970s they had presided over the revival of civic organisation which developed into the Western Cape Civic Association (WCCA), and helped to build trade unions such as the African Food and Canning Workers Union and the Western Province General Workers' Union. But in Cape Town, as in Durban, there were few younger township activists. One of the exceptions was Rosebery Sonto, who was the only active African member of CAYCO's first executive and was later elected CAYCO president. The absence of younger activists reflected in part the patriarchal authority of the Charterist veterans, who discouraged independent initiatives by younger people. More fundamentally, it mirrored the character of Cape Town's African population: more working class, less educated, and with stronger rural links than the African population of the PWV – all largely due to decades of severe influx control imposed in the Western Cape.

If the strength of the Charterist movement was that it had feet in both African and coloured areas, this strength was forever limited by the fragility of cross-racial unity. Key ANC activists – coloured and African – came together in an underground caucus widely referred to as the High Command. But there were few formal organisational links between coloured and African areas. The WCCA was initially part of

CAHAC, but soon went its separate way. Tensions also arose within CAYCO. Coloured Charterists may have espoused the rhetoric of African leadership, but this was not easy to effect in practice in an area where coloured people far outnumbered African people and, more importantly, there was a much larger number of dynamic, young, educated activists from coloured areas than from African townships. Many African Charterists were unsure about their brash young coloured counterparts. The fragility of the Charterists' non-racialism exposed coloured Charterists to charges of multiracialism – which, in the rarefied ideological atmosphere of Cape Town was considered tantamount to an endorsement of apartheid classification and hence of apartheid itself. The political situation was further complicated by the independent trade union movement. Leading officials in the African Food and Canning Workers' Union and Western Province General Workers' Union agreed with much of the socialist critique of nationalism put forward by the Unity Movement-influenced left but at the same time had links with the ANC through unionists such as Mpetha and Sidina.

In late 1982 these different groups – African and coloured Charterists, trade unionists and other non-Charterists – came together in the loosely constituted Disorderly Bills Action Committee to oppose the government's reforms. But conflict among the different ideological groups paralysed the committee.[33] Key Charterists were thus receptive to the idea of forming a Charterist-dominated front. Trevor Manuel liaised closely with the NIC and TASC networks, and went with other Charterists to Johannesburg for the TASC congress in January 1983. The Cape Town activists argued for the name 'UDF' in preference to the 'national democratic front' which, with its nationalist implications, would have been harder to canvass support for back in Cape Town. But, lacking clear mandates from their organisations and no doubt slightly unsure as to what kind of reception would await the idea of a front, they were unable to commit their organisations or participate fully in the initial steering committee.[26]

Key Cape Town activists drove back to Cape Town from the TASC congress in one minibus. Not surprisingly the main topic of conversation was how to work towards a united front in the Western Cape. Outside Beaufort West they stopped and argued it out in the shade of a tree. Coloured Charterists divided into three broad factions. One group, led by Manuel and Carolus, was closely associated with Gordhan and the NIC–TASC networks, and shared most of their views on strategy and organisation. A second faction was based around Issel (although he himself was banned and so could not attend the TASC congress). Issel, with deeper roots in BC, was critical of the 'opportunism' of the NIC. He favoured a more non-racial approach, and increasingly emphasised the importance of African leadership. Both these groups were powerfully positioned in the ANC underground. The third faction comprised UWC students or ex-students – including Hedley King and De Vries – who argued for a more theoretically coherent, but less immediately usable, Marxist approach. They were more attuned to some of the criticisms made by Neville Alexander, for example, but shared Alexander's weakness of detachment from mass action. Outside Beaufort West these different factions agreed to work together, ensuring that each was represented in the leadership of any structure formed.[27]

But this co-operative dedication to forming the UDF proved inadequate. Back in Cape Town the activists who had attended the TASC congress battled against widespread scepticism and opposition. Several activists, including some within the broadly Charterist fold, expressed their principled opposition to any multiracial approach, with or without the participation of white South Africans, or multi-class alliances. The proposed UDF was denounced as either a 'liberal' or an 'ethnic' Indian initiative. Other activists feared being sucked into a process directed from Johannesburg or Durban and over which they had little or no control. All were wary of exposing themselves to criticism from the unions or other non-Charterist, socialist critics.

When Moosa came to Cape Town in March on the last leg of his trip to revive enthusiasm for the UDF, he found that Cape Town's Charterists were reticent. At a small meeting organised by Issel, activists pointed to the perceived link between the revival of the 'ethnic' TIC and the UDF. Moosa was also taken, supposedly as a member of a local youth organisation, to a meeting where the proposed UDF was attacked as a 'PFP plot' – a plot hatched by the liberal Progressive Federal Party. Yunus Mahomed flew from Durban to help the dispirited Moosa. Together, in an all-night meeting, they persuaded Issel, Manuel and other key actors to resume their efforts at forming a regional UDF structure in the Western Cape. They also agreed that the front would be launched in Cape Town. Issel and Manuel thereafter organised meetings where more and more Cape Town activists were persuaded of the need to take part in the proposed front.[28]

While a growing number of young coloured activists were drawn into the initiative, there remained the problem of African involvement. The older township leaders were cautious, apparently in part because they did not feel themselves to be playing an adequately central role in the process. They thought that the struggle was really in the townships, and were not altogether persuaded of the need for legal and aboveground organisation and tactics. The trade unions were even less interested. FOSATU's workerist regional leader, Joe Foster, rejected the Charterists' overtures outright. The General Workers' Union and the African Food and Canning Workers' Union were initially more sympathetic, but later adopted a more critical position, as we saw in Chapter 3.[29] The unions' withdrawal of support meant that a regional UDF launch scheduled for mid-May had to be aborted.

At the urging of other regions, the Western Cape Charterists finally went ahead without the unions and launched the Western Cape region of the UDF on 24 July. The elected REC largely comprised educated coloured and Indian university students or professionals. These included Manuel and Carolus as secretaries, and Andrew Boraine, the recently unbanned former NUSAS president, and Rashid Seria, a journalist, and key figure in *Grassroots*, as treasurers. Among the additional members were De Vries, Presbyterian minister Chris Nissen, and Ebrahim Rasool of the Muslim Students Association and AZASO. Working-class ANC veterans filled the nominal leadership positions: Mpetha as president and Tinto as one of the vice-presidents, with civic leader Joe Marks from the coloured area of Steenberg as the other vice-president. Imam Solomons of the Muslim Judicial Council was also elected to the REC, although his presence was symbolic. The only young African activist was Baba Ngcokoto a former AZASO national organiser. The *de facto* representation of African areas soon declined, as Mpetha was too ill to attend meetings regularly, and was later jailed, whilst Ngcokoto's portfolio had to be taken over by De Vries.

Most of the Western Cape UDF's affiliates were based in Cape Town's coloured areas: civics under the umbrella of CAHAC, youth groups attached to CAYCO, and branches of Inter-Church Youth. Twenty or so civics and youth groups in Cape Town's African areas attended the UDF's national launch, as well as branches of COSAS and UWO, but these gave a slightly exaggerated impression of the UDF's strength in the townships. Many of these organisations were little more than names.

Although the formation of the UDF was more complex in the Western Cape than in most other regions, it was here that the UDF first developed strong sub-regional structures. A wide range of co-ordinating and executive (but not decision-making) roles were devolved from the REC and RGC to geographically defined regional and area committees. (The terminology is confusing: the Western Cape referred to its sub-regions as 'regions'.) Nine regional structures were planned, stretching as far as the Boland, although only five seemed to be operational by late 1983 and even these varied in strength. Several regions had a further tier of Area Committees. In the Cape Town region, for example, there were Area Committees in Bo-Kaap, Woodstock, Gardens, Observatory and Kensington. These sub-regional structures were unable to transcend Group Areas boundaries. A Townships Region was initially demarcated across these boundaries, but the different concerns and organisational methods of activists in the various areas soon led to the region splitting into two parts.[30]

Most non-Charterist groups stayed outside the new Front. Charterist activists had initially approached various members of the Unity Movement-linked left as well as the trade unions, but with no success. Dullah Omar, a lawyer and leading figure in the Thornhill Residents Association in Cape Town's Indian suburb of Rylands, was initially sympathetic but eventually declined nomination as a regional UDF vice-president, and the Thornhill Residents Association voted against affiliating to the UDF. Most other non-Charterist activists were more hostile. A range of Black Consciousness bodies, Unity Movement groups such as the Federation of Cape Civic Associations, and the Unity Movement-influenced group centred on Neville Alexander formed the rival Cape Action League (CAL). CAL launched savage criticisms of the UDF, but it soon became clear that its bark was worse than its bite.[31]

The initial Western Cape UDF was largely confined to Cape Town. The only REC member from outside Cape Town was David Petersen, a former Labour Party activist and close colleague of the late Hennie Ferrus from Worcester. The UDF had a number of affiliates in the Boland towns of Stellenbosch, Paarl, Wellington and Worcester, but almost none beyond. The REC subsequently worried about converting the REC into 'a truly W. Cape Exec'. Marks and Carolus from the REC, together with Cecil Esau from CAYCO, went on a series of trips outside Cape Town, primarily to the West Coast and Namaqualand.[32] Cape Town activists also helped to initiate organisation in the Southern Cape and Little Karoo, but as these were seen as a different region they are considered separately below.

THE BORDER

If the formation of the UDF was delayed in the Western Cape because of the dearth of working-class African involvement, in the Border and Eastern Cape the problem was that there was no core of Indian or coloured activists to drive the process. In neither the Border nor the Eastern Cape was there a strong Charterist presence in coloured or Indian areas, and African Charterists initially saw the UDF as having little immediate relevance to them. The UDF's Border and Eastern Cape regions were formally launched in October and December respectively, *after* the national launch in Cape Town. Thereafter the UDF had a rather different character in these regions from that elsewhere. Reflecting local conditions, the UDF served as forums of township-based organisations, more concerned with liberation than civil rights, and with much closer links to the ANC political and military underground. The identity of the UDF in these regions was by and large subsumed into the broader identity of the ANC or Congress Movement.

The core of radical organisation in the Border region was the South African and Allied Workers' Union (SAAWU). From its stronghold in the Border region, SAAWU forged a significant presence in Bloemfontein, in parts of Durban and in the PWV. Its leaders were integral to the ANC underground and in close contact with ANC officials in Lesotho. In contrast to FOSATU, they believed that unions should play an active role in the community. SAAWU assisted COSAS, made an abortive attempt to form a Border Civic Organisation, and in 1982 initiated the formation of an East London Youth Organisation. But their union and community work was constrained by brutal repression, especially in the Ciskei. SAAWU provided the primary links between the Border and Charterist networks in Johannesburg and Durban, especially after 1981 when Charterist groups around the country had campaigned for a consumer boycott of Wilson-Rowntree products in support of a strike at their SAAWU-organised factory. SAAWU leaders Thozamile Gqweta and Sisa Njikelana regularly spoke on political platforms in Johannesburg. Gqweta supported Boesak's call for a united front at the TASC congress in January 1983, and was part of the group which formulated a more concrete proposal.[33]

Besides SAAWU, there were a number of veterans of the ANC and MK from the 1950s living in the Ciskei. They were divided in their attitude to SAAWU. Some of them advocated a class-orientated Communist Party perspective. In jail on Robben Island they had clustered around Govan Mbeki. Others adhered to a more nationalist perspective on the struggle; they had followed Mandela's lead on the Island.[34] The most important of the ex-Islanders was Steve Tshwete, but other than Tshwete, few ANC veterans were involved in above-ground organisation.

In East London and in the university town of Grahamstown, which often considered itself to be part of the Border region, there were a few Charterist coloured and Indian activists. In East London there were also coloured activists within the broad Unity Movement tradition and in FOSATU unions. In late 1982 these different activists came together in an Anti-President's Council–Koornhof Bills Committee, which was probably similar to the Disorderly Bills Action Committee in Cape

Town.[35] The Border and Eastern Cape regions were represented at the TASC congress in January 1983 by a student from Rhodes University in Grahamstown, Devan Pillay.

After the TASC congress, contact between the Durban- and Johannesburg-based national network and the Border and Eastern Cape broke down. Pillay moved to Cape Town, and SAAWU leaders seem to have been preoccupied with their own work. There were no representatives from the Border or Eastern Cape on the initial national UDF steering committee. Moosa visited East London in March in order to revitalise the UDF initiative, and spoke to Njikelana. Although Njikelana personally expressed his support, SAAWU was distracted by ongoing unity talks with the other independent trade unions as well as a debilitating series of internal divisions. Some of the older African nationalists and ex-Islanders were contacted, but nothing came of this either.[36] It seems that most African activists saw the proposed UDF as an *ad hoc* structure for opposing constitutional reforms in Indian and coloured areas, and therefore considered participation in the UDF less important than building local organisation, the ANC underground or a mass working-class trade union movement. In May 'there was nothing' in the Border region, as former SASO leader Arnold Stofile found when he returned after a year's study abroad.

In June, Charterists from across the region and beyond gathered in Cradock for the funeral of Canon James Calata, who had been secretary general of the ANC in the 1930s and 1940s. Among the speakers were Gumede and Victoria Mxenge. Other prominent activists canvassed support for the UDF.[37] But the funeral did not lead to any firm decision to form a regional structure.

When the National Interim Committee met in Johannesburg at the end of July there was grave concern at the lack of progress in the Border – especially because the Border-based SAAWU was the largest of the Charterist trade unions and was needed to give credence to the prospective UDF's claimed commitment to the working class. Tshwete attended the meeting but was unable to allay this concern. It was decided that Ramgobin and Lekota should go to East London to mobilise support. But when Ramgobin and Lekota arrived, Gqweta and their other contacts in SAAWU were in hiding. At this time SAAWU was centrally involved in the organisation of a bus boycott in the Ciskei, which grew 'from a short-term struggle over a fare increase into a protracted political struggle that had as its focus the illegitimate Ciskei regime and its apartheid designers in Pretoria'. The Ciskeian state responded with severe repression, including vigilante attacks, the massacre of commuters at train stations, the declaration of a State of Emergency, the detention of over a thousand people including top SAAWU leaders, and the banning of SAAWU in the bantustan.[38]

In the face of SAAWU's preoccupation with struggles in the Ciskei, the task of organising the UDF in the Border fell on others: Tshwete, Stofile and Charles Nqakula, all three deeply involved in the ANC underground. Stofile, who worked at the University of Fort Hare, was active in regional sports associations, which he had used to build up an ANC underground in the interior of the Border region. Nqakula was national chairperson of the Media Workers' Association of South Africa (MWASA). In early August Nqakula invited about fifty Charterist or sympathetic activists, representing twelve organisations, to discuss the UDF. The participants agreed that they could not take a decision about forming a regional structure without clear mandates from their respective organisations, and so adjourned for a week. At a second meeting attended by representatives of just eight organisations – four days before the UDF's national launch in Cape Town – there was unanimity that a Border UDF structure should be formed, but that the UDF must not assume the role of the banned liberation movements.[39]

The crisis in the Ciskei had its toll on the Border's delegation at the UDF's founding conference and national launch in Cape Town on 20 August. Gqweta had been scheduled to speak at the launch, but could not attend after SAAWU leaders were detained in the Ciskei. In addition, the bus company contracted to provide transport from East London reneged at the last moment under pressure from the Ciskei government. Only a handful of Border delegates, including Tshwete and Stofile, succeeded in reaching Cape Town by other means. The only Border organisations present at the launch were therefore SAAWU and the Border delegation itself.[40]

On 23 August Tshwete and Stofile reported back to a third meeting. An interim committee was elected, with Tshwete as chairperson and Stofile as treasurer. This committee planned a regional UDF launch for 24 September in East London. Again, state repression intervened. Tshwete was detained, together with further SAAWU and COSAS leaders. The Chief Magistrate of East London banned all meetings of the UDF, SAAWU and COSAS over the weekend of 24–25 September. A second launch scheduled for mid-October was also banned. But by then the interim UDF leadership had made alternative plans, organising a clandestine meeting on the same day in Grahamstown. The Border UDF was thus finally launched, albeit at a venue outside the region and at a meeting attended by only six organisations. Most of the interim committee members were elected onto the new REC: Tshwete as president, Stofile as general secretary and Nqakula as publicity secretary. SAAWU's vice-president, Bangumzi Sefingo, was elected as UDF regional deputy president.[41]

The state's actions around the Border UDF's launch were characteristic of its brutal approach to policing dissent in the region. 'It is a well known fact', a UDF report later recorded, 'that repression in this area has always been excessive.' Examples of 'the obstacles placed in the way of the democratic movement' included denial of venues for meetings, detention and questioning of activists, banning of meetings, attacks on people involved in campaigns, waylaying of people coming from meetings and confiscation of materials, searches in homes of members and their offices, and the ban on all meetings of more than 20 people in the Ciskei. Repression was so severe that, the report claimed, 'there is no difference here between a banned and not banned organisation'.[42]

The regional UDF was also born amidst divisions within the Charterist movement along ideological and strategic lines. Several Charterist organisations did not attend the Grahamstown regional launch and contested the validity of the elections held there. These organisations included the East London Youth Congress, East London Women's Organisation and East London-based Release Mandela Committee. They were all tied to the more nationalist anti-communist strand in Border Charterist politics. There was, however, little racial division within the regional UDF, not least because the Charterist movement was so weak in coloured and Indian areas.

Progress towards forming a UDF regional structure was even slower in the Eastern Cape than in the Border. This region was not beset by the same level of repression but shared the Border region's wariness of what seemed to be an initiative affecting organisations in Indian or coloured areas. Port Elizabeth and Uitenhage had large coloured populations and a small Indian population – combined, they came to about half of the cities' African populations. But there was no existing Charterist organisation in the coloured and Indian areas, and the region had poor links with the national network driving the UDF initiative. Furthermore the Border and Eastern Cape were initially regarded as one region by the national leadership, who tried to maintain links with the whole region through their ineffective contacts in East London. It was only at the first meeting of the UDF's NEC in September that the UDF officially decided that the Eastern Cape and Border would comprise two separate regions,[43] and even after that their boundaries were disputed.

At the end of 1982 above-ground organisation in the townships of the Eastern Cape was more or less confined to African townships in the metropolitan hub of Port Elizabeth and Uitenhage. The driving force behind Charterist organisation was a group of educated young activists, many of whom had been politicised in the mid-1970s or particularly in protests in 1977. Some, such as Stone Sizani and Mike Xego, had then spent time on Robben Island. Others, such as Mkhuseli Jack, had come through COSAS and school boycotts in 1980–1. These younger activists linked up with older Charterists including ANC veterans from Robben Island like Edgar Ngoyi. They revived the dormant Port Elizabeth and Uitenhage Black Civic Organisations (PEBCO and UBCO), and in 1983 formed the Port Elizabeth and Uitenhage Youth Congresses (PEYCO and UYCO).[44] But they were not closely linked with the Charterist networks involved in the UDF initiative elsewhere. Instead they had closer ties with underground ANC and MK networks in Lesotho.

This growing organised Charterist strength in the townships was balanced by independent trade unions affiliated to FOSATU, especially in the auto industry. Many of the FOSATU unions' officials propounded a workerist position and wariness of political involvement – in part out of recognition of the conservative political allegiances of many of their coloured members. In 1979 PEBCO-linked workers had formed a breakaway union, the Motor Assembly and Components Workers' Union of South Africa (MACWUSA), but its membership never matched that of the major FOSATU unions. The key ideological division in Port Elizabeth–Uitenhage lay thus between a syndicalist trade unionism and a more militant, township-based African nationalism.

The coloured areas of Port Elizabeth and Uitenhage were strongholds of the Labour Party, and had no civics comparable to the Durban or Cape Areas Housing Action Committees. The Charterist movement was confined to a small group based around former students from the University of the Western Cape, including Derrick Swartz and Mikey Coetzee. These young coloured activists did provide, however, the strongest link between the Eastern Cape and national Charterist networks. But a tendency to see themselves as the purveyors of revolutionary truths, gleaned from an illicit reading of banned issues of *African Communist* and elsewhere, caused them to be viewed with unease by African township leaders. It took time for coloured and African activists to learn to work with each other.[45]

In January 1983 an Eastern Cape Co-ordinating Committee was formed in Port Elizabeth to co-ordinate opposition to the state's constitutional reforms. The Committee comprised 16 organisations, including PEBCO and PEYCO (although it had not yet been formally launched), a strong group of trade unions (including FOS-ATU), the Unity Movement-aligned Eastern Province Council of Sports, and the Eastern Cape Council of Churches. This Co-ordinating Committee, like similar committees in Cape Town and East London, did not survive for long. Led by the fervently Charterist interim leaders of PEYCO, the Charterist participants pulled out in response to the perceived domination of workerists opposed to the ANC and SACP.[46]

Having withdrawn from broad-based structures, the Port Elizabeth Charterists were slow to form their own umbrella body. There was a general ambivalence about or lack of interest in the UDF in the Eastern Cape, which was fuelled no doubt by the neglect of the region shown by the UDF's interim national leadership. Moosa skipped Port Elizabeth in his whistle-stop tour to revive the flagging enthusiasm for the UDF in March. Township activists were more involved in an initiative to form a regional civic structure. Even when interest began to grow, progress was inhibited by widespread uncertainty as to what precisely the UDF was going to be. Older African Charterists saw it as simply a revival of or a front for the ANC, and wanted to join it as individual members. Moreover, some of the Eastern Cape leaders argued that any regional structure should be built from the ground up, and not formed as an 'office-based' organisation controlled by 'unaccountable' individuals. They therefore concentrated on forming or reviving local organisation. In July and August Molefe, Ramgobin and Lekota all visited the Eastern Cape to encourage moves towards forming a UDF region.[47]

The Eastern Cape sent a small delegation to the UDF's founding conference and national launch. The national UDF leadership took the opportunity to prompt and direct the Eastern Cape activists at a meeting the following day. When they returned to Port Elizabeth, the Eastern Cape activists established an interim UDF committee which included Ngoyi, Swartz, trade unionist Dennis Neer, and the Indian civic leader Dr Previn Manilal. They also began to build new networks in Port Elizabeth, bringing in prominent church leaders and other people who had nothing to do with the ANC underground. In mid-September about a hundred local activists attended a workshop run in Port Elizabeth by national UDF leaders. Lekota and Molefe both travelled to the Eastern Cape to encourage regional activists. Their reports to the NEC must have been dispiriting, because the NEC decided in early November to hold its planned national conference in Port Elizabeth in order to raise the UDF's profile and generate some enthusiasm there.[48]

The Eastern Cape region of the UDF was finally launched on 4 December. The elected REC was headed by Edgar Ngoyi as president, with Uitenhage MACWUSA trade unionist Fikile Kobese as deputy president and Swartz as general secretary. Sizani and the white Rhodes University student Roland White were elected co-treasurers. The publicity secretary was Prince Msuthu, a former Islander and PEYCO activist. Manilal was elected as an additional member. Over a thousand people attended the public rally, which was addressed by Mpetha and Manuel from Cape Town, Ngoyi and Saki Macozoma, a former Robben Islander employed at the Eastern Province Council of Churches.[49]

The Eastern Cape REC was drawn only from the metropolitan centres of Port Elizabeth–Uitenhage, and indeed the Eastern Cape UDF was essentially limited to that area until early 1985. Whilst it was true that organisation was generally weak in other areas, there were important exceptions, such as Grahamstown and, increasingly, Cradock and Port Alfred. Regional co-ordination in the hinterland was largely provided through other networks. Activists in both the Cradock and Grahamstown areas sought at different times to have these areas included in the Border UDF region. Indeed, the Rhodes University Black Students Society affiliated to the Border rather than the Eastern Cape UDF.

Part of the problem over boundaries arose out of the ANC's underground networks. To a greater extent than in other regions, the UDF in the Eastern Cape and Border was based on underground structures. But the ANC underground was organised along lines of communication extending out from Lesotho and cutting across the UDF's preferred provincial boundaries. The ANC underground in Cradock, for example, was organised by Stofile, based in Fort Hare. Stofile recruited Matthew Goniwe, a teacher and (later) school principal who had spent five years in jail in the Transkei for being part of a Marxist reading group, and charged him with building underground structures in Cradock and the Karoo. But whereas Stofile and others in the Border sought to spread the underground's tentacles across the countryside, ANC activists in Port Elizabeth were preoccupied with building structures in the city itself. The result was that the Border UDF leadership had better contacts with places like Cradock and Grahamstown.[50]

THE OTHER REGIONS

At the time of the UDF's national launch, three UDF regions had been formed and RECs elected. What distinguished the Transvaal, Natal and Western Cape was the large number of coloured and Indian activists linked into nationwide Charterist networks. By the end of 1983 two further regions had been formed: the Border and Eastern Cape. For a while the UDF's national leadership thought of these as constituting one region together. As this suggests, the UDF had no overall plan for regional development. There was no certainty as to regional boundaries or even whether areas would comprise sub-regions under existing RECs or autonomous regions with their own RECs.[51]

The Orange Free State sent a delegation comprising two busloads of activists to the national launch. But thereafter there was slow progress towards forming a UDF regional structure. In September, at its very first meeting, the UDF's NEC decided that the Transvaal region, together with Molefe and Lekota, would undertake organisation building in the Free State. In 1984–5 Lekota ran several workshops for activists, and liaised closely with activists in Bloemfontein and in the corridor from Welkom through Kroonstad to Parys. A regional co-ordinating committee was finally formed immediately after the UDF's second NGC in late April 1985. In fact, as we shall examine later, regional co-ordination never really got off the drawing board in the Free State.[52]

The case of the Free State provide a clear, if extreme, example of the problems facing the UDF in regions where there was no clearly leading metropolitan centre which could serve as an acknowledged nucleus for Charterist networks. The Free State comprised a number of small and medium-sized towns, spread over the province. Organisation was no stronger in Bloemfontein than elsewhere; Bloemfontein had no black university (hence no AZASO presence), no media and no financial resources. The towns in the northern Free State were physically closer to Johannesburg than to Bloemfontein, and looked to the former for support, resources and leadership. Activists in Tumahole, the township outside Parys, felt that they were part of the PWV. Tensions between activists in Welkom, the largest town in the northern Orange Free State, and Bloemfontein, the largest town in the southern part of the province, persisted throughout the 1980s, and within the northern Free State there were long-standing rivalries between activists in Welkom and those from Kroonstad and Parys.

The Northern Transvaal – everywhere north of Pretoria – was also made the responsibility of the Transvaal REC, and was considered for a long time to be just a part of the Transvaal region. Transvaal REC member Moss Chikane from Pretoria was charged with building UDF organisation to the north of Pretoria. The core of organisation in the Northern Transvaal was based in Pietersburg; it comprised AZASO at the University of the North and associated civic activists in the Pietersburg townships. As Van Kessel writes: 'The UDF leadership in the Northern Transvaal was dominated by intellectuals and students.' Among the initial Northern Transvaal leadership were Louis Mnguni and Joyce Mabudafhasi, respectively lecturer and librarian at the University of the North.[53] In May 1984 a Northern Transvaal Co-ordinating Committee was formed, and in mid-year it began to produce its own Northern Transvaal version of *UDF News*. But it was not until February 1986 that an independent regional structure was established and an REC elected.[54]

One reason why the Northern Transvaal activists opted for autonomy from Johannesburg was what they saw as their neglect by the Johannesburg-based officials of the Transvaal UDF. A memorandum complained of being 'treated as a bantustan', and of being made to feel that 'their liberators would one day emerge from Johannesburg'.[55] These feelings were widespread outside the metropolitan areas. The Northern Transvaal was also typical of the non-metropolitan regions in that its successful activists often migrated to the metropolitan areas.

The situation was slightly different in the Southern and Northern Cape, where a high proportion of the population was coloured. Cape Town-based activists, including Issel, Manuel and Carolus, had made contact with a few individuals in the Southern Cape and Little Karoo prior to the national launch. Together with Reggie Oliphant, a teacher in Oudtshoorn, they visited many small towns encouraging people to form, at least, interim structures. Delegates from several towns attended the UDF's national launch in Cape Town. Later in the year a community newspaper, *Saamstaan*, was started. Based in Oudtshoorn, *Saamstaan* served the whole Southern Cape. In 1984 the Southern Cape was formally constituted as a sub-region within the UDF Western Cape, instead of as an autonomous region.[56]

The Northern Cape was linked more closely to Johannesburg than to Cape Town. Before 1983 Molefe and Vincent Mogane had built up links with young activists in townships outside Vryburg – such as Huhudi, galvanised into organisation by the threat of forced removal – and Kimberley. Indeed, Hoffman Galeng from the Huhudi Civic Association was actually elected to the Transvaal UDF's REC in August 1983. A Northern Cape consultative committee was reportedly formed by November 1983, and a regional launch was planned for January 1984. Cape Town-based UDF activists including Cecil Esau began to play a more prominent role in promoting regional co-ordination. Although the regional launch did not take place, three Area Committees were formed in early 1984, and the young Jomo Khasu was employed as regional organiser in mid-year. It was not until October that a regional steering committee was elected at a regional workshop in Kimberley. It comprised activists from the Vryburg and Kimberley areas, in both of which there was organisation in African and coloured or Indian areas. The chairpersons were Galeng from Huhudi and M. Chetty of the Kimberley Committee of Concern, and Khasu served as secretary. There was also a core of local Charterist organisation in Kuruman, but they failed to attend the meeting owing to transport problems. The report of the meeting recorded that organisational development had been slow because of 'the vastness of the region, the lack of resources, uneven organisational development, poor communication and co-ordination'.[57] The formation of a fully fledged UDF region was, it seems, not accomplished until early 1986.

Chapter Five
....

Opposing the Tricameral Parliament, September 1983–August 1984

In early September the twenty-odd members of the NEC met for the first time. The venue was Durban's historic Phoenix Settlement, established at the turn of the century by Mahatma Gandhi. The meeting represented a triumph in terms of bringing together diverse organisations from different parts of the country. It was a proclamation of non-racialism, attended by individuals from each official 'racial group' but as representatives of regional rather than racially defined structures. And it was a triumph for the ANC, because every NEC member was either aligned with or an underground member of it.

But the meeting was not merely a celebration. The NEC had, firstly, to clarify what the new Front was and how it would act in relationship to its affiliates. Uncertainty over these issues had been evident in the different regions and at the national launch. At this stage the UDF leadership saw the Front as a co-ordinating forum. Campaigns would be conducted by affiliates themselves. The UDF would strive to strengthen 'the Democratic Movement' – as it was phrased at a workshop days before – but could not claim itself to be 'the Democratic Movement'. The UDF was not a 'Freedom Charter Front' of Charterist organisations only, as some Charterist leaders had implied, but rather sought to build a more broadly encompassing political movement, albeit under Charterist direction.[1]

The NEC also had to decide how the Front would operate. As a co-ordinating body, the NEC would meet every other month. Day-to-day decisions would be left to the two national officials, Molefe and Lekota. As Molefe recalls, it was only at this meeting that it was 'accepted that we would have to work full-time, working for salaries'.[2] Salaries were paid for many months out of funds loaned to the Front by a white student activist, Jonty Joffe. A national office was established in Khotso House in Johannesburg, courtesy of the South African Council of Churches.

Much of the first NEC meeting was taken up with a discussion of how to oppose the government's constitutional reforms. The NEC decided that its first step would be to co-ordinate a massive public education programme, putting forward its criticisms of the reforms. In practice, the UDF's campaigns in its first few months were reactive and piecemeal, and there was no integrated public education programme. But the main thrust of the UDF's work was indeed publicity, even if it was conducted in a somewhat disjointed manner.

Even before the NEC met for the first time, the UDF had been drawn into a campaign at the regional level. In the Western Cape UDF affiliates opposed elections to the racially segregated local government structures in coloured areas, called management committees. Civic organisations campaigned for an election boycott, declaring that 'A vote for a management committee is a vote for apartheid'. The UDF itself provided speakers for meetings, and helped organise extra manpower to campaign in some areas. On election day voter turnout was very low in the Cape Peninsula but higher in the Western Cape interior and the Eastern Cape, where there was little radical organisation in coloured areas.[3]

Soon after, the UDF took up its first national campaign, over repression in the Ciskei. A mix of civic and political protest in the Ciskei had led to the imposition of curfews, the banning of SAAWU and other organisations in the bantustan, detentions, torture and killings. Molefe travelled to East London for the launch of the Border UDF, but the meeting was banned. Back in Johannesburg, he and Lekota announced a 'campaign of solidarity and support' involving, primarily, publicising the situation in the Ciskei. The fact that the campaign was announced by UDF officials rather than the NEC was indicative of the limited role that the latter could play if it only met bi-monthly and if important functions were devolved upon officials.

In November and early December the UDF was faced with elections for the new Black Local Authorities (BLAs) and other segregated local government structures in African townships. The BLAs were perceived as an integral component of the government's 'new deal'. Established under one of the Koornhof Bills, they were seen as a substitute for the representation of African South Africans in central government. UDF leaders also believed that 'the success of the boycott campaign against the Black Local Authorities ... was going to be decisive in terms of persuading the Indian and "Coloured" communities not to accept the constitution'.[4] The UDF and its affiliates campaigned for a boycott. When polls proved low in the elections, at least in the larger BLAs, the UDF claimed 'an overwhelming victory for democratic forces'.[5]

The anti-BLA campaign was conducted for the most part by local-level organisations. The Eastern Cape UDF regional secretary later noted that 'the most striking feature of the anti-BLA campaign in our region was that it was predominantly waged outside UDF'. When the UDF was involved, it did so largely 'in the name of affiliates'.[6] This was due partly to the fact that most of the BLAs were in regions or areas where the UDF had not been launched or remained detached from local level organisation, and partly to the belief that the UDF should leave the conduct of campaigns to its affiliates.

In all these campaigns the UDF's roles concerned overall co-ordination, and in particular the welding of locally based struggles into a cohesive national movement through the production of media and speeches made at campaign meetings. The young UDF was still unable to provide much co-ordination: its officials were over-stretched, and its NEC, RECs and RGCs met too infrequently. Moreover, the UDF's national and regional offices rarely operated smoothly. The Transvaal regional office, for example, was described by the regional co-secretary as not functioning 'properly': it was too small, ill-equipped, was not staffed by 'competent people', and was bedev-illed by poor communication between officials. Much of this was because, as Molefe later put it, 'our Front was still on very uncertain legs'.[7]

But the UDF played an effective role in the production of media, and in helping its affiliates produce media. In the Transvaal, for example:

There are pamphlets which were mainly to advertise meetings. There are posters which emphasise a mobilising message (Don't Vote!), while others ... emphasise on popularising the civic (Support SCA! [Soweto Civic Associ-ation]). Some pamphlets are educational in the sense of giving reasons why people were called on not to vote. Much of the media combines these purpos-es. But the most common purpose ... is mobilising people against the elections through the Don't Vote! call.[8]

Civic activists were taught media skills, and some of their publications were funded through the UDF. The Front also produced its own *UDF News* and pamphlets. The Transvaal region reported that it had distributed no less than 250 000 copies of an issue of *UDF News* focusing on the BLAs.[9] Some of the media were distributed through blitzes and door-to-door work – both methods which the UDF was to use extensively during campaigns in 1984.

The UDF used its media to draw local activists into an integrated, country-wide movement. Its anti-BLA campaign media, for example, 'aimed at knitting together [local] struggles into one stream' so that 'people from smaller isolated townships got to know that they are part of a broad movement opposing the same puppet struc-tures'.[10] The Ciskei issue was used to draw attention to the government's 'new deal' as a whole: 'The call for support is more than a call to halt the terror of the Ciskei authorities. It focuses our attention on a life of misery and starvation for the mass of South Africans, on the exclusion of the majority from the constitutional process, on the retention of the pass laws, the Group Areas Act and the Population Registration Act. The new constitution firmly entrenches these.'[11] They were drawn into a move-ment that was both increasingly coherent and more clearly purposive.

THE FRAGILE FRONT: REFERENDUMS ON THE NEW CONSTITUTION

The campaigns against local government elections and repression in the Ciskei were sideshows to the struggle over the Tricameral Parliament, which stood at the centre of the government's 'new deal'. The first public stage in the introduction of the Tricameral Parliament was a referendum on the reforms among white voters – and perhaps also among Indian and coloured voters. Such referendums posed a troubling dilemma for the UDF. The Front would clearly urge people to reject the reforms, but should this be done through boycotting referendums or through voting against the reforms?

The issue arose first with respect to the referendum among white voters to be held on 2 November. Parliamentary parties to the left and right of the National Party advocated a 'no' vote, as did Inkatha and other organisations involved in state structures.[12] The National Union of South African Students (NUSAS) was the UDF affiliate most directly affected by the referendum. NUSAS was wary of alienating large numbers of students on the 'liberal' university campuses and so wanted to campaign for a 'no' vote.[13] But this was contrary to the boycott position which was strongly entrenched within extra-parliamentary politics.

The UDF was concerned that any campaign among white voters should be integrated into a broader campaign among all South Africans. The Western Cape UDF thus proposed a series of campaigns, starting with a signatures campaign calling for a 'people's referendum' on the constitutional proposals, and climaxing with a regional rally.[14] But this did not address the specific question of what the UDF's white supporters should do. On this, the UDF leadership was divided.

Lekota supported NUSAS's position, urging white democrats to vote 'no':

> We have to decide how best we can stop the government in its tracks. We have to look at the strength of the whites we have with us and decide on how best their vote could be used. If, for example, we find that there are a sizeable number of our white supporters who could vote no and this vote could affect the outcome of the referendum, then perhaps they should be encouraged to vote. If they do not vote then perhaps the result would go in favour of Botha.[15]

But, he said, a boycott would be advisable in the case of referendums held among coloured or Indian voters. Tactics should be chosen on the basis of efficacy rather than ideology.[16] Other UDF leaders favoured a boycott position, not least because at this time the UDF and its affiliates were calling for boycotts of the elections for segregated local government institutions.

After a short discussion at the NEC's September meeting the UDF announced a noncommittal position to the press. It rejected any whites-only referendum in principle: 'If there is to be a referendum, then it must be for all the people of South Africa'; best of all, there should be a non-racial national convention to discuss the country's constitution (as the ANC had repeatedly demanded). People should show that they rejected 'the current process of apartheid legislation'. But the UDF declined to specify whether white voters should vote 'no' or not at all. NUSAS itself adopted a slogan 'No is not enough', which was catchy if ambiguous.[17]

The UDF was able to reach a workable compromise, primarily because white politics was not regarded as important enough to warrant fierce debate. But in practice UDF leaders and those affiliates directly involved endorsed a 'vote no' position. The UDF acknowledged 'the unique position within the Front of organisations seeking to win support in communities which have a solid voting tradition', and key UDF leaders implicitly endorsed the 'vote no' position. Some Western Cape UDF leaders explicitly called on UDF supporters to participate and either vote 'no' or spoil their ballot papers.[18]

The UDF scheduled a series of protests and events as an alternative to the whites-only referendum. This culminated in a People's Weekend on the eve of the referendum. An estimated 30 000 people attended events around the country – including meetings and rallies, concerts and even motorcades. The People's Weekend represented the first notable public defiance of the state since the UDF's national launch, and was the first major UDF event in the Transvaal, Natal and Eastern Cape.[19]

More important and more controversial than the referendum among white voters was the question of referendums among coloured and Indian voters. Throughout most of 1983 the government and the coloured Labour Party equivocated over whether to hold such referendums.[20] The UDF, on their side, equivocated over whether to call for referendums to be held, and whether to urge participation if they were held. While the NIC and TIC advocated that the UDF and its affiliates should demand referendums and actively campaign for a 'no' vote, other Charterist leaders opposed this strategy. After extensive discussion in informal meetings, the issue was raised in the NEC's second meeting held in Lenasia just days after the whites-only referendum. The delicacy of the problem was also readily apparent, with some NEC members expressing unhappiness over UDF leaders' *de facto* support for NUSAS's position.

Most NEC members favoured the NIC–TIC position on referendums among coloured and Indian voters. But the NEC recognised that some UDF leaders and affiliates would dissent, especially in the newly launched Border region whose representatives did not attend the NEC meeting, and in the Western Cape. According to the minutes:

> Noting the seriousness of the implications of the new constitution for the democratic movement, in particular the Coloured and Indian National Groups, the NEC decided to recommend to all regions that a special National Conference be held in Port Elizabeth from 16 to 18 December 1983. The Conference would determine the UDF response to both the referendum and elections for the tri-cameral parliament for Indians and Coloureds.

The NEC itself controversially recommended 'a call for a referendum', whilst restating the demand for a national convention. Meanwhile, the Labour Party began to back-pedal, describing referendums as unnecessary or 'time-wasting'. As Trevor Manuel said of the Labour Party leader, Allan Hendrickse: 'Quite clearly the man is scared'– scared, that is, of losing the referendum.[21]

Between 16 and 18 December, regional UDF delegations met in conference in Port Elizabeth. The NEC decided that its members should not play 'a leading role' in the debate 'so that at the end of the day we should not be accused of imposing our views on the regions', Molefe recalls. Notwithstanding their professed neutrality, the NEC sought to structure the debate through its input and intervention. Molefe, as national general secretary, spelt out the importance of the conference:

> we are gathered here ... [to] ... decide on very important questions in our his-
> tory. This now demands of us a very careful evaluation of our work, tactics and
> strategies. This conference promises, therefore, to be a truly momentous event
> in the life of our Front. Decisions and resolutions adopted by this conference
> are going to be decisive in terms of the future development of the UDF and,
> indeed, the way forward of the national democratic struggle in South Africa.[22]

In his address, Molefe set out the crisis facing the state, and the objectives of the
democratic movement. The purpose of this was twofold. The assessment of the situation framed the debate over strategies and tactics, whilst the reiteration of the
UDF's goals enabled Molefe to emphasise the importance of unity. The state was
attempting, Molefe argued, to restructure society through 'sophisticated methods of
divide and rule'; with big business, it sought 'to co-opt a tiny middle-class sector and
in this way to isolate the working class.' The UDF was formed, he said, to oppose and
overcome divisions among 'our people'. 'We see the unity of our people as paramount: it had to be fought for, it has to be defended.'[23]

Molefe reminded delegates of the UDF's general objectives, and then reviewed its
track record so far. This served to emphasise the importance of providing for the
diverse needs of the UDF's varied affiliates. 'The challenge facing this conference is to
evolve a programme of action which will allow scope for growth and development of
these organisations; a programme of action that will link our day-to-day work in our
organisations with the work of the UDF in a way that will build both.'[24] One of the
key difficulties facing the UDF was that 'the different aspects of the "New Deal".
affect different sections of our society differently'. Indeed, the state's intention was to
sow divisions. Molefe then posed the crucial question: 'How do we approach these
matters? Do we act as though we are affected similarly? Do we act as though divisions
on the basis of race are non-existent? On the other hand, do we through our practice
encourage and entrench these divisions?'[25] Molefe and other leaders sought to establish a basis on which the debate could proceed constructively and amicably, emphasising above all the importance of unity.[26]

But the differences within the UDF over strategies and tactics were too acute to be
put aside through appeals for unity. Tensions simmered during the early stages of the
conference. When the time came for the regions to present their views, the debate
became acrimonious; accusations of 'selling out' were bandied about. The Natal
region strongly supported participation and the 'no' vote, with support from the
fledgeling Northern Cape region. The Border region unanimously called for a boycott. The Western Cape, Eastern Cape and Transvaal were divided.

A straw vote was held, with an official result of 55–45 in favour of the 'vote no'
position. This was so close that the NEC decided that the issue should be referred to
a commission comprising representatives of each delegation and position. The commission sat through the night, and several times came close to physical violence.
Proponents of both sides of the debate threatened to pull out of the UDF if their

position was not accommodated. Eventually the commission recommended that 'the UDF allow its affiliates flexibility of tactics to show rejection of the referendum'. This recommendation would be referred back to the regions, and then back to the NEC for a final decision. In Molefe's words, this was 'the good old diplomatic way of saying we can't resolve this problem'.[27]

During the course of the debate three arguments were made for a 'no' vote. Firstly, a majority 'no' vote could frustrate the state's attempt to implement the constitution. As Lekota pointed out, a 'no' vote would place those leaders and parties which had opted for full participation in the Tricameral Parliament in a very difficult position. Although the government could disregard the referendum result – which had no statutory force – the resulting institutions would have lost legitimacy. Secondly, it was suggested that a 'no' vote would 'demonstrate solidarity of the coloured/Indian community with the African community'. Thirdly, 'A no vote can be used to mobilise … [and] can indicate the strength of the UDF.' It 'would strengthen local organisations and [the] UDF, [and] involve people directly through campaign and voting'. Overall, its proponents argued, a 'no' vote would enable the UDF most effectively to 'engage the enemy'. The 'no' vote argument was based on efficacy not principle, and was premised on two beliefs: that a majority 'no' vote could be delivered in referendums, and that the UDF should manipulate opportunities to deter repression.[28]

The opposing pro-boycott position was argued primarily on principled grounds. Participation in segregated referendums meant 'flouting' the principles of non-racialism or of 'non-collaboration' with apartheid. 'Whatever strategies we adopt should not go against our principles.' Participation in any structures or processes set up by the state, it was argued, served to maintain continued subordination, oppression and exploitation. The referendum advocates were accused of representing 'the sinister forces of reaction and middle-class prejudice and interest'. Whilst primarily a matter of principle, the argument had strategic bases. An argument influenced by Unity Movement thinking was that 'we must struggle to develop the class consciousness of working people', which required 'the breaking down of ethnic/racist prejudices'. A segregated referendum would arguably strengthen those prejudices. It would be a 'surrender to the divide-and-rule tactics of the regime'. There was also the question of whether a 'vote no' campaign could deliver the necessary majority 'no' vote.[29]

The pro-'no' vote and the pro-boycott positions differed on whether the boycott of state-initiated processes was a principle or a tactic. Implicitly criticising the pro-boycott position, Molefe wrote of the 'lack of understanding of the difference between tactics and strategies on [the] one hand and principles on the other' and 'between participation in the referendum and collaboration with the government'. More accurately, the question was whether boycotts were an inviolate or a flexible tactic, and the debate over this reflected deeper differences on the underlying character of the struggle. The pro-boycott position had greater faith in the insurrectionary potential of the working people, at least in the long term; this potential would only be realised through uncompromising, and often confrontational, activity. The pro-'no' vote position, by contrast, prioritised short-term gains which either visibly weakened the state or boosted opposition, or both of these. Such short-term gains, even if won on a terrain imposed by the enemy, could accumulate in a gradualist but successful long-term programme.

The rival positions drew on some of the contrasting political approaches or traditions which were uneasily combined within the UDF. The strategic debate of late 1983 mirrored debates in the 1940s and 1950s. In both periods anti-apartheid organisations argued over whether to seek incremental gains in the face of possibly worsening repression, perhaps even using government-created platforms to reach people or frustrate the government. Or should they employ a more principled, and essentially apocalyptic or revolutionary, approach? Given the composition of South African society, how far should the struggle focus on the organisational needs of more cautious groups, as Indian and coloured South Africans were seen to be? But there was one important difference between the 1950s and the 1980s. Most coloured Charterist leaders, whilst generally proponents of a gradualist strategy, were deeply uneasy about participation in state-initiated processes. Influenced by the Unity Movement and Black Consciousness, they espoused what Allan Boesak called the 'politics of refusal'. The UDF's Western Cape leadership did not come out in strong support of the Natal proposal.

The debate over the referendum raised, implicitly at the time, sensitive issues concerning race, non-racialism and multiracialism. Most Indian activists within the UDF supported the participation and 'no' vote position, and it was the Natal and Transvaal Indian Congresses that most forcefully advocated this stand. African and coloured activists were mostly opposed. The small number of white activists was divided. Whilst supporters of the two positions could not simply be distinguished on racial grounds – the Natal position was broadly supported by the region's African leadership, and by African leaders in prominent positions in the UDF such as Molefe – it was a common perception at the time that the issue was, among other things, a racial one.[30] Race was pertinent not in terms of who worked with whom – that is to say, of the non-racialism of the leadership – but rather in terms of the strategic implications of a *de facto* multiracial organisational alliance. Multiracialism favoured the adoption of gradualist or reformist strategies and tactics, which were seen as necessary in coloured and Indian areas. The goals of the African masses were thereby subverted, it was argued, their militancy was diluted, and African leadership was compromised. It was no coincidence that opposition to the 'no' vote proposal was led by a region – Border – where there was no significant Indian or coloured presence and so no difficult strategic choice had to be made.

The referendum debate also exposed problems in the relationship, or rather relationships, between the UDF and the ANC in exile. Both advocates and opponents of a referendum claimed a mandate from the ANC; indeed the differences within the UDF mirrored the ANC's own ambiguity. UDF leaders were encouraged in different ways by their underground connections with various ANC structures: those in Durban by their contacts with the ANC in Swaziland and London; some in Johannesburg with the ANC in Botswana and Lusaka; and Border UDF leaders with the ANC leadership in Lesotho. Overall, as Molefe puts it, there was apparently 'no central co-ordination' in the ANC. The ANC in exile consistently emphasised the importance of unity – and this emphasis was reflected in the contributions of senior UDF leaders in the Port Elizabeth conference. But the ANC did not clearly favour either position. Its contradictory signals exacerbated personal tensions within the UDF as protagonists accused each other of 'going against the Movement'. As was often to be the case, invoking a line from Lusaka served less to guide debate than to stifle it, and often aroused great bitterness.

The final decision was to be taken when the NEC met in Pretoria in late January 1984, after further discussion in the regions. By the time the NEC met the context had changed. Most observers assessed that the UDF could muster a majority of votes against the new constitution if referendums were held. In response, the Labour Party had asked the government to hold elections without a prior referendum.[31] Nonetheless, the NEC meeting again degenerated into heated argument. The NEC eventually adopted a three-point resolution, with the Border region, buttressed by fresh support from an ANC unit in Lesotho, formally dissenting. The UDF would call for a non-racial referendum, 'in which the majority of the people of South Africa may clearly state their opposition to the so-called "new deal."' At the same time, each affiliate should mobilise according to 'local conditions' and 'in accordance with the aims, objects and principles of the UDF' – not that these had ever been clearly defined. The UDF avoided taking a clear position, but allowed affiliates to participate in referendums if they so chose.[32]

The NEC's position represented a qualified victory for the 'vote no' advocates. But it might have been a pyrrhic victory if referendums had been held and dissenters had withdrawn from the Front in protest. As it turned out, the government announced in mid-February that there would not be any referendums among coloured or Indian voters. The UDF was thus let off the hook over what Molefe later said was 'perhaps the most divisive issue dealt with by the UDF'.[33] But it was a close thing, as Molefe acknowledges:

> It was threatening to split the UDF, which would have meant that we would not have provided [or] produced a formidable opposition and challenge to the state, if we had allowed the UDF to be divided on that issue ... I think that decision was a milestone decision in the sense that it averted a possible split with ghastly consequences for the UDF and for the entire struggle for democracy in this country. And I think, if anything, that conference demonstrated that the UDF had the capacity to deal with internal problems in such a manner that it did emerge united.[34]

The referendum debate revealed the absence of a 'common perception of tactical and strategic questions',[35] although it had brought some understanding of the different points of view. As some Cape Town activists reported after the December conference:

> Overall the conference was a success, its major value being in bringing together a range of individuals and organisations which have been active building the

UDF over the past half year and in giving delegates a national perspective on UDF activity. In this regard it was historically an extremely significant conference; not since the 1950s had there been such a representative gathering of South Africans striving to determine a common political programme.[36]

Furthermore, it was surely the UDF's confidence with regard to the referendums that led to the government's decision to proceed directly to elections. The UDF thus denied the state the legitimisation and political momentum which a successful referendum would have provided.

The UDF emerged formally united. But some activists were alienated from the Front, and some regions were said to be 'paralysed by the tensions generated by the debates'.[37] Critics of the UDF leadership began to point fingers at a supposed 'cabal' that caucused outside formal UDF decision-making structures and then pushed its decisions through into policy. The 'cabal' comprised, it was alleged, mostly NIC and TIC leaders, but had also drawn in figures such as Molefe, Frank Chikane and Molobi. Over the following years the strategic and organisational differences which arose in the referendum debate were to plague the UDF. In the meantime Molefe and other leaders emphasised that the UDF could accommodate disagreement. Organisations affiliated themselves to the Front on the basis of agreeing 'as little as five per cent' of the time, Molefe said, but their common opposition to the government's 'new deal' outweighed any disagreement on other issues.[38]

THE MILLION SIGNATURES CAMPAIGN

The People's Weekend at the end of October had been the UDF's alternative to and protest against the whites-only referendum. As the government continued to steer its constitutional reforms into place, it became clear to the UDF's leaders that they needed to embark on an altogether more ambitious campaign. Amidst the fractious hubbub of the Port Elizabeth conference, the UDF approved a 'Million Signatures Campaign', replicating one waged by the ANC in the aftermath of the Congress of the People in the mid-1950s.[39] One million signatures would be collected from the public, declaring opposition to apartheid and the government's constitutional reforms, and support for the UDF.

The Million Signatures Campaign (MSC) was a bold initiative. The UDF's profile would be raised, opposition to apartheid visibly demonstrated, and the new constitution and prospective participants within it discredited. In fact, only a third of a million signatures were collected in the five or so months between the campaign's launch at the end of January and mid-year, when it dragged to a halt. This was clearly a disappointing total in comparison with the target, and reflected the UDF's organisational weaknesses, the inexperience of its leadership, and differences over its priorities. But the campaign provided lessons on how to overcome these problems. It contributed to building the UDF's image and structures, and promoted non-racial politics. Overall, the campaign was an important episode shaping the development of the UDF.

The stated goal of the MSC was to demonstrate opposition to constitutional reforms, whilst indicating support for the UDF. It would serve as a non-racial 'people's referendum' proving, in Lekota's words, 'that the people unequivocally reject this constitution'. 'This will strengthen our cause both at home and internationally. Organisations overseas can cite the million signatures as proof that the constitution does not have the support of the masses.'[40] A second objective of the MSC was to publicise the Front and strengthen it and its affiliates. As Molefe later wrote:

We used this campaign to take the message of the Front to the people, to expose our local organisations to the masses and also to give our activists an opportunity to interact with the masses in schools, factories, townships, churches, squatter and resettlement areas ... Our aim was not only to get one million signatures, but to get one million people to know and accept the Declaration of the UDF. The campaign was seen as a way to educate UDF activists and to recruit new members as a way to build each of the affiliates of the UDF.[41]

Activists would be 'initiated in the streets of Johannesburg and Soweto', as Morobe put it. The UDF's 'message of non-racialism within a united South Africa' would be taken to 'people who [had] been largely unaffected by it so far', said Lekota.[42]

The campaign was largely focused on coloured and Indian areas. For one thing, it was seen as part of the struggle against the proposed Tricameral Parliament. For another, it was felt that building a non-racial movement required special efforts among the more cautious or conservative people in coloured and Indian areas. Many African people might be 'ready for freedom', it was argued, 'but we must be sure that all the people in our country are ready so that when we move, we move together'.[43] At the same time, the national UDF leadership considered that the campaign was relevant in African townships.

The UDF and its affiliates succeeded in calling for an effective boycott of the BLAs and community councils. The next phase of the campaign is to challenge the support and legitimacy of each councillor in each ward ... Affiliates will go on a signature campaign to prove that those councillors are unpopular and therefore unrepresentative of the residents. On the basis of the concrete support shown in the signature forms affiliates will call for the resignation of those serving in Black Local Authorities and community councils.[44]

The momentum of earlier struggles would be maintained, and township struggles would be directly linked to the struggle against the new constitution. In this way, some national UDF leaders believed, the campaign could help repair the divisions which had surfaced so bitterly in the referendum debate. As it turned out, most township activists remained aloof from the campaign, and divisions continued.

The MSC was novel in important respects. Like the UDF itself, the campaign sought to integrate the concerns of different South Africans into a common, if minimalist, position on national politics. It was by far the most substantial attempt at a nationwide political campaign on a non-racial basis since 1961, and it involved an active demonstration of support rather than, say, a passive election boycott. But the supposed target of one million signatures was enormous, requiring the signatures of about one in four African adults or alternatively two out of three coloured and Indian adults in the metropolitan areas where the UDF's affiliates were concentrated. Moreover, the campaign was derided by many township activists as a distraction from the insurrectionary challenge. And whilst the UDF's leaders envisaged the campaign as building organisation, it required considerable organisation to begin with.

The idea of an MSC was discussed sporadically during October and November, and was approved formally at the Port Elizabeth conference. Natal UDF officials drafted a declaration which signatories would endorse:

> We, the freedom-loving South Africans, declare for the whole world to know that: WE reject apartheid; WE support the struggle and unity of our people against the evils of apartheid; WE stand for the creation of a non-racial democratic South Africa free of oppression, economic exploitation and racism. WE say: NO to the new constitution because it will further entrench apartheid and white domination; NO to the Koornhof Laws which will deprive more and more African people of their birthright; YES to the United Democratic Front (UDF) and give it our full support in its efforts to unite our people in their fight against the constitution and Koornhof Bills.

The first signatory was UDF patron Allan Boesak in Pretoria on 22 January. A public launch was held the following day at a rally in Soshanguve, north-west of Pretoria. The national launch doubled up as a Transvaal regional launch, and the Western Cape followed two days later. In Natal the campaign was launched in February. Other regions lagged behind, reflecting a relative lack of interest in the MSC.

Although the UDF did not initially set up any specialist co-ordinating structure for the MSC, it soon became evident that the RECs, RGCs and NEC met too infrequently to provide adequate co-ordination. Morobe was belatedly appointed as full-time national MSC convener. Morobe and regional MSC co-ordinators formed a National Co-ordinating Committee. Even this was to prove insufficient, especially when state harassment intensified. As one regional secretary noted at the time, there was a 'lack of planning'.[45]

Just as there was little sense at the outset of how the campaign would be organised, there was also little sense of how long it would last. There was no sense of a 'deadline' by which the target of one million should be achieved, although Lekota told the press that the UDF hoped to reach the target within four months. By April it was clear that the campaign would have to be completed before August when elections were held for the coloured and Indian chambers of the Tricameral Parliament.[46]

Campaign organisation was provided in the regions by different combinations of regional and sub-regional structures. The most successful regions in terms of collecting signatures were the Western Cape and Border, where Area Committees and Units respectively provided effective sub-regional co-ordination – in the latter case, despite an apparently ineffective regional MSC committee. Organisation at the regional level alone proved inadequate in terms of collecting many signatures. In the Transvaal a Signatures Committee met weekly, but battled to persuade affiliates to get involved. Most signatures were therefore collected at special events rather than by affiliates.

Signatures were collected in four ways: at big meetings or special events, through house visits in residential areas, through blitzes in city centres, and in churches, at train stations and other public places. The first of these was favoured in regions where organisation was weak, or where affiliates were not enthusiastic about the campaign. The Transvaal had patchy success in setting up sub-regional MSC committees, and relied heavily on meetings and special events; one of these was a People's Festival where 6000 signatures were collected. In Cape Town signatures were collected in mosques and churches, at the Baxter Theatre, the Mowbray railway station, the University of the Western Cape, and at a high-school sports meeting in Athlone.[47]

House visits, generally in the form of a blitz on a residential area, were most successfully undertaken in Cape Town and Durban where the UDF could draw on traditions of civic activism. The first such blitz in Cape Town took place one Sunday in the coloured area of Heideveld and, to a lesser extent, in the old African location of Langa. About two hundred people were involved in collecting signatures. According to an account in *Grassroots*:

> People from all regions in Cape Town gathered together in their bright yellow and red UDF skippers. For an hour they listened to people talking of the problems and struggles that the Langa and Heideveld people experience in their day-to-day lives. Then they went out, to the homes, shops, pavements, to do the hard work of listening and talking.

Nearly four thousand signatures were reportedly collected in just a few hours.[48]

In Durban one of the most successful blitzes was conducted in part of KwaMashu township. The area, considered to be a Charterist stronghold, comprised about 1400 matchbox houses. One of the organisers was a young activist, Khetso Gordhan, the nephew of Pravin Gordhan:

> We got the local activists, we got a map from the township office, we confirmed that those were the number of houses. We broke that up into little blocks of thirty houses, or forty houses, with a little map of each section made out of the big map, and we would brief the local activists on how we were going to carry out the blitz, going door-to-door. And then we invited the key activists from the other townships, and our strongest area at that time was Lamontville, who would normally come with about fifty people, forty people. And then sort of ten each from Chesterville and Clermont and other places. And in the case of KwaMashu, I remember there were about a hundred and forty of us there on the Sunday. And we covered those 1400 houses, going in pairs, and collected over a thousand signatures for the campaign.[49]

Such blitzes generated enthusiasm among participants, resulted in many signatures, and played a major role in building a non-racial, mass movement. The Heideveld blitz garnered an unusual number of signatures. The KwaMashu blitz resulted in a thousand signatures, and most blitzes in Cape Town netted about four hundred.[50]

By the end of April 127 000 signatures had been collected, including 60 000 in the Western Cape but only 15 000 in the Transvaal. This disappointing performance was attributed to poor co-ordination between affiliates, and the limited involvement of NEC and REC members. The regions were encouraged to follow the example of the Western Cape and Natal in holding blitzes, not only door-to-door in residential areas but also in the city centre – a method tried first in Durban in March to boost a flagging campaign. The first blitz held in central Johannesburg in late April collected about 4500 signatures.[51]

With more blitzes and more volunteers, signatures were collected at a faster rate in May than before, bringing the total by the end of the month to about 216 000. But, as the national UDF office reported, gloomily, this left 'a staggering figure of 800 000 signatures still to be collected within the next two months. Going by our performance so far it may be said that if in four months we collected 200 000 signatures, in the remaining two months we shall add another 100 000 only. If this is indeed so we are deep in a crisis.'[52] The NEC decided that the MSC should be concluded before the August elections. It was also agreed that 'numbers were not important', but rather the priority was taking UDF organisation into new areas. Whatever the objective, greater effort was needed. Although a further 50 000 or so signatures were collected nationwide in June, the campaign slowed to a halt.[53]

The UDF could neither draw on the manpower nor provide the co-ordination required to collect anywhere near a million signatures. In most areas there were just too few active members of affiliates to collect the numbers of signatures required. Moreover, organisation was inadequate at the central as well as the local level. In May Lekota and Molefe wrote that 'The idea behind the UDF is to bring organisations together so that they co-operate in direct actions such as blitzes, house-to-house campaigning, etc. to bring to an end the isolation of one affiliate from another. But our observation is that in many regions our affiliates still operate in isolation from each other.'[54] RECs and RGCs were barely engaged in the campaign, and many NEC and REC leaders were failing to get involved in grassroots work. Indeed, the Transvaal regional co-ordinator reported that 'some affiliates – if not most – do not seem to have taken up the campaign in any serious way'. Organisational weaknesses were exacerbated by harassment by the police, who arrested activists, confiscated signature forms, and intimidated prospective signatories.[55]

A crucial problem concerned the lack of enthusiasm for the MSC among many African activists. Some indeed were openly critical of the campaign. This reflected the difficulty of putting together a campaign which appealed to both the more brazen and the more cautious sides of the UDF – a difficulty transformed into bitter differences during the referendum debate. Morale among activists was said to be low following the Port Elizabeth conference, and there was widespread scepticism about the UDF. Collecting signatures was derided as 'reformist':

Petitions [were seen] as the preserve of white suburbia. You know, whenever the council threatens their fences by building or enlarging the road or traffic lights etcetera, they would do those things. But in the townships the collection of signatures has never really been a widely used tactic. So in a sense it was like trying to introduce a new tactic to a political situation which traditionally had expressed itself through boycotts and even more militant forms of action than just merely collecting signatures. So one could then understand the position that some people were putting across that collecting signatures is reformist and uninspiring.[56]

In areas like Soweto UDF leaders had to 'sell' the campaign, and did so with only patchy success. In Alexandra, Youth Congress members helped to collect signatures in white areas but not in Alexandra itself.[57]

In Port Elizabeth, recalls the regional MSC co-ordinator, Stone Sizani, it was very difficult to persuade affiliates in African townships to incorporate the MSC into their own programmes. Many local activists saw the MSC as too 'intellectual' and not linked to the struggle for freedom. Mkhuseli Jack makes a similar point. Activists in Port Elizabeth, he says, were divided over the MSC. 'Some people were saying, "I don't sign for freedom, I will fight for it." It was very difficult.' There was also some discontent over the feeling that the campaign had been 'imposed from above'.[58]

In the Northern Transvaal, activists encountered a different obstacle. When youth activists tried to collect signatures they found that older people claimed to have signed the petition already – in 1955![59]

In the Western Cape 'not many signatures' were collected in the townships. In an effort to take the campaign into African areas, a major blitz was planned for the Crossroads squatter settlement. UDF leaders had to negotiate with the local shack-lord, Johnson Ngxobongwana, and to accede to his demand that his photograph be included in the pamphlet to be handed out. The Crossroads blitz was the only blitz in African areas in the Western Cape. Netting a massive 12 000 signatures, it was the most successful event of the campaign nationwide. It was also almost the last.[60]

The one region where collecting signatures in African townships was prioritised from the outset was Durban, where poor organisation and an assumed Inkatha presence meant that political support could not be taken for granted. The situation called for special preparation:

We spent hours with activists, saying: 'Now, if you go into a house, and some-body from Inkatha is there, what are you going to say?' And [we] had worked out an approach, which basically said that the UDF is not excluding anybody. It is inviting anybody who subscribes to the following principles and agrees with our vision to join. And that you didn't have to be a member to sign. That was the second key point that we were making: That you don't have to join the UDF to sign the form; that you could simply indicate your support for what it stood for.[61]

Khetso Gordhan recalls an Inkatha supporter in KwaMashu asking, 'What has this got to do with the Inkatha, and with the Chief?' The MSC volunteers told him, 'We are not challenging him, it is a new organisation, everybody is welcome to join it.' The man was persuaded to sign. Remarkably, the MSC was even taken into areas like Lindelani, a squatter settlement which later became an Inkatha stronghold.[62]

But despite successes like these, the MSC faded out before the Tricameral parliamentary elections in August. Immediately after the elections, Molefe sent a memorandum to the UDF regions noting that 'Our failure to collect even one-third of the targeted one million signatures reflects seriously on the abilities of the Front'.[63] Still no decision was made to end the campaign. In October the Western Cape UDF complained:

> It is very demoralising for our activists and many new people who have been drawn in as volunteers for the campaign to just allow the campaign to fizzle out. This also applies to those who had signed. We need to find a way of portraying the signature [sic] we have obtained as a victory despite the fact that we have not achieved our target.[64]

Neither the national nor the regional UDF found a way of doing this. The fate of the MSC illustrates one of the most common criticisms of the UDF by middle-level activists: that campaigns were taken up but never brought to a satisfactory conclusion before attention and energies were switched to a new issue.

It is easy to dismiss the MSC because of the low number of signatures collected relative to the target, and because of the role of the UDF's own deficiencies in this. One million signatures was over-ambitious, given the constraints of manpower and time. The symbolic impact of reaching the target was sacrificed. But the campaign was nonetheless very important in what it did achieve. One thousand or so activists were actively involved in a nationwide campaign on overtly political issues, and a third of a million people did sign a declaration of public opposition to the state and its reforms. The MSC easily surpassed other national campaigns of the previous twenty years in terms of popular involvement and impact.

UDF leaders, in subsequent assessments, focused on the MSC's contribution to building the UDF. Molefe later proclaimed the MSC to have been 'a very successful campaign' in terms of developing organisation through contact with the public. 'There were also many lessons to learn from this campaign. Activists discovered that dealing with the masses demands patience and a thorough understanding of their organisation and policies. There were valuable lessons for all of us.'[65] Regional activists broadly concur, pointing to important developments in terms of building organisation and networks. Khetso Gordhan, for example, points to 'the high level of interaction between different areas', the strengthening of 'the whole activist culture ... of dedication and hard work and ... non-racialism', and the consolidation of disciplined clusters of activists.[66]

Building teams and networks on a non-racial basis was a particularly important achievement. South Africa's extra-parliamentary resistance had long been fragmented along racial lines, reflecting the different political traditions and conditions in racially segregated living areas and schools. By contrast, the MSC, and especially the blitzes, brought together activists from different areas: 'people got to know each other much better, and began to understand the conditions in which other people work; that was quite useful'. The MSC took many coloured activists in Cape Town into Crossroads for the first time.[67]

As was so often the case, UDF leaders were their own strongest critics. The UDF may have 'consolidated' its area structures through the MSC but 'not enough thought had been given to how organisations could be built through the campaign'. There had often been 'little content' in blitzes, and rarely any follow-up. The UDF had failed to draw in the 'large "silent majority" – in the church, parents of school kids, on the sports field, we're just not reaching sufficient people or sufficiently'. There was, in Molefe's words, a glaring 'lack of thorough planning' and the MSC's objectives were 'often forgotten'.[68] The different goals were not entirely consistent:

> I think what was not made clear in the beginning of the campaign was, what was the emphasis of the campaign? Whether we were just targeting a million signatures or whether we wanted to build organisations. And there was a contradiction between these two objectives, which we certainly didn't recognise initially. We thought it was part of the same process. If you wanted to build organisation then you needed to go back into areas where you had collected signatures to consolidate the activists and recruit the people who showed keen interest and all that kind of stuff which took up a lot of time. Time which could have been spent collecting more signatures.[69]

These criticisms indicate the failings of the UDF at the time. It had been formed not long before and was feeling its way in terms of organisation, strategy and tactics. The MSC revealed that much had been achieved but at the same time indicated the huge gaps yet to be traversed. The UDF itself grew through the MSC: literally, in terms of its structures, personnel and relationship with supposedly sovereign affiliates; and more generally in terms of profile and stature. The UDF succeeded in seizing the fabled 'middle ground' of politics, and denying support to the state.

BOYCOTTING THE PARLIAMENTARY ELECTIONS

In mid-year the UDF turned its attention from the faltering signatures campaign to the elections for the new Tricameral Parliament. The elections were scheduled for the end of August: on the 22nd for the coloured House of Representatives, and the 28th for the Indian House of Delegates. In the absence of any prior referendums among coloured and Indian voters, the elections represented the crucial test of the legitimacy of the reforms. The UDF, its affiliates and other extra-parliamentary groups campaigned hard for an election boycott, and began to articulate publicly and prominently an alternative vision of a democratic South Africa.

Until mid-year the UDF barely discussed the forthcoming anti-election campaign. The Front was preoccupied with the signatures campaign and, as it later acknowledged, was unable 'to sustain two intensive campaigns with different profiles at the same time'. But the experience of the signatures campaign provided important lessons. The UDF 'must find ways of and commit itself to active forms of generating a *lively* campaign to boycott these elections', and must work with other extra-parliamentary groups. This was especially important given the scale of the challenge. Western Cape UDF leaders considered that they could not even count on the support of people who had signed the UDF declaration, as the Labour Party and state media had then been 'asleep'. The Labour Party was fielding several popular candidates in the elections and had the funds to pay campaign workers.[70]

A national planning meeting was finally held on 7 July. As in the case of the signatures campaign, the boycott campaign was co-ordinated by specialist national and regional committees together with the full-time UDF officials, and not by the NEC, RECs or RGCs. The degree of co-ordination provided by the UDF varied between regions. In Natal and the Transvaal the UDF's affiliates played the leading roles. In the Western Cape the UDF took on a bigger role through a regional Co-ordinating Committee that met almost every evening. The weaknesses of organisation in coloured and Indian areas in the Northern Cape and Border meant that entirely new structures had to be formed – a Committee of Concern and a Friends of the UDF group respectively. As in the Natal Midlands, these were thinly veiled UDF co-ordinating structures.[71]

The anti-election campaign finally got under way in mid-July, and rapidly accelerated into a remarkable programme of mass meetings and rallies in towns and cities across the country. Collinge aptly describes this as 'roadshow-style mobilisation' revolving around 'high-profile political leadership'.[72] One impressed journalist wrote that in just three weeks in August, TIC speakers 'addressed 19 meetings across the length and breadth of the Transvaal and spoke to about 10 000 people. None of the participating parties has reached anything like that number of potential voters.'[73] TIC and other speakers addressed meetings as far afield as Potchefstroom and Schweizer-Reneke in the Western Transvaal, Kimberley in the Northern Cape, Pietersburg in the Northern Transvaal, and Middelburg in the Eastern Transvaal. The campaign culminated with nationwide rallies on 19 August, attended by a total of 20 000–25 000 people.[74]

Speakers were carefully chosen for each meeting. Each platform comprised leaders from different racial groups, which was in itself a protest against the racial segregation underlying the new constitution as much as any previous apartheid policy. The UDF also brought in speakers from other regions so as to emphasise the national nature of the struggle. Religious leaders were often present to bestow respectability on the protests. For example, one meeting in Cape Town's Grassy Park was addressed by Boesak of the Dutch Reformed Church, Muslim Imam Solomons and the Anglican Rev. S. Luckett. Several meetings were held jointly with other extra-parliamentary organisations: the UDF and FOSATU held joint meetings in Port Elizabeth, whilst in Cape Town between four and five thousand people crammed into Athlone stadium for a rally jointly called by the UDF, independent trade unions and the Cape Action League.[75]

The predominant theme in the speeches at anti-election meetings, as well as in pamphlets and *UDF News,* was the importance of civil rights for all South Africans. This was articulated most clearly by Allan Boesak, who was the UDF's leading public speaker in this period. For Boesak, the Tricameral Parliament had to be opposed because 'It is morally wrong to accept for myself rights and privileges when such rights and privileges are denied others who are fellow South Africans. We must say once more: justice denied to one is justice denied to all.'[76] Boesak portrayed the UDF as a movement not unlike the American civil rights movement, and the struggle as a moral one. 'Let us not forget that every protest against injustice, every prayer for liberation, every act of compassion and love is an affirmation of freedom and a living sign of the kingdom of God.'[77] Boesak's appeals were echoed by other speakers. Imam Solomons, for example, told audiences that the constitution was contrary to the teaching of Islam that mankind was created equal.'[78]

Boesak's powerful oratory made him a cult figure. According to one journalist:

> Many political slogans have been chanted in the course of these elections. But none is uttered with such conviction as the cry of 'Boesak, Boesak, Boesak' from thousands of throats at a mass meeting. Sounding like a warcry, the chant punctuates just about every meeting addressed by Dr Allan Boesak ... An audience can be gently slumbering to the sound of lesser speakers. But when the crowd senses the presence of Dr Boesak arriving at the hall, the air becomes charged and the meeting begins in earnest.[79]

Lekota was another effective orator, especially among Afrikaans-speaking audiences. At one rally in Cape Town, Lekota spoke in Afrikaans, Xhosa and English, and helped to translate what other speakers said.[80]

Activists in the UDF and its affiliates also sought to challenge candidates standing for election, in part to distinguish the UDF's position from that of the candidates. This was especially important in Cape Town, where the Labour Party used anti-apartheid rhetoric and could draw on its sometimes militant history. UDF supporters heckled at and disrupted Labour Party meetings – so successfully that the Labour Party all but stopped holding election meetings. In coloured areas in the Eastern Cape, where the Labour Party was strong and UDF affiliates weak, UDF supporters were swiftly dealt with when they tried to use the same disruptive tactics. In Natal the NIC twice challenged Amichand Rajbansi – leader of the main party contesting the House of Delegates elections – to a debate, but on neither occasion did he turn up.[81]

During the first half of 1983 the state had allowed its critics considerable latitude, apparently out of concern that the elections should be seen to have been free and fair. But as election day drew closer the government became more repressive, ostensibly to counter intimidation. UDF campaigners were arrested and charged with diverse offences, there were a few intimidatory covert incidents, and finally, on 21 August, the security police detained 16 UDF leaders (including Lekota) and 19 other activists, mostly from the TIC, NIC and RMC. The Minister of Law and Order, Louis le Grange, said: 'It is a known fact that these people and their organisations plan to thwart free and democratic elections and are enthusiastically backed by the South African Communist Party and the African National Congress alliance, which openly seek the revolutionary overthrow of the democratic system in South Africa.' On the two election days the police brutally attacked demonstrators outside several polling stations.[82]

Turnout in the elections was low among coloured voters and very low among Indian voters. Overall, about one in five potential voters actually voted. An estimated 630 000 students boycotted classes at coloured schools, and many tertiary educational institutions were empty; but there was no worker stayaway. The UDF was jubilant:

> The results ... should remind the rulers that they can fool some of the people only some of the time, but no regime has succeeded in fooling all of the people all of the time. The government and its surrogates have suffered a humiliating defeat at the hands of the democratic movement ... Above all, the stay-away is a demonstration of popular support for the UDF.[83]

The following year, Molefe noted that 'we scored a major victory from which the present dispensation will never recover'. Even the Labour Party's national secretary admitted that the party's victory was 'hollow'.[84]

Although the poll was remarkably low, the UDF's claimed victory needed to be qualified in several respects. As one of the Western Cape UDF's affiliates pointed out: 'Probably there would have been a low percentage poll without UDF activity but the UDF provided an extremely important rallying point for people, showed its power to organise and work, and undoubtedly must have helped to educate the a-political or those who are lethargic about citizenship matters.'[85] Non-Charterist groups and the trade unions had also campaigned strongly against the elections, and deserved some of whatever credit was due. The polls were very uneven, with high polls outside Cape Town, Durban, Pietermaritzburg and Johannesburg reflecting the limits of UDF-affiliated organisation. There was, for example, a poll of almost 50 per cent in the Uitenhage constituency of Labour Party leader, Allan Hendrickse. Overall, more than a third of a million people voted – more coloured and Indian people than had signed during the signatures campaign.

The UDF's campaign was focused on coloured and Indian areas and generally failed to draw in African people. Earlier in the year the national UDF leadership urged that 'the campaign must be seen as a campaign of oppressed and democratic South Africans – not just the Indian and coloured sectors', and in June the NEC agreed to link the campaign with issues directly affecting African people. But these goals were not achieved. Nonetheless, the UDF-led campaign was important symbolically, helping 'to strengthen non-racial approach to struggle' and to revitalise political resistance in African areas. As the UDF regional secretary in the Border region claimed, 'the UDF had roused people who had gone to slumber since the end of the Black Consciousness-era in this region'.[86]

RETHINKING THE FRONT

The UDF's efforts at campaigning and organisation building during its first year raised a series of questions about the UDF itself. What was the UDF's goal, what was its alternative to the government's reforms? How was the UDF going to achieve that goal, how did it understand the mechanism of change and what strategies would it therefore employ? And, in the light of these, what was the UDF itself?

The UDF was formed around common opposition to the government's 'new deal'. The UDF's Declaration held up the 'vision of a united, democratic South Africa based on the will of the people'. 'We stand for the creation of a true democracy in which all South Africans will participate in the government of our country. We stand for a single, non-racial, unfragmented South Africa. A South Africa free of bantustans and Group Areas. We say, all forms of oppression and exploitation must end.' But none of the UDF's early documents indicated how this vision would be achieved.

UDF leaders were pushed into identifying an alternative process of constitutional reform as the government's own reform process unfolded. Thinking within the UDF revolved around the idea of a national convention – an idea inherited from the ANC. The ANC itself had been born in response to the exclusion of African leaders from the 'national' convention where the British colonies and former Boer republics had negotiated the constitution of the Union of South Africa. Whilst it was a legal organisation, the ANC repeatedly called for a fully representative national convention, most famously in 1961, partly in response to the National Party's 1961 constitutional reforms. In 1984, therefore, the UDF presented its call for a national convention as a response to a third undemocratic constitutional reform by the government of the day.[87]

The UDF first called for a national convention of popular representatives to draft a new constitution in about October 1983. In a letter to the Prime Minister, UDF co-presidents Gumede and Mpetha wrote:

> We sincerely believe that a speedy and harmonious solution to the country's problems can be found. To this end we call upon your Government not to implement the Constitution Act and not to enact the Koornhof Bills. We urge you to release all political prisoners unconditionally, to lift the bans on those who are silenced and restricted and to recall those who have been forced into exile by the inhuman and racist policies of successive White minority Governments. The chosen leaders of all our country's people can then sit together in an atmosphere free of fear and suspicion to work out a constitution based on the will of the people – a constitution acceptable to all.[88]

Having agreed in November on the need for a national convention, the NEC became more specific when faced with the Tricameral elections. In an NEC meeting in July 1984 'it was noted that calling on people to boycott elections is not enough, the UDF has to offer alternatives'. The NEC therefore called publicly for a national convention, with an accompanying set of preconditions: 'The unbanning of banned organisations; the return of exiles and release of all political prisoners; the demobilisation of the police and army; the suspension of the constitution, and dissolution of the bantustans; and the repeal of racist and unjust laws, including the pass laws and Group Areas legislation.' The national convention would be elected by all South Africans, would be sovereign, 'i.e. having the power to put into practice the constitution it draws up', and would meet in public, not behind closed doors.[89]

The call for a national convention was, however, not uncontroversial. The preconditions partially allayed lingering suspicions within the Charterist movement that some UDF leaders aspired to supplant the ANC leadership. But the call was still criticised, both within the UDF and by AZAPO and other non-Charterist groups, on the grounds that a national convention was a 'bourgeois sell-out' because it made the 'oppressors' party to the deliberations. A democratic constitution should be drafted by the people alone. The ever-cautious NEC referred the issue to the regions for discussion. The Transvaal UDF, for its part, resolved 'not to call for a national convention at this point in time' in order to preserve unity. The issue was put to one side.[90]

The UDF never explicitly set out how it would achieve the goal of a national convention. There were many statements of what the UDF should be doing in the short term. For example:

We know that without *mobilising* our people against every facet of apartheid; *organising* our people into democratic mass and political organisations; [and] *raising the consciousness* of our people, so that they can struggle more effectively for democracy, there can be no peace and freedom for all South Africans. Our task is to create the maximum unity of all patriotic forces through efforts like the United Democratic Front ... Our unity, organisation, mature consciousness and willingness to struggle will one day result in meaningful negotiations for the creation of a democracy based on the will of the people in which all shall live in peace.[91]

But there was little sense of how change would be effected in the longer term. What it meant by 'struggle more effectively' was not publicly clarified, and the link between increased organisation as well as more 'mature consciousness' and constitutional change went unstated.

Boesak, the premier UDF speaker of the time, presented a millenarian vision of change in his speeches. Faith and ideas were represented as being sufficient to change the world. 'Truth crushed to earth shall rise again,' Boesak claimed; 'no lie can live for ever'.[92] Faith would uphold the truth. Together with a willingness to sacrifice, even martyrdom, it would ensure the success of the struggle. Integrity was ultimately more decisive than power. The struggle was in large part a spiritual one.

Other key UDF leaders had a less millenarian view. Molefe, for example, envisaged the government and white South Africans eventually being persuaded of the justice or inevitability of the claims articulated by the UDF. According to Molefe: 'When I set out to oppose the government I was not under any illusion that it would change its attitudes and policies very easily. I knew that it was going to be a difficult task involving hard, long and patient persuasion of both the government and the white constituency.' But, Molefe continued:

> I am also aware of how over a period of time many whites shifted from their traditional positions of conservatism to supporting efforts to bring about changes, as a result of pressure and persuasion from those opposed to apartheid. I believe that I have a role to influence these shifts even further. As my ideas reach out to the white constituency, an increasing number of white people will withdraw their mandate from the government. Those who do not withdraw it will argue for change – genuine change from within the ruling party.[93]

Molefe pointed to instances where the state had given in to pressure, including forced removals that were abandoned, and the recognition of African trade unions in 1979. Pressure needed to be exerted on the government and its supporters, and the so-called political 'middle ground' won over. Faced with diminishing support, the government would accede to peaceful change rather than risk the apocalyptic alternative. Boesak himself sometimes put forward a similar view:

> We are saying to the South African government, 'We are using every method that we can possibly think of to non-violently mobilise the people and to do things that will make you realise that your violence will not change our minds and not deter us.' We are not appealing to their consciences, we are simply saying, 'You better take heed of this.' ... I believe very strongly that if the South African government does not take the UDF seriously as possibly the last mass non-violent effort in this country, then the only thing we will have left is the possibility of violent revolution. I have no doubt in my mind.[94]

In this view, as in Molefe's, it was assumed that the government would ultimately act reasonably and heed popular defiance.

These views of change might not have seemed plausible but they were perhaps the best available. Even the hard-nosed strategists in the NIC did not publicly propose a convincing alternative view of how change would come about. The obvious alternative, put forward by the ANC in exile, involved an armed struggle combined with internal insurrection in a revolutionary seizure of state power.[95] UDF leaders would not openly dispute the official ANC line. But Boesak argued strongly against violence, and Molefe apparently believed in private that revolution was neither realistic, at least not during 1983–4, nor desirable given the moral and strategic problems that would arise. Such views led to bitter arguments over specific tactics between Molefe and like-minded UDF leaders on the one side, and those leaders enamoured of strategies of armed struggle and revolution on the other.

Strategies and tactics were barely mentioned prior to or at the UDF's national launch. Only in late 1983 did the UDF begin to confront these – nearly tearing itself apart in the process. The crucial strategic choice lay between intensifying and broadening resistance. The former made more sense in terms of a strategy aimed at the revolutionary seizure of state power. The latter accorded better with a strategy focused on whittling away support for the state, leading to a situation where white South Africans would recognise that peaceful change was the only alternative to revolution. During 1983–4 the UDF's national leadership consistently emphasised this latter approach, seeing the UDF as a vehicle for forging the broadest possible unity against the proposed Tricameral Parliament rather than co-ordinating a revolutionary and direct onslaught on state power.

At the UDF's national launch, Gumede warned against 'adventurism' and 'rash actions'. A regional workshop in Cape Town in September advised against confrontational actions, although some affiliates warned against 'reformism'. Molefe emphasised a similar point in his secretarial report to the Port Elizabeth conference. The UDF, he warned, must not mistake 'the consciousness of the leadership for mass consciousness':

> This is important because we know that over the years, people have developed a scepticism and a fear of politics. We cannot pretend that the excitement the UDF has created has put an end to these feelings. We must take the prevailing consciousness as a baseline and take people through a process that will overcome their scepticism and fear.[96]

People must be drawn into organisation, he urged.

Many township activists saw the UDF as overly cautious and reformist, and believed that conditions were propitious for more militant actions and strategies. The UDF's township-based affiliates were, by and large, sceptical of the Million Signatures Campaign, and indeed maintained some distance from the UDF. Some activists lobbied the UDF to adopt more aggressive tactics including, in early 1984, a nationwide defiance campaign.

The defiance campaign was another tactic inherited from the ANC. In 1952 the ANC had waged a defiance campaign with considerable success in terms of mobilising people into the organisation. But a campaign of defiance of the pass laws in 1960 had a different conclusion: the Sharpeville massacre, and subsequent banning of the ANC and PAC. Most UDF leaders were therefore hesitant about the UDF taking up such a campaign in 1984. 'The UDF attitude', Molefe later wrote, 'was that as a front organisation, it was ill-advised at that stage to embark upon a campaign of defiance.'[97] According to the minutes of the NEC meeting in July 1984:

> No agreement could be reached as to whether the UDF could call for a defiance campaign. The emphasis made was that every action taken must win the UDF more supporters. That those involved must understand the implications of the action. It was accordingly recommended that the matter be discussed seriously by all Regions as it is likely to have far reaching implications for the UDF.[98]

Discussion of a defiance campaign was to be overtaken by the township revolt.

Issues like the national convention and the defiance campaign raised the question 'What was the UDF, and what was it for?' At its national launch there had been 'no clear understanding' of this question and a discussion paper written for the NEC in late 1983 was deemed to be inadequate.[99] Molefe later noted that the UDF had 'been grappling with the problem of developing a common understanding of front politics, as well as a common approach at the level of tactics and strategy'. He attributed the bitter disputes over the referendum debate to this uncertainty, which was itself the product of the youth of the Front.

> Most of those leading it as well as most of its affiliates are completely new to Front politics. Given the inherent strains and stresses of fronts, it can be expected that the UDF ... should manifest these problems most glaringly. Above all, most of our activists know very little about the Congress Alliance. They belong to the post-1976 era. It is therefore going to take a lot of persuasion on the part of those with experience or at least those who had the opportunity to study and discuss issues pertaining to fronts to educate our activists on these key questions.[100]

There was, however, little time for such discussion in early 1984.

The question 'What was the UDF?' soon became caught up with the question of the UDF's future after elections were held for the Tricameral Parliament in August 1984. Should the UDF continue, and if so, as what, and doing what? In June the NEC resolved that a workshop should be held after the August elections, 'to assist NEC members develop a common understanding of how a Front should function and also to deal with the contradictions within the Front'. When the national secretariat met soon afterwards, however, it considered that the 'problems within the Front' were sufficiently serious to warrant a workshop being held before the elections.[101] In July the NEC met for a workshop-cum-NEC meeting in Bloemfontein. It decided it could not take binding decisions about the UDF's future without mandates from the regions. Preoccupied with the anti-election campaign, the head office did not get round to writing formally to the regions until September. In a memorandum designed to guide discussion in the regions, Molefe wrote:

> The NEC notes that the structure and form of the UDF assumed at its inception were determined by conditions present at the time. The method of a tactical front was because of the need for the broadest possible unity. The NEC believes that it is still necessary to retain the UDF as a tactical front for it provides enough scope for the drawing [in] of more organisations particularly the unions. Nevertheless the NEC notes that not wishes but conditions will finally tell if the UDF should transform itself into another type of Front.[102]

The debate continued, but in practice the form of the front was already changing. Although the UDF was formed as a co-ordinating umbrella body, its own structures had grown during 1983–4. The UDF expanded its own personnel and structures whenever its affiliates proved inadequate at conducting campaigns agreed on within UDF forums. One aspect of this was the formation of sub-regional UDF structures in many areas and a second aspect was the growing number of full-time UDF personnel. In September 1983 the NEC decided to employ Molefe and Lekota full-time. In January 1984 they were joined by a national co-ordinator for the Million Signatures Campaign. Some of the regional secretaries were employed, and in mid-1984 the UDF began to employ regional organisers, starting with Jomo Khasu in the Northern Cape. An office administrator was appointed for the UDF head office, and Curnick Ndlovu and Billy Nair were employed in a Labour Unit to liaise with the unaffiliated independent trade unions. The NEC also agreed to employ a full-time official to take up the issue of forced removals, and discussed the appointment of a national organiser, although nothing seems to have been done about these.[103]

The employment of UDF officials required more funds. At first the UDF had operated on a financial shoestring. The national general secretary and publicity secretary were initially paid a meagre R600 per month, and NEC members had to drive to NEC meetings because air fares were too expensive. Funds were raised piecemeal, mostly from the UDF's wealthier Indian supporters in Durban. Major expenses drove regions into the red. This changed in 1984. Early in the year the co-treasurer, Cas Saloojee, went abroad to raise funds, and in May he and Morobe travelled to Sweden to collect, on behalf of the UDF, a human rights prize and the accompanying financial award. The UDF regions began to spend much larger sums, especially on the media.[104]

Given the structure of the UDF, most of the UDF's funds raised centrally were distributed to the regions. But the national treasurers, having raised the funds, were understandably concerned that funds be adequately accounted for. The increase in funding therefore involved greater accountability of the supposedly sovereign regions to the UDF head office. Finances were controversial from the outset in another respect. For example, the UDF helped to fund media produced for some civic organisations during the anti-BLA campaign in late 1983. 'This financial subsidy was a controversial issue – some civics were upset that they did not receive it. Other civics were content to rest on "UDF charity" (which UDF could not in any event afford financially).'[105] The UDF's control over expanding financial resources was to be a mixed blessing. While it enabled the UDF to shape and assist organisation building, at the same time it produced tensions within affiliates and between affiliates and the Front.

The need for international funding provided impetus to the UDF's efforts to develop its international contacts. Trips to Europe also allowed the UDF to maintain personal contact with senior ANC and SACP personnel. International contacts had a third significance: foreign governments and pressure groups were seen as an important source of influence on the South African state. This concern underlay the UDF's major activity in September and October 1984.

THE OCCUPATION OF THE BRITISH CONSULATE

In mid-September six UDF and NIC leaders took refuge in the British consulate in Durban in a very public protest against the state's practice of detaining its opponents without charging them with any criminal offence. Three of the six left after three weeks, but the other three remained inside the consulate for ninety days, only leaving in December after the government had acceded to domestic and international pressure and initiated a prosecution of leading political detainees.

Almost immediately after the detention of senior leaders of the UDF and its affiliates in late August, lawyers acting for the detainees applied to the Supreme Court to have the detention notices declared invalid. In early September the Pietermaritzburg Supreme Court declared that the detention notices in Natal were invalid because they had not provided reasons for the detentions. The government was compelled to release detainees, but immediately sought to redetain them with suitably revised detention notices. But seven detainees disappeared before the revised notices could be served on them. On 13 September five of them – Gumede and Ramgobin of the UDF, Sewpersadh and Naidoo of the NIC, and Nair – together with Paul David of the NIC, who had been in hiding for a month, took refuge in the British consulate in Durban.

The objective of the action was twofold: to draw attention to detention without trial, and to keep public attention on the UDF. NIC and UDF leaders decided that something quite dramatic had to be done. The British consulate was chosen because the British government was at the time seen as especially supportive of the South African government.

British officials made it clear that the fugitives were unwelcome, but could not evict them. After the first few days the fugitives were allowed visits only from doctors and lawyers – although this enabled them to stay in close contact with the NIC–UDF and, no doubt, the ANC. David recalls:

> Some of our friends came as lawyers: ... Zac Yacoob, ... Yunus Mahomed. So other of our friends would come, to advise us, so we were able to have some political discussions. And our doctors were carefully chosen as well, political activists who happened to be doctors. Mewa Ramgobin chose Jerry Coovadia who was a paediatrician. I remember on one occasion when Jerry came to visit Mewa, ... the Consul-General ... said, 'Mr Ramgobin, your paediatrician is here to see you.' It was so funny. And I chose Farouk Meer, who was an anaesthetist. Ja, but we thought these were reliable people who could relay messages accurately.[106]

Although the fugitives were not allowed press contacts, they managed to be interviewed over a two-way radio, and by shouting out of the window to journalists on the roof of a neighbouring building.

Conditions inside the consulate were 'no different to prison', says David. The fugitives slept on the floor because they were not allowed mattresses or pillows. Gumede suffered back problems as a result. There was no bathroom, so they were escorted to toilets for half an hour each morning, and otherwise used a chemical toilet in their room. The British officials tried hard to cajole and persuade the fugitives to leave. According to David, 'They tried rough, harsh methods and the gloved methods as well.' Some of the security guards 'were pretty nasty'; one guard 'threatened to throw me out of the window'. An official played the piccolo all night – 'He thought that this would irritate us, just scales, no tune whatsoever.' The British also brought in people to befriend the fugitives, again 'with the purpose of trying to get us out'.

On 10 December the government withdrew all the preventive detention notices. Lekota and Molefe were among the detainees released. Some detainees remained in custody, but would be charged and brought before the courts. The government's retreat from preventive detention represented a significant victory for protesters, their lawyers and their allies abroad. Two days later six thousand people gathered outside the consulate for the victorious emergence of the remaining three activists. 'David and Gumede never made it to the pavements. The police arrested them as the door of the lift opened and hurried them away ...'[107] Nair was not arrested, and was carried shoulder-high through the crowd in celebration. Days later the five fugitives, together with Transvaal UDF and RMC leaders Nkondo and Mokoena and Dr Essop Jassat of the TIC, were charged with treason.

The Natal UDF regional secretary later considered that the occupation had 'allowed the struggle and our demands to be publicised internationally. It also captured the imagination of our people. This campaign helped both to advance organisation and to politicise our community. Through the campaign we highlighted unjust security laws and detention without trial.'[108] Meer enthuses: 'In effect a lull that may well have followed in anti-system political activism after the elections, was not only arrested, but a new lease of life was injected into the anti-tricameral resistance, raising it to international proportions.'[109]

The action's principal strategist, Pravin Gordhan, modestly describes it as a 'brilliant' tactic. It eclipsed the launch of the Tricameral Parliament, and ensured that attention was focused on repression rather than reform. Molefe had spent most of September lobbying diplomats, but it was the consulate protest that provided the UDF with the opportunity to meet with a junior minister in Britain as well as the secretary general of the United Nations.[110]

But the protest also provoked dissent. It was criticised as a 'liberal' tactic, relying on the mediation of imperialist Britain rather than the revolutionary potential of the masses inside South Africa. And Gordhan was criticised for his forthright role. Transvaal regional secretary Moss Chikane privately noted that 'no coherent position' was ever explained to activists; 'as a result, when people started asking questions there was no decisive answers [sic] ... No gains in a progressive sense, only in the liberal sense.' Gordhan acknowledges that the protest made much more sense in the Durban context – where there was little protest in African areas and the action represented a logical extension of the struggle against the Tricameral Parliament – but would probably not have done so in the Transvaal where the focus of resistance had clearly shifted to the townships. Amidst state repression, however, the UDF provided little national co-ordination, leaving the regions more cut off from each other than at any time in the previous year.[111]

Controversy about international pressure in the struggle continued after the consulate protest. In early 1985 the UDF was deeply divided when UDF patrons invited American Senator Edward Kennedy to visit South Africa, and there was extensive discussion about international contacts at the UDF's national conference in April 1985. The controversy pointed to the ambiguity in the nature of the struggle. Interventions from governments and politicians in the advanced capitalist democracies made sense in terms of the struggle for democratic or 'liberal' rights but not in terms of a liberation struggle dressed up in anti-capitalist rhetoric.

The consulate occupation marked the end of the first phase of the history of the UDF. For eighteen months the UDF had campaigned against the government's 'new deal', seeking to discredit it both internationally and in the eyes of the coloured and Indian voters being wooed by the government. The occupation of the consulate served to emphasise that this package of supposedly democratic reforms came along with detention without trial and other distinctly illiberal forms of repression.

The successes of the election boycott and other campaigns notwithstanding, 1984 drew to a close with the government's constitutional reforms in place. But by this point the Tricameral Parliament was already a sideshow in South African politics. The main drama no longer involved the hearts and minds of coloured and Indian South Africans, but was focused instead on the state's authority in African townships. The township revolt was sweeping across the country.

The UDF's activities of 1983–4 played a significant part in this. The national and regional launches, NEC and REC meetings, UDF media, the Million Signatures Campaign and the election boycott all helped to build a nationwide political movement. The UDF articulated an alternative political vision and discourse which challenged the state and recast the debate on political change. There were limits to the UDF's success in building a united movement, as the debates over referendums and the proposed defiance campaign clearly showed. But South African politics had without doubt been fundamentally transformed.

The impact of the UDF was accurately assessed by its Western Cape regional secretary in early 1985:

> The UDF pushed back the frontiers of what was politically possible. We have seen how people's awareness has been heightened by the buzz of activities associated with the UDF. It is now far easier to link bread-and-butter issues to politics … This awareness has stretched throughout the breadth of our land … The UDF has awakened our people's determination to fight back, it has become the symbol of our people's will throughout the country.[112]

Chapter Six

The Township Revolt,
September 1984–September 1985

On Monday 3 September the newly elected coloured and Indian MPs joined their white counterparts in Cape Town for the inauguration of the Tricameral Parliament. At the other end of the country, in the African townships of the Vaal Triangle, residents participated in a stayaway from work and demonstrations in protest against rent increases. By the end of the day about thirty people had died in clashes between protesters, police and township councillors. As Lodge remarks: 'The longest and most widespread period of sustained black protest against white rule in South Africa's history had begun.'[1] By the end of 1984 almost 150 people were reported to have been killed in political violence, almost all of them in the PWV. By the end of September 1985 another 600 people had died as the revolt spread to the Eastern Cape, then through the northern Orange Free State and parts of the Eastern Transvaal, and on to East London, Durban and Cape Town. The government responded by declaring a State of Emergency in the PWV and Eastern Cape.

Government ministers blamed the township revolt on the UDF and charged its leaders with treason, although international attention seems to have deterred the government from banning the Front altogether. Sixteen leaders of the UDF or major affiliates – including five of the consulate fugitives – were prosecuted in Pietermaritzburg. These included Sisulu, Gumede, Ramgobin and Frank Chikane. In a second treason trial, mostly held in the dusty town of Delmas to the east of Johannesburg, Molefe, Lekota and Moss Chikane were charged together with civic and youth leaders from the Vaal Triangle. The prosecution alleged that UDF leaders had conspired with affiliates to promote revolution in the Vaal Triangle and elsewhere.

Contrary to the government's allegations, the UDF's *direct* role in the initial stages of the township revolt was limited. The UDF's national leadership was decimated by detentions in late 1984, and its regional leadership was often cut off from the townships where the revolt was concentrated. Then, too, the UDF was ill suited to playing an active role in local protests. It was generally seen as a co-ordinating forum for specific national campaigns. Despite efforts to project the UDF as an organisation for all

South Africans, to promote African leadership and to secure African participation in campaigns, the Front was still seen by many township activists as concerned with the political loyalties of coloured and Indian people in particular. Furthermore, its NEC had decided earlier in the year against adopting more confrontational tactics involving direct action. In addition, the UDF's decision-making procedures were cumbersome, inhibiting prompt responses in a rapidly changing situation. The UDF was forever 'trailing behind the masses', as Popo Molefe put it.[2]

Indirectly, however, the UDF played very important roles in both the genesis and spread of the revolt. The UDF-led campaigns of 1983–4 had reasserted the possibility of political changes far more fundamental than the government's 'reforms'. Resistance was revitalised across the country. Moreover, the revolt transformed the Front. It emphatically demonstrated the need for the Front to continue, even after the implementation of the reforms which it had been formed to oppose. It rendered more urgent the tasks of organisation building, strategic thinking, and political education in the townships, lest the revolt peter out like that of 1976–7. And it led to the organisational expansion of the Front, with a proliferation of structures at the sub-regional level and a growing number of employees. As a result of these changes, the UDF was better able to shape the further development of the revolt. In late 1985, and especially in early 1986, the UDF seized the initiative with an aggressive strategy of organisation building and political education centred on the concept of 'people's power'.

TOWNSHIP REVOLT

The Vaal Uprising, starting on 3 September, marked the beginning of a sustained revolt but it had been preceded by a series of localised confrontations elsewhere: in Pietermaritzburg in 1982, Durban and Mdantsane outside East London in 1983, Crossroads outside Cape Town, and in parts of the Free State, the East Rand, Atteridgeville outside Pretoria, and Cradock in the Eastern Cape in early and mid-1984. Protesters were killed in Tumahole in the northern Orange Free State in July, and on the East Rand in August. In each of these confrontations, and in the Vaal Uprising itself, protests were largely driven by discontent over local issues such as rent or bus fare increases or shack demolition. These issues represented material grievances and focused anger on the township councillors or bantustan authorities deemed responsible. But these local protests were not disconnected from the political struggles being waged at the national level. Civic grievances were closely tied to the 'Koornhof Bills' and the state's new dispensation for urban African people. Rents and service charges had become an issue because of the state's policy of making residents pay for the upgrading of their townships. The elections of new councils in late 1983 greatly intensified dissent since many of the new councillors broke their campaign promises by raising rates and service charges. Furthermore, the formation of the UDF, the reassertion of political resistance nationwide, the ever-rising stature of the ANC and growing access to its literature, and especially the elections to the Tricameral Parliament, were all factors that stimulated some people to become activists and play a leading role in civic protest.[3]

Whilst township activists may have been inspired by national political factors, there is little evidence of any organised co-ordination of their local protests. On the contrary, documentary and other evidence points to a remarkable lack of involvement on the UDF's part in township politics in 1984. The reasons for this lay in the character of the UDF at the time. The perceived purposes of the UDF, its organisational form, and its immediate preoccupations during 1984 all militated against its involvement in the growing tensions and dissent in the country's African townships.

The UDF was formed to co-ordinate affiliate-based campaigns around opposition to the state's reforms. Its national leaders were wary of the prospects of an insurrectionary strategy, at least given current levels of political organisation, and actively decided against adopting more confrontational tactics in early and mid-1984. The UDF was campaign-orientated. Although during 1984 it had taken on a more active role in campaign organisation than had initially been envisaged, the affiliates were still seen to be both sovereign and independent. It was up to affiliates to initiate, at least conceptually, any campaign, and to allocate to the UDF whatever co-ordinating role they felt to be appropriate.

In UDF-linked media and in the speeches of UDF leaders, the issues of rent increases and education were explained in terms of central government policies. Struggles over such issues were perceived as a way of mobilising and organising a wide range of people into active opposition to the government. But these issues were seen as the concerns of 'first-level' organisations: of civic and student associations, and not of the UDF as a second-level organisation. More importantly, the UDF, nationally and in the major regions, was focused on struggles in coloured and Indian areas, not in the African townships, and on broadening the struggle rather than intensifying it. Many township-based activists came to see the UDF as unconcerned with their revolutionary goals. Whilst supporting the UDF, they did not look to it for leadership or co-ordination in the townships, and sometimes actually discouraged UDF involvement. For a combination of reasons, therefore, the UDF was barely involved in township struggles during 1983–4.

The issues of housing and local government had been on the UDF's agenda because of their perceived roles in the state's reform strategy. The UDF had therefore helped to co-ordinate opposition to local government elections in the townships at the end of 1983, and repeatedly talked about a national conference on the housing issue. A conference was actually scheduled for mid-year in Durban, and the Western Cape UDF drafted a conference programme. The Western Cape region and its affiliate CAHAC, which organised in coloured areas, were particularly motivated because they saw housing as an issue to use in the struggle against the Tricameral Parliament. But the proposed conference was not held, and the campaign against the local government elections was not followed up.[4]

UDF national leaders thought that they should not initiate a national campaign over an issue central to some of its affiliates. As Molefe later explained:

> As far as the UDF was concerned the decision to take up a campaign around the question of housing could only be started once community and housing

committees consulted among themselves, first at regional level and then at national level. These consultations would then culminate in a national housing conference ...[5]

The initiative should arise 'from below': from affiliates via regional structures.

This view was reinforced by the problems the UDF ran into when it did intervene in the growing schooling crisis as students boycotted classes in protest over a mix of educational and political grievances. After an Atteridgeville student was killed by police in mid-February, the Transvaal REC mandated the regional co-secretary, Moss Chikane, to intervene. But Chikane's interference provoked complaints from COSAS. The minutes of an RGC meeting in April record:

It was apparent that this intervention created serious problems. After serious discussions on this, it was resolved that local organisations should discuss this issue among themselves, rather than debate this in the UDF General Council meeting. It was stressed that UDF should respect other organisations and their roles. To avoid further confusion UDF personalities should identify themselves and make it clear on whose behalf they speak. This is necessary to avoid confusion about the role of the UDF.[6]

The concern about the relationship between the Front and its affiliates was further buttressed by disagreements over strategies and tactics. The UDF leadership generally urged students to use the boycott as a tactic, to force the state to make concessions, and then to return to class. Some student leaders apparently saw the boycotts as incipient elements in a broader strategy of rebellion.

A further reason for the UDF's inaction on the housing and educational issues was the fact that there were no representatives on the RECs or NEC of those African townships where rent and schooling struggles were concentrated during 1984. None of the members of the Transvaal REC lived in African townships on the East Rand or Vaal Triangle, or in Atteridgeville (although affiliates in those areas sent representatives to RGC meetings). The Eastern Cape REC was drawn entirely from Port Elizabeth and Uitenhage; there was nobody from Cradock, Grahamstown or Port Alfred. And there was still no UDF regional structure at all in the Orange Free State.

UDF leaders were slow to recognise the significance of the growing number of protests sweeping through African townships. The minutes of Transvaal REC and RGC meetings do not record a single discussion of rent-related issues in the first eight months of 1984. In the Eastern Cape there were meetings about forming a regional civic structure, and a Crisis in Education Committee was established in November to deal with the growing schools crisis – but neither of these initiatives was closely linked to the UDF, which was not regarded as the appropriate vehicle for co-ordinating such township-based concerns.[7] When the UDF did get involved in the growing township crisis it was not because of rent or educational protests *per se* but because of state repression and the ensuing violence.

RESPONSES TO THE REVOLT

In the last months of 1984 the UDF was unable to respond decisively to the township revolt. As a result Charterist activists outside the UDF took the lead. The UDF's paralysis was primarily due to the detention of many of its leaders as well as officials in affiliates such as the NIC and TIC. The UDF itself noted: 'Repression mounted, and it found the UDF unprepared for it. Immediately after UDF big names were locked up in jails – the whole machinery of the UDF came to a standstill.'[8] The UDF's head office and the Transvaal regional office were thrown into disarray. Molefe initially evaded detention but had to operate semi-clandestinely. He too was detained in early October. The secretaries of the Western Cape UDF, Trevor Manuel and Cheryl Carolus, took over at the UDF's head office.[9] The Front was also distracted by the occupation of the British consulate in Durban.

Repression curtailed the UDF's ability to hold regular meetings, especially at the national level. The NEC and national secretariat met just once each in the last five months of 1984. At the NEC meeting in November the major item on the agenda was not the specific issue of formulating a strategic response to events in the townships but the general problem of the Front's form and direction.[10] Until this general problem was resolved, the Front's acting national leadership could hardly take it into altogether new activities. Regional structures could meet more easily. The Transvaal REC, for example, met almost monthly.[11] These REC meetings provided opportunities for sharing reports on local developments, starting a pattern of stocktaking which continued through the rest of the 1980s. But the REC lacked the capacity to take effective executive action.

Most senior UDF leaders were personally wary of rash and confrontational actions, as we have already seen. The lesson of 1976, as they assessed it, was that revolt was doomed to failure unless it was based in strong grassroots organisation and involved a wider range of constituencies than students or unemployed young men alone. On 13 September, in the week *after* the Vaal Uprising, Molefe sent a circular to the regions summarising the NEC's discussion of strategy in July.

> Although some affiliates may feel that the UDF is not militant enough and that its Declaration is too moderate, the considered view of the NEC is that whatever tactics we apply and whatever programme we develop, we must win support rather than push organisations and backward sections of our society into the hands of those forces working against us.[12]

Individual UDF leaders therefore took up issues such as state repression and the schooling crisis which could be used to embarrass the state and draw more constituencies into organised political activity. They generally did this through affiliates or other structures; doing so through the UDF itself would have been inappropriate. Thus the Detainees' Parents Support Committee monitored detentions, and the churches organised relief.

Individual UDF leaders were very active in responding to the education crisis.

Most urgently, they encouraged the formation of 'parents' organisations – more accurately, organisations of older residents concerned about the issue, preferably but not necessarily the parents of school students. A Soweto Parents' Committee was formed in October. This was not a UDF structure, since it was deemed important to involve non-Charterist activists, especially from AZAPO, but key figures were closely involved with the UDF, including Frank Chikane and Vusi Khanyile. In December the Soweto Parents' Committee convened two meetings for parents' committees from other parts of the country, and formed an Ad Hoc National Co-ordinating Committee. The parents' committees sent memorandums to and met with the Deputy Minister of [African] Education and Training in order to persuade the government to accept key student demands, especially for democratic student representative councils (SRCs).[13]

The UDF leaders' cautious emphasis on building organisation and unity was not, however, shared by all the UDF's affiliates. Many township-based activists within the Charterist movement preferred a more confrontational strategy. Some of these activists had been members of the Soweto study group in the early 1980s alongside people like Molefe and Frank Chikane who became key UDF leaders. But their strategic differences had since become apparent – in the debates over referendums in late 1983 and over UDF strategy in early and mid-1984, in their lack of interest in the Million Signatures Campaign and in tensions over the UDF's involvement in the schooling crisis. By September 1984 they were indifferent or even hostile towards the UDF, and they acted independently of its national and regional structures.

The pro-confrontationists not only were inspired by the events on the East Rand and Vaal Triangle, but also felt that they were doing the ANC's bidding. On the second day of the Vaal Uprising the ANC called on its supporters to 'intensify the struggle and ... open new fronts. We must render inoperative the ability of apartheid to exploit and oppress us further. The sharp confrontations now raging in Sharpeville, Evaton, Sebokeng, Lenasia and other areas must be widened and extended to other areas.'[14] Later in the month, ANC leader Thabo Mbeki said on Radio Freedom:

> The forces to carry out [our] offensive are daily demonstrating in action their readiness to march ever forward ... We must destroy the enemy organs of government. We must render them ineffective and inoperative ... In every locality and in all parts of our country, we must fight to ensure that we remove the enemy's organs of government ...[15]

The ANC repeated such calls over the following months. 'What is happening today ... in the African areas around the Vaal Triangle must be extended to cover the entire country,' it declared. The ANC's involvement in these events may have been 'confined largely to shouting from the sidelines', as Barrell puts it, but these 'rhetorical urgings' spurred on like-minded activists inside the country. The pro-confrontationists saw themselves as implementing the ANC's calls for mass-based direct action, or what was later termed 'ungovernability'.[16]

Both of these two approaches had strong advocates in Soweto, with each grouping deeply involved in the ANC underground. The group more closely linked to the UDF emphasised patient organisation building through house-to-house visits and workshops for activists. They focused on the Soweto Civic Association, and used its Inter-Branch Committee as a base. They were also prominent in organising around the schooling crisis. The second group, by contrast, sought opportunities for intensifying the revolution. They were clustered in the Release Mandela Committee (RMC), COSAS and sections of the Soweto Youth Congress (SOYCO), and included Oupa Monareng and Thami Mali. The tactic that they looked towards was the work stayaway, or general strike, in part because the 3 September stayaway in the Vaal Triangle had prompted the Vaal Uprising and they hoped that the same might happen in Soweto.[17]

The more cautious UDF activists were critical of the stayaway proposal. According to one SOYCO activist:

One comrade was saying: Look, the masses are not ready for a stayaway, and we cannot impose ourselves on the people. But we said: Look, this is a revolutionary situation, the masses cannot be ready on their own, they must be steered into readiness by a leadership which has read and studied the situation. So we were very confident that this stayaway is going to succeed ...[18]

The advocates of a stayaway, priding themselves on the labels 'militants' and 'radicals' bestowed on them by their critics, decided to go ahead. They issued pamphlets in the name of the RMC, calling for a stayaway in solidarity with people in the Vaal Triangle on Monday 17 September. For their part the key UDF-linked activists in Soweto, including Frank Chikane, Morobe, Pat Lephunya, Amos Masondo and Eric Molobi, were not involved in organising for the stayaway, and the Soweto Civic and its increasingly important Inter-Branch Committee were sidelined.

The stayaway was unevenly supported – by between a third and two-thirds of Soweto's workers – and was accompanied by coercion. As one organiser put it, people who went to work were later 'dealt with accordingly'. A more important problem was that the RMC's pamphlets did not specify how long the stayaway was to be, perhaps because its organisers hoped that it would be extended in the face of confrontation or insurrection, as in the Vaal two weeks before. On the Tuesday, UDF leaders Frank Chikane and Eric Molobi were apparently stoned on their way to work, and complained to the RMC-based 'steering committee'. The latter retorted that the people clearly wanted the stayaway to continue, and the leadership had no right to stop them. In practice, the stayaway quickly fizzled to a halt.

The RMC and COSAS-based activists immediately began thinking about a further, week-long stayaway. They recognised that they needed the support of trade unions.[19] On 10 October COSAS reportedly met with other organisations 'within the UDF' to discuss an approach to the trade unions. The two major independent union federations – FOSATU and CUSA – were then approached. The Central Committee of FOSATU discussed the matter on 20 and 21 October. Views on what that response should be varied within FOSATU, by union and by region. The Natal regions opposed positions that would alienate union members who supported Inkatha, whilst the Western and Eastern Cape regions were wary of what they denounced as political opportunism. Even within the Transvaal there were differences. In the heart of the metals industry in Germiston, unionists were watchful of political or township-based activity, in part because of the difficulties they faced in the workplace and in part because of the difficulties in organising in the area's townships. In areas such as Springs and Nigel where it was easier to organise in the workplace and the township, unionists favoured more active political involvement. This contrast was one factor in a split in mid-year within FOSATU's largest union on the East Rand, the Metal and Allied Workers' Union (MAWU).[20]

FOSATU's Central Committee resolved their dilemma by agreeing that 'community unrest' was 'a local issue and … must be dealt with at a local level'. The broader issues of unions' relationships with other organisations would be discussed later at a 'policy seminar'. (This was not dissimilar to the way in which the UDF had 'resolved' the referendum issue the previous year.) With regard to the stayaway, FOSATU's Central Committee agreed 'to support the students in their demands and also mandated the representatives from the Transvaal to represent FOSATU on the Stayaway co-ordinating committee'. These representatives would be led by Chris Dlamini, the FOSATU president, and included MAWU's Moses Mayekiso, who was regarded as a staunch workerist.[21]

At the same time, senior FOSATU trade unionists, including Dlamini, were involved in local developments in KwaThema, the township for Springs on the south-east Rand. School protests, and rivalry between COSAS and AZASM, led to a diverse group of people coming together in a joint parents–students committee. The group included Dlamini, other unionists, local AZAPO leaders and Charterist activists. KwaThema was one of the East Rand townships with almost no UDF or organised Charterist presence. At a public meeting in KwaThema on the same weekend as FOSATU's Central Committee meeting, it was decided to stay away from work on Monday 22 October in support of student protesters. It was proposed that the stayaway should be repeated weekly until the grievances had been addressed. The KwaThema activists already knew about the proposed regional stayaway, but it is not clear whether or how this affected their decision.[22] The success of the stayaway must have encouraged trade unionists, especially since they maintained a central role in its organisation and were not subordinated to populist politics.

Support for a region-wide protest grew when, on the day after the KwaThema stayaway, the state's security forces mounted an unprecedented operation in the Vaal Triangle. Six thousand troops and police surrounded and then searched the Vaal Triangle townships in Operation Palmiet. Heightened state repression seems to have persuaded sceptics that they had no choice but to support strong action in protest. On 27 October COSAS, the trade unions and other organisations met at Khotso House in central Johannesburg. There was some dissent over whether conditions were propitious for a stayaway, and a consumer boycott was proposed as an alternative. But the meeting finally agreed to hold a stayaway, though for two days only, on

5 and 6 November. An organising committee was formed, comprising Thami Mali and Oupa Monareng, and the unionists Moses Mayekiso of MAWU and Themba Nthlantla of the Charterist, non-FOSATU Municipal and General Workers' Union (MGWU).[23]

As far as planning the stayaway was concerned the UDF, disrupted and distracted, was not centrally involved. The initiative came from activists in COSAS, the RMC and SOYCO, who seem to have approached the trade unions directly. These initial advocates of the stayaway had poor relationships with the UDF leadership, whom they saw as overly cautious as well as being 'very hostile to cut-and-dried ANC positions' (by which they meant the insurrectionary rhetoric of Radio Freedom). Affiliates had the 'right' to initiate protests, they pointed out; the stayaway's advocates even claimed that they were 'protecting the UDF from itself' by implementing the ANC's call for ungovernability.[24] There does not appear to have been any discussion of any of the stayaways at regional or national UDF meetings during September and October. The regional stayaway was apparently first raised in a Transvaal REC meeting on 1 November – *after* Chikane had attended the planning meeting at Khotso House and just four days before the stayaway. Despite some reservations, the Transvaal UDF endorsed the call for a two-day stayaway.[25] The REC was largely bypassed, and then presented with a *fait accompli*.

Soon after the stayaway, Transvaal regional leaders provided a frank assessment of the UDF's position. When the 'crisis erupted' in the PWV: 'No quick UDF response came out. The masses expected UDF to give direction, UDF was not there to give direction, opportunists were there to seize the opportunity. We must address this question very seriously.'[26] These unnamed 'opportunists' must have been the RMC–COSAS activists. Subsequent UDF reports clouded its role in the stayaway. The secretarial report to the NGC in April 1985 recorded that 'most unions joined forces with the UDF in making that campaign the success that it ultimately became', but the stayaway was not listed as one of the UDF's own activities.[27]

The stayaway marked an important point in the growth of organised resistance. Despite last-minute detentions by the police, between 300 000 and 800 000 workers stayed at home for both days (according to the Labour Monitoring Group's estimate), making it the largest labour protest since 1961. The stayaway was uneven across the region, with the strongest support in those areas – the East Rand, Vaal Triangle and Atteridgeville – where protests, repression and confrontation had been most intense. Some 400 000 students boycotted classes, according to official figures; 23 people were killed. More important than the scale of the stayaway was the active involvement of the trade unions. For FOSATU, 'the events of November 1984 overshadowed many other important developments in what was a tumultuous year'.[28]

The UDF said that it was 'overwhelmed' by the stayaway's success. It showed the breadth of support for better education and reasonable rents. 'But the real issue is that people are no longer prepared to be ruled by other people. The underlying demand is that the Government should listen to the voice of the people and get rid of apartheid.'[29] The experience of the stayaway fed into a general strategic reassessment within the UDF, strengthening support for a bolder strategy focused on the town-

ships. But the UDF, together with FOSATU, moved quickly to quash calls for a further stayaway. Assessing that the protest showed that 'we have power in our hands ...,
that we can bring the machinery of this country to a standstill', some activists proposed a five-day stayaway in the last week of November. The UDF and FOSATU
made it clear that they would not support a second stayaway. UDF leaders believed
that the lesson of the stayaway was the need for 'sober leadership' to counter 'opportunists', for effective planning, for better discussion before public statements were
issued, and above all for 'adequate organisation'. Stayaways must be of 'manageable
proportions': regional, not national, and not insurrectionary.[30]

Unions, supported by the UDF called for a 'Black Christmas' as an alternative to a
further stayaway. The Black Christmas entailed the kind of protest favoured by the
UDF leadership. Molefe, who, along with Lekota, was released from detention in
December, later described it in court:

> The purpose of the campaign, as I understood it, was an appeal for calm during
> the period of Christmas, to demonstrate to the Government that the people
> were not happy with what had happened in the Vaal Triangle, and it was an
> appeal for solidarity with the families of people who had died, and those who
> had been in detention ... It ... appealed to ... residents not to be in a festive
> mood during the Christmas period, not to indulge in luxurious things ... buy-
> ing a lot of food, throwing parties, ... because the nation was mourning.[31]

Between 16 and 26 December, people were asked to refrain from public celebration
and from spending money on luxuries. The emphasis was on voluntary self-
sacrifice.[32] This was not, the UDF later clarified, a call for a general consumer boycott. Nor, clearly, was it the kind of revolutionary protest advocated by the more confrontational Charterist leaders.

REORIENTATING THE FRONT

In its first twelve months the UDF had presented itself as a campaign-orientated
front concerned, first and foremost, with opposing the establishment of the Tricameral Parliament. After the Tricameral elections the UDF entered an inevitable
period of hiatus as it sought not only to identify new campaigns or activities but also
to reorientate itself generally. There was never any doubt that the UDF would continue, but doing what, and how, were not clear. Crucially, there were no obvious
campaigns for the UDF to take up comparable to its campaign against the new constitution and the elections.

The Western Cape UDF later thought that this period was 'the most difficult in
the life of the Front', resulting from the UDF's lack of 'direction or programme
beyond our election campaign'. A series of meetings was held to evaluate the UDF's
work hitherto and chart its future direction. But activists were dispirited as well as
exhausted, and attendance at meetings was usually poor. In the Eastern Cape, 'disil-
lusion and incohesiveness [sic]' were said to have set in after August. The UDF

entered 'a period of intense introspection ...' In Natal and the Transvaal there was no shortage of activity, but the underlying question of the UDF's future remained unresolved. In November a Transvaal regional report urged the UDF to address the question 'Where is the UDF going to?' The Border region was least affected, because it had never been primarily election-orientated.[33]

Both the existing disagreements over the UDF and the uncertainty over its future role revolved around two related issues: the Front's character, and its form. With regard to its character, how would the UDF combine strategies of immediately intensifying the revolt with those of building opposition, either through broadening alliances against apartheid or through strengthening the organisations therein? With regard to its form, how would the UDF define the relationship between its structures and its affiliates? As soon as the elections were over, the UDF's national leadership sought to resume the debate over these issues, apparently in the belief that dissent arose from misunderstanding rather than from fundamental strategic differences. In September Molefe invited Tshwete to write a paper on 'united fronts'. The purpose was to help affiliates to develop 'a common understanding of front politics, as well as a common approach at the level of tactics and strategy'. Molefe also circulated to the regions a summary of the NEC's views on the UDF, as broadly agreed at the NEC's pre-election meeting in July. The NEC's view was that the Front should continue to 'win support rather than push organisations and backward sections of our society into the hands of those forces working against us', and remain a 'tactical front' so as to build 'the broadest possible unity' embracing 'particularly the unions'. Molefe's circular was intended to provide some guidance to the regions in their discussions.[34]

It soon became clear to both national and regional leaders that in fact the form of the Front had already changed. The UDF's structures were far less strictly accountable to its affiliates than had been envisaged at the outset, having gone beyond mere coordination in implementing campaigns. This was of particular concern in the Western Cape. The Western Cape REC considered that 'The working principles describe the UDF as a *front* comprised of affiliated organisations ... However, we have often been forced to operate as an *organisation*. The role of affiliates is thus diminished, especially when area/regional committees function well and in the height of intensive campaigns.'[35] Most activities were initiated by UDF structures rather than affiliates. 'There has been some tension between the need for us to respond quickly and efficiently on issues and the need for broad participation.' In March 1985 the regional secretary reported that the region was 'still battling with the question of how a front should operate and at times the differences between a front and an organisation have been blurred'. Problems in decision making were said to have led to 'confusion and disunity', and undermined the implementation of decisions.[36]

Most sections of the UDF agreed that it should be restructured into a tighter organisation. The Front's structures should enjoy more autonomy from its affiliates so as to allow for prompt decision making and interventions. As the Eastern Cape UDF put it, 'the REC should acquire a more functional, interventionist and dynamic leadership character'.[37] Tshwete, the Border regional president, provided an overtly vanguardist perspective on this:

As an executive committee we should be able to take decisions and formulate policy. This is important and allows you the privilege of influencing the course [of] events. It is a privileged position because the perspective of any executive at any level will always be wider than that of affiliates who necessarily must be able to see only as far as their limited affiliate horizons.[38]

(This vanguardist perspective was much closer to the way in which the ANC understood its own role, as Barrell shows.)[39] In early 1985 several regions streamlined their decision-making procedures, most thoroughly in Natal where the role of the RGC was severely curtailed. The national UDF did likewise at its national conference in April. This restructuring prompted some unsuccessful opposition. When the Western Cape REC proposed that a majority within the REC be sufficient for decision making, some affiliates argued that decisions should be based on consensus within the RGC.[40]

UDF leaders not only proposed making UDF structures more autonomous of affiliates, but also began to suggest that affiliates should be accountable to the UDF. Tshwete, for example, wrote that the leadership must consult with affiliates before making a decision, but 'once a decision has been struck it becomes immediately binding on all affiliates. No dissent will be allowed.'[41] While Tshwete's view, akin to the 'democratic centralism' characteristic of some left political traditions, was more rigid than that of most other UDF leaders, there was general agreement that affiliates should act in a more responsible or disciplined manner. According to a paper discussed at the NEC in November:

> Most of our affiliates do not have the experience of having worked in an alliance like the UDF. While we encourage affiliates to take up campaigns, we must bear in mind that the work of our affiliates will invariably have a bearing on the work of the rest of the Front. As affiliates, we should feel duty-bound to consult with or at least inform the rest of the Front about all campaigns we propose to tackle, particularly when campaigns will be mass-based.[42]

Even Molefe, a strong defender of the form of a front, felt that the UDF was 'ultimately responsible for everything done by our affiliates'.[43]

The move towards increased independence from affiliates began before September, and was indeed rooted in the fact that the Front was formed to execute tasks distinct from those of its affiliates. But the township revolt from September greatly accelerated this shift, as affiliates seemed to be acting independently of the Front. As the national secretariat put it in January, the UDF had to 'work out an approach that will ensure that the UDF does not trail behind the masses but lead them'.[44] The Transvaal regional stayaway played an important role in defining the new approach. According to Jeremy Cronin, a former ANC political prisoner and, from 1985, Western Cape REC member:

> We had very successfully boycotted the Tricameral elections and ... Black Local

Authorities, which was the project which had assembled the UDF ... [After that] there was a substantial strategic crisis of ... how to go forward ... And there were two threads coming through at that point. One was a return back into our affiliates, picking up on [everyday civic] issues ... But there were ... strong feelings that you couldn't just retreat back into that. You had to, at the same time, be focusing on the national political issue of state power. But we didn't know how to do that. We were lost, I would say. And what the stayaway did, ... [it] pointed to continuing mass surges, mass militancy. [It] also indi- cated that this heightened political climate had [also] affected quite dramati- cally the African townships ... [From] that November stayaway onwards, the real focus, the cutting edge of struggle, became the African township.[45]

This meant an important strategic shift. Rather than organising at the grass roots in order to transform popular consciousness and prepare for some subsequent polit- ical struggle, the UDF would involve itself in the existing political struggles being waged in the townships. And rather than struggling over the middle ground, it would harness the militancy of the most revolutionary sections of society.

One aspect of this shift was to reorientate the UDF towards African rather than coloured and Indian areas. In the Western Cape, for example, the UDF acknowl- edged that it had hitherto been preoccupied with coloured areas, such that 'Not enough had been done to generate substantial opposition from the African sector'. Even in this region, where a majority of the population were coloured, 'African working-class' leadership should be emphasised.[46] A second aspect of the shift was a renewed emphasis on organisation building. The UDF leadership understood that sustained and successful struggle required strong organisation, and worried that the high level of mobilisation in the Transvaal had no such basis. In mid-November the ex-Islander and Natal political leader, Curnick Ndlovu, presented a paper to the NEC in which he stressed the necessity of organisation building. Organisation, he wrote, played a 'vital role'. 'Our success must be measured against the criteria – to what extent have we mobilised *and organised* our people. The task of organising then will be an *added* task of the Front. Appropriate resources need to be allocated for this purpose.'[47] The Western Cape REC similarly argued that the UDF should build national political consciousness with 'systematic education and training of our activists', and develop local organisations.[48] Organisation building in African areas was to become a leading UDF activity.

The strategic shift also entailed a different overall role for the UDF. As a legacy of the struggles of 1983–4, the UDF had an uneasy relationship with many of the activists most closely involved in the township revolt. As Barrell puts it, 'the UDF was *leading from behind*'.[49] Henceforth, the UDF would not co-ordinate protests as much as co-ordinate the organisations which sought to direct resistance.

Most of the top UDF leaders were slow to embrace this strategic shift, and did so only as they became convinced that there was a real opportunity for revolutionary change. By March 1985, for example, the Western Cape REC began to describe the government as being in deep crisis, and credited mass defiance with pushing it into 'the weakest position since it came to power in 1948'. REC leaders abandoned their earlier caution and espoused an increasingly militant perspective.

It is often said that we have tried to march too far ahead of our organisations and that we have not done sufficient ground work. Yet we remember that our people will not wait until we believe we have adequately prepared the ground. The anger that is exploding all over the country bears testimony to our people's readiness for mass action, and we must be committed to taking this forward.[50]

In the Western Cape this meant that the UDF would no longer be so constrained by the perceived caution and conservatism of most of the coloured people – although most regional leaders remained wary of the revolutionary politics espoused by the most militant township activists.

The ANC's role in this strategic shift is not clear. Radio Freedom broadcasts advocated general insurrection, as we have already seen, inspiring some Charterist activists inside the country. Most of the top UDF leaders, with exceptions such as Tshwete, seem to have been wary of purely insurrectionary strategies. It is not entirely clear what the UDF leadership thought of the revolutionary rhetoric broadcast on Radio Freedom, nor what consultation took place between them and the ANC during the period of reorientation in late 1984 and early 1985. Whatever the content of Radio Freedom broadcasts, however, it seems that the ANC consistently recognised the need for a national co-ordinating structure, endorsed the UDF's emphasis on organisation, and supported activities which would enable the UDF to tread the fine line between legality and illegality.

The UDF's relationship with the ANC as well as the Front's strategic direction was raised in a debate over its adoption of the Freedom Charter. Adoption of the document could explicitly promote Charterism but might also undermine the continued building of a broader alliance under implicit Charterist leadership. Tshwete urged that the UDF adopt the Charter. In an apparent reference to the UDF Declaration, he denounced 'watered-down' alternatives as 'certainly a sell-out position'. UDF affiliates averse to the Charter 'need to be educated about it'. The NEC felt, however, that the Front itself should not adopt the Freedom Charter 'at this juncture'. The Front did not have the necessary ideological cohesion, and in fact wanted to attract organisations wary of or even opposed to the Charter and its perceived link to the ANC, including important trade unions as well as organisations based in white areas. The UDF Declaration and the Freedom Charter were not considered to be incompatible, however, as the Charter was 'a document of far greater stature'. A UDF workshop on the Freedom Charter recommended that there should be a campaign to popularise the Charter, but that the UDF, as a front, should play a supportive role and not actually lead the campaign.

In June the UDF declared its full support for the celebration of the Freedom Charter's thirtieth anniversary but, rejecting a proposal from the Border region, decided not to adopt the Charter itself. The celebrations were run by committees formed by UDF affiliates, not by the Front's regular structures. The UDF later claimed that over 400 000 copies of the Charter were distributed in the Western Cape, Natal and Transvaal.[51]

These debates took place in a context of ever-spreading confrontation between protesters and the state's security forces. Violent conflict continued across much of the PWV and northern Orange Free State, and spread to much of the Eastern Cape and parts of the Eastern Transvaal. As in the last months of 1984, the UDF played indirect rather than direct roles in this. At this time the UDF was extending its organisational reach across more and more of the country. In the Border region, for example, the UDF began to co-ordinate new affiliates in the small towns of the interior: youth structures in Queenstown, Mgwali, Sada and Fort Beaufort, and COSAS branches in Queenstown, King William's Town, Whittlesea and Fort Beaufort.[52] Through its national and regional structures and, in some areas, its local Area Committees, the UDF facilitated communication, and thus the replication of protests in hitherto quiescent areas. Activists were also sent to poorly co-ordinated areas such as the Eastern Transvaal to build political networks.[53] Funerals provided opportunities for high-profile UDF speakers such as Lekota to emphasise the links between local and national struggles. But protests could not simply be turned on at will. In Cape Town UDF leaders unsuccessfully tried to organise a bus boycott. And UDF meetings were not the only mechanism for inter-township contact. On the East Rand, for example, COSAS played a more important role in the intensification of protest.

Unlike the leadership in organisations such as COSAS, the UDF leadership was not unambiguously committed to the escalation of protest. Leaders like Molefe had very mixed views about student protests, for example, and were consistently opposed to indefinite school boycotts. Many UDF leaders favoured meeting with state officials to address some of the students' demands and facilitate the students' return to class. Molefe, among others, urged students to return to class, arguing that students could not achieve victory on their own and needed to work with parents committees.[54] Most COSAS leaders, in contrast, generally denounced meetings with state officials, and called for continued boycotts. Although many students returned to school in January 1985, it was reported in mid-February that as many as 70 000 students were still boycotting classes.

In March resistance exploded in the Eastern Cape. In late 1984 there had been some school boycotts and isolated clashes. In December 1984 the house of UDF regional vice-president Fikile Kobese was petrol-bombed, and his nephew killed. In the New Year school boycotts spread, and many township councillors resigned in the face of popular anger.[55] As elsewhere in the country, activists in the Eastern Cape were inspired by the November Transvaal stayaway. They may also have been motivated by the ANC's call in January for people 'to render South Africa ungovernable',[56] although this appeal may not have circulated much inside the country until the widespread distribution of an ANC pamphlet in April. It was not until March, however, that plans were made for a 'black weekend' comprising a consumer boycott and stayaway over the weekend of 16–17 March, followed by a full stayaway on Monday 18 March. In Port Elizabeth, as in the Transvaal, the stayaway call was made by

Charterist activists outside formal UDF structures; in Port Elizabeth's case it came from the local Youth Congress (PEYCO). The UDF seems to have been involved peripherally.[57] But in Port Elizabeth, in contrast to the Transvaal, the stayaway was called without FOSATU's involvement and proceeded without its support and despite consequent misgivings among some Charterist activists. The protests were unevenly supported, with near total support in Port Elizabeth's African townships, much weaker support in Uitenhage's African townships, and very little support in coloured areas in either city. Nonetheless, the protest emboldened the Charterist leadership. PEYCO's Mkhuseli Jack said that the stayaway demonstrated the effectiveness of the community-based organisations, and showed 'that we can hit at the white businessman if we like at any time'.[58]

Just a few days later politics in Uitenhage and the region was transformed. On 21 March – the anniversary of the 1960 Sharpeville massacre – twenty-odd people were killed by police on their way to a funeral, in what became known as the Langa massacre. This prompted further stayaways and violence in which the one remaining councillor and members of his family were killed. The popular mood was demonstrated by the size of crowds attending the funerals of unrest victims over the following weeks. An estimated 35 000 people attended one funeral in Uitenhage; 60 000 people attended another. The UDF's immediate response to the massacre was to condemn it, and call for a national day of mourning. The escalation of violence forced the UDF to restate its commitment to non-violence – albeit qualified in that the UDF refused to condemn what it called the 'defensive' violence of protesters against the state and its agents. The UDF also sought to repair its troubled relationship with the FOSATU unions in the Eastern Cape.

Not only was the UDF's role in the escalation of resistance more indirect than direct, but there is some evidence that the ANC itself played a limited role only. Lodge, in a survey of this period, records the hiatus in MK activity between September 1984 and February 1985. The deportation of ANC personnel from the frontline states, in terms of the Nkomati Accord signed between South Africa and Mozambique, and under South African pressure in Swaziland, greatly disrupted the ANC's forward command structures. The ANC had to concentrate on rebuilding its lines of communication into and inside the country. As Lodge notes, 'guerrillas have not been very active in the areas affected by the recent township unrest: there have been no attacks attributed to the ANC in the southern Vaal, none in the Eastern Cape, and only a few on the East Rand'.[59] The ANC, as much as – if not more than – the UDF, was 'leading from behind', in Barrell's words.

The UDF was also constrained by its own organisational weaknesses and distracted by other activities. Molefe later described the UDF head office at this time as being understaffed and chaotic: 'it was really difficult to get anything done properly'.[60] The UDF was caught up in activities over the visit to South Africa of American Senator Edward Kennedy and then the celebration of the award of the Nobel Peace Prize to Bishop Tutu. Kennedy was actually invited by Boesak and Tutu, who were both UDF patrons, and not by the UDF itself. Some affiliates, especially in the Western Cape, were very critical of Kennedy's visit, denouncing him as an agent of American capitalism and imperialism. The UDF, after some indecision, endorsed the invitation to Kennedy, but decided not to meet him formally during his visit. A celebration of Tutu's Nobel Prize was the UDF's biggest ever function in Soweto, and brought the Front new allies.[61]

As protest escalated across the country, the state intensified its attack on the UDF. National and Transvaal regional leaders were detained in raids on the night of 18 February. The detainees included one of the national presidents, Albertina Sisulu, national treasurer Cas Saloojee and Frank Chikane, along with trade union leaders from SAAWU. Seven of the new detainees were charged with treason, joining the eight leaders already charged in what was to become the Pietermaritzburg Treason Trial.[62] It was immediately apparent that this was to be the most important treason trial since the 1960s, and consequently it attracted wide international as well as national attention. The police missed both Lekota and Molefe. Lekota recalls that the next morning he went to Khotso House.

> I had parked my car and was reading a newspaper in the car ... [Popo Molefe] came up after he had parked his car. I then said he must go to the office, and 'I will be coming back later'. Then, almost a minute later, he came back, running, and he told me that there were police in the office ... I said to him: 'The last time, I was the first one to be arrested. You go there and find out what is going on. If anybody gets arrested, you get arrested first this time.' So he left his bag with me, and he went ... But apparently, halfway, he decided to phone our lawyers ... He discovered that people had been arrested in other parts. He came back ... From that day onward, I did not appear in public, did not address any public meeting or attend any public gathering ... I had just come out from a long period of detention ... and I was not keen to return to it again.[63]

For the next two months, Lekota and Molefe 'had to run the organisation from the corners of streets, dark rooms and buses'. Manuel and Carolus from Cape Town and Ndlovu and Nair from Durban took over many of Lekota's and Molefe's roles. At the end of March the state prohibited the UDF and a number of affiliates from holding indoor meetings.[64]

Despite the repressive context, the UDF proceeded with its planned regional and national conferences. Border was the only region to have already held an AGM. In March AGMs were held in the Eastern Cape, Transvaal, Western Cape and Natal. The atmosphere at the AGMs was celebratory. The UDF had led successful struggles against the Tricameral Parliament and, as the Border regional secretary, Arnold Stofile, reported: 'the winds of democracy and liberation are indeed sweeping through the dusty, famine-ravished tracts of land wherever our masses, sweltering in the heat of oppression, are to be found'. But the AGMs were also self-critical. Secretarial reports pointed to the poor performance in the signatures campaign, the poverty of organisation in many areas, and persisting problems of disunity.[65]

Elections were held for new RECs. Most of the existing officials and many REC members were re-elected. A small number were defeated in competitive elections, reflecting political divisions within the Charterist movement. In the Western Cape civic leader Zoli Malindi defeated the incumbent Oscar Mpetha for the regional presidency. In the Transvaal, a whole slate of candidates associated with Freeway House, including Moss Chikane, were defeated. Across the country, many of the older REC members chose to step down, or had already dropped out, to be replaced by younger activists; veterans of the 1950s gave way to 1970s activists, the products of secondary and even tertiary education.

The addition of new members to the RECs meant, in two important cases, that the UDF regional structures were extended to previously unrepresented areas. Until its AGM in March 1985, the Eastern Cape UDF was largely confined to the Port Elizabeth–Uitenhage area. At the AGM, two new REC members were elected. Cradock activist Matthew Goniwe, having been fired from his job as a teacher, was employed as a full-time 'rural' (small town) organiser. Mthiwabo Ndube from Port Elizabeth, a leading figure in the Eastern Cape Crisis in Education Committee, was elected as recording secretary. Both activists had strong links in the small towns. Through these appointments the Eastern Cape UDF developed a genuinely regional perspective, linking up with further small town leaders such as Gugile Nkwinti (Port Alfred), Dan Sandi (Grahamstown) and Thembile Bete (Alexandria).[66] Similarly, the new Transvaal REC was drawn from a much wider range of townships across the PWV. Neither the Western Cape nor Natal REC succeeded in broadening their membership in the same way. Under the new pattern the regional UDF leadership expanded much more easily in those regions dominated by African politics.

By the beginning of April 1985 the National Party government seemed to be under unprecedented pressure, both inside the country and internationally. Its constitutional reforms had been undermined, and the continued oppression of the African majority was now highlighted by protests in urban streets, schools and factories in several parts of the country. A top army general acknowledged the danger of the situation 'getting out of hand'.[67] Although the UDF may not have been quite the instigator that the state portrayed in the press and in court, it played an important role in linking local protest with the national political struggle. The upsurge in resistance opened up new opportunities for the UDF – but also posed new challenges. While the UDF leadership had the objective of political change, most of them sought to achieve it with the minimum of violence, using strategies and tactics that were morally defensible, and in a spirit of non-racialism. In April, the UDF held its first full national conference, or National General Council (NGC), to assess the Front's performance since its launch and to plan the roles it should play in the fast changing political context.

THE AZAADVILLE NATIONAL GENERAL COUNCIL, APRIL 1985

About three hundred delegates and observers from all over the country gathered over the Easter weekend in the Indian area of Azaadville, Krugersdorp, on the West

Rand for the UDF's first full NGC. The conference theme was 'From Protest to Challenge, From Mobilisation to Organisation', a slogan which Lekota had been developing since the end of the previous year, partly in response to the rash insurrectionism that had surfaced at the time of the November stayaway.[68] This theme indicated the direction in which the UDF leadership sought to move, presumably after consultation with the ANC.

The first task facing the NGC was to reformulate the UDF's stated objectives. At its launch the UDF had focused almost entirely on the new constitutional dispensation. It now needed a broader purpose. The NGC accordingly revised the statement of objects in the Front's Working Principles, to include the following:

The UDF shall strive towards the realisation of a non-racial, democratic and unfragmented South Africa, and to this end shall:
    3.1 articulate opposition to the legislative programme of the government in so far as such a programme conflicts with democratic principles,
    3.2 act as a coordinating body for progressive community, social, educational and other such organisations which subscribe to democratic principles
    3.3 articulate the social and political aspirations of the affiliates of the UDF and their members.

The NGC issued a set of 'immediate demands' to match its broadened role. These included:

- the abolition of the Tricameral Parliament, segregated local government and bantustans;
- the scrapping of the Land Acts, Group Areas Act, pass laws, and so-called security laws;
- an end to forced removals;
- the release of political prisoners and unbanning of political organisations;
- the disbanding of the security forces; and
- a unified education system.

The original UDF Declaration was, however, left unchanged. The NGC also declared that 'the UDF continues to represent and articulate the genuine needs and interests of all democratic South Africans'. But, it emphasised, the UDF should not be seen as 'the spearhead of the liberation struggle'.[69] As Curnick Ndlovu put it in his keynote address, the UDF was 'another link in the process of liberation'. The so-called Border clause in the 1983 Working Principles was retained.

This broadened role increased the need for the UDF to reform its own structures. Its experiences of campaigning, partial paralysis in the face of the township revolt, and state repression during 1984 had already persuaded the UDF leadership of the need to reform the Front to provide more effective political leadership. Popo Molefe described in his secretarial report how existing procedures prevented prompt decision making. 'At times this has meant that the Front has been unable to provide a lead on some issues, for example the current education crisis. Since it is essential that we are able to lead our people in every struggle they fight, we must find a way of taking quick decisions whilst maintaining maximum unity.' Molefe suggested that a smaller NEC would facilitate faster decision making and more effective co-ordination, and at the same time 'reduce the number of people who are exposed to state victimisation at any single point in time'.[70]

The NGC duly revised the UDF's Working Principles. The initially unwieldy NEC was massively slimmed down, reducing the number of regional representatives by two-thirds. The regions would be more fully represented in meetings of a National Working Committee, an extended NEC, to be held at least twice a year. The NGC would only meet every two years, rather than annually as (supposedly) hitherto. These changes ratified and accelerated the UDF's transformation from a merely co-ordinating front to an organisation operating with ever-increasing independence from its affiliates.[71]

A new slim NEC was elected. Molefe and Lekota (who surfaced from underground for the conference) were re-elected, but the jailed treason trialists were replaced. Azhar Cachalia, a Johannesburg-based lawyer from a family long involved in Charterist politics, was elected as national treasurer, and Curnick Ndlovu was elected to the new post of chairperson.

The NGC flagged changes in the UDF's activities that were even more fundamental than its structural reforms. Hitherto the UDF had been campaign-orientated, and a critical assessment of campaigns took up a large part of the secretarial report to the NGC. The 1985 NGC shifted the Front's focus to building organisation and training activists. This reflected three factors. Firstly, there was no single issue comparable to the Tricameral Parliament which could provide a focus for campaigning. Secondly, most UDF leaders considered that the popular mobilisation of the previous nine months was flawed by organisational weakness. As Molefe put it, repeating the words he had first used in January, 'organisations trail behind the masses' in many areas; mass action, he said, was more often 'spontaneous' than 'disciplined'.[72] Thirdly, the Front was not in a position to command the loyalty of many organisations at the fore of the township revolt. In view of all this, the UDF should exercise leadership through organisation building and political strategising.

The NGC identified the transformation from mass mobilisation to mass organisation as the major challenge facing the Front. Molefe elaborated in his secretarial report:

> We must deepen our organisation. Out of the mobilised mass support our current organisations must develop cohesive structures ... Our affiliates must develop the capacity to identify and to address the needs of the masses of our people. We must increase mass participation in our organisations. Skills must not be limited to a few people, but rather spread and be shared.[73]

The 'quality' of activists and leaders needed to be raised, he said, and action against apartheid should be 'disciplined'. As Billy Nair later summarised:

- consolidation and creation of organisation is our strongest defence [against repression];
- education in our ranks is crucial;
- we should not be overtaken by our people;
- specific conditions in areas should not be viewed as the general: our response should reflect a national perspective.[74]

It also meant that 'all forms of factionalism, regionalism, individualism and cliqueism must be stopped'.[75]

The NGC trod gingerly around the issue of education, reflecting the tensions during the past fourteen months between the UDF and its affiliate COSAS. The UDF's student-based affiliates would take the leading role in education struggles, including an Education Charter Campaign. The UDF would encourage other affiliates to support the students, and 'develop structures that will ensure effective participation in and support for student struggles'. It would also help to organise co-ordinating structures, but these would not have decision-making powers, presumably out of respect for the student-based affiliates' autonomy.[76]

The NGC also recommitted the UDF to further broadening the alliance against apartheid. This was now understood not so much as contesting the middle ground, as it had done in 1983, as in building unity among radical opponents of apartheid. An NGC Statement appealed to progressive forces to avoid mutual attacks and fragmentation. The importance of trade unions was emphasised over and over again. Molefe's report included a call for campaigns for political prisoners, clearly designed to accommodate both the Transvaal-based and Natal RMCs. Most importantly, perhaps, the NGC committed itself to building the UDF 'so that it reflects the centrality and leadership of the African masses in our struggle'.

One of the major concerns of the NGC was the question of the UDF's international links. These had long been a source of dissent within the UDF. On the one hand, most of the UDF leadership saw international pressures as playing an important role in opposition to state repression, and cited the Durban consulate occupation as a major victory in this regard. On the other hand, many affiliates were strongly opposed to what they saw as imperialism and the American and British governments in particular, and regarded activities such as the consulate occupation as a distraction at best and supping with the imperial enemy at worst. Differences over this issue had been exacerbated by the consulate occupation and the Kennedy visit. In his report, Molefe made a point of distinguishing contacts with governments from those with progressive forces in other countries; the latter could help isolate South African internationally. Molefe defended Kennedy's visit to South Africa on the grounds that Kennedy was genuinely opposed to apartheid; Molefe even implied that Kennedy was in the 'anti-imperialist camp'. The NGC tried to accommodate both positions, fervently condemning imperialism, and especially American imperialism, in two resolutions whilst endorsing the UDF's international contacts in a third. The importance of international relations was highlighted soon after the NGC, when Arnold Stofile flew to New Zealand to oppose successfully a planned tour of South Africa by the All Blacks rugby team.

The NGC seems to have secured broad agreement within the UDF for its new strategic approach. There was little clarity, however, as to the precise contents of a programme of action, or indeed on the strategic direction in which organisation building should proceed. The criticism of opportunism was clearly not shared by all UDF leaders, let alone those Charterist critics who remained outside UDF structures – in COSAS, youth organisations, the Johannesburg RMC, and elsewhere. The NEC itself believed that there had been inadequate 'political content' and 'no clear public line emerged'.[77] The UDF was unable to provide clear strategic or ideological leadership. Only towards the end of the year did a sense of strategic direction emerge, over the notion of people's power.

ORGANISING NEW AFFILIATES

Organisation building was concentrated in two sectors: the youth and civic sectors. The youth were prioritised because of their prominence in the township revolt, and civics because they represented those older township residents whose involvement was considered necessary if a sustained and effective struggle was to be waged against the state.

The UDF had been considering a campaign around youth since mid-1984. The specific impetus arose from the decision of the United Nations to proclaim 1985 as International Youth Year (IYY), and the subsequent announcement by the South African government that it would organise activities as part of the UN focus on the conditions facing young people. UDF leaders thought that a campaign around IYY could perform three roles. Firstly, it would provide 'an opportunity to highlight the conditions of youth in S.A. and to place our struggle on the international agenda'. Secondly, it could be used to 'project extra-parliamentary opposition as a viable alternative to the current regime, and at the same time project the current regime's illegitimacy'. Thirdly, and most importantly, it provided 'an opportunity to educate our youth and to mobilise them to take up issues like unemployment, education and conscription' – linking the concerns of young African, coloured, Indian and white people. Faced with widespread mobilisation among sections of the youth, the UDF sought to build youth organisation and to reach out to non-political youth groups. In short, it was hoped that this campaign would provide the kind of integrative focus for youth organisation nationwide that the campaign against the Tricameral Parliament had done for the UDF itself.[78]

The problem facing the UDF was that most of its affiliated youth organisations in the townships favoured direct action over organisation, prioritised overtly political issues, were cynical of non-political youth groups, and seemed to be dismissive of the UDF's moderation. The very reasons why the UDF promoted a campaign around IYY were the reasons why the UDF, as an affiliate-based Front, would struggle to get it off the ground.

In November 1984 Charterist youth organisations from across the country had met in Lenasia, where they established an interim committee to co-ordinate an IYY campaign and prepare for the formation of a national youth organisation. A further conference was held in January outside Durban. It quickly became apparent that there were mixed feelings about both the proposed campaign and the UDF itself. The result was the formation of not one but two national co-ordinating committees. One committee, chaired by Dan Montsitsi, would co-ordinate IYY activities. Montsitsi, one of the 1976 student leaders in Soweto, jailed on Robben Island and active in the Soweto Youth Congress since his release, was close to people like Molefe, Molobi and Morobe. The second committee, chaired by Pretoria activist Deacon Mathe, would co-ordinate the formation of a national youth organisation. These committees represented two distinct approaches to youth organisation. The IYY committee was seen as a means of bringing non-political youth groups into a broad-based youth movement, in the expectation that they would become more overtly politicised. The national youth organisation proposed by Mathe's committee, by contrast, would be a federation of 'disciplined youth congresses' that had already adopted or were 'well disposed' towards the Freedom Charter. It would explicitly *not* be a 'conglomeration' of 'social, cultural, sporting and political youth groups'. The group around the second committee included activists linked to Freeway House in Johannesburg, and others who were critical of the UDF Transvaal and national leadership. The purge from the Transvaal UDF leadership of activists associated with Freeway House in March 1985 could only have exacerbated enmity.

The dispute led to disagreement over whether the IYY campaign should be conducted under the banner of the UDF at all. There was strong opposition to this at the January conference, although it was not clear what the alternative was in the absence of a national youth organisation. The UDF's leaders seem to have recognised that the campaign would get nowhere if it was not taken up under the banner of the UDF. After meeting with Mathe and Montsisi, Popo Molefe wrote to the regional secretaries insisting that the campaign be conducted in the UDF's name, although affiliates should lead the campaign:

> The UDF has already won a great amount of legitimacy both nationally and internationally. Many people and organisations ... will support anything that is associated with the Front. To give the IYY campaign publicity and to win even greater support for it we need to encourage our affiliates to conduct it under the banner of the UDF ... We have already started building the UDF as a vehicle to advance our struggle. The youth organisations in their campaigns, especially the IYY, must be seen to be part of this broad movement.[79]

But the UDF's regional structures do not seem to have paid heed to Molefe's exhortation.

The dispute within and between the UDF's affiliated youth organisations retarded the IYY campaign. A programme of activities was planned, including a National Youth Week around 16 June, and culminating in a National Youth Festival in December. But the response was poor almost everywhere. The campaign was finally killed off by repression under the State of Emergency from July: events were banned, and scores of youth activists detained.[80]

The UDF made better progress with respect to civic organisations, although this too was to fall victim to the Emergency.[81] After neglecting civic organisation and struggles during 1983–4, UDF regions became steadily more involved in the aftermath of the township revolt. Most notably, the Transvaal UDF held a workshop for civics, established a new civic-orientated service organisation, the Community Education and Information, or CEI, project, and elected a regional civic co-ordinator at its AGM. In the Eastern Cape the Cradock civic activist Matthew Goniwe was elected to the REC, and immediately began building and linking civic organisation in the Eastern Cape hinterland. In late April the Soweto civic, with the assistance of CEI, convened a workshop which was attended by civic activists from as far away as Cape Town and Durban. At this meeting it was apparently agreed that some kind of national co-ordinating body was needed.

The national UDF leadership responded slowly to these regional initiatives. Civic organisation was seen as something to be built from the bottom up rather than the top down. There was remarkably little discussion of township-based struggles over rents or housing, or of civics, at the NGC in April, although Goniwe convened an informal meeting of civic activists and suggested that a national structure for civics should be formed within the UDF. It seems that at this stage there was little clear perception of either civics' roles in overall UDF strategy or the UDF's role in building civic organisation. Some UDF leaders were thought to have reservations about the formation of a national civic structure, because such a body would primarily express African political aspirations and could easily become a vehicle for Africanist opposition to the more multiracial UDF. Nonetheless, after the Azaadville NGC, the UDF head office began to plan a national civic and housing conference for July. A weak response from UDF regions, and hostility from some civics, compelled the head office to postpone the conference.

This initiative was cut short by the imposition of the State of Emergency in July 1985. There were no further initiatives at the national level until the beginning of 1986. The UDF, weakened by detentions, was unable to provide extensive national co-ordination or direction. The one tactic which proliferated – the consumer boycott – was not regarded as a specifically civic tactic, required very limited national co-ordination, and did not prompt improved civic organisation. In the Eastern Cape, however, civic leaders were involved in innovative forms of organisation building which were to be of national importance in early 1986. A system of street committees was developed in Cradock under the direction of Goniwe, and replicated in the townships of Port Elizabeth. These provided a mechanism both for popular representation and for maintaining organisation when mass meetings were prohibited and it was difficult to distribute pamphlets. The periodical State of the Nation provided the following account:

each township is broken down into areas, and the areas into streets. In each street one or two people take responsibility for calling house meetings to discuss issues and problems. The street rep sits on an area committee, which co-

ordinates people's actions against whatever common problems there are. There
is also an elected executive committee of that area committee. The street committee structures have particular advantages for organising in the current climate ... They can withstand the most repression. Street reps can be low-profile
and will be protected by the people in the street. If the street rep is detained, the
street can appoint a new rep. In other words, since the community organisation is run at a mass level – rather than being an 'executive organisation' – there
will always be people to take over leadership responsibilities. And street committees provide a structure for training ... [and] also a structure through
which communication can reach every house within a short space of time.[82]

The example of Cradock was held up as a model:

Its system of street committees and house meetings ... has not only ensured
democracy, but has also developed the organisational and leadership skills of
the rank and file. As a result, the organisation has been able to continue with its
programme, in spite of killings and crackdowns on elected office-bearers and
key figures ... In many ways Goniwe's major achievement was his ability to
develop viable and appropriate forms of organisation which ensured program-
matic activity and made it possible to consolidate mobilisation into organisation.[83]

Civic organisations became involved in the administration of medical clinics and
crime prevention, and thus helped to meet immediate needs as well as forming the
embryo of future, democratic forms of goverment. Tragically, it was only after his
murder that Goniwe's efforts were appreciated beyond the Eastern Cape. In 1986
UDF leaders in the Transvaal incorporated the innovative organisational work of
activists in the Eastern Cape and Border into the strategic framework of 'people's
power'.
    Whilst organisation was being built in the major urban areas the rural areas
remained very patchily organised during 1984–5. Some of the UDF regions had
begun to extend their networks into the small towns in rural areas. The Western
Cape, especially, had been pushed into some activity by the presence of many
coloured voters in rural areas, and held some mini-conferences outside Cape Town.
The UDF's first regional organiser was employed in the embryonic Northern Cape.
In March 1985 Morobe was appointed as rural officer on the Transvaal REC, and
Johannesburg-based activists were soon to begin organising in the small towns of the
Eastern Transvaal. Goniwe was appointed as rural organiser in the Eastern Cape,
whilst the Border UDF established a presence in parts of the Ciskei. In May the NEC
approved the employment of a rural organiser for the Natal Midlands.
    Outside the Ciskei, however, the UDF's only significant organised presence in
bantustans was among university students. The rural areas proved very difficult to
organise, not least because activists were so caught up in the fast-changing politics of
the townships or were victims of state repression. At the Azaadville conference a

commission focused on the problems of organising the bantustans and rural areas. It proposed a national anti-bantustan campaign 'to promote national unity against ethnic division', and a campaign over forced removals.

The UDF also assisted in moves towards forming regional organisations for women. In the Transvaal the UDF helped the Federation of Transvaal Women to organise a workshop on the role of women in the struggle. In Cape Town it helped broker unity between two rival Charterist organisations. But UDF leaders lacked any clear strategy for mobilising and organising women. There were few strong women's organisations on the ground which could be brought together into regional structures, as was increasingly the case with civic organisations. Regional organisations tended to serve as political clubs for women activists rather than organisations concerned with issues that were of immediate concern to women in general.

The marginalisation of women as a constituency was mirrored in their marginalisation within the organisation. There were very few women among the top UDF leadership. All 16 members of the NEC elected at Azaadville were men, and only 9 of the 65 REC members were women. The only woman in the *de facto* top leadership was Cheryl Carolus.[84]

THE ESCALATION OF CONFRONTATION AND VIOLENCE

The state responded to escalating resistance and the UDF's renewed assertiveness with increased repression. In mid-April P.W. Botha verbally attacked the UDF in parliament, denouncing it as an extension of the ANC and SACP. Lekota, Molefe and Transvaal regional secretary Moss Chikane were detained. Later, together with almost twenty local activists from the Vaal Triangle, they were charged with treason in the Delmas Treason Trial. Meanwhile the first treason trial of UDF leaders was proceeding in Pietermaritzburg. The Pietermaritzburg trial had an importance beyond the leaders accused in it. As the UDF observed, the Front itself 'was in the dock: its ideas, its mode of operating, its very existence were being put under legal scrutiny'.[85] The state's strategy of prosecuting UDF leaders seems to have reflected its concern to delegitimise the organisation through the courts, rather than merely repress it through an executive banning order. Although foreign pressure provided the UDF with some protection, the Front did have to replace its top leaders, who were clearly not going to be available again for some time. Moosa took over most of Molefe's work and Morobe took over as acting national publicity secretary. Carolus, Manuel, Nair, Ndlovu and Yunus Mahomed provided back-up.

Repression took a more sinister turn in the Eastern Cape, where the police preferred more direct or physical methods than detention and trial. In early May three PEBCO leaders disappeared after leaving a regional UDF meeting. Over a decade later the Truth and Reconciliation Commission revealed that these three men – Sipho Hashe, Champion Galela and Qaqawuli Godolozi – had been abducted and executed by the security forces. In June Matthew Goniwe and three other Cradock activists were murdered after leaving a UDF meeting – again, by the security forces. At the time there was no proof, but the UDF nonetheless voiced the widespread belief and accused the government of responsibility for the assassination or disappearance of these and other political activists around the country. On the ground, too, the security forces were engaged in routine brutality.[86]

At the same time there was a proliferation of violent clashes between supporters of the UDF and those of AZAPO. The UDF and its affiliates accused AZAPO of acting in cahoots with the state. Evidence later emerged that the security forces were indeed involved in sponsoring such so-called 'black-on-black' violence.[87] But most AZAPO activists were as opposed to the apartheid state as UDF activists were. They were denounced, however, because many Charterist activists assumed that 'If you're not for us, you're against us'. In this view, the UDF and ANC embraced the whole of the 'people's camp', and anyone else must therefore be part of the 'ruling camp'. When AZAPO, increasingly politically marginalised, turned to desperate criticism of the UDF and ANC, it reinforced the belief of Charterist activists that AZAPO was on the enemy's side.[88]

The worst clashes occurred in the Eastern Cape in April and May. They were triggered by the actions of Charterist youth at a major funeral in KwaNobuhle, outside Uitenhage. AZAPO supporters were ordered to remove their T-shirts, and Charterists refused to read out a message from AZAPO's national president. Although national UDF and AZAPO leaders denounced this action and emphasised their common opposition to the government, this message was not heeded on the ground. There were attacks and counter-attacks, hostages were taken and houses burnt out, and there were assassination attempts on local leaders. AZAPO's Port Elizabeth leadership not unreasonably claimed that 'the UDF is out to eliminate AZAPO entirely'. One AZAPO supporter was killed at the house of the UDF regional president, Edgar Ngoyi. The UDF's NEC had a meeting with AZAPO leaders, and together they blamed the violence on 'elements who were interested in undermining and diverting the heroic struggles'. But violence continued on the ground.[89]

The conflict with AZAPO in the Eastern Cape and elsewhere seems to have solidified a new UDF identity in the townships affected. Participants in conflict and protest did not identify themselves in public only as PEBCO and PEYCO supporters, in the case of Port Elizabeth for example, but also as UDF supporters, or even as members of the UDF. The UDF was no longer something 'out there'. This was probably in part due to the higher profile of the UDF's regional leadership at the time, and the national UDF's increased engagement with township struggles. But it also reflected the partisan edge to conflict on the ground, and the need to declare a supra-local allegiance to the ANC in a legal way. The other region where the identity of 'UDF supporter' would become similarly important was Natal, as members or supporters of UDF affiliates clashed violently with the rival Inkatha movement.

Meanwhile resistance continued to escalate. This was fuelled by the ANC, which distributed inside the country 'several thousand copies' of an important statement made by the NEC of the ANC in late April. The statement characterised the moment as revolutionary, with 'growing ferment from below' and 'deepening crisis from above'. There was, it continued, a real possibility of a decisive national insurrection. Youth and other militants were called on to take up arms and establish no-go areas closed to the state. 'Make apartheid unworkable! Make the country ungovernable!', it urged. But, Barrell argues, the ANC did not have the political structures inside the country to provide adequate direction. Indeed, Mufson suggests: 'the urgency of the ANC pamphlet was more of an attempt to keep pace with, rather than inspire, events unfolding in the townships'. The result was a somewhat chaotic escalation of protest.[90]

The townships of Duduza on the East Rand and Kagiso on the West Rand provide good illustrations of the way in which the UDF, the ANC and local factors combined in mid-1985. In Duduza secondary school students had boycotted classes in late 1984, clashes occurred around funerals, and workers joined in the Transvaal regional stayaway. Isolated protests gave way to general confrontation in February 1985, prompted by police repression of a civic protest over municipal services. Conservative township residents, together with the police, began petrol-bombing activists' houses. In May a local COSAS leader and her sister were killed in one such attack. In this situation students responded to the ANC's call to arms. A group sought to obtain hand-grenades with which to attack the vigilante leaders. But there was no ANC structure in the township, and the local students had poor contacts elsewhere. A state agent, formerly in the ANC, offered them booby-trapped hand-grenades. In June, four students killed themselves, and others died in neighbouring townships, in abortive attacks.[91] In many townships like Duduza, the 'UDF' meant a handful of local individuals in irregular communication with regional-level activists in the big cities, with uneven links to student and youth militants, and prone to repeated periods of detention by the police. The ANC's underground structures were generally even more nebulous.

In an effort to strengthen organisation, the UDF promoted the formation of area committees. The East Rand Area Committee, which encompassed Duduza, was still in the process of being set up. On the West Rand, however, the UDF Area Committee had been meeting more regularly from late 1984. It was to play a significant role in the development of resistance in Kagiso. In June it organised a Soweto Day commemoration service, which attracted six or seven hundred people, a reflection of the heightened politicisation prevailing in much of the country. Following an apparently incendiary speech by the chairman of the UDF Area Committee who was also in the ANC underground, local youth attacked, looted or burnt two beerhalls, four councillors' shops or houses, and several vehicles.[92] While the presence or absence of UDF and ANC links shaped the precise ways in which local factors and regional or national political dynamics combined, an enthusiasm for action extended far beyond the organisational reach of the UDF or ANC.

Funerals provided perhaps the most important medium for the UDF to exert influence on local-level politics at this time. Wherever people were killed by the security forces, political funerals became major rallying points. The UDF was called on to assist with speakers, publicity, and funds for transport and funeral expenses. UDF leaders used these occasions to promote their views on resistance, and to build or strengthen organisational networks. According to the UDF Eastern Cape publicity secretary, Stone Sizani: 'Speakers address the people on the local authorities and the general wrongs of what the police and army are doing. Other speakers comment on the role of the church, the principal role of the workers, and the central role that the UDF is playing.' But, Sizani added, 'it is difficult to operate from the streets and the graveyard'.[93]

On 20 July UDF leaders and mourners from all over the country gathered in Cradock for the funeral of Goniwe and his three colleagues. The funeral represented a symbolic moment, in terms of the number and range of mourners, the public display of ANC and SACP flags, and the speeches made. The crowd was estimated at over 70 000. Over 500 people came from Cape Town, for example. The importance of the event was recognised by the presence of many foreign diplomats and messages from others, as well as leaders of the liberal parliamentary opposition, the Progressive Federal Party. The display of flags indicated the increasingly confident defiance of the state and the strength of identification with the ANC and, in the Eastern Cape at least, the SACP. When the red flag, with hammer and sickle, was unfurled, 'people looked at it in disbelief', recalled a witness, 'it was huge'.[94] Photographs of churchmen, including Boesak, against the backdrop of ANC and SACP flags were published in newspapers over the next few days.

At the same time, the churchmen called strongly for restraint. Boesak began his speech with a list of the many forms of state terrorism, and urged white South Africans to put pressure on the government. But he ended his speech with an appeal for restraint and non-violence, exhorting the audience to 'raise a sign of hope' rather than avenging deaths with 'more senseless violence and hatred'. 'So raise a sign of hope and continue the fight for justice and for peace ... Raise a sign of hope and do not give in to hatred and violence, but seek peace and genuine reconciliation ... Raise a sign of hope and the God of peace and justice shall be with you – and we shall have our freedom!'[95] Boesak called for consumer boycotts to be implemented all over the country. In Boesak's mind it was the non-violent use of buying power, rather than violence, which would win freedom.

During Goniwe's funeral, UDF leaders received word that the government was going to declare a State of Emergency later that day. Sizani actually announced this during the funeral service. After the funeral, most of the top UDF leaders drove to Tshwete's home in the Ciskeian village of Peelton, anticipating that they were marginally safer in the 'independent' Ciskei.[96] The next day P.W. Botha declared a State of Emergency in terms of the 1953 Public Safety Act in 36 magisterial districts in the PWV and Eastern Cape. This was the first declaration of a State of Emergency since 1960, indicating the gravity of the crisis facing the state. By declaring an Emergency, Botha empowered himself to issue a battery of repressive regulations. The police were granted wide powers of arrest and detention, authority to close off areas and impose curfews at any time, and exercise control over the media. Days later, the police were given further powers to control funerals.[97]

Gathered in Peelton, the UDF leadership 'didn't really know what to do', recalls Valli Moosa; 'we didn't know how to respond'. Strategic thinking within the UDF had been driven by Lekota, who was by now in detention. The stand-in leaders were still finding their feet and lacked authority. It seems that the UDF had no contingency plan. Moosa and Morobe decided not to return to Johannesburg immediately, but rather to go to Durban where there was no Emergency, and lie low for a while.[98] The wisdom of this became apparent when the police stopped buses returning from Cradock to Johannesburg, and detained over a hundred activists. Many others were picked up in police raids on their homes, some immediately, others soon enough. Mufson summarises the typical experiences of the UDF Eastern Cape leader, Henry Fazzie:

> Fazzie evaded the dragnet for weeks. The police had pictures of Fazzie at every road block so the soldiers would recognise him. But Fazzie disguised himself. He dressed himself as a minister. Police searched Fazzie's own home and failed to recognise him, one story went. Fazzie even flew on the state-owned airline using a false name. But within a few weeks, Fazzie was captured, as were thousands of others.[99]

The UDF later described the Emergency as

> a desperate attempt by P.W. Botha to break the unity and organisation of our people ... [It] was an admission of defeat by the regime. It was an admission that the cosmetic reforms and the 'politics of consensus' had failed. It was an admission that it, the regime, was ruling over an unwilling people and hence could only rule by using excessive force. Above all, it was an admission that the political initiative had passed from the hands of the state to the people.[100]

But the UDF was hit hard by the State of Emergency, notwithstanding its upbeat, morale-boosting public statements. 'In some parts of the country our contact networks broke down, many organisations were unable to meet, fear and a sense of disillusionment set in.'[101] Moosa and Morobe returned to Johannesburg soon, having got 'as bored as hell' in Durban, Moosa says.

> We arrived in Johannesburg and didn't know what to do with ourselves. Everybody we had worked with had been arrested. Homes and offices were watched. We ducked and dived. The UDF wasn't equipped to go underground. It had no underground machinery to fall back to – that was the province of the ANC ... It did lead to a tremendous amount of inefficiency. We spent a lot of time trying to keep out of jail, keep in contact with each other ..., keep the organisation ticking over.[102]

While the Emergency did not quell resistance, it weakened the UDF's capacity to provide direction. According to the Transvaal activist Mpho Mashinini, who was detained almost immediately:

> The leadership was picked up and no one was outside to direct things. There was no UDF to tell people what action to take. It was left to people's own

hands. As a result it changed the pattern of daily struggle. More people were mobilised and conscientised than ever before. It was amazing the stories we heard from those coming into prison for fourteen day stretches [short spells in detention].[103]

The one form of protest that UDF affiliates and other organisations could and did embark on, to great effect, was the consumer boycott.

CONSUMER BOYCOTTS

Consumer boycotts became the most widely used tactic of protest against state repression in the second half of 1985. The boycotts targeted white-owned shops, sometimes excluding shops owned by progressive whites and sometimes including shops owned by black collaborators with the state. Earlier in the year they had been employed in many of the small towns of the Eastern Cape, typically over localised grievances. In mid-July a boycott was implemented in Port Elizabeth, attracting widespread media attention. Between late July and mid-August boycotts spread across the country's major urban areas: East London, Pretoria, Johannesburg, Cape Town, Pietermaritzburg, as well as many smaller towns. Of the major urban centres only in Durban was there no sustained effort to organise a consumer boycott. These boycotts combined national and local demands.

Whilst boycotts quickly spread across the country they were not centrally co-ordinated. It is not clear whether they were even discussed at a national UDF meeting.[104] Their rapid spread was due to other factors: the call made for consumer boycotts at the Cradock funeral, media coverage of the first boycotts, and regional-level and sub-regional-level organisation. The evident success of boycotts in some areas prompted activists to replicate them elsewhere. Within the Eastern Cape, the UDF and other regional networks made provision for news of boycotts to spread from town to town. 'Local organisations were asked by activists from other towns to follow a regional line. Sometimes local activists felt obliged to launch a boycott because surrounding towns had done so.'[105] UDF activists were widely involved, but the boycotts were not a concerted UDF campaign in the same way as the campaigns of 1984.

In most areas boycotts were organised by ad hoc campaign-based consumer boycott committees, with varying involvement by UDF leaders. There were several reasons for these committees being at least partly independent of the UDF. Firstly, many of the UDF's formal organisational structures broke down in the first months of the Emergency. Secondly, the membership of *ad hoc* committees was less easily identifiable, and was less vulnerable to detention or harassment. This also helped the UDF to tread the thin line between legality and illegality. Thirdly, trade unionists, non-Charterist political groups and Charterists outside the UDF could join with UDF activists in *ad hoc* committees. In some areas the consumer boycott committee was little more than a disguised UDF Area Committee. In Pretoria, for example, the key consumer boycott organiser was the local UDF organiser, who had hitherto been accountable to the UDF Area Committee and REC. It was the Area Committee which took the decision to launch a boycott. In other areas, such as Cape Town, the active involvement of groups not affiliated to the Front meant that the committees remained independent, often too much so for the UDF's liking.[106]

There were areas where the call for consumer boycotts was not heeded, or where local activists found no support when they tried to start them. This was the case, at least until later in the year, on the West Rand beyond Soweto and on the East Rand, both areas where the UDF and local organisation remained weak. The East Rand UDF Area Committee, for example, had not progressed beyond 'talking about bringing the East Rand townships together'.[107]

Boycotts appealed to a wide range of activists. For some, boycotts were 'one of the last available options for non-violent political protest' against state repression.[108] Boycotts were advocated in part to restrain people from resorting to violence against the state. The accompanying 'demands' typically included an end to the State of Emergency and the withdrawal of the South African Defence Force from the townships – factors which would reduce levels of violence. The non-violence of the tactic was particularly important to Boesak and other church leaders. A second view was that they formed part of a general insurrection, part of the ungovernability called for by the ANC. Some of the leading members of consumer boycott committees were committed insurrectionists, and there was discussion within the UDF national leadership on whether the boycotts should be seen in this way.[109] Both the defiant and the insurrectionary views were, however, increasingly hampered by tactical considerations. White businessmen, targeted by the boycotts, sought to negotiate settlements, pushing boycott organisers to formulate short-term demands. At the same time, organisers began to recognise that boycotts often petered out, and it was politically and organisationally better to call a boycott off before this happened, especially if concrete short-term gains could be won. UDF activists, particularly in the Eastern Cape, began to develop a strategic framework to explain the use and purposes of the boycotts. This emphasised their roles in organisation building and in compelling white businessmen to put pressure on the state.[110]

As the UDF itself acknowledged, the consumer boycotts did not result in the lifting of the Emergency or the withdrawal of troops from the townships. 'Yet the boycotts are above all a story of resistance, an example of the people's determination to continue speaking when all other avenues of protest have been closed off.'[111] The boycotts also had a downside. Intended to build organisation through non-violent protest, they often undermined organisation through brutal enforcement. This was due in part to the problems of launching boycotts when it was impossible to hold mass meetings or do door-to-door work to consult and inform people.[112]

Consumer boycotts played an important part in the growth of resistance in the Western Cape. In the first half of 1985 there had been little overt protest in the region. In February renewed attempts by the state to forcibly remove people from Crossroads to Khayelitsha provoked violent clashes, and in March the UDF organised protests against the Langa massacre. But it was not until Goniwe's funeral and the declaration of a partial State of Emergency that resistance escalated. REC leaders felt that it was their duty to respond to these events. They encouraged student protesters, first at the University of the Western Cape and soon afterwards at many coloured secondary schools. They also took up the call for consumer boycotts, a tactic which had a long tradition in the region.[113]

The UDF convened a meeting in August of affiliates and other organisations, at which a Western Cape Consumer Action Committee was formed. This included representatives of non-Charterist groups such as the New Unity Movement, Cape Action League, the Federation of Cape Civic Associations and FOSATU-affiliated trade unions. A consumer boycott was launched on 20 August. There was some debate and confusion over what shops were being boycotted. The initial agreement seemed to be all white-owned shops. But non-Charterist groups called for a selective boycott of national chain stores, as part of a more specifically anti-capitalist approach. In September the Consumer Action Committee voted to adopt such a selective boycott, although the UDF and most of its affiliates remained unhappy about this. In many areas the old blanket boycott continued to be enforced.[114]

Amidst spreading school boycotts and the consumer boycott, Boesak announced a protest march from Athlone Stadium to Pollsmoor Prison, for 28 August. The march was of immense symbolic importance, perhaps the most important event since the anti-election campaign of almost exactly one year before. A non-violent and tightly focused tactic, justified on religious as much as political grounds, was to be employed in protest against state repression, and in demand of the release of political prisoners. The UDF threw its weight behind the event. The police detained six REC members, driving the rest into hiding. On 28 August itself the police prevented the march with a substantial show of force. This provoked widespread clashes in the townships and some coloured areas, and at least 28 people were killed in three days. Protests quickly escalated. In early September almost five hundred coloured schools and colleges were closed by the government, and the UDF and COSATU jointly called a two-day stayaway. As in other parts of the country, brutal and often indiscriminate policing played a key role in the intensification of resistance, and served to strengthen the consumer boycott. But the detention of its senior leadership caught the UDF unprepared. As a position paper noted: 'We in the Western Cape, were not prepared for this onslaught and are not used to operating under such repressive conditions. This has led to some breakdown of communication between our areas; a lack of direction and sometimes even a sense of despondency.'[115]

Events proceeded differently in the squatter camps of Crossroads where the consumer boycott was physically enforced. The boycott exacerbated tensions arising from the prospect, after years of struggle, of a selective upgrading of the area. The Crossroads warlord, Ngxobongwana, reached some kind of agreement with state officials, whilst Charterist 'comrades' and allied squatter leaders in the smaller camps around Crossroads prepared to challenge his authority. Cole writes:

> militant youths from the black townships often ruthlessly dealt with residents suspected of not supporting the campaigns. There were, for example, numerous reports of militant youths forcing residents to drink fish oil, or swallow

washing powder, as punishment for not following the 'correct line'. The actions of these 'comrades' alienated a large percentage of residents from the townships and surrounding squatter camps.[116]

Ngxobongwana and the security forces were to exploit this opportunity, mobilising many Crossroads residents against the youth and their allies.

Consumer boycotts may also have played a role in the escalation of resistance and confrontation in East London. In 1983–4 conflict had simmered, erupting occasionally, in Mdantsane, East London's new township across the border in the Ciskei. Conflict had arisen over a bus boycott, which was finally called off in early 1985. SAAWU, which had played a leading role in the boycott, was weakened by divisions and the arrest and prosecution for treason of its top leaders. When, at the end of July, a consumer boycott was called, focus shifted to East London's old location, Duncan Village. School students began to boycott classes. On 11 August activists from all across the Border region, including Duncan Village, descended on King William's Town for the funeral of the Natal UDF activist Victoria Mxenge. Mxenge was the second UDF REC member to be murdered in as many months. The keynote address at her funeral was given by Tshwete. His speech was very different from the call for restraint made by Boesak in Cradock just three weeks earlier. 'If we have to liberate ourselves with the barrel of a gun,' Tshwete said, 'then this is the moment.'[117] A Ciskei soldier was killed by the crowd at the funeral. Soon after activists from Duncan Village returned home, various administrative buildings were torched. That weekend eight of the nine schools were burnt down, and the township councillors fled. Some 32 people were killed, and 138 injured over the weekend. According to Ntsebeza, the uprisings involved a combination of 'political youth' and 'the unruly youth', although the Residents' Association was quick to try to provide direction and discipline to the uprising through the development of a system of street committees.[118]

Areas such as Duncan Village may have become no-go zones for state administrators, but heavy policing made it very difficult for regional activists to leave such areas. The security forces were especially keen to get hold of Tshwete. Tshwete was smuggled through police cordons to speak at one of the mass funerals in Duncan Village and then spirited over the border into Lesotho. According to the account Tshwete gave to Mufson:

> He shaved his heavy beard and his head, tucked his glasses under the seat of the car, and fixed a new photo to a forged passport. Border officials held him for an hour while they examined his passport. They asked Tshwete if he had any other names. 'It was tense,' Tshwete said. Eventually they let him go. When he later opened his suitcase, Tshwete realised how lucky he had been. A friend had packed his suitcase and included a jacket with a UDF brochure in the breast pocket. If the border officials had found the brochure, it would have tipped them off that the inarticulate bald 'migrant' was more than he seemed.[119]

The Border UDF leader Nqakula also left for Lesotho. Tshwete soon surfaced in

Lusaka, as a top ANC leader, whilst Nqakula took over the position of chairperson of the ANC's Lesotho Revolutionary Political-Military Council.

NATAL

Protest and conflict also increased in Natal and KwaZulu during 1984–5. The first areas affected were the highly politicised township of Lamontville in Durban, Hambanathi outside Tongaat (around the issues of rent increases and incorporation into KwaZulu), and in the Richard's Bay and Empangeni area of northern Natal (around bus fare increases). In July and August 1985 conflict spread to the sprawling shack settlements of Inanda outside Durban and in Pietermaritzburg's Imbali township.[120]

In some respects these local conflicts resembled those occurring across South Africa. Civic, educational and overtly political grievances pitted African protesters against the state and its local allies. In Natal, as in the industrial areas of the Reef and the small towns of the northern Orange Free State, local leaders in official institutions – township councils, school committees, bantustan chiefs – were themselves the immediate focus of much popular anger, and felt threatened by the emergence of independent and vocally critical political leadership. But the political landscape of Natal and KwaZulu was complicated by three features of the region. First, many of these councillors and chiefs were part of Inkatha. At the time of the UDF's formation Inkatha had been trying to redefine its role in national politics. Its institutional base in the KwaZulu bantustan state, and the social character of key constituencies of supporters, pulled it in an increasingly reactionary direction.

Secondly, fewer people were mobilised by grievances such as rent increases in Natal–KwaZulu, in comparison to other regions, primarily because rents were low in townships within KwaZulu. Education was the primary focus of protest. In the absence of parental mobilisation over rents and housing, parents could easily be mobilised against rebellious youth. Thirdly, there remained deep social, cultural and political differences between Indian and African people. During 1983–5 the UDF had greatly strengthened the practice of non-racialism within extra-parliamentary politics, and its campaigns against the National Party's constitutional reforms had ensured that Indian South Africans were not seen as having been co-opted into the apartheid state. But the major role played within the UDF by organisations and leaders from Indian areas contributed to a perception, even within some UDF affiliates, that the Front was dominated by a predominantly Indian cabal.

In 1983 opposition to incorporation into KwaZulu had led to protests and conflicts in townships such as Lamontville in Durban and Hambanathi outside Tongaat. The fast-deteriorating relationship between the UDF and Inkatha fuelled local antagonisms. In mid-1984 Inkatha supporters attacked the houses of dissident civic leaders in Hambanathi, killing one and driving others out of the township. For a while, events in Richard's Bay, up the north coast, seemed to belie this trend. Commuters began to boycott the local bus service in January 1985. Although there was no organised UDF presence, Inkatha and the local FOSATU unionists initially worked together. Soon differences emerged, and Inkatha labelled the unionists UDF. In May 1985 violence escalated again in Hambanathi. Amidst rising tensions, the Natal UDF decided against following the lead of other UDF regions in calling for regional consumer boycotts. Not only would it have been very difficult to identify the target of the boycotts because of the high number of Indian-owned shops in central Durban and other places, but there was also a high risk of a violent backlash.[121]

At the beginning of August the UDF regional treasurer, Victoria Mxenge, was murdered. Nobody was ever prosecuted but the murder seems to have been carried out by the police. COSAS immediately called for a week-long stayaway and for shops to close from Monday 5 August. School boycotts affected KwaMashu, Umlazi, Clermont and Lamontville, and then Inanda. Police intervention led to widespread riots. Rampaging youth targeted Indian-owned businesses and houses and over a thousand Indians fled their homes in Inanda. Inkatha leaders, including Wellington Sabelo from Umlazi and Thomas Shabalala from Lindelani, led vigilante groups which brutally repressed the youth in KwaMashu and Umlazi, but failed to do so in Inanda. The Gandhi Settlement in Phoenix, venue of the first UDF National Executive meeting in 1983, was burnt down.[122] There was a widespread fear of a repeat of the 1949 Durban riots, in which African crowds had killed many Indian people.

Underpinning these events was the distraction of the regional UDF leadership from local-level developments. De Villiers writes that, even in townships such as Lamontville and Hambanathi, the local leadership 'became cut off from day-to-day community concerns and was swallowed up in broader national UDF activities. Generally, the largely Indian intellectual middle-class leadership of the UDF made little progress trying to organise from the top down'.[123] Sitas echoes this view:

apart from the boycott campaign against the elections [the UDF] initiated no other mass action in Durban: rather, most energy was absorbed at a national level and [it] did not develop a coherent grassroots approach to consolidate its base ... [In mid-1984] the UDF and especially the NIC were at the helm of historical events. The tragedy was that the rhythms of national confrontation put severe strains on local consolidation, but at the same time very little effort was put into translating the broad mobilising style of the earliest campaigns into a coherent grassroots structure.[124]

Amidst rising violence, UDF affiliates were unable to operate successfully, and many people were intimidated into passivity. The activities of the youth also alienated many older township residents. De Villiers concludes:

Township people, aware of the dangers of being associated with the UDF, are concerned to distance themselves from the organisation. The UDF has little attraction for them: it appears to be Indian-led, with a predominantly radical, and by implication, violent, young membership ... As they see it, to belong to the UDF now almost certainly means having your home burnt down, and possibly death. With the UDF leadership in detention, and a weak organisational infrastructure, the UDF is unable to defend itself and its supporters against the combined onslaught of Inkatha and the state.[125]

The only organisational growth occurred among the youth, with the formation or formalisation of youth groups in a number of areas and increased contact between them through the Youth Forum centred on Diakonia. The need to develop African leadership was recognised. One of the goals of the Youth Forum was to nurture broader leadership, in part out of recognition of the UDF REC's failure in this respect. A workshop was held in Mariannhill to consider the issue of African leadership.[126] Improved organisation was, however, to fall prey to further escalating violence.

Violence had the effect of reducing support for Inkatha in urban areas: Meer put Inkatha support in KwaMashu at 32 per cent before the 1985 violence, and just 5 per cent afterwards, and in Inanda at 29 per cent before and 4 per cent afterwards. Support for the UDF rose correspondingly in African areas.[127] The violence also produced large numbers of refugees, and left 70 dead. The UDF condemned the attacks on Indians as the work of criminals but was unable to come up with a more robust response.

It was in the Natal Midlands, rather than down on the coast, that the UDF had to confront the issue of violence most directly. During 1983–5 there was no overt UDF sub-regional structure in the Natal Midlands, although a Committee of Concern served as a *de facto* UDF co-ordinating structure. Local Charterist activists had formed the Committee of Concern rather than a fully fledged UDF body because of the lack of 'respectable' older leaders, both African and Indian, willing to take up high-profile UDF positions at the time. The Pietermaritzburg Committee of Concern had participated in the Million Signatures Campaign and had opposed the Tricameral parliamentary elections. As in Durban, overt political organisation other than Inkatha was concentrated in Indian rather than African areas.[128]

In February 1985 the Committee of Concern formally reconstituted itself as a UDF sub-regional structure. The Midlands UDF leadership intentionally reflected the UDF's professed non-racial character. The veteran Natal Indian Congress activist A.S. Chetty was elected as chairperson. Three co-secretaries were elected, one from each racial community, but one dropped out, leaving the Imbali teacher and activist S'khumbuzo Ngwenya' and the white student activist Martin Wittenberg. Beneath the overt sub-regional structure were covert cells or caucuses, comprising twenty or so members each. One operated in Indian areas, another among UDF-friendly trade unions. The third, operating from late 1984, drew in township activists, including Ngwenya and Mdou Ndlovu from the Imbali Youth Organisation.

Almost immediately the Natal Midlands UDF was given a boost by the state's decision to hold the treason trial of UDF leaders in Pietermaritzburg. Activists and students from local townships attended court sessions, and met with the trialists. This contributed to a rapid expansion of youth, civic and student organisation, especially in Imbali and Edendale. The new organisations affiliated to the UDF. There was also an upsurge in protest in local schools, to the dismay of many older people. In Sobantu, the old location situated in the heart of Pietermaritzburg, the local UDF-aligned civic was strongly opposed to 'insubordinate' students boycotting classes, and tried to force students back to school.

Despite these changes, the pace of protest in mid-1985 was not set by UDF affiliates but rather by a trade union which was generally critical of the UDF. The Metal and Allied Workers' Union (MAWU) organised the workforce at the Sarmcol factory in Howick, just outside Pietermaritzburg, and therefore had a strong presence in the local township of Mpophomeni. Although an elderly MAWU organiser had been elected as vice-president of the UDF sub-region in February, he was too inactive to provide a link between organisations that were generally wary of each other. But when Sarmcol's workers went on strike, and were dismissed at the end of April, MAWU was compelled to turn to the UDF for assistance, especially in its efforts to deter scab labour. In mid-July MAWU took the lead in calling for a sub-regional stay-away in support of the strikers. When this failed to resolve the industrial dispute, MAWU called for a consumer boycott.

In Natal as a whole, the UDF leadership had decided against calling for consumer boycotts, recognising that the tactic could backfire, given the generally poor state of organisation in African areas, widespread political conservatism and support for Inkatha, and the danger of exacerbating racial tensions. These misgivings proved prophetic in the Natal Midlands. As in several other parts of the country, consumer boycotts provoked popular discontent with and reaction against progressive organisations. When young men enforced compliance with the boycott in Imbali and the Edendale valley, in the name of the UDF, Inkatha members of the local council and school committee were provoked to action. The home of the chairperson of the Imbali Civic Association, Robert Duma, was attacked. Inkatha-led vigilantes forced school students back to school, and patrolled the area. UDF activists were told to leave the township, or risk being killed and having their houses burnt down. The consumer boycott petered out.

When the Midlands UDF leadership later reflected on these events, they recognised that the mobilisation of early 1985 had led them, and local-level activists, to overestimate their own organisational strength. They had confused student mobilisation with general organisation. 'We continued as if everyone had joined us.'[129] At the same time they had underestimated Inkatha's disruptive potential. Although Inkatha had no public profile comparable to those of UDF affiliates in townships such as Imbali, it retained a local leadership and support base. Moreover, these local leaders were threatened by Charterist mobilisation, both institutionally, in the sense that they controlled structures such as the community council and school committees, and personally. As has been wryly noted, the 'feeling of personal insecurity … must have been sharpened by the fate of "collaborators" in the Eastern Cape', a fear no doubt played on by local police. UDF leaders also underestimated Inkatha's ability to control a township with small numbers of supporters, given the connivance (whether non-interference or selective interference) of the state's security forces.[130] Nonetheless, events in Imbali were later replicated elsewhere.

The expulsion of UDF-aligned civic and youth activists from Imbali emasculated organisation in the one African area where there had been a UDF presence. Furthermore, this occurred at a time when, nationally as well as regionally, the UDF was shifting its attention to township-based struggles. The result was that the UDF in Pietermaritzburg was thrown into confusion. The UDF sub-region's response was limited by the insistence among Imbali activists that their problem could be dealt with locally. A Crisis Committee was formed, with the participation of groups both outside and affiliated to the UDF. The Committee provided material support that included accommodation for township activists on the run, assistance in applications in court for interdicts restraining vigilante leaders, and media coverage.

THE TOWNSHIP REVOLT: OPPORTUNITIES AND DILEMMAS

While the intensification of resistance provided anti-apartheid leaders with a golden opportunity to advance the cause of democratisation, the revolt also posed grave dilemmas, especially about the form of popular protest. Most of the UDF leadership favoured a disciplined intensification of resistance, meaning that violence should be defensive only, that organisation should be built, and that people should be persuaded rather than coerced to support protests. For some leaders, this emphasis reflected moral concerns; for others, it reflected strategic considerations, in that sustainable and effective resistance required a broad and well-organised base.

In promoting discipline, however, the UDF had weak direct influence and an uncertain level of moral capital. Crucially, the UDF, contrary to the state's allegations, had not orchestrated or directed the initial township protests. It had underestimated the prospects for revolt, and its character and structures were inappropriate for proactive involvement. At a time of enormous disruption due to detentions and trials, the UDF had to extend and strengthen its links to local level activists in the African townships caught up in the revolt, and thereby effect a shift 'from mobilisation to organisation' in order to move 'from protest to challenge', in the words of the Azaadville NGC theme. The necessary change in the relationship between the UDF and the grass-roots was recognised by Lekota, after the NGC. 'The struggle must be placed in the hands of the people. We are not here to struggle on behalf of the people but with them.' The UDF, Lekota said, would 'not hesitate to take our activists and march in the streets'; 'we will not be satisfied with making press statements'.[131]

The UDF sought to provide direction to the revolt, adopting a more vanguardist approach and building organisation on the ground. The UDF itself thus became ever more like an organisation and less like a front. The UDF described itself as being 'a national political structure which would lend cohesiveness to resistance, but at the same time organise the unorganised areas. That is why the UDF today plays both the role of a front in certain parts of the country and the role of an organisation in other parts.' The UDF leadership saw the African townships as under-organised: 'Without strong, mass based democratic organisations we will not attain victory.'[132]

Most UDF leaders sought to promote change through ways that were non-violent, as an alternative to insurrection. Most were wary of confrontation, and were prepared to enter into talks, even with the state, in order to promote change. All this prompted disputes with some of the UDF's affiliates. COSAS, for example, was strongly critical of UDF-backed parents' committees when they held meetings with the Minister or officials from the Department of Education and Training. In April 1985 Lekota spelt out the UDF's public support for a negotiated settlement at the national level:

> We in the UDF seek a negotiated settlement because we believe that the less bitter the methods adopted to resolve the present problem, the easier will be the process of reconciliation ... The reason for the existence of the UDF is to help the various sections of the public to learn to live together, to move towards a democratic society with all participating.[133]

But the UDF's position on violence was far from clear cut. Officially, the UDF was committed to non-violence, although it would not dissociate itself from the ANC's qualified endorsement of violence, especially after Mandela rejected an offer of release by the government, which made his release conditional on renouncing violence. But as the violence perpetrated by the state intensified, so it became harder for UDF leaders to criticise popular violence. Steven Mufson, in his *Fighting Years*, provides an excellent summary of the dilemmas facing UDF leaders. Popular violence was often defended on the grounds that such violence was itself defensive, but not all the targets of popular violence were themselves perpetrators of violence. Priests such as Tutu and Boesak were sometimes criticised in private for their opposition to violence: 'Clerics want to come from above the struggle,' one UDF leader complained to Mufson; 'they say "don't do violence because we know what's best for you."' Frank Chikane, himself a priest, told Mufson that violence was not an 'option', but was 'the necessity of the situation'. 'You have to defend yourself.'[134]

UDF leaders went furthest in endorsing violence in the Eastern Cape and Border, advocating violence as a way of hitting back at the enemy and contributing to liberation. At one funeral, Sizani said:

> When the youths die they do not die, but fall in the battle. We ... must take over their spears, their AKs and go forward. When one nation subjugates another the first thing they do is disarm them. They disarm us and bring in their armed forces to kill and shoot us. They expect us to take it lying down. To wear black robes and mourn. To pray and ask God to liberate us. We say enough is enough. Now is the time to hit back. So that is why we say *amabutho* must ever be strengthened, must ever be organised. They must be mobilized to hit more and most effectively.[135]

Even incidents such as the killing of a soldier at the Mxenge funeral in King William's Town were not condemned by UDF spokesmen.

More than ten years later, when making their submission to the Truth and Reconciliation Commission, a delegation of UDF leaders insisted that the UDF's policy had been, quite clearly, one of non-violence. Violence by UDF supporters, they said, was an 'unintended consequence' of protests, in the context of state violence and insufficient political maturity on the part of some of the UDF's supporters. Restrictions on the UDF hampered its efforts at political education, which would have reduced levels of popular violence. But, the delegation admitted, UDF leaders had made 'reckless statements' which were understood as encouraging people to use violence. The delegation hinted at a further factor: the UDF lacked the organisational capacity to stop violence, and more energetic attempts to do so would have undermined the UDF's capacity among many of its supporters.[136]

As the revolt, and repression, continued, there was a subtle shift in the predominant discourses used by UDF leaders, from a focus on rights to a focus on power. Part of this was an explicit denial that the struggle was a civil rights struggle. According to Moosa, there was no space for 'civil rights type of stuff' as more militant tactics became the norm. The shift was reflected most clearly in the rhetoric of leaders from the Eastern Cape and Border, and was least evident in the rhetoric of UDF leaders in the Western Cape and Natal. The shift was certainly not total: individual leaders and the NGC continued to present the struggle for liberation in terms of a struggle for peace; and Boesak and others advocated consumer boycotts as a non-violent and moral form of protest. Lekota, whilst advocating mass action, dedicated the UDF to finding 'ways in which our people, in action and in practice, can say "no,"' echoing the discourse used by Boesak in 1983–4.[137]

For most of this period, the UDF remained on the margins of the revolt, lacking a clear perspective or strategic direction. Nominally, the UDF set out clear objectives: to promote the international isolation of the South African state, to isolate the state from the people, and to divide senior and junior partners in the Tricameral Parliament and cause it to collapse.[138] In practice, the UDF lacked a clear strategy to build on the township revolt to achieve these objectives. The detention of Molefe and Lekota, the escalation of confrontation on the East Rand and Eastern Cape, and the State of Emergency, all hindered attempts to develop a clear strategy, or to effect the approach adopted at the NGC. It was not until late 1985 and especially early 1986 that the UDF was able to formulate a more incisive approach, enabling it to play a more decisive role in the swelling tide of resistance.

Chapter Seven
....

People's Power,
September 1985–June 1986

RESISTANCE AND REPRESSION

By September 1985 protest and confrontation had spread to every major urban area
in South Africa. The escalation of the township revolt across much of the PWV and
Eastern Cape had prompted the imposition of a State of Emergency in those regions
in July. In August major riots and confrontations occurred in East London and Cape
Town, and protest and violence increased in the Natal Midlands and Durban.
Consumer boycotts had spread from the small towns of the Eastern Cape through
most of the country's metropolitan areas, and into towns in the northern Orange
Free State and elsewhere. August was the most violent month in the current period of
revolt, with independent monitors estimating that a total of between 150 and 200
people were killed in political violence. Many parts of the country, including Soweto
and some other townships in the PWV, remained quiet. But the overall picture was
unmistakably one of burgeoning revolt.[1]

Underlying these outbursts of dissent, township politics were being deeply transformed through a combination of local and regional factors. Not satisfied with wide
legal powers of detention and control, the state's security forces engaged in increasingly brutal forms of repression. In some areas repression subdued overt dissent, but
in many other areas it served as a powerful mobiliser of opposition. The polarisation
of township politics cut away the fragile support base remaining to township councillors. Some resigned. Others defied protesters, apparently siding with the state; a
few were murdered, whilst many fled their townships. The discrediting of township
councillors was matched by the rising stature of and support for alternative civic
organisations. In parts of the Eastern Cape, grassroots street committees were being
formed. At the same time, township activists were increasingly interconnected
through regional networks. Activists in more quiescent townships sought to instigate
boycotts and other tactics being employed elsewhere. Regional and local factors thus
came together, generating protest, repression and further protest.

The state was increasingly seen to be vulnerable. The economy was in evident crisis, especially when, in August, the value of the rand collapsed and the Johannesburg Stock Exchange was closed temporarily. Some members of the government seemed to favour major reforms, although P.W. Botha dashed expectations in his 'Rubicon speech' in August. Prominent business leaders and journalists visited the ANC in Zambia for talks in September. And, although it was not known at the time, the Minister of Justice, Kobie Coetsee, visited Mandela in November, the first purposive direct contact between the government and the top ANC leadership.

In exile, the ANC seemed revitalised. Changed conditions inside South Africa and internationally more than offset the earlier setbacks in the frontline states. The ANC emerged from its June consultative conference in the Zambian town of Kabwe with renewed confidence and sense of direction. Henceforth it would promote a 'people's war', in which MK cadres would work closely with people on the ground. There was a sharp increase in MK attacks within South Africa from mid-1985, albeit with rising casualties among MK cadres.[2]

Inside the country, however, the UDF was in considerable disarray, reeling from the effects of a battery of repressive measures. Many of the UDF's initial national leadership were on trial for treason in Pietermaritzburg. Molefe and Lekota were awaiting trial for treason; bail was refused, and the actual trial began in Delmas in November. One of the Transvaal regional secretaries, Chikane, was awaiting trial with them. Six other NEC members were detained in August and held in Pretoria whilst the police unsuccessfully endeavoured to assemble evidence for a third treason trial. The six comprised Yunus Mahomed, who was also Natal regional secretary, Curnick Ndlovu, Titus Mafolo, Zoli Malindi from Cape Town, Johnny Mohapi from the Orange Free State, and Xundu. They were later joined by UDF patron Allan Boesak. Another NEC member, Eastern Cape UDF president Ngoyi, was imprisoned in the Eastern Cape, awaiting trial for murder. Manuel was detained in late October, and Jomo Khasu, Northern Cape regional secretary, was detained too. Only four NEC members avoided detention: Cachalia, the national treasurer; Moosa, Transvaal regional secretary and *de facto* acting national general secretary; and Stofile and Swartz, regional secretaries for the Border and Eastern Cape respectively.

RECs were also hit hard by detentions under the Internal Security Act or the Emergency. Two REC members – Goniwe and Mxenge – had been murdered. Only two members of the Eastern Cape REC remained free. In the Western Cape, 12 out of 14 REC members were detained. Nationally, 43 out of 80 UDF office-holders were reportedly detained or on trial.[3] Among the more than five thousand other activists detained in the first three months of the emergency alone were many leading members of UDF affiliates who played important roles, formally or informally, at the regional level.

The detention of leaders was not the only aspect of repression. Besides a general ban on outdoor meetings, the government had moved against indoor meetings during 1985. The UDF and many other organisations were prohibited from holding meetings in much of the country. In many areas not formally covered by the State of Emergency there was what Coleman and Webster describe as 'an undeclared state of emergency'. A key UDF affiliate, COSAS, was banned altogether in August.

Not surprisingly, such a high level of persecution had a serious effect on the UDF. Morobe was frank in an interview later in the year: 'With two Treason Trials, hundreds of our activists detained, our meetings banned, offices raided, and those remaining constantly hounded by the security police, survival has been high on our list of priorities.' It seems that there was no major UDF meeting until late October, three months into the Emergency. The National Civic Conference planned for the end of August was cancelled, and activities around International Youth Year and the formation of a national youth organisation floundered. Activity was also curtailed at the regional level.[4]

Even leaders who avoided detention found that life underground and forever on the run was debilitating. According to Sizani,

> It is difficult living from one house to the next. You are kept busy looking out for soldiers and the security branch ... It is difficult in the sense that if you do not have transport, or enough resources to keep you going, you have to fall back on your friends, your comrades, or supporters of the organisation ... It is only because of the hope we have of achieving what we are fighting for, that one feels the strength to go on. Hope keeps us going.[5]

Nonetheless, the UDF managed to maintain a minimal level of activity at national and regional levels. At the national level, Cachalia, a lawyer, remained free and able to play an important role. Moosa acted as national general secretary and Morobe as national publicity secretary, with assistance from Manuel and Carolus especially. At the regional level, a second tier of activists outside the RECs could sometimes fill the gap. In the Western Cape, for example, Naseegh Jaffer served as *de facto* regional organiser. In some regions such as the Eastern Cape the detention of UDF leaders meant that regional co-ordination was provided by Charterist activists outside formal UDF structures. Service organisations such as the Johannesburg-based Detainees' Parents Support Committee and the Community Education and Information project (CEI) served to monitor state repression, facilitate co-ordination and help to build organisation.

The situation began to improve from October, with the gradual release of NEC and REC members, and with a process of adaptation on the part of UDF leaders to operating under semi-underground conditions. Mahomed, Ndlovu and Nair were released in October; Xundu and Manuel in November (although Manuel was restricted). Charges were withdrawn against 12 of the accused in the Pietermaritzburg Treason Trial in December. Most detained Western Cape leaders were released at the end of the year. These leaders returned to find that second-tier activists had learnt new ways of operating in repressive conditions.[6]

Whilst national and regional organisation was disrupted by repression, resistance and conflict continued on the ground. The death toll in political conflict in the last four months of the year dropped somewhat from the very high level of August, but still averaged over three deaths a day. Specific events attracted considerable attention.

In November, for example, the police shot dead 14 people at one meeting in Queenstown, and 17 in a demonstration in Mamelodi. Boycotts continued sporadically at the local level, but there was little in the way of concerted national or regional protest.

The easing of repression towards the end of the year enabled UDF and allied leaders to provide some national co-ordination to resistance. Inspired by the continued use of consumer boycotts in the Eastern Cape, and angry at the massacres in places like Mamelodi, Charterist leaders called for a new round of consumer boycotts as part of another Black Christmas. In late November and early December boycotts began across much of the Witwatersrand, Pretoria and the Vaal Triangle, as well as parts of the Northern Transvaal. Most boycotts were co-ordinated by local consumer boycott committees, generally comprising UDF leaders alongside groups or activists not active in or even affiliated to the UDF. There were several reports of attempts to form a national consumer boycott committee. Most of the boycotts were called off in early January, with the threat of resuming them at the beginning of February unless some conditions were met. One reason for this was that boycotts were often not as non-violent as intended. Coercion replaced organisation, undermining support for the tactic and for the local political leaders associated with it. In some areas, including Kagiso, the civic leaders who called for the suspension of boycotts were 'overtaken by a groundswell of militancy', and the boycotts continued.[7]

At the same time there were fresh initiatives over the school boycotts that continued in many parts of the country. As the school year drew to a close it was clear that examinations would be a fiasco. The national initiative earlier in the year had run out of steam, and a fresh start was needed. In Soweto, civic leaders convened a meeting in October at which a Soweto Parents' Crisis Committee (SPCC) was formed. Among the civic leaders involved were several closely linked to the UDF: Mogane, Molobi, Khanyile, the Rev. Tsele and, especially after charges were dropped in the Pietermaritzburg Treason Trial, Frank Chikane. The SPCC met with the Deputy Minister of Education and Training twice and the Deputy Minister of Law and Order, and made preparations for a national consultative conference to chart a way forward to securing a resumption of schooling at the start of 1986. In the UDF's view the SPCC played a vital role 'in giving direction to the struggle against Bantu education', and the Front played a 'central role' in organising the national conference, or so the UDF itself later claimed.[8]

At the very end of December, perhaps as many as a thousand delegates and observers from about 150 organisations met at the University of the Witwatersrand in Johannesburg. The keynote address was delivered by Fr Smangaliso Mkhatshwa, a member of the ANC underground and secretary of the Southern African Catholic Bishops Conference. The ANC sent a message supporting the call for students to return to school. The conference resolved that students should do so, subject to the state meeting specific demands. These included the unbanning of COSAS, ending the State of Emergency and recognising student representative councils elected by the students themselves.[9] Whilst the conference was not strictly a UDF initiative, the approach adopted was very much in line with that of the UDF. As with the consumer boycott committees, the desire to include non-Charterist groups as well as Charterists critical of the UDF militated against the initiative being taken under the UDF's banner, even if the state had lifted its prohibition on public UDF gatherings.

One indication of the UDF's resurgence in late 1985 was the publication in November of the first issue of its new theoretical journal, *Isizwe*. Hitherto the UDF had scarcely been involved in political education. But by late 1985, the UDF later explained:

> The rapid expansion of the UDF's ranks has created the need for a publication that can assist in introducing greater theoretical clarity amongst activists and members of affiliates. Isizwe is aimed mainly at activists; however it is also designed to serve as a forum for debate and exchange of views within the Front.[10]

The first issue of *Isizwe* provided a lengthy statement of the need to build disciplined organisation. The opening article charted 'The Tasks of the Democratic Movement in the State of Emergency', which entailed, above all, isolating the enemy and strengthenening popular organisation.

> Without organisation, our struggle will risk becoming chaotic, we will not be able to learn from our victories and from our mistakes. Each day will be a new day. But above all, we need to understand that mass-based democratic organi- sations are not a luxury, not something that we can talk about because we think 'democracy' is a nice word: It is an absolute necessity for the survival of our struggle, that we develop well-knit, cohesive mass organisations.[11]

Political strategy was here reduced to organisation building. This represented a reaf- firmation of part of the theme adopted at the NGC earlier in the year, 'From mobili- sation to organisation'. This reflected both a defensive concern to ensure the survival of the Front in the face of state repression and the more assertive goal of providing direction to an otherwise wildly insurrectionary movement. A further article thus discussed the importance of discipline. But *Isizwe* provided no sense of how to move 'from protest to challenge', as the NGC had also envisaged.

The general lack of strategic direction was also reflected in the presentations to the SPCC conference in December, and in the UDF's New Year message delivered by Morobe at the start of 1986. The UDF rather weakly called on people to 'intensify the struggle against the apartheid state'.[12] The UDF's lack of strategic direction paralleled, and no doubt also reflected, a similar deficiency within the ANC.

But the context was of one of great political change. The visit by businessmen to the ANC in September was followed by visits by the parliamentary opposition, the Progressive Federal Party (PFP) and, over the following months, by a series of other groups. In October 1985 the nations of the British Commonwealth, at their summit meeting in Nassau in the Bahamas, temporarily settled their deep differences over sanctions with an agreement to send a team of 'eminent persons' to South Africa to evaluate the situation. There seemed to be a real prospect of negotiated change.

Indeed, inside the country there was much talk about a national convention, which some ANC and UDF leaders had espoused until recently, and the PFP and Inkatha had discussed the formation of a 'National Convention Alliance'.

As importantly, the long process of unity talks among the independent trade unions finally resulted in the formation of a new, broader union federation, the Congress of South African Trade Unions (COSATU). This new federation comprised the old FOSATU unions, together with the UDF-affiliated and other ANC-aligned unions, and the massive National Union of Mineworkers (NUM). The formation of COSATU was to greatly strengthen opposition politics inside the country, and bring the mainstream of the union movement firmly into the Charterist fold. The ANC and ANC–UDF activists such as Billy Nair inside the country had played some part in the formation of COSATU, leaning on the Charterist unions to participate. At least two members of the six-man executive, Chris Dlamini and Sydney Mufamadi, were underground ANC and SACP members, whilst a further two, Jay Naidoo and Elijah Barayi, were clearly aligned with the Charterist movement.[13] Mufamadi, the assistant general secretary of the new federation, was also a member of the UDF Transvaal REC.

CONSULTATIONS WITH THE ANC

The UDF found new direction in the New Year after senior leaders held detailed talks with the ANC's top leadership in Stockholm, Sweden. The UDF delegation comprised Stofile, Moosa, Carolus, Mahomed and Raymond Suttner, a member of the UDF Transvaal REC. They spent three days in discussions with an ANC team that included ANC president Oliver Tambo, Alfred Nzo, Thomas Nkobi, Thabo Mbeki, Aziz Pahad and Mac Maharaj. The meeting was to have a considerable effect on the UDF. As the UDF's acting general secretary cryptically put it in a report later in the year, 'The trip to Stockholm in January marked a significant departure from previously held views.'[14]

UDF leaders had been in intermittent contact with ANC leaders since its formation. There had been occasional meetings in Europe or America, and steady communication through underground channels. UDF leaders would generally report on their activities, and ANC leaders would give them encouragement, patting them on the back, as one UDF leader put it. The ANC would also send very general advice, such as a reminder of the importance of unity during the divisive 1983–4 referendum debate. On occasion different ANC structures would send conflicting messages of affirmation and support to activists inside the country, as was the case in the referendum debate. But not until January 1986 was there a substantial and detailed dialogue on strategies and tactics.

It is not clear who took the initiative in arranging the meeting in Stockholm, or precisely what the motivation was. We can speculate that four factors were pertinent. Firstly, both the ANC and the UDF might have been concerned about the apparent lack of direction on the latter's part. Secondly, the ANC might have been concerned to ensure that the UDF understood the new strategic approaches which it was employing: the more aggressive 'people's war' strategy formulated at Kabwe, as well as its growing interest in international diplomacy as a way of bringing the South African government to the negotiating table. Thirdly, the ANC was probably worried that it was out of touch with the situation inside the country and had become aware that insurrectionary rhetoric might be short-sighted. Finally, the ANC may have wanted to demonstrate its endorsement of the UDF in the face of divisions within the Charterist movement inside the country.[15]

The meeting began with the ANC outlining its analysis of the political situation. The crux of the analysis was that, as the UDF delegates reported back, the state was 'in disarray' and the democratic movement 'must intensify' its struggles. The ANC's public analysis at the time involved a twofold strategy. On the one hand the ANC advocated 'people's war', especially in its Radio Freedom broadcasts. On the other hand, it looked towards some kind of a negotiated settlement, *before* state power was seized through force. The ANC's expanding diplomatic contacts and its meetings with various South Africans raised the prospect of the enemy camp weakening polit-ically, if not militarily. According to one press report at the time, the ANC had raised the prospect of a moratorium on violence in a series of private meetings. The ANC reportedly believed that such concessions could pave the way to a negotiated settle-ment although P.W. Botha could not take the leap himself, and the National Party would need to replace him, perhaps with cabinet minister Gerrit Viljoen.[16]

In practice, the emphasis was on intensifying pressures inside the country. The ANC was partly trapped within its own bellicose rhetoric and the triumphalist insur-rectionism of many of its internal supporters. But its leaders, like the UDF's leaders, recognised the need for stronger and more extensive organisation if resistance was to be effectively escalated. Broader political constituencies should be organised in urban areas, and regional and national co-ordination improved. In its statement on 8 January the ANC praised what it described as the 'rudimentary' establishment of people's power in parts of the Cape. The ANC told the UDF that if it wanted to expand its work it should not rely on volunteers, but should employ full-time organ-isers. This was particularly important in rural areas, in part because of the perceived importance of these areas in expanding the armed struggle.

The ANC leaders urged the UDF to formulate a new Programme of Action. This should include campaigns for the establishment of non-racial local government, and a national rent strike for the release of political prisoners and against the govern-ment's proposals for 'reformed' influx control. The UDF should also work with COSATU, whose secretary, Jay Naidoo, had met with the ANC in December. Overall, the UDF should aggressively seize the initiative at this time of crisis for the govern-ment. The ANC leadership also urged the UDF to weaken the enemy camp political-ly. It should expand the democratic movement among white South Africans. Finally, the ANC emphasised the need to establish proper co-ordination between the UDF and ANC, but suggested that senior UDF leaders should avoid underground work for their own protection.

The UDF delegation respected the leadership of the ANC officials. But there were still practical difficulties in demarcating the division of roles between the UDF and the ANC. One of these concerned the UDF's external role. The ANC clearly expected groups inside South Africa to engage with the international community, and the UDF had to maintain direct contact with funders. How could internal groups do this so as to complement but not substitute for the ANC itself, as the UDF's Working Principles required? This issue arose at the Stockholm meeting, briefly causing some discomfort. According to Stofile:

> One of the things that stunned us in our very first meeting with the ANC was when Mac Maharaj said: 'Tell us, why is it necessary for the UDF to have an office of foreign affairs in Europe?' And so I said: 'What are you talking about?' They said: 'Well, we have got a proposal, we've got names of people, who are busy lobbying for the establishment of an office for UDF foreign affairs, in Sweden.'[17]

It transpired that some NIC and TIC leaders had floated the idea of overseas representation, without consulting the UDF's NEC. The issue had been discussed at the Azaadville conference, where a resolution had been adopted approving of the UDF 'consolidating and developing' its international contacts 'in accordance with the objectives and principles of the UDF'. The latter were, as ever, undefined but included explicitly in the resolution the reconfirmation that the UDF was not a national liberation movement. The NIC–TIC members' action was seen by Stofile and others as a violation of the UDF's resolution. The issue seems to have been resolved with a commitment by the UDF leaders not to establish any kind of external mission.

The January meeting rejuvenated the UDF. The NEC met almost immediately, and agreed to take immediate action on a range of issues. Rural organisers should 'be employed before next meeting'; a meeting would be held to promote national co-ordination of civic organisations; consumer boycotts should be brought under the control of RECs; problems in the establishment of a national Parents' Crisis Committee should be sorted out; meetings would be held with COSATU and the SACC, and with business leaders and foreign embassies.[18] In short, a lot of organisational work and improved co-ordination was needed before a national consumer or rent boycott were possible, or the other major campaigns suggested by the ANC could be taken up. Given this envisaged organisation building, the UDF would be able to reassert its leading role in providing direction to the struggle inside the country.

The reinvigoration of the UDF was reflected in a secretarial report dated February 1986.

> The Front is poised to enter into a new and decisive phase … We are on the brink of a new era in our struggle. The strength and sacrifice of our people, their will to be free, cannot be crushed. Now, there can be no turning back … today, seven months after the declaration of the State of Emergency, far from being smashed, we stand more confident than ever.

With continued mobilisation, organisation and discipline, the democratic movement would 'move forward to people's power'.[19]

The Stockholm meeting was also important in that it led to Swedish funding for the UDF. The UDF delegation was ostensibly invited to Sweden by the International Centre of the Swedish Labour Movement (AIC). It also met with the Swedish Ministers of Foreign Affairs and of Development Aid. The employment of full-time paid organisers, as suggested by the ANC, was to be financed largely by the Swedish government through the AIC.

The UDF was not alone in consulting with the ANC. In December, COSATU's Jay Naidoo had met with the ANC in Harare and discussed the relationship between the unions and the ANC.[20] In December the SPCC had visited Lusaka to discuss with the ANC the position to be set out at the national education conference at the end of the month. In March 1986 COSATU visited the ANC once again.

THE STRATEGIC FRAMEWORK OF PEOPLE'S POWER

The January meeting reinvigorated the UDF, but it did not provide a clear or catchy strategic framework within which UDF leaders, affiliates and supporters could understand their own parts. Over the following months the UDF found the framework it needed. As Zwelakhe Sisulu put it in March: 'The development of people's power has caught the imagination of our people.'[21] 'People's power' provided the UDF with the framework to carry forward its 1985 conference slogans of 'From protest to challenge' and 'From mobilisation to organisation', engaging with township protests after over a year of strategic confusion. The UDF was thus able to re-establish itself in a central position in opposition politics.

People's power had several roots. The first was in the strategic formulations of the ANC in exile. In this, people's power was contrasted with state power, and seen as the intended outcome or goal of the struggle for liberation. The goal would be achieved through armed insurrection. The UDF echoed the ANC's usage, adopting the slogan 'Forward to people's power' during the State of Emergency.[22] The second root of people's power lay in organisational developments on the ground, especially in the Eastern Cape. Activists such as Goniwe had pioneered new forms of grassroots civic organisation in response to the resignation of township councillors and the collapse of municipal services and other aspects of local state administration. These grassroots structures – street and area committees – grew in importance in late 1985. For one thing, they provided the necessary organisation to exercise some control over the direct action of the *amabutho*, or youth. For another, they enabled civic organisation to survive the detention of civic leadership and restrictions on public meetings. Thirdly, the concept of 'people's power' grew out of responses to the schooling crisis, and especially the talks between the ANC and the Soweto Parents' Crisis Committee.

In the first months of 1986 the ANC's insurrectionary perspective and organisational developments inside the country were combined in a reformulated understanding of people's power. In January the ANC acknowledged, perhaps for the first time, that some kind of people's power was actually being established in parts of South Africa.

In some parts of the country, having destroyed the puppet organs of government imposed on us by the apartheid regime, we have reached the situation
where even the enemy has to deal with the democratic forces as the legitimate
representatives of the people. The establishment of people's power in these
areas, however rudimentary and precarious, is of great significance for the further advancement of our struggle.[23]

The fact that the 'enemy' was forced to negotiate with 'democratic forces' was presumably of particular interest to the ANC, as it indicated both the weakness of the
state and a direction in which local struggles could usefully move. But other sections
of this statement suggest that the ANC still saw people's power as a goal to be
achieved through armed insurrection: through 'people's war', the goal of 'people's
power is within our grasp'. National UDF leaders also began to refer to people's
power, although still more as a goal than as something with immediate strategic and
organisational significance.

Developments on the ground, especially in the Eastern Cape, gave new substance
to people's power. Not only were street and area committees being formed across the
Eastern Cape, but regional leaders began publicly to ascribe a new strategic importance to them. These regional UDF officials were ahead of both their national counterparts and the exiled leadership of the ANC. In mid-January UDF officials in the
Eastern Cape were quoted as saying that street committees were the first step towards
replacing official state structures. Whilst some activists emphasised their role in facilitating civic activity, explicitly comparing them with the 'M-Plan' drawn up by
Mandela in 1953, others referred to 'liberated zones'. Furthermore, the extent and
ambitions of the Eastern Cape experience began to filter up to the Reef through personal contacts, and through meetings held as part of a concerted move towards
forming a national civic co-ordinating forum. In townships such as Alexandra,
activists seized on street committees or comparable structures 'to encourage discipline in our society, conscientising people of the struggle, to ensure mass control of
the struggle and proper democracy', to draw in 'reluctant parents' alongside younger
militants, and later to deal with the consequences of confrontation. By February a
Conservative Party member of parliament claimed that the ANC and UDF had
already taken over 27 townships in the Eastern Cape.[24]

Neither the UDF nor the ANC could claim the credit for the formation of street
committees and other manifestations of people's power. These were primarily a
response to conditions on the ground, shaped by deep-rooted traditions of localised
self-government and self-help. But the UDF and the ANC played a central role in
formulating an organisational strategy of people's power, both at a conceptual level
and in terms of co-ordination and networking. The UDF provided organisational
and conceptual links between disparate localised struggles and the overall struggle
for national political change, and thereby greatly boosted local-level developments.

UDF leaders and underground ANC leaders in Johannesburg acknowledged that
they had learnt from developments on the ground. According to Suttner, who was a
key figure in UDF political education work:

Until recently we have not clearly understood the relationship between the vision of a new society, as found for example in the Freedom Charter, and the possibility of starting to create that society now. In the past rather flimsy ideas for starting to implement the Freedom Charter were offered. People's power itself was generally conceived as something for the future. Now … we have a more dynamic conception. It is something we are learning from the creativity of the masses.[25]

People's power represented a marriage between the ANC's emphasis on armed insurrection and the organisational developments spreading across the country, and a direct link between present struggles and liberation.

The discussion of people's power took off in March, taking advantage of the easing of repression after the State of Emergency was lifted early in the month. The UDF dedicated its media to promoting people's power. The second issue of *Isizwe* opened with an article, 'Building People's Power', which seems to be the first detailed written discussion inside the country of people's power as a concrete organisational strategy. The article started with the Freedom Charter's call that 'the people shall govern', and continued to examine how this task could be realised even before the seizure of central state power.

It is true that the fullest consolidation of people's power is still in the future. It is true that control over central state power is the key to many things … Nevertheless, the building of people's power is something that *is already beginning to happen in the course of our struggle*. It is not for us to sit back and merely dream of the day that the people shall govern. It is our task to realise that goal now.[26]

The *Isizwe* article discussed street committees and people's courts – 'organs of people's power' concerned with self-government and dispute settlement – and specific activities such as street cleaning. These, together with their trade union-organised counterparts in the workplace, would help to build a different kind of political system based on popular participation.

From the outset the UDF saw the new strategy of people's power as a mechanism for promoting discipline and organisation, and not just for confronting the state, as UDF leaders were especially worried about the wanton use of force in people's courts. In a section on 'lessons, problems and difficulties', *Isizwe* advised:

Organs of people's power must be democratic and they must be under political discipline. In several cases militant youth, or others, have taken the initiative and set up independent people's courts. While the idea behind such independent attempts was well intended, the results have often been negative. Such courts must be rooted in organisation that enjoys the support of the great majority of the township, zone or street where the court is to operate. If this is not the case, such courts will be resented by the community. They will be imposing an

external discipline. It is especially important to ensure that there are democratically elected persons in these courts, and that it is not just the youth who are
represented in them. Where the level of organisation does not permit this, then
it is an error to proceed with the formation of such courts ... If these organs are
not deeply-rooted in democratic, political organisation then they are open to
corruption or hijacking by criminal elements.[27]

Isizwe also argued against dismissing the structures and activities of 'people's power'
as 'reformist'; they needed to be assessed in terms of the political context and the
potential for 'advancing the struggle'. Rubbish collection, creating public parks, or
running a soup kitchen could be progressive activities.

This theme was central to the first big national conference of 1986, held in the
name of the National Education Crisis Committee (NECC) in Durban over the
Easter weekend. The keynote address was presented by Zwelakhe Sisulu. Sisulu, the
son of jailed ANC leader Walter Sisulu and UDF co-president Albertina Sisulu, was
close to many UDF leaders but had never held office within the Front, perhaps
because he was a journalist (the editor of the Catholic-backed newspaper, *New
Nation*). 'We stand today', Sisulu told the conference, 'at a crossroads in our struggle
for national liberation.' The state had lost the initiative to the people, and the ANC
had come to be seen as 'the primary actor on the South African stage' by elements
from the 'white ruling bloc' as well as 'the people'. But Sisulu immediately inserted a
caveat: 'We are not poised for the immediate transfer of power to the people. The
belief that this is so could lead to serious errors and defeats. We are however poised
to enter a phase which can lead to transfer of power. What we are trying to do is to
decisively shift the balance of forces in our favour.'[28]

Sisulu contrasted the situation of 'ungovernability' in mid-1985, in the Eastern
Cape and East Rand, with that of early 1986 when 'the people had actually begun to
govern themselves in a number of townships.' 'In a situation of ungovernability the
government doesn't have control. But nor do the people ... In a situation of people's
power the *people* are starting to exercise control.'[29] People's power involved the formation of structures 'which were controlled by, and accountable to, the masses of the
people in each area.' This would dissolve the distinction between the people and their
organisations, and hence would stop state repression rolling back 'the gains made
through ungovernability'. Sisulu continued to discuss the need for discipline and
accountability, echoing *Isizwe*'s concern about coercion in people's courts. He discussed the struggle for people's education in some detail, and concluded with a call
to broaden the struggle, reaching into unorganised areas and constituencies, including white South Africans and teachers, as well as deepening organisation.

The theme of building people's power was taken up in the rush of meetings and
conferences that followed the lifting of the State of Emergency in March. Within the
space of three months the UDF held two major national conferences, many organisational and educational workshops, and regional civic meetings. According to one
of the 'input' papers at a regional civic conference convened by the UDF in Cape
Town in April: 'It is through civic struggles that we are going to establish people's

power. It is through civic struggles that we are going to build structures that are deeply rooted in the community. Here we are going to challenge the authority of the state and provide the alternatives.'[30] The papers pointed to the experience of Eastern Cape townships:

> In P.E., Cradock and elsewhere, our civics are built street by street and house by house so that nobody is excluded from the process. Today therefore, civics which are thus organised can implement important decisions like stayaways, rent boycotts and consumer boycotts within a matter of days ... This is the road from mobilisation to organisation – our civics lead that road.[31]

UDF media promoted the same messages. The April edition of a new publication, *UDF Update*, proclaimed that 'advancing people's power is no longer merely a slogan'. *SASPU National* discussed people's power in detail for the first time, reporting on Alexandra, Mamelodi, the Eastern Cape and elsewhere. The small Eastern Cape seaside town of Port Alfred also began to feature in press reports.[32]

People's power represented a retreat from the more triumphalist and insurrectionary claims of many activists, especially in youth organisations. *Isizwe* included an article on 'the errors of populism', arguing that 'emotional mobilisation' was no substitute for 'solid organising'. People's power also represented a renewed emphasis on the importance of non-military factors in the South African struggle. This was clear when contrasts were drawn between the form of people's power in South Africa and its form in the liberation struggles fought in Mozambique and Angola in the early 1970s. The military strengths of the South African state meant that people's power would take a very different form from the liberated zones in the Portuguese colonies. In South Africa people's power would involve people taking political and administrative control over their own lives in townships, schools and factories, despite the state's military superiority.[33]

The ANC in exile did not explicitly endorse these arguments. It remained committed to a view of change hinged upon the armed seizure of state power, and saw the building of people's power inside the country primarily in terms of political support bases for MK and a people's war. UDF leaders, by contrast, attached greater importance to a wider range of pressures on an increasingly isolated state. Their understanding of people's power therefore involved a slightly different emphasis from that of the ANC. Organs of people's power could contribute to change through either serving as the basis for a new state or further weakening the apartheid state; both of these promised to push the National Party government further into a corner. People's power also incorporated the UDF's emphasis on organisation, presenting it as necessary to sustain the militancy of ungovernability in acceptably democratic ways. People's power was, however, unambiguously about power. A discourse of power had conclusively replaced discourses of rights within the UDF. The brilliance of the discourse was that it combined an emphasis on power with a fundamental concern with organisation building. By mid-1986 people's power had taken on an appealing coherence, rescuing both the ANC and UDF from the dilemmas of uncontrolled insurrectionism.[34]

The doctrine of people's power provided an overall strategic framework which was crucial in giving direction to struggles inside the country. Within this framework the UDF national leadership sought to build a stronger basis for resistance through organisation building and political education. These would address the unevenness of political organisation around the country. The discussion of people's power generally focused on areas where organisation was strongest – the Eastern Cape and individual townships elsewhere. In most other parts of the country, even localised people's power remained an objective only, albeit in the short to medium term rather than the long term. The UDF national leadership remained cautious, rather than ambitiously seeking to implement people's power everywhere and immediately.

TOWNSHIP ORGANISATION AND PROTEST

After the Stockholm meeting with the ANC, and greatly strengthened by the ANC's backing, the UDF adopted a more assertive approach to the co-ordination of political organisation and protest in the townships and, patchily, the rural areas. This entailed bringing the Charterist movement, with the exception of two sectors, under the general umbrella of the Front. The two exceptions were the trade unions, most of which were now under COSATU, and organisations in the educational sector, which would be organised in parallel with the UDF, in part to deter repression, in part to defuse student criticism of the Front's moderation, and in part to draw in non-Charterist leadership. The UDF sought to build organisation on sectoral and regional bases, invested in political education and restructured the UDF. The medium-term goal was to launch co-ordinated campaigns on a nationwide basis, using rent and consumer boycotts, stayaways and negotiations in support of medium-term demands such as the establishment of non-racial local government, and the obstruction of the government's proposed reforms of influx control. All this was to be undertaken in terms of the evolving strategic framework of people's power.

The capacity of the UDF to effect this approach was shaped by the changing conditions on the ground. Immediate localised crises repeatedly distracted UDF national and regional leaders from their more strategic goals. Typically, a confrontation in one or other township would result in an urgent call for medical and legal assistance, and then for help in organising funerals. Funds would have to be arranged, generally through the South African Council of Churches, and speakers scheduled. If the confrontation continued, then regional or national leaders might intervene to try to defuse the situation, negotiating with the security forces and sometimes restraining the more confrontational comrades. Independent monitors estimated that almost eight hundred people were killed in political violence in the first five months of 1986, which meant a lot of funerals. In the Transvaal, arranging speakers for funerals was on the agenda for almost every REC meeting during this period. On one Saturday in February, for example, the UDF had to organise speakers for four major funerals – in Atteridgeville, Mamelodi, Jouberton and Sekhukhuneland in the Northern Transvaal.[35]

Crises were disruptive even when the UDF had patchy links to the leading local organisation in the area. One such case concerned Alexandra, in Johannesburg. Alexandra remained largely quiescent long after protest had erupted elsewhere across the Reef, but in February 1986 it too exploded in a spate of violence. The houses of policemen were attacked; the police retaliated very brutally, prompting further anger and reaction. Leaders of the UDF-affiliated Youth Congress described the township as having become ungovernable. The price, however, was high: the death toll over six days reached 19 according to the police, or 46 according to civic and church monitors, almost all of them killed by the security forces. The mass funerals were organised by a committee initiated by the chair of the Civic Association, a UDF affiliate. Repression intensified. In April barely disguised policemen attacked activists' houses, killing at least five people. Resistance intensified, and activists began to describe Alexandra as a liberated zone.[36]

Alexandra was, indeed, one of the few townships outside the Eastern Cape where activists could credibly speak of people's power, using the discourse developed by the UDF. Ironically, the UDF's involvement was unusually indirect, in that the UDF-affiliated Civic Association was not at the forefront of the struggle on the ground. In February a rival Alexandra Action Committee had been formed, led by the unionist Moses Mayekiso. Mayekiso had long been critical of the populist politics of the Charterist movement, and the Action Committee did not forge strong links to the UDF. When the Action Committee proved to be much more active and more progressive than the old civic, the Alexandra Youth Congress switched allegiance to it. It was the Action Committee and Youth Congress which spearheaded the formation of yard, block and street committees in Alexandra.[37] Nonetheless, UDF leaders were caught up in the crisis in Alexandra.[38]

This was an exhilarating period, with new organisations and protests appearing across the country. Most organisations were loosely affiliated to the UDF; many of them had been critical or wary of the UDF before participating in the UDF's sub-regional structures. The rapidity of change and spread of activity meant that a large part of any UDF meeting was taken up with reports from the different areas. Consider the following extracts from the Transvaal regional secretary's notes of an organising meeting in early May. The organiser for the south-east Rand, which included a small corner of the Orange Free State, reported: 'Ratanda Youth Congress being launched; May Day rally in Ratanda; two shot in Balfour on May Day, 86 arrested; Villiers visited – no structures; Standerton – met Zakhile Congress Party and Zakhile Youth Congress – CB [consumer boycott], enforcing of CB alienated community from organisations.'[39] The East Rand organiser reported: 'New structures: Women's groups in Vosloorus and Tsakane; Wattville Civic formed; Wattville Youth Congress launched last Sunday; shebeeners structure in Wattville – want to join Front; E. Rand Chamber of Commerce to be met; May Day [rallies held] in Tsakane and Daveyton; A.C. [Area Committee] Exec established.'[40] Through such reports, regional leaders were able to take stock, try to identify trends and patterns, and look for initiatives which might serve as examples or lessons for other areas. Reports and stock-taking were also a source of encouragement and inspiration.

The proliferation of local organisations and protests in townships across the country underscored the need for improved regional and national co-ordination. The UDF focused its efforts on civic organisations, which were the only bodies at the local level which could perform an adequately integrative role. Within the overall strategic framework of people's power, civics would provide the participatory organisation in residential areas corresponding to trade unions in the workplace and student organisations in the schools. Civic co-ordinating structures could step into the breach if the UDF were banned, as several UDF leaders feared. Civics could also help to keep the youth in check.

This represented in part a retreat from, or antidote to, the triumphalist immediatism of the youth. UDF leaders were wary of repeating the 'mistake' of 1976, when, as they saw it, insufficient organisation and too narrow a social base had undermined sustained protest. In 1985–6 there had already been indications that the zeal of the youth had alienated many older residents, prompting what was seen as counter-revolutionary vigilantism. Sisulu's speech at the NECC conference explicitly warned against exaggerating the imminence of revolution, and this was touched on again in May:

> We must develop an ability to understand the views and consciousness of the millions of people whose efforts will one day bring about change. We should be able to implement decisions with the active and willing participation of *all* our people, i.e. youth, workers, students, women and residents. It is only in this way that the struggle can be intensified.[41]

Civic organisation could provide the necessary integrative organisation at the local level. Strong grassroots civic organisation also made it difficult for the state to repress organisation. Finally, civics would play a central role in tactics such as consumer and rent boycotts, which the UDF national leadership and ANC leaders abroad wanted to take up nationwide.

In the first half of 1986 the UDF organised a series of inter-regional meetings and workshops which were intended to result in the formation of some kind of national co-ordinating structure for civic organisations. An initial meeting was held in February in Port Elizabeth, at the New Brighton home of the regional UDF and civic leader, Henry Fazzie. A larger meeting took place in March in Durban. There it was agreed that a national planning committee would be appointed by the NEC of the UDF, that regional conferences would be held in April, and a national conference would take place in May. The NEC appointed NEC member Titus Mafolo to convene the national planning committee. Mafolo, from Atteridgeville, had been a founding member of *The Eye*, Pretoria's community newspaper, and had been elected to the Transvaal REC in March 1985. Through *The Eye* he had long been involved in civic issues. The UDF also asked the Johannesburg-based Community Education and Information project (CEI) to employ and co-ordinate civic organisers and run educational workshops for civics.[42]

Progress towards regional co-ordination was not smooth in all regions, even after the lifting of the State of Emergency in March. Most progress was achieved in the Western Cape, where a regional conference was held in April. In the Transvaal CEI organised a series of civic workshops, leading to a full conference in May. In the Eastern Cape and Border repression continued to impede the development of regional co-ordination. An Eastern Cape regional conference was banned. Further consultation took place through new UDF sub-regional co-ordinating structures. State harassment meant that a Border regional conference was adjourned without completing its discussions; it was due to be completed in May. It is not clear whether there were any meetings in Natal.[43]

These national and regional meetings revealed differences in the perceived roles of civics and of a national civic co-ordinating structure. Some civic activists envisaged a national civic co-ordinating structure which could bypass what they saw as an overly reformist and moderate national UDF. They seem to have resented the UDF assuming a guiding role. There were also difficulties in linking the overall civic-building project with the specific and immediate concerns of individual civics. The UDF's general position emphasised the centrality of civic struggles to the establishment of people's power, their integrative role at the local level, and the exemplary importance of developments in the Eastern Cape. In practice, however, many civics faced immediate problems, with the concept of people's power providing little more than overall strategic direction. In the Transvaal workshops, the M-Plan and street committees were discussed more in terms of self-defence against reactionary vigilantes and other forms of repression than of establishing alternative structures of control over the townships.[44]

The slow progress at the regional level meant that the national civic conference had to be postponed to the end of May. Deliberations took place within the framework of an overall strategy of building people's power, but focused on a range of specific and practical problems. Indeed, the focus of the conference was not so much on building a national civic structure on the basis of existing organs of people's power, as seems to have been envisaged at the first meeting in February, as on the unevenness of organisation and the diverse pressures on civics on the ground.[45]

The question of building a national framework for local organs of people's power was complicated by the variety of understandings of precisely how local organs of people's power should be structured. In some areas civics served as umbrella bodies for all local structures, including the youth, student, women and sometimes worker sectors. In other areas, by contrast, civics were seen as a sector, and in some cases were regarded as quite conservative, with township-level co-ordination taking place within other structures, generally informal activist forums. UDF leaders seem to have regarded civics as sectoral in the sense of corresponding to student organisations and trade unions, but supra-sectoral in that they played an integrative role within the township, 'welding parents and youth together'.[46] This raised a dilemma with regard to national co-ordination. Should it be based on civics, or on whichever local structures were most broadly based?

The conference also raised a number of issues of concern to building people's power. Both the Eastern Cape and Border regions reported problems at the grassroots level. In the Eastern Cape, 'political education of street committees' was said to be 'desperately needed', and action needed to be taken to overcome racial divisions. In some areas in the Border, 'street marshalls' were said to be 'superseding street committees'. Furthermore, the Eastern Cape region was divided over the issue of negotiations, with Port Alfred activists criticised for negotiating with officials of the white municipality about forming some kind of a non-racial municipality. The variety of conditions and problems facing civics in different parts of the country worked against the adoption of an unambiguously militant strategy based upon people's power and co-ordination independent of the UDF.

In true UDF style, the conference seems to have accommodated varied points of view by proposing both organisation building and protests, the latter to include national rent and consumer boycotts. The overall emphasis was on intensifying the pressure on the state through protests such as rent boycotts in an organised and disciplined way, more than on usurping state power through building alternative administrative structures *per se*. A new co-ordinating committee was set up at the conference, with Nkwinti as an informal convener.[47]

The ultimate goal of building organisation at local, regional and national levels was to facilitate co-ordinated, broad-based and sustainable protests across the country as a whole. In January the ANC had imagined nationwide consumer boycotts, rent boycotts, and campaigns over local government and the government's pass law reforms. Whilst there were a huge number of localised protests in the first half of 1986, by mid-year the UDF had not reached the point at which it could comfortably call for and actively co-ordinate nationwide protests other than stayaways. An examination of the different forms of protest and prospective campaigns provides an indication of the character of township politics at the time, and of the strengths and weaknesses of the UDF.

Inside the country there were strong pressures at the local level for protests against repression and over civic, educational and political grievances. From abroad, the ANC broadcast over Radio Freedom general exhortations to intensify resistance. In April, for example, Radio Freedom urged that 'the spirit of ungovernability must live on and must now be sustained by mass actions of resistance and defiance … We boycott all white-owned shops, we boycott rent payments, we boycott tax payments and intensify our armed struggle. Apartheid cannot be reformed; it must be crushed by the might of the people.'[48] This broadcast also called for strikes and stayaways, and industrial sabotage. Stayaways were the one form of protest co-ordinated at the national level and supported across the country during this period. The UDF and NECC publicly backed COSATU's call for a nationwide stayaway on May Day. This was the first nationwide stayaway called since the early 1960s, and it proved to be the largest-ever stayaway in South African history up to then. The Labour Monitoring Group estimated that 1.5 million workers stayed at home – an estimate derided by COSATU as far too conservative. The UDF's support was particularly important in the Eastern Cape, where non-Charterist unions and Charterist organisations put their previously bad relations behind them.[49] A nationwide stayaway was also being organised for 16 June.

There were many stayaways at the local level, with little evident co-ordination. One source lists 18 towns where there were one or more stayaways between February and May, and this list omits many other known cases.[50] Many of these were called by activists with an apparently insurrectionary perspective, suggesting that the ANC's call was reaching an audience. For example, a week-long stayaway was held in Witbank. A similar week-long stayaway was proposed in the Vaal Triangle, though this was shortened to two days only.

Consumer boycotts also continued intermittently in many areas in early 1986. Most of these seem to have been organised locally with little overall co-ordination, despite another call by the ANC for a nationwide consumer boycott.[51] Local conditions seem to have favoured a locally tactical rather than a generally insurrectionary use of consumer boycotts, and this undermined the prospect of national co-ordination towards national goals. At the beginning of the year the UDF sought to bring consumer boycott committees under direct REC control, but it is not clear whether this was successful. The UDF does not seem to have proceeded beyond talking about a nationwide boycott.

Rent boycotts were another matter. Originating in the Vaal Triangle, the tactic drew strong support from the Border UDF leadership. Rent boycotts were seen as a way of targeting the state directly, in comparison to consumer boycotts which targeted white retail business. Rent boycotts were easier to sustain than consumer boycotts and did not have the drawback of encouraging coercive enforcement. In May 1986 there was much talk about rent boycotts, as a way of 'going for the state'; the idea of a national rent boycott was discussed at length at the national civic conference in Cape Town. On 1 June a boycott was formally called in Soweto, and other areas looked like following suit.

The UDF also considered campaigns around specific issues. One of these was the demand for non-racial municipalities. The ANC had made the point in its 8 January statement that the struggle must be expanded outside the townships into the whole urban area: 'For every town and every city, there must be one local authority, elected by all residents, both Black and White, on the basis of one person one vote.'[52] The call was taken up all over the Eastern Cape and elsewhere, and workshops were held. The UDF also proposed a campaign against the government's reforms of the pass laws. A government White Paper on Orderly Urbanisation and subsequent draft legislation proposed to reform influx control so as to make urban residence dependent on housing. The UDF denounced these reforms as 'merely an attempt to embellish the grand design of apartheid and make it more acceptable to the people'.[53] There was some discussion of a campaign, perhaps including the burning of passes as in 1960 and jointly organised with COSATU. But the plans seem to have been cut short by the State of Emergency.

The UDF's moves towards national co-ordination of protests and nationwide campaigns thus came to little in the first half of 1986. The only nationwide protest was the stayaway, organised primarily by COSATU. The UDF's attempts to co-ordinate consumer boycotts nationally did not make any progress, and its plans for nationwide rent boycotts and campaigns against the reform of influx control were interrupted by the State of Emergency. It was in the realms of organisation and net-work building, political education, and the elaboration of an overall strategic frame-work that the UDF had most impact.

The UDF played an important if indirect role in continuing education struggles. Leaders of the Front helped to steer the formation of a National Education Crisis Committee (NECC), to take over from the Soweto Parents' Crisis Committee the co-ordination of action over the escalating schools crisis. The NECC was formed in March, and formally assumed a leading role at the conference in Durban where Sisulu gave the keynote speech on people's power. The NECC's members included UDF-linked activists such as Khanyile, Molobi and Tsele, as well as UDF regional officials such as Mabudafhasi of the Northern Transvaal and Ndaba Gwabaza of Natal. The UDF also formed a Commission on People's Education to prepare for an alternative educational curriculum. This commission was convened by Curtis Nkondo and included among its members Sisulu, Mkhatshwa, Pravin Gordhan and Stofile. The UDF, NECC and Commission of People's Education had a high profile, but continued to have sometimes tense relationships with militant student groups.[54]

THE BEGINNINGS OF RURAL REVOLT

Most political organisation and protest remained concentrated in the metropolitan areas. The rural areas continued to be weakly organised, although protest and con-flict escalated dramatically in some areas, most of all in Sekhukhuneland in the ban-tustan of Lebowa, north-east of Pretoria. In the 1950s Sekhukhuneland had erupted in open revolt against the imposition of Bantu Authorities, and in the early 1960s proved fertile ground for recruitment into MK. In early 1986 revolt broke out in the region once again and it briefly became a no-go zone for the apartheid state. But extensive mobilisation and resistance were not accompanied by robust organisa-tion.[55]

The UDF had a co-ordinating committee in the Northern Transvaal from as early as May 1984, and had held a major anti-election rally in the Pietersburg township of Seshego in August. But the UDF was slow to develop a permanent structure in the region. In early 1985 the UDF convened a series of small conferences to prepare for the launch of a Northern Transvaal region,[56] but it was not until February 1986 that an REC was finally established. One reason for this was the lack of formal organisa-tion in the region. The only other areas of concerted organisation were around the University of the North, including the neighbouring township of Mankweng, and in the Steelpoort valley on the southern boundary of Sekhukhuneland, where student and youth organisation were linked to union organisation in local mines. Even in the largest town, Pietersburg, organisation was weak.

The REC formed in early 1986 was drawn from the University of the North on the one hand, and the ranks of the resurgent ANC underground on the other. The regional chairman, Peter Nchabaleng, was a veteran ANC activist from the 1950s who had spent eight years in jail on Robben Island. Although he was acquitted of charges of organising the ANC in 1978 in the same trial as Joe Gqabi, he was and remained the key leader in the ANC underground in the Northern Transvaal. His eldest son left the country to join the ANC in 1982, and another son, Elleck, was jailed on Robben Island from 1978 to 1984. Two other REC members had recently returned from Robben Island: Peter Mokaba and Thabo Makunyane. The two other senior members of the REC both worked at the University of the North: Louis Mnguni (vice-chairman) and Joyce Mabudafhasi (secretary). Mnguni, Mabudafhasi and Mokaba all lived in Mankweng, the township serving the University of the North. The leadership was entirely African.

The Northern Transvaal leadership felt a strong sense of isolation, to the extent that they believed themselves neglected by the Johannesburg-based UDF leadership. Moss Chikane seems to have assumed the primary role in liaising between Johannesburg and the Northern Transvaal, until his defeat in the Transvaal REC elections in March 1985 and subsequent detention and trial for treason. In March 1985 Morobe was appointed as Transvaal rural organiser, but he was almost immediately pulled into other work. Van Kessel reports that it was in response to this apparent neglect that the Northern Transvaal leadership decided to form a separate region rather than simply an area committee within the Transvaal UDF region.[57] There is likely, however, to have been a further reason. Elleck Nchabaleng worked for one of the Freeway House organisations that had a tense relationship with the Transvaal UDF. In March 1985 activists linked to Freeway House, including Moss Chikane, were all defeated – some say purged – in the Transvaal REC elections. This could only have reinforced suspicion of the Johannesburg-based Transvaal UDF leadership.

The Northern Transvaal UDF remained isolated even after the formation of the REC. According to one of Peter Nchabaleng's sons, Morris: 'Organisations like the UDF were not very familiar to us. We were close to the UDF because my father became president, but we were having problems because you would find that maybe a member of the UDF would only come after some months'.[58] According to Van Kessel, 'the formation of a separate Northern Transvaal region did not bring the expected flow of resources from Johannesburg, nor did it stop the flow of activists to Johannesburg'. The UDF did not even have its own office.[59]

The region as a whole, however, was not immune to the tide of revolt sweeping across the rest of the country. AZASO, at the University of the North, urged its members to organise in rural areas in the university holidays, or after graduation. But such pockets of organisation were dwarfed by the reverberations of resistance elsewhere – in the PWV, in Witbank and Middelburg to the south, and then in the region itself. According to Elleck Nchabaleng, young people 'got the UDF from newspapers and heard about the formation of youth congresses, so they just got together and called themselves *macomrades* without any politics at all …'[60]

Between February and April much of Sekhukhuneland was turned into a no-go zone for the state. In April the UDF boasted that 'the people … had established entrenched structures of people's power' in place of discredited chiefs. The UDF exaggerated in reporting its appropriation of Sekhukhuneland to the cause of people's power. The revolt never progressed beyond the stage of ungovernability, driven by unemployed, young men out of school, with no countervailing organisation. Even Peter Nchabaleng, an ANC as well as UDF leader, had limited influence, mitigating perhaps rather than preventing an orgy of witch killing in April. The UDF claimed some 63 affiliates, but most of these seem to have been affiliates of the Sekhukhuneland Youth Organisation, minimally linked to the parent body, let alone the UDF itself. The UDF had little role in this insurrectionary movement. According to REC member Makunyane, the youth in many areas 'were doing things in the name of ANC or UDF without these organisations ever knowing'. When asked what UDF campaigns had been taken up, one youth activist paused in thought before eventually replying that they had 'participated in the campaign to make the country ungovernable and to set up alternative structures'.[61]

In mid-April the state wrested back control of Sekhukhuneland through massive and brutal repression. Nchabaleng was detained in the middle of the night. In the words of his wife, the police told him, 'Last time it was Robben Island, this time we are going to kill you.' This is exactly what they did, beating him to death in the Schoonoord police station. Mabudafhasi was injured when her house was fire-bombed. Mokaba's house was also firebombed, and his brother injured.[62] There were mass detentions and the remaining leaders were driven into hiding.

As on previous occasions, such brutality by the state pushed UDF leaders to an open questioning of their commitment to non-violence. The UDF NEC, in a press statement after Nchabaleng's death, concluded: 'It is also important to note that the UDF has been called upon by many of its affiliates to review its non-violent stance in the wake of unmitigated violence against its officials. While at this point we are still committed to non-violent methods, we will not be able to ignore these calls forever.'[63] Precisely which affiliates had lobbied the UDF remains obscure, and there is no evidence of any discussion of violent alternatives. The UDF's stance reflected internal pressures rather than a clear assessment of possible alternatives.

Sekhukhuneland was not the only rural area to experience escalating opposition to the bantustan administrations. There was also resistance to the incorporation of Moutse into the KwaNdebele bantustan, and within KwaNdebele to the proposal that the bantustan accept 'independence' (as four bantustans had already done). While the existence of overarching political organisation in these areas requires further research, there is little evidence of any involvement by any UDF structure.

The 1986 Sekhukhuneland and Moutse–KwaNdebele revolts put the rural areas on the political map in a way unprecedented since the 1950s. Hitherto the UDF had made rhetorical gestures towards rural areas; now there was good reason to take action. Following Nchabaleng's death, Charterist activists from the rural areas began to develop their nascent political networks into a more formal organisation, later to be launched formally as the Northern Transvaal People's Congress (NOTPECO). According to a NOTPECO document, the Congress was formed when UDF organisers recognised that:

- Rural communities are politically backward as a result of which there is no co-ordination between them and urban communities. This was highlighted by the lack of co-operation between 'hostel-dwellers' who are in the most [sic] people from the rural areas, and surrounding communities in the urban areas during stay-away calls. During these times there was always confrontation between the urban people and the innocent or ignorant 'hostel-dwellers'.

- Rural communities need to be educated about their position and plight.
- Rural communities need to be mobilised and organised.
- Rural people staying in urban areas need to be politicised so that they in turn go back to their communities to organise and form civic and village committees.
- There is urgent need to narrow or bridge the gap between rural and urban development.[64]

Johannesburg-based UDF activists attended a series of preparatory meetings in villages in the Northern Transvaal. The emphasis on linking urban and rural areas through migrant workers recalled similar relationships in the 1950s.[65]

RACE AND VIOLENCE IN NATAL AND CAPE TOWN

In many parts of the country activists in UDF affiliates experienced repression not only directly at the hands of the security forces, but also at the hands of reactionary vigilante groups. In the bantustans, these were often linked to bantustan regimes; in townships, to remaining township councillors who had resisted pressures to resign. In some areas, vigilante groups enjoyed significant popular support. This was the case in areas of Natal and KwaZulu, where Inkatha had a mass base, and in Cape Town. In both parts of the country the regional UDF leadership, dominated by Indian and coloured activists, struggled to comprehend the political dynamics in African areas.

In Durban, the UDF undertook in 1985–6 to transform itself into an African-orientated movement, in line with the UDF as a whole. This posed chronic and severe organisational problems, in part because of the apparent weaknesses of political organisation in most African areas. JORAC had served as the key affiliate in the townships, but in 1985–6 JORAC declined almost to the point of collapse. JORAC's participation in the UDF's REC and RGC became increasingly sporadic: its initial representative, Ian Mkhize, resigned in early 1986, and JORAC later ceased sending a representative altogether. The Natal Organisation of Women (NOW) grew in areas such as Umlazi and KwaMashu, but lacked a decisive voice within the regional leadership. Youth organisations also proliferated, first in areas such as Clermont, Umlazi and KwaMashu, and then on Durban's periphery. But this sector remained fragmented and divided, with two rival co-ordinating structures: a regional committee supposedly organising the International Youth Year and preparing for the formation of a national youth organisation, and the Youth Forum. The former was aligned with the UDF, whilst the latter was critical of the Front, not deciding to affiliate until March 1986. In May 1986 youth organisations were officially united under an umbrella Natal Youth Organisation. But the unification conference evoked controversy, with Youth Forum activists bitter at what they saw as their undemocratic marginalisation. Whilst the Natal Youth Organisation represented youth on the UDF

REC thereafter, some youth structures continued to feel unrepresented.[66]

Dissenting youth and student activists, alienated or feeling excluded from the UDF, became the pillars of rival Charterist networks. In Lamontville, a Youth Congress was formed as an explicit rival and challenge to the UDF-linked Masibosane Lamontville Youth Organisation, by mostly ex-COSAS and Youth Forum-linked activists, reflecting a combination of personal ambition, strategic difference and legitimate criticism. Many ex-COSAS activists were recruited into MK, and denounced the UDF leaders as liberals or reformists, who would not 'talk war'.[67]

Problems within sectors reinforced the perception that the REC did not represent the Charterist movement in Natal and was run by a cabal. The leading role of Indian activists in the existing leadership – or cabal – reinforced the view that African leadership in particular was being excluded. In consequence African activists on the REC were denounced as puppets of the implicitly Indian cabal. Mkhize says he resigned from the REC because resources and power were monopolised by a small core of UDF leaders based in the NIC. The NIC had a 'very sophisticated organisational machinery' which they did not make available to the movement as a whole. 'There was a strong sense, especially among the older Africans, that they were being marginalised, that the UDF was NIC-controlled.'[68]

The issue of African leadership was raised in late 1985 and early 1986 by youth activists, particularly from Clermont and Chesterville, along with activists from Umlazi, all of whom were outside the REC.[69] As violence escalated, demands for African leadership grew, as it was African communities which were most affected by violence. A growing number of older African activists believed that the UDF had mishandled its dealings with Inkatha. Some were themselves stung by Inkatha's allegations that the UDF was controlled by Indians, and reacted by denouncing the cabal.

Tensions in the region rose following the launch of COSATU in December. At the launch, new COSATU president Elijah Barayi delivered a strong speech on bantustan leaders, presumably including Buthelezi. This added to the belief among Inkatha leaders that they were under attack. Some local Inkatha leaders responded viciously. Thomas Shabalala, a member of Inkatha's Central Committee and a KwaZulu bantustan MP, controlled the Lindelani shack settlement in Durban. Residents of Lindelani paid a levy that financed a core of vigilantes which Shabalala used in his fight against 'the UDF'. Shabalala told one newspaper that he longed 'for the day when there will be open war between the UDF and Inkatha – it will prove who is who in the political battle'. Similarly, Inkatha leaders around Pietermaritzburg organised vigilante groups that targeted local UDF-aligned civic, youth and student leaders.

The outbreak of violence in the Natal Midlands in August 1985 led to a period when the sub-regional UDF was simply 'running around like chickens with [their] heads cut off', but in early 1986 the UDF recovered. In large part this was because the Natal Midlands UDF leadership included prominent and credible African leaders such as Ngwenya, Thami Mseleku and Reggie Radebe. By March UDF activists felt confident enough to consider holding major events. The first opportunity was provided by the death in exile of SACP leader Moses Mabhida. Mabhida had come from the Midlands, and it was proposed that his funeral be held in the area. The Midlands UDF supported the proposal, believing that they could organise a huge funeral, larger than that of Goniwe and fellow activists in Cradock the previous June, and thereby reassert the UDF's vitality. This view was supported by some other Natal activists, who argued that a strong display of support at the funeral would challenge the claims which Buthelezi repeatedly made to regional leadership. But some Durban-based activists, including UDF national co-president Archie Gumede, opposed the suggestion, fearing a brutal response from the state and Inkatha. Mkhize, for example, argued against the proposal, recalling the attack on the Victoria Mxenge memorial service the previous year.[70]

The issue was debated back and forth during March. The ANC left it to the UDF to decide. In a series of RGC-type meetings, a majority of Natal UDF leaders came out in favour of holding the funeral. But at each meeting perhaps a third of the participants strongly opposed the idea. Each side claimed to represent the people; the minority accused the majority of packing the meetings; and so on. One of the UDF sub-regional co-secretaries recalled that it was the first time he had seen the UDF being ripped apart. Mabhida's family expressed a wish for a trouble-free funeral. When the police imposed severe restrictions, after initially prohibiting the funeral outright, it became clear that this wish could only be met if the funeral were held abroad. In the end, therefore, the funeral was held in Mozambique with a memorial service in Pietermaritzburg. Even this service, however, was the largest UDF public event since before August.

Slowly, organisation revived, although activists were still subject to attack by vigilantes. Ngwenya, for example, was abducted and badly assaulted in February, and in May survived an attack on his house after defending himself with an assegai. A pamphlet issued by the Inkatha Youth Brigade in May warned all 'UDF members' to leave Imbali.[71]

Another area in which the regional UDF leadership had little understanding of or influence on the political dynamics in shack settlements was Cape Town, where violent conflict erupted in mid-1986. Squatter struggles revolved around Old Crossroads. The state had finally agreed to upgrade part of Old Crossroads, but wanted to remove many households to Khayelitsha. The UDF denounced the whole initiative, but had little grasp of the internal dynamics that generated division within the Old Crossroads area. Up to mid-1985 the squatter leadership was broadly aligned with the UDF and ANC. Power in Old Crossroads was held by Ngxobongwana, who was nominally chairperson of the UDF-affiliated Western Cape Civic Association, but he broke with the UDF in July 1985. Most of the various satellite squatter camps on the periphery of Old Crossroads provided safe havens to MK cadres. Several factors combined in 1985 to sow discord. First, younger Charterist activists began to challenge the patriarchal authority of Ngxobongwana and his headmen. At the same time, the coercive implementation of consumer boycotts alienated many residents, generating support for Ngxobongwana. Secondly, the state wooed Ngxobongwana, making it clear that the upgrading of Old Crossroads depended on moving the residents of the satellite camps to Khayelitsha. In May 1986 Ngxobongwana's *witdoeke* vigilantes, supported by the security forces, conducted what Cole describes as 'one of the most brutal and well organised forced removals ever to take place in South Africa's history'. One hundred people died, and 70 000 were made homeless, amidst the systematic destruction of the satellite camps.[72]

The UDF was slow to respond to the crisis. Cole writes that 'Although many activists from progressive organisations assisted the relief agencies as volunteers, the UDF took a full week to issue a public statement, despite the fact that what had happened was a direct and blatant attack on organised resistance to the state.'[73] The incident also indicated a fissure in the regional Charterist leadership. The UDF REC was dominated by educated coloured activists with poor contacts in the townships and shack settlements. Some of the younger African activists with better links were on the REC, but increasingly dedicated their efforts to the MK underground. There was little co-ordination between the two groups and their respective political approaches. In Cape Town, as in Durban, there were no prominent African activists able to command support from across the racial divide.

RESTRUCTURING THE UDF: CENTRALISATION AND DECENTRALISATION

In the first half of 1986 the UDF further restructured itself in response to the changing political context. The need increased for security in the face of repression, and the availability of financial resources combined with a concern to co-ordinate more fully local protest and organisation.

The first factor behind this restructuring was the experience and further prospect of sustained repression. The ability of the UDF to continue operating under the Emergency – holding meetings, producing media, and even sending delegates abroad to meet with the ANC – reflected an adaptation to working wholly or partially underground. As Moosa said in an interview just after the Emergency was lifted in March:

> Over the seven months of emergency, we have devised ways and means of operating that enable us to withstand extreme repression. We have adapted our organisation and structures – and these methods will stay with us. The lifting of the Emergency does open up new space for us, but only in a few areas. We will take advantage of this and come out into the open again. But we won't go back to the way we were working before the State of Emergency. Next time the state clamps down on us, they'll find it much more difficult to weaken us … Not all our work will be as public as it was before. We will maintain a public presence – this is very important to us. But people won't necessarily know when our committees meet or even who makes up those committees.[74]

In May the UDF warned: 'Let us not forget the lessons of the emergency. We must be able to continue operating effectively even under the hardest repressive conditions.'[75] National UDF leaders were constantly concerned about security, wary of further repression. The national civic conference in late May, for example, was organised highly clandestinely: many participants did not know where they were meeting, few people were allowed out of the conference until it ended, and all documents were collected at the exit.

A second factor driving the restructuring of the UDF was the massive growth in financial resources that became available after the Stockholm trip. This would make it possible for the UDF to employ full-time organisers as well as to expand its media and political education activities.

The changing nature of political struggle was the third factor in the UDF's restructuring. The UDF had initially been formed to co-ordinate national resistance to the constitutional reforms, an unambiguously national political issue. It had floundered in 1984–5, seeking to redefine its role in the face of the township revolt. Not until 1986 did it recover its sense of strategic direction, as we have seen, within the framework of people's power. The context in 1986 was very different from that of 1983, however. People's power was not only motivated by a sense of opportunity, so that significant strategic gains could be made through seizing political or administrative control at the local level. It was also motivated by a sense of weakness: the scale of resistance was misleading, given the weakness of organisation and the narrowness of its social bases. The strategy of people's power meant that the UDF had to intervene actively and decisively in building organisation and conducting campaigns at the local level, so as to build a more robust and sustainable national movement. This required a restructuring of the Front itself.

This restructuring involved simultaneous centralisation and decentralisation, possible because both occurred amidst massive expansion. A wide range of newly assumed roles and activities were devolved to sub-regional structures and personnel. At the same time, there was increased central authority, especially through control over financial resources. The concern with security meant a delineation of public from secret activities, encouraging both decentralisation, as local personnel and structures had less contact with the regional level, and centralisation, as communication and decision making at every level were concentrated in fewer channels or hands.

The key organisational change in early 1986 was the decision to employ many more full-time organisers. After the Stockholm trip the UDF decided to 'flood the country with organisers'. UDF organisers or co-ordinators would work in demarcated areas or sub-regions, and would be primarily accountable to the sub-regional structures. Some organisers would have specific responsibility for the civic and youth sectors, whilst others would have a more general brief. The Transvaal, which included the Northern and Eastern Transvaal, was provisionally divided into 19 areas in May, with a total allotment of 45 co-ordinators and organisers. The PWV was divided into five areas, with a sixth area formed when Johannesburg and Soweto were separated.[76]

The employment of locally based organisers was accompanied by a proposed restructuring of RECs, which, it was suggested, should comprise representatives of sub-regional structures alongside sectoral representatives and the elected officers. The Transvaal REC, for example, would comprise representatives of the key sectors –

students, women, youth and civics – and of six area committees, plus the elected president, three vice-presidents, general secretary and assistant, treasurer, and media and education officers, making a total of 19 people. It was later suggested that there should also be representatives of the white, coloured and Indian sectors, and a regional organiser. The locally based organisers would 'attend RECs from time to time'. Once the REC was thus restructured there would be little need for RGC meetings.[77] The Natal REC considered a similar restructuring, but the proposal does not seem to have got off the drawing board. Decentralisation was probably taken furthest in the Eastern Cape, where the REC comprised just four people, and Border.

The activities of UDF area committees (or zonal structures as they were called in the Border region) remain a largely unresearched topic. It is not clear how extensive they were in the first half of 1986. They seem to have been well established in parts of Cape Town, where they had already taken over some of the functions of individual affiliates. They were also active across most of the PWV and in parts of the Eastern Cape and Border. The Natal Midlands seems to have been the only part of Natal with an active sub-regional structure at this time, although there were moves afoot in both Durban and northern Natal. What any of these were actually doing, how often they met, how they were organised, and how they related to affiliates on the one side and regional UDF structures or personnel on the other, remain obscure.

The other side to restructuring was the representation of the sectors. In 1985 several RECs had been elected with sectoral representatives, but the sectors had been loosely or informally constituted. The 1986 proposal was that the affiliates in each sector would elect a representative to the REC, as well as being represented on a non-sectoral basis through Area Committees. This required organisation in each sector. The UDF aspired to building such organisation at regional and national levels. The UDF had been making some progress in terms of civic co-ordinating bodies, as we have seen. It had much less success in the other sectors. Various student organisations, such as the Transvaal Students Congress, were formed after the banning of COSAS. But these were of uneven strength, and their relationship with UDF RECs and national leadership was generally poor. The youth sector was also disappointing. The detention of many youth activists in mid-1985 forestalled the faltering steps towards national co-ordination. April 1986 had been suggested as a possible launch date for a National Youth Organisation, but April passed with little progress in any region, let alone nationally. The only region to show progress was Natal, where rival youth groups had been bludgeoned into unhappy unity. Youth organisers insisted that they were moving towards a national workshop, but needed resources to employ full-time organisers and produce a newsletter.[78] There was only slightly more progress towards forming a national women's organisation, with some consolidation of women's organisations in the regions.

At the same time there was a process of centralisation in the UDF, as the powers of the head office and national leadership expanded. The UDF head office controlled the financial purse strings. Cachalia, the national treasurer, sought to establish proper financial accountability within the UDF. He complained that only one region submitted proper financial statements, and that regional treasurers did not seem to be accountable to RECs. Henceforth the regions must prepare full financial statements, and raise 20 per cent of the UDF's budget. Regions that did not do so would not receive financial allocations from head office. Financial accountability meant, in practice, a broader accountability to head office. Organisers were instructed to provide monthly reports to show that they were indeed working. This led to the national treasurer becoming *de facto* their supervisor. Affiliates were instructed to submit budgets and foreign funding proposals so that the UDF could prevent overlap or inconsistency, but this meant that the head office came to approve affiliates' activities and employment practices.[79]

The other nationally based activity was political education and media. These activities had gone semi-underground during the State of Emergency, and stayed there after the Emergency was lifted in March. One team produced *UDF Update* and a series of leaflets, out of a small and secret office in central Johannesburg.[80] Another group produced *Isizwe*. Suttner, who was involved in *Isizwe*, also ran political education classes for activists. There was some discussion about appointing a national education officer. The Community Education and Information project, *de facto* a UDF structure, was also involved in political education. All these were controlled, in practice, by the UDF head office.

National UDF leaders were struck, however, by their apparent organisational weaknesses. As the national secretary reported in May: 'We are buckling at the centre. Our ability to initiate, generalise on situations and make the correct assessment speedily is severely constrained by this weakness.'[81] The strength of local dynamics and the 'tremendous unevenness both between and within regions' made it difficult to provide effective national co-ordination or to conduct nationwide campaigns.

This restructuring, and the more general trend towards a more integrated and, in some ways, centralised structure, gave rise to the criticism that the UDF was behaving more like a party than a front. It was accused of intervening in the affairs of its affiliates, and making decisions on its own which should have been made by its affiliates. Critics pointed out that some affiliates had withered as their leaders and energy had been absorbed by the UDF, and concluded: 'The front needs to limit itself and its objectives.' This criticism was most strongly made by affiliates involved in the UDF at the outset, mostly based in coloured, Indian or even white areas. In the Western Cape, REC members were said to be 'not organisationally based'.[82]

The UDF leadership itself acknowledged that the relationship between affiliates and the Front had changed: 'We find ourselves increasingly sitting uncomfortably between being a front and an organisation.'[83] But, UDF leaders insisted, changed conditions required new practices:

The front is more than the sum of its parts. Does leadership not have a task of advancing understanding and capabilities of affiliates beyond their immediate limitations? At the very least, leadership is responsible for thorough and ongoing political assessment at a national level and for outlining a range of options and responses that may be fed back into the various affiliates.[84]

The leadership adopted an increasingly vanguardist self-perception in response to the township revolt: it was up to the UDF to provide the strategic 'line' and build the 'correct' kind of organisation. UDF leaders spoke of 'democratic centralism', warning against 'loose individuals [and] service units'.[85]

The UDF responded with a re-commitment to participatory decision making and accountability. The NWC in May adopted four 'organisational guidelines'. Firstly:

> Always involve the maximum number of people in any decision. The UDF should not merely obtain mandates from officials of its affiliates, but must ensure that as far as possible structures like street committees and democratic SRCs are also consulted. Decisions must be reported back to the grassroots structures.[86]

Secondly, the restructuring of RECs to comprise representatives of constituencies was necessary to enhance democratic representation. Thirdly: 'Not only should RECs be accountable, every affiliate must be fully accountable to its membership.' Finally, there must be 'constant evaluation and reflection on our activities ... at every level'.[87]

The UDF leaders may have been committed in principle to democratic procedures, but conditions were far from conducive for such procedures in practice. The growth of the Front, in terms of financial resources and personnel especially, would have put a strain on decision-making procedures even in the absence of any repression. Given the extent of formal and informal repression, and the perceived urgency of building more robust and sustainable political resistance, it was deemed more important to ensure that the Front was effective than that it be democratic. Restructuring provided for greatly enhanced efficacy in national, regional and sub-regional co-ordination and organisation building.

Having seemed on the verge of eclipse in 1985, the UDF retrieved the leading role in political developments inside the country. It did this not through drawing affiliates in by making its procedures more participatory, but on the basis of delivering the goods: a strategic framework which enabled activists to understand their localised activities in terms of a countrywide challenge to the apartheid state; enhanced sub-regional, regional and national co-ordination, within distinct sectors as well as on an overall basis; political education material; and financial resources.

NEGOTIATIONS AND THE ANC

As the revolt escalated, the stature and importance of the ANC grew visibly. The ANC came to be seen, by conservative foreign governments and sections of the South African political and economic elites as well as by ANC supporters in townships and elsewhere, as an indispensable element in any lasting political settlement in South Africa. And a settlement was increasingly seen as necessary for economic stability or growth. In late 1985 and early 1986 a steady stream of groups openly visited the ANC in Zambia or met with them in Zimbabwe. P.W. Botha had himself offered

Mandela his release earlier in 1985 – on terms which Mandela refused – and in November the Minister of Justice, Kobie Coetsee, initiated direct, albeit clandestine, contact with Mandela.[88]

During early 1986 the unbanning of the ANC and the release of its jailed leadership became the focus of external and internal initiatives. The external initiative involved the Eminent Persons Group, or EPG. The EPG had its origins in a summit meeting of the nations of the British Commonwealth, held in Nassau in the Bahamas in October 1985. Strong demands for sanctions against South Africa were resisted, in particular by the British government. Eventually an agreement was reached whereby an Eminent Persons Group would be sent to South Africa to evaluate the prospects for change and to 'initiate a process of dialogue' leading to democratisation. The EPG recognised that the unbanning of the ANC and the release of its jailed leadership were virtual prerequisites for any meaningful dialogue. Unless a deal could be arranged whereby the South African government would make these 'concessions', the EPG's mission would fail.[89]

The members of the EPG themselves made a series of brief visits to South Africa, visiting the government in Pretoria and Nelson Mandela in prison. Up until mid-May it appeared that the Group was making progress, securing loose agreement from both ANC and government leaders over a 'possible negotiating concept'. This would have involved unbanning the ANC, a mutual suspension of violence, and direct talks between the ANC and the government. But the initiative was dramatically scuppered when South African security forces launched raids into three frontline states against supposed ANC targets. Observers assumed, at the time and since, that hard-line members of the government had won the day, and ordered the raids with the intention of terminating the EPG initiative. The Group left South Africa in protest on the day after the raids. Three weeks later they published their report, which was very critical of the South African government. At about the same time the government Bureau of Information published a report of its own, entitled 'Talking to the ANC', which denounced the ANC as a communist-controlled revolutionary organisation. There seemed little prospect for further dialogue.

The EPG initiative posed a troubling dilemma for the UDF. On the one hand, the EPG had the guarded support of the ANC. On the other, the initiative represented an arguably reformist international intervention driven by a country – Britain – previously denounced by UDF leaders as imperialist. In 1984 and 1985 there had been some controversy within the UDF over whether the demand for a national convention was too reformist; now the EPG was holding up the prospect of negotiations with the government. Not only were negotiations several steps behind even the national convention proposal, but this was the government that was prosecuting several UDF leaders, was held responsible for assassinating some more, and had detained most of the rest. Initially, the UDF leadership had misgivings about meeting with or assisting the EPG, but after discussions with the ANC it was agreed that they would do so. The EPG met formally with the UDF in March and May, and there was more extensive contact through officials of the Commonwealth Secretariat. These contacts led to what one UDF leader called some 'political relaxation' on the UDF's side, and the EPG mission 'became the main thing' for a while for some of the UDF's leaders.[90]

Most of the top UDF leadership – like much of the exiled ANC leadership – were not entirely comfortable with the emphasis on foreign-mediated negotiations. Waldmeir records that the exiled ANC and internal UDF leaders were actually relieved when the EPG initiative broke down.[91] Whether or not this was true, the EPG initiative did put the issue of negotiations on the agenda in a concrete way for the first time, and changed perceptions within the UDF of the role that foreign powers could play in them.

Spurred on by the external initiative perhaps, the UDF took up the call to 'Unban the ANC' and release Mandela and other prisoners inside the country. Events included a Release Mandela rally, held in Cape Town in March. Amidst speculation that Mandela might be released at any time, the UDF formed a National Planning Committee, to be co-ordinated by Ndlovu and including COSATU and the South African Council of Churches as well as UDF structures. By taking up the issues of the ANC and political prisoners, the UDF trod again on the toes of its long-disaffected affiliate, the Johannesburg-based Release Mandela Campaign. The price of the UDF's rising profile was resentment among some of the UDF's Charterist critics.[92]

The government's raids into the frontline states in May, and the collapse of the EPG initiative, changed the political context. The UDF decided at its NWC conference in late May to call for the total international isolation of South Africa. The UDF wrote an open letter to the EPG, arguing that the government's various repressive actions indicated that it was not interested in a peaceful transition to genuine majority rule. The letter called for 'the total isolation of the apartheid regime, politically, economically and culturally'.[93] To help police this, the UDF formed a Sports and Culture Desk.

The collapse of the EPG initiative suggested that any changes in South Africa would result from direct pressure on the government. As Trevor Manuel said, 'We don't think our struggle will be determined at Lancaster House in London. The people of South Africa will resolve the problem.'[94] The NWC conference approved plans for a campaign for the unbanning of the ANC and release of political prisoners to be launched on 5 June. In a press statement, the UDF pointed to the ANC's stature internationally and inside the country, and insisted that 'there can be *no* solution to the country's problems without the involvement of the ANC'. The government must create 'an appropriate climate for discussions and negotiations' by releasing political prisoners, unbanning the ANC and other proscribed organisations, and allowing exiles to return.[95] But the government did the opposite: the Minister of Law and Order banned all meetings from 4 to 30 June, ruling out events planned for 5 June. The following week the government declared a nationwide State of Emergency.

AVOIDING A REPEAT OF 1976–7

The township revolt of 1984–5 was more widespread in geographical scope, more inclusive in terms of its social support bases, and more effective in terms of pressure on the state than the earlier 1976–7 uprising. But there was a real possibility in 1985 that the township revolt would fail to sustain itself in the face of state repression, just as the earlier one had failed. The achievement of the UDF in 1985–6 was to ensure that resistance intensified rather than diminished. For sure, the UDF could not claim sole credit for this, but it played the leading role.

The lesson of 1976, as learnt by activists in Soweto and elsewhere, was that mobilisation was not sustainable without strong and widespread organisation. The theme adopted by the UDF in early 1985 – 'From mobilisation to organisation, From protest to challenge' – represented the intention to move beyond a repeat of 1976. Through most of 1985 the UDF failed to deliver on this, largely because of the disruptive effects of formal and informal repression. Resistance escalated, but generally through increased mobilisation without any significant strengthening of organisation.

From the end of 1985, however, the UDF retrieved its leading role in political developments inside the country in part because it was widely seen to be at the helm. Perceptions became, to some extent at least, reality. The UDF itself referred to its position in terms of the Gramscian concept of 'hegemony', meaning that its approach and ideas had become generally accepted as correct, had become commonsensical. At the end of May the UDF's national leadership itself made the following self-assessment:

> Enormous strides have been made in imprinting the hegemony of the UDF position on virtually every development in resistance in the country. Our work has forced the South African Struggle continuously high up the international agenda … The UDF has grown phenomenally into parts of our country which were previously unorganised.[96]

The UDF was seen to be providing a national integrative framework across much of the country: in more and more areas individuals began to think of themselves as 'UDF people', and many Charterist activists and organisations which had been critical of the UDF now worked with it. The UDF also established closer ties with the trade union movement, meeting with the national leaders of the newly formed COSATU in February 1986. The UDF's role was recognised internationally, the EPG attaching a priority to meeting it. And when in May the British opposition Labour Party proposed a top-level trip to South Africa, they sought an invitation from the UDF.

The elaboration of the strategic framework of people's power was central to the nascent hegemony of the UDF. People's power was presented as a stage in the struggle for democracy and liberation beyond the stage of ungovernability. This, together with its explicit focus on power, made it attractive to insurrectionists on the streets. But its emphasis was very much on organisation and discipline – the priority of those sections of the Charterist movement inside the country which had come to the fore in the UDF. People's power required extending the social base of resistance beyond the youth, and indeed subordinating the militancy of the youth to the concerns of more cautious sections of the community. In the schools, people's power meant that students should return to class: their role was to seize control of the classroom and appropriate this space for people's education, not to seize control of the streets.

The concept of people's power was promoted extensively through the UDF's own media, including its new political education journal, *Isizwe*, as well as through the alternative and even commercial media. This gave rise to the analysis that the Front was serving increasingly as an 'ideological centre'. It is more accurate to refer to this role during this period as strategic rather than ideological, but it remains true that the UDF was centrally concerned with symbolic aspects of political struggle. These symbolic aspects were, nonetheless, important. Given the military weaknesses of the anti-apartheid movement, it was essential that the UDF and the ANC in exile find ways of shaping perceptions of the struggle. The concept of people's power allowed the UDF to encourage the perception both in the state and in the townships that there was a powerful challenge to the state. Revolutionary rhetoric notwithstanding, no parts of the country were liberated to the extent that the security forces were excluded altogether, and the collapse of elected councils in the townships did not mean the complete collapse of the local state. Liberated zones were not springboards for armed incursions into enemy-occupied territory. But the fact that state authority was severely curtailed was important because the perception that state power was compromised was important in itself.

While the strategic framework of people's power was central to the UDF's re-emergence at the forefront of resistance, the goal of sustainability required concrete organisational development as well as symbolic politics. Early 1986 was a period of remarkable organisational expansion within the UDF. At the national level, meetings and conferences were held regularly and frequently, resources increased, and progress was made with regard to sectoral organisation. At the regional level, organisation was streamlined and one new region, the enormous Northern Transvaal, launched. At the sub-regional level, area and zonal committees took on a new importance, working closely with newly appointed organisers, helping to establish new affiliates, and re-integrating into the UDF many township-based organisations that had operated independently over the past 18 months. The UDF also improved its relationship with the trade union movement. People's power provided an opportunity to link political and workplace struggles, since it readily embraced notions of workplace democracy.

There remained important limits to the UDF. As the consumer boycotts showed, it was still difficult to set up national co-ordination; a proposed national consumer boycott committee was never formed. Tensions persisted in the education sector, with student groups remaining wary of the UDF. Sections of the Charterist movement became still more disaffected, especially in Durban and Cape Town. The UDF also trod a fine line between promoting discipline and retaining credibility among more militant groups. The result was continuing ambiguity in its position on political violence. An example of this was the UDF's failure to condemn immediately the killing, by UDF supporters at a UDF meeting in Mitchell's Plain, of an ordinary member of the public, Moegsien Abrahams.[97]

By mid-1986 it seemed that the UDF was on the verge of leading an unprecedented escalation of pressure on the apartheid state. On the UDF's immediate agenda were intensified struggles in the bantustans, countrywide rent and perhaps consumer boycotts, and campaigns for the release of political prisoners and the unbanning of the ANC, as well as continued organisational development. For many, it seemed that revolution was just around the corner. In a political sense, the state was in a deep crisis. But in a military sense, the state still retained a superiority of coercion that was more than sufficient to preserve the core of state power. This was evident in the deployment of troops in areas such as Alexandra and KwaNdebele in May. It was to become much more obvious with the reimposition of a State of Emergency, this time across the whole country, in June.

Chapter Eight

A Holding Operation:
Surviving the State of Emergency,
June 1986–February 1988

THE STATE OF EMERGENCY

In the early hours of the morning of Thursday 12 June the South African Police carried out raids in townships and suburbs across the country. The next day newspapers estimated that 1200 people had been detained. Although the Minister of Law and Order initially described the raids as 'normal operations', State President P.W. Botha later announced to a joint session of the Tricameral Parliament that he had declared a further State of Emergency, effective from the previous midnight. Botha accused the ANC and UDF, together with other 'radicals and anarchists', of planning large-scale unrest so as to undermine and replace government institutions with alternative structures.[1]

The new Emergency differed from the earlier one in 1985–6 in terms of the scale and scope of repression. The earlier Emergency had only covered parts of the country; the new Emergency was nationwide. Unprecedented numbers of people were detained. In mid-August the government named over 8500 detainees who had been held for over thirty days. The number in detention at any one time fell slightly thereafter, levelling off at about five thousand. But the total number of people crept up, reaching an estimated 16 000–20 000 by the end of the year.[2]

The detainees ranged from national leaders to members of local street committees, from important cadres in the ANC underground to worshippers in two church congregations detained *en masse*. The UDF and its affiliates were the primary targets of detention. According to one report, fifty national and regional UDF leaders had been detained by August. One difference between this and the previous State of Emergency was the large number of local activists caught up. In Oudtshoorn's Bongolethu township, for example, over one hundred people were detained; in Duncan Village, about three hundred. Another difference was that detainees were held for much longer. Trade unionists were not exempt, especially those with close links to the ANC or to township organisations. By the end of July 320 union officials or elected leaders were known to be in detention. The entire northern Natal COSATU regional executive was detained, as well as every regional organiser and many leading shop stewards. Equipment at trade union offices was confiscated by police, and some offices had to close when all their staff were detained or in hiding.[3]

The thousands of activists who escaped police raids were faced with the strain and difficulty of operating underground. Baskin's description of trade union activists applies equally to those of the UDF: they 'developed irregular movements, sometimes changed appearance, avoided places usually frequented, and rarely slept at home'. COSATU's Central Executive Committee met for the first time under the Emergency in the unlikely venue of the Carlton Hotel:

> It was a strange gathering. Ordinary COSATU activists kept a careful watch for signs of police activity in the vicinity. Some monitored street corners. Others kept an eye on the hotel lobby. The ... delegates came in unusual attire. Most wore suits and ties and carried briefcases. Some had rapidly grown beards and moustaches or now wore spectacles to help alter their appearance. Yet other delegates arrived wearing overalls. None wore the T-shirts with fighting slogans which, until a few weeks previously, had been standard unionist garb. A few of the most sought-after delegates decided it would be wisest not to come to the meeting at all, and sent others in their place.[4]

Whilst some COSATU leaders were targeted by the state, the trade union movement as a whole was treated mildly by comparison with the UDF. Initial UDF executive meetings were held even more clandestinely than those of COSATU.

In time, activists developed whole new ways of working underground. According to one:

> a whole new life developed in the underground. People had contact with each other, worked with each other, and they were a whole new society that had no contact with the previous society ... You never went to places like Khotso House, and you never went to any public meetings. There was a whole sort of sub-culture that actually functioned underground, parallel to the remaining things that were open.[5]

Morobe operated underground for more than a year, 'the longest period of underground activity by a high-profile political leader in two decades', as Mufson points out.[6]

But living this life and operating underground was not an easy experience. The strain took its toll, sooner or later. Many activists were caught by the police when they were tempted to relax their security. Western Cape REC members Tinto and Malindi avoided detention for more than six months before being detained on brief visits to their own homes: Tinto had returned home to visit his wife and newly born daughter, Malindi to collect his diabetes medicine. The fear of police informers could be debilitating, and was manipulated by the police accordingly through insinuations and misinformation about activists.[7]

The UDF's style of operation was affected not only by the detention and threat of detention of its activists, but also by a whole battery of other restrictions. The state sought to control the mechanisms used by the UDF to reach the public. Prior to the Emergency, in April, the government had reimposed a blanket ban on outdoor public meetings and a partial ban on indoor meetings, in terms of the Internal Security Act. From June, the police used Emergency regulations to ban and restrict many meetings and funerals not already covered. Restrictions were also imposed on specific organisations and individuals. Most severely, in the Western Cape the police prohibited the UDF and 118 other named organisations from holding meetings, issuing pamphlets or publications, and making press statements. This was successfully, although only temporarily, challenged in court. Night-time curfews were imposed in many areas, especially in the Eastern Cape and northern Orange Free State. Political T-shirts, flags and so on were prohibited in other areas. In October the UDF was declared an affected organisation, and prohibited from receiving foreign funding.[8]

The state also imposed restrictions on the media. Emergency regulations prohibited filming or taking photographs of unrest situations or of the security forces, and the publication of any 'subversive statement', a term defined so widely as to include even criticism of the State of Emergency. Severe penalties were attached to violations of the regulations. 'The immediate effect of these regulations and police orders was to limit severely what could be published.'[9] For the UDF, which had come to use the media extensively, both commercial and alternative, these restrictions proved very disruptive.

The severity of repression under the Emergency exceeded what was needed to prevent overt political demonstration. In the short term, it checked disaffection among the National Party's white supporters. More importantly, the Emergency provided the means for the state to regain the initiative in terms of political change. Even pro-reform state officials supported the use of repression, recognising that 'where once there could be no security without reform, now there can be no reform without security'.[10]

Repression played both symbolic and real roles. Just as the UDF sought to build a broad unity against the government to demonstrate the inevitable failure of anything less than full democratisation, so the state sought to demonstrate the inevitable failure of the UDF-led challenge. At the same time, just as the UDF mobilised resistance around material grievances, so the state sought to weaken resistance through developmental projects shielded by repression under the State of Emergency. The state greatly increased the resources it allocated to township development, and expanded the opportunities for private sector involvement. Townships such as Alexandra in Johannesburg were targeted for selective upgrading. But these developmental initiatives were undertaken behind the repression of resistance. In some cases, whole townships were finally and forcibly removed, such as Langa in Uitenhage. More generally, opposition was silenced. As one journalist reported from Cradock, 'revolutionary graffiti is the only visible link between the militant, tightly organised Karoo community of 1984–1986 and the bruised Lingelihle of today.'[11]

Although not unexpected, the State of Emergency caught UDF leaders in various degrees of readiness. Acting general secretary Moosa narrowly escaped capture, despite taking some precautions. Together with Suttner and Momoniat, he had spent the previous night in a cheap hotel in Hillbrow rather than at home. Suttner was due to fly to Zimbabwe, ostensibly to attend a law conference but actually to consult the ANC and get advice on what to do – the senior UDF leaders did not have sufficiently good links with the ANC underground to ensure reliable communication. They agreed that Suttner would only go if there had been no raids. But they overslept the next morning, and rushed to the airport without even phoning their homes or looking at the morning headlines. Only after Suttner had walked into the international departures section of the airport did Moosa glance at the newspapers and read that an Emergency was about to be declared. He phoned his lawyer, Krish Naidoo, who told him that all the office buildings used by the UDF and its major affiliates were surrounded by the security forces. Moosa and Momoniat immediately went into hiding. Suttner was, however, stopped and detained.[12]

The first concern of those UDF leaders who had evaded detention was to find out who else was on the run, make contact and take stock of the situation. But the UDF head office and Transvaal office were perforce closed, with their entire full-time office staff in detention. Through Krish Naidoo and other links, Moosa was able to make contact with Morobe, who had also avoided detention. This process of restoring contact was, in Moosa's words, 'very *ad hoc*'.[13] But other activists were able to use prearranged plans. For example, Community Education and Information activists had arranged to meet at a specified day and time at the Johannesburg Zoo.

> And we met on that day, and we ... set up a way of keeping in touch with each other, and then lay low for about six weeks. We didn't do anything. We just sat in 'solitary confinement' in our various hiding places for six weeks and waited. Because I mean it was bad then ... Eventually Valli [Moosa] got us together, but this was long afterwards, about two months after. And he said that what we needed to do was we needed to find people, ... to re-establish contact with people, anybody we could find ... We managed to pull together a meeting of about ten or twelve people to try and find out what was happening, to try and find out who was left, to make contact between people who were left.[14]

It was some time before middle-ranking activists in the Transvaal regrouped, but a skeleton NEC was able to meet within the first month of the Emergency. In fact, according to Moosa, the NEC could meet without interruption throughout the State of Emergency. Its membership was more fluid and informal than hitherto, however, depending on who was available. The regular members during the first year of the Emergency included Moosa (acting general secretary, except between January and April 1987, when he was detained), acting publicity secretary Morobe, co-presidents Sisulu and Gumede, Frank Chikane, Nair, UDF chairperson Ndlovu, Natal secretary

Yunus Mahomed, and other regional and youth representatives.

NEC meetings had generally started with regional reports, taking stock of the situation. Under the Emergency, with severe repression and limited news in the media, stocktaking became especially important. The first meeting for which any documentation is available seems to have taken place in the first half of July. Moosa's notes on three of the UDF's regions present a picture of general repression.

> *E.C.* [Eastern Cape]: Stone [Sizani] & [Edgar] Ngoyi detained ... Street Comms being detained. Seems like state is preparing for a mass trial. Massive SADF presence. Homes of key people petrol-bombed. More than 800 people arrested. Rent boycott launched this month ... *Natal:* a few hundred detained ... Pmb [Pietermaritzburg] was hit very hard – but many released now. Empangeni – unionists detained ... Most of REC in hiding ... *W.Cape:* REC is intact and operational ... Good communication and contact with African areas. Peninsula not hit too hard, but bad in outlying areas ...[15]

Border activists reported to a subsequent meeting: '*Border:* REC members in Ciskei functioning. Unit structures intact. All organisers out. Office closed. 1 or 2 leaflets produced per month ... Little co-ordination with National office. Press coverage very poor. Lucille [Meyer]'s house destroyed ...'[16] A full discussion was held at a major meeting, probably in early September:

> *Natal:* Many breakdowns below REC level ... Maritzburg Area Comm. functioning well. REC meets once in two weeks. Detained portfolios are being replaced ... Office is open and manned by President and administrator ... *Cape:* ... 2 [REC] members inside. Meets fortnightly. On weekly basis 3 different national groups meet. Weekly meeting of 7 regional co-ordinators ... Scaled-down GC [General Council] held recently (of 18 people) ... 4 UDF newsletters distributed at mass level. REC is full-time. Activists moving around quite freely ... *N.Transvaal:* REC started meeting 3 weeks after emergency. REC meets either weekly or fortnightly ... Problem of transport ... Many affiliates crushed. Gen. secretary non-functional. Office never used. *E.Cape:* No REC. Reg[ional] co-ord[inating] comm[ittee] consists of existing organisers has been established and met once. *Border:* ... REC meets fortnightly. GC to be held soon ...[17]

The situation in the Transvaal was generally poor. When civic activists regrouped in August, they found that 'Soweto was actually in a much better position than anywhere else at this point. But the East Rand was badly hit. West Rand was badly hit, the Vaal was badly hit. Whereas in the first emergency they were taking like the top ten, this time they were taking like 200, 300 people at a time.'[18]

As these notes and recollections indicate, regional structures were disrupted to different degrees. The situation in Cape Town was clearly easier than in the Eastern Cape. The UDF later acknowledged that state repression of its regional structures had been particularly disruptive:

> Regional structures play the crucial role of facilitating co-ordination and democratic interaction between local affiliates and the Front at a national level. Our inability to maintain regional structures has impaired the co-ordination and democratic interaction within the Front. This has been one of the main weaknesses of the Front over the past year.[19]

Communication between national and regional levels had often been poor, and within regions the zonal or sub-regional structures functioned unevenly. In the Northern Transvaal, according to regional vice-chairman Thabo Makunyane, 'The UDF never was a very strong organisation; what was missing was a link between the structures. And then the structures became static. No new leadership was coming up.'[20] Without a second layer of activists, the UDF could easily fragment into its discrete components.

Whilst repression was severe, in most regions many leading activists had escaped detention and could continue to mobilise protests. Apparently underestimating the degree of disruption in the regions, the UDF national leadership initially seems to have planned to continue with the tactics identified before the Emergency. Just days after the Emergency, an estimated 1.5 million workers observed a national stayaway on 16 June to mark Soweto Day – as had been planned previously. The NEC discussed rent boycotts, which had been called for at a special UDF conference in Cape Town two weeks before the Emergency, and decided that planned national meetings for women's organisations and the sports sector should go ahead. Even some of the confusions which characterised the pre-Emergency period were reported at NEC meetings. For example, people in some areas were apparently confused about street committees. 'We need to write papers' – guides – noted Moosa.[21]

The UDF did promote one new campaign, although it was not related to the Emergency as such. In early June the government had tried to rush security legislation through parliament that would provide for draconian powers without having to impose a State of Emergency. In a rare moment of defiance, MPs in the Indian House of Delegates and the coloured House of Representatives had held up the legislation, but the government had then bypassed them, imposing the State of Emergency. The UDF drew up plans to lobby the MPs to resign.[22]

The first activity directly related to the Emergency was undertaken by COSATU. The trade unions called for a Day of Action on 14 July. It is not clear what UDF involvement there was in this. The key action was a stayaway, which was very poorly supported. Overall, Baskin considers, 'the Day of Action was a failure.'[23] The UDF, for its part, seems to have limited its immediate response to setting up meetings with a range of groupings to prepare for some unspecified future action. Besides meeting with UDF affiliates and allies (COSATU, the National Education Crisis Committee and the churches), the UDF leaders controversially met with business leaders. In mid-August, Morobe and others met with key business leaders Tony Bloom (Premier Milling), Julian Ogilvie Thompson (Anglo American), Basil Hersov (Anglo-Vaal) and Zach de Beer (Anglo American and PFP member of parliament).[24]

Morobe, the UDF's acting national publicity secretary, repeatedly dismissed the effects of repression in statements to the press. On the UDF's third anniversary in August, Morobe stated:

> The UDF has not only survived the most severe repression but has grown into a powerful mass movement. The democratic movement has not been crushed. While widespread detentions have hit some areas hard, many activists foresaw the Emergency and took the necessary precautions. They have been able to avoid detention and remain active, if covertly. Our organisations are stronger and deeper than before and are thus better able to replace activists detained, killed or forced into exile ... We are still intact and able to hold meetings at national level. But the UDF power basis is at the local level, where there is more intimate contact with the community ... So far they have failed to enforce the quiescence they desire ... Students are becoming angrier by the day and the effects of that anger are being carried over to the rest of the community.[25]

Morobe did concede, however, that the 'days of Mitchell's Plain are over', meaning that the days of mass public rallies were past. Whilst Morobe was right to emphasise that state repression had failed to suppress political organisation and action completely, he was disingenuous in suggesting that it had made no difference. The UDF had in fact been severely disrupted. It soon became clear to UDF leaders that they could not simply hold to their existing strategies and tactics, formulated prior to the Emergency. As Moosa later put it, the UDF would only be able to run a 'holding operation' during 1986–7.[26]

THE CAMPAIGN FOR NATIONAL UNITED ACTION

After establishing new forms of clandestine co-ordination and communication, and recognising the need for an innovative approach, the UDF called for a Campaign for National United Action. The campaign was jointly taken up by the UDF and COSATU, together with the NECC, the South African Council of Churches (SACC) and the Southern African Catholic Bishops' Conference (SACBC). Its primary aims were to oppose the Emergency publicly, to revive the momentum of national resistance, and to broaden the scope of resistance by forging a close working alliance with COSATU. The campaign, including a 'Christmas against the Emergency', was essentially symbolic, and the primary audience was local-level activists.

The campaign seems to have been conceived within the UDF leadership. Moosa later wrote: 'An analysis of the situation ... led the Front to conclude that its very survival and indeed the survival of its affiliates on the ground, rested in the unity of all democratic forces. It was this realisation that led the Front to launch the Campaign for National United Action.'[27] The aims of the campaign, according to a workshop report circulated among UDF regions and affiliates, were:

1. To fight back against the repressive conditions imposed by the state of emergency; to open up space to organise further, in order for the progressive movement to take the political initiative.
2. To engage in joint action between various sectors of our people, locally, regionally and nationally.
3. To build organs of people's power in the townships, factories, schools, universities, etc.
4. To deepen the political consciousness of both the masses and our activists.[28]

The report added: 'The main emphasis of the campaign is to strengthen the unity of the progressive movement.' Seven broad national demands were suggested. These included an end to the State of Emergency, the unbanning of the ANC, no eviction of rent defaulters, and a set of worker-related demands. But the precise demands were unimportant. An article in the UDF's own *UDF Update* neglected even to mention them. The purpose was not to achieve demands but to 'galvanise all democratic forces in the country'.[29]

The campaign hinged upon the alliance with COSATU, with the UDF looking for 'structured contact' between the UDF and COSATU at the regional and local levels. COSATU hesitated before agreeing to participate in the campaign, telling the UDF that the 'July 14 setback makes it difficult to take any quick decision'. COSATU agreed, however, 'that there should be united action against [the] emergency' and that it was 'important to strengthen and formalise links and contacts between UDF and COSATU at a local level'. UDF–COSATU meetings were soon held in some of the regions, starting with the Natal Midlands and Northern Transvaal, although the alliance did not develop smoothly everywhere. The UDF Border region repeatedly complained to the NEC about the bitter divisions within COSATU in the Eastern Cape and Border. In the Western Cape UDF leaders were worried about what they called 'workerist domination' within COSATU.[30]

The Campaign for National United Action was finally launched by the UDF, together with COSATU, the NECC, SACBC and SACC, at a press conference in October. The press conference introduced a new trio of faces representing the democratic movement: Morobe, Mufamadi and Molobi, from the UDF, COSATU and NECC respectively.[31] All three were from the political grouping that came together in Soweto in the early 1980s; all three were closely linked to the ANC, with Morobe and Molobi having spent time on Robben Island. Mufamadi was a UDF REC member as well as COSATU official. Molobi had never held formal office in the UDF, but was very close to the UDF leadership. Personal ties helped cement organisational alliances. All three were African, reflecting a continuing commitment to African leadership.

The UDF later described the campaign as creating the basis for this alliance through 'unity in action at a national, regional and local level'. The campaign represented 'a phenomenal alliance of democratic forces'. The national leaders repeatedly emphasised the importance of action and unity at the local level: 'The programme for the campaign must be built on the ground in order to make National Unity a reality.'[32]

But no guidance was initially provided as to what the content of the campaign should be. In other words, the campaign was formulated so as to embrace any actions, according them a national significance, but did not suggest any particular focus.

It was perhaps the lack of a specific focus that led the UDF and its allies to call for a 'Christmas against the Emergency' as part of the Campaign for National United Action. The UDF, COSATU, NECC and SACC called on people to observe a set of essentially symbolic practices for ten days, from 16 to 26 December. The overall theme was 'to rededicate ourselves to the struggle for national liberation'. People should partake in two two-hour candle vigils, read a Unity Pledge in churches, avoid drunkenness, and so on. The UDF and allies asked that major sports fixtures and music festivals be suspended, called on people not to shop in town, and appealed to shebeens to close, at least at night. A 'special appeal' was made to 'young militants to exercise maximum possible discipline'; activists must 'ensure that the campaign is explained to the people well before December 16'. The UDF later claimed that the Christmas campaign had been 'highly successful mainly in the Transvaal and Eastern Cape'. One success was that 'For the first time the structures of the UDF, COSATU, NECC and SACC engaged in united action at a local level'.[33]

The message that resistance had not been crushed either in practice or in spirit was central to the overall campaign. This was the upbeat message that the UDF repeatedly sought to convey through the media. For example, the 'Comment' in *UDF Update* in November stated:

> As 1986 draws to an end the UDF and the democratic movement can look back
> with pride at the massive blows struck against the apartheid regime. No longer
> is the prospect of victory ... a distant dream. Today we can say with confidence
> that the day of our liberation is in sight ... Despite all its efforts, the regime's
> attempts to reverse the tide of history has been a dismal failure.[34]

In strategic terms, the campaign represented a return to the UDF's strategy of the early 1980s. The UDF and its new allies were in practice less concerned with directly challenging the state, as perhaps in the pre-Emergency period of people's power, but rather sought to demonstrate that the democratic movement remained strong and united, thereby asserting the impossibility of the state resisting fundamental change.

The UDF was surely correct to view the significance of the campaign more in the fact that it took place at all, thereby registering continued defiance, than in the numbers of people actually involved. But the campaign nonetheless suffered from two important weaknesses. Firstly, the UDF was largely constrained by the limits of the media. Its own media production was disrupted by the Emergency. The first post-Emergency issues of *UDF Update* and the UDF-aligned *SASPU National* were dated November and November/December respectively. Only *Grassroots*, in Cape Town, appeared regularly. Besides *UDF Update* and the theoretical journal *Isizwe*, no national publications were produced in 1986–7, 'due to difficulties in communication, printing and distribution'. UDF leaders warned against relying on national propaganda: 'While national propaganda has an important role to play, the most crucial form of propaganda is that which is published at a local level ... It is only with local-ly based and decentralised production and distribution of propaganda that we would be able to counter the apartheid propaganda strategy.'[35]

In practice, regions and affiliates seem to have been able to do little in the first six months of the Emergency. The UDF was therefore forced to make use of the com-mercial press, including the very sympathetic *New Nation*. Morobe fed a constant stream of statements to the media. But in most regions the UDF struggled even to secure coverage in the commercial media. At an NEC meeting in September 1986, propaganda was reported to be 'very weak' in Natal, Border and the Northern Transvaal. Only in the Western Cape were REC members said to have 'close connec-tions with certain journalists'. These comments were echoed later in the year, with only the Western Cape region apparently producing pamphlets, although its media on National United Action was said to be 'very poor'.[36]

Use of the media was further limited by state regulations. The restrictions on the media imposed in June were streamlined and further tightened in December. The definition of 'subversive statements' was widened to include not only statements promoting protest or organisation but also those merely reporting on these. The publication of blank spaces or of text obscured by thick black lines was prohibited so as to conceal the extent of censorship. As if these were not enough, still more regula-tions were gazetted to plug any remaining gaps. Three newspapers – the *Weekly Mail*, *Sowetan* and *City Press* – were prevented from publishing statements concerning specifically the Campaign for National United Action. In January 1987 the *New Nation* was similarly restricted.[37]

The second, and more important, weakness of the campaign was the lack of any clear programme of action. A range of protests did continue at the local level, despite (or, in some cases, fuelled by) repression under the Emergency. But these were bare-ly integrated into any national strategy. This is not to say that there were no discus-sions of strategy. For example, strategy was discussed at an NEC meeting in September, where a general approach of both intensifying and broadening resistance was mapped out. Intensification involved rent boycotts, campaigns against apartheid structures – in practice, sending letters to MPs in the House of Delegates – and planned campaigns around the Sharpeville Six, who were political prisoners on death row for their part in killings in the Vaal Triangle in 1984. Broadening involved building alliances, especially with COSATU, and (controversially) forging a closer relationship with big business. But this hardly amounted to a programme of action. It was more of a list of what was known to be happening, a report-back, than an inte-grated strategy. Under the circumstances, little more was possible. And most of what was reported was not protest, but rather story after story of repression, smear cam-paigns, and so on.[38]

Registering continued defiance was of undoubted importance, providing encour-agement to activists whose spirits flagged, and maintaining some pressure on the state, but it hardly amounted to a persuasive strategy for achieving political change. Uncertain as to how to proceed, internal leaders sought further guidance from the ANC in exile. Since January the ANC had been regarded as the font of all strategic wisdom. Suttner was detained *en route* to the ANC in June; in July the NEC discussed a 'trip abroad' – with Moosa scribbling a note, 'also suggest to COSATU'.[39] The full range of contacts with the ANC thereafter remains unclear, the only confirmed visitors being youth leaders Deacon Mathe and Peter Mokaba, who consulted with the ANC in Harare, but there clearly were extensive contacts, especially during 1987.

The ANC's position can probably be determined from a document entitled '1987: What Is to Be Done?', allegedly drafted by the ANC's National Executive Committee and Political-Military Council in October 1986, but of unproven authenticity. The document called on the democratic movement to avoid simply defensive actions. It identified a need, as apparently had already been mooted, for 'a very broad summit meeting of democratic and anti-apartheid leaders', as well as campaigns in the white population, in the bantustans, and over political prisoners.[40]

The ANC document also identified a series of 'major problems' within the democratic movement inside the country. The frankness of this acknowledgement suggests that the document is authentic.

a.　Sharp divisions and conflict within the leadership of the UDF
b.　The failure of the UDF to work out a programme of action and a set of strategic and tactical objectives
c.　The emergence of contradictions between the national leadership of the UDF on the one hand and regional and local collectives on the other
d.　In some cases, the weakness of the UDF's affiliates and the failure of the Front to attend to this question
e.　Divisions within COSATU …
f.　[Concerning failures within the churches]
g.　The inability to ensure concerted joint actions over time among all the social forces that constitute the democratic movement
h.　The failure of ANC people within the democratic movement to solve organisational and political questions relating to the combination of legal and illegal work
i.　The sporadic nature of contact between ourselves and the leadership of the democratic movement.

Indeed, repression under the Emergency served to reopen many of the divisions which had come to the fore during 1984–5. The strategic framework of people's power had provided a way of drawing together under the UDF's umbrella the different strands of the Charterist movement. But the strategic framework fell apart in the face of mass detentions and the extraordinary difficulty of holding large meetings. The rival strands of the Charterist movement began to send separate delegations to the ANC, and used different lines of communication. Over the next few years tensions were to increase steadily.

In response, the ANC advocated unity, as it always had, but did so in conjunction with a strategic vision which was itself unconvincing and hence a source of disunity. As Barrell writes: 'Operationally, the ANC was stuck in a profound strategic hiatus, if not crisis. Across the gamut of its operational activities, it showed no sign of a break-through, although conditions were more favourable than at any time since the resort to armed struggle in 1961.'[41] The ANC had failed to infiltrate large numbers of military cadres into South Africa, had only a limited tactical influence on internal protesters and, above all, had made no significant progress in building integrated political-military command structures inside the country. ANC strategy was simply to repeat its past efforts.

Several years later, Moosa told journalist Patti Waldmeir that by 1987 he had become unhappy with the ANC's 'romantic approach to revolution'. 'Whenever I met with ANC leaders,' he told Waldmeir, 'the question I asked over and over was, How exactly are we going to take over?' Moosa recalled voicing his unhappiness at a meeting with the ANC held near London:

> We said, we've done everything, and we can do a bit more of everything, but there is a stalemate. We were saying, something else now needs to happen. The Boers are killing us, and it's not conceivable that we are going to be able to overrun Pretoria ... We were *attacked* by the [ANC] leadership for even suggesting that there could be a stalemate. We were given a lecture on insurrection and sent back to prepare for it. And of course, that's what we did.[42]

But the UDF leadership, and the COSATU leadership too, were not committed insurrectionists. They were willing to work towards unity, and were certainly willing to support a wide range of defiance and protest action, but they were wary of the insurrectionism advocated by some sections of the Charterist movement. The ANC, however, was slow to recognise that the promise of people's power had dissipated.

One tactic which burgeoned in mid-1986 was the rent boycott. At a conference just prior to the State of Emergency, UDF regions and affiliates had agreed to promote rent boycotts across the country. In this they were inspired by the success of the rent boycott in the Vaal Triangle, which by November 1986 had caused local government in the area to run up a deficit of R46 million, growing by R2 million each month. In June a boycott began in Soweto. The state's attempts to suppress the boycotts through force merely served to strengthen them. Boycotts also began in the Border region. By February 1987 rent arrears in townships across the country had reached R178 million.[43]

'UNBAN THE ANC'

In the second half of 1986 the UDF's public activities had been largely symbolic, concerned more with marshalling the UDF's supporters than with challenging the state. At the beginning of January, probably spurred on by the ANC itself, the UDF once again seized the initiative. On 8 January 1987, on the 75th anniversary of the ANC's birth, whole page advertisments calling for its unbanning appeared in sixteen newspapers. The action, which the UDF saw as part of its Campaign for National United

Action, may have involved very few people, but it had a powerful effect, encouraging the UDF's supporters and exposing divisions within the 'ruling bloc'.

The unbanning of the ANC and other organisations had been a goal of the UDF since its formation. Action on the demand had been discussed at the January 1986 meeting with the ANC in Stockholm, and formed part of the Programme of Action adopted at the NWC Conference in May 1986. In June 1986, just before the imposition of the Emergency, the UDF, supported by COSATU, NAFCOC, SACC and the Black Sash, had demanded publicly that the ANC be unbanned, and linked this demand to the planned protests on 16 June and 26 June. Unbanning the ANC was also one of the seven demands in the Campaign for National United Action.

The advertisments constituted a symbolic protest, but were nonetheless very powerful. Apart from the sixteen newspapers they appeared in, three more papers were prevented from publishing the advertisement by security police, and several others refused to publish them. Moosa later wrote:

> The advertisment made a tremendous impact both at a mass level inside the country and internationally. In the face of a plethora of media restrictions and the declaration of the UDF as an affected organisation, the advertisement served to boost the morale of UDF supporters and demoralise those in government and other supporters of the regime who assumed that the State of Emergency had succeeded in silencing the Front. In this sense, it was a psychological victory.[44]

The impact of the action was reflected in the rapidity of the state's response. The Commissioner of Police issued a prohibition under Emergency regulations on advertising or reports in the media which promoted the image of a banned organisation. Although the prohibition was ruled invalid in the Supreme Court later in the month, the government immediately amended the regulations to permit this kind of prohibition. The advertisements clearly irked P.W. Botha especially. In February he alleged that the advertisments had been paid for by First National Bank (FNB), and appointed a compliant judge to run a commission of inquiry. It turned out that the advertisments, costing about R150 000, had been paid for by an Indian businessman, in part through a loan made available by FNB on the direct instructions of its chief executive, Chris Ball. The 'Ball affair' served to reveal the disaffection among the English-speaking business elite with the government, as well as the government's paranoia.[45]

The government soon responded to the UDF's call for the unbanning of the ANC. P.W. Botha announced in January, on the day after the 'Unban the ANC' advertisments had been published, that elections would be held for the House of Assembly, the House elected by white voters only. At the end of January the date was set for 6 May. The central theme in the elections was the threat posed by the ANC. The elections posed two dilemmas for the UDF and its allies. Firstly, as in the 1983 referendum, the UDF had to advise its white supporters and sympathisers on their response. Secondly, it sought activities which would demonstrate the power of the UDF and the ANC as well as popular dissatisfaction with the whites-only elections. The UDF's capacity to respond was, however, impaired by the detention of Moosa from January to April.

In advising white voters, the UDF was typically evasive. Whilst it could not approve of participation in the elections, it did not explicitly call for a boycott. 'White UDF supporters and democrats' should instead strive to 'bring meaning to the politics of non-racialism'. In general, the UDF sought to refocus attention on the broader context, describing the elections as a 'farce' because 'the minority of South Africans will elect a Parliament that will attempt to determine the future of the majority of South Africans'.[46] In the event, the elections returned a greatly strengthened National Party on the basis of a right-wing shift in the white electorate. The PFP was ousted by the Conservative Party as the official opposition.

Protest against the elections as a whole was undertaken in conjunction with COSATU. The UDF and COSATU called for a two-day stayaway on 5 and 6 May 1987. The stayaway was supported by over one million workers on both days. Support was strongest among African workers in the Eastern Cape, and weakest among coloured and Indian workers in other regions. The two-day stayaway was later described as 'the biggest action of its kind in the history of our struggle'. 'A mood of optimism swept across the country', showing 'that the masses were far from defeated' and attesting to the 'new capacity gained through the Campaign for National United Action ...'[47]

In fact, the alliance between the UDF and COSATU was not without difficulties. Within COSATU, some trade unions argued for a more cautious approach, in part for fear that the state would unleash the kind of repression on the trade unions that it had already dealt the UDF and its affiliates. UDF leaders also complained that COSATU had twice failed to turn up to meetings with them: 'This has resulted in the inability to organise and decide on issues.'[48]

Soon after the election the UDF identified various weaknesses in the Campaign for National United Action:

While unity is being forged at a national level, it is not being built adequately at the regional and local levels. This campaign will be ineffective unless we are able to reap its benefits at a local level. It is also an observable fact that not all regions and affiliates are participating evenly in the campaign. The campaign must take on a truly national character – its potency lies in its ability to mobilise all sections of the people into united action.[49]

The Campaign had involved only three episodes: the Christmas against the Emergency, the January advertisments, and the May stayaway. These had an overly national and even international focus. There was no Programme of Action showing how local structures and activities fitted into the national campaign. And in most areas organisation at regional and local levels was in a very parlous state.

THE DEVELOPMENT OF SECTORAL AND REGIONAL ORGANISATION

Perhaps the most striking development of early 1987 was the formation of the South African Youth Congress (SAYCO). In May the UDF referred to SAYCO as an 'inspiration, not only to the hundreds of youth congresses around the country, but the Front as a whole'.[50] The formation of SAYCO was the outstanding success in the UDF's general development of the different sectors. The UDF had begun to emphasise this in 1985, following the lead of several RECs which had restructured themselves around the representation of the different sectors in order to facilitate co-ordination and accountability. The Programme of Action adopted at the UDF's NWC Conference in May 1986 had called for the formation of national organisations in the women's, youth and civic sectors. The Emergency increased the urgency of forming such national structures – but at the same time made it still more difficult to do so.

Building national co-ordination in the youth sector had long been held up by divisions within youth organisations, personal, ideological and tactical.[51] In July 1986 a national interim co-ordinating committee was elected at an underground consultative conference in Cape Town. Peter Mokaba, former Robben Islander and publicity secretary of the Northern Transvaal UDF, was elected as interim national education officer with a brief to solve the bitter divisions which persisted in some regions. Together with Deacon Mathe, Mokaba consulted with the ANC in Harare. The ANC's backing seems to have facilitated progress. A planning workshop was held at Broederstroom west of Pretoria in October.

Finally, in March 1987, delegates from youth organisations around the country met at the University of the Western Cape to launch SAYCO. SAYCO adopted a federal structure, with ten regional youth congresses comprising 1200 affiliates, over half a million signed-up members and a support base of two million. SAYCO thus claimed to be the biggest youth grouping of its kind in South African history. SAYCO made its commitment to Charterism and militancy quite clear. It adopted the slogan 'Freedom or Death: Victory is Certain', and its colours combined those of the ANC and COSATU. Mokaba was elected president.[52]

Charterist women's organisations had a similarly difficult history, particularly in the Western Cape and Border regions. By May 1986 several regional organisations had been formed, and stalwarts of the former Federation of South African Women (FEDSAW) had formed a national working committee to work towards the relaunch of the organisation. FEDSAW had been formed in 1954 as a federal structure for women organised within the various racial components of the Congress Alliance, such as the ANC's Women's League. Although never banned, FEDSAW effectively lapsed around 1963. Reviving FEDSAW was a clear and open commitment to Charterism. In the Programme of Action adopted by the UDF's NWC in May 1986, the UDF stated that it was 'committed to the revival of the Federation of South African Women' during 1986. 'Women's organisations should be formed where none exist and should affiliate to regional structures, which need to be built and strengthened to pave the way for a strong national structure.' UDF regional structures were urged to assist: 'the task of organising women should not be seen as the task of women alone'.[53]

Before the imposition of the State of Emergency it had been proposed that FED-SAW be relaunched on 9 August – Women's Day, and the thirtieth anniversary of the famous FEDSAW march on Pretoria. But disruption ruled out an August relaunch. A two-day national conference was planned for early 1987, to develop a common understanding of the nature of the women's movement as well as to establish a national co-ordinating structure. Eventually, in April 1987 a national structure was formed. This was not FEDSAW but a UDF Women's Congress, which set 'itself the task of uniting the broadest range of democratic women under the umbrella of the Federation of South African Women'.[53]

Attempts to form a national co-ordinating body for civics had gone on even longer than initiatives on either youth or women, but it would not be until 1992 that a national structure was finally formed. During 1986–7 attempts continued, but in vain. Building co-ordination among the civics was especially difficult because of the peculiarly ambiguous character of the sector. Civics claimed to be more than just activist groupings, and should not, it was therefore believed, be formed 'from above'. Rather, they needed to be formed on the basis of strong local, or at least regional, structures. Unfortunately, the State of Emergency hit civics especially hard. Local structures were devastated, and regional structures largely incapacitated. In the Transvaal co-ordination was undertaken through the Community Education and Information project, which formulated a three-phase strategy:

> Our first phase was to make contact and get information. The second phase was to do training work with what was, by and large, a completely new layer or second generation of civic leadership. And the third phase was to reconvene a civic conference in the Transvaal, and re-elect a new civic leadership for the Transvaal which could co-ordinate.[55]

A regional conference was held clandestinely in Lydenburg in 1987. But an interim regional co-ordinating committee was not elected until about April 1988. Most other regions seem to have been even less organised, and plans for a national meeting were repeatedly postponed.[56]

The unambiguous success story in national organisation building was, of course, COSATU. The unions that joined together to form COSATU had included several affiliates of the UDF, which in some regions had been seen as a sector, with a labour representative on the REC. But the strongest unions in COSATU had never been UDF affiliates, and had a history of antipathy and even hostility to the UDF. COSATU itself was committed to political action at local and national levels, but its relationship with the UDF remained undefined during 1986 and the first half of 1987. Whilst COSATU was a success, and was in some respects stronger than the UDF during this period, there were regions where the UDF became involved in help-ing develop COSATU organisation. This was especially the case in the Eastern Cape and Border regions, where COSATU experienced severe difficulties in unifying.

COSATU's Eastern Cape regional structure was not launched until February 1987, well over a year after COSATU had been formed. As late as November 1987, the Border UDF region reported to the NEC that there were 'two COSATU structures in existence', and requested that the NEC ask COSATU's national leaders to intervene.[57]

The educational sector was a major cause of concern for the UDF leadership during 1986–7. Huge numbers of students stayed out of school in the second half of 1986. The challenge to the UDF's affiliates was how to organise for students to return to school under conditions which the organisations and the students could agree on as being acceptable. This would have been a difficult task in a free climate. Under the Emergency it was all but impossible, with most of the leadership of the National Education Crisis Committee in detention and with constant provocation of students by the security forces. Early in the Emergency the UDF's national leadership met with the remnants of the Crisis Committee to discuss the education crisis. A national education conference was proposed, 'to create space' and 'draw in everybody'. But the Emergency left little space for such a conference, and it soon became clear that the NECC was in such disarray that it could do little itself. Student organisation had also been weakened by state repression. In May 1987 the UDF noted: 'While regional structures exist, regional and national co-ordination has broken down and organisation at the level of the local student congresses is weak.'[58]

There were also important developments in some of the non-metropolitan regions. Nine UDF regions were represented at the NWC in May 1987, including, besides the six formally constituted regions, the Orange Free State, the Northern Cape and the Eastern Transvaal. The Northern Cape had been hit hard by detentions, setting back progress towards a formal regional launch. Co-ordination had always proved more difficult in the Orange Free State. The region was divided between the north, focused on the townships of Welkom, Kroonstad and Parys, and the south, focused on Bloemfontein. A regional committee was eventually elected in April 1986 but apparently excluded activists from the southern Free State. Ironically, repression strengthened linkages within, but not between, the two sub-regions, as activists from different townships were thrown together either in detention or in internal exile in Johannesburg. In July 1987 an umbrella Free State Youth Congress was launched – at a conference in Durban, because of the difficulties of meeting in the Free State itself. The Eastern Transvaal grouping seems to have comprised primarily civic activists organised through the Community Education and Information project. A Far Northern Transvaal Co-ordinating Committee was also formed in 1987, to cover Venda, the townships around Louis Trichardt and Messina, and the northern parts of Gazankulu.[59]

One area where organisation developed was in the Northern Transvaal. In August the Northern Transvaal People's Congress (NOTPECO) was formally launched at a secret meeting. NOTPECO defined itself as a 'political umbrella organisation' for migrant workers, both at home in the villages of the Northern Transvaal and in the industrial hostels of the Reef and parts of the Eastern Transvaal. A key figure in the initiative was C.W. (Wilfried) Monama, who was employed by the UDF as a regional organiser as well as serving as acting chairperson of NOTPECO. Monama was a veteran of the ANC and the Sebatakgomo movement in the 1950s. Under Monama's direction, NOTPECO adopted a position strongly opposed to chiefs, advocating instead elected village councils. UDF leaders were reported to be critical of Monama, accusing him of 'hijacking' NOTPECO, turning it into a personal fiefdom and, worst of all, dabbling in ethnic politics.[60] Perhaps in response to NOTPECO, other UDF and ANC activists initiated the formation of a Congress of Traditional Leaders of South Africa (CONTRALESA) in September 1987. CONTRALESA was initially based among chiefs in KwaNdebele and Moutse who were opposed to KwaNdebele 'independence', and to the bantustan system in general. But they were not, of course, opposed to the chieftainship. The differences between NOTPECO and CONTRALESA reflected a difficulty which the UDF and ANC were to face again and again: what position to adopt on chieftainship whilst opposing the bantustan system.

'BUILDING THE FRONT'

On 29–30 May 1987 about two hundred delegates from all nine UDF regions met in Durban for a National Working Committee conference. The conference was held in great secrecy – even changing venues in mid-conference. It provided the first opportunity for a full-scale assessment of the UDF's performance during the Emergency, and of the path forward. What became clear was that many UDF structures had transformed themselves to cope with Emergency conditions, and that this transformation needed to be recognised and directed. The conference came up with a new political approach.

The national leadership presented a 28-page secretarial report to the conference, comprising the longest-ever national assessment of the UDF.[61] It began with an optimistic analysis of the political context. Notwithstanding the state's strategy combining repression, limited development and bogus constitutional reform, the strategic initiative was deemed to have remained in the hands of the democratic movement. Invoking the slogan adopted by the UDF in 1985, the report boldly claimed that 'Over the past two years the struggle has indeed moved from Protest to Challenge. Apartheid rule is being challenged on every front.' Such bold claims were perhaps intended to revive flagging spirits. Moreover, the UDF claimed to have 'become the vehicle which embodies the political aspirations of the broad masses. Every sector of our movement' looks towards the Front for political expression and leadership.' As the ANC itself had acknowledged, this was far from the case. The report also put a positive spin on the UDF's campaigns over the past year.

The report provided a more accurate survey of the UDF's own structures. At the national level, the NEC had been hard hit by repression. Two NEC members were still on trial, eight were in detention, one had gone into exile, and two others 'had been withdrawn by their regions'. Only five remained, requiring that new members be nominated by the regions or co-opted. The regions had also been hit hard; only two (the Western Cape and Border) had been able to hold AGMs. Zonal and area structures existed in most regions but functioned very unevenly. Communication was often poor between the national leadership and the regions, and between regional leaders and sub-regional structures.

In terms of sectors, the UDF's youth affiliates had adapted most easily to the Emergency, and had succeeded in launching SAYCO. The Women's Congress had also been formed. The situation was very different among school students: 'regional and national co-ordination has broken down and organisation at the level of the local student congresses is weak'. The National Education Crisis Committee and its regional structures, teachers' organisation and the civics were weak. COSATU had 'grown in leaps and bounds'. But organisational growth on the sports and cultural fronts, in white areas, and in coloured and Indian areas was poor. Indeed, in coloured and Indian areas there had been 'a general backward slide over the past two years'.

The conference adopted a long Programme of Action around the theme of the conference, 'Defend, Consolidate and Advance'. The Programme opened with a call to 'discuss, explain and popularise the Freedom Charter'. This call was based on a recognition that the UDF had changed significantly over the previous two years, during the period of people's power and then under the Emergency: 'The UDF has since its inception moved from the position of opposing only the President's Council proposals [for the Tricameral Parliament] of 1983 and the Koornhof Bills to addressing a broad range of political issues. The Front now needs to adopt a comprehensive political programme.' UDF structures should discuss the Freedom Charter, 'with a view to the UDF itself adopting' it. A second major development had been the alliance with COSATU.

> More and more, the rank and file members of COSATU and the affiliates of the Front have united in action around common issues and campaigns ... Our task now is to consolidate and strengthen this unity at every level. In particular we need to work towards a more structured relationship with the trade union movement. The united front needs to be built at a local level. Zonal and area structures of the UDF must be transformed into united front structures, in which all sectors are represented, especially workers, youth, women, students and civics.

'Build the united front!', proclaimed the Programme of Action. As part of this, the different sectors – women, civics, students and the National Education Crisis Committee, and cultural workers – needed to be strengthened. At the same time, the democratic movement needed to be broadened. The Programme of Action called for intensified efforts in organising among white, coloured and Indian South Africans, and throughout the bantustans. It also called for a 'national conference of all Anti-Apartheid forces', as well as appealing to white people to 'stay and contribute' to the democratic movement.

Overall, the thrust of the Programme of Action was in calling for organisation to be strengthened and broadened. The only discussion of specific campaigns concerned a National Anti-Death Squads Campaign and a continuation of the Campaign for National United Action. The latter should include two weeks of action in June against the anticipated reimposition of the State of Emergency. There was no explicit call for a stayaway because, Morobe suggested, the UDF had sensed that in some areas support for a stayaway was still low after the massive stayaway on 5 and 6 May.[62] Although the Programme of Action called for action over ending the Emergency, the UDF leadership anticipated that the Emergency would only be lifted 'if we abandon the struggle for freedom'. 'The days of relatively ample legal space are gone for ever.'

Two weeks after the NWC, Morobe was interviewed by the *Weekly Mail*. Morobe argued that the state was trying to force the UDF to turn to violence.

I think our task remains to engage apartheid legally and in an open way. To the extent that there is space for us to do that, I think the UDF will continue to do that. It is a matter of crucial strategy for us that we continue exploring those avenues that are open to us even at the legal level. Our strength as the UDF lies on the basis that we conduct our struggles non-violently.

Morobe insisted that 'our strength and support base has actually broadened over the past twelve months' but at the same time described the Emergency as a period of 'tactical retreat' for the UDF. 'It is going to be a long and hard struggle.'[63]

In mid-June the Emergency was reimposed, as expected. Despite the NWC's call, it seems that protest was muted. Several important UDF leaders were released from detention, including Mafolo. New and broader restrictions were imposed on the media, in order 'to curb the present flood of revolutionary propaganda'. The government appointed publications censors, with extensive powers of seizing media and even closing media down.[64]

The two major decisions taken at the NWC concerned the adoption of a comprehensive political programme, exemplified by the Freedom Charter, and the establishment of mechanisms for the structural participation of the trade unions in a united front. The implementation of both decisions was clearly going to be shaped by the position taken by COSATU. In mid-July COSATU met for its second National Congress, marked by strong debate. Some unions supported the Freedom Charter enthusiastically, others with qualifications, and still others not at all. Some unions believed that alliances should only be built with organisations committed to an anti-capitalist as well as an anti-apartheid position, which would rule out many UDF affiliates and possibly the UDF itself. Other unions, led by the National Union of Mineworkers, 'called for the broadest possible alliance around democratic and anti-apartheid demands such as those expressed in the Freedom Charter'. As Baskin writes, 'unity did not run deep' within COSATU. The Congress eventually carried a political resolution that called for the adoption of the Freedom Charter as a 'guiding document' and for 'disciplined alliances' with 'democratic and progressive organisations'. But whilst the resolution called for 'permanent structures at local, regional and national levels' with COSATU's allies 'in a united front alliance', the evident disunity within COSATU meant that this would not be pushed too hard.[65]

Morobe was one of the guest speakers at the COSATU congress. In his speech,

Morobe began to discuss some of the ways of implementing the ideas raised at the NWC. This speech provided the basis for a widely influential statement of the UDF's views on restructuring, published later in the UDF's journal *Isizwe* under the title 'Build the Front'. The published version started by noting that the NWC had

> enabled the UDF collectively to take stock of the situation and to note some of the significant shifts and developments in the character of the Front, and the tasks before it. Many of these shifts and developments have been under way for some time ... But our *understanding* of these developments has often lagged behind practice itself.[66]

The statement called for 'boldness and imagination', rather than being locked into existing ways of working which were no longer appropriate.

> If we go simply on to the defensive, passively trying to hold what we have built, then we will be defeated. We must constantly advance, develop imaginative programmes of action that keep the enemy stretched nationally and off balance. On the other hand, if we advance militantly, without also carrying our defensive and consolidating tasks, we will become a narrow group of activists – an easy and isolated target for the regime.

It invoked an old UDF strategic perspective in the new context: 'The political key to defence lies in broadening to the maximum the people's camp, while isolating to the maximum the apartheid regime.' It also restated the UDF's commitment to public activity:

> We have mastered many of the techniques of secret, underground work ... While developing these skills, we must not confuse our *tactical* adoption of some underground methods with the *strategic* underground methods that organisations like the ANC have chosen. For [the] UDF, tactical use is made of some underground methods in order *to continue open, mass-level work*.

The need for changes within the UDF thus occurred within an overall framework of continuity.

Crucially, the new context required new practices. Building the Front meant, as in the past, strengthening the UDF's own structures, organisationally and ideologically. But at the same time it meant 'deepening the unity in action between the UDF and its natural allies' – non-affiliates such as COSATU and the South African Council of Churches – and 'broadening the UDF's political and moral influence over the widest possible range of South Africans': in other words, building the Front by working with structures and constituencies outside as well as within the Front. The article provided one eye-opening illustration: Afrikaans-speaking white workers! These might be drawn into temporary alliances with the UDF over some economic issues, even if they differed fundamentally on social and political issues.

One section of the article covered the character of the united front at the local level, calling for 'the development of *political centres* at every level from the zone, or small township upwards. Such political centres will gravitate around the UDF, but will not necessarily be exclusively UDF ... At the local level, *the political centre is the heart and engine of the united front of organisations*.' This kind of structure had already developed in some areas.

> By 'political centres' we are referring to organisational collectivities that are capable of providing political leadership, that are able to strategise, to lead ... The concept of 'political centre' means that all our co-ordinating structures – the zonal, area and township structures, our RECs and the NEC – must be more than the simple sum of their parts. A township co-ordinating committee, for instance, must not simply be a bureaucratic recording of mandates from its affiliates.

The idea of political centres represented a further step away from the original conception of the UDF as a front for affiliates. Political centres would play an interventionist as well as a co-ordinating role.

The article was both controversial and ambiguous. The controversy primarily concerned the perception that the article was calling for the UDF to be transformed from a front into a party-type structure, which would impinge on affiliates' autonomy. The debate about this seems to have distracted attention from another issue: the ambiguities in the UDF's new approach on crucial organisational questions. To what extent was the UDF to remain a co-ordinator, and to what extent was it to become simply a participant in the united front? Would the different sectors be participants in both the UDF and the united front? At the local level, would the UDF disappear, as its affiliated sectors and non-affiliated allies formed political centres? Or would the political centres be co-ordinated through the UDF? Were civics just a sector? In some areas civics had historically served as just these kinds of political centre – for example, in Port Alfred, where the other sectors had been represented on the civic executive. How would these political centres relate to the activist forums which had operated in other parts of the Eastern Cape including Port Elizabeth? At the regional level, how would the weakness of COSATU's regional structures be accommodated? In short, a range of organisational ambiguities remained unaddressed. These were later to pose difficulties for organisations like Community Education and Information, charged with building civic organisation in particular but increasingly distracted into building general structures.

By the time *Isizwe* published 'Building the Front', the UDF had been set back further by the detention of its two key officials. Morobe and Moosa were finally caught by the police on 22 July, seized in a pre-dawn raid by police wearing balaclavas in Port Elizabeth. In subsequent interrogation, the police accused them of coming to Port Elizabeth to reorganise rent boycotts. 'The detention of two of our leading people has brought the UDF into difficulty,' acknowledged Billy Nair.[67] Mafolo took over the running of the UDF's national office, with assistance from Momoniat,

Molobi (until he was detained in December) and Samson Ndou. Several trade unionists also assisted, although this caused some tensions with and within COSATU.

An increasingly important figure within the UDF was Azhar Cachalia, the national treasurer, because of a rapid expansion in the volume of financial resources available to the UDF during the first eighteen months of the nationwide State of Emergency. By 1987, Anthony Marx reports, the UDF itself had an annual budget of over R2 million, and employed about 80 staff. The bulk of this funding came from abroad, from the Dutch church agency NOVIB and the Swedish labour movement. This staff included an army of regional and sectoral organisers, and media and office staff. By November 1987 the Southern Transvaal region employed two paid officials and six paid organisers (two of whom were in detention). The Northern Transvaal region employed nine paid organisers. Seven organisers were employed in the Border region.[68]

The growth in funding prompted the state to impose more and more stringent restrictions. In October 1986 the state declared the UDF an affected organisation, which meant that it was prohibited from receiving foreign funding. The UDF challenged its proclamation as an affected organisation in court, winning its case in May 1987. The state proposed further curbs on foreign funding in August 1987. Although Cachalia said that the UDF had been 'plunged into debt' by these restrictions, the UDF's donors remained generous; its problems were really logistical. Cachalia had to find innovative ways of accessing funds. These included complex deals with sympathisers who wanted to get money out of the country. Such people would give the UDF rands, in return for which the UDF's foreign donors would deposit funds into European bank accounts. The UDF also formed the Friends of the UDF, which was chaired by businessman Tony Bloom, to raise funds. Until late 1989 the UDF's own records identify large sums received as 'cash'.[69]

The sums channelled directly through the UDF were dwarfed by the sums given to its affiliates through other means. Foremost among these channels was the Kagiso Trust. This was established in 1985 by the South African Council of Churches and the Southern African Catholic Bishops' Conference in order to channel funds allocated by the European Community to its Special Fund for the Victims of Apartheid. It started with just two staff and a limited budget, but grew rapidly, opening regional offices in Johannesburg, Cape Town and Durban in 1987, and in Port Elizabeth the following year. Large sums were allocated to civic organisations and advice offices, which were, in 1987–9, often regarded as fronts for civics in repressive times. Between January 1987 and March 1988 the Kagiso Trust granted almost R900 000 to civics and advice centres in Natal, almost R300 000 in the Transvaal, and about the same in the Western Cape. Civic organisers in the Transvaal also received funds through the Community Education and Information project. Between July 1987 and July 1988 this project spent over R230 000, raised through the UDF, including R85 000 on salaries and almost R100 000 on miscellaneous transport costs.[70]

Cachalia had little say over the UDF's policy with regard to funds but he had considerable discretion over their allocation. The threat of confiscation by the state meant that he could hardly use a bank account in the UDF's name, nor could he keep detailed financial records. Many of the UDF's local donors, who were giving rands to the UDF as a foreign exchange scam, handed over cash, which Cachalia stored in a shoe box in the safe of the legal firm where he worked. 'For a couple of years I ran the UDF literally out of my back pocket ... People would come to me and say, 'I am the UDF organiser in the Northern Transvaal and I have not received a salary in the past three months.' What should I do? There was no way of checking. I had to rely on my instincts and trust people's honesty.'[71] These practices contributed to organisational tensions within the UDF. Some organisers resented not receiving larger sums. Cachalia's ability to disappear and return with bundles of cash fuelled the perception that the UDF had infinite resources. This soon led to further discontent among activists who felt that they were not receiving their fair share.

The UDF leadership was also viewed as exerting influence over allied funding agencies such as the Kagiso Trust. Activists and organisations that were refused funds from these other agencies, or at least not granted the amounts they felt they deserved, tended to blame the UDF. NOTPECO, for example, applied for funds through churches and the Kagiso Trust as well as the UDF itself. Its applications were not modest: it asked for R60 000 from the UDF, and R70 000 from the Kagiso Trust. Monama seems to have blamed the UDF for not providing money or helping with fund-raising.[72]

Discontent over finances was soon focused on the supposed cabal controlling the UDF. The domination of these activists explained, in some critics' minds, the UDF's reluctance to fully embrace militant tactics. Senior African UDF leaders, such as Molefe (notwithstanding the fact that he was on trial) and Morobe, were dismissed as stooges. At some point during 1987 accusations regarding the cabal seem to have begun to circulate again, this time involving national officials such as Moosa and Cachalia, regional officials such as Yunus Mahomed, and key activists behind the scenes such as Gordhan and Momoniat. Morobe began to be referred to dismissively as 'Murphy Patel'.

One of the key critics of the supposed cabal was Aubrey Mokoena. Initially drawn into the UDF, Mokoena had soon become disillusioned with the Front's leadership and helped to set up the Johannesburg-based Release Mandela Campaign as a counterweight within the Charterist movement. Through 1984–6 tensions had persisted. The UDF's necessarily clandestine operations under the State of Emergency fuelled resentment, generating broader support for Mokoena. Mokoena seems to have found support among the leading members of SAYCO, who had their own criticisms of the UDF, and probably also from Winnie Mandela. In late 1985 Mrs Mandela had returned to Johannesburg from Brandfort in the Free State, where she had been banished since 1977, to Johannesburg, although her banning order was not fully lifted until 1986. Whilst in Brandfort she had never been drawn into UDF activity. Indeed, using some of her extensive financial resources, she had built a network of personal patronage and loyalties in the Free State that inhibited the establishment of a regional UDF structure. Back in Johannesburg she had little sympathy for the organisation-building emphasis of the UDF leadership. As Gilbey writes, 'She saw herself as an independent entity who didn't need a mandate to do and say as she pleased.' Mokoena, perhaps encouraged by Mrs Mandela, finally lodged a complaint about the cabal with the ANC leadership in exile in 1987. Little seems to have come of this complaint, and the cabal saga continued to bedevil the UDF.[73]

ORGANISATION AND VIOLENCE IN NATAL

The UDF set itself the goal of building tight organisation in which affiliates participated through sectoral representatives, but in practice repression made participation difficult, and this resulted in organisation being dominated by small clusters of activists. Discontent with cabals intensified as the Front handled ever greater financial resources. Such discontent was especially acute in and around Durban. The leading role of Indian activists in the Natal regional leadership reinforced the view that African leadership in particular was being excluded by the cabal.

The issue of African leadership in Natal had been raised in 1985–6 by youth and civic activists outside the REC.[74] As violence escalated, demands for African leadership increased, as it was African communities that were most affected by violence. Unhappiness grew under the Emergency, as the formal channels of decision making and implementation were subverted. The Natal region of the UDF held no elections after March 1985, and was thus denied fresh legitimacy.

Sandy Africa, who assumed the role of regional secretary, describes this as 'a period when practising accountability was very, very difficult'.[75] Affiliates were not kept informed about the new procedures adopted in the face of state repression. 'We entered into a period of illegality, where much was not even explained to the UDF's affiliates, sometimes even to the REC, where decisions were made largely by those of us who ..., *de facto* or otherwise, were permanent on the executive, whether we were the proper members or not.' Organisation became more and more centralised, with the REC generally just rubber-stamping decisions made by the secretariat.

> For example, it was not possible to talk about the organisation of a stayaway, or a consumer boycott, or any such illegal activity, during that period ... The UDF did have a base from which it operated, but it was never known to any but the members of the secretariat. So there developed this highly centralised situation. The REC was correctly accused of being too centralised ... The secretariat almost became a kind of inner, secret core ... Its members were known but how it went about its business was not really disclosed. Things just happened, and people were asked not to question how it was possible, for example, for a hundred thousand pamphlets to reach different parts of Durban. The important thing was that it happened, that affiliates would distribute them, and the stayaway was called.

The REC 'was forced to operate ... [in an] increasingly narrow way'. Regional leaders sought to preserve 'the UDF as a co-ordinating centre', but the changing context posed major difficulties. Not only were regional leaders and structures particularly vulnerable to repression, but at the same time,

> in spite of violence, organisation was growing: youth organisations were springing up all over; NOW [Natal Organisation of Women] was developing more branches; civic structures were being developed; and so on. Organisation at the local level was certainly growing. The problem was that the UDF as a co-ordinating centre was failing to address the question of how to make the regional structures more representative and more in touch with what the local structures were saying and doing.

The REC proposed the establishment of a hierarchy of sub-regional co-ordinating structures. Each sub-regional Area Committee would send a delegate to the REC. But this system never became operational, and REC and RGC meetings continued to be poorly attended.

From the outside it seemed that there was a small cabal monopolising power. 'And because there were no real co-ordinating structures, there was always the feeling among some affiliates or some structures that they were being excluded. It was very difficult to satisfy everyone, and at the same time ensure that the meetings were not known about by the police.' Activists 'out there' were left 'on their own, with not so much support from the centre', Africa recalls.

One organisational change which was effected, in Natal as elsewhere, was the employment of sub-regional organisers. These were mostly youth activists, charged with building youth organisation in their respective areas. The employment of organisers often exacerbated organisational tensions. Appointed by the REC without broad consultation in the sub-region concerned, some of the organisers were inappropriate, and there was inadequate accountability to whatever sub-regional organisations already existed. Furthermore, the impression was given that the REC had extensive financial resources, which it used to extend its own patronage. In the Midlands, organisational culture was transformed by the injection of funds.

A growing number of Charterist activists, feeling themselves excluded from the REC-based 'cabal', withdrew from the UDF and sought alternative co-ordinating networks. The NOW leader and UDF REC member Nozizwe Madlala was released from almost one year in detention in December 1987. She found the Charterist movement riven by deep divisions and bitterness:

> I spoke to people and I remember feeling quite depressed about the situation, because it felt to me like the people were being very negative ... And I felt at that stage it would be very difficult to bring people together again. It felt to me like there was anger, and I felt also that people were misdirecting their anger ... Rather than people pooling together their strengths and ... playing a leading role, they were withdrawing ...[76]

The UDF was, as a result, becoming less and less of a co-ordinating structure.

Repression had a disruptive effect on organisation at the local level. At the beginning of 1987 the UDF organised a sub-regional workshop in the Natal Midlands to
take stock of its strengths and weaknesses, and to formulate an appropriate strategy.
Overall, participants reported, there was little support for Inkatha in the sub-region,
but the considerable support for the UDF was not reflected in any local organisation.
The first 'general strategic objective' identified at the workshop was telling: 'adapt
structures to cope with repression'.[77]

During 1987 there was a steady expansion of organisation, especially among the
youth. This, however, proved threatening to local Inkatha leaders, and thus precipitated further violent conflict. In the peri-urban areas around Pietermaritzburg, especially, Inkatha and UDF-aligned youth groups vied for territorial control. In July and
August Inkatha began to recruit members more energetically than hitherto. This
sparked the formation of embryonic 'defence committees' in 'UDF' areas. From
September, Inkatha recruitment became more coercive still. 'All-out war' swept
through Edendale and further up the Vulindlela valley outside Pietermaritzburg. In
contrast to the more piecemeal violence of 1985–6, the Inkatha-led violence of late
1987 prompted rapid organisational growth among its opponents. Defence committees were consolidated or formed, drawing in older residents, especially shop stewards in the COSATU unions as well as youth. Defence committees often provided the
basis for civic structures:

> the need for defence was one of the strongest motivating factors for people to
> become organised. The [Inkatha] vigilantes did not recognise neutrality – any-
> body who refused to join Inkatha was by definition UDF. Anybody who was
> UDF was the enemy and a legitimate target for attack. With this outlook on life
> the vigilantes achieved what the UDF on its own had failed to do – it politicised
> entire communities.[78]

Inkatha vigilantes were even forced out of areas such as Ashdown. Such successes
may not have been strategised beforehand, but the lesson was not lost. As UDF
activists later wrote, it became clear 'that only the strength of mass organisation and
the willingness of the people to defend themselves was going to guarantee the survival of progressive organisations'. Subsequent UDF–COSATU strategy therefore
prioritised building or consolidating mass organisation.[79]

The successful resistance against Inkatha prompted further state involvement. It
has been speculated that the state feared Natal would follow the example of the
Eastern Cape into a situation of ungovernability. The security force presence in the
Midlands was increased in October, and the police increased their harassment of
organisation. In November the police netted the leadership of the sub-regional youth
co-ordinating structure as well as UDF co-secretaries Ngwenya and Wittenberg. By
the end of 1987 almost all the UDF leaders from African areas were in detention.[80]

The escalation and spread of violence prompted the churches to initiate a peace
initiative, as well as a further exchange of correspondence between Buthelezi and
Gumede (for the UDF). The most important of the peace initiatives was brokered by

the Pietermaritzburg Chamber of Commerce. In November a joint UDF–COSATU delegation met with an Inkatha delegation at Pietermaritzburg's Imperial Hotel. Midlands UDF secretaries Wittenberg and Ngwenya were released from detention to enable the UDF to participate. This first meeting 'went surprisingly well' and 'ended cordially'. With the assistance of the Chamber of Commerce, the UDF and COSATU even secured permission to hold a report-back rally at Pietermaritzburg's Wadley Stadium.[81]

Before a second meeting was held, however, Inkatha's attitude to peace talks had changed. When Inkatha met again with COSATU and the UDF in Pietermaritzburg in December, their delegation included several national leaders. At the outset they insisted that the COSATU–UDF delegates repudiate an article critical of Buthelezi than had been published in a periodical produced by a small group of exiled Trotskyists who had been expelled from the ANC. The UDF–COSATU delegation pointed out that the periodical in question had not been circulated in Pietermaritzburg, had nothing to do with COSATU, the UDF or their structures, and did not reflect their policies or views. The Inkatha delegation did not accept this position. The meeting ended.[82]

Inkatha's new position was articulated in a bellicose speech made by Buthelezi several days later:

> I am now coming close to believing that the only reconciliation that there will ever be in this country is the reconciliation of the most powerful with those who pay homage to the most powerful. We are talking about a life and death struggle. We are talking about all-or-nothing victories. We are talking about the final triumph of good over evil.[83]

The new position was further articulated and converted into action at an Inkatha rally in January. V. Mvelase, a member of Inkatha's Central Committee and the KwaZulu government's 'chief urban representative', said that the only way to end the violence was to drive COSATU and the UDF out of KwaZulu into 'Xhosa areas'. The UDF and COSATU were, he said, 'Indian' organisations, and their supporters must go to live with the 'Indians'. Any 'Indian' who failed to move or repent, he was reported to say, should be killed. Similar fighting and racist rhetoric was repeated by other Inkatha speakers. After the rally, a body of men raided 'UDF'-controlled Ashdown. The Inkatha offensive was later termed 'Operation Doom'. The security forces played their part, with an estimated 700 detentions between November 1987 and January 1988 in the Pietermaritzburg area.[84]

COSATU and the UDF also launched a second strategy, through COSATU. As a result of investigations by COSATU head office, lawyers were sent to prepare urgent applications for interdicts restraining key Inkatha leaders from violence. The first papers were served on 2 November. The interdict applications served a dual purpose: if successful, they might indeed restrain Inkatha; at the same time, the interdict applications, backed up with memorandums and press conferences, served to publicise Inkatha attacks and the connivance of the security forces.[85]

A NEW 'MIDDLE GROUND': ORGANISING AMONG WHITE SOUTH AFRICANS

The UDF's concern to broaden as well as intensify the front increasingly involved attempts to attract white South Africans away from the 'enemy camp' and into the 'people's camp'. While the first such attempts had preceded the imposition of the nationwide State of Emergency, the initiatives gathered momentum during 1987 and into 1988.

The UDF's work among white constituencies had accelerated during 1985 and early 1986. In its 1986 New Year message, the UDF had called on whites to 'ditch Botha and join the democratic movement in our struggle for a just and peaceful South Africa'. Hitherto, activity among white South Africans had been concentrated on the issue of conscription into the army, with the lead being taken by the highly effective End Conscription Campaign. Now the UDF sought to appeal to a wider range of white groups. The UDF was further prompted by the ANC, which entertained a growing number of white visitors, including businessmen, newspaper editors, opposition members of parliament, students and churchmen. It was evident that support was growing among white elites for radical political change. In February the leader of the parliamentary opposition, Van Zyl Slabbert, resigned from parliament, and soon visited the ANC. In June the chairman of the Broederbond met with top ANC officials including Mbeki and Maharaj at a Ford Foundation conference in New York.[86]

Any campaign in white areas required the UDF to co-ordinate with its leading white affiliate, the Johannesburg Democratic Action Committee (JODAC). After meeting with JODAC in March 1986, Moosa noted: 'Moderate extra-parliamentary group emerging. This terrain is being shifted. Therefore need to run "UDF call to Whites" campaign. [There] has been no clear call to those who potentially would support us.'[87] Although the UDF itself was thought to be 'taken more seriously by ordinary whites than JODAC', it was agreed that JODAC would organise a 'UDF Call to Whites' campaign on behalf of the UDF. The campaign was launched in April. Two thousand people attended a meeting in Johannesburg; the speakers included Slabbert, Beyers Naudé and Morobe.[88] The UDF's May 1986 Programme of Action, under a heading 'Call to Whites', noted:

> More and more whites are losing confidence in the ability of the government to secure a peaceful future for them. This has resulted in many whites looking towards the democratic movement for an alternative. Our task is to spare no effort in welcoming such people and calling upon others to join the democratic movement. Every region should investigate the possibility of initiating this campaign.[89]

In June, as part of its Unban the ANC campaign, the UDF described the ANC as representing 'the aspirations of the oppressed people and white democrats'.[90]

Under the State of Emergency from mid-1986 the UDF was unable to spare much of this promised effort, but the scale of repression and the inadequacy of the

National Party's vision led to further realignments among key groups of the white intelligentsia and, more ambiguously, the English-speaking business elite. These included, in March 1987, the formation of the Five Freedoms Forum by a range of white left and liberal organisations. In May the UDF noted the 'important shifts' taking place within white politics, with 'dissension from the white laager':

> The last Whites elections have given impetus to the process whereby more and more whites are becoming disillusioned with parliamentary politics. The so-called middle ground between the Nationalists and the democratic movement has caved in. Those Whites who are opposed to Apartheid rule now have no option but to make a decisive break with White minority rule and become active participants in the struggle for National Liberation.[91]

Some affiliates were organising successfully among white South Africans – such as NUSAS on Afrikaans campuses – but area-based affiliates such as JODAC were deemed disappointing. Overall, performance had 'not matched the spirit' of the 1986 NWC statement. There was a need for 'guidance on a new initiative'. Included in the Programme of Action adopted at the 1987 NWC was a commitment to '*intensify* the UDF Call to Whites Campaign', particularly in the Afrikaner community, and to 'support the process of convening a national conference and establishing a broad national organisation of white democrats'. There should also be more national co-ordination between those UDF affiliates in white areas.

There were further signs of political change among white South Africans later in 1987. The Institute for a Democratic Alternative in South Africa (IDASA), formed by Slabbert after his resignation from parliament, led a large group to meet with the ANC in Dakar in July. A number of senior members of the Progressive Federal Party resigned from the party though not from parliament.[92] But the UDF recognised difficulties in drawing anti-apartheid white people into the struggle. A UDF position paper noted: 'There is ... a significant constituency of whites who would accept the need for a negotiated solution with the democratic movement as opposed to fighting it out to the bitter end. These people are searching for alternatives and a political home ... If organised [they] could become a powerful force for change.'[93] But this constituency, it went on, does 'not currently see the UDF as offering a viable way out of the present malaise', and could easily be lured into support for more conservative initiatives linked, for example, to Inkatha. 'The challenge that faces us is to provide both a political direction and a home to this grouping. To take up this challenge we have to embark on a process which begins with where they are at. We need to address their fears and concerns and provide direction in a language and style to which they can relate.'[94] As JODAC later put it: 'Democrats working in broad white politics may have to march to a different drum from those working in the oppressed communities or in UDF affiliates.'[95] Here was a restatement of the old, essentially multiracial approach of the Congress movement: appeal to and organise people in terms to which they can relate, terms reflecting the racial division of South African society.

The UDF increasingly emphasised the need to enter into broader alliances than hitherto. As a subsequent document continued, such alliances mean 'working with forces and groups whose line is not the same as ours' but who share a common goal in ending apartheid. The UDF's approach to white South Africans should be to work with groups who would probably never join the UDF or subscribe to its 'full programme'. Put starkly, the UDF's strategy 'must include strengthening and supporting each and every initiative which weakens the main enemy, that is the National Party, the government, and the neo-fascist right-wing forces', so as to build 'the broadest possible anti-apartheid front'.[96]

Alliances with capitalists, and even 'imperialist forces', were defended on the pragmatic grounds that they contributed to the struggle for political change. This strategy reflected the continuing reorientation of the UDF towards an unambiguous concern with power, and more specifically state power. In defending the campaign against critics within the democratic movement, signals were being given – perhaps for the first time – of the capitalist nature of the post-apartheid society envisaged by the UDF leadership. 'There should be no illusions about the extent to which a post-apartheid society will rely on capital's knowledge and resources,' wrote JODAC.[97]

The UDF also began to recognise a growing problem in coloured and Indian areas, where UDF affiliates had struggled 'to come to terms with the situation of heightened conflict in the African townships'. There had been poor participation in coloured and Indian areas in the Campaign for National United Action. The 1987 NWC Programme of Action included a commitment to rebuilding organisation and increased activity in these areas. A 'national gathering' should be held to 'plan strategy'.[98] But organising in these constituencies was of declining relative importance. The middle ground had shifted, and was now occupied by white dissenters from the 'ruling bloc'.

TOWARDS BANNING

Repression under the countrywide State of Emergency in South Africa was not particularly brutal by comparison with undemocratic regimes elsewhere in the world, but it was brutal by South African standards. It was estimated that 25 000 people had been detained under Emergency regulations by February 1988. Over 1200 were known to be in detention at the end of 1987, including almost 400 people who had been in detention since June or July 1986.[99] In addition, public meetings were tightly controlled, foreign funding was restricted, and the media were heavily censored.

In the face of this repression, the UDF could do little more than mount a 'holding operation', as Moosa puts it. Its only major public campaign was the 'campaign for united mass action', which had been intermittent even in late 1986 and early 1987 before faltering thereafter.[100] In late 1987 the UDF continued its protests against repression with an Unlock Apartheid Jails campaign, calling for the unconditional release of all political prisoners and detainees, and supporting the SAYCO-led Save the Condemned Patriots campaign, opposing the death sentence on convicted political prisoners. The UDF had some success in building organisation, especially with the formation of SAYCO. But the UDF's own national and regional structures were too disrupted to do much. Unable to operate openly, they became increasingly vulnerable to accusations of cabalism.

The UDF's holding operation, however, was successful. The UDF not only continued to operate and to meet, even holding a national conference in May 1987, and directing a network of organisers across much of the country. It also maintained a public profile, helping to keep repression under the national and international spotlight. It took advantage of the tumult in white politics to draw important sections of the white elite away from the apartheid state. It began to forge a substantive alliance with the trade unions, through COSATU. This was manifest especially in the Natal Midlands, where the UDF and COSATU engaged jointly in peace talks.[101] Crucially, the UDF together with its allies demonstrated that the state could do no more than stem dissent. As in 1983–4, the UDF showed the limits to the state's capacity and options.

The UDF did not, however, challenge the state, as it had done in 1985–6. The Emergency revealed the UDF's lack of a viable strategy for effecting political change. The promise of people's power could not survive intensified repression. And whilst the UDF turned to the ANC for strategic direction, the ANC itself had no convincing answer. Certainly, rebuilding organisation, strengthening alliances, mobilising among white elites – all of these might help, but none could break the stalemate between anti-apartheid groups and the apartheid state.

In January 1988 the UDF issued a New Year message that merely extended the holding operation. Prospective campaigns for the coming year included opposition to the municipal elections scheduled for August, a renewed call to whites, a further call on Tricameral parliamentarians to 'abandon collaboration', yet another call for strengthened organisation, and action against the ongoing treason trials.[102]

In fact, the underlying political context was changing. During 1987 talks resumed between Kobie Coetsee and the jailed Nelson Mandela. In November the government released the veteran prisoner Govan Mbeki, although he was confined to Port Elizabeth and restricted from public speaking. At about the same time talks had begun in England between the ANC and members of the Afrikaner elite with very close connections to the National Party government. As Waldmeir puts it, these were 'talks … about whether to talk … about talks'.[103] But they were talks nonetheless, and reflected a growing recognition that a negotiated settlement might be the only kind of settlement available.

For the state, exploring the possibility of a negotiated settlements did not mean easing up on repression. The total number of detainees may have fallen, but they were well chosen. In December 1987 the *de facto* UDF leadership was further depleted by the detention of Molobi. In January the government moved to close the *New Nation* newspaper temporarily, finally doing so in March, after a court ruling. Then, on 24 February, the Minister of Law and Order effectively banned the UDF and 16 other organisations in terms of a new Emergency regulation. The only actions permitted to these organisations were the maintenance of their accounting books and taking legal advice.

Chapter Nine

The Mass Democratic Movement, February 1988–January 1990

The effective banning of the UDF, its key affiliates and other organisations, together with new restrictions on the Front's leaders, was paradoxically an acknowledgement of the weakness of the apartheid state. Twenty months of a countrywide State of Emergency – with mass detentions, restrictions on political activity and media censorship – had failed to create the political situation that the government deemed necessary for its reform programme to succeed. Internationally, the state was under mounting pressure to negotiate with the ANC; domestically, there was spreading disaffection among white political and economic elites; and the UDF, its affiliates and the unions had not been reduced to the desired level of quiescence. Notwithstanding this new level of repression, the pressures placed on the state inside the country were in fact to grow during 1988 and even more in 1989.

Although the UDF could not operate openly between February 1988 and January 1990, when its NEC decided to 'unban' the organisation, it did continue to operate: in practice if not in name; unevenly, for sure; and only weakly during 1988, before growing in confidence and assertion in 1989. The first strand in UDF activity comprised maintaining or rebuilding its own structures and affiliates, and engaging in discrete campaigns against repression, municipal elections and in defiance of racial segregation. Through these campaigns the UDF and its allies eroded the scope of repression, challenged and undermined the efficacy of state reforms, and exposed the moral weaknesses of the state.

The second strand in UDF activity comprised building new and broader political alliances. Central to any broader alliance was the Congress of South African Trade Unions (COSATU), which was only partially restricted in February 1988 and could therefore operate more easily and openly than the UDF. During 1988 the relationship between the UDF and COSATU was solidified, as were the relationships between both of them and the ANC. In 1989 the links between the UDF and COSATU were semi-formalised through the Mass Democratic Movement (MDM). At the same time, the UDF and, more broadly, the MDM forged new links with disaffected white elites as well as with some black participants in the bantustan system.

The beginning of this period may have been marked by intensified repression, but the defining feature of the time was the growing momentum of moves towards a negotiated settlement. This involved, first and foremost, the ANC rather than internally based organisations. In May 1988 Nelson Mandela embarked on a series of detailed talks with a team of government officials, and was given a telephone to maintain contact with the ANC in exile. After being transferred from Pollsmoor Prison to Victor Verster Prison in December 1988, he met regularly with UDF and other political leaders from inside the country. In July 1989 Mandela met with P.W. Botha. In exile, the ANC continued to talk to Afrikaner intellectuals, who mediated between them and the NP government, and then began to talk to state officials directly. Further progress followed when F.W. de Klerk ousted the ailing Botha as President in September. The following month he ordered the release from prison of the top ANC leadership excepting Mandela. The momentum which the talks assumed marked an important shift in the loci of political change. No longer were political developments driven by events in the streets but by talks near Cape Town and abroad; no longer by the UDF or other internally based organisations, but by the ANC.

How fast and how far the political scene had changed was made clear by other events at the end of 1989 and the beginning of 1990. In December 1989 the MDM convened a massive Conference for a Democratic Future. The following month, the Kagiso Trust hosted a conference entitled 'From Opposing to Governing: How Ready is the Opposition?' Also in January, the UDF's NEC declared the Front to be 'unbanned' and resumed public activity. Finally, and most dramatically, in February the government unbanned the ANC and the other exiled liberation movements, and lifted restrictions on the UDF, its affiliates and leaders.

THE EFFECTS OF REPRESSION

The restrictions imposed on the UDF and 16 other organisations on 24 February 1988 prohibited them from performing almost all activities. The UDF was *de facto* banned. At the same time COSATU was prohibited from involvement in anything other than employment and workplace concerns. The restrictions were issued under Emergency regulations, were reimposed along with the State of Emergency in June, and would presumably remain in force until the Emergency was eventually lifted. Restrictions were also imposed on many individual activists. These included UDF national presidents Albertina Sisulu and Archie Gumede, UDF national treasurer Azhar Cachalia, and many regional UDF leaders, especially in the Western Cape.

State officials did not divulge their reasons for intensifying restrictions. A senior police officer blandly described the purpose of the restrictions as 'to enable the security forces to ensure the safety of the public and to maintain law and order more efficiently'.[1] Two explanations were put forward at the time. The first saw the restrictions as a symbolic gesture aimed at the NP's white supporters, who seemed to be defecting in large numbers to the Conservative Party. The second saw them as a way of preventing the UDF and other restricted organisations from derailing the state's reform programme.

Whatever the immediate motivation, state repression was understood by its opponents to be part of a coherent, overall counter-revolutionary strategy. The restrictions were seen as the major element in the state's repressive battery, which also included the Labour Relations Amendment Bill to weaken the trade unions, as well as threatened controls over foreign funding and university-based protests, and further attacks on the press. Repression would be accompanied by attempted reforms, comprising a proposed National Council, continued township upgrading projects, and the much-heralded countrywide municipal elections to be held in October 1988. But, the UDF and its allies concluded, the state's actions were born out of its political weakness rather than its military strength. The state lacked any viable vision of the future. There remained, therefore, a continued need to conduct political struggle, even if the form of organisational activity had to change. This was acknowledged in UDF working papers reportedly circulated in June 1988. Anticipating that the State of Emergency would remain for several years, these proposed that the 'mass democratic movement should master the techniques of secret and underground work' in order to be able to continue with above-ground activity.[2]

The UDF was unable to respond to the new restrictions speedily or effectively, primarily because so many of its leaders were in jail. Some of them, like Mpetha and Stofile, were serving prison sentences, and some were still on trial – Molefe and Lekota – but most were in detention under Emergency regulations. These included Moosa, Morobe and Manuel, behind-the-scenes leaders such as Zwelakhe Sisulu and Molobi, as well as a host of regional leaders including the entire Eastern Cape UDF leadership. Many of them were released during 1988 but were then served with restriction orders under the Emergency regulations. This was the fate of Sisulu, Molobi, Suttner and Mokoena.[3]

With the banning of the UDF, some of its former activities were taken up by, or in the name of, unbanned affiliates. Advertisements were put in the press demanding 'UNBAN THE UDF', and calling for a National Day of Protest on 21 March, Sharpeville Day, in the name of 'unbanned UDF affiliates'. When Mandela was receiving medical treatment in mid-year, an advertisement proclaimed: 'The UNITED DEMOCRATIC FRONT affiliates wish NELSON MANDELA a speedy recovery.' Affiliated bodies such as the Natal Indian Congress played an important role in, for example, challenging aspects of the restrictions in court. Supposedly new structures were formed to get around the restrictions. A Committee for the Defence of Democracy was set up to protest against the new restrictions, until it too was banned. In the Eastern Cape, a Special Committee against Repression was formed to step into the vacuum left by the formal banning of the UDF. Ad hoc committees also claimed public responsibility for organising specific events, such as a concert and a football match to celebrate Mandela's 70th birthday.[4]

In practice, the effect of the February restrictions was not so much to change the work that individual activists were doing as to make it far harder for them to co-ordinate with each other. Cachalia, for example, continued to receive and dispense funds from his legal offices in Johannesburg. But the restrictions made it far more difficult to meet, even clandestinely. Moosa later said that the state had 'targeted our structures of communication and co-ordination, which led to [their] weakening and breakdown'. Many activists and organisations were beginning to feel isolated. 'Much of the energies of those who weren't detained was taken up by maintaining a holding position.'[5] Numbers of activists from small towns sought refuge in the bigger cities, and this often caused tensions in their relationships with those colleagues who stayed behind. Media production was also hard hit by the 1988 restrictions, although small teams continued to operate clandestinely, and a new journal, *Phambili*, soon filled the space left by *Isizwe*, which could not be produced legally.

BROADENING THE STRUGGLE

The new wave of repression left the UDF unable to provide much of a lead for the six or so months following February. It was COSATU and its affiliated unions, taking advantage of their relatively limited restrictions, which played the leading role in the debate over how to maintain the momentum of the struggle, and in particular how the struggle should be broadened. And it was within COSATU that debates about the character and limits of political alliances had to be resolved. While disaffection among white political and economic elites threw up the possibility of a much broader alliance against apartheid than hitherto, some unions feared that drawing liberal white South Africans and business groups into an alliance would compromise their commitment to radical social and economic transformation.

Sections of the trade union movement seem to have largely agreed with the UDF that a loosely structured 'united front' should be formed of a wide range of organisations opposed to apartheid. This view seems to have been held within most of the COSATU national leadership, and especially within the leadership of the National Union of Mineworkers. NUM's general secretary, Cyril Ramaphosa, had a long history of association with UDF and progressive church leaders from his days as a Christian student leader at the University of the North. Under his leadership, NUM argued for the inclusion of multi-class organisations, and even organisations based among bourgeois white South Africans, in a united front against apartheid. The alliance would be structured upon agreed tactics and short-term or medium-term demands rather than ideological consensus.

As in previous periods, this view of broadening the anti-apartheid alliance was opposed by groupings advocating a more radical approach. In 1988–9 opposition came from trade unions committed to socialist transformation and critical of the two-stage theory put forward by the SACP, this theory holding that the second stage of transition to socialism should await the first stage of transition to bourgeois democracy. The leading proponent of this criticism was the metalworkers' union, NUMSA, arguing that the new alliance should comprise anti-capitalist rather than merely anti-apartheid organisations, should include non-Charterist as well as Charterist groupings, and should have permanent structures. The relationship between NUM and NUMSA, and between their respective leaders, Cyril Ramaphosa and Moses Mayekiso, were to remain strained throughout the following years.

COSATU took the first step towards rebuilding an alliance on the same day that the Emergency restrictions were imposed – 24 February. Its Central Executive Committee agreed to call a special national congress to discuss state repression and possible responses, and to invite representatives of 'the community' – the UDF and its affiliates. COSATU's Special Congress was held at the University of the Witwatersrand in May 1988. The 1500 delegates included 120 'guests from the community' – from UDF affiliates, church and sports organisations – with full speaking rights. The conference was therefore more than just a gathering of trade unions. It pulled together what was left of the democratic movement to assess conditions and chart a way forward.[6]

The mainstream Charterist position was presented at the COSATU Special Congress by NUM. It called for a united front, based upon the 'fighting alliance' of UDF and COSATU but also including other mass-based organisations 'whose political programmes are not incompatible with those of COSATU's affiliates'. The front would try to 'unify the broadest possible section of the South African population', and would focus on action rather than debate. The rival position was presented by the metalworkers' and chemical workers' unions (NUMSA and CWIU). They argued for a 'broad front' of working-class organisations, with permanent structures. The NUMSA–CWIU position would have excluded many UDF affiliates, and clearly superseded the UDF, whilst the NUM position would accommodate the UDF and its affiliates. Not surprisingly, UDF speakers at the congress argued against the NUMSA–CWIU proposal. A third position called for a very broad anti-apartheid conference to discuss united action against repression, rather than a structured alliance. This would accommodate both non-Charterist opposition organisations, in the Black Consciousness tradition, for example, and emerging groups of white South Africans outside the UDF.[7]

While the debate was to some extent a re-run of the divisions at COSATU's 1987 congress, this time there was more common ground and a general awareness of the urgency of reaching compromise. The congress eventually did adopt a compromise resolution, based on the third proposal but incorporating elements of the other two. COSATU and its allies would work on a programme of action and organise an anti-apartheid conference. The conference would include non-Charterist and multi-class organisations. The congress also resolved, with some opposition, to hold three days of 'peaceful national protest' against repression on 6–8 June. It was clearly understood that this protest would hinge upon a stayaway, although Emergency restrictions precluded an explicit call for one.

The stayaway was supported by an estimated 2.5–3 million workers on the first day, with a slight drop in support on the second and third days. Support was strongest in the PWV region and Natal, and much less so in the Western Cape. The scale of the stayaway confounded sceptics within and outside the democratic movement, and strengthened ties between unions and other organisations. As COSATU's general secretary, Jay Naidoo, said, the protest illustrated how 'unity is forged in action'.[8]

Although the call for a stayaway had been supported by the Charterists within COSATU more strongly than by, for example, NUMSA, the UDF's *Phambili* later assessed the action quite critically. According to *Phambili*'s analysis, the stayaway had successfully demonstrated popular power and divided the ruling block, but had also exposed organisational weaknesses, including a lack of support among coloured or Indian workers, 'inadequate strategising between COSATU and community organisations', and inadequate propaganda. *Phambili* warned:

> The militancy and political awareness of the masses must not be confused with a preparedness to back any action, no matter how rash or ill-considered ... We should be careful not to be overconfident and embark on campaigns which do not correspond to the mood of the people. We should remember that the pace of a column is not determined by the fittest and fastest soldier but by the slowest and weakest.[9]

Faced with repression by the state on the one hand, and the socialist demands of NUMSA on the other, the UDF once again emphasised the need to broaden the alliance against the government, drawing in relatively conservative groups. Slowing the pace of the column to that of the slowest soldiers was a change from the UDF's position in 1985–6, and a return to its position of 1983–4.

The importance of broadening the alliance whilst paying special attention to the needs of its slower and weaker components was raised again in a discussion document, apparently drafted from within the UDF in mid-year. The document represents the first full statement of the UDF's perspective in the new political context. It begins with an analysis of the situation:

> We are seeing in our country today more and more polarisation between apartheid forces on the one hand and the democratic forces on the other ... While many and different structures are involved in the fight against and defence of apartheid, the two main protagonists in this conflict are clearly the ANC and the government.[10]

The document proceeds to discuss the 'mass democratic movement', introducing a new term into political discourse:

> There are many organisations in the country who share with the ANC a vision of a unitary, non-racial and democratic South Africa. These organisations, organised mainly under the UDF and COSATU, use above-board, open and legal ways to fight apartheid ... These organisations together with the ANC are referred to as the mass democratic movement. Mass because of their mass approach to work and the mass support they enjoy, democratic because they believe in and employ accountable and democratic methods in their work. Most of these organisations see the Freedom Charter as their guiding document.[11]

The challenge facing the mass democratic movement (or MDM, as it came to be called) during the State of Emergency was twofold: 'Firstly, they should continue to deepen and strengthen their grassroots structures ... Secondly, we must deny apartheid forces any chance of gaining more junior partners amongst our people. Thus we should win over in a disciplined and systematic way, groups which are seen to be on the middle ground.' In other words, the various groups opposed to apartheid but outside the MDM needed to be drawn into a broader alliance.

The Anti-Apartheid Conference (AAC) proposed at the COSATU Special Congress would provide an opportunity to build a broader alliance. Even before the conference, the document advised, 'we should begin to work together and commit ourselves to a closer working relationship ... The conference should be the place to cement and give impetus to unity.' The document emphatically rejected the NUMSA position: 'It must be clear that we do not envisage the setting up of a structure/structures to replace the UDF at the conference ...' This argument was taken up in an article published early the following year by a COSATU unionist. The conference, he emphasised, had not been intended to replace the UDF, nor to replace the 'fighting alliance' between the UDF, its affiliates and COSATU.

> Rather, its intention was to broaden the base of opposition to apartheid. The AAC aims to reach out to elements who are not yet fully committed to our liberation struggle, as well as reach out to organisations with whom we have political differences ... The democratic movement and the majority of our people are under heavy attack ... To resist these attacks, to defend our rights to organise, and to speak out we need to mobilise the broadest possible range of forces ... The AAC is based on the concept of building a tactical and strategic alliance with the aim of winning short-term and medium-term goals. It is an alliance of forces who may have differing long-term aims and interests.[12]

The range of organisations invited to the conference was indeed broad and controversial. The UDF document suggested that invitations should be extended to business groups (including the black National African Federated Chamber of Commerce, sports groups including the National Soccer League, bantustan-based groups including the ANC-orientated Inyandza movement of Enos Mabuza in KaNgwane, and white bourgeois groups including the National Democratic Movement, which comprised white members of parliament, alongside the Five Freedoms Forum and the Black Sash.[13] Inviting such a range of groupings was unprecedented, and met with strong resistance in some unions and COSATU regions. Sydney Mufamadi, who served as convener of the AAC planning committee, explained the organisers' position on bantustan-based groups:

> It seems inconceivable to some that having taken a principled stand against the bantustan system, we can invite opposition parties from the bantustans. However, we cannot wish bantustans away. We have to tackle them as part of our objective reality ... Most of the activities of our people in the bantustans

have not taken place under the auspices of the mass democratic movement. To sit back and wait for the day when all the people in the bantustans will shout the slogans we are already shouting within COSATU will amount to a dereliction of leadership duties … If we are to broaden our political and moral influence … [then the bantustans are] a terrain we have to contest.[14]

Similarly, he added, the mass democratic movement should try to dislodge white liberals 'from the trenches of the enemy'. Links between the democratic movement and white business leaders were greatly strengthened in August when 37 MDM leaders met with 40 prominent business leaders and academics in Broederstroom, leading to the formation of the Consultative Business Movement as a forum for business leaders in favour of political and social change.[15]

Clearly threatened, the state banned the conference on the very eve of its opening in late September. Organisations in the Black Consciousness and Unity Movement traditions had already pulled out, objecting to the presence of groups from the bantustans, the National Soccer League, and so on. The police detained conference organisers in Cape Town, raided COSATU offices in four regions and, soon after, imposed restrictions on Mufamadi and other COSATU leaders most centrally involved in the initiative.

Soon after the conference was banned, the Cape Town-based left magazine *New Era* interviewed two pseudonymous members of the AAC planning committee. They elaborated on the analysis presented in the UDF document on the AAC in mid-year. One assessed the context as 'a state of unstable equilibrium, where objectively the conditions are favourable for a great leap forward, but subjectively we find ourselves not yet in a position to take full advantage of the situation.' The MDM must 'maximise the process of unity' in order to better resist repression and to 'harness' and 'give direction to' groups 'like taxi-drivers and businessmen' and former sections of the 'ruling bloc' who were now opposed to apartheid. The second MDM leader concurred, saying: 'the most reactionary sector of the ruling bloc must be isolated', so as best to 'shift the balance of forces in favour of the people'.[16]

The AAC proposal was not abandoned. Nine months of extensive discussion and debate, particularly between different trade union groupings, led to the revival of the proposal in mid-1989, and eventually the holding of the Conference for a Democratic Future in December 1989. The term MDM also re-emerged, and entered popular discourse in a way which it never had in 1988.

MUNICIPAL ELECTIONS

Through 1988 the UDF and MDM had their sights firmly set on the municipal elections due to be held in October across the whole country excepting, of course, the bantustans. For the first time, municipal elections would take place among all racial groups on the same day, disguising the racially structured inequality between them in a pretence of equality. These elections were the only concrete expression of any proactive political project on the state's part, with the government presumably hoping that the elections would produce a credible group of black councillors to serve as the core of a counter-revolutionary political initiative. The elections would also serve, as Moosa later said, 'as a test of the extent to which the Emergency had succeeded' in crushing resistance. The government, he added, 'predicted that the turnout at the polls would be huge. It also predicted that now that the so-called trouble-makers were either in jail or too intimidated to do anything, the masses would support the puppet structures.'[17] The elections thus had symbolic and practical importance beyond the local level.

The UDF held a meeting in August in Durban to settle upon a strategy for its campaign against the municipal elections. Mafolo drafted a paper on behalf of the NEC. He recalls:

The paper was saying that obviously the struggle had actually rendered the policy of minority rule ineffective and so on, and the aim of the elections was to try and revive that. The other argument then was that we brought the upgrading of some townships ... Whilst the regime wanted to use that as a way of appeasing people, the fact of the matter was that that was actually a victory on the part of the people, because that was exactly what the UDF had been fighting for ... We must, even in our propaganda, inform people that this would not have happened had it not been for the struggles of the people through the UDF and so on. Secondly, we should try to [persuade] the clerics, the Tutus and so on, to mount a campaign against the municipal elections, and also other high-profile people who were not detained at that time ... [But] they were also very, very cautious given the level of repression at that time. In fact only Tutu ... was able to come out clear against the elections.[18]

Repression also led some people to propose that the UDF should consider participation in the elections. According to one argument:

The relentless repression of the past few years has smashed and weakened our structures. Repression will continue, thus we will not be able to have an opportunity to revive structures and be in a position to effectively oppose the municipal elections and continue with the struggle. We should therefore use the space provided by the elections to propagate our views.[19]

The UDF prepared another paper dealing with the participation issue. Most of the paper dealt with other, more clearly fatuous arguments for participation. The argument that participation could provide needed space was dealt with somewhat cursorily. Firstly:

If our analysis is correct that the state is out to crush the mass democratic movement, what makes us think that it will let it thrive within its own structures? Even if we were able to contest seats in these elections, the space gained will be short lived. Even the puppet local authorities have been threatened this year that they would be disbanded because they have not done enough to collect rents.[20]

Secondly, the boycott of segregated institutions was described as being not merely a tactic but a broad strategy, 'i.e. part of a general coherent approach to build united opposition and move towards one person one vote'. The UDF did make an exception in the case of white areas, explaining that the 'strategies and methods used in the enemy camp will always be different from those used in the people's camp'. After the UDF's allies in groupings such as the Five Freedoms Forum argued strongly in favour of participation, the Front merely insisted that 'no affiliate can participate as a UDF structure and no UDF activist can stand as a candidate'.[21]

These arguments indicated the sense of weakness that pervaded the UDF at the time. The UDF's ambition was to minimise the legitimacy and credibility of elected local government. There seems to have been no significant support for a more ambitious strategy. With hindsight, a more aggressive strategy could have greatly intensified the crisis facing the state. Such a strategy might have entailed, for example, candidates campaigning under slogans such as 'Unban the ANC', followed by a complete boycott of the institutions by elected councillors. But such a strategy would only have made sense if the UDF had been certain it could mobilise and demonstrate overwhelming popular support and that the moment was a turning-point of some sort – conditions which some UDF activists felt had existed at the time of the divisive referendum debate in 1983. Instead, senior UDF activists were perhaps unsure of their organisational capacity to mobilise strong support, and seem to have anticipated an extended period of repression. Few would have predicted the major political changes that were to take place just one year later.

It is unclear precisely how the elections were opposed, and how support for a boycott was mobilised. Moosa later said that there had been no national co-ordination; the boycott was the result of the 'large number of localised initiatives' together with a pervasive popular scepticism of the state. Given the constraints on the UDF and COSATU, it was left to the churches to take a public stand against the elections. Notwithstanding Mafolo's scepticism, a number of church leaders defied Emergency regulations and called on people not to vote.[22] Civic organisation on the ground was very uneven after two years of heavy repression, although most civic activists had been released from detention, and the links between local and national levels were often weak.

The election results were interpreted positively by both the state and its opponents. On the one hand, the state could point to polls of 45 per cent, 35 per cent and 25 per cent in coloured, Indian and African areas respectively, counting only wards where seats were contested. On the other hand, opponents pointed out that these polls were of registered voters only, and registration rates had been low. Only between 5 and 10 per cent of eligible African voters had voted, for example. The results certainly did not support the state's claim that they demonstrated the legitimacy of and support for the 'extension of democracy' at the local level. The overwhelming majority of voters, especially of African voters, had stayed away, and most of the votes that were cast were for candidates who campaigned on a populist ticket critical of state policy. Above all, the elections did not provide the state with credible allies in African townships. But the results were also worrying for the democratic movement. No fewer than 280 000 coloured and Indian people voted, with generally higher polls than in previous local elections. This should have provided a warning of ebbing popular support for the UDF. Furthermore, no fewer than 370 000 African people had voted, with significant polls in some areas such as Khayelitsha. This pointed, at the very least, to deficiencies in the reach of UDF and allied media, and in the scope of organisation.[23]

The municipal elections did not allow the state to regain the political initiative in the country's African townships. The combination of urban development and repression had failed to generate a political payoff. This encouraged UDF-aligned leaders to adopt new strategies over the continuing crisis of urban development and rent boycotts. Non-payment of rents, including service charges, by township residents had now reached serious dimensions. According to official figures, rent arrears stood at almost R500 million in August 1988 – in Soweto alone, arrears were creeping up to R200 million. Local councils had resorted to evicting boycotters and cutting off electricity and even water to an entire area when non-payment reached a certain level. In response to these local problems, to the expressed willingness of the newly elected council to negotiate a settlement, and to a perceived national political opportunity, civic leaders in Soweto appointed a delegation to meet with the Soweto Council. The Soweto People's Delegation was led by Frank Chikane, and included also Ramaphosa, Albertina Sisulu, Archbishop Desmond Tutu and others. The use of such high-profile people would, it was envisaged, both attract publicity and reduce the likelihood of detention. The delegation could not operate under the auspices of the Soweto Civic Association because the latter had been banned in 1988 although it continued to meet clandestinely.[24]

The Soweto People's Delegation met with the Soweto Council for the first time in December 1988. Early the following year it commissioned research on Soweto's finances. Through the rest of 1989 and into 1990 talks proceeded between the delegation and, first, the Soweto Council and, later, other tiers of government. The concept of the 'people's delegation' was adopted in other areas in 1989, notwithstanding criticism by, for example, NUMSA unionist Mayekiso. The profile of the delegation, combined with a preparedness to negotiate an end to rent boycotts, seems to have provided sufficient protection against repression, allowing civic leaders to regain the political initiative at the local level.

REVITALISATION

The success of the campaign against the municipal elections helped to revitalise the UDF and MDM. Moosa later recalled that 'towards the end of [1988] we began to see the first sign of a turn in events'; by early 1989 'it finally became clear to all of us that the Emergency had failed'.[25] Although restrictions compelled the UDF to continue to operate more or less covertly, its revitalisation was clearly reflected in a strengthening of the MDM, organised along the broad lines envisaged by the UDF.

A second factor contributing to this revitalisation was the dramatic escape from detention of Moosa and Morobe, the UDF's acting general secretary and publicity secretary. Together with Vusi Khanyile, chairperson of the National Education Crisis Committee, they escaped to the American consulate in September, before being allowed to leave their sanctuary in October without any of the restrictions that constrained other UDF leaders and with a degree of immunity from re-detention.

Morobe later described the escape as 'one of the highest moments of my life ... We grew up seeing these things in movies. It never occurred to me that one day I would be the one to jump prison walls and dash for safety.'[26] The decision to try to escape had been taken after they were nominally 'redetained' when the State of Emergency was renewed for another year in June. According to Moosa:

> On June 9 1988, those of us in Diepkloof were redetained ... We got the feeling that we would remain in detention without any recourse to justice for an endless period of time. It was also clear that the government was not prepared to listen to the whole range of voices inside the country and around the world who were demanding the lifting of the state of emergency. In this situation the only option we had was to use a creative way to secure our freedom.[27]

Escape was the 'only dignified response to our continued incarceration', after the failure of their attempts to secure release through official channels.[28] The three men feigned illness, and were taken under guard to Johannesburg Hospital for treatment. They escaped from the hospital and made their way to the American consulate in the Kine Centre in downtown Johannesburg.

Although 'the American consulate officials were reluctant to allow us to remain in the first hours of our arrival there', the so-called 'Kine 3' were to remain in the consulate for over a month. The escape was a massive publicity coup – at least until the consulate forbade press interviews. The Kine 3 coolly rejected a succession of offers made by the South African government, desperate to defuse the situation: they could have safe passage out of the country, they could be allowed out if they agreed not to talk to the press, and so on. They demanded their release without restriction or threat of redetention. When this was conceded by the government, they stayed in the consulate to highlight the continuing detention of other activists.[29]

The occupation of the American consulate harked back to the occupation of the British consulate in Durban in 1984. Both attracted considerable publicity in South Africa and abroad. They reflected the UDF's emphasis on political struggle, using public events to further isolate or divide pro-apartheid forces. But there were important and telling differences between the two occupations. First, the international context was very different. In 1984 five of the six refugees were arrested and tried for treason after they left the British consulate. In 1988 the Kine 3 could secure their release not only without charges, but also without restrictions. Secondly, the local context had changed. Whilst the international status of the UDF had improved, the local context had worsened, for the Kine 3 were released into a situation where the

UDF and other organisations were still banned. Moosa and Morobe were forced to adapt to this new context. Not until the second half of 1989 were they able to defy outright the restrictions on activity.

The escape of Moosa and Morobe was followed by one setback. In November judgment was finally delivered in the marathon Delmas Treason Trial. The judge found that the UDF had acted as the internal wing of the ANC, had sought to make the country ungovernable and overthrow the government through violence. Lekota was sentenced to twelve years' imprisonment, and Molefe and Moss Chikane to ten years each. The state was widely expected to follow up the judgment by holding a mass trial of Eastern Cape UDF activists.[30] But the state was curiously unable to use what was, from its point of view, a much welcomed judgment. The judgment's criminalisation of the UDF was politically undermined by three factors. Firstly, the judgment was derided in many circles, including liberal ones. Secondly, it was already evident that the Delmas Treason Trial conviction would not be replicated in a second major treason trial of Moses Mayekiso and other Alexandra activists. In December Mayekiso and his co-accused were released on bail. The following April they were to be acquitted, with the judge implicitly criticising the state's decision to charge them with treason at all. And, thirdly, the ANC was by now clearly a central player in the fast-changing South African political scene. Criminalising the UDF for being a front for the ANC was of little importance when many groups, including foreign governments as well as South African business leaders and parliamentary parties, and the South African government itself, were now in direct contact with the ANC. The MDM could therefore happily expand its contacts with the ANC in the period following this supposed criminalisation of the UDF.

The new sense of direction within the UDF was clear in the New Year statement issued by the 'non-banned affiliates of the UDF' in January 1989. The statement opened with an acknowledgement of the confusion within the MDM, asking whether the MDM was on the retreat, marking time or advancing. The statement listed various setbacks but also a series of advances, including both continued protest and political gains in terms of extending 'its political and moral influence' and isolating the government. 'It is clear that the mass democratic movement has forced the government on to the defensive. They are now marking time in a vain attempt to implement meaningless constitutional schemes and to stem the tide of change. Clearly, the mass democratic movement is on the advance.'[31] Although it had 'not taken full advantage of the favourable objective conditions', the strategic initiative was firmly in its hands. The UDF reiterated the strategic programme adopted in 1987: 'Defend, Consolidate and Advance'. Its interpretation of this emphasised the strengthening and extending of unity, both with fraternal organisations like COSATU and with 'forces in the middle ground'. The government must be isolated, and the moral and political influence of the MDM spread still further.[32]

More important were protests by detainees. During 1988 there had been a few localised hunger strikes in protest against aspects of detention. In January 1989 detainees embarked on a mass hunger strike, demanding their unconditional release. Altogether 644 detainees had been on hunger strike by the end of April, according to the government – with independent monitors putting the figure higher, at almost 800. As many as 130 were hospitalised. The hunger strike was called off when the government promised to release a 'substantial number' of detainees – and before a single hunger striker died. Most detainees were, indeed, released in early 1989. This represented an enormous boost to the UDF and the MDM more broadly.[33]

The victory of release was qualified slightly by the imposition of restrictions on over five hundred of the released detainees. When Trevor Manuel, for example, was released in February, his restrictions included house arrest between 6 p.m. and 6 a.m. and confinement to the Wynberg (Cape Town) magisterial district. He had to report to the police twice daily, and was prohibited from preparing anything for publication. He could not attend any UDF or civic activities, could not address large gatherings and could not give interviews.[34]

NEGOTIATIONS AND THE ANC

The revitalisation of the UDF in late 1988 took place at the same time as it became clear that the locus of opposition politics had shifted decisively from internally based organisations to the exiled or jailed ANC. From the UDF's formation in 1983 until mid-1986 organisation and protest inside the country had proved more important than the largely ineffectual activities of the ANC in exile. Even in 1986–7, the ANC's strategic bankruptcy had led it to attach most importance to the intensification of resistance inside the country. In 1988, for the first time, the initiative clearly shifted to the ANC, as talks between it and the government gained momentum – and talks were the exclusive preserve of the ANC.

Discussion between the ANC and the apartheid state took place on two tracks, focused on the jailed Mandela and the exiled ANC leadership. In 1987 Kobie Coetsee resumed his intermittent and hitherto rather directionless contacts with Mandela. These led in May 1988 to the first of an intensive series of talks between Mandela and a team of officials led by the director of the National Intelligence Service, Niel Barnard, whom Waldmeir describes as P.W. Botha's 'top strategic thinker'. On the second track, Afrikaner intellectuals with close links to the NP government continued their meetings in England with ANC leaders led by Thabo Mbeki. At some point in 1988–9 – when exactly is not clear – direct contact was initiated between the National Intelligence Service and exiled ANC.[35]

The impetus to talks arose from the conjuncture of a number of factors. Within the government there appears to have been a growing recognition that its choice lay between a holding operation – maintaining the current unstable position with continuing repression – and embarking on talks in order to achieve a negotiated settlement of some kind. Internationally, the government was under heavy pressure to negotiate. P.W. Botha was perhaps willing to defy foreign powers – including friendly powers such as the United States and Britain – but even he agreed to a meeting with Mandela in May 1989. By then, however, he was already losing his authority. In January he suffered a stroke, as a result of which he gave up the NP leadership whilst holding on to the presidency of the country. His successor as NP leader was F.W. de

Klerk. Although regarded hitherto as conservative, De Klerk was committed to reaching a negotiated settlement from the moment of his elevation to the NP leadership in February 1989. In August De Klerk was to oust Botha as president.[36] The role of political protest and organisation inside the country during 1987–8 was primarily to limit the government's room to manoeuvre, although of course hanging over the government was the fear of a resurgence of revolutionary protest as in 1984–6.

It is not clear precisely how fully informed Mandela and the exiled ANC leadership kept the UDF leadership. Mandela himself did not keep even his closest comrades in jail or in exile fully abreast of his talks, and he in turn seems to have had incomplete information on external developments. Political organisations inside the country were the last to be brought into the ring. From late 1988 there was certainly no shortage of opportunities for the ANC to keep the internal leadership informed. In October leaders of the Natal and Transvaal Indian Congresses had met with the ANC in Lusaka, and this was followed in November by a delegation from the South African Council of Churches. Then, in December 1988 the government moved Mandela from Pollsmoor Prison to Victor Verster Prison, outside Paarl, where he was given his own cottage and allowed visitors as he pleased.[37] UDF and other MDM leaders were able to visit him there. In January 1989 Moosa and Morobe travelled to Lusaka, ostensibly to attend a conference convened by the African America Institute, and to London, as part of an international diplomatic tour. They were thus able to hold detailed discussions with the ANC leadership.

Events inside the country soon tested the efficacy of communication between the ANC and the MDM. For some time political and religious leaders in Soweto had been becoming more and more concerned about the brutality of the Mandela United 'Football Club' based at Winnie Mandela's house in Soweto. Formed in 1986, the club served as bodyguards to Mrs Mandela – and terrorised residents of the area.[38] During 1988 tensions between members of the club and local residents had escalated, culminating in local school students burning down Winnie Mandela's house. At this point Nelson Mandela himself instructed that a Crisis Committee be formed to deal with the situation. The committee comprised Frank Chikane, Mufamadi, Rampahosa, Mokoena and Sister Bernard Ncube – all Soweto residents of high standing. Whilst the committee attempted to persuade Winnie Mandela to disband the club, the crisis deepened. In January 1989 it became clear that members of the club had murdered at least one youth activist. Eventually the Crisis Committee recognised that it had been unable to persuade Winnie Mandela to rein in her thugs; indeed, evidence was coming to light implicating her directly in acts of brutality. In February, following a meeting of the top MDM leadership and flanked by UDF co-president Gumede and COSATU president Barayi, Morobe read a statement to the press. Winnie Mandela was said to have 'abused the trust and confidence which she had enjoyed over the years'. The statement described her as a victim of repression, but went on to say: 'The Democratic Movement has uncompromisingly fought against violations of human rights from whatever quarter. We are not prepared to remain silent where those who are violating human rights claim to do so in the name of the struggle against apartheid.' The statement expressed outrage at the so-called football team and its reign of terror. The MDM called on people to ostracise her.[39]

Through most of this crisis there had been close consultation between internal leaders and the ANC. The Crisis Committee stayed in close contact with the ANC. In January Frank Chikane was briefing Tambo in London, and the committee's lawyer briefed him again in Lusaka, whilst Mandela was kept informed through his lawyer. But both Mandela and the ANC leadership in exile felt that the MDM press statement went too far. Morobe, together with COSATU's Jay Naidoo, was called urgently to Lusaka for two days of further discussions.[40] Although the MDM leaders seem to have been supported at the time, Morobe especially was made to pay for his role later.

Nor were meetings between the internal leadership and the ANC entirely effective in clarifying the situation with regard to negotiations. This became evident in March. Mandela sent a detailed memorandum to P.W. Botha setting out his position on negotiations. Rumours of this reached Govan Mbeki, who was still restricted to Port Elizabeth. Mbeki, a long-standing critic of Mandela's approach to politics,[41] was prompted to share his doubts with other political leaders inside the country. According to Sparks, 'word moved through the grapevine that Mandela's behaviour was suspect and that UDF members should not respond to invitations to visit him in Victor Verster Prison.' Sparks then quotes Boesak: 'There was a huge debate about it. People were worried, because they didn't know what Mandela was talking to the government about ... He had not consulted, and there was no greater sin in the UDF.'[42]

The crisis was solved by the ANC's Mac Maharaj. In 1988 he had returned to South Africa incognito, as part of the top-secret Operation Vul'indlela (Vula) to build a new integrated political and military machinery controlled inside the country. Using a laptop computer and modem, Maharaj was able to open new and direct lines of communication between South Africa and the ANC in exile. Maharaj obtained the full Mandela memorandum and showed it to UDF leaders in Johannesburg and to Mbeki in Port Elizabeth. 'When they saw the full text of the letter they realised they had misread Mandela's intentions. Within days we were able to sort the matter out. I sent a message to Mandela explaining how the trouble had arisen. He promptly sent invitations to Govan Mbeki and the others involved to come and see him.'[43]

This, and perhaps other misunderstandings, prompted the UDF, ANC and COSATU to convene a fuller meeting in Lusaka in June 1989. According to the official record of the meeting, as reported in the press, the three organisations identified the following immediate concerns:

> Our struggle is to take control of the process and ensure that negotiations, should they come about, are genuine and serious. For this reason it is imperative that:
> • We should all have the same agreed positions both inside and outside South Africa.
> • We have a strategy to remain in control so those who intervene have to deal with our position.
> • Our position should become an all-Africa position. This is crucial to our

ability to influence the rest of the world ... The world must deal with our
proposal rather than us having to deal with another initiative ...
We have to find ways of using the issue of negotiation to further divide/disrupt
the ruling class rather than have the issue divide us ... Also we have to ensure
that we do not demobilise the masses and that there is widespread consultation
among our people.[44]

From the ANC's side, the purpose of such meetings seems to have been not so
much to keep the UDF leadership fully informed as to indicate to the UDF the roles
that it should play in the changing political context. Information seems to have been
shared on a need-to-know basis. First, the UDF and other organisations were
charged with the task of building support within the country for a strategy that
included, centrally, talks with the enemy. Secondly, the UDF and other organisations
had to maintain pressure on the state inside the country. And, finally, they could
assist in intensifying international pressure.

UDF leaders energetically canvassed support for negotiations over the following
months. These issues were raised at a South African Council of Churches conference
in July. Soon after, Moosa and Frank Chikane spoke at COSATU's national congress.
Moosa told delegates that 'FW de Klerk has realised that ... either he enters into genuine negotiations with the ANC now, or he gets swept away by the rising tide of mass
militancy and action'. Frank Chikane said that popular resistance had pushed the
state 'to a point where it has no option but to talk about talks'. Morobe spoke at
length on negotiations at a 'consultative conference' held by the Transvaal Indian
Congress, also in July.[45]

Many commentators seem to have taken it as axiomatic that the UDF – and the
MDM more generally – was hostile to the kind of negotiations being pursued by the
ANC. There is certainly some evidence of suspicion. Apart from the tensions around
Mandela's March memorandum, some opposition to 'secret negotiations' was
expressed at the COSATU congress. Baskin reports that it was rumoured at the congress that Mandela was meeting with the government. NUMSA leader Mayekiso said
he believed that a solution would be reached through negotiations, but he did not
'believe that negotiations are near'.[46] Some of the unions were especially likely to be
suspicious, given their history of scepticism about the multi-class character and
nationalist project of the ANC and UDF. Suspicion, however, is not the same thing as
hostility. A series of UDF leaders had repeatedly emphasised support for a negotiated settlement, and this was not mere rhetoric. There may have been a problem selling a compromise settlement to particular constituencies of activists at the local
level, but not at the national or regional levels of the UDF.

Indeed, support among UDF and MDM leaders for a strategy involving negotiations probably strengthened during 1989, as they were drawn into diplomatic activity. In January 1989 Moosa and Morobe left South Africa, followed later by Khanyile.
Although their passports were endorsed for the United States only, they also visited
Sweden, the Netherlands, Germany and Canada, and, the press reported, 'are also
understood to have spent some time in Moscow', as well as Lusaka. In London they

had a long meeting with the British Deputy Foreign Secretary, Lynda Chalker. In June Albertina Sisulu led a UDF delegation to meet the British Prime Minister Margaret Thatcher, the new American President, George Bush, the French President, François Mitterrand, and the Swedish Prime Minister. The delegation included Mafolo, Ndlovu and Cachalia. The meeting with Thatcher was apparently the first between internal South African opposition leaders and a British prime minister since ANC founder Sol Plaatje and other leaders met with Lloyd George in 1919! Both meetings thus indicated the newly elevated status of the MDM and ANC. In July Cachalia and Molobi met with the Belgian Foreign Minister, and in August a large MDM delegation met with the Zambian and Zimbabwean Presidents, Kenneth Kaunda and Robert Mugabe, in Harare.[47]

Prospects for a negotiated settlement were given a boost in August, when the Harare Declaration was adopted at a meeting of the Organisation of African Unity in Harare. The declaration specified five preconditions for negotiations: lifting the State of Emergency, removing restrictions on political activity, releasing all political prisoners, legalising banned organisations and stopping all political executions.[48] The ANC had achieved the 'all-Africa position' it had aspired to.

Inside the country, UDF leaders sought to rebuild the organisation that had been weakened by the Emergency. Moosa set up an African Scholarship Trust, with an office in Johannesburg. On the surface, the Trust processed applications for bursaries granted through churches and other bodies. In practice, it served as a front for MDM organising.[49] The UDF also prepared budgets in the name of the MDM. Its budget for the 1989 calendar year provided for 158 employees, with total expenditure nearing R8 million.

BUILDING THE MASS DEMOCRATIC MOVEMENT

In mid-1989 the term Mass Democratic Movement began to be widely used among political organisations, in the media and even by government ministers, albeit with the prefix 'so-called'. After it had first surfaced a year before, the term had been used little during the months in late 1988 and early 1989. This may have been because it denoted a particular view of the alliance between COSATU and the UDF which was being challenged from within the trade unions by proponents of an anti-capitalist rather than an anti-apartheid front. An anti-apartheid front that included bantustan-based groups and 'liberal-capitalist collaborators' was said to rob 'the working class of its political independence and organisation', replacing 'its historic mission (striving for socialism) with the struggle to "win the moral high ground."'[50]

One argument for building broad alliances was put forward by Andrew Boraine, a former UDF NEC member. Boraine extended the old UDF and ANC argument about the middle ground. Broad alliances served, firstly, as a 'short-term defensive strategy', facilitating organisation building and opening up legal space. Alliances must complement and strengthen, rather than take the place of, organisation building. Secondly, he argued, alliances served to isolate apartheid. The MDM should provide leadership and direction for groupings which became disaffected from the

National Party government, and prevent them becoming forces of reaction in the future. But it was imperative, Boraine argued, that the different interests and aims within any alliance be recognised. 'Alliances should therefore be built around specific issues on which there is agreement.'[51]

The Charterist axis comprising the former UDF and the major part of COSATU were predominant, as their critics recognised.[52] In about April, COSATU and 'community based organisations' – the former UDF – met to chart a way forward for the MDM. Discussions were held over five issues: building the MDM under conditions of repression, negotiations, the ANC's Constitutional Guidelines, organising in the white community and building an anti-apartheid coalition. Activity was to focus on building organisation and alliances, in part through campaigns against repression and the remaining institutions of 'minority rule'.[53]

The meeting recommended that co-ordinating committees should be set up at national, regional and local levels. Further discussion took place at the joint UDF–COSATU–ANC meeting held in Lusaka in early June. The MDM assessed its own weaknesses: 'our inability to effectively implement programmes of action, ineffective communication with the grassroots, our dependence on foreign funds, our failure to make use of favourable conditions, and our inability to effectively counter enemy propaganda.' Thinking about 'the way forward', the MDM proposed a programme of action that was 'capable of firing up the imagination of the people and building up action to increasingly higher levels'. More concretely, the meeting suggested a 'defiance campaign with a mass character'.[54]

The general dominance of the anti-apartheid position was apparent at COSATU's third national congress. The congress was attended, as the previous congress had been, by representatives of what Jay Naidoo called the 'broader democratic movement' led by Moosa. The congress adopted two resolutions concerning alliances. First, it resolved to reconvene the anti-apartheid conference not later than October, recognising the importance of isolating apartheid and winning over all anti-apartheid forces. The convening committee would be led by COSATU and the UDF but with the full involvement of the churches, the National Council of Trade Unions (NACTU) and AZAPO. The objections of NUMSA were accommodated in a clause recording that 'At this stage we do not envisage inviting representatives of companies and big business.' Secondly, noting that its 1987 congress resolution on building the mass democratic movement had not been put into practice, COSATU reaffirmed its commitment to 'the strategic alliance of COSATU and UDF as crucial for unifying a wide range of anti-apartheid organisations from all classes and sectors of our people'. The emphasis should be on building a non-sectarian, grassroots-based civic movement. The congress also endorsed flexibility in tactical alliances at the local and regional levels but rejected 'any strategic alliance with representatives of big capital and participants in apartheid state structures'.[55]

Interviewed after the congress, the re-elected COSATU general secretary, Jay Naidoo, reiterated the importance of rebuilding the MDM, and especially building the civic movement. The goal was a restructured as well as a strengthened MDM.

> We would like to see the MDM transformed into a more co-ordinated structure of national sector organisations of youth, students, women, civics, and so on … This would facilitate structured and disciplined alliances with COSATU at local, regional and national levels.[56]

There was, Naidoo continued, 'general agreement within the MDM on this rebuilding process, much of which is going on around concrete struggles'. He added:

> What is clear to us is that there is a new mood of defiance among the people at the moment. It could be clearly seen at our congress. As a reflection of this, the MDM as a whole is opting for major mass campaigns in the next few months ahead. It is through these campaigns that the masses are going to create the legal spaces for their organisations. People are saying that they are not going to be bound by the State of Emergency.[57]

Curiously, besides brief references to opposing the Labour Relations Amendment Act and the Tricameral parliamentary elections, there was no discussion of specific campaigns in either the congress resolutions or the Naidoo interview.

The police later produced a draft resolution on a National Defiance Campaign, which was apparently not discussed at the congress. The draft envisaged three phases of protest: firstly, against segregated medical facilities; secondly, against other segregated facilities; and finally, against the banning and restriction of organisations and individuals. The campaign would culminate in a week of 'militant mass action', during the week of the Tricameral parliamentary elections.[58] In practice, the successive phases identified in this draft resolution were only to begin after the dates suggested, but the draft resolution makes it quite clear that planning for the defiance campaign had already gone far beyond the proposal raised at the June meeting with the ANC.

UDF leaders also made an effort to clarify what the MDM was. According to Morobe, the MDM:

- recognises the ANC as the vanguard in the national democratic struggle
- has organised formations like the UDF, COSATU, which form a strategic alliance
- has a mass approach to organisation thus involving the masses actively, purposefully and consistently in their struggles
- has or sought to have accountable leadership
- engages in alliances and campaigns on the basis of unity in action and united mass action behind a common programme.[59]

But there clearly remained some confusion, particularly within COSATU, as to what the MDM was. The report of a COSATU–UDF meeting (undated, but in September or early October) sought to 'clear up any confusion which may result from an incorrect view of the difference between a *movement* and an *organisation or federation of organisations*. The report described the 'core' of the MDM as COSATU, the UDF and their 'tried and tested allies', mass-based student, youth, women and civic organisations. This core had a unified ideological position based on commitment to the Freedom Charter, non-racialism, democracy and accountability, a commitment to working-class leadership, and so on. There were also 'forces that cluster around the MDM core', which might not have adopted the Freedom Charter, for example, but 'share with UDF and COSATU the basic principle and broad aim of a democratic, non-racial and unitary South Africa'. With regard to structures the report was emphatic: 'The MDM is not an organisation but a movement. It has no permanent structures.' But the document identified the need to build 'permanent structures to co-ordinate and streamline the functions of the MDM core, at a national, regional and local level', that is, to restructure the core of the MDM.[60]

The MDM had its critics, of course. Black Consciousness leaders denounced the MDM as neither mass nor democratic, arguing that it had been established without any democratic consultative process. They accused it of being led by a rich elite, whose 'values are entirely bourgeois' and who sought to use the MDM to 'achieve bourgeoisdom without the taint of apartheid'.[61]

VIOLENCE AND PEACE IN NATAL

In Natal UDF and COSATU activists faced not only state repression but also escalating violence from Inkatha. From late 1987 violent conflict coursed across the region. Almost a thousand people were killed in 1988 and thirteen hundred in 1989 in what Matthew Kentridge called South Africa's 'unofficial war'. The 'UDF' was one of the sides in this war: participants and observers spoke of 'UDF members', and above all of 'UDF areas'. People were killed for wearing a 'UDF' T-shirt or using 'UDF' greetings, or – far more often – just living in a 'UDF area'.[62] But there is no evidence that the UDF was a hierarchical, military formation. Many of the local leaders of UDF-affiliated organisations on the ground were involved in 'defence committees', but their relationship to the UDF regional or even sub-regional leadership was generally one of allegiance and identification rather than subordination and accountability. Later, at the beginning of the 1990s, some regional ANC leaders appear to have been involved in the distribution of weapons. But in the late 1980s the UDF, as a set of regional and sub-regional structures and personnel, played more limited, reactive roles, primarily concerned with peace initiatives. As the UDF's close ally COSATU put it in early 1989, organisation was 'poor' and their supporters were 'undisciplined'.[63]

State repression and Inkatha violence were not, of course, unconnected. As the Minister of Law and Order, Adriaan Vlok, put it: 'The police intend to face the future with moderates. Radicals, who are trying to destroy South Africa, will not be tolerated. We will fight them. We have put our foot in that direction and we will eventually win in the Pietermaritzburg area.'[64] The state would act against the UDF-aligned 'radicals' and support the Inkatha-aligned 'moderates'. There were almost no Inkatha supporters or leaders among the many detainees in the region, even though the police claimed they detained people not on a partisan basis but according to who was a threat to public order.[65] Police units operated as hit-squads, most notoriously in the Trust Feed massacre, where they ironically ended up killing Inkatha supporters by mistake.

The UDF's capacity to respond on a regional or even sub-regional level to the conflict with Inkatha was restricted by intense state repression. The February 1988 restrictions pushed the UDF in Natal further underground, which accentuated tensions around the regional 'cabal'. Even in the Natal Midlands, where a coherent sub-regional UDF leadership existed prior to the State of Emergency and 1988 restrictions, the UDF was weakened by divisions exacerbated by repression. The sub-regional leadership was almost completely detained in early 1988, including both co-secretaries Wittenberg and Ngwenya, as well as key Imbali-based leaders such as Reggie Radebe and Thami Mseleku. Wittenberg was released in July 1988, but Ngwenya and other African leaders were not released until 1989. In their absence a new leadership emerged, including Sipho Gqabashe of COSATU, Denis Sithole, a former teacher, Cassius Lubisi, a former student leader, and John Jeffrey, part of the COSATU legal team. This replacement leadership was soon riven by division.

Divisions within the Charterist movement in the Natal Midlands were shaped by external factors. First, some local activists were caught up in the plans of Aubrey Mokoena, of the Johannesburg-based Release Mandela Campaign, to build a national Charterist network outside and alternative to the UDF. Secondly, the veteran ANC and SACP leader Harry Gwala was released from jail on medical grounds in November 1988. Gwala became the nucleus of another rival Charterist leadership, allying with the post-1988 leaders against the mid-1980s leaders, such as Ngwenya, when he was eventually released, and drawing support especially from those areas politicised after 1987. In Durban the divisions were more local in origin. Discontent continued with the supposed cabal based in the Natal Indian Congress, especially as the cabal's members extended their control over financial resources. Older and more conservative township leaders led by Archie Gumede formed a group called *izingwevu*. Buthelezi continued to play on divisions within the Charterist movement. In a letter to Gumede, he accused Natal Indian Congress members of fanning the flames of 'black-on-black' confrontation.[66]

In the face of repression and, to a much lesser extent, division, COSATU assumed a more prominent role in regional politics. It organised a series of legal applications for court interdicts restraining vigilante leaders in the Pietermaritzburg area. The interdicts, brought in the name of 'ordinary citizens caught in the escalating and widening cycle of violence', involved serious and well-documented allegations of violent activities, including murder and arson, carried out by senior Inkatha leaders. The applications also documented the failure of the police to take action against named and identified Inkatha leaders.[67]

Their interaction over the interdict applications led to COSATU and Inkatha agreeing, in September 1988, to an accord governing the action of their members. The accord provided for the establishment of a neutral Complaints Adjudication Board to examine alleged breaches of the accord. But Inkatha soon ceased to co-operate, eventually prompting the formal withdrawal of COSATU. The UDF, being banned, could not formally be involved in the Accord with Inkatha or the Board. But Buthelezi later criticised the UDF's non-participation in the Board as evidence of its insincerity over peace. COSATU and UDF leaders retorted that COSATU had signed the accord and established the Board with the full support of the UDF:

> UDF leadership were informed of the proposal from the outset and endorsed it. Within the time constraints placed by the need to settle to [sic] court action UDF affiliates in the Pietermaritzburg area were consulted and endorsed the proposal. It was also known that UDF affiliates acknowledged that they were unable to consult all affiliate structures in the conditions imposed by the State of Emergency and the restrictions. However, the support for the proposal was quite clear and during the negotiations we canvassed the idea of joining UDF affiliates or UDF itself to the accord. It was decided that this was impractical.[68]

In an interview, however, COSATU leader Thami Mohlomi pointed to the problems that arose with regard to the Complaints Adjudication Board:

> Immediately after the first peace initiative, people were detained and the UDF was restricted ... That had a psychological effect on the youth who began to see the exercise of negotiation as futile. What peace can you make when you are being detained and restricted? The situation was very bad ...
> Some tensions began to arise between COSATU and UDF structures. Some leaders of UDF had been informed about the peace processes, but they were unable to convey that down to the rank-and-file membership because of the restrictions. So when the youth saw on TV and in the newspaper that COSATU and Buthelezi had signed an agreement, they naturally felt that they had not been properly consulted.[69]

In order to strengthen communication over peace initiatives, COSATU and the UDF formed a Joint Working Committee. The committee's core comprised, initially, Sandy Africa, Yunus Mahomed and Diliza Mji from the UDF, together with Jeffrey Vilane, Thami Mohlomi, Alec Erwin and Jayendra Naidoo from COSATU. As it was concerned with the entire Natal region, regional representatives also attended; these included Sipho Gqabashe from Pietermaritzburg and Willis Mchunu from northern Natal. National COSATU and UDF leaders, including Morobe, sometimes attended.

During 1989 the Joint Working Committee emerged as the key regional political decision-making structure, replacing the UDF REC. As it grew in importance, so its organisational structure became the subject of increased debate. Among its short-comings were inadequate links to local structures and inadequate representation of areas such as the towns of northern Natal, where there was a wave of protest during 1988–9, the south coast and some parts of Durban. In fact, the key strategic differences within the MDM in Natal were not so much between the UDF and COSATU as between activists in different areas. Pietermaritzburg leaders were said to be opposed to any meeting between the MDM and Inkatha, arguing that Inkatha could be defeated militarily, whereas Durban-based leaders favoured talks. After an MDM delegation consulted with the ANC in exile, it was agreed that the MDM should support peace talks.[70]

The major stumbling block to peace talks was Buthelezi. Talks were stalled whilst he insisted on meeting in Ulundi, despite his earlier statement that he would 'go to the ends of the earth to secure peace in Natal'. Finally, five-a-side talks began, with the MDM delegation comprising Naidoo and Erwin from COSATU; Mchunu, active in both unions and civic organisation in northern Natal; Gqabashe, similarly active in Pietermaritzburg; and Mji from the UDF. The UDF had a problem selecting a representative in the delegation: the REC comprised mostly Indian and coloured people, but it was agreed that the representative must be from an African area. Mji, a doctor, was chosen even though he did not attend REC and rarely attended RGC meetings. Recognising the need to keep their constituencies on board, COSATU and the UDF initiated a newsletter, *Ubumbano*, as well as holding joint meetings, workshops and rallies in the region. In July Morobe spoke at the first open-air rally in the province in over eighteen months. Full formal talks continued to be held up by Buthelezi's intransigence. Inkatha agreed to a meeting of delegations led by the presidents of the ANC, UDF, COSATU and Inkatha, and an accompanying peace process, but Buthelezi then held up these proposed talks with further demands. In September 1989 Buthelezi imposed a moratorium on top-level talks between Inkatha and the MDM, although peace talks proceeded at the local level.[71]

THE DEFIANCE CAMPAIGN

In August the UDF, together with its allies in the MDM, embarked on its first sustained mass protest since the Emergency began. Thousands of people across the country engaged in acts of civil disobedience, defying laws that segregated public and workplace facilities on racial grounds, as well as the Emergency restrictions placed on political activists. Through this Defiance Campaign the UDF and MDM were able to regain the political initiative, in part through seizing the moral high ground, as well as invigorating popular protest and helping to build fresh political organisation.

The idea of a defiance campaign arose in the ANC–UDF–COSATU meeting in Lusaka in early June. Frequent comparisons were drawn with the ANC's 1952 Defiance Campaign. There were important common features. The 1989 campaign was intended to rebuild mass organisation around the UDF and MDM just as the ANC had grown into a mass movement through the 1952 campaign. In addition, both campaigns were presented in terms of moral politics, or what Boesak had previously termed the 'politics of refusal'. The MDM described the 1989 campaign in the following way:

This is to be a peaceful programme of non-violent mass action, directed against apartheid laws and addressing the immediate needs and demands of our people. We are saying that we can no longer jail ourselves, nor accept seg-

regation and racial division, nor stand silent in the face of the crushing economic problems of the mass of our people.[72]

But there were also important differences. The 1989 campaign was intended not only
to mobilise people and indicate popular opposition to the state, but also to contest
the state's claim to be 'reformist'.

> While the government talks of democracy and an end to apartheid, it refuses to
> let us speak and sends its police to prevent our peaceful protests against segre-
> gation and apartheid laws. We hope that the world will take note of the true
> face of reform, and see the true colours of FW de Klerk, and listen to the voice
> of the majority of South African people.[73]

The UDF, as ever, had an eye on the international arena. Moreover, the 1989 campaign took place at a time of extraordinary weakness on the part of the state,
notwithstanding the apparent weaknesses of the MDM.

The campaign was accompanied by various demands. On one level, these were
deceptively straightforward: 'The solution to the situation is simple: throw open the
doors of all segregated facilities to all the people of South Africa.'[74] On another level
the demands were clearly more fundamental: 'We call for the unbanning of our leaders and organisations, release of all political prisoners and the return of exiles, the
end to the state of emergency, the withdrawal of the security forces from our townships and schools, and the abolition of all unjust and repressive apartheid laws.'[75] On
a third level, the demands were not particularly important at all. The campaign was,
above all, symbolic.

The campaign was couched in the language of civil rights, and the organisers
made a point of consulting with church leaders as well as involving them in individual protests. Leading churchmen endorsed the campaign. Boesak and Tutu issued a
joint statement, proclaiming that 'Laws and regulations which empower the government to restrict people's freedom of movement, their freedom to assemble and their
freedom of speech are evil.' Defying beach apartheid was, as the MDM put it, part of
making 'all God's places in South Africa open for all God's children'.[76]

The first phase of the Defiance Campaign comprised protests against the racial
segregation of hospitals. On 2 August black patients successfully presented themselves for treatment at hospitals reserved for white people. In Durban, two thousand
protesters gathered at Addington Hospital to support the nearly two hundred actual
patients. In Johannesburg, Pretoria, Krugersdorp and even Welkom there were much
smaller protests, and in the Cape apparently none at all at this stage. The protests
may have involved small numbers of people but attracted considerable local and
international attention, and the presence of foreign diplomats was seen as one reason
for the passivity of police. Later, a spokesman for the UDF-aligned National Medical
and Dental Association assessed the protests: 'The Campaign succeeded in publicising to the world that petty apartheid in health care still exists. Secondly, we managed
to get a foot in the door by getting black patients admitted to white hospitals.' But the

further objectives – of desegregating health care in practice and in policy – would require further pressure.[77]

UDF leaders spoke of further protests against the segregation of medical facilities, but the focus of the Defiance Campaign was to shift to a different aspect of segregation and a different region: beach apartheid, and the Western Cape. There had been no protests at Western Cape hospitals, but the Defiance Campaign had kicked off when 18 leading UDF activists, including almost the entire UDF REC, publicly announced that they would disregard their restriction orders. Two weeks later, the protests against beach apartheid began. On 19 August the MDM planned defiance at the whites-only beach at the Strand. A massive police presence, including roadblocks, prevented many protesters from reaching the beach. Those that did, including Archbishop Tutu, were eventually cleared off the beach by police with dogs and sjamboks. Journalists were detained, and film confiscated. Over a thousand protesters re-gathered on another 'whites-only' beach at Bloubergstrand. The brutal response of the police was a public relations disaster for the 'reformist' government. Two cabinet ministers later criticised the police. De Klerk clearly gave orders that future protests should be policed more 'softly'. When an estimated five to seven thousand protesters gathered on Durban's South and Addington beaches, the police were ordered not to use dogs or sjamboks.[78]

The state did not sit back entirely, however. Many top leaders were detained, including Moosa, Manuel, Ndlovu, Mafolo and many regional leaders from Cape Town and Durban. The state banned meetings scheduled for the UDF's 6th birthday in August, when UDF activists planned to declare the Front 'unbanned'. Such repression prompted some national leaders to advise Cape Town activists, who were especially brazen in their defiance of restrictions, not to push too fast lest the state be provoked to much greater repression and disorganise MDM structures that were slowly regaining their strength. But Cape Town activists were confident in their organisational capacity, and pushed ahead.[79]

The Defiance Campaign took many different forms across the country. In Pretoria the campaign focused on segregation in the municipal bus service. Protests were organised by the churches as part of a Standing for the Truth campaign. In the Border region, people marched on whites-only schools. At the same time, the trade unions called on their members to defy racial segregation and discrimination in the workplace. A black mineworker was shot dead by a white supervisor after sitting on the chairs reserved for white staff in a canteen, and drinking out of a whites-only teacup. The campaign fused into protests against the new Labour Relations Act which the government proposed to enact.[80] These all had some impact. But nationally and internationally these were soon overshadowed by protests against the Tricameral parliamentary elections.

The Defiance Campaign concluded with protests against the elections to all three chambers of the Tricameral Parliament on 6 September. An MDM statement described the parliament as 'discredited' and added that 'no amount of sweet-talking can coax us into accepting it as a democratic and legitimate structure'.[81] The major event was a two-day stayaway, involving more than three million workers. As Jay

Naidoo pointed out, more South Africans protested through staying away from work than actually voted in the elections. But the smaller protests and the police reaction attracted even more national and international attention. A march in central Cape Town on 2 September was dispersed by police using water cannons with purple dye; Boesak was among the many marchers arrested. Protests in Mitchell's Plain and elsewhere were broken up with great brutality, prompting criticism by a police lieutenant, Gregory Rockman, who described the riot police as behaving like 'wild dogs' with a 'killer instinct'. (Rockman lost his job, but his allegations were justified in court). On election night itself, Cape Town's townships became battle zones, with 23 people allegedly killed and over a hundred injured by the security forces. Internationally, this police action prompted very critical media coverage.[82]

Once again, De Klerk ordered that demonstrations should be policed with more restraint. He also gave permission for a mass march in Cape Town, on 13 September, and clearly instructed the police to hold back. An estimated 30 000–50 000 people, including the mayor of Cape Town and Democratic Party MPs, marched through Cape Town in protest against security force actions. Tutu and Boesak addressed the crowd from the balcony of Cape Town's City Hall, adorned with the flags of the ANC and UDF. 'Loop Kaapstad Oop' (Walk Cape Town Open) proclaimed the posters. The success of the Cape Town march led to further marches being held elsewhere over the following days, with protests against repression and racial segregation fusing with opposition among workers to a proposed new Labour Relations Act. An estimated 20 000–25 000 people marched in central Johannesburg. Some 80 000 people marched in Uitenhage; 40 000 in East London; 20 000 in Durban; 50 000 in Port Elizabeth. There were marches in small towns also: 8000 people marched through Oudtshoorn, 7000 in Secunda. ANC (and even SACP) flags were flown at many of these marches.[83]

The marches symbolised the success of the Defiance Campaign. The campaign had struck at the government's weakest spots: racial segregation and police brutality. In the face of greatly increased pressure from abroad and from white economic and intellectual elites inside South Africa, the new President, De Klerk, was certainly not willing to allow police brutality in defence of racial segregation. Confronted by mass defiance of racial segregation, he promised to repeal the relevant Separate Amenities Act. Nor was De Klerk prepared to sanction police brutality in the suppression of peaceful demonstrations of support for the ANC. Negotiations with the ANC had reached the stage when the question was more when, rather than whether, the ANC would be brought into open political life. There was no point in incurring international and local costs through repressing popular support for a course of action that the government itself was contemplating.

In the aftermath of the Defiance Campaign the political situation changed rapidly. In September the National Intelligence Service met with the ANC's Thabo Mbeki and Jacob Zuma in Switzerland. In October De Klerk released Walter Sisulu and all the other jailed top ANC leaders excepting Mandela himself. The MDM organised receptions for the released prisoners under the slogan 'ANC Lives, ANC Leads'. Whilst the ANC was now clearly at the centre of opposition politics, other supportive organisations were being revitalised: UDF regions began to hold long overdue AGMs and employ yet more organisers, and the National Education Crisis Committee held national and regional conferences with the theme of 'Preparing to Govern'. In December a UDF delegation openly met with Mandela. Molefe and Lekota were released from jail after their appeal against conviction of treason was upheld; they resumed their posts in the formally banned UDF, with Moosa and Morobe moving to assistant general secretary and assistant publicity secretary respectively. As Carolus put it after the Western Cape UDF held its AGM in December: 'The overwhelming feeling was that the Front had battled through over three years of harsh repression ... and had emerged victorious.'[84]

The Defiance Campaign helped to revitalise local organisation and militancy at a time when talks between the ANC and the government had reached a crucial point. As the MDM itself declared, the campaign had demonstrated 'to our people' once again that it was possible to resist apartheid, and had rendered the State of Emergency 'virtually unworkable'.[85]

CONFERENCE TIME: ANTICIPATING POLITICAL CHANGE

As 1989 drew to an end it became ever clearer that fundamental political change was in the offing, and that negotiations would play a major part in this. The UDF was involved in two conferences concerned with aspects of the anticipated transition. First, through the MDM, the Front was involved in a Conference for a Democratic Future, initially planned for October but finally held in December. The conference was to focus on the roles of negotiations, popular protest and international action in the final stages of the struggle against apartheid. Secondly, through the Kagiso Trust, the Front was involved in a conference in January on the theme of 'From Opposing to Governing: How Ready is the Opposition?'. Just eighteen months before it had been almost inconceivable that either conference could have been held: the state would not have allowed them, and the UDF–MDM would not have imagined the themes worthwhile. That the two conferences took place was evidence of the rapidity and extent of political change since about September 1988.

The Conference for a Democratic Future (CDF) was, in some respects, the successor to the proposed Anti-Apartheid Conference, which the state had banned in September 1988. Support had grown within COSATU for an anti-apartheid, as opposed to an anti-capitalist, coalition. In June 1989 the MDM announced that the CDF would be held later in the year, and a Convening Committee was established. The Committee comprised two leaders from each of the UDF, COSATU, AZAPO, the churches, and the smaller Black Consciousness-aligned trade union federation, NACTU.[86]

Morobe expressed the significance of the conference in terms of its breadth, and hence its prefigurative potential:

The remarkable nature of this conference is the diversity of those who will attend. This is not a conference of any one particular tendency within the liberation movement, but of all the people for all the people. It is a democratic conference and minor differences emerging among the participants would be part of the democratic process ... The CDF is a forerunner of genuine people's assemblies, a dry run, giving people an inkling of what a future and genuinely democratic parliament might look like.[87]

This supposed breadth had to be limited in order to mollify critics within the trade unions and the Black Consciousness movement. The MDM leadership agreed, therefore, that participation should be based on acceptance of a 'Unifying Perspective' and an accompanying policy statement. The Unifying Perspective listed a set of political rights acceptable to all opponents of apartheid. But the policy statement was more restrictive. Participants in the CDF were required to 'be associated both in principle and deed with the oppressed and exploited and be committed to the destruction of all apartheid structures', to 'be committed to the unification of our country' and to 'commit ourselves, our organisational structures and the people of this country to mass action for the total eradication of oppression and exploitation'. Organisations such as the Consultative Business Movement, liberal parties in parliament and 'progressive' bantustan leaders such as Transkei's General Holomisa could attend as observers but not as full participants. Inkatha was not invited, and did not apply to attend. Despite agreeing to the above position, NACTU pulled out of the CDF shortly before it began, although some of its officials and affiliates decided to defy the federation and participate.[88]

The purpose of the conference was set out in a booklet distributed within the MDM beforehand. The conference would examine the role of negotiations, draw up a programme of mass united action to defeat apartheid ('the most ambitious programme of mass action to date', said Morobe),[89] and consider the role of international pressure, especially sanctions. The conference would help to forge broad consensus among internal organisations, and emphatically demonstrate to the outside world the views of 'the majority of South Africans' on these issues. The MDM booklet included a discussion paper on 'negotiations as a terrain and method of struggle'.

The conference was enormous, with almost 4500 people from over 2100 organisations packing into the venue at the University of the Witwatersrand. It reportedly cost R1 million, a massive sum for the time.[90] But it was curiously unmomentous. One reason for this was the divisions that were apparent from the outset. The keynote addresses were given by recently released Walter Sisulu and AZAPO's Itumeleng Mosala. Whilst Sisulu was positive about negotiations, focusing on the need to ensure that they were democratic and participatory, Mosala came across as much more wary, even hostile. It was resolved that a new constitution should be drawn up by a fully representative Constituent Assembly, but the Black Consciousness organisations were unwilling to accept the Harare Declaration. A more important reason for the limited importance of the conference was inherent in its public character. Positions on negotiations adopted in the full glare of public attention were primarily of symbolic importance: the more important positions were being presented and argued over in the continuing bilateral talks between the government and the ANC.

The Kagiso Trust conference held the following month had a much lower profile but was perhaps at least as significant as the CDF. Since 1986 the Kagiso Trust had been dispensing money from foreign governments to anti-apartheid groups inside the country. Until 1989 it paid little attention to the uses to which its funds were put, but then its donors began to exert more pressure on it to ensure that its funds were used constructively. At the same time, civic and political leaders – most visibly in Soweto, through the Soweto People's Delegation – had been drawn into local negotiations with state structures over rent boycotts. Facing an opportunity to table their demands for ending rent boycotts, they were pushed to thinking through issues of administration and development in very concrete terms. On top of this, the prospect of a negotiated settlement at the national level raised the question of what would follow, and how the hitherto extra-parliamentary opposition would manage government.

The opening speech at the conference was given by the UDF's Trevor Manuel, under the title of 'Preparing to Govern'. Manuel separated his discussion of the 'readiness to govern' into, first, 'securing power' and, secondly, 'retaining power'. With regard to the former, Manuel warned against 'all the glib talk about our strength'. The promise of negotiations could seduce people into passivity. He contrasted South Africa with countries like East Germany, where there had been marches of as many as half a million people (or ten per cent of the population). With regard to retaining power, Manuel bemoaned the lack of serious grappling with the challenges of transition: 'We lack the boldness to differ with our constituency, to challenge and debate key issues. We lack the boldness to move our constituency in the direction that secures our future. We lack the boldness required for transformation.'[91] Another UDF speaker at the conference, Morobe, went even further:

> We remember only too well the situation in the townships during the period described as a 'period of people's power', [when local government structures] … could no longer function. We had very strong civic associations springing up in almost all the areas, but a serious problem obtained: Community Councillors left their jobs, and a huge vacuum was formed. We did not know what to do with the Community Council structures, we did not know what to do, in fact, with the authority, the power, that had already come into the hands of the people. Perhaps history is on our side in that liberation did not come then. At least it has given us yet another chance to be able to reflect and to develop our positions to even stronger heights.[92]

Manuel's response was primarily political. He called for stronger organisation (reviving the old UDF refrain) as a requirement for 'a smooth transition'. 'I would like to suggest that the most important requirement is ORGANISATION; organisation which is solid, impervious to state strategy, organisation which is rooted and accountable, organisation which is capable of regenerating leadership at all levels.'[93] But he also called for 'more intensive strategising which takes account of the fine balancing act which the period of transition requires of us – the fine balancing act required between destroying and, already at this stage, beginning some sort of process of reconstruction.'[94]

Development was put more squarely on the agenda in a speech by Eric Molobi, who was a trustee of the Kagiso Trust, and one of several UDF-linked activists to have moved to the Trust; others included Vincent Mogane and Stone Sizani. Molobi told the conference that in order to challenge the government effectively, the extra-parliamentary opposition needed to acquire expertise in developmental fields. With reference to the Kagiso Trust in particular, he said:

> We must change our outlook and begin to consider development as the biggest challenge. We have to begin to think of ourselves, in a sense, as a department of a government-in-waiting, meaning that as an alternative funding agency we will be dealing with areas that should be dealt with by the present government but which it is incapable of or unwilling to deal with.[95]

Indeed, development was to become central to UDF activity during the following year.

The two conferences, although overshadowed by the spectacular unbanning of the ANC and release of Mandela so soon afterwards, were in their own ways turning-points. The CDF was held not only in public but also on a scale altogether unprecedented for the UDF and its allies. It indicated clearly that the Emergency had lost its bite. It also indicated, whatever the rhetoric of some speakers, the subordination of mass action to the requirements of the negotiation process. The Kagiso Trust conference indicated the beginnings of a major mindshift in the thinking of the leaders of the UDF and its allies, as they began to anticipate becoming a government with the responsibilities that were to go with it.

CONCLUSION

The period 1988–9 was bounded by a repressive clampdown at the one end and an unprecedented upsurge in expectations of political change at the other. In February 1988 the UDF had been banned, and through most of 1988 UDF leaders had expected that repressive conditions would continue to govern their conduct for the indefinite future. Through 1989 they embarked on a series of defiant actions that eroded the impact of the state's restrictions, just as talks between the government and the ANC were raising the prospect of fundamental political change as an imminent probability. By the end of 1989 the UDF was on the verge of resuming full and public political activity.

These shifts were to some extent the result of the activities of the UDF, its affiliates and allies, especially COSATU, inside the country: their (very qualified) resilience in the face of repression raised the level and hence the political costs of repression required to ensure quiescence; their opposition to municipal elections severely constrained the state's ability to recruit legitimate collaborators; and their seizure of the political initiative over rent boycotts and urban development secured them a leading role in urban politics. The Defiance Campaign exposed both the segregationist underbelly of a supposedly reformist government and the state's continuing predilection for brutality. By forging a close alliance with the labour movement, the UDF was able both to harness the strength of the unions' support bases and to take advantage of their relative exemption from repression. By building alliances with disaffected white economic and intellectual elites, the UDF further eroded the moral and political position of the government.

But these activities were of secondary importance compared to the effects of the changing political environment. The government was under enormous international pressure to negotiate with the ANC. Its various lines of communication with the ANC had led it to believe that some kind of negotiated settlement with the ANC was not only possible but also acceptable. Conditions inside the country were important not so much in terms of determining the most important political developments in the near future – the legalisation of the ANC and beginning of direct talks – but rather in shaping the prospective bargaining positions of the ANC and the government in such a transitional phase. The government's position would be strengthened if it could recruit collaborators; weakened, if there was an upsurge in popular protest and ANC-aligned organisation.

Chapter Ten

The Dissolution of the UDF, 1990–1

The prohibition of the African National Congress, the Pan Africanist Congress, the South African Communist Party and a number of subsidiary organisations is being rescinded ... the Government has taken a firm decision to release Mr Nelson Mandela unconditionally.[1]

The unbanning of the ANC and other organisations, announced by F.W. de Klerk in his speech opening parliament on 2 February 1990, marked the start of the period of transition that was to take South Africa from apartheid to a non-racial, multi-party democracy. This transition brought a fundamental transformation of South Africa's extra-parliamentary opposition. Most obviously, the ANC was transformed into a political party focused on contesting democratic elections and governing South Africa. To get to that position the ANC openly rebuilt its structures inside the country, held regional and national conferences, engaged in full-scale negotiations over constitutional change and other issues, prepared policies, and then in 1993 was drawn into the executive activities of government.

Less dramatically, the UDF faded away before finally disbanding formally in August 1991. There was a certain inevitability to the organisational shift from the UDF to the ANC. As Peter Mokaba, president of SAYCO, argued: 'the UDF has no distinct platform apart from that of the ANC ... It has adopted the Freedom Charter as a principle ... Its membership must become part of the ANC ... Now that the ANC can operate legally, the UDF is redundant.'[2] The organisational shift seems more inevitable still with hindsight, as it corresponded to or reflected broader changes: from anti-apartheid defiance and confrontation in the 1980s to the politics of negotiation, development and reconstruction in the 1990s. The dissolution of the UDF seems just part of these changes: a logical, unavoidable, even unremarkable event.[3]

But at the time the future of the UDF was far from clear, and there was persistent and widespread support for the UDF's continuing to operate in some form. In the first half of 1990 many UDF and ANC leaders agreed that the UDF should continue to co-ordinate socio-economic struggles whilst the ANC assumed responsibility for political struggles. Later it was argued that the UDF should be transformed into a non-partisan co-ordinating structure for organisations in civil society involved in developmental struggles. Not until early 1991 did it become clear that the Front could not continue, however thoroughly transformed. The UDF was dissolved not by design on the part of the top ANC or UDF leadership, but because of the breadth and depth of opposition and even hostility to the UDF leadership and the UDF as a co-ordinating body. Diverse groups within the broad Charterist movement saw the UDF as the vehicle of leaders whom they did not like and who, they were pretty sure, did not like them either – as a body which pursued strategies and tactics that they disapproved of, and which controlled resources that should be reallocated elsewhere. The final chapter in the history of the UDF is the story of an attempt to transform the Front to play new roles in new times, an attempt that was frustrated by the political forces unleashed under the umbrella of an unbanned ANC.

THE UDF IN EARLY 1990

The ANC was unbanned just as the UDF itself was being revived. At the end of 1989 the UDF's structures were in disarray after more than three years under a nationwide State of Emergency and two years of effective banning. Amidst the resurgence of political protest and defiance in the second half of 1989, MDM leaders had quietly charted the organisational revival of the Front. At the national level several planning meetings were held, although most top activists were distracted by preparations for the Conference for a Democratic Future. But the UDF quietly began to revive its regional and even sub-regional structures. Regional organisers were employed, and AGMs were held in most regions: the Southern Transvaal in October, the Western Cape in December, the Eastern Cape in January 1990, and Northern Cape in February. The Pretoria Area Committee resumed public activity in about October 1989, and a Bloemfontein Action Committee was formed in November with the intention of building regional organisation in the Orange Free State. Natal was the only major region where the UDF was not resurrected, although regional organisers were employed here. In Natal most of the Front's roles had been taken over by a Joint Working Committee nominally comprising COSATU and the UDF but in practice increasingly independent of the latter. The revival was both encouraged and facilitated as repression eased off. Restrictions were rescinded on over a hundred people, including UDF treasurer Cachalia, whilst Molefe, Lekota and Stofile were all released from jail.

In mid-January 1990 the NEC of the UDF met publicly for the first time since 1986, in open defiance of the state's restrictions. 'By its action', Molefe later wrote, 'the UDF was challenging the Government, claiming its inalienable right to articulate the aspirations of the oppressed freely and peacefully.'[4] The meeting was primarily concerned with the practical aspects of rebuilding UDF structures and resuming public activity. Molefe and Lekota formally resumed their posts. An outline programme of action was drawn up, and it was agreed that this would be discussed in a consultative forum of the MDM in February and then formally adopted at a conference of the UDF's National General Council (NGC) in April. The NEC suggested that the UDF's strategy should take advantage of the momentum generated by the Conference for a Democratic Future, engaging 'the middle ground and broader anti-apartheid forces at all levels, including the "homeland" leaders, more effectively'. The Defiance Campaign would be intensified.[5]

The UDF's challenge was explicitly spelt out at a press conference following the NEC meeting. The UDF would resume its political activities in order, it said, to intensify the struggle. According to Morobe, 'In what we see as a challenging period ahead of us, we have decided to claim our rights, to engage in open opposition activities. We owe it to our people that the leadership of our movement is openly available at this crucial movement in the struggle for freedom and democracy in our country and the world over.'[6] Cachalia added: 'Since the UDF's restriction there have been no public campaigns under the UDF banner. We merely concentrated on holding the organisation together. Now we will resume high-profile activities such as those prior to the restrictions.'[7] Soon after this, UDF leaders accompanied released ANC leader Walter Sisulu and other ex-prisoners to consult with the exiled ANC leadership in Lusaka. Plans were made for a UDF delegation to meet Mandela in jail in February.

The state's response was typically bureaucratic. Adriaan Vlok, the Minister of Law and Order, spelt out the formal channels through which the UDF could apply to have its 1988 restrictions lifted.

> The regulations ... made allowance for the UDF to apply to the Minister to carry on with its activities and operations. I therefore invite the UDF to let me have the necessary representations. However, should the UDF violate the restrictions placed on it without permission, it could be a transgression of the emergency regulations and the alleged infringement will be investigated in the normal course and handed in to an attorney-general for a decision.[8]

But, just two weeks later, the restrictions on the UDF were formally lifted as part of F.W. de Klerk's sweeping political liberalisation.

De Klerk was expected to announce some kind of an initiative in his speech opening parliament on 2 February 1990, but almost everyone was taken by surprise when he announced the unbanning of the ANC, PAC and especially the SACP. Indeed, De Klerk had organised a massive publicity effort to downplay expectations. Even the ANC was taken by surprise.[9] De Klerk also announced the rescinding of Emergency restrictions on the UDF and 32 other organisations, on almost 400 former detainees, and (incompletely) on the media.

De Klerk had decided to unban the ANC, it seems, almost as soon as he assumed the presidency in August 1989, and the cabinet agreed at a *bosberaad* at the beginning of December.[10] While we await a fully persuasive analysis of why De Klerk, hitherto regarded as conservative, accepted in late 1989 the need for boldness, existing accounts sketch the key elements of an explanation. First, the internal political situation had reached a kind of stalemate, in which opponents of apartheid did not believe they had the capacity to seize state power but the government was unable to secure either a sufficient level of popular quiescence or credible collaborators to bolster indirect rule in the urban areas. Under considerable pressure both internationally and from local business and the intellectual elite, the government had recognised that it needed, at the very least, to reform the political system. But reforms were failing to generate political support among African people in the short term, whilst, it seems, the security chiefs pointed to the difficulties of managing a piecemeal process of change. This led to De Klerk realising, as Sparks puts it, 'that you cannot reform an oppressive system, that if you start to relax it you have to go the whole hog'.[11]

At a deeper level, De Klerk's decision reflected the underlying social changes identified in Chapter 1. There had been enormous growth in the size of the African urban industrial working class and of the nascent, upwardly mobile African middle class, both classes were not only frustrated by the social and economic restrictions of apartheid but also excluded from political citizenship. It was these classes that had provided the backbone of the independent trade union movement, the civic and youth organisations, and of the UDF itself. The state was totally unable to solve the fast-growing 'urban African' problem. As the declining labour-repressive agrarian elites lost influence over the state, so the state sought more subtle and less overtly racist ways of protecting inequality and privilege.

The unbanning of the ANC provoked elation within the UDF leadership but also aroused suspicion and wariness. The State of Emergency and Internal Security Act remained in force, political trials continued, and the future of many political prisoners remained obscure. The UDF believed that the government was attempting to seize back the moral high ground, restore confidence in the economy, and demobilise opposition, but had only partially embraced the need for change. The government wanted to remain 'the pivot of all political processes and the dispenser of concessions … De Klerk, having only jumped in the Rubicon, is yet to cross it. Caught midstream, he will just have to contend with the swirling tide for democracy.' The UDF boldly concluded: 'The structures of the UDF should be maintained. There can be no question of the UDF disbanding at this stage.'[12]

The UDF's plans for formulating a programme of action and resuming public activity were thrown into confusion by these dramatic events. The first NEC meeting after De Klerk's speech was largely taken up with assessing the new situation and planning immediate responses, including practical arrangements for rallies and so on. The NEC briefly discussed the UDF's future strategy, emphasising the contest over the middle ground, and identified a number of specific campaigns to be taken up. But the meeting recognised that key issues were no longer clear, and one of these was the future of the UDF itself.[13] The scheduled two-day MDM Consultative Forum was cancelled, and the NGC scheduled for April was downgraded to the status of a national workshop.

An immediate challenge facing UDF leaders, along with other MDM leaders, was to organise for Mandela's release from jail. The task was complicated by the need to liaise not only with Mandela himself but also with Winnie Mandela, who had a strained relationship with key MDM leaders. A National Reception Committee (NRC) had already been formed, with Morobe and Cachalia from the UDF, trade unionists, including Ramaphosa as chairman, and church leaders such as Frank Chikane. It seems that the committee was caught on the hop by the suddenness with which Mandela was released. Mandela was given very little notice of the date and time of his release. Just hours before, he phoned 'a number of people from the ANC and the UDF to come to the cottage to prepare for [his] release and work on [his] speech'; these included Ramaphosa and Manuel.[14]

After leaving prison, Mandela addressed a rally on Cape Town's Grand Parade that evening. The following afternoon he addressed a huge welcome rally at Johannesburg's FNB stadium. Mandela's Cape Town speech has been strongly criticised by Waldmeir: 'Radical UDF leaders, profoundly suspicious of De Klerk, had penned a speech from hell, a speech without warmth, vision or humanity; a speech for the political warpath.' With an audience of millions across the country and the world, this was 'a missed opportunity of epic proportions'. The speech was unconciliatory, calling for the intensification of the struggle; it was not, in Waldmeir's view, the speech of a statesman.[15] Whatever the merits of the speech itself, its authorship cannot simply be attributed to 'radical UDF leaders' alone. Firstly, the speech seems to have been an NRC effort, not only the work of UDF leaders. Secondly, the call to intensify the struggle was one being made in January by sections of the ANC leadership in exile. The ANC was itself unsure how to respond to the rolling political liberalisation inside the country. Thirdly, Mandela himself says that he 'spoke from the heart'[16] – not words describing a speech entirely penned by others. The view that the struggle should be intensified was widespread, reflecting a similarly widespread suspicion of De Klerk and, probably, a recognition that political organisation and protest was still limited inside the country as a result of the long period of repression.

The important role played by certain UDF leaders in the Reception Committee did not automatically translate into influence within the ANC. Winnie Mandela, especially, harboured a grudge against those UDF leaders associated with the MDM's condemnation of her and her 'football club' the previous year. According to Gilbey, Winnie Mandela sought to ostracise Cachalia, and it was widely rumoured at the time that she had demanded that Morobe be thrown off the plane carrying her husband and herself to Johannesburg the day after his release. Mrs Mandela was to be rehabilitated quickly within the ANC.[17]

The ANC required the services of some of its most experienced underground members in the job of rebuilding itself above ground after February, however, and many senior UDF leaders were thus pulled into top ANC positions. Gumede, Lekota, Molefe, Stofile and Suttner became members of the ANC's Internal Leadership Core (ILC), formed to complement the ANC's NEC in exile. Moosa also moved across as secretary of the ILC. Among the ANC's interim regional conveners appointed in April were UDF leaders Lekota (southern Natal), Manuel (Western Cape), Stofile (Border), Makunyane (Northern Transvaal) and Khasu (Northern Cape). These regional conveners also served on the ANC's ILC. Gumede and Carolus were members of the ANC delegation that met with the government in Cape Town in May in the first open direct negotiations. Ndlovu was also drawn into ANC work, which included helping the ANC's Jacob Zuma make the initial arrangements for the return of ANC exiles and the release of the remaining political prisoners.[18]

The UDF leadership was severely denuded through this transfer into the fledgeling ANC. But the fact that the ANC did not simply take over the UDF, use it as a convening structure, or even take over its offices – the ANC opened a head office in Johannesburg in March – indicated important differences between the organisations. One reason for this was, as Lodge suggests, the need for 'insurance against the Government changing its mind about the ANC's freedom'.[19] At least as important were the internal politics of the Charterist movement inside South Africa. Notwithstanding the overlap between the ANC's ILC and the UDF, key sections of the Charterist movement were either outside the UDF, in COSATU for example, or were actually hostile to it. The latter included some of SAYCO's leaders, most Durban-based leaders, Harry Gwala in Pietermaritzburg, Aubrey Mokoena and the Release Mandela Campaign leadership, Govan Mbeki, civic leaders in several regions, and (of course) Winnie Mandela herself.

The big question facing the UDF was what, if anything, it should do now that the ANC was being rebuilt. The ANC's ILC advised that it was up to the UDF's structures themselves to decide on the UDF's future. Charterist critics of the UDF proposed that it and its affiliates should simply disband and join the ANC. But the predominant view through the first half of 1990 was that the UDF should continue, with newly demarcated roles for it and the ANC. The UDF NEC suggested in March that

- the ANC should assume National Political Leadership;
- the UDF should retain its presence at national, regional and local levels;
- the policy positions of the UDF should be informed by those of the ANC;
- the UDF should participate fully in the establishment of ANC branches ...;
- the ANC should be requested to brief the UDF on all important developments and vice versa.[20]

The NEC's position on the interim role of the UDF was broadly endorsed by the UDF's regions and affiliates at its National Workshop in April, and reconfirmed by the NEC in July. The UDF 'cannot continue to exist as in the past', particularly since key affiliates such as SAYCO were already merging into the ANC. Pending further discussion on the UDF's long-term future it 'should continue to play the role of co-ordinating campaigns such as land, rent and other issues'. It should also help to build the ANC. It should no longer act as any kind of political vanguard, nor should it provide political co-ordination. These roles should be played by the ANC, or by a new patriotic front embracing the ANC and other anti-apartheid groups to carry forward and extend the alliance building of the Conference for a Democratic Future.[21]

The UDF's proposed role combined uneasily two very different components. On the one hand, the UDF would continue to co-ordinate its affiliates, mobilise mass action over issues that were not national political issues, and develop sectoral organisation, all on a supposedly non-partisan basis. UDF and ANC leaders talked of people having dual membership of the ANC and UDF, to the supposed benefit of each. As Carolus put it:

> We can foresee that there will be a much closer working relationship with the ANC now that the organisation has been legalised. This will obviously strengthen both organisations. The UDF has never seen itself as substituting the role the ANC has played and continues to play, despite being banned. We foresee that the ANC will take its rightful place in the community, and one which the UDF has never occupied.[22]

At the same time, the UDF would make a priority of building the ANC. 'All UDF structures (national, regional, and local) and members must help in the building of the ANC and SACP', proclaimed the UDF at the start of its 'organisational development' programme adopted in April.[23] In July the NEC noted: 'The building of the ANC cannot happen without the full participation of the UDF. All UDF structures and affiliates should be encouraged to double their work in building the ANC. Campaigns should be used to recruit for the ANC.'[24] When NEC members raised their concern over 'the possible "bleeding" of the UDF' as the ANC poached its staff, they were reminded that the 'UDF should always remember that the ANC needs the best cadres to re-establish itself'.[25]

In other words, the UDF and ANC were to remain separate but with very close links; they would engage in different activities but in synchrony; and the UDF would be ostensibly non-partisan whilst serving the interests of the ANC. This balancing act required much closer liaison than was achieved. The UDF's NEC raised its concern 'about inadequate communication between the ANC and UDF structures' and 'strongly urged those UDF members on the ILC to report consistently to the UDF structures on every decision taken by the ANC'. In practice, the attempted parallel development of ANC and UDF structures was both confusing and unworkable. The 'doubling of work' in building the ANC meant that UDF work was neglected, and the UDF's role remained obscure, almost mysterious. As Molefe later noted, the April 1990 decisions 'had a negative impact on the organisational capacity of the UDF and its affiliates', particularly because 'it was unclear what role the UDF was going to play'.[26]

REBUILDING THE UDF

From the end of 1989 through the first half of 1990, UDF leaders sought to strengthen affiliates and rebuild structures weakened by repression. In Molefe's words:

> Although the State of Emergency did not break the resilience nor dampen the fighting spirit of our people, it left many affiliates in a bad state of disorganisation. No regular meetings could be held. Many experienced activists were either detained or killed by the agents of the regime. Scores left the country. All these impacted upon the organisation of the UDF and its affiliates.[27]

This was true at regional as well as national levels. The Eastern Cape regional secretary noted, for example, that the region had 'been in a mess over the past five years'.[28]

The UDF leadership's first concern was to re-establish its national office. During early 1990 the UDF's national leadership was in constant flux, with the loss of Lekota, Moosa and Ndlovu to the ANC, and of Morobe, who went to study abroad. By July, therefore, Molefe was the only senior national leader continuing to perform UDF work full-time. Molefe desperately asked other NEC members to do more than just attend meetings.[29] After that the situation improved: Titus Mafolo was employed as publicity secretary, Pat Lephunya as national civic organiser, and Cas Coovadia joined to improve financial management.

In most regions, as at the national level, there was an enthusiastic spurt of organisation building in the first half of 1990: offices were opened, equipped and staffed, leaders were elected, and budgets and programmes of action were drafted. Generous funding from abroad continued despite the unbanning of the ANC. Most regions had about half a dozen organisers and administrative staff, although the Southern Transvaal employed no fewer than 15 organisers. In total, about 40 people were employed by the UDF regions during 1990–1. But the rebuilding of the UDF was also beset by problems. Regional meetings, in contrast to national meetings, were held irregularly and often poorly attended. Elected leaders and paid employees prioritised building the ANC and neglected UDF work, whilst divisions or hostility severely undermined the UDF in several regions. The high point of UDF regional organisation was reached in mid-1990 when successful Regional General Councils were held in most regions, and several sub-regional structures were active.

Sub-regional structures were revived or formed in several areas. In the Eastern Cape zonal structures were formed in the Albany area around Grahamstown in late 1989, followed by the Midlands around Cradock, and Tsitsikamma, which included Uitenhage, in early 1990. In the Southern Transvaal region the Pretoria Area Committee organised an impressive range of activities. This Area Committee was somewhat anomalous, however, as it operated semi-independently of the Southern Transvaal region, almost as an additional region in the Transvaal. In the Orange Free State, there were active Area Committees in Bloemfontein and Welkom, although their rivalries prevented them from forming an overall regional structure.

Organisational revival often brought political differences out into the open, as rival sections of the Charterist movement sought to consolidate power in various institutions. Such differences within or involving the UDF inhibited its organisation building in the regions and at the national level. There were important differences between UDF regional structures and, variously, regional reception committees in late 1989 and early 1990, interim ANC regional or sub-regional structures, the UDF's own affiliates, and later the slowly emerging regional civic groupings. In some regions there were tensions between sub-regional UDF structures – for example, in the Eastern Cape, between the UDF and affiliates in Port Elizabeth, between the UDF and ANC in Uitenhage, and later in 1990 between the new Eastern Cape Civics Organisation and the UDF. In the Orange Free State, the Bloemfontein Area Committee was criticised by certain affiliates, opposed by the Welkom Area

Committee, and ignored by the ANC regional leadership. The Pretoria Area Committee clashed with local youth and student organisations, while in Natal the ANC
provided a home for the many critics of the regional UDF leadership, which rapidly
atrophied.

There was also progress in reinvigorating sectoral organisation. SAYCO held a
national congress in April, with nearly two thousand delegates representing eleven
regions, including a new regional structure in the Transkei. The congress did not formally resolve to merge into the exile-based ANC Youth Section but it did decide to
restructure itself as a unitary organisation, and this would facilitate any merger.
Another congress resolution was that the UDF should be phased out. The UDF also
sought to rebuild a national women's organisation, as the UDF Women's Congress
had collapsed. Together with COSATU, the UDF organised two women's conferences, in March and May. Later in the year, however, the UDF's women's affiliates
merged into the ANC's Women's League, just as SAYCO merged into a relaunched
ANC Youth League. With the *de facto* disaffiliation of these two sectors, the UDF
had, to use Molefe's word, 'shrunk' considerably. The UDF also assisted with the
relaunch of COSAS. In addition, there were important initiatives in the civic sector.[30]

The active UDF leadership was small but tightly knit and very industrious. This
helped to perpetuate old rivalries and hostilities, which were given fresh impetus by
the new political opportunities opened up by the unbanning of the ANC. Old divisions within Charterist politics came into the open in 1990, with bitter denuncia-
tions of the alleged cabal controlling the UDF. In the words of its most vocal critic,
Mokoena: 'The cabal is a secret clique of activists who have been doing what is perceived as good work on the surface, but with a hidden double agenda.'[31] We have
examined how the criticism of the 'cabal' grew, especially during the State of
Emergency, and we saw how UDF leaders accepted some of the criticisms. The controversy took on a new importance, however, in the context of uncertainty over the
respective roles of the ANC and UDF.

Controversy surrounding the 'cabal' imposed itself on the UDF's agenda as soon
as the Front was revived at the beginning of 1990. Some UDF leaders, including (it
seems) Lekota, were unhappy about the participation of the UDF in the MDM's
denunciation of Winnie Mandela the previous year. In January the UDF NEC
appointed three of its members as part of a delegation to meet with Winnie Mandela.
At a head office meeting in late January, Morobe was rebuked for his role in the
MDM condemnation, and it was agreed that the UDF would release a statement dis-
owning the MDM's position.[32]

The cabal issue came into the open in June 1990 when Mokoena attacked the
'cabal' in an open letter to the ANC. Mokoena's letter came in response to a document, supposedly written by the 'cabal', which allegedly argued for the continued
existence of the UDF, called for the isolation of Molefe, Lekota and Mokaba, and criticised SAYCO. Mokoena argued that the UDF had deviated from its original role and
character: 'It had always been our understanding that the UDF was a *front* of organisations and *never* an organisation in itself. However, certain functionaries of the
UDF cherished ambitions and aspirations that the UDF should be an organisation

... that the UDF should exist as a parallel structure to the ANC.'[33] For Mokoena, the UDF's existence undermined the ANC and retarded the struggle; it must, therefore, be dissolved. Mokaba and SAYCO were also strongly critical of the 'cabal', and called for the UDF to be disbanded.[34] A SAYCO document explained how the UDF had deviated under the pressure of repression:

> What began as precautionary, tentative and protective measures ... snowballed and became monsters and dinosaurs of over-centralisation ... Factionalism was the inevitable consequence, backed by the stifling of genuine debates, concentration of resources and decision-making in fewer and fewer and sometimes faceless hands and the unequal and undemocratic distribution of such resources. The Front was infected by a serious case of cancer called the cabal ... The Front tended to operate like an organisation and not as a Front of organisations.[35]

Leadership had ceased to be accountable, SAYCO alleged, and principles such as African leadership had been abandoned. The cabal issue was widely reported in the press.[36]

The ANC reportedly responded to the issue by appointing a commission of inquiry chaired by Govan Mbeki, himself no friend of the UDF leadership. His report does not seem to have been made public. The UDF itself seems to have ignored the issue for the most part. Mokoena's letter was raised in an NEC meeting in September, but discussion was postponed pending consideration in the regions and sectors, and again postponed in November because the necessary documents had not been circulated to all regions.

The issue resurfaced again in November when a group of political prisoners on Robben Island wrote a critical analysis of the UDF leadership in Natal, the region where the cabal was based, although the paper avoided using the term 'cabal' itself. The paper was read to the first congress of the ANC's southern Natal region. It asserted that the democratic movement had 'serious weaknesses', including its 'lack of leadership on the ground', its 'detachment from the masses' and internal organisational problems:

> The UDF as it existed in the region was plagued by in-fighting, factionalism, clique-ism and uneven distribution of resources. It would appear that it failed to adhere to proper democratic principles ... The issuing of political decrees without proper discussion and broad consultation with the people has done more harm than good. The difficulties experienced with the state of emergency have been carefully appreciated but they provide no justifiable basis to abdicate from exercising accountable leadership and direction.[37]

The paper concluded that 'it is crucial ... to ensure that these problems are not transferred to the ANC'. The paper was authored by ANC members involved in MK in Natal in the mid-1980s, and several of them had been critical of the UDF regional leadership even at that time. In 1990 their criticisms had some effect: the ANC's new REC included many ex-Islanders, and key 'cabalists' (including Pravin Gordhan) failed to gain election.

UDF leaders began to address the allegations more fully. Moosa wrote a short response which condemned what he saw as half-truths, lies and racism in the accusations, although he acknowledged organisational and communication failures under the Emergency. In February 1991 the NEC discussed criticisms of the 'cabal' attributed to Mokaba in a newspaper report (he denied making the comments). The NEC 'agreed that internal differences should not be debated through the mass media' but rather 'in the proper forum of the UDF'. The first full public response came from Popo Molefe, in his secretarial report to the UDF's NGC in March 1991. Molefe acknowledged that repression under the State of Emergency had severely affected the UDF's operations and led to a corruption of decision-making procedures. But UDF leaders denied having any double agenda and did not agree that the UDF needed to be dissolved.

Whilst most of the alleged cabalists survived the criticisms, the dispute undermined the UDF's future existence as a unifying co-ordinating structure. Some of the key figures in the alleged 'cabal' cooled off abroad. Morobe studied at Princeton in the United States from mid-1990 to June 1991. He denied having been sidelined: 'I had reached a point where I was burnt out and no longer had a sense of accomplishment.' Cachalia followed him the year after, while Molobi moved to the Kagiso Trust. Several alleged leaders in the 'cabal' in Natal were excluded from the ANC leadership. Yet many figures in the 'cabal' prospered within the ANC, including Moosa and Ramaphosa.[38]

The cabal issue resurfaced intermittently in early 1991, particularly during Winnie Mandela's trial on kidnapping charges, and again in 1997 when the Truth and Reconciliation Commission held hearings on Winnie Mandela and her Mandela United Football Club. In court Mandela accused 'so-called UDF leaders' of convicting her of murder before she was brought to trial, and named Gumede, Cachalia, Moosa and Morobe. Cachalia responded: 'The UDF has never retracted the statement distancing itself from Mrs Mandela's actions, and I stand by it today' – a somewhat incomplete statement in the light of the argument within the UDF in early 1990. Gumede also said he had no regrets.[39] As Mrs Mandela herself was maginalised within the ANC, her criticisms of the former 'cabal' lost influence.

As with many other disputes within the Charterist movement over the years, it is not easy to distinguish the arguments that were really important from those that were just rhetoric. It seems implausible that the UDF leaders' style of operation was the real issue. Certainly, under the State of Emergency the UDF leaders did operate with much less consultation than at the outset, and they could not easily be held to account for their use of funds and other resources. But the critics of the 'cabal' operated in much the same way in their own organisations, and there was actually wide support for the UDF operating more like an organisation under the Emergency. The UDF leaders' real 'crime' may have been to try to keep resources out of their critics' hands, for a mixture of strategic, organisational and personal reasons. It is hard to avoid the conclusion that the criticisms levelled at the 'cabal' were motivated by the critics' resentment that they did not control the UDF themselves; it was, after all, the most important political structure within the Charterist movement inside the country. Similarly, the UDF leaders were certainly guilty of failing to promote African leadership as much as they might. But how much of their critics' hostility was derived from the fact that they themselves had been marginalised, with personal anger disguised in the rhetoric of violated principles? What is least clear is how far these animosities and resentments were just personal, and how far they reflected strategic differences – with the UDF leadership marginalising people whom they saw as strategically mistaken.

UDF CAMPAIGNS

At the start of 1990 the UDF charted an ambitious programme of action, based primarily on its existing strategy of engaging the political middle ground. But during the year the UDF made little progress in implementing its programme. In March 1991 Molefe noted there had been little mass action in the year following the unbanning of the ANC. 'Nationally the Front has not taken up any major campaigns.'[40] One reason for this was that the UDF's capacity to campaign was constrained by its organisational weaknesses, its personnel and structures stretched and often confused by the needs to build different organisations. Secondly, several planned activities were taken over by the ANC or sectoral co-ordinating structures. Thirdly, the perceived imminence of a change of government led several leaders to question the wisdom of protests that might pose difficulties for the next, presumably ANC, government.

The first major issue taken up by the UDF was continuing violence. The UDF's Southern Transvaal region intervened to defuse internecine violence in Brits between different, supposedly UDF-aligned factions, and in Katlehong among taxi-drivers. In Brits, for example, the UDF set up a commission of inquiry, held a peace rally, reconciled the rival factions, and presided over the launch of a civic organisation.[41] The violence in Natal was a much more serious matter. UDF structures had been involved in peace initiatives since 1987 but there had never been a national campaign covering the Natal violence. In May the UDF with other groups organised a week of mass action against violence, including a successful national stayaway and a rather inconsequential peace conference. The Natal violence was soon overshadowed by an explosion of violence on the Reef, focused on migrant hostels. The UDF considered a range of possible responses, but most of these were more appropriately undertaken by the ANC: suspending negotiations with the government, calling for international pressure, or forming defence units, for example.[42] From mid-year the UDF ceded activity regarding violence and peace to the ANC.

At the beginning of the year the UDF had envisaged a range of campaigns in urban areas. These would include campaigns over land for residential settlement, crime, rents and service charges (through intensified rent boycotts and negotiations), organisation building down to street committee level, and non-racial municipalities. The occupation of land by homeless people was identified as a priority at the National Workshop in April. Amidst a proliferation of localised land occupations, the UDF sent delegations to meet with provincial officials and then with the government minister. But, Molefe considered, the land occupation campaign 'was not taken up vigorously' at the national level.[43]

In practice, the UDF's agenda shrank with respect to struggles over socio-economic issues just as it had with campaigns over violence. The shift to a more developmental thinking had begun even before February 1990, and continued into mid-1990. The UDF co-sponsored a workshop on funding in Harare, and approved participation in the Independent Development Trust, the government-established but otherwise independent organisation charged with spending R2 billion of public money on development. The prospect of a change of government forced the UDF's leaders to consider the effects of their campaigns, since it would be a democratic government which would inherit the consequences of continued defiance. Uncontrolled or spontaneous protests became a cause for concern. For example, although the Land Occupation Campaign was sometimes described in terms of a well-organised occupation of carefully identified land, in practice there were 'spontaneous' as well as 'controlled' occupations. This led Eastern Cape UDF leaders to warn in July: 'We should be cautious that the land we occupy now may be such that they are in areas that might force a future democratic government to remove people out of these occupied areas.'[44]

The problem was posed most starkly by rent boycotts. In his report to the UDF NGC in March 1991, Molefe raised the need to reassess rent boycotts:

A democratic government might come to power sooner than is expected. Yet the long rent boycott seems to be moving towards a culture that people do not have to pay for services. Should this culture be entrenched, the future democratic government is going to be in serious trouble. Contradictions between it and the communities will deepen to the detriment of all.[45]

Molefe called for a shift in orientation 'towards the reconstruction of a new South Africa. This entails serious efforts on our part to normalise the situation in the townships. The challenge that faces us is how to normalise the situation without impinging upon the right of the communities to engage the regime through mass action.'[46] As we shall see, Molefe and the other remaining members of the UDF's national leadership increasingly prioritised issues of reconstruction and development, and sought to build civic organisations so as to meet these challenges.

Not only was there wariness within the UDF about some of its best-established tactics, but the new context raised the further problem of formulating alternative policies. Should this be the responsibility of the UDF, the ANC or of individual civics or civic umbrella structures? With respect to land occupation, the UDF decided that it was up to the 'civics, in consultation with the ANC', to develop a policy position.[47] The initial allocation of responsibilities in this case was confirmed when an assertive regional civic structure was formed in the region – the Southern Transvaal – where land occupations were most numerous. The division of responsibilities was less clear with regard to local government. Both the ANC and UDF organised conferences in late 1990, the former around the problems of transforming local government, the latter focusing more on the implications for civics.

In practice, the UDF's major campaign in 1990 concerned not socio-economic issues or violence, both of which raised issues more appropriately dealt with by other organisations, but rather the political issue of challenging bantustan authorities. This was ironic in view of the UDF's cession of overtly political issues to the ANC. But the ANC continued to be subject to acute repression in some bantustans, especially Bophuthatswana, Ciskei and Venda. Indeed, throughout the 1980s the UDF itself had struggled to maintain any direct presence in the bantustans, with the exception of parts of the Ciskei. In the late 1980s, however, events in KwaNdebele, KaNgwane and elsewhere raised the possibility of securing the bantustans for the 'people's camp' and weakening thereby the National Party government in Pretoria.

The UDF's draft programme had proposed holding mass marches in support of the demand for reintegration into South Africa, as well as 'deepening and extending' the 'organisation of traditional leaders under the MDM'.[48] During 1990 popular protest certainly burgeoned in the bantustans, and unprecedented political mobilisation took place among ANC-aligned students, civil servants and urban residents, especially in the Transvaal bantustans. Civil servants stayed away from work for six weeks in Gazankulu, and for five weeks in Lebowa. The intransigent Bophuthatswana regime was forced to declare a State of Emergency after rallies and marches attended by as many as 100 000 people swept through its Odi and Moretele districts. UDF structures and affiliates played a leading role in several bantustans. In Bophuthatswana, for example, political co-ordination was provided by the Anti-Bophuthatswana Co-ordinating Committee, which operated as a UDF sub-regional structure; its leaders attended NEC meetings and received funds from the UDF.

Some bantustan elites saw the writing on the wall and began to woo the ANC and its allies. The military government in the Transkei, in power since December 1987 and declining in popularity, had allowed the reburial in the bantustan in October 1989 of Chief Sabata Dalindyebo, the ANC-aligned paramount chief of the Tembus, who had died in exile three years earlier. The funeral was attended by the UDF's Morobe, NUM's Ramaphosa and SAYCO's Mokaba. In November the military government formally unbanned the UDF. Lacking affiliates, the UDF did not, however, establish a strong presence in the Transkei, and the ANC soon assumed a much more important role. In KwaNdebele, MDM-aligned chief James Mahlangu finally became chief minister in April, and the Lebowa government forged an unholy alliance with the ANC later in the year. Coups removed hostile regimes in the Ciskei and Venda.

One bantustan where the UDF was active in trying to build alliances was the Ciskei. UDF national and regional leaders met with and expressed support for the leader of the Ciskei coup, Oupa Gqoza. There was some tension between grassroots protest and UDF meetings with bantustan leaders, since the latter angered some of the UDF's bantustan-based affiliates. They complained of a lack of consultation, and reported that 'the masses have been demoralised ... People do not understand why the comrade leaders are meeting the people who are perpetuating the bantustan system'.[49] But engaging with the bantustan leaders made good sense in national political terms, and only Bophuthatswana, KwaZulu and QwaQwa retained close ties to the government.

The UDF's closest relationship was with Enos Mabuza, the Chief Minister in KaNgwane. In March, following protests in other bantustans and looting in the Ciskei, the UDF issued a statement saying, 'We cannot allow the dissolution of KaNgwane as Mabuza has clearly shown he is on the side of the people.' The UDF, Lekota said, counted Mabuza as an ally, and added: 'The dismantling of the homelands has to be a guided process and we cannot allow the situation in KaNgwane to deteriorate into anarchy and chaos. People must understand structures that exist today will be needed tomorrow to build the new South Africa.'[50] Mabuza's government became a kind of reference point. In Gazankulu, for example, the people were later said to be 'prepared to settle for a Mabuza-style of government'.[51]

The UDF's overall strategy was spelt out in August at a conference on the bantustans organised by the Front:

In dealing with the bantustan leaders we should try to win over those who are sympathetic, neutralise those who are ambivalent and intensify the struggle against those who are hostile. We must strive at all times to democratize the bantustans and isolate the racist South African regime in the process. The government is constantly trying to win the bantustan leaders to their side ... We need to deny the government this opportunity.[52]

The conference was attended by 150 people from nine bantustans. It reached agreement on a principled rejection of the bantustan system, the importance of building the ANC, and a range of activities including political education, land and housing struggles, and campaigns against repression. The conference also discussed the issue of meeting with groups operating within bantustan structures. It was agreed that national leaders should not meet with such groups or leaders without first consulting with local MDM organisations, and local leaders must be included in any delegations. Alliances should only be formed with bantustan leaders if they met a set of conditions, including a commitment to 'a non-racial, united and democratic South Africa free of bantustans', and to free political activity.[53]

The UDF's efforts achieved mixed results. Gqoza proved to be an unreliable ally in the Ciskei, soon turning against the UDF and ANC. In the far Northern Transvaal, however, the UDF and ANC together succeeded in winning over important constituencies. The UDF's biggest success was in Bophuthatswana, where the UDF, through the Anti-Bophuthatswana Coordinating Committee, provided an umbrella for growing localised organisation. Although Bophuthatswana's president, Lucas Mangope, remained in power until March 1994, the organisation building and protests of 1990–1 paved the way for the upsurge in resistance that swept Mangope away.

Apart from the bantustans, the UDF was scarcely involved in mass action in 1990. This was not inevitable. An opportunity was missed in early 1990 for campaigns of mass defiance over the kinds of issues central to UDF struggles in the past, such as the continued segregation of certain public facilities and especially local government, using tactics of non-violent direct action with which the UDF was familiar. Nelson Mandela might for example have called for mass defiance at the massive celebratory welcome rallies he addressed after his release. The absence of mass action 'allowed a regime that had been routed and was on the retreat to regroup', according to Molefe. 'We allowed President De Klerk to recapture the initiative that his predecessor P.W. Botha had lost to the Democratic Movement.'[54] There were at least two reasons for this. Firstly, the ANC had assumed responsibility for overall political strategy, but it was caught up in organisation building and negotiations; if the ANC had not been unbanned, then it is very likely that mass action would have been organised under the auspices of the MDM, with the UDF playing a leading role. Secondly, both ANC and UDF leaders held quite cautious beliefs about change in 1990. Both were wary of mass action, and considered preparing for power a more urgent task than intensifying pressure. For both these reasons, the unbanning of the ANC ironically had a temporarily demobilising effect outside the bantustans.

DEBATING THE UDF'S FUTURE

Between February and April 1990 the view that the UDF should continue to operate with a revised agenda predominated over the challenge made by the anti-cabalists calling for the UDF's dissolution. But the fact of the challenge ensured that there would be further debate. The NEC requested that the regions consider the future of the Front, and report back to a meeting of the National Working Committee (NWC), comprising the NEC as well as additional representatives from regions and sectors. Between July and the end of the year there was intense debate, during which the options narrowed down to two basic alternatives: the Front must either disband altogether or be transformed into what was later to be called a 'developmental front'.

When the NWC met in September diverse views were aired. There was general agreement that some kind of co-ordination outside the ANC was still needed, but little agreement on what kind or on the UDF's role in it. The Northern Transvaal favoured the disbanding of the UDF, and its replacement with a 'broad front at a higher level' – which seems to have meant a patriotic front comprising the political movements and their allies in the 'people's camp'. The Border, Northern Cape, Orange Free State and Eastern Cape regions felt, however, that the UDF should continue to play a co-ordinating role, perhaps on a broader front. There were, as ever, diverse views in the Western Cape. ANC representatives, led by Walter Sisulu, favoured the continuation of the UDF. SAYCO was particularly emphatic that the UDF must disband. A special commission was appointed to explore the matter further, and a national conference was proposed for February 1991 to take a final decision. 'In the meantime', the NWC agreed, the UDF should do the following:

1. Continue the co-ordinating function
2. Develop organisations where they don't exist
3. Build a national civic, COSAS, teacher unity and other formations
4. Campaign around violence.[55]

This interim programme represented a further shift from mass action to organisation building.

Between November and March the range of options was narrowed down to two. The NEC prepared a report setting these out. The first option was that the UDF disband entirely. The arguments for this were that the ANC needed the experience of UDF activists; the UDF's continued existence would confuse 'the masses'; and its co-ordinating roles could be performed by either the ANC or specific sectoral structures (especially the proposed national civics structure). The second option was that the UDF transform itself into an overall co-ordinating front for organisations in civil society concerned with development and reconstruction. The arguments for this were, first, that many local organisations remained, and should continue to be, independent of the ANC or any political party, notwithstanding the fact that they had generally been aligned with it. Secondly, sectoral organisations within civil society would benefit from some broader co-ordination – a broad front, including organisations which were not aligned with the ANC, and excluding the ANC and other political parties. Thirdly, the basis of the front should be shared strategic goals, as the UDF had held in 1983, rather than principled or merely tactical unity.[56]

The UDF chose between these options at a conference of its National General Council (NGC), held in KwaNdebele in March 1991. Although Molefe and other national leaders clearly favoured the second option,[57] the NGC resolved to disband. Affiliates and activists would 'devote energies to the building of the ANC into a mighty force'. At the same time the NGC recognised the need for a developmental front. As Mafolo put it: 'our members feel strongly that we must not fall into the trap of Eastern Europe, where everyone was consumed in the party. While building the ANC as the main force, we must also ensure that the organisations of civil society will be central towards the search for a true democracy.'[58] Some kind of 'broad social movement of organisations outside of political parties' should be formed. But the proposed front would be entirely new, not a transformed UDF.[59]

What decided the debate over the future of the UDF? One factor was the irretrievably partisan image of the UDF within the extra-parliamentary opposition, most clearly manifested in the UDF's adoption of the Freedom Charter. It was hotly disputed whether or not the UDF's past association with the ANC ruled out its being transformed into a front for ostensibly non-partisan structures. Molefe, for example, argued that the UDF could do so provided it distanced itself from the ANC and the Freedom Charter. The Southern Transvaal UDF regional secretary, Paul Mashatile, countered that 'the front's key personnel and activists on the ground are too closely identified with a particular position'. A broader, non-partisan front could only be formed by 'publicly dissolving the present structure and initiating a new one'.[60]

The state of UDF organisation in the regions was a more crucial factor, since the

UDF's collapse from within left little alternative for it but to disband. The UDF could hardly be transformed if there was little prospect of the necessary future components existing. In most parts of the country what regional organisation there was fell apart rapidly from mid-1990. By September, regional officials were giving the NEC sombre reports. The Southern Transvaal region, to take one example, tried to hold an AGM but too few delegates attended to render it quorate. Only one Area Committee (Pretoria's) remained functional, none of the organisers submitted progress reports, and there had been no campaigns since July. 'Briefly,' the regional secretary concluded, 'the UDF in the S. Transvaal is in a state of complete collapse.' The Southern Transvaal was by no means unique. REC and other regional meetings in the Eastern Cape were repeatedly postponed because of poor attendance, and most of the Area Committees stopped functioning. Regional leaders reported that 'there was an obvious disintegration of the UDF. Many UDF activists are busy doing tasks of building the ANC.'[61]

There were successes. The Pretoria Area Committee and Anti-Bophuthatswana Co-ordinating Committee had promoted unprecedented organisation building and mobilisation in the Pretoria area and neighbouring bantustans. The Eastern Cape UDF convened a series of meetings on development. The Border UDF had assisted in the formation of a Border Civics Congress. But, overall, the weaknesses and gaps outweighed these successes.

The situation was accurately summarised in Popo Molefe's characteristically frank secretarial report to the NGC in March 1991. 'Today,' he told delegates, 'the UDF is at its weakest in the entire history of its existence.'

Very few regional councils meet regularly. Most of the zonal structures have collapsed. There is nothing that provides for joint strategising and joint decision-making. Leaders no longer operate on the basis of sufficient mandates, nor are they sufficiently accountable because meetings are irregular.[62]

The Natal region had 'completely collapsed due to internal tensions and contradictions', and the Orange Free State region had never formally constituted itself. Molefe reported that the RECs of the Southern Transvaal, Northern Transvaal and Northern Cape regions were not meeting regularly, nor were RGCs convened.

The collapse of UDF structures was accelerated as more UDF leaders and officials were pulled into the expanding ANC. Many were elected onto new ANC RECs at the ANC's regional conferences held in late 1990. The Western Cape ANC REC included a long list of UDF REC members: Christmas Tinto as ANC regional president, Hilda Ndude as vice-president, Amos Lengisi as secretary, Bulelani Ngcuka as treasurer, Trevor Manuel as publicity secretary, together with Dullah Omar, Chris Nissen, Mildred Lesia and others. In the Eastern Cape, three out of six UDF REC members were elected to the ANC REC. These included the only two active members: Edgar Ngoyi, UDF chairperson, and Gugile Nkwinti, UDF secretary, elected as the ANC's regional vice-president and secretary respectively. Molefe was elected vice-chairman, and Saloojee treasurer, of the ANC's PWV REC.[63]

A further factor in the collapse of UDF structures was the growing lack of direction. The general uncertainty about the future role of the UDF had been compounded by the lack of mass action. According to Molefe: 'The absence of mass action left many structures inactive and activists redundant. It became meaningless for them to attend meetings which did not produce any definite programmes of mass action. Consequently many activists stopped to attend meetings.'[64] Finally, and perhaps most important of all, the collapse reflected the burden of resentment and hostility shouldered by the UDF's leadership. This enmity increased in the second half of 1990, as the formation of new organisations and the redefinition of existing ones opened up new opportunities for struggle over resources and political influence. The dissolution of the UDF was, in significant part, the easy way out of the quagmire of Charterist politics at the time. Faced with widespread hostility and lacking support, advocates of the transformation option floundered.

THE CIVIC SECTOR AND DEVELOPMENT

Development or 'reconstruction' became the focus of UDF strategy in the second half of 1990, and the UDF's future role (if it had one) was increasingly seen in terms of co-ordinating developmental struggles – although 'development' remained very ill-defined. As civic organisations would play a leading role in development on the ground, the UDF invested considerable effort and resources into building organisation and co-ordination in the civic sector. But many activists based in the civics believed that national and regional civic co-ordinating structures, and not a transformed UDF, should be responsible for developmental activities. Indeed, emergent civic sectoral leaders were among the most fervent opponents of the UDF's continuation in any form. The civic sector and development were therefore keenly contested terrains during the UDF's last year.

During 1990–1 the UDF national leadership sought to nurture a forward-looking civic movement based on strong local-level organisation. The Front appointed a national civic co-ordinator, Pat Lephunya, and an assistant for the Western Cape, Zohra Ebrahim, and convened a national civics workshop. Molefe, together with the civic co-ordinators and Cas Coovadia, who was working at the UDF head office, invested considerable energies in this project. The need for a forward-looking movement was set out in a paper written by Coovadia in May. Civics, Coovadia argued, had to do more than just protest about living conditions. 'If civic organisations do not begin to have a more developmental approach now,' he warned, 'we will be unable to address these massive problems in the future.' Civic activists urgently needed education and training in fields such as urban administration, housing, transport and health. The NEC endorsed participation in the government-established Independent Development Trust in order to influence development policy. In the Eastern Cape the UDF formed a regional Development and Funding Forum (ECDAFF) to bring together community-based and developmental service organisations.[65]

The UDF views on the civic sector were set out in presentations to the workshop.

These reiterated the need for a developmental approach which would serve as the basis for a robust national civic movement. As one UDF discussion paper boldly declared, the current period could 'best be characterised as "a struggle for Development and Reconstruction."' The paper identified some necessary features of civic organisation building, implicitly pointing to civics' existing shortcomings:

- We will need a national campaign, with massive resources made available to build an effective *National Civic Movement* ...
- We need to professionalise our civics, with organisers [and] proper report backs ... We need to develop a system of institutionalising the participation of the people and ensuring an internal democracy within our civics.
- We need to advance our education and training work ... Development workers need to be trained ...[66]

In another presentation to the conference, Lephunya warned of the 'slackness and lack of commitment' prevailing in many civics towards grassroots organising.[67] The UDF head office view emphasised the consolidation of civic organisations, improving their internal organisational procedures and the skills of their personnel, before civic co-ordinating structures could be formed at the regional or national levels. At the same time, however, the UDF recognised that a national civic structure could help nurture local civics, and 'prevent the government from manipulating weaker civic associations', as Molefe noted.[68]

This view was spelt out repeatedly over the following months. Popo Molefe wrote that 'the issues of development and reconstruction have assumed priority'.[69] Lephunya emphasised the need for 'making the shift from primarily "protest/boycott" tactics to a mix between this and a development and reconstruction perspective ... It is no longer enough to destroy apartheid. We now have to begin rebuilding what apartheid has destroyed.'[70] He also stressed the importance of 'strong grassroots structures and broad representivity', with federal regional and national structures, in order to ensure that 'the struggle is not removed from the local level'. The NEC decided to accept funds from USAID to run workshops 'to empower people with skills on issues of development', and pressed the RECs to appoint full-time regional civic organisers.[71]

The UDF head office's approach was challenged, however, by activists in the new regional civic structures. The Eastern Cape Civics Organisation (ECCO) and the Civic Association of the Southern Transvaal (CAST), formed in August and September 1990 respectively, were dominated by civic activists antipathetic to the UDF leadership. Many were elected on the basis of militant rhetoric, and were hostile to innovative strategic thinking such as the UDF's 'reconstructionist' perspective. They favoured the rapid formation of a unitary national civic structure, with its own resources and fully independent of the UDF, and saw the UDF's emphases on development and consolidating sub-national civic structures as foot-dragging. In October 1990 ECCO and CAST leaders decided to proceed with forming an interim national civic body, on their own if necessary. The National Interim Civics Committee was established in February 1991. Its chairperson was Eastern Cape activist Thembile Bete, who had been nominated but not appointed as a national civic co-ordinator in 1990 and had clashed repeatedly with the regional UDF leadership. The committee set about planning a national consultative conference for civics, developing national policy positions and looking into the availability of external funding.[72]

The decisions taken at the UDF's NGC in March 1991 represented a victory for the opponents of the UDF leadership. The UDF would be quickly disbanded, and its remaining cars, office equipment and other assets transferred to civic structures, apparently regardless of their organisational strength and understanding of 'development' and 'civil society'. There was one exception to this picture. In the Eastern Cape the regional UDF secretary had built up ECDAFF as an alternative developmental umbrella body to ECCO, much to the latter's chagrin. Overall, however, the UDF dissolved amidst disagreement or ambiguity about civics' roles, and at a time when civic organisation was generally weak. This was to plague the civic movement in the following years.

THE DISSOLUTION OF THE UDF

The decision to disband the UDF, taken at the NGC conference in March 1991, does not seem to have been greeted with great joy or excitement by its leadership. Zohra Ebrahim recalls that 'it was all so sad. It was only when we went home that we realised what had happened'.[73] The UDF was not disbanded because of any universal recognition that it had achieved its objectives, or that the need for an organisation like it had passed. Nonetheless, once the decision had been taken, there was great pressure on the UDF to wind up its affairs rapidly. This meant, above all, transferring its financial assets to sectoral organisations and terminating the employment of its far-flung staff. During this time civic leaders in several regions were manoeuvring to establish a national civic organisation as a successor to the UDF. But the UDF's leaders were reluctant to transfer assets to weak structures, especially as they regarded some of the emergent leaders of the civic movement with a certain amount of suspicion. The UDF leaders therefore set themselves a further, final task: to strengthen civic organisation.

In order to identify the UDF's assets and liabilities and to assess whether civic structures were 'politically and administratively ready to receive such assets', Molefe and Coovadia toured the regions at the end of April. They found, almost everywhere, further evidence of the collapse of the UDF's structures, including widespread administrative and financial chaos. This made it difficult to trace even major assets. The UDF regions supposedly possessed fifteen vehicles. Two of these had been sponsored by churches. Of the remaining thirteen, only three were still working. Three others were unroadworthy, two were believed to be in the possession of the police, and five had been written off in accidents or otherwise 'lost'. Few vehicles had been insured. Most regions had a few items of office equipment, and little of this had been insured – the Orange Free State region faced a legal claim for over R100 000 for office equipment which had been rented, not insured, and stolen. The total value of the

UDF's assets was estimated at less than R150 000.[74]

Nor were Molefe and Coovadia impressed by the state of civic organisation. After their tour they reported back to the NEC:

> Our assessment of the civic movement nationally is a very bleak one. It is our contention that our structures on the ground are generally weak or non-existent. The only region that, in our opinion, has a strong and viable regional structure is Border. We believe the Northern Cape is progressing well and should grow into a strong region.[75]

But elsewhere there was generally little civic co-ordination, and civics on the ground were often weak.

> Our overall assessment is that a lot more effort needs to be expended on building the civic movement. We are very wary of launching a national structure in the immediate future, given the weaknesses we observed in virtually every region. We believe the assets of the UDF should be transferred to the civic movement, but we fear that most regional structures are not yet in a position to administer the assets. We also have doubts whether a national structure formed in the immediate future would have this capacity.[76]

Molefe and Coovadia proposed that the UDF transfer its assets into a Civic Trust. Molefe – who was no stranger to civic organisation – was said to have been very disappointed by what he saw and heard on his trip.[77]

However sceptical they were, the UDF leadership had but limited influence over the process of forming a national civic structure. At a national civic conference convened by the UDF and the National Interim Civics Committee in May 1991, the UDF leaders could do little more than exhort civic leaders to face the challenges of violence, non-partisanship, democratic organisation and a 'culture of development'.[78] Overriding the UDF leaders' views, as well as some dissent within the civic movement, the conference resolved to launch a national civic structure as early as August. Within the civic movement itself, opposition to the predominant approach often came from areas where UDF leaders were prominent in local civic organisation.[79]

There was widespread speculation following the May conference that the formation of a national civic organisation resulted from a rift in opposition politics. But the press misunderstood the nature of the rift, assuming that the institutional separation between the state (to be occupied by the ANC) and civil society (identified with the civics) corresponded to the political dispute. The press eagerly seized on remarks made by leaders such as Archie Gumede, who described the ANC's leadership as an 'elite', and explicitly talked of the need for 'checks and balances' as the ANC came closer to involvement in government.[80] Gumede, however, had nothing to do with the civic initiative. The UDF's national treasurer, Cachalia, responded to this 'mischievous' speculation.

It is widely known that there have been concerns expressed within MDM structures about the lack of consultation between the leadership of the ANC and its
supporters. In fact, this criticism was made by the ANC itself at its consultative
conference in December last year. But this is not why a national civic body is
being launched. It is certainly not being formed in opposition to or in competition with the ANC.[81]

There were indeed sharp personal and political animosities surrounding the formation of a national civic body, but these concerned the details of the process involved
and the strategic direction in which civics would travel rather than the institutional
separation *per se*.

The only area in which the UDF leadership had some influence over the civic
movement was finance. The UDF-appointed national civic co-ordinators tussled
with regional civic structures over the control of funding and funding applications.
The UDF undertook to discuss the question of continued funding for the sectoral
organisations with the UDF's major financial backer, the Swedish labour movement.
But the civics were slow to obtain major international backing. The Kagiso Trust,
many of whose top staff were former UDF officials or had been closely linked to the
UDF leadership, put increasingly severe conditions on grants to civics, insisting on a
higher standard of financial accountability and organisation. The UDF also quar-
relled with the existing regional civic structures – CAST in the Southern Transvaal
and ECCO in the Eastern Cape – over funds. The UDF told CAST that it should raise
its own funds, and that the UDF might assist in funding campaigns but would not
pay for car hire and such expenses. In turn CAST alleged that the UDF was holding
back funds. In the Eastern Cape the UDF had long fought with ECCO over funds. In
1991 the UDF transferred its assets to ECDAFF, not ECCO, and asked the sponsor of
its two cars to do likewise. The weakness of COSAS also led the UDF to propose
transferring funds into a Trust Account.[82]

The final task facing the UDF was the retrenchment of its staff and closure of its
offices. There was some uncertainty as to how many employees the UDF had. Molefe
and Coovadia counted between 22 and 26 staff in seven regions, in addition to the
handful of staff at head office. The NEC decided that regions should close their
financial books at the end of April, although some regional employees would continue to work on specific tasks until June. After staff raised the question of severance
pay, the NEC agreed to pay one month's severance pay to those employees who
remained unemployed in July, subject to the availability of funds. This was a sensible
solution, since most staff were immediately employed by the ANC or other structures, with only a few experiencing even temporary unemployment.

Just as many UDF employees were re-employed by the ANC, so many UDF
regional and national leaders took up leading positions in the former liberation
movement. Fourteen former national or regional UDF office-holders were elected to
the ANC's NEC in July 1991: Lekota, Stofile, Molefe, Albertina Sisulu, Suttner,
Manuel, Carolus, Omar, Moosa, Nair, Mokaba and Mufamadi, together with
Tshwete and Cronin (who had been office-holders before going into exile). In addi-

tion, MDM leader Ramaphosa was overwhelmingly elected as secretary general. Molefe was narrowly defeated by former exile Jacob Zuma in the election for deputy secretary general. Former UDF activists occupied important positions within the ANC, with Carolus, Manuel, Molefe, Lekota and Moosa all presiding over departments or commissions. Mokaba was elected Youth League president, and Sisulu deputy president of the Women's League. Many former UDF leaders had already been elected onto the ANC's RECs at the end of 1990, although divisions within the Charterist movement had led to the exclusion of many previously prominent UDF leaders in Natal and the Western Cape.

By contrast, there were few former UDF leaders in the leadership of the new regional civic organisations, and their absence was even more conspicuous in the leadership of the South African National Civic Organisation (SANCO) formed the following year. Of SANCO's executive, only one person, Lechesa Tsenoli, had been involved in UDF leadership – he had served on the Natal REC for several years. SANCO was dominated by civic activists from the Southern Transvaal and Eastern Cape who had either long been critical of the UDF's populist approach – Moses Mayekiso for example – or been alienated from the UDF during disputes over how to run organisations, as was the case with several of SANCO's leaders from the Eastern Cape. Civic leaders who had been prominent in the UDF either moved on to the ANC, or moved into more explicitly development-orientated organisations such as the Kagiso Trust.

The NEC held its final meeting on 14 August in Johannesburg. The agenda was short. The NEC's last decision was to commission a book on the history of the UDF, to be 'rigorously researched', as the minutes record. UDF chairperson Curnick Ndlovu closed the meeting with a tribute to the UDF's leaders for their selfless contribution to the struggle – a struggle which, he emphasised, was not yet over: 'tough battles still lay ahead'. The meeting closed at 3 p.m. Morobe, who had recently returned to South Africa after a year studying in the United States, told the press that there was a feeling of accomplishment rather than of sadness at the meeting. Just over a week later the ANC hosted a rally in Cape Town to celebrate and applaud the UDF. The rally was held at the Rocklands Civic Centre in Mitchell's Plain where the UDF had been publicly launched exactly eight years before. Finally, the UDF held a cocktail function in Johannesburg, at the Carlton Hotel, which was a venue not without irony. As Morobe explained: 'At the height of repression in the past we used to meet in the basement of the Carlton Hotel. So it is fitting that we hold the farewell on top of the hotel – 30th floor – so that the world can see.'[83] After eight decisive and largely successful years, the UDF was just history.

ASSESSMENT

The period from the UDF's revival at the start of 1990 to its decision to disband the following year was a tumultous one. The political situation was ever changing – the rebuilding of the ANC, the onset of negotiations, an escalation of political violence on the Reef and in Natal, all following on each other in rapid succession. The tumult of the time perhaps helps explain the sudden shift within the Charterist movement from predominant support for a continued UDF in the first half of 1990 to the decision that the Front would disband in March 1991.

Four specific factors determined the fate of the UDF. Firstly, it suffered a drain of key personnel into the ANC at both national and regional levels. Whilst the ANC slowly built its own structures after being banned for three decades, the UDF struggled to rebuild its structures, which had been suppressed for under four years. This imposed severe constraints on the UDF's capacity to perform further tasks.

Secondly, the UDF's agenda shrank more than had been expected. The changing context meant that various issues initially seen as the concern of the UDF came to be regarded as political and hence the ANC's concern. Socio-economic issues such as land settlement raised questions of post-apartheid policy, and became the responsibility of the ANC as the government-in-waiting. Thirdly, the anticipation of an imminent post-apartheid future resulted in the revision of the UDF's strategies and tactics, with a strategic emphasis emerging on development and reconstruction and a tactical shift away from defiance. These were not the strategies and tactics historically associated with the UDF, and the UDF's efforts to popularise them undermined its own existence.

Fourthly, the UDF's leaders and structures suffered from the hostility of large sections of the Charterist movement, including some erstwhile affiliates. Eventually it was the enmity of the rising civic movement, the complete collapse of the UDF in regions such as Natal, and opposition from other sections of the Charterist movement that forced the UDF to dissolve rather than transform itself. Overall, the dissolution of the UDF seems to have had less to do with its relationship with the ANC, either before or after the ANC's unbanning, than with the unanticipated effects of the changing political context.

Chapter Eleven

Conclusion:
Turning the Tide

At the UDF's national launch in 1983 Frank Chikane expressed his hope that the day would be recorded in history as an event that would 'bolster the tide of the struggle'. Almost eight years later, Walter Sisulu told the UDF's final national conference that the Front had indeed 'decisively turned the tide against the advances being made by the [National Party] regime'. The metaphor of the tide is apt in the task of understanding the impact of the UDF on South African politics. It conjures up images of the fundamental pressures and forces in a society rather than the more superficial events – even those that are supposed historical 'turning-points'. As the UDF's founders themselves recognised, the struggle for democracy and freedom depended not on single events, however momentous, but on the shifting balance of political power.

The UDF was formed at a time when the balance of power was not irredeemably tilted towards either the apartheid state or its opponents. The state remained immensely powerful in military and economic terms, notwithstanding a long-term decline in profit rates and the more immediate economic downturn since 1981, but underlying processes of social and economic change together with the resurgence of internal resistance since the mid-1970s had undermined the state's ideological and political positions. As key state actors themselves recognised, the political future of the country and of the dominant white minority depended on a successful political strategy: military might and economic power were insufficient. The apartheid state therefore sought to rebuild its ideological and political foundations around a package of major policy reforms. These were intended to draw (or co-opt) Indian and coloured South Africans, together with some sections of the urban African population, into support for a reformed but still racially non-egalitarian system. The reforms were also intended to foster acquiescence among a broader range of the African population. At the same time, a series of deals with the frontline states strengthened the state's position in the southern African region. These changes thus threatened to tilt the balance of power markedly towards the state; as Boesak put it in

January 1983, 'apartheid's crisis has become our crisis'. The formation of the UDF, its founders hoped, would help first to forestall this prospective shift, and then perhaps to carry forward the faltering momentum of resistance – to stop the advancing 'tide' of counter-democratic politics, and then turn it round.

With hindsight it is clear that the tide flowed strongly against the state from the end of 1983. Prospective opposition from the newly formed UDF first led the government to discard the idea of referendums among coloured and Indian voters to legitimise the process of constitutional reform. Then the elections to the new coloured and Indian houses of parliament were largely boycotted. This and other protests discredited the government's 'new deal', both within South Africa and internationally. The township revolt from the second half of 1984 forced the state onto the defensive, pushing it to use brutal repression, which served to highlight the moral poverty of even 'reformed apartheid'. The strategic framework of people's power enabled the forces of revolt to be harnessed more effectively, and channelled into a direct and potentially sustainable challenge to the apartheid state. In response the government was able to stem the tide of resistance only by imposing a level of repression that was unprecedented in South Africa, although mild by comparison with many other anti-democratic regimes. But resistance adapted and continued at a level sufficient to render the state's strategy of repression unsustainable. In mid-1988 the first talks were held towards some kind of a negotiated settlement. Amidst a dramatic (if uneven) revival of popular protest during 1989, the move towards a negotiated settlement speeded up, leading to the government's decision to unban the ANC. By the early 1990s, as Lodge writes, the slogan *amandla* (power) was no longer just an aspiration; it had became an assertion.[1]

ASSESSING POLITICAL ORGANISATION IN PERIODS OF CHANGE

What role did the UDF play in this turning tide? What impact did the UDF have on the process of democratisation and liberation in South Africa? How can one isolate the roles and impact of an organisation like the UDF from those of other factors – ranging from the international context to the pressures exerted by highly fragmented groups at the local level, from divisions within ruling elites to the broad dynamics of social and economic change? Answers to such questions are, to some extent, only conjecture. They depend on counterfactual scenarios which themselves rest on multiple assumptions and defy easy specification. Presumably in part for this reason, analytical histories of political organisations generally tend to avoid explicit assessment in their concluding chapters.

The role played by political organisation in periods of political change may, however, be too important to circumvent. The importance of organisation is an empirical question, within the limits of the kind of 'empirical' research possible. Certainly, organisation should not be assumed to be a key factor – even when political activists and strategists themselves generally act as if it is. Some actors' emphasis on organisation no doubt sometimes reflects a concern to strengthen or protect their own power within opposition politics. In other cases, actors' emphasis on organisation may prove to be futile. In the South African case, Barrell shows how the ANC's interminable restructuring never led to the adoption of an effective strategy and appropriate organisation.[2]

One context where one might expect that political organisation would play an especially important role is during periods of political transition. As O'Donnell and Schmitter, Huntington and others have argued, liberalisation and democratisation are typically uncertain and indeterminate processes: 'unexpected events, insufficient information, hurried and audacious choices, confusion about motives and interests, plasticity, and even non-definition of political identities, as well as the talents of specific individuals, are frequently decisive in determining the outcomes'.[3] Political organisation – including ideas and discourses, strategies and tactics, leadership and networks – play an important role in determining the outcome of these processes. While specific social, economic and international factors may constitute necessary conditions for successful democratisation, they are not sufficient. As Huntington writes: 'Economic development makes democracy possible; political leadership makes it real.'[4] This is not to say that political organisation is isolated from broader factors, whether material, ideological, international or other, but rather that the effects of the structural context are generally mediated through the political realm. This renders the choices made by political actors consequential. Organisations can perceive pressures and opportunities in diverse ways, and then exercise a degree of choice in how they respond to the perceived pressures and opportunities.

Curiously, studies of transition rarely focus on the character of political organisation, despite the acknowledged importance of political factors. One reason for this has already been mentioned: the necessarily speculative nature of any assessment of the role and impact of particular organisations. More important, perhaps, is the general absence of an outstanding, above-ground political organisation in such periods of transition. Non-democratic regimes typically do not permit public, mass-based and determinedly subversive opposition organisations. South Africa was an exception to the general pattern, for reasons that we shall begin to delineate in the section on opportunities below. To emphasise the distinctiveness of the South African case, and thus of the UDF, consider the experiences of communist-ruled Central and Eastern Europe. The anti-communist revolutions of 1989, more or less coincident with democratisation in South Africa, occurred without organisations comparable to the UDF. The one possible exception was Poland, where Solidarity remained a key player even during the years of martial law after 1981; the military were eventually left with little option but to negotiate with it in 1989. Whilst perhaps not unique, therefore, the UDF is certainly at one end of the spectrum of political organisation in periods of transition.

Few studies of South Africa assess directly and explicitly the significance of political organisation in the transition. The few that do typically criticise the ANC and the UDF from the left. McKinley, for example, condemns the ANC and UDF for their failure to promote a more revolutionary outcome.[5] According to their view, the structural conditions were favourable for a revolution, but the leadership was derelict. A careful study of the 1980s provides little support for this view. For sure, the UDF leadership did indeed at times seek to rein in the militancy of sections of the population; the UDF was indeed weakly committed to a socialist vision of transformation; the UDF was willing to enter into or support negotiations, and offer compromises in the course of them. But accounts such as McKinley's ignore very real political obstacles to radical change. The street militancy that the UDF sought to rein in was rarely linked to the organised working class or any clear socialist project; there were important strategic costs to such militancy, as well as considerable direct costs to the people living in the townships concerned; the UDF certainly sought to intensify the pressure exerted on the state in other ways; and, above all, the practice and prospect of state repression placed severe restrictions on the UDF and other organisations. The 'moment' of the mid-1980s had much less revolutionary potential than is often imagined. Political organisation, including the UDF, needs to be assessed in terms of what it did achieve, and not simply dismissed for failing to achieve observers' revolutionary dreams.

THE ROLES AND IMPACT OF THE UDF

The 'role' played by the UDF in turning the tide was neither monolithic nor static, but rather varied between regions and changed over time. As the political landscape was transformed, so the UDF too was transformed, organisationally, strategically and above all in its relationships with the ever-changing smorgasbord of organisations, groups and individuals arrayed against the apartheid state.

The UDF was formed, first and foremost, to co-ordinate and hence intensify opposition to the state's reforms. From the outset the UDF stamped its mark on political developments – notwithstanding its initially reactive and piecemeal activities and its deep internal divisions surfacing around the Port Elizabeth conference. The UDF played a minor role in mobilising opposition to new local councils in African townships. More importantly, it was the threat of action by the UDF and key affiliates that deterred the government from holding referendums among coloured and Indian voters over its constitutional proposals. The importance of this should not be underestimated: referendums would have helped to legitimise the new constitution, internationally and domestically, in part through the spurious symmetry of allowing coloured and Indian as well as white voters the opportunity to approve or reject the proposals. The Million Signatures Campaign demonstrated popular opposition to the reforms, even though the campaign fell far short of its goal of a million signatures. Moreover, the campaign involved an active demonstration of support, through signing a petition, and not just the passive demonstration involved in (for example) boycotting an election. This campaign allowed the UDF to capture a significant part of the so-called political middle ground. The election boycott was a triumphant success, with low polls and public opposition, especially in the important metropolitan areas, thereby undermining the political value of the government's project. Finally, the occupation of the British consulate in Durban focused international attention on detention without trial, further undermining the reformist image that the government sought to project. By the end of 1984 the Tricameral Parliament and African township councils were discredited. The government had failed to secure political advantage from its reforms – largely thanks to the scope of opposition co-ordinated through the UDF.

The UDF's existence and activities served to 'push back the frontiers of what was politically possible'. As Morobe later said, 'We managed to get people to stand up and fight for their rights without any fear and actually challenge authority.'[6] Perhaps it was the government that unwittingly put politics on the table, but it was the UDF that overcame the previously widespread fear and wariness of politics. Its opposition to the constitutional reforms demonstrated not just the efficacy of protest but also the possibility of challenge.

Whilst primarily concerned with opposition to the government's reforms, the UDF also posed the outline of an alternative approach to politics. For the most part this was somewhat abstract: the goal was a non-racial, democratic, unitary South Africa, and the appropriate interim institution was not some multi-cameral parliament but rather a national convention. Not surprisingly, this did not seem to catch the popular imagination. But UDF speakers also put forward a more appealing alternative, couched in the universalist language of rights and morality: in Boesak's words, 'we want all of our rights, we want them here, and we want them now ... Now is the time!' Here was a vision and a rallying cry, simultaneously a demand and an expression of impatience.

The twelve or so months between mid-1983 and mid-1984 also saw the construction of a country-wide movement. The two national conferences of 1983 gave the movement some momentum; NEC meetings provided for inter-regional co-ordination; RECs and RGCs provided for regional co-ordination. The growth of this movement was reflected in, and in turn strengthened by, the Million Signatures Campaign, which involved on a sustained basis perhaps a thousand activists in collecting signatures, building cross-racial contact and developing organisational experience. It is easy to criticise the campaign – as UDF leaders themselves did – but it was the first nationwide campaign on this scale since the 1950s.

The importance of the formation of the UDF in terms of building political networks is evident from comparison with the deep fragmentation of opposition politics prior to 1983. Then, some networks did exist, but they were very patchy. Inter-regional contact and debate were limited to individual connections, interspersed with very rare opportunities provided by conferences such as the 1981 Anti-SAIC conference in Durban. Even at the regional level, key activists sometimes did not even know each other. The formation of the UDF ensured the institutionalisation of regular inter-regional and intra-regional co-ordination.

For sure, the Charterist movement was scarred by multiple tensions after 1983: across racial lines in many areas; between more nationalist and more socialist strands of Charterism, in East London for example; between groups plugged into different resource bases, including the battles around Freeway House in Johannesburg; between individuals with different lines of communication to 'the' ANC, especially during the referendum debate; between regions, notably over the election of a president, and also during the referendum debate; and within regions between metropolitan and non-metropolitan areas. But most of these tensions were the products or results of improved co-ordination, problems that would not have arisen in a more fragmented context; they were the inevitable frictions associated with building a movement out of disparate components.

Symbolically, the existence of a nationwide front, its campaigns and its media helped to integrate the disparate parts of opposition politics into a larger whole. Activists in smaller townships were encouraged to see themselves as part of a broad movement, and to regard the various aspects of state policy as part of a larger state strategy. The UDF did not seek explicitly to construct a Charterist movement but helped to secure the construction of Charterist near-hegemony. Non-Charterist strands of opposition politics were emphatically sidelined, with the exceptions of Inkatha, whose base lay increasingly within bantustan state structures, and the independent trade union movement, whose political role was muted at the time.

There were clear limits to the UDF's achievements in this initial period. Much of the impetus to the formation of the UDF came from the specific political needs of apartheid activists in coloured and Indian areas. In terms of leadership, concerns, discourses and strategy, the UDF was orientated primarily towards coloured and Indian politics. This fuelled dissent or at least a sense of distance among some activists from African areas, notwithstanding the UDF's rhetorical commitment to the 'primacy of African leadership'. Perhaps it was the very success of the UDF in advancing the Charterist cause, sidelining rivals in order to secure its claimed position as the 'only' body representing 'all' sections of the population, that subsequently allowed sections of the Charterist movement to adopt a hostile attitude toward the Front.

If opposition to the government's reforms largely frustrated the government's political project, thereby forestalling any shift in the balance of forces in the state's favour, it was the township revolt of the mid-1980s that decisively tilted the balance of forces away from the state. In the Delmas Treason Trial, UDF leaders Molefe and Lekota were initially convicted for their parts in the township revolt. The UDF was found to have been party to the instigation of revolutionary violence. This judicial interpretation is perhaps not surprising: governing elites, including judges, rarely appreciate the ways in which localised political, social and economic conditions can give rise to burgeoning revolt; to do so would be to acknowledge their collective failure to address these causes. Instead, governing elites typically look for conspiracies and agitators.[7]

The UDF's own leadership was taken by surprise by the initial revolt. Certainly the UDF sought the collapse of the apartheid state but, as its own leaders acknowledged in internal documents, the UDF was at the margins of the revolt. Indeed, the sites of the initial revolt were areas with particularly weak direct links to the UDF: Tumahole, Atteridgeville, the East Rand, the Vaal Triangle, Cradock. Even those townships with stronger links to the UDF – including Soweto, Mamelodi, as well as the townships of Port Elizabeth, Uitenhage and Cape Town – were slow to be drawn into the revolt.

Much of the initial impetus to the revolt came from issues which the UDF had neglected: rents and service charges, housing, urban development, and even the roles and responsibilities of elected township councillors. The UDF was clearly and emphatically opposed to the reform of African local goverment, since elected township councils seemed a substitute for full democratic rights. But the Front was not integral to the widespread, locally based opposition to councils and councillors. The UDF was also somewhat distant from the schooling crisis, in part because COSAS resisted UDF involvement. The organisational form of the UDF as a front meant that, at this stage, it could only be involved in issues if the relevant affiliates sought its assistance. Township-based organisations either opposed the UDF's intervention or at least had not sought it.

Indirectly, however, the UDF played an important role in the genesis of the revolt. As Lodge puts it, the Front 'inspired an insurrectionary movement'.[8] Two factors helped to transform localised discontent over civic and educational issues into a nationwide political movement. First, the existence and prominence of the UDF served to encourage local-level activists to link their struggles into the national political struggle. This is presumably what Lodge means when he writes of the 'inspirational' role of the UDF. Secondly, state repression played a powerful politicising role. It is surely likely that the heightened mobilisation around the UDF's campaigns in 1984 was an important factor in the state's often heavy-handed approach to policing in the second half of the year. The fact that township protests coincided with UDF-led resistance to the Tricameral Parliament meant that many police, as well as National Party politicians, were likely to regard civic protests as part of a political conspiracy and then to use a high level of force to 'contain' them.

Revolts may seldom be instigated by political organisations, but revolts typically provide unprecedented opportunities for political organisations to extend their organisational and ideological reach and power. The UDF was initially not well placed to take advantage of the opportunity posed by the growing revolt. Most of its leaders were deeply wary of insurrectionary or confrontational tactics; indeed, the Front had decided against them earlier in 1984. Some UDF leaders saw violence as morally suspect; others saw it as potentially counterproductive, a threat to sustained revolt; most favoured instead extended organisation building. The UDF came to be seen as overly conciliatory and insufficiently supportive of the insurrectionary project favoured by some activists and promoted by the ANC through its Radio Freedom. It was only with escalating violence by the state against its opponents that senior UDF leaders began to endorse the use of 'counter-violence' for ostensibly defensive purposes.

The UDF's capacity to seize the political initiative became hampered by repression. In August 1984 and February 1985 its leadership was decimated by detentions. Top leaders were prosecuted in two treason trials. In the Eastern Cape an REC member and other activists were abducted and murdered. In Natal an REC member was assassinated. In July a State of Emergency was imposed across most of the Eastern Cape and PWV, and later extended elsewhere; the Emergency regulations were used to detain activists at all levels and impose a complete clampdown on political meetings. In August a further round of detentions seemed to herald a third major trial, although in fact this never took place. The effect of this was, not surprisingly, very disruptive. Although resistance was spreading across the country, it was difficult for the UDF to provide direction. The Front sought to reorientate itself to the new conditions and opportunities. It adopted a more vanguardist approach and streamlined its organisational structures. Discourses of power replaced discourses of rights. But the Front lacked any overall strategic direction, and lacked the authority to retrieve its position at the helm of the Charterist movement inside the country.

In early 1986 the UDF succeeded in seizing the political initiative, both within the Charterist movement and in the politics of the country as a whole. It did this through developing the strategic framework of 'people's power'. By providing direction it helped to intensify and, more importantly, sustain popular insurrection. The impetus to people's power came from several sources: from burgeoning violence and the education crisis, which was deemed to require urgent intervention; from the Eastern Cape, where street committees had been formed at the very local level to provide direction to political struggle amidst pervasive repression; and from the ANC, which continued to preach popular insurrection over Radio Freedom. The UDF's ascendancy was made possible by its endorsement by the ANC – not least at their meeting in Stockholm in January – as playing an integrative role in the Charterist movement inside the country.

The goal of people's power, as Zwelakhe Sisulu put it, was to shift decisively 'the balance of forces in our favour'. 'Protest' should be transformed into a sustainable 'challenge'. The strategic framework envisaged converting the situation of ungovernability, in which the state was unable to control the townships, into one in which the people governed themselves. What this meant in practice was a massive programme of organisation building, enlarging the social bases of resistance, and integrating the disparate parts of the Charterist movement. It involved a clear retreat from the more triumphalist and insurrectionary claims of some activists, and a return to the emphasis of political rather than military factors. The brilliance of 'people's power' lay in its retention of the discourse of power. Through developing and promoting this strategic framework, through conferences, meetings and an expanded media, the UDF retrieved its leading role in political developments inside the country, at the same time as reducing the risk of the mid-1980s revolt spluttering to a halt in the same way as its predecessor of 1976–7.

It is important here to acknowledge the role of the ANC in the UDF's resurgence. UDF leaders generally saw themselves as subordinate to the ANC in exile, although subordinate in the sense more of a subordinate partner than of a subordinate in a straightforwardly hierarchical command structure. In practice, however, the UDF was often the tail that wagged the ANC dog. The ANC simply did not have the capacity to provide detailed direction and co-ordination for political initiatives inside the country, and it was these rather than the muted activities of MK that were driving forward the prospect of political change. Mufson quotes an unidentified UDF leader who was angry at his treatment on one occasion by the exiled ANC: 'The ANC had done a lot of ambassadorial tasks we could not have done. But we unbanned the ANC at home ... I'm an equal in the struggle, if not more.'[9] Where the ANC was decisive was in buttressing the leading role of the UDF inside the country. Faced with dissent or scepticism from important sections of the Charterist movement inside South Africa, the UDF could have its leading role confirmed only by endorsement by the ANC. While the ANC needed an integrative vehicle like the UDF to develop the capacity of the Charterist movement to sustain the revolt, the UDF needed the endorsement of the ANC to play this role. (When, in 1990–1, the ANC's endorsement ceased to be unambiguous, the UDF fell prey to its detractors.)

The state countered the challenge of people's power with an unprecedented clampdown. In July it imposed a country-wide State of Emergency. By the end of the year an estimated 20 000 people had been detained; some were to remain in detention until 1989. The state was unable, however, to secure significant political or ideological gains despite its clear military domination. 'Despite all its efforts, the regime's attempts to reverse the tide of history has been a dismal failure,' the UDF claimed. The National Party government failed to build a significant organised support base in African areas, and failed to erode the support enjoyed there by the ANC and the Charterist movement. The system of elected township councils failed to generate a credible set of conservative, pro-government African political leaders. Those councillors who refused to resign in the face of popular anger fled their townships to live in protected isolation far from their supposed constituents. As a result the National Party was to enter negotiations with the ANC in 1990 devoid of any significant allies in African urban areas. Only among coloured and Indian South African did it bolster its support, laying the basis for its electoral success among these voters in the 1990s.

The UDF's role in boxing in the government is hard to assess. The rhetoric of the Front's leadership was brave, but the reality was that organisation was badly battered, especially at the regional level. In Moosa's words, the UDF sought to conduct a 'holding operation'. Its campaigns were muted, and much of the impetus came from co-organisers in COSATU and the churches. The UDF's own media were disrupted, and its coverage in the commercial press was circumscribed by the press's caution in the face of Emergency regulations. What the UDF did provide was a minimal organisational network across the country, recharged on occasions such as the clandestine 1987 National General Council in Durban, financed through the fast-growing revenues available from Europe, and given some direction through the media. Above all, perhaps, its recommitment to continued public political activity helped to inject into opposition politics an element of continuity from the heady days of the mid-1980s. The late 1980s would not be like the early 1960s, when all efforts had been diverted to the embryonic armed struggle; political struggle was to remain central to the struggle for democracy and freedom. The UDF thus forged a nascent alliance with COSATU and re-engaged the so-called political middle ground, targeting disaffected white political and economic elites. It also played an important part in the rising profile of the ANC, through the Unban the ANC activities and its adoption of the Freedom Charter.

The political strength of the state's opponents became more visible during 1988, notwithstanding the *de facto* banning of the UDF and other organisations early that year. Popular support was demonstrated through the mass stayaway in June, and this was followed by plans for a broad-based Anti-Apartheid Conference, which was banned by the state at the last possible moment. In October the government gave in to international and local pressure, allowing UDF leaders Moosa and Morobe unrestricted freedom after they had escaped from detention and taken refuge in the American consulate in Johannesburg. In January 1989 the government revealed the limits to its political will when it conceded a *de facto* end to mass detention in the face of detainees' hunger strikes.

The key development in this period was, of course, the government's recognition not only that the crisis would be resolved politically rather than militarily, but that unilateral political initiatives were insufficient and that the political agenda now hinged upon negotiations with the ANC. As multiple lines of communication were opened between the government and the ANC, the UDF was transformed more clearly into a component of the ANC's strategy. Its role was to maintain political pressure on the government inside the country, discrediting it, chipping away at the margins of its support, and building support for the kind of transformation envisaged by the ANC. The UDF played this part with outstanding success. The UDF-led Defiance Campaign simultaneously strengthened resistance and weakened the state: participation in protest grew rapidly, as public defiance demonstrated the possibility once again of active protest, whilst the campaign embarrassed the government by highlighting racial segregation and police brutality. The marches raised the spectre of escalating defiance, comparable perhaps to the huge marches that were at that very moment rocking Communist Party rule in Central and Eastern Europe. The Campaign, followed by the Conference for a Democratic Future, strengthened the ANC-led opposition politically, and it was this political terrain that was all important.

Walter Sisulu was quite right to note, in his speech to the final UDF conference, that the Front had placed the 'central question of political power on the agenda'. In 1983–4, when the state sought to present its reforms as extending democracy, the UDF redefined them as exclusionary and anti-democratic. In early 1986 the Front drew together disparate protest and defiance into an explicit challenge to state power. In 1988–9 it pushed the government into actions which acknowledged that the future would be resolved politically, not militarily. Further, in each of these periods the UDF defined the nature of the political game as involving not the government and its allies and supplicants, but rather the government and the extra-parliamentary opposition – the ANC and its internal supporters and allies. Thus Mandela was right to praise the UDF, on his release from prison in 1990, for ensuring that 'none of the reformist strategies of the Government have succeeded'.[10] But he might have gone further: the UDF, along with other groupings, had ensured that there was no realistic possibility of any reformist strategy succeeding without the full co-operation of the ANC.

LIMITS TO CHANGE: THE PROCESS, FORM AND OUTCOME OF DEMOCRATISATION

The onset of negotiations between the ANC and government in 1990 and, four years later, the successful completion of the formal process of democratisation, marked by democratic elections, may be considered as underlining the achievements of the

UDF. Yet, in several respects, each of these events was somewhat less than the UDF had publicly aspired to. Firstly, the process of designing a new South African polity was not what the UDF had envisaged. Secondly, the form of post-apartheid democracy differed from the vision set out by some UDF leaders in the mid-1980s. In addition, some critics of the UDF point to the failure to reach a socialist outcome.

From 1983 the UDF called publicly for an alternative process of constitutional change that involved a national convention. As it turned out, the post-apartheid interim constitution was not designed in a national convention but through multilateral and bilateral negotiations among political parties. The country's 1996 constitution was finalised by a democratically elected Constitutional Assembly in the form of parliament, but within guidelines set during the earlier multi-party talks. Furthermore, in 1984 the UDF had set out several preconditions for a national convention, which were not met prior to the start of talks between the ANC and the government in 1990, including the demobilisation of the security forces and the repeal of all racist and unjust laws.[11]

The appeal of a national convention faded with the growing power of the township revolt. The ANC, whilst still a legal organisation, had long advocated a national convention. The concept was put forward again in the 1980s primarily as an alternative to the Tricameral Parliament: a national convention would be inclusive and representative of all South Africans, in contrast to the Tricameral Paarliament. The township revolt transformed the political terrain in such a way that it seemed possible that state power could be seized. The conception of the struggle in terms of power supplanted a conception in terms of rights; the national convention proposal was damned as a compromise with the oppressors. The democratic alternative to the state's constitutional initiatives was not some national-level bargaining forum but the network of representative structures built at the grassroots, from street committees upwards. The UDF embraced and directed this alternative through the strategic framework of 'people's power'. A paper on 'Towards a People's Democracy', widely distributed in 1987, referred to the 'expansion of the democratic process' and did not mention a national convention. Locally based initiatives would serve to fashion a democratic South Africa even before the transfer of 'political power to the majority had taken place'.[12] In so far as there needed to be a national initiative, this was satisfied by the demand that the ANC be unbanned. It was unnecessary to demand that the ANC and government actually sit together at a negotiating table. Similarly, a national convention was not mentioned in the secretarial report to the UDF's National Working Committee conference in May 1987, nor in any of the conference resolutions.

Similarly, the form of South Africa's democratisation was not what the UDF had committed itself to in the immediate aftermath of people's power. In 1987 the UDF set out a vision of democracy that involved far more participatory elements than were later provided in the post-apartheid institutions of representative democracy. Enthused with people's power, and influenced by accounts of Nicaraguan democracy under the Sandinistas, the UDF declared that it was opposed to the existing parliamentary institutions not only because most of the population was excluded, but also 'because parliamentary-type representation in itself represents a very limited and narrow idea of democracy'.

> Our democratic aim therefore is control over every aspect of our lives, and not just the right (important as it is) to vote for a central government every four to five years. When we speak of majority rule, we do not mean that black faces must simply replace white faces in parliament. A democratic solution in South Africa involves all South Africans, and in particular the working class, having control over all areas of daily existence – from national policy to housing, from schooling to working conditions, from transport to consumption of food. This for us is the essence of democracy. When we say that the people shall govern, we mean at all levels and in all spheres, and we demand that there be real, effective control on a daily basis … In other words, we are talking about direct as opposed to indirect political representation, mass participation rather than passive docility and ignorance, a momentum where ordinary people feel that they can do the job themselves, rather than waiting for their local MP to intercede on their behalf.[13]

In its strongest form, this kind of vision was based on a glorified understanding of both people's power in South Africa, on the one hand, and the experience of socialist democratisation in Nicaragua and elsewhere, on the other.[14] The reality of people's power in South Africa – and of democracy under the Sandinistas in Nicaragua – was more complex and fragile than imagined.[15] The decline of this vision, however, was not so much due to the growth of any critical analysis of such South African or Nicaraguan experiences, but rather to the shifting balance of power in South Africa in the face of state repression and popular demobilisation from June 1986.

Faced with a perceived stalemate under the State of Emergency, UDF leaders became more open to alternative processes of change and forms of democratic outcome. Although some affiliates remained opposed to any kind of negotiation, including even the idea of a national convention, in which the 'oppressors' would be represented, the senior UDF leadership was willing to accept both the ANC's lead in embracing negotiations and the goal, at least initially, of a representative democracy for all South Africans. Some UDF leaders hastily accepted this as reality, and denounced as utopian any more participatory vision. For others, it seems, this acceptance involved a measure of disappointment. It is easy to see such disappointment as an inevitable part of the process of democratisation. Huntington, controversially, considers disappointment as 'an essential first step in the process of democratic consolidation', because the health of democracy as a political system depends on 'the premise that governments will fail and that hence institutionalised ways have to exist for changing them'. In Huntington's view: 'Disillusionment and the lowered expectations it produces are the foundation of democratic stability. Democracies become consolidated when people learn that democracy is a solution to the problem of tyranny, but not necessarily to anything else.'[16]

In South Africa the more substantive view of participatory democracy that had been widespread in 1986 gave way, at least among the UDF leadership, to a procedural view of democracy emphasising elections and representative government. In their comments at the Kagiso Trust's 'From Opposing to Governing' conference in January 1990, both Morobe and Manuel intimated that the radicalism and expectations of the UDF's supporters needed to be tempered. Similarly, in describing the preceding Conference for a Democratic Future as akin to a 'genuine people's assembly' and a 'genuinely democratic parliament', Morobe was endorsing a more or less conventional view of representative democracy.

The appeal of an essentially procedural view of democracy probably reflected the ANC political elite's concern to control state power from the top (perhaps for progressive purposes) and the partial demobilisation of protest inside the country, as well as a recognition of the need to reassure white and other minority South Africans, economic elites and the international audience. If the formal transition had begun in mid-1986, rather than early in 1990, the impulse towards a more participatory form of democracy would have been far stronger, for better or worse. All the same a weak version of the more radical vision of democracy did persist in South Africa, surfacing somewhat confusedly in the Reconstruction and Development Programme adopted by the ANC as its election manifesto in 1994, and expressed intermittently by critics on the left. It must be acknowledged that former UDF leaders have not been prominent among the visible supporters of such a vision.

In some respects, the South African experience was not dissimilar to that of other contexts where people were struggling against oppressive regimes. In Central and Eastern Europe under Communist Party rule, 'democracy' was widely understood as the antithesis of the existing political and economic system; that is, in terms of freedoms from state and party authority, and economic opportunities through free markets. In South Africa liberation generally meant rights and representation for all, decentralised power, and a redistributive economic alternative. To some extent, the vision was contingent on the existing system. In South Africa, as in Central and Eastern Europe, a more precise picture of social and institutional arrangements did not begin to take shape until democratisation became imminent.

A more striking dissonance between 1980s rhetoric and 1990s outcome concerns the extent of social and economic transformation. In the early and mid-1980s certain elements of socialist rhetoric were widespread within the Charterist movement, as well as within the movement's growing range of allies in the labour movement. This has led many scholars to the view that 'the UDF's capacious ideological umbrella also sheltered socialists', as Lodge writes.[17] But should apparently socialist rhetoric be taken at face value? Lodge himself tends to caution, believing that 'a substantial proportion of the UDF's working-class following was inspired by a socialist vision' whilst suggesting that the 'ideological predilections of the largely middle-class leaders of the movement' are harder to pin down. Certainly, it is not clear that a hostility to perceived exploitation or even the intermittent use of class in popular discourse is sufficient to warrant categorising a movement, organisation or individual as 'socialist'. The hostility to capitalism among many UDF leaders seems to have been rooted in the perception that capitalism and apartheid were intimately linked, and that capitalists were opposed to democratisation. In other words, social and economic radicalism was rooted at least as much in perceptions of the battle lines around democratisation and liberation as vice versa. When capitalist elites appeared ready to throw their support, albeit conditionally and self-interestedly, behind the ANC and UDF, so most of the top UDF leaders welcomed their support and shifted away from socialist rhetoric.

Even among the broader movement as a whole inside the country, it is easy to exaggerate the extent and depth of radicalism. Radical discourse was often highly contingent on the context. Unfortunately, there is almost no research on popular political culture in the 1980s. Research conducted in the early 1990s tends, however, to deflate assessments of popular radicalism. Surveys of public opinion suggest that few African voters regard themselves as particularly 'left-wing' or 'radical'. Most voters combined radical views on some issues with conservative views on others, so that Johnson and Schlemmer (no radicals themselves) regarded ANC supporters to be 'social democrats'. Research conducted by Charney soon after the 1994 elections found little evidence of revolutionary sentiment: people wanted to 'prod the system, not smash it'. Most African voters regarded the election in a purely political sense, and did not expect any rapid emancipation from economic wants. Certainly, trade union members may be committed to democratic procedures that are more radical than mere accountability through elections, as Maree suggests, using post-1994 survey data; but even this section of the population is committed to representative democracy, which they seek to make more democratic, rather than replace it altogether. As the SACP intellectual Mzala suggested, perhaps the best way of understanding the socialist rhetoric and ideology of the 1980s is as 'populism about socialism', based more in anti-apartheid sentiment than any clear socialist vision.[18]

The UDF leadership generally articulated the view that the UDF was engaged in a 'national democratic struggle'. Its goal was a changed political system rather than a changed society, (political) democracy rather than socio-economic equality. The UDF Declaration refers to the Front's goals as a 'true', unitary and non-racial democracy. Its demand that 'all forms of oppression and exploitation must end' was appealing but vague. Many self-conscious socialists, whether in the labour movement or elsewhere, tended to remain outside the UDF; those who were active in the UDF tended to subordinate socialist goals to democratic ones. For sure, most UDF leaders held strong beliefs in justice that extended beyond formal political equality, but justice was generally conceived in terms of rights and responsibilities rather than public ownership of the means of production. Beliefs in justice were infused with liberal conceptions of rights, including, especially, freedom from discrimination, together with a religious morality.

The UDF should not be regarded as synonymous with the broader movement – or movements – of popular resistance in the 1980s. It was not even coterminous with the Charterist movement, large parts of which declined either always or sometimes to acknowledge the UDF as the overarching co-ordinating structure for Charterists inside the country. In so far as the UDF was integral to a broader movement, that movement was primarily a 'people's movement', as Boesak put it in 1983, standing for freedom and democracy, and proclaiming a message of hope and freedom, more than for radical economic or social change. Its successes thus corresponded to its objects.

OPPORTUNITIES

While the UDF's successes, and their limits, were in part the product of tactical and strategic choices made by the UDF leadership, the prospects of success were shaped by the changing structure of opportunities facing the UDF. Crucially, the UDF was formed during a period of liberalisation on the state's part, as the state sought to reconstitute its political and ideological foundations. Liberalisation entailed new political openings and a lowered level of state repression. The changing international context also shaped the prospects of success, with growing international pressure on the South African government and growing acceptance of the ANC. The impact of the UDF was also dependent, in large part, on the organisational basis provided by its many affiliates. The social structure of South Africa had changed in ways that facilitated the formation of collective organisation in the workplace, residential areas and educational institutions. Finally, the government faced elite disaffection and struggled to maintain a broad anti-democratic alliance: democratisation for its part offered growing benefits to some important elite groups, but growing costs to others.

Authoritarian regimes seeking to reconstitute their political bases often tolerate political liberalisation prior to – or as an attempted alternative to – full democratisation. Liberalisation typically involves the relaxation of controls over political communication, association and activity, thus providing openings for opposition movements. 'Liberalizing authoritarian regimes may release political prisoners, open up some issues for public debate, loosen censorship, sponsor elections for offices that have little power, permit some renewal of civil society, and take other steps in a democratic direction, without submitting top decision-makers to the electoral test.'[19] In many cases, including most of contemporary Africa, political liberalisation has been a government response to political pressures, especially from below, but sometimes from the international arena. Often, political liberalisation has not led to democratisation – which suggests that it can serve as an alternative for incumbent regimes.[20]

In South Africa the UDF was formed amidst a general political liberalisation, itself the result of political pressures from within the country and international factors. The constitutional reforms were part of this liberalisation, but more important for opposition was the accompanying relaxation of repression. Although the ANC remained banned, a significant degree of freedom of assembly and association was permitted during 1983–4, except in the bantustans. While outdoor political meetings were banned, indoor meetings and conferences were generally permitted, with rare exceptions – notably in the Border region. The UDF itself was not banned. The Million Signatures Campaign was tolerated: not without illicit interference, but tolerated nonetheless. Restrictions on many individuals were lifted. The mainstream commercial media reported on the anti-apartheid opposition with growing impunity, and the explicitly anti-apartheid alternative press – community newspapers such as *Grassroots* – burgeoned, being only partly fettered.

The effect of this political opening was to strengthen the national, rather than local, focus of opposition activity. Had there been a higher level of repression it is likely that more localised and sporadic activities would have been far more predominant. Overt activities at the national level required a higher degree of freedom. (Such national level activity was facilitated, and perhaps even made possible, by the technology of the telephone and improved inter-city road and air transport.)

Liberalisation involved the curtailment of repression. Repression in South Africa had always operated within political limits, its use being governed by political considerations. Even in the late 1980s, when the South African state was widely referred to as the 'security state', politics had primacy. The military and police never had the scope to conduct the kind of dirty war practised in, for example, Argentina after 1976, El Salvador and Guatemala after 1979, or Algeria in either the 1950s or 1990s.[21] As many people 'disappeared' or were murdered in Argentina as were detained in South Africa. In Guatemala over 21 000 people were murdered between 1978 and 1986. In El Salvador 55 000 people were murdered over the same period; no fewer than 31 000 people were murdered in 1980–1 alone.[22] An equivalent dirty war in South Africa would have entailed the death of all of the activists who were 'only', in the event, detained and often tortured.[23] This would, surely, have transformed the character of resistance in South Africa. There were considerable variations within South Africa in the level and brutality of repression, with the worst atrocities concentrated in the Eastern Cape. Nonetheless, of about one hundred top national and regional UDF leaders, only three REC members, Goniwe, Mxenge and Nchabaleng, were killed by the police or army, with one other senior leader, Ngwenya in Pietermaritzburg, killed by Inkatha leaders.[24]

Repression was particularly muted at the time of the formation of the UDF. This was the result of two related shifts in state strategy, linked to political liberalisation. First, the state adopted what has been termed the 'Rabie Strategy', named after the judge who chaired a commission of inquiry that led to the promulgation of the 1982 Internal Security Act. Under the Rabie Strategy, threats to internal security would be responded to as crimes, through the courts and by the police. The Internal Security Act tightened up the criminalisation of political offences such as subversion, as well as making provision for detentions, bannings and other restrictions. Secondly, the South African Police Commissioner from June 1983, Johann Coetzee, favoured a strategy of stealth over one of confrontation. 'Believing that the UDF was too powerful to crush and that banning it would merely force it underground, he was reportedly behind the government's relatively tolerant attitude to the organisation in its first years.'[25] Coetzee sought to weaken anti-apartheid groups by fomenting divisions. This strategy had the additional intended benefit of legitimising the government's constitutional reforms: allowing meetings to be held in protest against the elections would, it was envisaged, legitimise the elections themselves. The state thus allowed its opponents considerable latitude to organise in 1983–4. Bannings were lifted, meetings and conferences tolerated. Few activists were detained without being prosecuted.[26] Of course, the state engaged in propaganda and a range of dirty tricks against its internal opponents, but these stopped far short of the high level of brutality exercised by many other repressive regimes. Protests in townships – most notably in the Vaal Triangle in September 1984 – were dealt with by the use of force. But organisations themselves were allowed the space to operate.[27]

The Rabie–Coetzee strategy was not, of course, a success. The UDF itself embarrassed the state at the end of 1984, when its leaders occupied the British consulate in Durban and demanded that detainees be charged or released. The state's attempts to criminalise the UDF and its leadership were conspicuous failures: the core of the Pietermaritzburg Treason Trial collapsed; the Delmas Treason Trial degenerated into a farce; preparations for a third major UDF trial in 1985, and of Eastern Cape UDF and other Charterist leadership in 1988–9, came to naught; and Edgar Ngoyi was acquitted on a murder charge. Of over a hundred UDF national and regional officials, none were successfully convicted for activities linked to the UDF. There were some convictions for non-UDF activity: Mpetha was convicted of charges concerning incidents prior to 1983; Stofile was convicted of assisting MK, though on flimsy evidence, in a Ciskei court; several regional UDF leaders were jailed for MK-related activities. For sure, much of the UDF leadership was diverted by prosecution, but neither they nor the Front as a whole were successfully criminalised. Indeed, trials could serve a mobilising purpose, providing a focus for nationwide publicity and local organisational development, as in the case of Pietermaritzburg in early 1985.

The partial liberalisation of 1983–4 was brought to an end in 1985–6, as the state sought to retain a firmer grip on politics and society. A blanket ban was imposed on specified political organisations holding meetings indoors in a growing number of magisterial districts. Political leaders were detained under the Internal Security Act or – from July 1985 in parts of the country – under the State of Emergency. The government extended its controls over the media.[28] But even then, divisions within the state kept some options open to the opposition: at the local level, officials were often willing to negotiate with civic leaders; the Department of Education and Training was willing to talk to its critics.

In mid-1986 the level of repression was stepped up with the imposition of a countrywide State of Emergency. Detentions and restrictions replaced prosecution as the primary strategy for containing opposition leaders, whilst force was used to disperse people on the streets. This reflected the failure of the earlier strategy: instead of justifying executive action on prior legal conviction, the government was forced to rely on executive condemnation to justify its more repressive approach. Security remained, nonetheless, subordinate to reform. By this stage, however, the UDF had established itself, and state repression could only legitimise it. Escalating repression also increased the importance of the media – and the UDF took advantage of both improved coverage in the commercial press and the opportunities that increased funding opened up for its own media production. The UDF was also able to work with and through organisations which were less subject to repression: the churches and trade unions especially.

At the end of the decade repression eased off once more, again in response to both internal protest and international pressure. The government lacked the political will to maintain the more repressive strategy of the mid-1980s. The number of activists in detention fell, although the remaining detainees included much of the core national and regional leadership of the UDF and its major affiliates. When Morobe and Moosa took refuge in the American consulate in Johannesburg in late 1988, the state agreed to allow them to leave without restrictions. Faced with hunger strikers protesting against continued detention without trial early in 1989, the state conceded that mass detention would be discontinued; in deciding to release detainees, the cabinet apparently overruled the advice of the State Security Council.[29] Hunger strikes can be an expression of political weakness, as in Ireland, in the early and late twentieth century;[30] in South Africa, however, they were an expression of political strength. Similarly, faced with the burgeoning mass marches, the police were ordered to desist from their initial brutality; the government was not worried by the possibility of defections, as in parts of Central and Eastern Europe at this time, but rather by the political costs associated with highly public police brutality. At the end of the decade, as at the beginning, the UDF was shaped by the political opportunities opened up by liberalisation.

Non-violent protest is far more sensitive to the opportunity structure than violent protest. Severe repression raises the costs of non-violent collective action, rendering it almost impossible to sustain; conversely, greater institutional responsiveness to such action has a mobilising effect. The openings of 1983–4 and 1989 were crucial in facilitating the demonstrations and defiance of those periods. The only non-violent protests that endured in the more repressive environment of 1985–8 were passive protests: consumer boycotts, the Black Christmas campaigns, stayaways and rent boycotts.

While liberalisation was driven in large part by the government's need to accommodate internal political protest, it was also a response to the international context. The South African economy had long needed foreign capital. Although investors are rarely very concerned about democracy *per se*, they do demand a degree of stability, which in turn, in the South African context, was widely seen as requiring a more accommodating political strategy on the state's part. Moreover, the policy of constructive engagement on the part of the United States and, in practice, Britain depended on the credibility of the South African government's reform programme. When the South African government chose to retreat from reform in 1986, most dramatically through its dismissal of the Eminent Persons Group initiative, it embarassed and greatly weakened the support of its foreign sympathisers. At the same time, the Cold War began to wind down, reducing perceived stakes in regional conflicts like those in southern Africa. Relations soured between the United States and Britain on the one hand and South Africa on the other. Both the American and British governments shifted towards the endorsement of the ANC as indispensable to a peace settlement in South Africa. The United States intensified economic pressure with the 1986 Comprehensive Anti-Apartheid Act, whilst the British held off heavy sanctions by agreeing that the European Commission fund the 'victims of apartheid' through the Kagiso Trust.[31]

The South African government's diplomatic weaknesses were compounded by military setbacks in Angola. In 1987–8 South African troops incurred heavy casualties among mostly white troops, trying to protect its ally (or surrogate), UNITA, in and around Cuito Cuanavale in southern Angola. Whilst the battle cannot be considered a clear military defeat, the costs of fighting in Angola had risen to a level which the politicians were unwilling to endure. The battle thus provided further impetus to the South Africans to negotiate a political settlement not only for Angola but for Namibia too. With the Soviet and American governments reducing their support for their surrogates in the region, and pushing for a settlement instead, peace accords were quickly signed in December 1988.[32]

Skocpol and others have shown how military defeat is often a key element in weakening the state, providing opportunities to the regime's opponents.[33] The South African military had not been defeated; nor was there much likelihood of its being seriously weakened by defections or resistance to conscription, notwithstanding the efforts of the End Conscription Campaign.[34] Indeed, the Angolan–Namibian settlement represented a setback for the ANC, which had to withdraw its bases still further north and away from South Africa. Some sections of the military seem to have remained gung-ho about their capacity to maintain internal repression. It was the civilian rulers whose confidence in the military was dented. Military power no longer provided a bulwark behind which the international pressures for democratisation could be resisted. With the Cold War winding down, the 'third wave' of democratisation would soon sweep over South Africa's borders.[35]

The international context was also important in that the UDF, its affiliates and allies enjoyed considerable funding from abroad. Foreign funds vastly exceeded the meagre sums that these organisations could hope to raise locally. Even the trade unions, which raised fees from their members, relied heavily on foreign funding. The collapse of the rand also helped, inflating the rand value of foreign donations.

The UDF was able to take advantage of the political liberalisation and the international context because there was a base of existing organisations and networks on which it could build. The organisational base of the UDF reflected the character of South African society in the 1980s: professional organisations with fast-growing black membership; community organisations in settled urban areas; student organisations in the burgeoning secondary and tertiary educational sectors; and youth organisations bringing together highly politicised, well-educated activists and unemployed school-leavers. The power of the UDF was rooted in the growth of the settled black urban population, comprising both the urban industrial working classes and the aspirant black middle classes. Without this patchwork of organisations the UDF would not have been possible: a national association of individual activists along the lines of the Release Mandela Committee, for example, would have been too easy to suppress.

The possibility of the UDF was also premised on the existence of the ANC, in terms of both its political traditions – which remained alive, in many parts of the country, into the early 1980s[36] – and its expanding political underground. The actual relationship between the UDF and the ANC may not have been the neatly hierarchical one alleged by the state, but it was certainly true that the formation of the UDF and the subsequent maintenance of unity, albeit fragile and strained, depended on the glue provided by loyalties to the ANC.

The changing social and economic structure of South Africa eroded the ability of the National Party to maintain a broad anti-democratic alliance. The hitherto enduring elite alignment that had sustained apartheid collapsed. For some rural elites – especially in sectors that remained dependent on state patronage, through price support for example – and for poorer white, coloured and Indian people, social and economic changes were profoundly threatening. The National Party thus faced a growing disaffection and defection to rival parties to its right. At the same time, economic elites whose well-being depended more on the market than on the state viewed the costs of apartheid, including the prospect of chronic instability, with growing concern. To them, as to many such elites in the advanced industrialised world before them, democratisation seemed preferable to revolution. Having learned to live with trade unions, key business elites viewed the ANC with suspicion but with diminishing hostility. Businessmen sought to negotiate deals with civic leaders at the local level, whilst big business opened up lines of communication with the ANC in exile. Intellectual elites were also increasingly disaffected from the National Party – as was reflected in visits to the ANC by Afrikaner students, academics, newspaper editors and others, as well as the ideological struggles within the Dutch Reformed Church and Broederbond.[37]

In summary, the UDF was very much the product of its context: of liberalisation on the part of the state, of international pressures, and of the growth of anti-apartheid organisation and elite disaffection amidst fundamental socio-economic changes in society. But whilst such opportunities may make action possible, actors also create their own opportunities. The organisational structure of the UDF and its choices of strategies and tactics were important factors shaping its impact on the course of South African politics.

ORGANISATION AND RESOURCES

The organisational structure of the UDF was an important factor in its capacity to weather adverse conditions and maintain political pressure on the state. Many commentators have suggested that the Front's 'shell-like' structure reduced its vulnerability to repression. More importantly, the organisational form of the Front allowed for the degree of flexibility required for acting in very different modes as conditions demanded – sometimes in a vanguardist mode, taking the initiative and pulling its affiliates along, and sometimes in a more co-ordinating role, linking sovereign affiliates together. The organisational form of the Front varied not only over time, but also between and even within its constituent regions.

The form adopted by the Front was unusual in comparative terms. It was not a mere purposive alliance of competing parties, as the popular fronts had been in the 1930s. In South Africa one political movement, the ANC was hegemonic within opposition politics. But the ANC was banned and unable to operate in the legal and public space provided by the state's political need to be seen as tolerant of non-violent opposition.

The Front could be flexible because its form, and indeed its functions, remained somewhat indeterminate, open to varied interpretation. This inevitably meant that the organisational structure and practices of the Front were a matter of continuing dispute and rancour. The Front was formed with little clarity as to how it would operate. It had no constitution. Its Working Principles insisted that affiliates retained their autonomy but did not provide any concrete guidance on how the Front would operate. In the face of repression as well as its leaders' concern to strengthen the movement against apartheid, the Front adopted more and more of a vanguardist role – prompting repeated criticism, as we have seen. Its leadership remained insistent, however, that the Front was committed to democratic practices. In the UDF's 1987 paper 'Towards a People's Democracy', five 'basic principles of our organisational democracy' were identified:

1. Leadership must be elected and recallable.
2. Leadership must be collective (and leadership skills must be developed).
3. Leadership must exercise their initiative, but act according to democratic decisions.
4. Leadership must report back regularly and fully to organisations, areas, etc.
5. There must be constructive criticism and self-criticism through regular evaluations.[38]

In practice, the UDF adhered to this democratic model unevenly and intermittently, although generally through no choice of its own. At least initially, its leadership was elected. Its national office-holders were elected in 1983, and again in 1985. Regional leadership was elected in 1983, again in 1984 in the case of the Border region, and again in all major regions in 1985. Some of the regional elections were fiercely competitive. Thereafter, elections were not held regularly. In the Western Cape, elections were held in 1987 and 1989, but in other regions they were only held in 1989, and in Natal it seems they were not held again at all. This was primarily due to repression. The detention or prosecution of elected leaders ensured that in practice leadership roles were played by non-elected leaders from most of 1985 to 1989. At the national level, for example, Morobe, Nair and Mafolo were not even members of the NEC as constituted in 1985. In the face of the constraints on elected representation, the UDF reorganised many of its executive committees so that subordinate structures or sectors sent representatives, rather than elected specific individuals. Repression also curtailed the capacity of the Front's leadership to operate collectively. Until mid-1985, or even late 1985, the NEC retained decision-making power at the national level; thereafter, much power shifted in practice to key officials: Moosa as acting secretary, Morobe in charge of publicity, and Cachalia as treasurer. The same constraints existed at the regional level.

The Front also acted creditably in terms of the last two of the basic principles identified above. The UDF maintained an impressive level of reporting-back and of self-criticism, given the constraints under which it operated after 1985. As is clear from preceding chapters, UDF leaders carried forward an impressive tradition of self-critical reflection on their performance and that of the Front. In public, UDF speakers adopted a celebratory tone, even during the height of repression and disorganisation in 1986–7. Within the organisation, however, the UDF's own leaders were among the most focused of its critics. It was Molefe who reported to the 1985 national conference that political organisation was 'trailing behind the masses', and who identified a series of weaknesses in the Front's performance. It was Moosa, the acting secretary general in Molefe's absence, who reported to the 1987 NGC that the Front had been unable to maintain its regional structures. And it was Molefe, again, who told the 1991 NGC that the Front was then 'at its weakest in the entire history of its existence'.

It was with respect to the third of the basic principles listed above that the practices of the UDF diverged furthest from the stated goals. Decisions were rarely made on the basis of mandated positions, and the national leadership exercised considerable latitude. Most of the major decisions made after 1984 were taken without extensive discussion and consultation among affiliates or even regional structures. Co-ordination took the form of injunctions from above: help with this campaign, use this tactic, avoid the errors of both populism and workerism, and so on.

Faced with this situation it is not surprising that the leadership of the Front came in for some vicious criticism from ANC-aligned activists as well as from their opponents. It was also no surprise that most of these Charterist critics did not seek to contest control of the Front from within but rather voted with their feet and challenged it from the outside. For all its achievements, the leadership of the Front was not sufficiently accountable to the affiliates to persuade critics to voice their opposition through internal channels. Whilst further research is required on this, it seems that the only times that incumbent UDF office-holders were defeated in elections were when the leadership core supported the challenge, as in both the Western Cape and the Transvaal in 1985, when Oscar Mpetha and Moss Chikane respectively were unseated in competitive elections. With no prospect of being able to contest the UDF leadership successfully, critics were driven to snipe from the outside.

Criticism of the UDF leadership was focused on the so-called cabal. Dissent within the UDF had emerged during the referendum debate in late 1983, grew in 1984 amidst strategic differences – these included the Million Signatures Campaign, the proposed defiance campaign, the calls for a national convention, stayaways or general strikes, and finally the occupation of the British consulate – and cohered during the Pietermaritzburg Treason Trial. Aubrey Mokoena, who had been a member of the initial NEC, and others began to build the Johannesburg-based Release Mandela Campaign as an alternative forum for leadership in the Charterist movement. Later, supported by Winnie Mandela and sections of the youth movement, Mokoena voiced more strident criticisms of the 'cabal' controlling the UDF, and even complained to the ANC in exile. In 1990, the criticisms became public when he wrote an open letter to the ANC leadership, alleging 'treachery' and 'treason' on the part of the UDF leaders involved in the cabal.

Its accusers conjured up a vision of the UDF that resembled, in some respects at least, the classic analysis of the oligarchic tendencies in organisation formulated by Max Weber and Robert Michels at the beginning of the twentieth century. According to Michels's 'iron law of oligarchy', as 'democratic' organisations develop social and economic bases in society, so they inevitably become bureaucratised, and power becomes concentrated in the hands of a few leaders. The organisational leadership grows increasingly concerned to maintain the organisation, prone to adaptation to the existing power structure in society, and retreat from the organisation's original goals.[39] The critics of the 'cabal' in the UDF did not level the second of these charges at the time, although they have done so since 1991;[40] they did level the first and third of these charges.

There is certainly evidence that the UDF became bureaucratised. At the outset, charismatic leadership clearly played a major part. Most notably, Boesak played an inspirational role both in the formation of the Front in 1983 and in some of its campaigns and activities up to the time of the banned march on Pollsmoor Prison in 1985. Boesak was never an office-holder in the UDF (he was, formally, a patron only), but many members of the Front's initial NEC were more charismatic than bureaucratic. As the Front grew, however, and was transformed into an increasingly coherent organisation, so bureaucrats assumed greater authority. Molefe was perhaps the first of the senior bureaucrats; when he and the charismatic Lekota were detained, their places were filled (temporarily) by Manuel and Carolus, and later and for much longer by Moosa, Morobe and Cachalia, all of whom were effective bureaucrats.

It is less clear, however, that there was much 'goal transformation'. Certainly, under the State of Emergency the UDF leadership invested considerable effort in maintaining and strengthening organisational structures, both of the Front and its affiliates. But such organisation building was actually one of the UDF's original goals; the lesson of 1976 was that organisational development was necessary if sustained pressure was to be exerted on the apartheid state. Moreover, most of the strategies and tactics employed by the UDF at the outset were retained. From late 1989 many UDF leaders were conspicuously wary of confrontational tactics. But such wariness was evident from 1983, and in so far as there was a shift in 1989 it took place in a context in which it was believed (rightly) that the UDF had already effectively secured its goal of democratisation, in that the state was locked into a path that would lead precisely there.

In addition, oligarchic tendencies were by no means confined to the UDF 'cabal'. The critics of the 'cabal' were vulnerable to the same charges. Indeed, there was a strong current of vanguardism within opposition politics, including the diverse Charterist movement. Barrell has shown how ANC strategic thought in exile revolved around a conception of its role as the 'detonator' that would spark an irresistible insurrection.[41] The most striking vanguardist statements made by UDF leaders were not made by 'cabalists', but by leaders such as Tshwete, who argued that the UDF's top leadership had a perspective superior to the leadership of its affiliates.

The UDF did develop a bureaucratic leadership; the 'cabal' did wield considerable power through their control of financial and other resources; they did advocate a less immediately confrontational strategy than some of their critics. But they did not do so from an explicit strategy of subverting the organisation or through any conspiracy to monopolise power for personal gain. Rather, they were the products of the context. Moreover, the allegations were part of a contest for power in which the accusers themselves sought to secure the leading role in the internal Charterist movement, sought to control resources, and sought to determine the strategies and tactics to be employed. The contest was fuelled further by a degree of resentment towards non-Africans in leadership positions, and by the complexity of relationships with the ANC, with various sections of the internal Charterist movement using different lines of communication and each claiming a superior mandate.

Control over resources was central to many of the disputes within the UDF. As the Front's resources grew, so disputes intensified. In 1983 the UDF's income depended largely on donations. The two national treasurers, Ramgobin and Saloojee, were especially successful in raising donations from Indian businessmen in Natal. The total budget was limited. Up to mid-October 1983, for example, the Western Cape region spent just over R30 000 – one-third of which was on the national launch, and another third on printing media and posters. Then the UDF began obtaining funds abroad, as prizes, such as the Swedish 'Let Live' human rights award, or grants. By the end of 1984 the national office had distributed R175 000 to the regions, and some regions were able to supplement their share through their own fund-raising. Required to produce a budget for foreign donors, the UDF began to think grandiosely, drafting a budget motivation with a price-tag of R455 000 to cover the next six months. Such ambitions were only slightly premature. From 1986 the UDF received massive funding from abroad, enabling it to employ more and more organisers. By 1989–9 the UDF had an income of about R1.7 million, excluding grants for specific expenses such as the Conference for a Democratic Future (cost: R417 000). In 1990–1 the UDF's income rose to about R4.8 million; in real terms, taking inflation into account, this represented about ten times its budget for its first year. By this stage the single largest item of expenditure was salaries. All these figures exclude the income received separately by the UDF's affiliates for their own purposes.

The growing availability of funds affected both strategies and politics within the UDF. It enabled the regions to employ teams of organisers. It paid for the production of media. It paid for airfares for the leadership, bought cars, and settled their telephone bills. It paid for some of the transport and accommodation needed at national conferences. In the last eighteen months or so of the UDF's existence, it paid for computers and fax machines. Funding thus enabled activists from across the country to come together for co-ordinating and decision-making meetings, and for organisers to spread out across much of the country, promoting organisational development and protest. Funding was thus crucial to the project of building a nationwide political movement. Funding was perhaps most important during the Emergency, when it enabled the UDF to continue to provide some national leadership through media and organisers, even when many of its organisational structures and affiliates were in disarray.

Funding also affected the internal politics of the UDF, as we have already seen in the cabal allegations. Cachalia, national treasurer from 1985, freely admits that he had considerable autonomy to decide whom to pay and whom not. And, as he himself warned in January 1990: 'As foreign money washes into our organisations, the executives in our organisations become less and less responsible or accountable to the masses.'[42] The accrual of power to the UDF's financial controllers was balanced, to some extent, by the flow of funds to UDF affiliates. Funds from the European Commission and other foreign donors were channelled, often through intermediaries such as the Kagiso Trust, to civic organisations, advice offices, and youth organisations. Thus, whilst the national treasurer became more powerful within the Front, some of its major affiliates became more autonomous from the Front. The concentration of power was accompanied by a diffusion of power.

Although the inflow of funds after 1985 seemed immense and had important political ramifications for the UDF, it must be acknowledged that the sums involved were small compared to those of other mass organisations. The ANC is reported to have had a budget of US$50–100 million per annum whilst in exile; back in South Africa in 1991, the operational costs of the ANC's administration were put at R4 million per month; in 1993 the ANC announced a fund-raising target of R168 million for its election campaign.[43] These sums dwarf the income of the UDF. The trade union movement also commanded much more extensive resources than the UDF. It is difficult to obtain figures for union finances, but by the mid-1990s the unions affiliated to COSATU were employing an estimated 1500 people.[44] The progressive churches also had considerable budgets in the 1980s, and substantial funds were directed to legal firms for defence in political trials and to service organisations for development-related work.

Funds were the most conspicuous resource enjoyed by the UDF, but they were not the only resources. Personnel also comprised a crucial resource. The UDF's leadership included people – some of them lawyers – with a wealth of administrative and professional skills and who, generally through family or education, had networks of contacts with a wide range of skills and resources. When Goniwe needed to get from Cradock to Port Elizabeth for a UDF REC meeting, he could persuade his good friend Sparrow Mhlauli to drive him and others there in Mhlauli's car (assistance that would cost Mhlauli his life, as it turned out).

LEADERSHIP

The character of the UDF's leadership has been the subject of extensive debate. Left critics of the UDF's pan-class approach to politics implied that its leadership was middle class, dominated by 'petty bourgeois intellectuals,'[45] rendering it ripe for a post-election sell-out to business.[46] In response, Swilling asserts that 'a high proportion of the UDF's leadership are (or have come) from poor working-class backgrounds'; he suggests that, of 62 REC members for which he had evidence, about half were in 'economic positions that can be defined as working class'; the other half were in professional occupations or were students.[47] Lodge interprets the same data differently. 'Socially, UDF leadership is heavily middle-class': the number of NEC–REC members in professional, religious or technical occupations greatly outnumbered those classifiable as workers. Lodge notes the absence of 'people from middle-level management, modern commercial occupations, township business, and petty trading'. The UDF leadership, he emphasises, 'belong to an intellectual middle class rather than an entrepreneurial one', and therefore he concludes that 'a disproportionate share of the original national leadership came from a radicalized middle-class intelligentsia'.[48] Anthony Marx concurs with Lodge: both the Black Consciousness and Charterist movements were 'to a large extent led by the black middle class and aspirants to it'.[49]

These contrasting assessments arise in part from Swilling's apparent conflation of class origins with class position. Certainly, many of the UDF's leaders – including almost all of its African leaders – came from impoverished, working-class backgrounds. Popo Molefe, for example, grew up in a very poor family in Soweto. His father was a labourer, his mother a domestic servant. His schooling was interrupted several times when his family could not afford his school fees, and he eventually reached Standard 10 in 1976, aged 24. Prior to being employed by the UDF, he was a printing machine operator for Kodak. Leaders such as Molefe were born in South Africa's cities, generally of working-class families that had moved there from rural areas. Similarly, Matthew Goniwe's father was a labourer, and his mother a domestic worker – but he went to high school and on to Fort Hare University, becoming a teacher.

Focusing on class origins obscures the importance of class mobility. From the 1940s onwards, South Africa underwent extraordinary social and occupational change. Children like the young Popo Molefe had the opportunity, which most of their parents had not had, to complete primary schooling and go on to high school. Graduating from high school, students like Molefe were able to secure jobs as skilled or white-collar workers that had not existed a generation previously. For Molefe, working as a machine operator was a transitory stage in a path of upward occupational mobility. In his case, Molefe became a professional activist; eleven years after working as a machine operator he became Premier of the North West Province. Similarly, Stone Sizani, a UDF REC member in the Eastern Cape, was employed as a skilled technician, and is thus classified misleadingly as a worker by Swilling.[50] After several years as a professional UDF activist, Sizani became the Eastern Cape manager of the Kagiso Trust, studied overseas, and then worked as an executive in the Independent Development Trust. Few UDF leaders had any significant experience of blue-collar working-class employment, and these were mostly confined to the older generation of 1950s veterans such as Ngoyi and Fazzie in the Eastern Cape. The younger activists may have had passing experience as skilled workers but were for the most part professional activists. Some had already broken into professional occupations by the time they became UDF leaders – for example, Goniwe was a teacher; and the Natal secretary, Joe Phaahla, was a doctor. Professionals and quasi-professionals played key roles at regional and national levels.

The UDF leadership was most clearly middle class in Natal and the Western Cape.

In Natal, Lodge classified only two out of sixteen REC members as workers; this regional leadership was 'largely middle class and professional'.[51] Similarly, in the Western Cape, Swilling classified only three out of twelve REC members as working class.[52] In Natal the UDF regional leadership was drawn heavily from sections of the Indian middle class and a relatively well-established African middle class. In the Western Cape the UDF leadership included mostly coloured activists, many with post-secondary education. In both cases, a large majority of REC members had experience of tertiary education. Most UDF leaders in these two provinces may not have been African, but they too were drawn from sections of the South African population that were enjoying marked upward mobility.

The importance of high school education led Brewer to identify the driving force of opposition politics as 'educated labour', borrowing the phrase from Habermas.[53] But in also describing this social group as a 'radicalised middle class',[54] Brewer obscures the significance of mobility. The key African social group in the UDF leadership comprised people with working-class origins, radicalised at high school or university, and thereafter set on a path of upward occupational mobility, but who, because of residential segregation and the late development of urban African middle-class housing estates, remained in close contact with their working-class families and neighbours.

The UDF leadership was conspicuously not drawn from certain social groups. As Lodge and others note, there were very few leaders from the 'old' or entrepreneurial middle class; in so far as they were middle class, they were 'new' middle class. Secondly, few if any of the UDF leadership came from peasant or other backgrounds in deep rural areas. The sons, let alone daughters, of peasants or migrants rarely had the opportunity to get to high school in the 1960s or 1970s, and thus had few opportunities to move into a leadership position in the cities, where political organisation was concentrated. Thirdly, and most importantly perhaps, there were very few UDF leaders with any sustained experience on the shop floor. Workers made it into leadership positions in the trade unions but not in the UDF. To take just one example, the leadership of unions in the metalworking industry included Moses Mayekiso and Enoch Godongwana, both of whom came from the Transkei to work in factories on the Reef. Both later became involved in community issues, in Alexandra and the East Rand respectively. But neither became involved in the UDF. While the African UDF leadership had working-class roots and links, it was generally not in or to the industrial working class in particular.

The social character of the UDF leadership had some clear implications for the Front. While Anthony Marx rightly warns against assuming that 'a leader's family background or current professional status determines his or her class sympathies',[55] their experiences surely shaped their political horizons and skills. Even though some of them came from poor backgrounds, few of the UDF's leaders spoke the language of the poor: their schooling, and in the late 1980s their dress, set them apart. Their experiences of upward educational and occupational mobility, but continuing direct and indirect racial restrictions, must have influenced their visions of the goals of the struggle, making them more likely to subordinate 'economic transformation to end-

ing racial discrimination and national domination', as Marx puts it.[56] Resisting affiliation to the UDF in 1983, and remaining wary for the following two years, some
trade unionists seem to have dreamed of a blue-collar worker leadership in the struggle for political change. Such dreams ran up against the reality of rapid social change,
with political leadership slipping into the hands of classes based not in industry but
in the service sector, and not in the working class but in the fast-growing black middle classes.

The racial and gender composition of the UDF's leadership is easier to identify.
Despite an oft-stated commitment to the primacy of African leadership, the roles
played by coloured, Indian and even white activists were disproportionate to the
racial composition of even the metropolitan population. The prominence of people
such as Gordhan, Yunus Mahomed, Manuel, Carolus, Moosa and Cachalia all too
easily fuelled racist allegations about cabals. Such allegations, as we have seen, be-
little the importance of very capable African leaders. The gender composition of the
UDF leadership was a much more serious cause for concern, although (tellingly) it
never surfaced as a major controversy at the time. Less than one in ten of the UDF's
leadership was female; the proportion in the top leadership was even lower. The UDF
leadership was also distinctively urban, and mostly metropolitan. Almost none of its
leaders came from the bantustans or farming areas.

The final important point about the UDF leadership is its relationship with the
banned ANC. Most of the titular leaders of the Front were drawn from the ranks of
older leaders, veterans of the 1950s, who remained firmly rooted in the working
class. Most of the provincial and national secretaries, by contrast, were drawn from
the younger generation of upwardly mobile activists. As the UDF grew as an organisation, expanded its media production, controlled greater funds and relied ever
more heavily on modern communications technology, so the relative power of the
younger generation increased, fuelling perceptions among the newly marginalised
that the more tightly knit bureaucrats were operating as a cabal.

Social differences were also one factor in the highly complex nature of the relations between the UDF and the ANC. Whilst this remains a topic requiring further
research, as is the related topic of relations between the UDF and SACP, some key
features are clear. Firstly, most – if not all – of the top UDF leadership saw themselves
as part of the ANC underground inside the country, whether formally or informally,
to use Barrell's distinction.[57] A significant number of UDF leaders had spent time in
jail for ANC or MK-related activities or had joined the ANC whilst in jail.[58] Others
had long-standing personal links to the Congress movement.[59] Many of the younger
African UDF leaders had grown up in an environment where they learnt ANC songs,
read Mandela's old speeches, and generally saw the ANC as 'the mother body', as
Molefe recalls;[60] in many cases, especially in Soweto, their links to the ANC had been
forged upon the events of 1976.

ANC leaders made bold claims to journalists about the coherence of the ANC.
Mufson records being told by Mbeki that 'The ANC exists in two parts: in South
Africa and outside South Africa. No major decision on strategy or important tactics
can be reached without consultation with the other part.'[61] Tshwete told Mufson that,

when he was inside the country, he communicated with the ANC in exile about once a week.[62] In practice, however, communication and consultation was never easy. As Tshwete emphasised, there were many informers, and this made it difficult to communicate safely. Furthermore, communication channels between the many parts of the ANC underground and the ANC in exile were very fragmented. The ANC's formal lines of command to its formal political and military underground structures were divided, not only between the different bases in the frontline states (Botswana, Lesotho, Swaziland, Mozambique) but also at times between political and military structures. Moreover, many UDF leaders were not in the formal underground; for security reasons, several top leaders including Molefe had cut direct links[63] – though no doubt retained indirect links. The result was that there was a multiplicity of lines of communication between the UDF and the ANC. UDF leaders relied on whatever lines they felt most comfortable with. This became clear in late 1983, during the debate over referendums on the constitutional reforms, and again in late 1985 over school boycotts. Both sides in the debate claimed that their positions had been endorsed by or came from the ANC in exile. This complexity facilitated, and was in turn entrenched, by deepening divisions with the internal Charterist movement.

The complexity of the relationship between the ANC and UDF can only have been complicated by the additional presence of the SACP within both organisations. The character and activities of the SACP inside the country remain an entirely unresearched topic. The importance of the topic is indicated by the role played in parts of the UDF by Charles Nqakula, initially Border UDF convener and then publicity secretary; Jeremy Cronin, editor of *Isizwe*; and Raymond Suttner, who ran political education classes in Johannesburg, especially during 1985–6. All of them were revealed as prominent members of the SACP after 1990. Indeed, when the SACP announced publicly for the first time the names of its internal Central Committee in July 1990, the list of 22 people included Cronin, Billy Nair, Mufamadi and even Carolus.[64]

STRATEGIES AND TACTICS

During the eight years of its existence the UDF employed or endorsed an extensive repertoire of tactics. These included, in roughly the chronological order in which they were used, election boycotts, media campaigns, protest meetings, festivals, petitions, diplomatic occupations, hosting international visitors, overseas publicity, stayaways from work, protest marches, mass vigils, political funerals, consumer boycotts, rent boycotts, creating parallel institutions ('people's power'), media and political education production, negotiations and meetings, civil disobedience, overseas diplomacy, land occupations and (selectively) violence. These can be divided into three main categories: protest and persuasion, non-cooperation and direct challenges.[65]

The bulk of the UDF's efforts fell into the first two categories. Its direct challenges to the state were confined to developing the strategic framework of people's power in 1985–6, its tangential and vacillating involvement in land invasions in 1990–1, and its very selective endorsement of violence. The reason for this lay in the predominant strategic thinking within the UDF, which itself reflected an assessment of the relative strengths of the state and opposition.

The UDF faced throughout its existence a choice between two broad political strategies. These were repeatedly conceptualised in terms of the metaphor of the speed of a military column. This metaphor had been used by the ANC in the early 1970s, drawing perhaps on earlier use by Mandela and others in the 1950s. A column could march at the speed of its slowest members: the logic of this was that it would arrive on the battlefield with the greatest possible numbers, and thus with the greatest possible strength. Alternatively, the column could advance at the speed of its fastest members: the logic of this was that it would arrive at the battlefield as soon as possible, would retain the initiative, and would therefore be able to exert great pressure on opponents at their moment of vulnerability. In the early 1970s the ANC had advocated the more cautious approach:

> The speed of a column on the march is determined by the pace of the slowest and the weakest soldier and not the fittest and fastest. The most advanced sections should, therefore, at all times, seek to advance the least developed ones, keeping in the forefront the principle of the greatest and highest unity of the people and at all times fighting all tendencies to 'go it alone' through impatience and contempt for the less developed forces of the revolution.[66]

In the 1980s the UDF oscillated between these two approaches. During 1983–5 the dominant view was that it should draw as many people and groups as possible into an anti-apartheid alliance. As Molefe put it in late 1983, the UDF should not 'mistake the consciousness of the leadership for mass consciousness'; rather, he argued, 'we must take the prevailing consciousness as a baseline and take people through a process that will overcome their scepticism and fear'.[67] In 1985–7 the opposite view predominated: the people were deemed ready for action, and the UDF should carry forward rather than restrain their defiant impulses. Then, in the face of state repression in 1988, the UDF reverted to its initial, more cautious approach. 'We should remember that the pace of a column is not determined by the fittest and fastest soldier but by the slowest and weakest.'[68] There was one difference between the initial and post-1988 periods: prior to 1985 the Front had sought to compete with the National Party government for the loyalties of coloured and Indian South Africans; after 1987 it sought to pull disaffected white economic and other elites away from the government.

Throughout, however, the UDF defined its role as strengthening the tide of resistance rather than playing a crudely vanguardist role. Even during the rise and peak years of the township revolt, from 1984 to 1986, the UDF emphasised organisation building and the maintenance of discipline within the anti-apartheid movement rather than an immediate explosion of direct action. UDF leaders sought to channel the insurrectionary militancy of the youth in constructive and sustainable directions, and on many occasions sought even to rein it in. 'People's power' was an exercise in self-discipline as well as a mechanism for exerting pressure on the state. What was dropped in 1985–6 was not the emphasis on organisation building but the privileging of alliance building over intensifying resistance. While many of the more con-frontation-orientated leaders agreed that alliance building was important, in practice they made alliance building dependent on the tactical compromises being forged by prospective allies, not by the democratic movement.

The tactics of protest–persuasion and non-cooperation were determined in part by spiritual and moral concerns. Boesak, who wielded great influence in 1983–5, articulated a millenarian view in which moral integrity would lead, in some unde-fined way, to political victory. In the case of Molefe, moral concerns were integrated into a more strategic vision. Strategy and morality coincided in persuading Molefe that 'a mature political approach must try to reach accommodation with whites'. UDF tactics often involved self-sacrifice and austerity. In calling for a Black Christ-mas, for example, the UDF explicitly asked for 'self-sacrifices in order to strengthen the solidarity and unity of our people'.[69] The churches played a very important indi-rect role in the development of strategic thought among the UDF's leaders – just as they did in the American civil rights movement and in Solidarity in Poland.

The strategic importance of alliance building combined with an embracing morality to underpin the rhetorical invocation of the 'nation' in the speeches and writings of UDF leaders. As Anthony Marx shows, the concept of 'nation' was central to the mobilisation of the Charterist movement and the UDF. This concept enabled the UDF leadership to transcend the divisive politics of race and class.[70]

Violence posed a dilemma for the Front's leadership. Some opposed recourse to violence on moral grounds, others on strategic ones. But, faced with brutal state repression and widespread popular protest, more and more UDF leaders began to endorse violence, albeit very selectively. Defensive violence was understandable, it was said. The UDF pointedly declined to condemn the killing of a Ciskei policeman and a (mistakenly) suspected informer at UDF-organised funerals, and was slow to criticise necklacing. Cachalia explained this in an interview with Van Kessel:

> Perhaps we should have come out with a clear position on necklacing. But many of the people involved in necklacing were not part of formal UDF struc-tures. They were the so-called *amaqabane*, comrades, people who felt them-selves to be part of UDF or ANC without formally belonging to any structures. We did not speak out against necklacing because we did not want to alienate those people.[71]

Even at the height of the township revolt, however, UDF leaders did not appear to turn to thinkers who advocated violence. Martin Luther King remained an inspira-tion; Fanon and the American Black Power leadership did not. South Africa's transi-tion – up to 1990, and excepting Natal – was not particularly violent. Given the importance of morality and especially non-violence in the thought of many UDF leaders, it is perhaps surprising that the UDF did not embark on a more extensive programme of civil disobedience. There was, after all, the precedent of the Defiance Campaign of the 1950s, which had proved an enormous success, transforming the then legal ANC into a truly mass organisation for the first time. Until mid-1989,

however, the UDF's engagement in active civil disobedience was limited to the occasional march, the most important of which – the 1985 Pollsmoor march – was prohibited. In 1984 the UDF had discussed the possibility of a defiance campaign but
hesitated on the grounds that even this was too strident a tactic for a 'front organisation', and might lose the UDF supporters. Having misread the moment, UDF leaders
were rapidly overtaken by events. Had they had time to take stock, early 1986 might
have been a propitious time for a defiance campaign, but the UDF leadership was
preoccupied with people's power. The Border UDF discussed an anti-pass campaign
but there is little record of any organised activity. Not until 1989 did the changing
political situation reopen the possibility of a campaign of civil disobedience.[72]

Underlying the UDF leaders' unease with a defiance campaign was, perhaps, the
complexity of the UDF's support bases. As it did not have formal membership, and
operated in part as a front of autonomous organisations, it is difficult to be precise in
discussing the UDF's 'support bases'. Lodge observes that, 'in one essential sense, the
UDF is a working-class movement':

> In a social context in which a black bourgeoisie scarcely exists, in which mem-
> bers of petty bourgeois or middle-class groups at best constitute a thin layer,
> and in which the rural population is largely proletarianised or at least depen-
> dent on wage labour, any popular organisation has to have a working-class
> base.[73]

As we have already seen, analysing social class in South Africa in such broad brush-
strokes omits important points. Although there remains a paucity of research on the
social bases of the many and varied organisations that affiliated to the UDF, it seems
likely that their active membership was drawn heavily from the upwardly mobile
members of working-class families. The affiliates' active membership did not, for the
most part, comprise blue-collar workers, and certainly not farmworkers, the rural
poor, domestic workers or mine-workers. Rather, they comprised people in white-
collar occupations or studying, with the prospect of entering such occupations. The
participants in specifically UDF activities were even more likely to be drawn from
these sections of the population. In the case of the Defiance Campaign of 1989, it is
likely that support was derived primarily from the coloured and Indian middle classes. Thus, whilst a defiance campaign in the mid-1980s might have been powerful
symbolically, it might also have reinforced a sense of detachment from the UDF in
some poorer, mostly African areas – undermining the UDF's ambition of achieving
the leading role, providing overarching co-ordination and direction within the
Charterist movement inside the country.

But this explanation cannot suffice. There were occasions when large numbers of
poor and working-class black people engaged in public collective action. The UDF's
own affiliates were involved in marches in protest against rent increases, unrespon-
sive councillors, and so on. In 1990 there was a series of protest marches against
bantustan administrations. Furthermore, the trade union movement organised mass
action on several occasions. Why did the UDF not organise any nationwide cam-

paigns of mass demonstrations? One answer is the UDF leadership's aversion to violence: the lesson of marches in, most notably, the Vaal Triangle in September 1984 and in Mamelodi in November 1985, as well as at countless funerals, was that marches very often prompted police repression, which often led to uncontrolled popular violence.

But again, this explanation does not suffice. It cannot explain why the UDF was, for the most part, opposed to mass action akin to the 'mass strike' advocated in the writing of the German Marxist Rosa Luxemburg. Such action would entail, primarily, mass non-cooperation rather than active and public defiance. In November 1984 the UDF leadership had argued strongly against the proposal that two-day stayaways be lengthened to, or followed by, indefinite work stoppages. In early 1985 the ANC floated a similar idea, but the internal leadership pointedly declined to take it up. The strategic framework of people's power was developed in 1986 in part as an alternative to an insurrectionary mass or general strike. In mid-1989 the idea surfaced again in discussions between the ANC, UDF and COSATU but was not used. Such proposals were opposed by the unions, as well as by the UDF, owing to a conservatism rooted in an assessment of the weaknesses of the democratic movement. The UDF leadership was consistently concerned that the experience of 1977 not be repeated, whilst the union leadership was concerned that their involvement in politics should not prejudice their organisational gains in the workplace. Extended defiance was not deemed conducive to the kind of organisation building that was in turn considered necessary if democracy and freedom were to be won. Repression may have been limited in comparison with Latin America for example, but it nonetheless served to deter many people from confrontation. In view of this, extended defiance would have been unsustainable and ultimately counterproductive.

THE LEGACY OF THE UDF BEQUEATHED TO THE ANC

What lasting impact did the UDF make on South African politics? In what ways, if at all, are post-apartheid politics marked by the imprint of the UDF? How would politics be different if there had been no UDF – if, for example, political change had occurred without any political organisation and mobilisation above ground inside the country? These questions bring us to a general question we can ask in contexts besides the South African one: how does the character of a major political organisation or movement prior to democratisation affect political life in the subsequent democratic era?

The legacy of the UDF is most directly visible within the political party that absorbed most of its leadership and supporters: the ANC. Unbanned in 1990, the ANC rebuilt its organisation inside the country, played the leading role in negotiations over the terms of constitutional change, and ran a victorious election campaign in early 1994. With 62 per cent of the vote, the ANC formed by far the largest party in the post-apartheid Government of National Unity, and its leader – Nelson Mandela – became the first President of democratic South Africa.

UDF leaders have played prominent roles in the ANC since 1990. The interim

ANC conveners in five of the key regions were former UDF office-holders, and UDF activists were prominent in most (but not all) of the ANC RECs elected in late 1990. When the first ANC NEC was elected in mid-1991 after its unbanning, former UDF leaders were prominent but not to the same extent as at the regional level. Over a quarter of the elected NEC members had been office-holders in the UDF.[74] A long list of UDF activists were elected as ANC MPs in 1994, and more besides elected to the provincial legislatures. Some acceded to key positions in the national government. Manuel became Minister of Trade and Industry and later Minister of Finance; Tshwete became Minister of Sport; after a spell as deputy minister, Moosa became Minister of Provincial Affairs and Constitutional Development; Omar became Minister of Justice; Mufamadi became Minister of Safety and Security. Other UDF leaders assumed office in the provinces. Molefe and Lekota became Premiers of the North West and Free State provinces respectively; later Lekota was 'redeployed' to the Council of Provinces after bitter struggles within the Free State ANC. Stofile, after a spell as ANC Chief Whip in the National Assembly, became Premier of the Eastern Cape. Many of the provincial ministers were former UDF leaders. Carolus, who was said to have decided against a government appointment, served as the ANC's assistant general secretary from 1994 and acting general secretary in 1997, before being appointed High Commissioner in London in 1998.

These former UDF activists were not the bearers of a single, monolithic political tradition. In the early 1990s there was much discussion of the difficulties the ANC would face in reconciling its different groups of leaders: the internal leadership, the exiles, and the Robben Island prisoners. But these groups had overlapping membership: some of the UDF activists had been prisoners, including Lekota, Tshwete and Nair, and others had been exiles – such as Tshwete and Cronin; most had been in the ANC underground, in one way or another. Moreover, as has been emphasised throughout this book, the UDF was a heterogeneous organisation: vast strategic and ideological differences existed between, for example, Molefe on the one hand and Mokaba on the other.

Notwithstanding the heterogeneity within the UDF, is it possible to identify ways in which activists' experiences within the UDF before 1991 shaped their contributions to the ANC thereafter? Former UDF leaders shared a common experience of and commitment to organisation building, and a commitment to non-racial or multiracial organising. These, however, were not unique to the former UDF leaders. The UDF, after all, had inherited existing traditions of organisation building and non- or multiracialism. What distinguished the former UDF leaders from most other ANC leaders was their experience of public organising above ground in South Africa in the 1980s – an experience that was recent and rooted in conditions that existed in South Africa in the 1980s, but not in the 1950s or 1960s. The ANC leaders of the 1950s had the experience of organising over issues such as the pass laws and restrictions on livestock, which were no longer on the agenda of the 1980s or 1990s. The UDF leadership also had the experience of using modern technology to appeal to settled urban constituencies comprising (increasingly) secondary-school-educated people in white-collar occupations.

The prominence of former UDF leaders gave rise to further allegations about the 'cabal', long after the UDF had dissolved. Most of these allegations were made by Winnie Mandela, who blamed the 'cabal', said to include Moosa, Morobe, Cachalia and Ramaphosa – the last of whom had never been a UDF office-holder but was closely linked to the UDF through the MDM and National Reception Committee – for ostracising her in 1989 because of the murderous activities of her football club. Mandela attacked the 'cabal' during her trial on charges relating to kidnapping and murder in 1991. When her alleged lover and subordinate within the ANC, Dali Mpofu, was sacked by the ANC in 1992, he also blamed the 'cabal'.[75] The following year Mandela, by then separated from her husband, hit out at the absence of democracy within both the exiled ANC and the internal UDF prior to 1990. 'The UDF, hampered by emergency and security legislation, was unable to develop a democratic tradition. In that situation the tendency for small groups to make decisions on behalf of the people became wide-scale, and all regions suffered.'[76] There were still ambitious, power-hungry, 'elitist dictatorships' within the ANC, she wrote, urging that these be 'eliminated'. The cabal issue arose again in 1997 when Mandela was called before the Truth and Reconciliation Commission.

The continuing attacks by Winnie Mandela may have contributed to the decision of two of the alleged cabal leaders – Morobe and Cachalia – to cease playing prominent roles in the ANC in the 1990s. Morobe, towards whom Winnie Mandela was, it is said, especially aggressive, went on to become chairman of the Fiscal and Finance Commission rather than run for elected office. Cachalia became a senior official in the Department of Safety and Security. But they were certainly not alone among former UDF leaders in choosing to pursue more bureaucratic than political roles. Among other prominent ex-UDF activists who chose similarly were Frank Chikane, although he ended up in Thabo Mbeki's Deputy Presidential office; Molobi and Sizani, who were recruited into the Kagiso Trust and later the Independent Development Trust; Andrew Boraine, who became chief executive of the Cape Town City Council; and Zac Yacoob, who was nominated as a Constitutional Court judge. For activists who saw their UDF leadership roles as involving co-ordination and facilitation and providing strategic direction, such choices made good sense. Indeed, the experience of leadership in the UDF in general can be seen as providing organisational rather than more orthodox public political skills.

Activists from the UDF as well as from the trade unions had organisational skills which their counterparts from exile or jail had (at best) not practised for many years. It was not surprising, therefore, that the ANC appointed former UDF activists Molefe and Lekota to run its election campaign in 1994. They were assisted by Khetso Gordhan, among others. After the elections the task of running the ANC as a party was entrusted to activists with recent experience of organising inside the country: Ramaphosa and Carolus.

The character of the ANC's 1994 election campaign reveals another aspect of UDF influence: an explicit strategy of contesting the political middle ground rather than relying on its existing support base. In the election context, this meant reaching out to undecided coloured and Indian voters, and not just mobilising the existing, overwhelmingly African support base. The ANC jettisoned its initial election slogan, Now Is the Time, when it became evident that its triumphalism was off-putting to coloured and Indian voters, and adopted instead the more universal slogan, A Better Life for All. The ANC spent a disproportionate share of its campaign expenditure in the Western Cape, and most of its expenses there were targeted on coloured voters. For sure, this emphasis reflected political considerations: victory in the Western Cape depended on winning the support of coloured voters, and the ANC dearly wanted to win this province.[77] But the presence of former UDF leaders was a contributing factor in the ANC's strategic choices.

The influence of the UDF is visible most strongly perhaps in the Western Cape. In this province the ANC faced the same strategic dilemmas that the UDF had in the 1980s: whether to focus on the province's small African population or to build support among the coloured majority. With the shift to electoral politics, winning votes became all-important, strengthening the advocates of a multiracial rather than a narrowly Africanist approach. The challenge facing the ANC was to overcome the perception among many coloured voters that the ANC was a movement for African people – in contrast to the UDF in the 1980s.[78] In part because so few coloured Congress activists returned from exile, the multiracial approach was led by former UDF leaders; the Africanist approach was spearheaded by activists from MK. Repeated interventions from the ANC's national leadership helped to ensure that provincial leadership was passed from one former UDF leader to another: Tinto, Boesak, Nissen, Omar and Rasool.

Ironically, given the prominence of ex-UDF leadership in the ANC, calls for the revival of a UDF-like movement were strongest in the Western Cape. Intermittently between 1992 and 1996 there were calls for the formation of a progressive, broadly ANC-aligned organisation or movement for coloured people. This impulse was fuelled by a feeling among many coloured ex-UDF activists that they 'were just pushed aside, left by the wayside or ignored', as Boesak put it in 1992.[79] More importantly, the ANC was unsuccessful in the contest for coloured support. The NP's strength in coloured areas – reflected in the national and local election results – gave rise to calls for an unambiguous return to the UDF politics of the 1980s. The experiences of the 1980s were painted in romantic, nostalgic shades: 'If the UDF's support in the 1980s was anything to go by, the ANC should easily have won the Western Cape in the 1994 elections.'[80] What the ANC needed to do was to become a 'home for coloureds as it is for Africans' – as, it was said, the UDF had done through its moral appeal, its strong emphasis on local organisation around bread and butter issues, and its diverse leadership.[81] The influence of the UDF, albeit glorified, was thus important in both calls to reform the ANC and to form some kind of supplementary organisation. It remains an open question whether the ANC could have campaigned more effectively.[82] But, contrary to the assumptions of both ANC activists and academic observers,[83] it is far from clear that the UDF did enjoy such widespread support among coloured people in the 1980s. As we saw in earlier chapters, there is evidence that support for the UDF in coloured working-class areas declined after 1984–5; the constituencies mobilised thereafter – mostly middle-class, in the Defiance Campaign

– were precisely the constituencies that continued to support the ANC in the 1994–6 elections.

The influence of the UDF was perhaps weakest in Natal, notwithstanding the important role played by Natal activists in the formation and subsequent leadership of the Front. As we have seen, the UDF in Natal withered sharply after 1986, with the focus of Charterist politics shifting elsewhere. In 1990 UDF-linked leaders were marginalised in elections for the first ANC REC after the ANC's unbanning. In contrast to the Western Cape, Natal politics in the early 1990s were dominated by competition for the support of African voters, between Inkatha on the one hand and the ANC on the other. In this contest, the ANC chose to embrace a version of Zulu-ness, challenging Inkatha's former monopoly. Few former UDF leaders were equipped to play a part in this competition.

Ideologically, the UDF strengthened one strand of the Charterist movement. The UDF was, for the most part, steeped in the tradition of the Congress Alliance, with its emphases on non-racial leadership and multiracial strategy, on alliance building and aspiration to occupy the political middle ground, and on a discourse of rights. The UDF served to strengthen this tradition, although it was far from paramount in the mid-1980s. There were strong continuities between the ideology associated with the UDF and that of the ANC in the 1990s. The ANC emphasised unity, nation building and reconciliation; divisive ideologies, including those focused on class, were downplayed. It would probably be mistaken, however, to attribute this primarily to the influence of the UDF. The personality of Nelson Mandela and the pressure of global economic and diplomatic forces were clearly important, and probably more so. Moreover, some aspects of the ideologies linked to the UDF have endured less well than others. The rights discourse of 1994 soon gave way to a more results-orientated discourse; the embrace of multiracial diversity appears to be wilting in the face of Africanisation.

In organisational terms, the UDF bequeathed to the ANC a political culture of robust internal debate and self-criticism. This was a tradition which the UDF had inherited from the ANC from the 1950s, but which appeared to have weakened within the ANC amidst the conditions of exile and guerrilla warfare. Some ANC leaders returning to the country seemed to be taken aback by the demands for consultation and the spirited criticisms made at regional and national levels. In the absence of detailed research into the ANC after 1990 it is difficult to assess how widespread and lasting was this culture of debate and criticism, but it was very evident in provinces such as the Western Cape.

Finally, we need to ask whether the UDF left a legacy to the ANC in terms of strategies and tactics. As we have already suggested, the dominant position within the ANC remained one that emphasised alliance building and contesting the so-called middle ground, through nation building and reconciliation. But, as the ANC drew closer to state power in 1990–3, and then exercised it, the specific strategies and tactics of the 1980s were deemed increasingly inappropriate. As we saw in Chapters 9 and 10, even UDF leaders in 1989–90 began to express reservations about the long-term repercussions of rent boycotts and of direct action, and UDF leaders had been critical of chronic school boycotts from the outset. For the ANC, social and political change would be effected through the state – which, after 1993–4, they controlled – rather than on the streets. ANC leaders sought to end rent boycotts (with very uneven success), to demobilise the youth, and were very critical of sit-ins and the coerced 'detention' of officials by discontented students and others.

The ANC's change of perspective from 1993 is not difficult to understand, whether or not we agree with it. What is harder to understand is the ANC's failure to utilise the strategies and tactics of the 1980s in the transitional period of 1990–3, when it might have chosen to maintain the pressure on the National Party government. In 1990–1 especially, the ANC seems to have lost the momentum that had built up inside the country in 1989–90. In the absence of careful research on the ANC in this period, we can only speculate why the ANC did not employ, for example, a defiance campaign against the remaining vestiges of racial discrimination and segregation. Was it because of the essential conservatism of the veteran ANC leaders? Were they distracted by the demands of organisation building and negotiations? Did they underestimate the remaining pitfalls along the route to democracy, and hence underestimate the need for countervailing pressures? Whatever the reason, the strategies and tactics of the UDF were not adopted by the ANC, even before its accession to formal power, and South Africa's venerable tradition of organised non-violent direct action and defiance seems to have run dry.

THE LEGACY OF THE UDF BEQUEATHED TO POST-APARTHEID POLITICS IN GENERAL

The lasting impact of the UDF was not confined to the ANC alone. The whole character of the overall post-apartheid political system reflects, in some respects, the influences of the UDF. The legacy of the UDF can be seen in the character of South African democracy, the contours of political society and the chequered emergence of civil society.

The struggles of the 1980s, and the role played by the UDF within these, bequeathed lasting understandings of democracy. The UDF played an important role in promoting the salience of rights, and of political and economic alternatives based on rights, within popular conceptions of democracy. Discourses of rights were paramount in the UDF at the outset. Although married and to some extent subordinated to discourses of power in 1985–6, they were resurgent at the end of the decade. Rights played a more important part in the South African struggle for democracy, and in the political system that resulted, than was the case in many other liberation contexts. Notwithstanding the protestations of Charterist activists, there was a strong element of the civil rights struggle in the Charterist movement – with the consequence that South Africa became a constitutional democracy in which the Constitution and Bill of Rights, rather than parliament, were sovereign.

Moreover, the Front also helped to promote a more pluralist political system through its recognition and acceptance of disagreement. The Front was based on the understanding that disagreement over many things did not preclude common action towards the central goal of democratisation. Indeed, the form and rhetoric of a front served to institutionalise this disagreement. The UDF thus did not seek to instil a single hegemonic conception of Charterism within even the Charterist movement; as we have seen, the history of the UDF was one of chronic diversity and disagreement. Moreover, it sought to work together with some non-Charterist groups in the much vaunted political middle ground without simply dragooning them into a Charterist frame. The UDF's emphasis on alliance building needs to be qualified: at the national level as well as on the ground, AZAPO was treated as a minor player (which indeed it was), whilst Inkatha was shut out altogether, with serious consequences. In general, however, the UDF looked out to prospective allies.

In their analyses of the discourses of the left in the 1980s, Glaser and Steinberg draw our attention to the prevalence of elements intolerant of disagreement and diversity. Glaser argues that the theory of 'national democratic struggle' included an 'authoritarian subdiscourse' that emphasised the homogeneity and collective will of the people and sometimes treated 'dissent as alien and divisive, even treasonous'. The anti-apartheid opposition failed, he suggests, to appreciate the importance of political pluralism and civil liberties – of free expression, association and political choice. It is indeed easy to find evidence of such discourses, especially in civic struggles in South Africa's black townships.[84] But such discourses were far from universal among the UDF's national and – in most areas – regional leaders. There was throughout a parallel discourse, emphasising diversity (especially on a multiracial basis) and disagreement. Pluralist discourses may have been subordinate across large swathes of anti-apartheid politics, but at the national level they were very strong, almost hegemonic.

The domination of party politics by the ANC perhaps disguises the extent of political pluralism in the new South Africa. It is in the realm of civil society that this pluralism is more easily visible. 'Civil society' was discovered as a concept in the early 1990s, as a wide variety of people sought a political arena independent of party politics and especially the overwhelming party political strength of the ANC. Civic organisations, trade unions and the media attempted to define their political roles in terms of civil society. Some drew on Gramscian understandings of civil society, bolstered by the examples of anti-authoritarian movements in Central and Eastern Europe. But these had short-lived relevance: the 'anti-politics' of democrats in Central and Eastern Europe was hardly applicable in a context where democrats engaged with, rather than circumvented, state power, seeking rights in a (just) state rather than freedoms from an (oppressive) state. The inauguration of representative democracy at national and, later, local levels in South Africa led to the withering of this kind of civil society. Other activists and groupings promoted a more Anglo-American conception of civil society, often without realising the etymology of their approach. In this, civil society was complementary to the formal political system, rather than defined in opposition to it. The UDF, through its pluralist emphases on rights and diversity, in practice promoted this kind of civil society: civil society as a pluralist arena, as Glaser advocates.[85]

One other aspect of post-apartheid politics in South Africa that reflects the stamp of the UDF concerns the moral boundaries to politics. In the 1980s political and religious leaders repeatedly called for morality in the struggle on the grounds that it was prescriptive. In Lekota's words: 'In political struggle, the means must always be the same as the ends. How else can one expect a racialistic movement to imbue our society with a nonracial character on the dawn of our freedom day? A political movement cannot bequeath to society a characteristic it does not itself possess.'[86] This was echoed by Goniwe, who wrote that 'if we are instruments of change, we must epitomise the society we want to bring about'.[87] Most UDF leaders sought to promote non-racialism, an appreciation of rights and a tolerance of difference. Church leaders were drawn in. Of course, emphasising morality and building on the legitimacy of the churches was strategic, drawing attention to the weaknesses of apartheid and building a broad political movement. But it nonetheless had the effect of strengthening the moral strands within opposition politics, strands that remained after 1994. The role of clerics and theology in the Truth and Reconciliation Commission, and of the Commission in general, is testimony to the enduring importance of morality in South African politics.

Against this, Kane-Berman has argued that the protests of the 1980s were profoundly immoral in that they led to generalised violence thereafter. He attributes the rising crime and disorder of the early 1990s to the encouragement of boycotts, defiance and 'people's war' by the UDF, ANC and so forth in the 1980s.[88] What Kane-Berman overlooks is the repeated attempts by UDF and some ANC leaders to confront the tendencies towards violence and disorder during the 1980s. As we have seen, some UDF leaders were preoccupied with the problem of ensuring that protests were orderly; internal leaders persuaded the exiled ANC to support their calls on students to return to class; people's power was a way of strengthening discipline and organisation as well as of seizing local power. UDF and ANC leaders expressed misgivings about the long-term effects of boycotts and violence.

In all these respects the UDF inherited ideas and tactics, discourses and strategies from the ANC and the Congress Alliance in the 1950s, and then modified and strengthened them before bequeathing them to the ANC and the political system in general in the 1990s. Nonetheless, in so far as post-apartheid South Africa enjoys a pluralist political system and culture, with a recognition of the importance of rights, this was in part due to the rhetoric and practices of the UDF in the 1980s.

Appendix:
Interviews Conducted

Aboobaker, Goolam (10 Feb. 1994, Cape Town)
Abrahams, David (5 Aug. 1993, Cape Town)
Africa, Sandy (20 Sept. 1992, Durban)
Badat, Saleem (4 Feb. 1992, by telephone)
Bete, Tembile (25 Nov. 1992, Port Elizabeth)
Bonhomme, Virgil (11 July 1992, Durban)
Cachalia, Azhar (14 Oct. 1992, Johannesburg; Nov. 1998, Johannesburg)
Carolus, Cheryl (13 Oct. 1992, Johannesburg)
Carrim, Yunus (17 Sept. 1992, Pietermaritzburg)
Cherry, Janet (25 Oct. 1992, Grahamstown)
Chetty, A.S. (8 July 1992, Pietermaritzburg)
Coetzee, Mikey (13 July 1993, Cape Town)
Cole, Josette (25 Feb. 1992, Cape Town)
Coovadia, Cas (15 Dec. 1992, Johannesburg)
Creecey, Barbara (23 March 1993, Johannesburg)
Cronin, Jeremy (3 Aug. 1998, telephone)
David, Paul (7 July 1992, Verulam)
De Vries, Johny (14 Oct. 1992, Johannesburg)
Dlamini, Baba (7 July 1992, Durban)
Du Plessis, George (26 April 1992, Reiger Park)
Ebrahim, Zohra (20 Aug. 1992, Cape Town; 3 Dec. 1992, Cape Town)
Gordhan, Khetso (14 Oct. 1992, Johannesburg)
Gordhan, Pravin (30 March 1992, Durban; 12 July 1992, Johannesburg; 30 Nov. 1993, Durban)
Gumede, Archie (11 July 1992, Pinetown)
Issel, Johny (22 June 1992, Cape Town; 12 March 1993, Cape Town)
Jaffer, Nazeegh (19 June 1992, Cape Town)
Jantjies, Cyril (27 March 1992, Johannesburg)

Jeffrey, John (Pietermaritzburg)
Jele, Josiah (23 April 1992, Johannesburg)
Kappa, Liso (19 Nov. 1992, Cape Town)
Kotswane, Benny (9 Dec. 1992, Botshabelo)
Lephunya, Pat (27 April 1992, Johannesburg; 12 Jan. 1993, Soweto; 2 Feb. 1993, Soweto)
Luckett, Syd (18 Sept. 1992, Pietermaritzburg)
Madlala, Nozizwe (18 Sept. 1992, Durban)
Mafolo, Titus (24 March 1993, Pretoria)
Magqabi, T. (25 Nov. 1992, Port Elizabeth)
Mahomed, Yunus (30 March 1992, Durban; 6 July 1992, Durban: 9 July 1992, Durban; 1 Dec. 1993, Durban)
Malebo, Sekgopi (22 April 1992, Bloemfontein)
Malindi, Zoli (17 Aug. 1992, Cape Town)
Mamdoo, Feizal (2 March 1993, Johannesburg)
Manuel, Trevor (4 July 1992, Johannesburg)
Marks, Joe (21 Aug. 1992, Cape Town)
Mashatile, Paul (28 April 1992, Johannesburg)
Masondo, Amos (22 Feb. 1990, Germiston)
Matona, Tsediso (21 Aug. 1991, Cape Town)
Mditshwa, Monde (29 April 1992, Johannesburg; 30 April 1992, Johannesburg)
Meyer, Lucille (Cape Town)
Mji, Diliza (29 Nov. 1993, Durban)
Mkhize, Ian (18 Sept. 1992, Durban; 29 Nov. 1993, Durban)
Mlonyeni, Themba (1992, Cape Town)
Mofolo, Titus (24 March 1993, Pretoria)
Mogane, Vincent (18 Aug. 1993, Johannesburg; 22 Aug. 1993, Johannesburg; 16 Feb. 1994, Johannesburg; 18 Feb. 1994, Johannesburg)
Mogase, Nomi (2 July 1992, Johannesburg)
Mohamed, Professor I. (26 March 1992, Johannesburg)
Mohapi, Johny (Bloemfontein)
Mokaba, Peter (27 April 1992, Johannesburg)
Molefe, Popo (28 April 1992, Johannesburg; 4 July 1992, Johannesburg; 22 April 1993, Johannesburg)
Moloi, Super (29 April 1992, Johannesburg)
Momoniat, Ismail (16 Feb. 1994, Johannesburg; 18 Feb. 1994, Johannesburg)
Monareng, Oupa (28 April 1992, Johannesburg; 29 April 1992, Johannesburg)
Moosa, Valli (25 April 1992, Johannesburg; 17 Aug. 1993, Johannesburg)
Morgan, Kim (1 July 1992, Johannesburg)
Morobe, Murphy (27 March 1992, Johannesburg; 26 April 1992, Johannesburg)
Mpetha, Oscar (June 1992, Cape Town)
Mseleku, Thami (1992, Pietermaritzburg)
Naidoo, Kumi (6 July 1992, Durban)
Nair, Billy (30 Nov. 1993, Durban; 1 Dec. 1993, Durban)

Ndebele, Sbu (1 Dec. 1993, Durban)
Ndlovu, Curnick (9 July 1992, KwaMashu)
Ndlovu, Mdou (10 July 1992, Pietermaritzburg)
Ndou, Samson (1 July 1992, Johannesburg)
Ngwenya, Jabu (23 April 1992, Johannesburg)
Nissen, Chris (21 Aug. 1992, Cape Town)
Njikelana, Sisa (9 April 1992, Johannesburg)
Nkomfe, Mandla (Johannesburg, 1992)
Nkomo, Dr A. (24 April 1992, Atteridgeville)
Nkondo, Curtis (27 June 1992, Eldorado Park)
Nkondo, Reavell (3 July 1992, Johannesburg)
Nkwinti, Gugile (26 Nov. 1992, Grahamstown; 27 April 1993, Port Elizabeth)
Ntombela, Simon (1 April 1992, Durban)
Oliphant, Reggie (12 Dec. 1995, Cape Town)
Oliphant, Vuyisile (30 Sept. 1993, Cape Town)
Oosterwyk, Trevor (24 June 1992, Cape Town)
Pillay, Nava (24 March 1993, Pretoria)
Radebe, Reggie (18 Sept. 1992, Pietermaritzburg)
Ramgobin, Mewa (9 July 1992, Verulam)
Ramokgopa, Nat (30 April 1992, Johannesburg)
Rasool, Ebrahim (7 Sept. 1992, Cape Town)
Rhodes, Wilfried (June 1992, Cape Town; 15 Nov. 1992, Cape Town)
Saloojee, Cas (18 Feb. 1994, Johannesburg)
Sathekge, Matthews (1994, Pretoria)
Scott, Mpho (1 April 1992, Durban)
Sidina, Wilson (20 Aug. 1992, Cape Town; 28 Aug. 1992, Cape Town)
Simmers, Veronica (18 Feb. 1993, Cape Town)
Sizani, Stone (27 April 1993, Port Elizabeth)
Solomon, Marcus (15 July 1993, Cape Town)
Sonto, Rose (27 Aug. 1992, Cape Town; 18 Nov. 1992, Cape Town)
Stofile, Rev. Arnold (26 April 1993, Fort Hare)
Tsenoli, Lechesa (30 March 1992, Durban; 1993, Bloemfontein)
Williams, Noel (15 Feb. 1993, Cape Town; 16 July 1993, Cape Town)
Wittenberg, Martin (30 March 1992, Pietermaritzburg; 5 July 1992, Pietermaritz-
    burg; 10 July 1992, Pietermaritzburg)
Wort, Logan (19 June 1992, Cape Town; 24 June 1992, Cape Town)
Xundu, Rev. M. (27 April 1993, Port Elizabeth)

Endnotes

The references below include the following five categories of source: (1) interviews: these are listed in an Appendix; (2) books, articles and theses, which are listed in the bibliography; (3) newspaper reports; (4) evidence in political trials (especially *State vs Baleka and 21 others*, i.e. the Delmas Treason Trial, henceforth identified as *Baleka*; (5) documents drafted for the defence lawyers mostly in *Baleka* and some in *State vs Ramgobin and others*, i.e. the Pietermaritzburg Treason Trial; and (6) UDF and other organisational documentation.

There is no composite catalogue of extant documentation of the UDF. A very large number of documents for the period up to early 1985 are included in the exhibits of *Baleka*; the best collection of these (together with the evidence) is at the University of the Witwatersrand, and there is an excellent catalogue of this collection by Michelle Pickover. Most of the UDF documents referenced below are the minutes of, or secretarial reports (Sec. Rpt) presented to, meetings of the National or Regional Executive Committees (NEC, RECs), National or Regional General Councils (NGC, RGCs) or National Working Committee (NWC). UDF regions are identified as follows: Tvl (Transvaal), WCp (Western Cape), ECp (Eastern Cape), NTvl (Northern Transvaal), Ntl (Natal), Bdr (Border), OFS (Orange Free State). Other documents are, wherever possible, identified with the catalogue number in the University of the Witwatersrand collection (e.g. *Baleka* exhibit XX.11). There is no cataloguing system at all, as far as I am aware, of UDF documents after early 1985. Many of these documents are in the South African History Archive (SAHA) Trust, which is now also housed in the Historical Papers collection at Wits. Other documents are in the Mayibuye Centre at the University of Western Cape. For many documents, either the author or the occasion remains unclear. One valuable source is a set of notebooks kept by Moosa, as acting general secretary, in 1986; these are referenced below as 'Moosa notebook' followed by a #.

The documents drafted for the defence lawyers in *Baleka* and *Ramgobin* are identified by number (e.g. *Baleka* Defence Doc. #2). These refer to the following:

Baleka Defence Doc.

#1.   'The United Democratic Front' (Molefe)
#2.   'Personal Statement' (Molefe)
#3.   'Document on the United Democratic Front' (Molefe et al.)
#4.   'Notes on consultation re the United Democratic Front', with M. Chikane.
#5.   'My Perspective on the Allegations' (Lekota)
#6.   'The Seventeen Campaigns' (Molefe)
#7.   'Statement on the United Democratic Front and Vaal Triangle'
#8.   'Statement on United Democratic Front National Secretariat Meetings'
#9.   Consultation with Allan Boesak.
#10. 'Some notes on the call … '

Ramgobin Defence Doc.

#1.   'History of the Transvaal Anti-PC Committee' (Prof. I. Mohamed)

#2.   'Statement' (Aubrey Mokoena)
#3.   'Statement' (Prof. I. Mohamed)

The following abbreviations are used:
BD   *Business Day*
CH   *Cape Herald*
CT   *Cape Times*
Cit   *Citizen*
CP   *City Press*
DD   *Daily Dispatch*
DN   *Daily News*
EP   *Evening Post*
EPH   *Eastern Province Herald*
FM   *Financial Mail*
GCP   *Golden City Press*
JSAS   *Journal of Southern African Studies*
NW   *Natal Witness*
RDM   *Rand Daily Mail*
SAIRR   South African Institute of Race Relations
SALB   *South African Labour Bulletin*
SAR   *South African Review*
Sow   *Sowetan*
SotN   *State of the Nation (SASPU National)*
SStar   *Sunday Star*
ST   *Sunday Times*
STrib   *Sunday Tribune*
WIP   *Work in Progress*

CHAPTER 1
THE UNITED DEMOCRATIC FRONT, FREEDOM AND DEMOCRACY IN SOUTH AFRICA

1. A video-recording of the launch was submitted as exhibit M26 in *State vs Ramgobin*; speeches were transcribed in the accompanying 'Transcript of speeches at National Launch of the UDF, Rocklands, Mitchell's Plain, Cape Town 20/8/83'.
2. 'Transcipt of speeches at National Launch ...' Boesak's speech was also published as 'God Bless Africa' in Boesak, *If This is Treason*. See also *Baleka* Defence Doc. #9.
3. As Bundy pointed out soon after, in 'Around which Corner?'.
4. Huntington, *The Third Wave*.
5. Walter Sisulu, speech at UDF NGC, 1991.
6. 'Transcript of speeches at National Launch ... '
7. Gerhart, *Black Power in South Africa*, pp. 11–16; Carter, 'African Concepts of Nationalism in South Africa'; Kuper, 'African Nationalism in South Africa, 1910–1964'.
8. My argument here is influenced by Gerhart's analysis, in *Black Power*, pp. 39–44, although I am not persuaded by the details therein.
9. Walshe, *The Rise of African Nationalism in South Africa*; Willan, *Sol Plaatje*; Lewis, *Between the Wire and the Wall*; Marks, 'John Dube and the Ambiguities of Nationalism'; Swan, 'Ideology in Organised Indian Politics, 1891–1948'.
10. Beinart and Bundy, *Hidden Struggles in Rural South Africa*; Hill and Pirio, 'Africa for the Africans'; Bradford, *A Taste of Freedom*; Edgar, *Because They Chose the Plan of God*.
11. Delius, 'Migrant Organisation, the Communist Party, the ANC and the Sekhukuneland Revolt, 1940–1958'; Sapire, 'African Political Organisations in Brakpan in the 1950s'; Glaser, '"When Are They Going to Fight?"'; Lodge, 'Political Mobilisation during the 1950s'.
12. Marx, *Lessons of Struggle*; see also my 'The Development of Strategic Thought'.
13. Simkins, *Four Essays on the Past, Present and Possible Future Distribution of the African Population of South Africa*, Essay 2, Table 1.
14. Matthew Chaskalson, 'Rural Resistance in the 1940s and 1950s'; Lodge, *Black Politics in South Africa since 1945*, Ch. 11; Delius, *A Lion Amongst the Cattle*, Ch. 4.

15. Bonner, 'African Urbanisation on the Rand'.
16. Ibid., pp. 128–9.
17. The official Riekert Commission reported that there was 'no reliable data' – *Report of the Commission of Inquiry into Legislation Affecting the Utilization of Manpower* (Chairman: Riekert), RP32/1979 (henceforth Riekert Report), p. 17, para. 2.55.
18. Jill Nattrass, 'The Impact of the Riekert Commission's Recommendations on the "Black States,"' p. 79; also *Riekert Report:* 17, paras. 2.58.
19. Data calculated from Simkins, *Four Essays*, pp. 71–2, Table 5.
20. Bundy, 'Street Sociology and Pavement Politics, p. 312.
21. Glaser, 'Youth Culture and Politics', p. 111; 'The City of Soweto'; *Informa* (May 1985); *Hansard*, House of Assembly, 19 June 1985, col. 1946.
22. Glaser, *Youth Culture*, p. 111; see also Glaser, '"We Must Infiltrate the Tsotsis."'
23. SAIRR *Survey* 1962, p. 195; *Survey* 1971, p. 289; *Survey* 1983, p. 460.
24. For examples, see Glaser, 'Youth Culture'; Seekings, 'Political Mobilisation in Tumahole'; Michael Tetelman, 'We Can: Black Politics in Cradock', Chs. 4 & 5.
25. Seekings, 'Quiescence and the Transition to Confrontation', Ch. 2; see further, Crankshaw, *Race, Class, and the Changing Division of Labour under Apartheid*.
26. Seekings, 'Quiescence'.
27. Analysis of coloured and Indian politics in the 1970s and 1980s is uneven, but see Jung, 'Political Identities in Transition', Ch. 6; Goldin, *Making Race*; Desai, *Arise Ye Coolies!*
28. SAIRR *Survey* 1961, 1962, 1971, 1983.
29. Lodge, 'The United Democratic Front', p. 206.
30. The UDF's 1983 Working Principles provided for affiliation by national organisations (clause 5.3); this provision was removed in 1985. RGCs and RECs were not specified in the national 1983 Working Principles.
31. Popo Molefe, 'What is the UDF?', typescript of a speech written for a meeting in Northern Cape (nd, but *circa* Dec. 1983).
32. UDF WC, 'Circular to all affiliates and regional committees', signed C. Carolus (regional secretary), 27 Aug. 1984.
33. UDF WC, sec. rpt to AGM, March 1985.
34. UDF, *Phambili* (Oct. 1988), quoted in Baskin, *Striking Back*, pp. 289–90.
35. UDF NGC 1991, sec. rpt (Molefe), pp. 3–5.
36. For an overview, see Seekings, 'Township Resistance in the 1980s'.
37. UDF, press statement, 27 Feb. 1991, p. 2.
38. Sisulu, speech at UDF NGC, 1991.
39. Melucci, quoted in William Gamson, 'The Social Psychology of Collective Action', p. 57; see also Eyerman and Jamison, *Social Movements*, pp. 2–4; Klandermans, 'The Social Construction of Protest'. Former UDF activist Graeme Bloch has recently argued that the UDF needs to be understood primarily in terms of the construction of meaning: Bloch, 'The United Democratic Front: Lessons of the 80s; Prospects for the 90s'. Bloch points to a range of factors which I believe are of great importance, but unfortunately his analysis remains suggestive and sketchy.
40. This is how Mark Swilling defines his own use of the term 'affiliation' – 'The United Democratic Front and Township Revolt', fn. 8.
41. Conflating the movement and the organisation is a common mistake across the political spectrum. The state constructed a conspiratorial analysis of the whole township revolt around the alleged revolutionary activities of the UDF. But in a series of treason trials state prosecutors were unable to demonstrate causality through specific organisational contacts, and therefore concentrated instead on speeches, media and slogans. Several academic studies tend towards conflating the movement with the organisation. Swilling ('The United Democratic Front and the Township Revolt'), for example, uses the terms 'UDF' and the 'UDF's affiliates' interchangeably. Lodge (in 'Rebellion: The Turning of the Tide') refers to 'the UDF revolt'. Both misinterpret the relationship between UDF structures and UDF affiliates.
42. Hunt, *Politics, Culture and Class in the French Revolution*, p. 2.
43. Kentridge, *An Unofficial War*.
44. Price, *The Apartheid State in Crisis*; Lodge, 'Rebellion'.
45. Van Kessel, 'Beyond Our Wildest Dreams'.
46. Barrell, *MK: The ANC's Armed Struggle*; 'Conscripts to Their Age'; '"The Turn to the Masses."'
47. Marx, *Lessons of Struggle*.

48. Baskin, *Striking Back*; see also numerous articles in *SALB*.
49. Seekings, *Heroes or Villains?*; Ntsebeza, 'Youth in Urban African Townships, 1945–1992'.
50. Seekings, 'Civic Organisations in South Africa's Townships'; 'The Development of Strategic Thought' and other contributions to Adler and Steinberg (eds.), *From Comrades to Citizens*; Van Kessel, 'Beyond Our Wildest Dreams'.
51. Including: Van Kessel, 'Beyond Our Wildest Dreams' (Cape Town, the West Rand and the Northern Transvaal); Delius, *A Lion amongst the Cattle* (Northern Transvaal); Carter, 'Comrades and Community'; Cole, *Crossroads*; Tetelman, 'We Can' (Cradock); Ntsebeza, 'Youth in Urban African Townships'; as well as my own work on different parts of the PWV and northern Orange Free State: see, especially: 'Quiescence' (on the PWV); 'From "Quiescence" to "People's Power"' (on the West Rand in particular); and 'Political Mobilisation in Tumahole' (on the northern Orange Free State).
52. Mufson, *Fighting Years*.
53. Sparks, *Tomorrow is Another Country*; Waldmeir, *Anatomy of a Miracle*.
54. *State vs Baleka and 21 others*. See Moss, *Shouting at the Crocodile*.
55. See Carter, 'Comrades and Community', p. 38.
56. Feit, *Urban Revolt in South Africa*, p. xi.
57. Gerhart and Karis (eds.), *From Protest to Challenge*.
58. This issue is discussed in South African contexts by Bozzoli, *Women of Phokeng*, pp. 7–11, and by Van Onselen, 'The Reconstruction of a Rural Life', pp. 506–10.

CHAPTER 2
THE ORIGINS OF THE UDF

1. Boesak's speech was later published under the title of 'The Present Crisis in Apartheid' in Boesak, *Black and Reformed*. His comment was made in *Baleka* Defence Doc. #9.
2. Hirson, *Year of Fire*; Marx, *Lessons*.
3. Marx, *Lessons*, pp. 75–84; Mokoape, Mtinso and Nhlapo, 'Towards the Armed Struggle'; Frederickse, *The Unbreakable Thread*, Ch. 14; interviews with C. Nkondo and Issel.
4. Bishop Manas Buthelezi (chairman of the Black Parents Association), interview in *Star*, 14 Aug. 1976, quoted in evidence in *State vs Twala & 10 others*, transcript p. 2433.
5. Interview with Mogase. Gqabi also linked up with activists in the Northern Transvaal: see Delius, *A Lion Amongst the Cattle*, pp. 176–9.
6. This account of the study group is based on interviews with Mditshwa, Mogase, Molefe, Monareng, Moloi and Ngwenya; and I. Mohamed, C. Nkondo, R. Nkondo and Ndou for the 1980–1 period.
7. Khetsi Lehoko, quoted in Marx, *Lessons*, p. 101. Gqabi and others draw on their experiences in the Northern Transvaal as well as Soweto; see Delius, *A Lion Amongst the Cattle*, pp. 179.
8. Quotations from interview with Monareng.
9. Quotations from interview with Issel. See also interviews with Solomon and Nissen.
10. Interviews with P. Gordhan and Y. Mahomed; Barrell, 'Conscripts'.
11. Interview with Mditshwa.
12. Interviews with Ngwenya, Molefe, Mogane and Lephunya.
13. Quotations from interviews with Molefe by Barrell, quoted in 'Conscripts', and by Anthony Marx, *Lessons*, p. 103. See also Molefe, *Baleka* Defence Doc. #1; my interviews with Molefe, Ngwenya and Moloi.
14. This section is based on Barrell, 'Conscripts' and '"The Turn to the Masses."'
15. Barrell, 'Conscripts'. The ANC's report is partly reproduced in Karis and Gerhart, *From Protest to Challenge*, vol. 5, pp. 720–34. The Report presaged, in general terms, the form of the UDF.
16. Barrell, '"The Turn to the Masses,"' pp. 85–6.
17. My interviews with C. Nkondo and Moloi; interview with Manthata by Anthony Marx, quoted in *Lessons*, p. 96; see further, *Lessons*, Ch. 3.
18. These debates are discussed in interviews conducted in 1990 by Rory Riordan with ex-Robben Islanders from Port Elizabeth, including Saki Macozoma, Mike Xego, Patrick Madalane, Mzimkulu Madinda, Lulamile Mati, Cecil Mkalipi and Mpumi Odolo. See also Marx, *Lessons*, pp. 97–9.
19. Interview with Mogase. See also my interviews with Ngwenya and Moloi.
20. Interviews with C. Nkondo and Molefe. See also *Post*, 15 Jan. 1980; *RDM*, 24 Jan. 1980; Marx, *Lessons*, pp. 89–91.
21. Interviews with David, P. Gordhan and Gumede.
22. Interview with Issel.

23. Interviews with Molefe, Mogane and Lephunya.
24. Interviews with Manuel, Issel, Jaffer and Solomon.
25. Interview with Molefe. See also interview with R. Nkondo.
26. Interview with Monareng.
27. Interview with Moosa.
28. Interviews with Molefe, Ngwenya and Monareng.
29. Interview with Molefe.
30. Interviews with Molefe and I. Mohamed. Janet Cherry recalls debates at this time over the Nicaraguan and other experiences with broad and 'principled' fronts.
31. Popo Molefe, 'The Black Worker and the Demands of Our Time', address to the annual national conference of the South African Council of Churches – *Baleka* exhibit DA.13; see also interview with Molefe by Barrell, 4 July 1992, in 'Conscripts'.
32. Barrell, 'Conscripts'; interviews with Momoniat and Molefe by Barrell.
33. Interview with Molefe.
34. This section is based on my interviews with Molefe, Gumede, R. Nkondo. C. Nkondo. Njikelana, Monareng, Ndou, Kota and Y. Mahomed. The exact dates of events remain unclear.
35. Gilbey, *The Lady*, pp. 134–5.
36. Interview with Momoniat.
37. Interview with Molefe
38. Interview with Morobe.
39. A 'national' meeting was held in Bloemfontein in November. Barrell writes that the ANC was promoting this general initiative ('Conscripts'). Many of the civics formed in 1981 proved short-lived, for example the Border Civic Organisation in East London (see my interview with Njikelana) and the East Rand People's Organisation (see my 'Quiescence').
40. Molefe, *Baleka* Defence Doc. #2, pp. 45–6.
41. Interview with Mogane.
42. Interview with Saloojee.
43. Barrell, 'Conscripts', Ch. 6; Dollie, 'The National Forum'; Pillay, 'Trade Unions'; I. Mohamed, *Ramgobin* Defence Doc. #1; *RDM*, 20 Oct. 1982; my interview with Saloojee.
44. My interviews with Momoniat and Saloojee; interview with Momoniat by Barrell.
45. Molefe, 'The United Democratic Front', *Baleka* Defence Doc. #2, p. 2.
46. Interview with P. Gordhan.
47. *CT*, 7 Jan. 1983; 'Labour Party', *WIP*, 25 (Feb. 1983).
48. ANC 71st anniversary statement, 8 Jan. 1983; published in *Sechaba* (March 1983).
49. Barrell, 'Conscripts'; interviews with Momoniat and Saloojee by Barrell.
50. Interview with Momoniat.
51. Interview with Saloojee.
52. I. Mohamed, *Ramgobin* Defence Doc. #1.
53. Interview with Momoniat by Barrell.
54. Interviews with Saloojee and Momoniat.
55. Interview with Saloojee by Barrell.
56. *Baleka*, Judgment, p. 726.
57. Interview with Maharaj, published in the ANC's *Sechaba* (March 1984).
58. Barrell, 'Conscripts'.
59. Interview with P. Gordhan.
60. Interview with Momoniat.

CHAPTER 3
'THE FREEDOM BREEZE': THE FORMATION OF THE UDF

1. Interview with Saloojee.
2. Transvaal Anti-SAIC Committee, *Speeches and Papers Delivered at the Congress* (booklet produced by TASC), pp. 3, 11.
3. Interviews with Saloojee, Momoniat, Aboobaker and Badat.
4. N.G. Patel, address to TASC congress, in transcript of a video of the TASC congress, *Ramgobin* exhibit, pp. 98–9.
5. Interview with Saloojee.
6. 'Statement by the Commission of the Feasibility of a United Front against the Constitutional Reform

Proposals' (*Baleka* Exhibit AL.32).

7. The parallel was inappropriate, because the Philippine NDF operated underground.
8. 'Statement by the Commission ... ' (two versions) (*Baleka* Exhibits AL.32 and C.49); TASC congress transcript, p. 129; interview with Saloojee.
9. Interview with Momoniat.
10. Interview with Molefe.
11. Lekota, quoted in Barrell, 'The United Democratic Front', p. 10.
12. The cases for and against the revival of the TIC were argued in 'Editorial', *WIP*, 25 (Feb. 1983); 'TIC Revived', *WIP*, 26 (April 1983); and 'The Transvaal Indian Congress', *WIP*, 28 (Aug. 1983).
13. Interviews with Cachalia and Moosa.
14. Molefe, *Baleka* Defence Doc. #3.
15. Chikane, *Baleka* Defence Doc. #4.
16. UDF, 'Inter-regional executive meeting', 30–31 July 1983, handwritten notes (possibly written by Andrew Boraine); Chikane, *Baleka* Defence Doc. #4.
17. Molefe noted this perception in an address to the NUSAS July Festival earlier that month: Molefe, 'Responses to State Strategy', in NUSAS, *Beyond Reform: The Challenge of Reform* (NUSAS, 1983), p. 29.
18. Interview with Y. Mahomed.
19. Molefe, *Baleka* evidence, p. 13198.
20. Lekota, *Baleka* Defence Doc. #5.
21. Interview with Momoniat.
22. UDF, 'Press Update', 12 Aug. 1983; see also the different figures in CH, 20 Aug. 1983.
23. Interviews with Ramgobin and Saloojee.
24. UDF, 'Memorandum to exec members from secretariat', 4 Aug. 1983, handwritten (possibly by Trevor Manuel) (*Baleka* Exhibit C.45).
25. Interview with Molefe.
26. Interview with Aboobaker; also discussions with Leila Patel and Donald Skinner.
27. Molefe, *Baleka* Defence Doc. #3, p. 3.
28. UDF Declaration (1983).
29. UDF, Working Principles (1983), clause 6.1.
30. Zille, 'UDF'.
31. Interviews with Saloojee and Momoniat.
32. Interview with Molefe.
33. Interview with Molefe; Molefe, *Baleka* Defence Doc. #1, p. 17.
34. The one possible exception was Dr R.A.M. Salojee.
35. The following account of the national launch is drawn from the 'Transcript of speeches at UDF National Launch', and the UDF's own 'Report on National Launch Conference' (*Baleka* Exhibit D.3); Boesak's speech was published as 'God Bless Africa' in his *If This Is Treason*; see also the press during the week of 17–22 Aug. 1983.
36. *Argus*, 21 Aug. 1984, quoted in Philip Smith, manuscript on Alan Boesak's theology, untitled and undated.
37. White democrats were only accepted after long struggles. In the Western Cape, Trotskyist and other ultra-left groups broke with the emerging Charterist movement over the issue, because they advocated a more class-bound 'unity of the oppressed'.
38. Boesak, 'God Bless Africa', p. 41.
39. For different contributions to this debate, see 'GWU on the UDF' and 'MGWUSA on the UDF', *SALB*, 9, 2 (Nov. 1983); for theoretical debates, see 'Class Alliances: The "Economic" and "Political" Struggle', *Social Review*, 21 (Aug. 1983), 'Workers and Politics: Another View of Class Alliances', *Social Review*, 22/23 (Dec. 1983), and 'Debating Alliance Politics', *WIP*, 34 (Oct. 1984). See also Pillay, 'Trade Unions'.
40. UDF, 'Inter-regional executive meeting', July 1983, notes; also interview with Ramgobin.
41. 'Transcript of speeches at UDF National Launch; UDF, 'National Launch'.
42. UDF, notes on UDF–FOSATU meeting, Wilgespruit, 17 Sept. 1983, and on UDF–AFCWU meeting, Benoni, 3 Sept. 1983 (included in *Baleka* Exhibit C.52); 'Summary of [FOSATU] Central Committee meeting, 15/16 October 1983', and minutes of the same meeting. Within FOSATU, opposition was led by Freddie Sauls from Port Elizabeth. The unimportance of the UDF as far as FOSATU was concerned is indicated by the lack of any discussion of the UDF in FOSATU's *Annual Report* for 1983.
43. Interviews with Nair and C. Ndlovu.

44. Maré and Hamilton, *An Appetite for Power*; Forsyth, 'The Past in the Service of the Present'.
45. F. Chikane, in 'Transcript of speeches at UDF National Launch', p. 3; UDF, National Interim Committee, July 1983, notes.
46. Molefe, *Baleka* Defence Doc. #6, p. 111.
47. The history of the South African Black Alliance is covered in Maré and Hamilton, *An Appetite for Power*, pp. 157–63. On Inkatha's opposition to the constitutional reforms, see SAIRR *Survey* 1983, pp. 50–3.
48. *RDM,* 26 Jan. and 29 Sept. 1983; SAIRR *Survey* 1983, pp. 52–3.
49. Martin Challenor, 'Business Built on Stones', pp. 105–9; Maré and Hamilton, *An Appetite for Power*, pp. 192–6; UDF NEC 10–11 Sept. 1983, minutes.
50. *RDM* and *Star,* 4 Nov. 1983; UDF Tvl, 'What is Inkatha up to?' (pamphlet, *Baleka* exhibit AK.1); the NEC later criticised the Transvaal Media Committee for issuing this pamphlet without consulting either national or regional publicity secretaries (UDF NEC 5–6 Nov. 1983, minutes).
51. Letter, Buthelezi to Gumede, 10 Nov. 1983; *Star,* 10 Nov. 1983; letter, Gumede to Buthelezi, 12 Nov. 1983.
52. Telex, Buthelezi to Gumede, undated (in response to Gumede's telex to Buthelezi, apparently dated 28 Nov. 1983); letter, Buthelezi to Gumede, 15 Dec. 1983.
53. UDF NEC 21–22 Jan. 1984, minutes. Letter, Gumede to Buthelezi, 30 April 1984.
54. Letter, Gumede to Buthelezi, 7 May 1984; letter, Buthelezi to Gumede, 22 May 1984; Lekota, in *Black Sash* (Aug. 1984).
55. Maré and Hamilton, *An Appetite for Power*, p. 148.
56. Ishmael Mkhabela (AZAPO publicity secretary), quoted in *The Leader,* 28 Jan. 1983, itself cited in Barrell, 'The United Democratic Front', p. 10. Mthembu, presidential address, and Mkhabela, address to AZAPO's 3rd Annual Congress, 4–6 Feb. 1983 (*Baleka* Exhibit B.2), pp. 12 and 37; interviews with Momoniat and Cachalia.
57. 'Statement by the Disorderly Bills Action Committee on the proposed formation of a United Democratic Front' (undated, probably May–June 1983).
58. Neville Alexander, speech at launch of National Forum, published as 'Nation and Ethnicity' in *WIP,* 29 (Aug. 1983); *CAL Newsletter,* 1, 1 (Aug. 1983); Western Cape Youth League, pamphlet (undated, Aug. 1983); *GCP,* 5 June, 26 June and 17 July 1983; *Sow,* 22 June, 24 June 1983. See further Barrell, 'The United Democratic Front', and Dollie, 'The National Forum'.
59. UDF, 'Inter-regional executive meeting', July 1983, notes.
60. M. Chikane, *Baleka* evidence, pp. 17018–21.
61. Ibid.
62. Mabasa, presidential address to AZAPO's 4th Annual Congress, 8–9 Jan. 1984 (*Baleka* Exhibit B.18), p. 6. The reference to 'a chameleon-like attitude' concerned the Indian organisations, who argued for participation in ethnic referendums over the new constitution – see Ch. 5.
63. Ibid. See further *RDM,* 5 and 10 Jan.; *Sow,* 9, 10 and 11 Jan. 1984; Anton Harber, 'The AZAPO Conference', *WIP,* 30 (1984).
64. UDF Nat. Sec. meeting, 10–11 March 1984, minutes, p. 3; UDF Tvl RGC 14 April 1984, minutes; transcript of videotaped proceedings, Regina Mundi, 16 June 1984 (*Ramgobin* Exhibit V.10); M. Chikane, *Baleka* evidence, pp. 17021–3; Molefe, *Baleka* evidence, pp. 13496–8; *RDM/Soweto News,* 22 June 1984.

CHAPTER 4

'SIYAYA': FORMING THE UDF IN THE REGIONS

1. Molefe, *Baleka* Defence Doc. #1, p. 9.
2. Lekota, *Baleka* Defence Doc. #5; M. Chikane, *Baleka* Defence Doc. #4; UDF, National Interim Committee, July 1983, record.
3. For examples, see Cole, *Crossroads,* and Seekings, 'Quiescence'.
4. Interview with Momoniat.
5. M. Chikane, *Baleka* evidence, pp. 16962–9; M. Chikane, *Baleka* Defence Doc. #4; interview with Momoniat.
6. M. Chikane, *Baleka* evidence; Seekings, 'Quiescence', Chs. 4 and 8.
7. M. Chikane, *Baleka* evidence; M. Chikane, *Baleka* Defence Doc. #4.
8. See Mokoena, *Ramgobin* Defence Doc. #2.
9. Interview with Momoniat.
10. Ari Sitas, 'Durban, August 1985'.

11. Interview with Ramgobin.
12. Interviews with P. Gordhan, David, Y. Mahomed, Bonhomme, Wittenberg and Carrim; interviews with S. Badat and K. Naidoo by J. Frederickse; 'A Brief History of the Durban Housing Action Committee (DHAC) and Joint Rent Action Committee (JORAC)' (*Baleka* Exhibit Y.10).
13. See Moodley, 'South Africa's Indians' and 'Structural Inequality and Minority Anxiety'; Carrim, 'Trade Unionism in Natal'; Charney, 'Minority Group Politics'. Ginwala provides a more romantic view of Indian politics in 'Indian South Africans', but this view is belied by political developments after mid-1985.
14. Interviews with Tsenoli, Scott, M. Ndlovu, Dlamini and Ntombela.
15. Sitas, 'Durban, August 1985', p. 92; see also John Brewer, 'The Membership of Inkatha in KwaMashu'.
16. McCarthy and Swilling, 'Transport and Political Resistance'; Challenor, '"Business Built on Stones"'; Reintges, 'Rents and Urban Political Geography'; interviews with Tsenoli, Mkhize, Gumede and Xundu.
17. Interview with P. Gordhan.
18. Interview with Bonhomme.
19. The committee is listed in UDF, 'National Launch' (booklet), although the names of the co-secretaries are omitted.
20. Interviews with David, Bonhomme, C. Ndlovu and Y. Mahomed; Lekota, *Baleka* Defence Doc. #5.
21. Interviews with Chetty and Wittenberg.
22. Sitas, 'Durban, August 1985', p. 102.
23. Challenor, '"Business Built on Stones,"' pp. 105–9; Maré and Hamilton, *An Appetite for Power*, pp. 192–4; McCarthy, 'Black Local Government Issues in Natal'; UDF NEC 10–11 Sept. 1983, minutes.
24. Sitas, 'Class, Nation and Ethnicity'; also Mike Morris, 'Lessons from Mayday'.
25. Interview with Gumede.
26. Interviews with Manuel and Aboobaker; see also Friedman, *Building Tomorrow Today*, p. 458; Pillay, *Trade Unions and Alliance Politics*.
27. Interviews with De Vries and Kota.
28. Accounts of these events differ: interviews with Moosa and Aboobaker; Pillay, 'Trade Unions', Ch. 6.
29. Interview with De Vries; Pillay, 'Trade Unions'.
30. UDF WCp REC, 6 Oct. 1983, 29 Feb. 1984 and 8 March 1984, minutes; UDF WCp RGC, 22 March 1984, minutes; T. Manuel, 'Memorandum to affiliates and regions' (13 Jan. 1984); UDF WCp, 'Report of the Regional Commission' (undated, *circa* March 1984); interviews with Sidina and Rasool.
31. Pillay, 'Trade Unions'; CAL Newsletter, 1, 1 (although unnumbered, and undated) and 1, 2 (Aug. 1983); interview with Ebrahim. See also 'Cape Action League; Challenging the Clichés' (interview with CAL media officer Armien Abrahams), *WIP*, 35 (Feb. 1985).
32. UDF WCp REC, 25 April 1985, minutes; interview with Marks.
33. Interview with Njikelana; Johann Maree, 'SAAWU in the East London Area, 1979–81'; Ntsebeza, 'Youth in Urban African Townships', pp. 110–16.
34. Ntsebeza, 'Youth in Urban African Townships', pp. 118 and 122.
35. *People's ECCO* (newsletter of the Eastern Cape Co-ordinating Committee), 1 (Feb. 1983).
36. Interviews with Moosa and Njikelana; discussion with Pillay; Avril Joffe, 'SAAWU Conference Briefing'; Friedman, *Building Tomorrow Today*, Ch. 13.
37. Interview with Stofile; but see Tetelman, 'We Can', pp. 173–4.
38. UDF, National Interim Committee, July 1983, report; Lekota, *Baleka* Defence Doc. #5; interview with Ramgobin. On the bus boycott, which ended through negotiations in March 1985, see Swilling, 'Urban Social Movements', and '"The Buses Smell of Blood."'
39. UDF Bdr, 'Report to UDF Special Conference' (Dec. 1983) (*Baleka* Exhibit AM.13); interview with Stofile.
40. Interviews with Stofile and Coetzee; UDF, 'National Launch'.
41. UDF Bdr, 'Report to UDF Special Conference'; UDF Bdr, 'Annual Secretarial Report' (*Baleka* Exhibit C.48); *DD*, 24 Sept. 1983; *RDM*, 15 Oct. 1983; interview with Stofile.
42. UDF Bdr, 'Annual Sec. Rpt'.
43. UDF NEC 10–11 Sept. 1983, minutes.
44. Interviews with Sizani and V. Oliphant; interviews with M. Jack and Nkala by Rory Riordan.
45. Interview with Coetzee.
46. *People's ECCO*, 1; interview with FOSATU Eastern Cape regional committee, *SALB*, 11, 1 (Sept. 1985); interview with Sizani. The press reported that this was a response to the call for a UDF, but it

seems unlikely (*SE*, 29 May 1983; *RDM*, 4 June 1983).

47. Interviews with Nkwinti, Sizani, Coetzee, and Molefe; Lekota, *Baleka* Defence Doc. #5.
48. UDF, 'Port Elizabeth – workshop on 14 August 1983', report (*Baleka* Exhibit C.73 – note that the report misdates the workshop); interview with Coetzee.
49. UDF ECp, Report on regional launch; *EPH*, 5 Dec. 1983.
50. Interviews with Stofile and Nkwinti.
51. UDF, 'Report, Future Programme, Budget Proposals: Motivation for Funding' (Nov. 1984) (*Baleka* Exhibit C.53), Appendix A.
52. UDF NEC 10–11 Sept., minutes; Molefe, *Baleka* Defence Doc. #7.
53. Van Kessel, 'Beyond Our Wildest Dreams', pp. 184–7.
54. UDF NTvl, *UDF News*, 1, 1 (*Baleka* Exhibit W.6); report on Northern Transvaal UDF regional meeting, Feb. 1985, and invitation to conference, March 1985 (*Baleka* Exhibit ABA.42); Van Kessel, 'Beyond Our Wildest Dreams', p. 183.
55. Quoted in Van Kessel, 'Beyond Our Wildest Dreams', p. 182.
56. Interview with R. Oliphant. The UDF's fund-raising document from November 1984 recorded that the UDF South Cape region was launched in July 1984, but other evidence suggests that it remained a sub-region under the Western Cape. There was no separate South Cape representation at the UDF's 1985 NGC.
57. UDF NEC Nov. 1983, minutes; UDF, 'The Northern Cape Regional General Council Question' (undated, *Baleka* Exhibit AM.14); UDF NCp, 'Report of Northern Cape Regional Workshop' (undated, *Baleka* Exhibit U.8).

CHAPTER 5

OPPOSING THE TRICAMERAL PARLIAMENT

1. UDF NEC 10–11 Sept. 1983, Durban, minutes; *Sow* and *RDM*, 14 Sept. 1983. See also UDF, Workshop 8 Sept. 1983, Cape Town, minutes; and interview with Molefe.
2. Interview with Molefe.
3. *CH*, 3 Sept. 1983; *STrib*, 11 Sept. 1983; SAIRR *Survey* 1983, p. 248; interviews with Rhodes and Rasool.
4. UDF NEC Nov. 1983, minutes.
5. UDF, Sec. Rpt to NGC 1983 (Molefe), p. 8.
6. UDF ECp, 'Regional Report', 14 March 1985 (*Baleka* Exhibit AAZ.9); UDF Tvl, 'Report to the NEC' 21 Jan. 1984.
7. Quotations from M. Chikane, *Baleka* evidence, and UDF, Sec. Rpt to NGC 1983 (Molefe). See also UDF Tvl, 'Report to the NEC', 21 Jan. 1984; UDF WCp, 'Report to the national office on assessment of the Front' (undated, *circa* Oct. 1984); UDF ECp, 'Regional Report', March 1985.
8. UDF Tvl Media Committee, 'Report on Campaign against Local Authority Elections in 1983' (April 1984) (*Baleka* Exhibit AM.2), p. 1.
9. UDF Tvl, Sec. Rpt to RGC, 10 Dec. 1983 (*Baleka* Exhibit N.3).
10. Ibid.
11. Baba Ngcokoto (UDF WCp publicity secretary), 'Unrest in the Ciskei: UDF's view', *CT*, 1 Oct. 1983.
12. SAIRR *Survey* 1983, pp. 78–87.
13. Molefe actually suggests that some NUSAS leaders believed that 'progressive "no" votes, together with those of the liberals and the far rightwing could effectively stop the constitution at base one' – Molefe, *Baleka* Defence Doc. #3, p. 15.
14. UDF WCp Workshop, 8 Sept. 1983, minutes.
15. *CH*, 3 Sept. 1983.
16. *Argus*, 24 Aug. 1983.
17. UDF NEC Sept. 1983, minutes; *RDM*, 14 Sept., 19 Oct. 1983; *Cit*, 14 Sept. 1983.
18. *CT*, 28 Oct. 1983.
19. Estimates of attendance vary, as ever: Barrell, 'The United Democratic Front'; *CP*, 5 Nov. 1983; *RDM*, 31 Oct. 1983; *UDF News*, 1, 3 (Oct. 1983), p. 1; UDF Tvl, Rpt to NEC, 5 Nov. 1983 (*Baleka* Exhibit E.2); UDF WCp, 'Report to the national office on assessment of the Front' (undated, *circa* Oct. 1984); *Grassroots*, 4, 8 (Oct.) and 4, 9 (Nov. 1983).
20. SAIRR *Survey* 1983, pp. 23 and 38.
21. UDF NEC, Nov. 1983, minutes; UDF Tvl RGC, 10 Dec. 1983, minutes; SAIRR *Survey* 1983; *CH*, 17 Nov. 1983.

22. UDF NGC 1983, Nat. Sec. Rpt, p. 1.
23. Ibid., pp. 1–2.
24. Ibid., p. 4.
25. Ibid.
26. Speech, untitled and undated, by Eric Molobi, p. 2; UDF Ntl, 'Report to the Natal Regional General Council of UDF on the Port Elizabeth conference held on 17/18 December 1983' (*Baleka* Exhibit T.15), p. 1.
27. Interview with Molefe.
28. Quotations from UDF reports on the conference, press reports and interviews.
29. I. Mohamed, *Ramgobin* Defence Doc. #1 and #3; I. Mohamed, 'UDF and the new South African constitution' (*Baleka* Exhibit AL.6); E. Daniels, 'Why we cannot participate in an election/referendum related to Botha's constitutional proposals' (*Baleka* Exhibit AL.7); Molefe, *Baleka* Defence Doc. #3, pp. 18–19; UDF, 'Report of the National Conference' (Molefe), p. 3.
30. See, for example, interviews with C. Nkondo and Stofile. Stofile says that it 'tended to be a racial cleavage'; he suggests that the African leadership from Natal were less than totally supportive of the NIC 'vote no' position.
31. *RDM*, 20 Jan. 1984; SAIRR *Survey* 1984, pp. 26–7.
32. UDF NEC 21–22 Jan. 1984, Sec. Rpt, pp. 2–3, and minutes; UDF, 'NEC press release on the coloured and Indian referendum', 25 Jan. 1993; *Sow*, 26 Jan. 1984; *EPH*, 26 Jan. 1984.
33. Molefe, *Baleka* Defence Doc. #3, p. 16.
34. Interview with Molefe.
35. UDF NEC Jan. 1984, Sec. Rpt, pp. 2–3.
36. UDF WCp, 'Reportback [to] Cape Town region', p. 5.
37. UDF NEC 1 June 1984, 'Officer's report to the NEC' (Molefe) (*Baleka* Exhibit T.9); UDF Tvl AGM 9 March 1985, Sec. Rpt, p. 3; I. Mohamed, *Ramgobin* Defence Doc. #1, pp. 15–16.
38. Molefe, 'What is the UDF?', speech written for meeting in the Northern Cape (undated, *circa* Dec. 1983).
39. Lodge, *Black Politics*, p. 74.
40. *Star*, 21 Jan. 1984; *NW*, 7 June 1984.
41. UDF NGC 1985, Sec. Rpt (Molefe), pp. 9, 16.
42. Interview with Morobe; Lekota, in *RDM Extra*, 20 Jan. 1984.
43. *Grassroots*, 5, 2 (Mar. 1984).
44. UDF NEC Jan. 1984, Sec. Rpt.
45. M. Chikane, handwritten notebook (*Baleka* Exhibit AM.3), p. 11; interviews with Morobe, C. Ndlovu and K. Gordhan.
46. *Star*, 21 Jan. 1984; *EPH*, 16 April 1984.
47. UDF NCp, Rpt on MSC (handwritten) (*Baleka* Exhibit AL.44); UDF Tvl Signatures Committee, Rpt, 10 March 1984 (*Baleka* Exhibit C.88).
48. *Grassroots*, 5, 2 (Mar. 1984).
49. Interview with K. Gordhan. Curnick Ndlovu provides a very similar account (interview). He suggests that there were about a hundred people, comprising about fifty from KwaMashu, thirty or more from Lamontville, twenty from Clermont, and some university students.
50. UDF WCp and Ntl, MSC documentation.
51. UDF WCp, Ntl and Tvl, MSC documentation; see also UDF Nat. Sec. meeting, April 1984, records, and *RDM*, 1 May 1984.
52. UDF NEC, 1–2 June 1984, Rpt from national office (*Baleka* Exhibit T.9).
53. UDF Ntl, Circular to affiliates (Ndlovu, undated but *circa* mid-June 1984) (*Baleka* Exhibit AL.39); UDF MSC Committee, 3 June 1984, minutes; UDF NEC June 1984, minutes; interview with K. Gordhan.
54. 'MSC Report'; letter, unaddressed, from Lekota and Molefe, dated 4 May 1984 (*Baleka* Exhibit AL.157).
55. UDF Tvl RGC 14 April 1984; UDF Nat. Sec. meeting, 28 April 1984, notes (handwritten); *RDM*, 1 May; *Sowetan Sunday Mirror*, 24 June 1984.
56. Interview with Morobe.
57. Interviews with Monareng, Lephunya and Morobe; Charles Carter, '"We Are the Progressives."'
58. Interview with Sizani; interview with Jack by Rory Riordan.
59. Delius, *A Lion Amongst the Cattle*, p. 183.
60. UDF WCp MSC Committee, 13 May 1984, notes (handwritten); UDF WCp 'Khayelitsha committee',

21 May 1984, minutes; UDF WCp REC, 13 June 1984, minutes; Cole, *Crossroads*, p. 98, citing *CT*, 12 June 1984; interviews with Sidina, Marks, Sonto and Rhodes.

61. Interview with K. Gordhan.
62. Ibid.; interview with C. Ndlovu.
63. UDF, Memorandum to all regional secretaries on 'The Million Signatures Campaign', by Molefe, dated 31 Aug. 1984.
64. UDF WCp, 'Report to the national office on assessment of the Front' (undated, *circa* Oct. 1984); also UDF WCp, Assessment of organisation, by T. Manuel (handwritten, June 1984).
65. UDF NGC 1985, Sec. Rpt.
66. Interview with K. Gordhan.
67. Ibid. See also interviews with Nkwinti, Morobe, Bonhomme, Tsenoli, Rhodes and Malindi.
68. UDF WCp, 'Report to the national office on assessment of the Front' (undated, *circa* Oct. 1984); also Assessment of organisation, by T. Manuel (hand-written, June 1984); interview with Molefe.
69. Interview with K. Gordhan.
70. UDF WCp, 'Preparation for the UDF Annual General Meeting', 7 Jan. 1985 (circular from REC); UDF, circular to regional secretaries, re 'Anti-election campaign', signed Popo Molefe, 2 July 1984 (*Baleka* Exhibit AL.77); UDF NEC June 1984, Nat. Office rpt; UDF WCp, 'Assessment of organisation', by T. Manuel (June 1984).
71. UDF NEC 21 July 1984, minutes. The National Committee comprised Molefe and Lekota, Nieela Hoosein (from P.E.), Yacoob (from Durban), Khasu (from the Northern Cape), Manuel (from Cape Town) and Andrew Hendricks (from East London) – Molefe, *Baleka* Defence Doc. #8. UDF WCp REC 27 June 1984, minutes; also interview with Rasool.
72. Collinge, 'The United Democratic Front', p. 257.
73. Gary van Staden, in *Star*, 24 Aug. 1984, quoted in Collinge, 'The United Democratic Front'.
74. List of Transvaal meetings in Anti-Constitution Campaign, 18 July 1984 (*Baleka* Exhibit AL.25). See also press reports on 20 Aug. in *DN, NW, Star* and *Cit*. For the UDF's claims, see *Star*, 22 Aug., and *FM*, 24 Aug. 1984.
75. *Argus*, 7 Aug.; *DD*, 21 Aug.; *EPH*, 21 and 22 Aug. 1984.
76. Boesak, 'The Present Crisis in Apartheid: A Reply to the South African Government Proposal for a Three-Tier Parliament', address given at the Transvaal Anti-SAIC Committee conference, Johannesburg (Jan. 1983), published in Boesak, *Black and Reformed*.
77. Boesak, speech at NIC meeting, Ladysmith, 1 Aug. 1984.
78. *CT*, 23 July 1984.
79. *Argus*, 21 Aug. 1984, quoted in Philip Smith, untitled manuscript.
80. *Argus*, 10 Aug. 1984.
81. UDF WCp REC 16 May 1984, minutes; *Star*, 5 July; *EP*, 9 July 1984.
82. *Argus* and *RDM*, 21 Aug.; *Star*, 22 Aug. 1984.
83. UDF, 'Statement on apartheid elections held on 28 August and related events' (Molefe) (*Baleka* Exhibit AL.151).
84. UDF NGC 1985, Sec. Rpt (Molefe); *RDM*, 24 Aug. 1984.
85. MIRGE, 'Memorandum from MIRGE concerning the way ahead for UDF', undated (5 pp.).
86. UDF Ntl, 'Report on National Secretariat Meeting held on 10th March 1984'; UDF NEC June 1984, minutes; UDF, 'Report of UDF Evaluation Workshop held on 4 November 1984' (*Baleka* Exhibit AL.76); UDF Bdr, Sec. Rpt.
87. *Baleka* Defence Doc. #10.
88. Letter, Gumede and Mpetha to the Prime Minister, dated 25 Oct. 1983 (*Baleka* Exhibit DA.21); UDF NEC Nov. 1983, minutes; *RDM*, 19 Oct. 1983. It is unclear why Sisulu was not a co-signatory of the letter.
89. UDF NEC July 1984, minutes; UDF, 'Some notes on the call for a National Convention' (undated) (*Baleka* Exhibit C.18).
90. *Baleka* Defence Doc. #10; UDF Tvl Special GC, Aug. 1984, minutes.
91. TIC (?), 'Congress prospective [*sic*] on the constitutional proposals', paper presented at the South African Institute of Race Relations, undated (*Baleka* Exhibit C.75), p. 11.
92. Boesak, 'The Present Crisis' (*Black and Reformed*, p. 130). See also *If This Is Treason*, p. 83; 'Raise a Sign of Hope', funeral address in Cradock, 20 July 1985, published in *If This Is Treason*, p. 108; and 'A Christian Response to the New Constitution', speech in Durban, 21 May 1983, published in *If This Is Treason*, p. 27.
93. Molefe, *Baleka* Defence Doc. #1, pp. 71–2.

94. Interview with Boesak by Philip Smith, quoted in Smith, untitled manuscript.
95. See Barrell, 'Conscripts'.
96. UDF National Conference, Dec. 1983, Nat. Sec. Rpt (Molefe).
97. Molefe, *Baleka* Defence Doc. #1.
98. UDF NEC July 1984, minutes, para. 7.4.
99. UDF, Report on National Launch Conference; UDF NEC Sept. 1983 and Nov. 1983, minutes.
100. Molefe, letter to Steve Tshwete, 'Re: paper on front', 13 Sept. 1984 (*Baleka* Exhibit C.3).
101. UDF NEC June 1984, minutes; UDF, 'Circular to all NEC members', by Molefe, 10 July 1984 (*Baleka* Exhibit AL.80).
102. UDF NEC, 'The Future of the UDF – Some NEC Views', unsigned (but drafted by Molefe) and undated (but *circa* mid-Sept. 1984).
103. UDF NEC Jan. 1984, Sec. Rpt; NEC June 1984 and July 1984, minutes.
104. Interviews with Saloojee and Y. Mahomed.
105. UDF Tvl Media Committee, 'Report on Campaign against Local Authority elections in 1983', April 1984 (*Baleka* Exhibit AM.2), p. 4.
106. Interview with David.
107. Meer, *South Africa*, p. 3.
108. UDF Ntl AGM 1985, Sec. Rpt, pp. 4–5.
109. Meer, *South Africa*.
110. Interviews with P. Gordhan, Molefe and Morobe.
111. Interviews with Nair, P. Gordhan.
112. UDF WCp, AGM 1985, Sec. Rpt.

CHAPTER 6
THE TOWNSHIP REVOLT

1. Lodge, 'Rebellion', p. 65.
2. UDF Nat. Secretariat meeting, 12–13 Jan. 1985, minutes; UDF NGC 1985 Sec. Rpt, p. 16.
3. Challenor, '"Business Built on Stones"'; Cole, *Crossroads*; Seekings, 'Quiescence' and 'Political Mobilisation in Tumahole'; Swilling, '"The Buses Smell of Blood."'
4. UDF NEC Sept. 1983, Nov. 1983, Jan. 1984 and June 1984, minutes; UDF National Secretariat meeting, Johannesburg, 10 March 1984, minutes; UDF WCp (with CAHAC), 'National conference for civic organisations', circular to all UDF regional secretaries, by T. Manuel, 16 April 1984 (*Baleka* Exhibit AAZ.1); UDF, 'Circular to all regions', by Molefe, 3 Sept. 1984 (*Baleka* Exhibit X.9); UDF WCp RGC, 29 May 1985, minutes (including notes on a report from the NEC meeting of 4–5 May 1985).
5. Molefe, *Baleka* Defence Doc. #6.
6. UDF Tvl RGC 14 April 1984, minutes; M. Chikane, *Baleka* Evidence, p. 17016.
7. 'Eastern Cape Crisis in Education Committee report to second national conference of parents' committees, Johannesburg, 6 April 1985'; interview with Nkwinti.
8. UDF NEC Nov. 1984, 'Secretarial report from the Transvaal'.
9. Interviews with Molefe, Creecey and Lephunya; M. Chikane, *Baleka* Evidence p. 17034; UDF Tvl, 'Emergency UDF Working Document', 25 Sept. 1984 (*Baleka* Exhibit C.118).
10. UDF NEC Nov. 1984, minutes.
11. UDF Tvl REC meetings were held on 11 Sept., 14 Oct., 1 Nov. and 7 Dec.
12. UDF NEC, 'The Future of the UDF – Some NEC Views'.
13. These early initiatives around parents' committees are curiously overlooked in accounts such as Johann Muller's 'People's Education'. I rely on copies of original SPC documentation, and the testimony of Bishop Manas Buthelezi in *Baleka*, 17–18 May 1988.
14. Quoted in Barrell, 'Conscripts'.
15. Quoted in ibid.
16 Ibid., 'Conscripts'; interview with Monareng.
17. This account of strategic differences between Soweto and the stayaway is based on interviews with Morobe, Monareng, Lephunya and Ngwenya.
18. Interview with Monareng.
19. My account here is based on interviews with Monareng, Lephunya, Mditshwa, Morobe, Mogane and Molefe. My interpretation differs from that of the Labour Monitoring Group (LMG) with regard to the strategic approaches and planning processes involved. See LMG, 'The November Stayaway'; also, Swilling, 'Stayaways'.

20. On the East Rand, see Von Holdt, 'Trade Unions'; Swilling, 'Workers Divided'; also FOSATU, 'Transvaal Regional Report to the Central Committee of 20/21 October 1984'.

21. FOSATU Central Committee meeting, 20–21 Oct. 1984, Johannesburg, minutes, p. 18.

22. Interview with Jantjies; see also LMG, 'The November Stayaway'.

23. FOSATU, 'Meeting between the COSAS, UDF re 27.10.1984 in Khotso House Johannesburg'; interview with Monareng.

24. Interview with Monareng.

25. UDF Tvl REC 1 Nov. 1984, minutes, and handwritten notes (*Baleka* Exhibit C.82); interview with Lephunya.

26. UDF NEC Nov. 1984, 'Secretarial Report from the Transvaal'.

27. UDF NEC Nov. 1984, 'Input on Organisational Aspects of UDF' (*Baleka* Exibit C.5).UDF NGC April 1985, Sec. Rpt. The stayaway was not listed as a UDF activity in the secretarial report to the Transvaal UDF's AGM in March 1985.

28. FOSATU, '1984 Annual Report'.

29. *Star*, 6 Nov. 1984.

30. *SE*, 11 Nov., *FM*, 16 Nov., quoted in SAIRR *Survey* 1984, p. 76. UDF NEC Nov. 1984, minutes, p. 3; interview with Molefe; Collinge, 'The United Democratic Front', p. 255; 'UDF calls ... ', *Sow*, 21 Nov. 1984; Lekota, quoted in *WIP* (Feb. 1985).

31. Molefe, *Baleka* evidence, pp. 13230–1, quoted in Moss, *Shouting at the Crocodile*, pp. 131–2.

32. *Star* and *Sow*, 13 Dec. 1984; *CP*, 23 Dec. 1984.

33. UDF WCp AGM March 1985, Sec. Rpt; UDF ECp AGM March 1985, Sec. Rpt, p. 5; UDF ECp, Regional Rpt, 14 March 1985 (*Baleka* Exhibit AAZ.9); UDF NEC Nov. 1984, 'Secretarial report from the Transvaal' (*Baleka* Exhibit J.2).

34. Letter, Molefe to Tshwete, 13 Sept. 1984. Tshwete, the Border UDF president, had at times been critical of the UDF's tactics, but was also a veteran Charterist. Molefe seems to have expected that Tshwete's familiarity with the history of the Congress Alliance would lead him to support the UDF's overall strategic approach. UDF NEC, 'The Future of the UDF – Some NEC Views'.

35. UDF WCp, 'Circular to all affiliates and regional committees', signed C. Carolus (regional secretary), 27 Aug. 1984.

36. UDF WCp, 'Report to the national office on assessment of the Front' (undated, Oct.? 1984); UDF WCp AGM 1985, Sec. Rpt, part 2, p. 1. See also UDF WCp REC, 'Preparation for the UDF Annual General Meeting', circular dated 7 Jan. 1985.

37. UDF ECp, Regional Report, 14 March 1985; UDF NEC Nov. 1984, 'Input on organisational aspects of UDF'.

38. Tshwete, 'The United Democratic Front and the struggle for national democracy', undated paper (*circa* mid-Oct. 1984).

39. Barrell, 'Conscripts'.

40. MIRGE, 'Preparation for the UDF AGM', 2 Feb. 1984; UDF WCp AGM 1985, minutes, pp. 2–3. The treasurer also questioned the way in which the UDF operated; it relied too much on the media, which was expensive, and spent large sums on attending national meetings – UDF WCp AGM 1985, Treasurer's Rpt.

41. Tshwete, 'The UDF ...'.

42. UDF NEC Nov. 1984, 'Input on organisational aspects of UDF'.

43. UDF, 'Memorandum to all [regional] secretaries' about International Youth Year, signed Molefe, 13 Feb. 1985. Molefe and the NEC seem to have been concerned to rein in the more militant affiliates, whilst Tshwete was probably concerned to pull along the more cautious ones.

44. UDF Nat. Sec., 12–13 Jan. 1985, minutes.

45. Interview with Cronin, by Barrell, quoted in Barrell, 'Conscripts', Ch. 8.

46. UDF WCp, 'Report to the national office on assessment of the Front' (undated, *circa* Oct. 1984); see also UDF WCp, 'Circular to all affiliates and regional committees', signed C. Carolus (regional secretary), 27 Aug. 1984. During the 1980s the demographic composition of Cape Town itself changed; by the end of the decade there were as many African as coloured people in the area.

47. C. Ndlovu, 'Input on political aspects of the Front', p. 2.

48. UDF WCp, 'Report to the national office on assessment of the Front'. Several of these suggestions were mirrored in the assessment offered by MIRGE, 'Memorandum from MIRGE concerning the way ahead for UDF'.

49. Barrell, 'Conscripts', Ch. 8.

50. UDF WCp AGM 1985, Sec. Rpt.

51. Letter, Molefe to Tshwete, 13 Sept. 1984; Tshwete, 'The UDF ...', p. 6. UDF NEC Nov. 1984, minutes. See also Molefe, 'Two Documents'; UDF, 'The Freedom Charter: Workshop Paper' (*Baleka* Exhibit C.97); UDF NWC June 1985, Resolution.
52. UDF NEC Feb. 1985, Sec. Rpt from Bdr Region (*Baleka* Exhibit C.11).
53. Interview with Mogane.
54. See, for example, transcript of Molefe's speech at Boipatong, Feb. 1985.
55. *EPH*, 7 Jan. 1985; information from Rory Riordan.
56. Anniversary statement of the NEC of the ANC, 8 Jan. 1985, quoted in Lodge, 'Rebellion', p. 76.
57. Neither the Eastern Cape REC nor any of its individual members seems to have issued any public statements before, during or after the protests. The UDF later acknowledged that the protests had been organised by UDF affiliates rather than the UDF as such.
58. Pillay, 'Community Organisations'; interviews with FOSATU leaders in *SALB*, 11, 1 (Sept. 1985). Stofile claims that the stayaway covered much of the Border as well (interview).
59. Lodge, '"Mayihlome!"' p. 231.
60. Molefe, *Baleka* Defence Doc. #1, p. 42.
61. Collinge, 'The United Democratic Front'; UDF Tvl AGM 1985, Sec. Rpt (*Baleka* Exhibit T.25), p. 4.
62. *Sow*, 20 Feb.; *RDM*, 22 Feb. 1985.
63. Lekota, *Baleka* evidence pp. 17745–6, quoted in Moss, *Shouting at the Crocodile*, pp. 146–7.
64. Lekota, quoted in *Star*, 7 April 1985; UDF Tvl AGM 1985, Sec. Rpt, p. 4; *CP*, 31 March 1985.
65. UDF Bdr, Annual Sec. Rpt (Nov. 1984).
66. UDF ECp AGM 1985, Sec. Rpt (*Baleka* Exhibit AAZ.6); interviews with Nkwinti and Sizani.
67. General Van Loggerenberg, quoted in Mufson, *Fighting Years*, p. 104.
68. Interview with Lekota, by Karen Jochelson, in *WIP*, 35 (Feb. 1985), p. 2.
69. UDF NGC 1985, Statement.
70. UDF NGC 1985, Sec. Rpt.
71. The UDF itself attributed this to inadequate organisation, but this is hardly a sufficient explanation – UDF NEC 4 May 1985, minutes.
72. UDF NGC 1985, Sec. Rpt, p. 16.
73. Ibid., p. 19.
74. UDF NWC 8–9 June 1985, minutes, pp. 1–2.
75. UDF NGC 1985, Statement, quoted in UDF, 'On Discipline', *Isizwe*, 1, 1 (Nov. 1985), p. 24.
76. UDF NGC 1985, Resolution on Education; UDF NGC 1985, Report from commission on education, recorded in handwritten minutes.
77. UDF NEC May 1985, minutes.
78. Quotations from 'The International Youth Year' (*Baleka* Exhibit AB.15); UDF NGC 1985, Sec. Rpt; UDF, Statement, quoted in *Cit*, 13 Nov. 1984. See also interview with Morobe.
79. This description of the proposed national youth organisation is from 'Decisions taken after reports of discussion on N.Y.S.', document from January 1985 youth conference (*Baleka* Exhibit AB.12). UDF, Memorandum to regional secretaries from head office, signed by Molefe, 13 Feb. 1985, on 'International Youth Year' (*Baleka* Exhibit AB.10).
80. 'Brief Report to Regions', by Dan Montsitsi, undated (but *circa* late Aug. or Sept. 1985).
81. This and the following paragraph are based on UDF NEC May 1985, minutes (handwritten); un-titled document, undated (probably May–June 1985), typed, 12 pp., on the proposed national housing conference; UDF WCp RGC 29 May and 5 June 1985, minutes; UDF WCp, circular letter re 'Preparation for National Conference of Civics'; handwritten draft of letter from T. Manuel, undated (early May 1985?); UDF NWC 8–9 June 1985, minutes; UDF WCp, Circular letter re 'Preparation for National Conference of Civics', to secretaries of WCCA, CAHAC, UWO, dated 17 June 1985, signed W. Rhodes (for co-ordinating committee); UDF, 'National Civic Conference: Information Bulletin No. 1'; circular memorandum, from C. Carolus (UDF National Office) to regional co-ordinators of the National Civic Conference, dated 10 July 1985, re National Civic Conference; UDF Tvl WR Area Committee, Workshop for KRO, record; interviews with Lephunya and Xundu.
82. *SotN*, (Oct.–Nov. 1985), p. 13.
83. *SotN*, Supplement (Oct.–Nov. 1985), pp. 29, 31.
84. Carolus, curiously, had no elected position at this time, according to the list of NEC and REC members provided in the official 1985 NGC booklet. The nine REC members were Albertina Sisulu and Amanda Kwadi (Transvaal); Victoria Mxenge, Sandy Africa and Nozizwe Madlala (Natal); Miranda Qwanyashe, Zoe Kota and Mildred Lesia (Western Cape); Lucille Mayer (Border).
85. UDF, Sec. Rpt Feb. 1986, p. 3.

86. Black Sash, 'Police Conduct'.
87. This was amply documented in the work of the Truth and Reconciliation Commission after 1994.
88. AZAPO opposed and disrupted Kennedy's visit, and fiercely denounced the call for a national convention spearheaded by the UDF (*STrib*, 7 April 1985).
89. UDF NEC May 1985, minutes; UDF NEC, open letter to AZAPO, signed by Samson Ndou, dated 6 May 1985; press reports between 15 April and 27 May 1985.
90. Barrell, 'Conscripts', Ch. 8; Mufson, *Fighting Years*, p. 104.
91. Seekings, 'Identity, Authority and the Dynamics of Violent Conflict'; Barrell, 'Conscripts', Ch. 9.
92. Seekings, 'From "Quiescence" to "People's Power."'
93. Sizani, quoted in *SotN* (May 1985), p. 8.
94. *EPH*, 22 July 1985. Mono Badela, quoted in Mufson, *Fighting Years*, p. 113.
95. Boesak, 'Raise a Sign of Hope' (*If This Is Treason*, p. 108).
96. Interviews with Moosa, Morobe and Stofile.
97. SAIRR *Survey* 1985, pp. 455–60.
98. Interviews with Moosa and Morobe.
99. Mufson, *Fighting Years*, p. 113.
100. UDF, Sec. Rpt Feb. 1986, pp. 4–5.
101. Ibid., p. 4.
102. Interview with Moosa.
103. Mashinini, quoted in Mufson, *Fighting Years*, p. 116.
104. No national UDF documentation has survived from this period, and leaders give contrasting views in interviews (see my interviews with Morobe and Moosa). The most likely occasion would have been the emergency, post-funeral meeting in Peelton.
105. Helliker, Roux and White, '"Asithengi,"' p. 35; interview with Morobe.
106. Interview with Moosa; discussion with Sathekge; Mufson, *Fighting Years*, p. 125. More information is required on UDF Area Committees to assess adequately the UDF's role in consumer boycotts.
107. Interview with Jantjies; Seekings, 'From "Quiescence" to "People's Power."'
108. UDF, Sec. Rpt Feb. 1986, p. 11.
109. Interview with Moosa.
110. White, '"A Tide Has Risen, A Breach has Occurred."' See also interview with Moosa.
111. UDF, Sec. Rpt Feb. 1986, p. 11.
112. Interview with Moosa.
113. *Grassroots*, 6, 6 (Aug. 1985); interview with Rasool; Pillay, 'Trade Unions'; Hall, 'Resistance and Rebellion'; Nekhwevha, 'The 1985 Schools Crisis', pp. 6–7; .
114. Obery, Jochelson and Carrim, 'Consumer Boycotts', pp. 17–20; *Grassroots*, 6, 7 (Sept. 1985).
115. UDF untitled, undated position paper (*circa* Sept. 1985); this paper noted that 'We have relied far too much on police brutality to mobilise people into not buying from white shops'. See further, Hall, 'Resistance and Rebellion', pp. 14–15; *Grassroots*, 6, 7 (Sept.) and 6, 8 (Oct. 1985).
116. Cole, *Crossroads*, p. 120; see also interviews with Malindi and Sonto.
117. Tshwete, quoted by Murray, *South Africa*, p. 324.
118. Ntsebeza, 'Youth in Urban African Townships', pp. 135–40.
119. Mufson, *Fighting Years*, p. 207. Tshwete says he left the country in November, according to *Sechaba*, April 1986. But other sources point to his leaving earlier in the year, in September.
120. Events in Natal are examined in Reintjes, 'Rents'; Sitas, 'Durban, August 1985'; Forsyth, *Pietermaritzburg Conflict Chronology*; Hughes, 'Violence in Inanda'; Gwala, 'Rebellion in the Last Outpost'; Byerley, 'The Empangeni/Richards Bay Bus Boycott'.
121. Interview with Y. Mahomed.
122. Sitas, 'Durban, August 1985', pp. 105–12.
123. De Villiers, 'UDF under Attack', p. 34.
124. Sitas, 'Durban, August 1985', pp. 103–4.
125. De Villiers, 'UDF under Attack', p. 34.
126. Interview with Tsenoli; Naidoo, 'The Politics of Youth Resistance in the 1980s'.
127. Meer, *Resistance in the Townships*, p. 263.
128. This account is based on interviews with M. Ndlovu, Chetty, Carrim and Wittenberg; see also Forsyth, *Pietermariztburg Conflict Chronology*, and Wittenberg et al., 'The Crisis in Pietermaritzburg'.
129. Interview with M. Ndlovu.
130. Wittenberg et al., 'The Crisis in Pietermaritzburg'.

131. Lekota, quoted in *Star*, 9 April 1985 and *RDM*, 9 April 1985.
132. UDF NEC Nov. 1984, 'Input … on political aspects of the Front'. The dual role as front/organisation, depending on the level of formal organisation locally, was repeated in UDF Sec. Rpt Feb. 1986, p. 9. UDF Sec. Rpt Feb. 1986, p. 2.
133. *Weekend Post*, 6 April 1985.
134. Mufson, *Fighting Years*, pp. 79–103; quotations from pp. 101–2.
135. Sizani, quoted in ibid., p. 97.
136. UDF, Submission to Truth and Reconciliation Commission, May 1998; see also Mufson, *Fighting Years*, pp. 123–6.
137. C. Ndlovu discussed this in his address to the NGC in April (and again in 1986 in in a memorandum sent to foreign embassies). Interview with Moosa. Lekota, quoted in *RDM*, 9 April 1985.
138. *Star*, 9 April 1985.

CHAPTER 7
PEOPLE'S POWER

1. *SotN*, issue entitled 'In a State of Emergency' (Oct.–Nov. 1985).
2. Lodge, '"*Mayihlome!*"' and 'The African National Congress'; Barrell, 'Conscripts'.
3. *WM*, 6 Sept. 1985, cited in Lodge, 'Rebellion', p. 79; *WM*, 25 Oct. 1985.
4. Coleman and Webster, 'Repression and Detentions'. Morobe, quoted in *SN* (Dec. 1985). *SStar*, 8 Sept. 1985. Unfortunately, no national and very little regional UDF documentation has survived for the seven months between June 1985 and January 1986. This seems to be in part due to repression, which deterred leaders from keeping records, and in part because there were not many meetings to be recorded.
5. Sizani, quoted in *WM*, 25 Oct. 1985.
6. *SStar*, 8 Sept. 1985; *BD*, 1 Nov. 1985.
7. Quotation from Van Kessel, 'Beyond Our Wildest Dreams', p. 314. See also *Star*, 9 Jan. 1986, *SN*, 6, 3 (Dec. 1985) and Seekings, 'From "Quiescence" to "People's Power,"' pp. 26–30.
8. UDF, Sec. Rpt Feb. 1986; Muller, 'People's Education'; interview with Mogane.
9. Programme and Resolutions, Conference convened by SPCC, University of the Witwatersrand, 28–29 Dec. 1985.
10. UDF, Sec. Rpt Feb. 1986, p. 17.
11. UDF, 'The Tasks of the Democratic Movement …', *Isizwe*, 1, 1 (Nov. 1985), p. 16.
12. UDF, quoted in report from SAPA/BBC, 4 Jan. 1986.
13. Baskin, *Striking Back*, pp. 60–6.
14. UDF NWC May 1986, Sec. Rpt. My account of this meeting is based on interviews with Stofile, Y. Mahomed and Moosa.
15. Mufson, *Fighting Years*, pp. 248–9.
16. *ST*, 12 Jan. 1986.
17. Interview with Stofile.
18. UDF NEC *circa* Jan. 1986 (Moosa notebook #1).
19. UDF, Sec. Rpt Feb. 1986.
20. Baskin, *Striking Back*, p. 74.
21. Sisulu, 'People's Education for People's Power'.
22. See, for example, the introduction to the first issue of *Isizwe* (Nov. 1985).
23. ANC, 'Attack! Attack! Give the enemy no quarter', annual anniversary statement by the NEC of the ANC, 8 Jan. 1986, published in *Sechaba* (Mar. 1986), p. 11.
24. Minutes of meeting on 5 Feb. 1986, by Richard Mdakane (later secretary of the Alexandra Action Committee), quoted in Judgment, *State vs Mayekiso and 4 others*, Supreme Court, Witwatersrand Local Division case no. 115/89, pp. 29–30; Carter, 'Community and Conflict', pp. 120, 124, 137; Jochelson, 'Reform, Repression and Resistance', pp. 7–8; *WM*, 17 Jan. 1986; Barrell, 'Conscripts', Ch. 9.
25. Raymond Suttner, 'Popular Justice', seminar paper presented at the University of the Witwatersrand, *circa* May 1986; an earlier version of this paper was presented at a conference in Cape Town in mid-April.
26. UDF, 'Building People's Power', *Isizwe*, 1, 2 (March 1986), p. 2.
27. Ibid., pp. 8–9.
28. Sisulu, 'People's Education for People's Power', p. 98.
29. Ibid., p. 105.

30. UDF WCp Regional Civic Conference, 26–27 April 1986, 'Input: Programme of Action', p. 2.
31. Ibid.
32. *CP*, 27 April 1986. Not until 1987, however, was the Port Alfred experience reported in the 'progressive press'; *SotN* (April 1987), pp. 18–19.
33. *Isizwe*, 1, 2 (Mar. 1986). UDF NWC May 1986, handwritten notes (Moosa notebook #2).
34. Differences of interpretation persisted – even within the ANC itself. See Mashinini, 'Dual Power'; Mzala, 'Building People's Power'.
35. See notes in Moosa notebook #2.
36. Carter, 'Community and Conflict'.
37. Ibid., but see also Mayekiso, *Township Politics*. Carter relies primarily on evidence in *State vs Mayekiso and 4 others*; the accused had obvious reasons to downplay their political links. But, whilst disputing Carter's account, Mayekiso himself downplays the roles of the ANC and UDF in his own book, written after1994.
38. See the explanation of low attendance at a regional civic workshop: UDF, 'Report of National Planning Meeting of Civic Organisations', 14 May 1986.
39. UDF Tvl, 'Organising Meeting', handwritten notes in Moosa notebook #2.
40. Ibid.
41. UDF NWC May 1986, 'Organisational Guidelines', p. 14.
42. See handwritten notes in Moosa notebook #1 on meetings of the UDF NEC (mid-Jan. 1986?), Nat. Secretariat (probably early Feb.), Tvl REC meeting (probably Feb.), and undated notes (early March 1986). Also 'Report on Meeting held in p. E. on 01/02/1986', signed 'Comrade Noël' (Noël Williams of the Atlantis Residents Association); UDF, 'Report of National Planning Meeting of Civic Organisations, 1 March 1986', minutes of meeting, 6 pp.; document on the Community Education and Information Project, signed Barbara Creecey and dated 17 May 1990; and interviews with Williams, Xundu, P. Gordhan, Moosa, Creecey and Mafolo.
43. UDF, 'Report of National Planning Meeting of Civic Organisations', 14 May 1986; UDF NEC 9 May 1986, handwritten notes (Moosa notebook #2; *SN* (April–May 1986); interviews with Sidina, Williams, Rasool.
44. UDF WCp, Regional Civic Conference, April 1986, 'Input' papers; 'Minutes of civic workshop, 26/27 April 1986'; miscellaneous handwritten notes of Transvaal UDF meetings, including REC meetings (March–May 1986) (Moosa notebooks); interviews with Williams, Xundu and Mafolo.
45. This account is largely based on handwritten notes taken at the conference by (I think) Nazeegh Jaffer, supplemented with information from interviews with Mamdoo, Williams and Mafolo. The conference was held in Hanover Park, in Cape Town, under tight security: participants were not allowed to leave the venue during the course of the conference, and all documents were collected at the end.
46. UDF WCp, Regional Civic Conference, April 1986, 'Input: The Importance of Civic Organisation'. On different models of civic organisation, see *SotN* (April 1987) (Port Alfred); UDF WCp, 'Report on Visit to Rural Areas', undated (mid-April 1986) (Oudtshoorn); and Boraine, 'Mamelodi', p. 157. See also my interviews with Creecey, Nkwinti, Mafolo and Lephunya.
47. Interviews, Mafolo, Creecey, Nkwinti. The Committee included two representatives per region, including Nkwinti and an activist from De Aar (Eastern Cape), Mogane and Mafolo (Transvaal), Jabu Sithole and Pravin Gordhan (Natal), and others. Creecey was brought in, in an administrative capacity.
48. ANC, Radio Freedom from Addis Ababa, in BBC *Monitoring Report*, 15 April 1986.
49. Baskin, *Striking Back*, pp. 121–8. See also Adler, 'The Season of Stayaways'.
50. Indicator, *Political Conflict*, pp. 130–1.
51. ANC, Radio Freedom from Addis Ababa, in BBC *Monitoring Report*, 15 April 1986.
52. ANC, 'Attack! Attack!'.
53. UDF NWC May 1986, 'Influx control – the 1986 model', summary of paper presented at the NWC.
54. UDF NEC Jan. 1986, handwritten notes (Moosa notebook #1); UDF NEC 5 May 1986 and NWC May 1986, handwritten notes (Moosa notebook #2); UDF Memorandum, presented to selected diplomatic corps (15 April 1985).
55. Delius, *A Lion Amongst the Cattle*.
56. UDF NTvl Regional Conference 3 Feb. 1985, Report (by F. Mohlala) (*Baleka* Exhibit ABA.42).
57. Van Kessel, 'Beyond Our Wildest Dreams', p. 182.
58. Nchabaleng, quoted in Delius, *A Lion Amongst the Cattle*, p. 182.
59. Van Kessel, 'Beyond Our Wildest Dreams', p. 183.

60. Nchabaleng, quoted in Delius, *A Lion Amongst the Cattle*, p. 184.
61. T. Mokanyane and D. Monakedi, quoted in Van Kessel, 'Beyond Our Wildest Dreams', pp. 187, 207.
62. Van Kessel, 'Beyond Our Wildest Dreams', p. 229; *CP,* 13 April, *Sow* and *Star,* 14 April 1986.
63. UDF NEC Press Statement 16 April 1986.
64. 'Formation and History of NOTPECO', unsigned and undated document.
65. Delius, *A Lion Amongst the Cattle.*
66. SAYCO/Natal had set up a funding arrangement with Kagiso Trust which bypassed head office, and seemed to privilege Natal over other regions (interview with Dlamini).
67. Interviews with Tsenoli, Dlamini and Naidoo.
68. Interview with Mkhize.
69. Interview with Madlala.
70. This account is based on interviews with Wittenberg.
71. *Echo,* 22 May 1986.
72. Cole, *Crossroads,* p. 115.
73. Ibid., p. 139.
74. Moosa, interviewed in *WM,* 20 March 1986.
75. UDF NWC May 1986, Report, p. 14.
76. UDF, 'Organising meeting', 20 May 1986, handwritten notes (Moosa notebook #2). Moosa reported to the NEC in May that there were 14 organisers – presumably in the Transvaal alone.
77. This restructuring was first discussed in the Transvaal as early as late January, and was probably due to be finalised at the AGM scheduled for June. The AGM did not take place, due to the reimposition of a State of Emergency.
78. UDF NEC 9 May 1986, and a subsequent meeting between Moosa and Deacon [Mathe?], handwritten notes (Moosa notebook #2).
79. UDF NEC meeting 9 May 1986 and NWC May 1986, handwritten notes (in Moosa notebook #2).
80. Interview with Morgan.
81. UDF NWC May 1986, Sec. Rpt.
82. De Villiers, 'UDF: Front or Political Party?'; UDF NWC May 1986, notes.
83. UDF NWC May 1986, Sec. Rpt.
84. Graeme Bloch, 'The UDF', p. 27.
85. An indication of UDF thinking is a statement in a report in May: 'The ability of the UDF to determine the correct issues and use them to deepen the state crisis are above serious reproach' – UDF NWC May 1986, Sec. Rpt, p. 3.
86. UDF NWC May 1986, 'Organisational Guidelines'.
87. Ibid.
88. Waldmeir, *Anatomy of a Miracle*, pp. 90–4; Sparks, *Tomorrow is Another Country*, pp. 24–5.
89. On the EPG visit see Mufson, *Fighting Years*, pp. 253–5; Waldmeir, *Anatomy*, pp. 95–7; Sparks, *Tomorrow*, pp. 33–6.
90. UDF NEC Jan. 1986 and Nat. Secretariat *circa* March 1986, handwritten notes (Moosa notebooks #1 and 2); interview with Y. Mahomed.
91. Waldmeir, *Anatomy*, p. 97.
92. Meeting between UDF NEC and Release Mandela Campaign members, *circa* 12 May 1986, handwritten notes (Moosa notebook #2).
93. UDF NEC, letter to the EPG, included in UDF NWC 1986, Report, pp. 10–11.
94. *WM,* 5 June 1986. The UDF NWC Report also recorded: 'We are now in a much stronger position to choose allies and dictate the terms of the relationships' with foreign initiatives such as the EPG.
95. UDF, 'Unban the ANC!', included in the UDF NWC 1986 Report, pp. 7–9.
96. UDF NWC 1986, Sec. Rpt.
97. The UDF did issue a press statement later, on 27 May. Abrahams had been incorrectly identified as an informer, and killed at a UDF rally.

CHAPTER 8
A HOLDING OPERATION: SURVIVING THE STATE OF EMERGENCY

1. *Star,* 12 and 13 June, *CT,* 13 June 1986.
2. *WM,* 22 Aug. 1986; Webster, 'Repression and the State of Emergency'.
3. Lodge, 'Rebellion', p. 88; Mufson, *Fighting Years*, pp. 262–3; Baskin, *Striking Back*, Ch. 8; Green, 'Trade Unions and the State of Emergency'.

4. Baskin, *Striking Back*, pp. 134, 140.
5. Interview with Creecey.
6. Mufson, *Fighting Years*.
7. Ibid., pp. 265 and 271–2.
8. Webster, 'Repression and the State of Emergency'; SAIRR *Survey* 1986, pp. 830–8; *WM*, 10 Oct. 1986. The government later said that 49 meetings were banned under Emergency regulations between June 1986 and February 1988 (SAIRR *Survey* 1988/89, p. 545).
9. Armstrong, '"Hear No Evil,"' pp. 202–4; SAIRR *Survey* 1986, Vol. 2, pp. 838–9.
10. The words are from the sceptical reformist and Stellenbosch academic, Willie Breytenbach, quoted in Swilling, 'The Politics of Negotiation', p. 19. See also *Observer* (London), 20 June 1986.
11. *WM*, 24 June 1986. See, more generally, Andrew Boraine, 'Managing the Urban Crisis'; Cole, 'State Urban Policies'; Jochelson, 'Reform, Repression and Resistance'.
12. Interviews with Moosa and Momoniat.
13. Interview with Moosa.
14. Interview with Creecey.
15. UDF NEC undated (mid-July), handwritten notes (Moosa notebook #4).
16. UDF NEC undated (late July or early Aug.), handwritten notes (Moosa notebook #4).
17. UDF NEC undated (early Sept.), handwritten notes (Moosa notebook #4).
18. Interview with Creecey.
19. UDF NWC May 1987, Sec. Rpt, p. 13.
20. T. Makunyane, quoted in Van Kessel, 'Beyond Our Wildest Dreams', p. 244.
21. UDF NEC June, July, Sept. 1986, handwritten notes (Moosa notebooks #3 and #4).
22. UDF NEC July, Aug. 1986, handwritten notes (Moosa notebooks #4 and #5).
23. Baskin, *Striking Back*, p. 142. Baskin does not mention any consultation with the UDF, and implies that the decision was taken by the COSATU Central Executive Committee alone.
24. Handwritten notes, undated (Moosa notebook #4). The Western Cape UDF later 'strongly condemned' the meeting, believing that the 'support of the bourgeoisie will not help us' – UDF NEC Sept. 1986, handwritten notes (Moosa notebook #5). The Western Cape, here, was clearly out of line with the predominant ANC–UDF strategic position.
25. Morobe, quoted in *WM*, 22 Aug. 1986.
26. Interview with Moosa.
27. UDF NWC 1987, Sec. Rpt, p. 23.
28. UDF, 'Campaign for United National Action: Workshop report for discussion amongst all affiliates and regions', undated (document submitted in *Baleka*, in state's response to the defence's third bail application).
29. UDF, 'Uniting for National Action', *UDF Update*, 2, 3 (Nov. 1986) p. 3.
30. UDF NEC Aug. and Sept. 1986, handwritten notes; UDF NEC meeting with COSATU, 17 Aug. 1986, handwritten notes (Moosa notebooks #4 and #6). The campaign was sometimes referred to as the 'Campaign for National Unity', to which was sometimes added 'Against Apartheid and the Emergency'.
31. *WM*, 3 Oct. 1986.
32. UDF NWC 1987, Sec. Rpt, in NWC Report, p. 23; 'Uniting for National Action', *UDF Update* (Nov. 1986).
33. UDF, 'Christmas against the Emergency', *UDF Update*, 2, 3 (Nov. 1986), pp. 1–2; pamphlet issued by UDF and allies (document submitted in *Baleka* [Wits collection G2.1.15]); UDF NWC 1987, Sec. Rpt, p. 23; UDF NEC 29–30 Nov. 1986, handwritten minutes; Lodge, 'Rebellion', p. 99.
34. UDF, 'Comment', *UDF Update*, 2, 3 (Nov. 1986), p. 8.
35. UDF NWC 1987, Sec. Rpt, p. 27.
36. UDF NEC Sept. 1986, and UDF Publicity Secretariat Nov. 1986, handwritten notes (Moosa notebooks).
37. Armstrong, '"Hear No Evil,"' pp. 205–8; SAIRR *Survey* 1986, Vol. 2, pp. 839–42.
38. UDF NEC Sept. 1986, handwritten notes.
39. UDF NEC July 1986, handwritten notes (Moosa notebook #4).
40. This document was submitted in the *Baleka* trial (Wits collection G.2.3.1 pp. 866–82).
41. Barrell, 'Conscripts', Ch. 9.
42. Moosa, quoted in Waldmeir, *Anatomy*, pp. 82–3. Waldmeir implies that this meeting was held in 1987, but this description might be of a meeting held in January 1989. Moosa was detained from January to April 1987, and again from July 1987 until the end of 1988. It is known that he visited

London in January 1989. I have been given a similar description of a meeting where the idea of a defiance campaign was raised, which dates it at early 1989.

43. Chaskalson, Jochelson and Seekings, 'Rent Boycotts'. See also statements by E. Matthysen of the Lekoa Town Council, in *Baleka* (Wits collection G2.1.16, G2.3.5).

44. UDF NWC May 1987, Sec. Rpt, p. 22.

45. Botha's anger was evident in speeches in parliament – see, for example, *FM*, 13 Feb. 1987. See further, SAIRR *Survey* 1987/88, pp. 388–1 and 818–19.

46. Morobe, quoted in *CT*, 21 March 1987, as quoted in SAIRR *Survey* 1987/88, pp. 777–8.

47. UDF NWC 1987, Sec. Rpt, pp. 9, 24. See also '5–6 May Stayaway 1987', *SALB*, 12, 5 (July 1987).

48. UDF Bdr, 'A brief report of proceedings in the recently held UDF National Executive Council', dated 12 May 1987, para. 6. On the debate within COSATU, see Baskin, *Striking Back*, pp. 188–90.

49. UDF NWC 1987, Sec. Rpt, p. 24.

50. Ibid., p. 13.

51. See, for example, the UDF–IYY National Co-ordinating Committee's 'Brief Report to the Regions', signed D. Montsitsi, undated (Oct. or Nov. 1985).

52. Niddrie, 'New National Youth Congress Launched'; *NN*, 12 April 1987.

53. UDF NEC March 1986, minutes; UDF NWC 1986, Programme of Action, para. 2. For the history of FEDSAW, see Walker, *Women and Resistance*.

54. UDF NEC July 1986, handwritten notes (Moosa notebook #4); notes on miscellaneous meetings Aug.–Sept. 1986 (Moosa notebook #6); UDF NEC Nov. 1986, handwritten notes, p. 10; UDF NWC 1987, Sec. Rpt, p. 15.

55. Interview with Creecey.

56. Interviews with Creecey, Mamdoo and Mogane.

57. Baskin, *Striking Back*, pp. 118–20 (Baskin says little about developments after mid-1986); UDF NEC Nov. 1987, handwritten minutes.

58. UDF meeting with NECC, undated (July–Aug.?), handwritten notes (Moosa notebook #4); UDF NEC Sept. 1986, handwritten minutes. UDF NWC 1987, Sec. Rpt, pp. 15–18.

59. UDF OFS regional meeting, Welkom, 27 April 1986, report; UDF NWC and NEC May 1986, handwritten minutes; UDF NWC 1986, Sec. Rpt; *WM*, 31 July 1987; Van Kessel, 'Beyond Our Wildest Dreams', p. 244.

60. NOTPECO Draft Constitution; Van Kessel, 'Beyond Our Wildest Dreams', pp. 208–12.

61. UDF NWC 1987, Sec. Rpt. The quotations that follow are all from this report.

62. Morobe, in *WM*, 12 June 1987.

63. Ibid.

64. SAIRR *Survey* 1987/88, pp. 820–9.

65. Baskin, *Striking Back*, p. 216.

66. 'Build the Front', *Isizwe*, 2, 1 (Sept. 1987). This was later reproduced as a discussion paper and widely distributed.

67. *WM*, 11 and 18 Sept. 1987.

68. *WM*, 8 May 1987; UDF NEC 21 Nov. 1987, handwritten notes; Marx, *Lessons of Struggle*, pp. 139–42.

69. SAIRR *Survey* 1986, Vol. 2, p. 818; SAIRR *Survey* 1987/88, p. 777; Marx, *Lessons of Struggle*, p. 140; Van Kessel, 'Beyond Our Wildest Dreams', p. 57; interview with Cachalia.

70. Information from Kagiso Trust; Audited account for CEI, 1 Jul 1987–31 July 1988, by Douglas & Co., dated 29 June 1989, p. 3.

71. Cachalia, quoted by Van Kessel, 'Beyond Our Wildest Dreams', p. 57; inter72. NOTPECO documentation; Van Kessel, 'Beyond Our Wildest Dreams', p. 210.

73. Gilbey, *The Lady*, p. 144. The ANC Commission reported in 1989.

74. Interview with Madlala.

75. This section is from my interview with Africa.

76. Interview with Madlala.

77. *Baleka* Exhibit (Wits collection G3.8.1.14). The meeting was probably in January or early February 1987. Records of the meeting – transparencies used on an overhead projector – survived because an 'undisciplined' activist, who had failed to destroy the records, was caught by police. The police then produced copies of the records in court, alleging that the records constituted a insurrectionary plan. According to UDF secretary Martin Wittenberg, they were prepared during the workshop, as conditions in each area were described, and strategic objectives were identified.

78. Wittenberg et al., 'Crisis in Pietermaritzburg'; see also Kentridge, *An Unofficial War*, and COSATU–UDF Memorandum on Violence in the Pietermaritzburg Area (undated, but *circa* Nov. 1987).

79. Maritzburg Collective, 'Violence and the "Peace Process,"' p. 2.
80. Wittenberg et al., 'Crisis in Pietermaritzburg'.
81. Letters, Buthelezi to Gumede, 18 Aug. 1987, and Gumede to Buthelezi, 28 Aug. 1987. 'Notes on a meeting held at the Imperial Hotel at 16h00 on 24 November 1987 between the parties to the peace process', with 'joint press release' annexed; *WM*, 20 Nov., 27 Nov. 1987; Maritzburg Collective, 'Violence and the "Peace Process,"' pp. 6–7.
82. See document, 'Inkatha/UDF peace talks', signed Musa Zondi (Inkatha Youth Brigade), dated 9 Dec. 1987; 'press statement from the COSATU–UDF delegation to the meeting of 9 December 1987'. The articles, in *Inqaba wa Basebenzi* (Oct. 1987) were very critical of the UDF's participation in talks and agreements with Inkatha – and were almost as rude about Gumede as Buthelezi! See also Baskin, *Striking Back*, p. 334.
83. Buthelezi speech, quoted in Baskin, *Striking Back*, p. 334.
84. Aitchison, 'The Civil War in Natal'; Baskin, *Striking Back*, p. 34; affidavits in *Phineas Zondo and 19 others vs Inkatha, V.V. Mvelase and 5 others*, Supreme Court, Natal Provincial Division, interdict application, Feb. 1988.
85. COSATU–UDF Memorandum on Violence.
86. UDF quoted in BBC/SAPA report 4 Jan. 1986. Waldmeir, *Anatomy*, pp. 63–64.
87. UDF meeting with JODAC, undated, handwritten notes (Moosa notebook #1).
88. Ibid.; *Star*, 8 April; *WM*, 17 April 1986. There are indications that some kind of national workshop was held for UDF structures and affiliates in white areas in early 1986 (SAIRR *Survey* 1986, p. 178, citing *Star*, 27 Jan. 1986).
89. UDF NWC 1986, Programme of Action, para. 7.
90. UDF, Unban the ANC, press statement, 5 June 1986.
91. UDF NWC 1987, Conference Report, pp. 10, 22, 23, 34.
92. SAIRR *Survey* 1987/88, pp. 706–8 and 764–5; Matisson, 'Meeting the ANC', pp. 3–5.
93. UDF, 'UDF Call to Whites', undated discussion paper (between June and Oct. 1987), p. 2.
94. Ibid.
95. JODAC, 'Winning White Support', pp. 7–9.
96. UDF, 'UDF Discussion Paper', untitled and undated (but soon after Oct. 1987), pp. 7–9. See also 'Taking the Struggle into the Ruling Bloc', *Phambili* (April 1988).
97. JODAC, 'Winning White Support', p. 31; see also 'Taking the Struggle'.
98. UDF NWC 1987, Conference Report, p. 35.
99. *WM*, 19 Feb. 1988.
100. UDF NEC 13 Feb. 1988, report.
101. The alliance fell short of the permanent structured relationships envisaged in key documents – UDF NEC 21 Nov. 1987, handwritten notes, and UDF NEC 13 Feb. 1988, report.
102. UDF, 'New Year Message of the United Democratic Front – January 1988', signed Albertina Sisulu (police transcript of document, *Baleka* Exhibit [Wits collection G.4]); see also UDF NEC 13 Feb. 1988, report.
103. Waldmeir, *Anatomy*, p. 77.

CHAPTER 9
THE MASS DEMOCRATIC MOVEMENT

1. *WM*, 26 Feb. 1988.
2. *WM*, 10 and 24 June 1988, cited in SAIRR *Survey* 1988/89, p. 707.
3. SAIRR *Survey* 1988/89, p. 547.
4. *WM*, 11 March, 18 March, 25 March; *NN*, 17 March, 21 July, 28 July, 11 Aug., 25 Aug. 1988.
5. *NN*, 2 June 1989.
6. Von Holdt, 'COSATU Special Congress'.
7. Ibid.; Baskin, *Striking Back*, Ch. 17.
8. Baskin, *Striking Back*, p. 290.
9. *Phambili* (Oct. 1988), quoted in Baskin, *Striking Back*, pp. 289–90.
10. UDF, 'Anti-Apartheid Conference', undated and unsigned, but apparently drafted between mid-June and the beginning of August 1988.
11. Ibid. The term 'mass democratic movement' is reported to have been first used in the exiled SACP's *Umsebenzi*, in 1987. The term 'democratic movement' had been used inside the country since 1987.
12. J. Yembe, 'In Defence of the Anti-Apartheid Conference', pp. 16–17, 21.

13. UDF, 'Anti-Apartheid Conference'.
14. Mufamadi, quoted in Baskin, *Striking Back*, pp. 296–7; see also Yembe, 'In Defence of the Anti-Apartheid Conference'.
15. Nel and Grealy, 'The Consultative Business Movement'.
16. 'New Era interview with two members of the Anti-Apartheid Conference Planning Committee', undated (but *circa* Oct. 1988), transcript.
17. Moosa, quoted in *NN*, 2 June 1989.
18. Interview with Mafolo.
19. This is the summary provided as a prelude to the UDF's counter-argument, in 'Municipal Elections', *Phambili*, Oct. 1988, p. 18.
20. Ibid., pp. 19–20.
21. Ibid., pp. 20–4.
22. Moosa, quoted in *NN*, 2 June 1989. SAIRR *Survey* 1988/89, pp. 720–1.
23. SAIRR *Survey* 1988/89, pp. 512–15.
24. Ibid., p. 208. Swilling and Shubane, 'Negotiating Urban Transition'.
25. Moosa, quoted in *NN*, 2 June 1989 and in *South*, 8 June 1989.
26. Morobe, quoted in *ST*, 18 Aug. 1991.
27. Moosa, quoted in *South*, 8 June 1989.
28. *NN*, 15 Sept. 1988.
29. *NN*, 15 Sept., 22 Sept. and 20 Oct. 1988.
30. SAIRR *Survey* 1988/89, pp. 571–2; *NN*, 15 Dec. 1988. A senior police officer was reportedly sent to Port Elizabeth to liaise with the local attorney-general, and decide whether to press charges (*New African*, 10 April 1989).
31. *NN*, 26 Jan. 1989.
32. Ibid.
33. *NN*, 2 June 1989.
34. Ibid.; *Argus*, 18 Feb. 1989.
35. Waldmeir, *Anatomy*; Sparks, *Tomorrow*.
36. Waldmeir, *Anatomy*, pp. 51–6 and 108–40.
37. *NN*, 20 Oct. 1988; SAIRR *Survey* 1988/89, p. 721; Waldmeir, *Anatomy*, pp. 100–4.
38. This account is based on Gilbey, *The Lady*, pp. 150–225.
39. MDM, Statement on Winnie Mandela, 16 Feb. 1989.
40. Gilbey, *The Lady*, pp. 192–4; *CT*, 27 Feb. and 1 March 1989.
41. Buntman, 'Resistance on Robben Island', p. 125, refers to Mandela's and Mbeki's long-standing disputes over participation in apartheid institutions; they were, she writes, 'polar opposites in attitude and opinion'.
42. Boesak, quoted in Sparks, *Tomorrow*, p. 61.
43. Maharaj, quoted in ibid., p. 66. Mbeki was still confined to the Port Elizabeth magisterial district, so it is not clear whether he was allowed to visit Mandela.
44. Official text of COSATU, UDF and ANC meeting, Lusaka, 6 June 1989, as reported in *Argus*, 20 July 1989.
45. F. Chikane, quoted in Baskin, *Striking Back*, p. 347; Morobe, 'A Perspective on Negotiations', speech to TIC Consultative Conference, 30 July 1989.
46. Baskin, *Striking Back*, pp. 347–9.
47. *CT*, 5, 6 and 20 Jan., 17 June, 11 and 21 July; *Argus*, 6 Jan., 19 May; *NN*, 14 and 28 July; SAIRR *Survey* 1989/90, p. 758; the August MDM delegation comprised Mufamadi, Gomomo, Mayekiso and Mofokeng from COSATU; Morobe, Suttner, Carolus and Mluleki George from the UDF; Khanyile from the NECC; and SAYCO and other leaders (*NN*, 25 Aug. 1989).
48. Sparks, *Tomorrow*, p. 87; SAIRR *Survey* 1988/89. pp. 641–4.
49. Interview with Morgan.
50. Mlambo, 'Popular Front or United Front?', p. 27, quoting a view argued by JODAC in 'Winning White Support', p. 38.
51. Boraine, 'Building Broad Alliances', p. 35.
52. Mlambo, 'Popular Front'.
53. 'Report of meeting between COSATU and community-based organisations', undated and unsigned (*circa* April 1989).
54. Official text of COSATU, UDF and ANC meeting, Lusaka, 6 June 1989, as reported in *Argus*, 20 July 1989.

55. 'Resolutions at COSATU's 3rd National Congress', *SALB*, 14, 3 (Aug. 1989); Baskin, *Striking Back*, pp. 351–3; *NN*, 14 July 1989.

56. Naidoo interviewed in Carrim, 'COSATU Congress'.

57. Ibid.

58. The draft resolution was published in *Star*, 28 July 1989. It was made public amidst great controversy. Minister of Law and Order Adriaan Vlok alleged that an official COSATU document specified the use of violence – including the petrol-bombing of parliamentary candidates' homes – in the proposed campaign. Threatened with legal action, Vlok was forced to back down publicly, conceding that the document did not advocate or support any acts of violence nor did it refer to petrol bombs (*Star*, 26 July; *CP*, 6 Aug. 1989).

59. Morobe, quoted in *NW*, 4 Aug. 1989. See also *WM*, 11 Aug. 1989.

60. UDF–COSATU meeting, undated (Sept./Oct. 1989?), report.

61. Quoted in *NW*, 4 Aug. 1989.

62. Kentridge, *An Unofficial War*. See also SAIRR *Survey* 1989/90, pp. 251–2.

63. Quoted in Baskin, *Striking Back*, p. 339.

64. *NW*, 27 Feb. 1988, quoted in Baskin, *Striking Back*, p. 335.

65. Kentridge, *An Unofficial War*, Ch. 29.

66. Letter, Buthelezi to Gumede, 30 Nov. 1988 – in response to letter, Gumede to Buthelezi, 15 Nov. 1988, handwritten, asking for Buthelezi's help in lifting restrictions on the UDF. See also my interviews with Radebe and Mkhize.

67. John Jeffreys, 'Rocky Road to Peace'.

68. UDF–COSATU, 'An end to violence and peace in Natal', p. 2.

69. Mohlomi, interviewed in 'The Struggle for Peace in Natal', *SALB*, 14, 2 June 1989, pp. 70–1.

70. UDF Ntl–COSATU Joint REC meeting, 10 Sept. 1989; 'Report on the special joint regional congress of COSATU S. Natal, COSATU N. Natal and UDF Natal region held on 13 Feb. 1990 at Justice Hall, Durban'; interview with Africa.

71. *New African* 17 April, 15 and 22 May, 3 and 17 July 1989; letters, Buthelezi to Gumede, Morobe, Barayi, Naidoo, 10 May and 13 May 1989; interview with Africa; Baskin, *Striking Back*, p. 340; SAIRR *Survey* 1989/90, p. 253; and 'Report for consideration by a meeting of the presidents of the ANC, COSATU, UDF and Inkatha and their delegations', signed by (*inter alia*) Jay Naidoo, Murphy Morobe and Oscar Dhlomo.

72. *NN*, 11 Aug. 1989.

73. Ibid.

74. MDM, quoted in *Natal Post*, 2 Aug. 1989.

75. *NN*, 11 Aug. 1989.

76. Quoted *NN*, 11 Aug. 1989 and in *Natal Post*, 6 Sept. 1989.

77. *Argus*, 2 Aug.; *WM*, 4 Aug.; *Saturday Star*, 19 Aug. 1989.

78. *Argus*, 12 Aug.; *WM*, 8 Sept. 1989.

79. *Argus*, 28 Aug.; *CT*, 19 Aug., 5 Oct.; *South*, 21 Sept.; *NW*, 31 Aug. 1989; interview with Ebrahim.

80. *WM*, 1 Sept. 1989; Baskin, *Striking Back*, pp. 407–8.

81. *NN*, 11 Aug. 1989.

82. *FM*, 15 Sept. 1989.

83. SAIRR *Survey* 1989/90, pp. 225–7; *New African*, 18 and 25 Sept. 1989.

84. Quoted in *CT*, 6 Dec. 1989.

85. 'United Mass Action for People Power', in MDM, Discussion Papers for the Conference for a Democratic Future, undated (*circa* Nov. 1989).

86. The Committee included Moosa and Albertina Sisulu from the UDF. See Moosa, 'Circular to all regions re Anti-Apartheid Conference', dated 20 July 1989. See also Baskin, *Striking Back*, pp. 351–2.

87. Quoted in *New African*, 27 Nov. 1989.

88. SAIRR *Survey* 1989/90, p. 759.

89. Quoted in *New African*, 27 Nov. 1989.

90. Kagiso Trust, *From Opposing to Governing*, p. 12.

91. Ibid., p. 6.

92. Ibid., p. 27.

93. Ibid., p. 9.

94. Ibid.

95. Ibid., p. 25.

CHAPTER 10

THE DISSOLUTION OF THE UDF

1. De Klerk speech opening parliament, 2 Feb. 1990, quoted in Waldmeir, *Anatomy*, p. 142.
2. Interview with Mokaba, *Barometer* (March 1991), pp. 12–13.
3. See, for example, Suzman, *In No Uncertain Terms*, p. 243. The dissolution of the UDF is not even noted in accounts such as Sparks, *Tomorrow*, or Waldmeir, *Anatomy*.
4. UDF, 'A report of the UDF National General Secretary for the period August 1989 to December 1990' (Molefe), p. 2.
5. UDF NEC 13–14 Jan. 1990, minutes.
6. *Star*, 17 and 18 Jan. 1990; 'United Democratic Front press statement, 17 January 1990'.
7. Quoted in *Argus*, 23 Jan. 1990.
8. *Star*, 17 Jan. 1990
9. Waldmeir, *Anatomy*, pp. 142–4; Lodge, 'The African National Congress in the 1990s', pp. 49–50.
10. Ibid., pp. 142–3; Sparks, *Tomorrow*, pp. 99–107. De Klerk became acting president in August, and was formally inaugurated in September.
11. Sparks, *Tomorrow*, p. 108. See, in general, Waldmeir, *Anatomy*, pp. 132–6.
12. UDF NEC, 'Evaluation of F.W.'s speech', 8 Feb. 1990 (6 pp.). See also the UDF statement in *New African*, 5 Feb. 1990.
13. UDF NEC 8 Feb. 1990, minutes; UDF NEC 'Evaluation of F.W.'s speech'. The meeting was attended by Jay Naidoo and Sydney Mufamadi representing COSATU, and Eric Molobi representing the NECC.
14. Mandela, *Long Walk to Freedom*, pp. 547–8, 531.
15. Waldmeir, *Anatomy*, p. 157.
16. Mandela, *Long Walk to Freedom*.
17. Gilbey, *The Lady*, p. 224; Lodge, 'The African National Congress in the 1990s', pp. 53–4.
18. UDF NEC 29 April 1990, minutes, p. 2; *Argus*, 3 April 1990; *UM*, 5 April 1990; Mandela, *Long Walk to Freedom*, p. 569; Waldmeir, *Anatomy*, p. 158. The UDF NEC understood that Archie Gumede and Popo Molefe 'represented' the UDF in the ILC.
19. Lodge, 'Rebellion', p. 51. He suggests that another reason was the principled issue of 'community organisations' retaining their independence of any political party, but I am not sure whether this was pertinent at the time.
20. UDF NEC 24 March 1990, minutes, p. 1.
21. UDF National Workshop April 1990, report; *CT*, 7 and 9 April, *Argus*, 9 April 1990; UDF NEC 28 July 1990, minutes, p. 1. A Patriotic Front would include the UDF (UDF NEC 29 April 1990, minutes).
22. Carolus, quoted in *Argus*, 3 April 1990. B. Ngcuka refers to 'dual membership' in the same report.
23. UDF, Organisational Development Programme (April 1990).
24. UDF NEC July 1990, minutes, p. 3.
25. Ibid., p. 2.
26. UDF NEC 29 April 1990, minutes, p. 2; UDF NGC 1991, Sec. Rpt, p. 4.
27. UDF NGC 1991, Sec. Rpt, p. 3.
28. Letter, Gugile Nkwinti (UDF ECp secretary) to Azhar Cachalia (UDF national treasurer), 16 July 1990.
29. UDF NEC July 1990, minutes, p. 2.
30. Niddrie, 'SAYCO Eyes the ANC'; also *WIP*, 66 (May 1990), *WM*, 20 April; *NN*, 5 April 1990. Molefe, quoted in *Barometer* (March 1991), pp. 11–12.
31. Aubrey Mokoena, open letter 're: conspiratorial cabal document', addressed to Walter Sisulu (ANC), 5 June 1990.
32. UDF NEC 13–14 Jan. 1990, minutes; UDF head office meeting 23 Jan. 1990, minutes, p. 1. It is not clear that the statement was either drafted or released.
33. Mokoena, open letter.
34. *CP*, 20 Jan. 1991. In an NEC meeting Mokaba denied saying all this.
35. 'SAYCO Discussion Paper: Towards Restructuring the UDF: The Building of a Formidable Foundation for National Unity' (undated), pp. 1–2.
36. *Sow*, 23 Aug. 1990; *Star*, 19 Nov. 1990; *Vrye Weekblad*, 23 Nov. 1990. It was also discussed in detail in the right-wing *Freedom Bulletin* (No. 9 of 1990), published by the International Freedom Foundation.

37. 'Robben Islanders Take a Frank and Critical Look at the Political Situation in Natal – The Way Forward' (unsigned, undated), p. 5. See also *WM,* 23 Nov. 1990.

38. Moosa, untitled document on cabal allegations, apparently intended for release to press, undated (but *circa* Nov.–Dec. 1990). UDF NEC 16 Feb. 1991, minutes, p. 4. UDF NGC 1991, Sec. Rpt, p. 4. Morobe quoted in *ST,* 18 Aug. 1991.

39. *ST,* 21 April 1991. Hearings at the Truth and Reconciliation Commission, Cape Town, 5 May 1998.

40. UDF NGC 1991, Sec. Rpt, p. 4.

41. UDF, 'A report of the UDF national general secretary for the period August 1989 to December 1990', p. 3.

42. UDF, Memo from Molefe to UDF regional secretaries, 14 Sept. 1990.

43. UDF NGC 1991, Sec. Rpt, p. 4.

44. UDF, emergency national meeting, July–Aug. 1990, report.

45. UDF NGC 1991, Sec. Rpt, p. 13.

46. Ibid.

47. UDF, emergency national meeting, July–Aug. 1990, report.

48. UDF NEC Jan. 1990, draft programme of action.

49. UDF Bantustan Conference, 10–12 Aug. 1990, Report, p. 13.

50. SAIRR *Survey* 1990, pp. 501–2, citing *Star,* 14 March 1990.

51. UDF Bantustan Conference, Aug. 1990, Report.

52. Ibid., p. 13.

53. Ibid.

54. UDF NGC 1991, Sec. Rpt, pp. 3–5.

55. UDF NWC 22 Sept. 1990, minutes.

56. UDF NGC 1991, 'The Future of the UDF'.

57. Interview with Molefe in *Barometer* (March 1991), pp. 11–12.

58. *Star,* 5 March 1991.

59. *Argus,* 4 March 1991.

60. Interviews with Molefe, *Barometer* (March 1991), pp. 11–12, and Mashatile, *NN,* 30 Nov. 1990.

61. UDF NWC 22 Sept. 1990, minutes; UDF STvl, 'Report to head office', 7 Nov. 1990.

62. UDF NGC 1991, Sec. Rpt.

63. *CT,* 1 Oct., 4 Oct. 1990; *NN,* 19–25 Oct. 1990.

64. UDF NGC 1991, Sec. Rpt.

65. 'Discussion paper', untitled, for 'proposed launch of [Southern Transvaal] regional civic formation', unsigned (but by C. Coovadia) and undated (but *circa* May 1990). *South,* 2 Aug. 1990. See Gugile Nkwinti, 'The Eastern Cape Development and Funding Initiative (ECDAFI): Process and Strategic Objectives', dated 31 Jan. 1991.

66. UDF, 'Towards understanding the current political conditions: implications for the civic movement', discussion paper discussed at the UDF National Civics Workshop, Dec. 1990.

67. Lephunya, 'Civics', paper discussed at National Civics Workshop.

68. UDF, 'A report of the UDF National General-Secretary for the period August 1989 to December 1990' (Molefe), p. 9.

69. Ibid., p. 8.

70. UDF NGC 1991, 'Paper on National Civic Movement' by Lephunya, and 'Civics: Meeting the Challenges of South Africa', by Ebrahim.

71. Lephunya, 'Paper on National Civic Movement'; UDF NEC 17 Nov. 1990, minutes. p. 3. See also the circular to UDF regions, signed by P. Molefe and dated 21 Nov. 1990, re civics workshop to discuss collapse of BLAs. Lephunya and Coovadia had recommended the appointment of regional organisers in November (UDF National Civics Office, 'Presentation to NEC', 17 Nov. 1990), and Molefe endorsed this in December (Molefe, 'A report of the UDF National General-Secretary for the period August 1989 to December 1990', p. 9). In Feb. 1991 the UDF asked its regions to budget for full-time regional civic organisers (UDF NEC 16 Feb. 1991, minutes, p. 2).

72. National Civics Meeting, 16 Feb. 1991, minutes.

73. *Argus,* 4 March 1991.

74. 'Memorandum, re: visit to Sweden', by Azhar Cachalia, 18 April 1991; UDF NEC 18 May 1991, 'Report submitted by comrades Popo Molefe and Cas Coovadia'.

75. 'Report submitted by comrades Popo Molefe and Cas Coovadia', pp. 9–10.

76. Ibid.

77. Interview with Coovadia.

78. Molefe, 'Political Perspective', paper presented to the National [Civic] Consultative Conference, 10 May 1991.
79. For example, in Pretoria and Johannesburg (including Soweto) – Coovadia: interview.
80. *SStar,* 12 May 1991; *SStar,* 5 May 1991; *Saturday Star,* 11 May 1991.
81. *SStar,* 19 May 1991.
82. UDF NEC May 1991, Molefe–Coovadia report; interview with Coovadia.
83. UDF NEC 14 Aug. 1991, minutes. *ST,* 18 Aug. 1991; *Star,* 24 Aug. 1991.

CHAPTER 11
CONCLUSION: TURNING THE TIDE

1. Lodge, 'Rebellion', p. 30.
2. Barrell, 'Conscripts'.
3. O'Donnell and Schmitter, *Transitions from Authoritarian Rule,* p. 5; Huntington, *The Third Wave*; Bratton and Van de Walle, *Democratic Experiments in Africa.*
4. Huntington, *The Third Wave,* p. 316.
5. McKinley, *The ANC and the Liberation Struggle.*
6. Morobe, quoted in *ST,* 18 Aug. 1991.
7. There were exceptions, even in South Africa. The importance of material conditions in generating legitimate grievances and protest was recognised occasionally in government reports and in court; for example by Mr Justice Van der Walt in the Alexandra Treason Trial. See Abel, *Politics by Other Means.*
8. Lodge, 'Rebellion', p. 29.
9. Mufson, *Fighting Years,* p. 210.
10. Mandela, 'Discipline, loyalty our liberation', text of speech at FNB stadium, Johannesburg, 13 Feb. 1990, published in *Star,* 14 Feb. 1990.
11. See Chapter 5.
12. UDF, 'Towards a People's Democracy', p. 82.
13. Ibid., pp. 82–3.
14. One influential celebratory account was Black, *Triumph of the People.*
15. See Gilbert, *Sandinistas.*
16. Huntington, *The Third Wave,* p. 262.
17. Lodge, 'Rebellion', p. 132.
18. Mattes, *The Election Book*; Johnson and Schlemmer (eds.), *Launching Democracy*; Charney, 'Voices of a New Democracy'; Nattrass and Seekings, 'Growth, Democracy and Expectations'; Mzala, quoted by Bundy, 'Marxism in South Africa', pp. 62–3; Maree, 'The COSATU Participatory Democratic Tradition'.
19. Huntington, *The Third Wave,* p. 9. See also O'Donnell and Schmitter, *Transitions,* p. 7.
20. Bratton and Van de Walle, *Democratic Experiments,* pp. 117–19, 159ff.
21. The proliferation of death squads and conservative vigilantism in the mid-1980s prompted comparisons with Latin America, the Philippines and elsewhere (see Catholic Institute for International Relations, *States of Terror*; Van der Spuy, 'Literature on the Police'; Haysom, 'Vigilantes', p. 188).
22. Caceres, 'Violence, National Security and Democratisation', p. 110; Corradi, Fagen and Garreton (eds.), *Fear at the Edge.*
23. On torture in South Africa, see Abel, *Politics by Other Means,* Ch. 7.
24. Vigilantism in South Africa remained a largely localised phenomenon, with roots in local political divisions as well as in state sponsorship. The victims of vigilantism were local-level activists. Even in Natal, Ngwenya was the only senior UDF office-holder killed by vigilantes, although Dube was killed just prior to the formation of the UDF, Mkhize driven out of Hambanathi for fear of being killed, and – after the UDF was disbanded – Reggie Radebe was killed, all by vigilante squads linked to Inkatha.
25. Cawthra, *Policing South Africa,* pp. 26–7. Coetzee was head of the security police prior to his promotion as commissioner; his influence thus predated June 1983.
26. In 1983, 15 per cent of detainees were charged; in 1984 the proportion rose to 62 per cent – Coleman and Webster, 'Repression and Detention', p. 120.
27. The nature of the state's changing strategies with regard to repression has yet to be researched adequately. There are tantalising references in O'Meara's *Forty Lost Years,* as in Cawthra's *Policing South Africa.* Too many studies simply emphasise the brutality of policing, without carefully analysing how

policing changed over time or varied in different areas.

28. See Abel, *Politics by Other Means*, Ch. 8.

29. O'Meara, *Forty Lost Years*, pp. 398–9.

30. See Beresford, *Ten Men Dead*.

31. Clough, 'The Superpowers in Southern Africa'; Alden, *Apartheid's Last Stand*, pp. 188–9.

32. Ohlson, 'The Cuito Cuanavale Syndrome'; Seegers, *The Military*, pp. 252–61; Jaster, 'War and Diplomacy'; Clough, 'The Superpowers in Southern Africa'.

33. Skocpol, *States and Social Revolutions*; Therborn, 'The Rule of Capital'; Mann, *The Rise of Classes and Nation-states, 1760–1914*.

34. See Nathan, '"Marching to a Different Beat."'

35. The general effect of democratisation on any one country elsewhere in the world is indicated by Przeworski et al., 'What Makes Do Democracies Endure?', *Journal of Democracy*, 7, 2 (Jan. 1996).

36. Tetelman, *We Can*.

37. O'Meara, *Forty Lost Years*.

38. UDF, 'Towards a People's Democracy', pp. 84–5.

39. Michels, *Political Parties* (first published 1911). The seminal application of Michels's theory to social movement organisations was Zald and Garner, 'Social Movement Organisations'.

40. Note Winnie Mandela's accusations against ANC leaders who were seduced by the comforts of power.

41. Barrell, 'Conscripts'.

42. UDF National Treasury workshop, 27 Jan. 1990, minutes.

43. Lodge, 'State of Exile', p. 258, fn. 95; 'The African National Congress in the 1990s', p. 64; 'The African National Congress and its Allies', p. 23.

44. Filita, 'COSATU: Marching Forward', *SALB*, 21 (Feb. 1997).

45. I am not sure how often this claim was made explicitly. Swilling ('The United Democratic Front', p. 106) attributes to Callinicos the view that the UDF was 'dominated by an intellectual petty bourgeois leadership', but I cannot find any such explicit claim in the Callinicos article cited ('Working-class Politics in South Africa'). What Callinicos does do is cite, apparently approvingly, an assessment of the UDF in Cape Town (Silver and Sfarnas, 'The UDF', pp. 98–104) that refers to the leadership being dominated by 'intellectuals', and points out that the UDF's affiliates included some organisations such as churches and trade organisations that were 'petty bourgeois in membership and programme', and others (student and youth organisations) where 'the radical petty bourgeoisie probably [dominates] working-class elements' (pp.100–1, quoted in Callinicos, 'Working-class Politics', p. 63). The quoted passage does *not* claim that the (radical) petty bourgeoisie dominates the UDF as a whole. I fully concur with the limited empirical observations made by Silver and Sfarnas (and Callinicos) with regard to the UDF in Cape Town; indeed, Swilling himself seems to concur with regard to Cape Town.

46. McKinley, *The ANC and the Liberation Struggle*.

47. Swilling, 'The United Democratic Front', pp. 96–7.

48. Lodge, 'The United Democratic Front', pp. 207–8; 'Rebellion', p. 55.

49. Marx, *Lessons of Struggle*, p. 240.

50. Swilling, 'The United Democratic Front', p. 97.

51. Lodge, 'Rebellion', pp. 54–5.

52. Swilling, 'The United Democratic Front', p. 97. This is an ironic finding by Swilling, as it conforms with the assertions by Silver and Sfarnas as cited by Callinicos in the passage Swilling criticises. Lodge comes to a different assessment of the Western Cape regional leadership, as 'divided equally between workers and professionals' ('Rebellion', p. 55); it is not clear on what evidence Lodge does this.

53. Brewer, *After Soweto*, pp. 22–3, and 'Black Protest'.

54. Brewer, 'Internal Black Protest', p. 198.

55. Marx, *Lessons of Struggle*, p. 136.

56. Ibid., p. 240.

57. Barrell, 'Conscripts'.

58. The first category included Ngoyi, Fazzie, Tshwete, Nair and Ndlovu. Lekota was the most prominent member of the second category.

59. Albertina Sisulu; Cachalia; the older NIC stalwarts; J. Marks and W. Rhodes in Cape Town; Victoria Mxenge.

60. Interview with Molefe.

61. Mufson, *Fighting Years*, p. 206.

62. Ibid., p. 207.
63. Interview with Molefe. Stofile (interview) reports that other leaders were very angry with him when he was charged with harbouring MK cadres, as he had thereby allegedly compromised his above-ground political work.
64. *Sow,* 30 July 1990. The list also included three non-UDF trade union leaders.
65. This categorisation is borrowed from Ackerman and Krueger, *Strategic Nonviolent Conflict,* p. 6; I have relabelled their third category, which they term 'interventions'.
66. ANC NEC, Anniversary Statement (Jan. 1973).
67. UDF National Conference, Port Elizabeth (Dec. 1983), National Sec. Rpt (see Ch. 5).
68. *Phambili* (Oct. 1988), quoted by Baskin, *Striking Back,* pp. 289–90.
69. Interview with Molefe; UDF, Press Statement, 12 Dec. 1984.
70. Marx, *Lessons of Struggle.* See also McKinley, *The ANC and the Liberation Struggle.*
71. Cachalia, interviewed by Van Kessel in 1992 and quoted in Van Kessel, 'Beyond Our Wildest Dreams', p. 47.
72. Gail Gerhart has pointed out to me that the accepted wisdom within the ANC was that the 1952 Defiance Campaign had been a failure, and the tactic should not be repeated. It is possible, therefore, that the ANC discouraged consideration of civic disobedience in the mid-1980s.
73. Lodge, 'The United Democratic Front', pp. 206–7.
74. These were, in order of number of votes won, Lekota, Tshwete, Stofile, Molefe, A. Sisulu, Suttner, Manuel, Carolus, Omar, Moosa, Mufamadi, Nair, Cronin, Mokaba. These 14 – out of a total of 50 – were about half the number of people who had returned from exile. See NEC list in *Argus,* 8 July 1991.
75. *ST,* 17 May 1992.
76. *Argus,* 22 Feb. 1993
77. Eldridge and Seekings, 'Mandela's Lost Province'.
78. See, for example, Xayiya, 'Cape of Great Gloom'.
79. Quoted in *ST Cp Metro,* 11 April 1993. There were good reasons for this perception, given the numerical strength of the Africanist camp within the provincial ANC.
80. Ryland Fisher, 'Movement searches for soul of a people', *CT,* 2 Dec. 1996.
81. Ozinksy and Rasool, 'Developing a Strategic Perspective', pp. 43–4; Rasool, 'Now is the time for an ANC election plan', *CT,* 26 Sept. 1996.
82. See Eldridge and Seekings, 'Mandela's Lost Province'.
83. See, for example, Lodge, 'The African National Congress and its Allies', p. 40.
84. Glaser, 'Discourses of Democracy'. See also Glaser, 'South Africa and the Limits of Civil Society', and Steinberg, 'A Place for Civics'.
85. Glaser, 'South Africa and the Limits of Civil Society'.
86. Lekota, quoted in Mufson, *Fighting Years,* p. 3.
87. Goniwe, quoted in ibid.
88. Kane-Berman, *Political Violence.*

Bibliography

This bibliography does not include references in UDF and ANC publications, nor other documentation produced within the UDF or ANC.
The following abbreviations are used:

JSAS   *Journal of Southern African Studies*
SALB   *South African Labour Bulletin*
SAR   *South African Review* (Johannesburg: Ravan Press and South African Research Service)
WIP   *Work in Progress*
SAIRR   South African Institute of Race Relations
Survey   The annual *Survey of Race Relations in South Africa*, produced by the South African Institute of Race Relations, is referenced as *Survey*, followed by the year.

Abel, Richard, *Politics by Other Means: Law in the Struggle against Apartheid, 1980–1994* (New York and London: Routledge, 1995).

Ackerman, Peter and Christopher Krueger, *Strategic Nonviolent Conflict: The Dynamics of People Power in the Twentieth Century* (Westport: Praeger, 1994).

Adler, Glenn, 'The Season of Stayaways: Popular Protest in Port Elizabeth and Uitenhage in 1985–86', Unpublished paper (1992).

——'Shop Floors and Rugby Fields: The Social Basis of Auto Worker Solidarity in South Africa', *International Labor and Working Class History* (Spring 1997).

——and Eddie Webster, 'Challenging Transition Theory: The Labor Movement, Radical Reform and Transition to Democracy in South Africa', *Politics and Society* 23,1 (1995).

Aitchison, John, 'The Civil War in Natal', *SAR* 5 (1989).

Alden, Christopher, *Apartheid's Last Stand: The Rise and Fall of the South African Security State* (Basingstoke: Macmillan, 1996).

Armstrong, Amanda, '"Hear No Evil, See No Evil, Speak No Evil": Media Restrictions and the State of Emergency', *SAR* 4 (1987).

Barrell, Howard, 'The United Democratic Front and National Forum', *SAR* 2 (1984).

——*MK: The ANC's Armed Struggle* (Johannesburg: Penguin, 1990).

——'"The Turn to the Masses": The African National Congress' Strategic Review of 1978–79', *JSAS* 18,1 (March 1992).

——'Conscripts to Their Age: African National Congress Operational Strategy, 1976–1986', Unpublished D.Phil. thesis, Oxford University (1993).

Baskin, Jeremy, *Striking Back: A History of COSATU* (Johannesburg: Ravan, 1991).

Beinart, William and Colin Bundy, *Hidden Struggles in Rural South Africa* (London: James Currey, 1987).

Beresford, David, *Ten Men Dead: The Story of the 1981 Irish Hunger Strike* (New York: Atlantic Monthly Press, 1989).

Black, George, *Triumph of the People: The Sandinista Revolution in Nicaragua* (London: Zed, 1981).

Black Sash, 'Police Conduct in the Eastern Cape', Report (April 1985).

Bloch, Graeme, 'The UDF: "A National Political Initiative,"' *WIP* 41 (April 1986).

——'The United Democratic Front: Lessons of the 80s, Prospects for the 90s', Paper presented at SAIS conference, Johns Hopkins University, Baltimore (April 1992).

Boesak, Allan, *Black and Reformed: Apartheid, Liberation and the Calvinist Tradition* (Johannesburg: Skotaville and Maryknoll, NY: Orbis Books, 1984).

——*If This is Treason, I am Guilty* (Trenton, NJ: Africa World Press, 1987).

Bonner, Philip, 'African Urbanisation on the Rand between the 1930s and 1960s: Its Social Character and Political Consequences', *JSAS* 21,1 (March 1995).

Boraine, Andrew, 'Mamelodi: From Parks to People's Power', Unpublished Honours dissertation, University of Cape Town (Jan. 1987).

——'Managing the Urban Crisis, 1986–1989: The Role of the National Management System', *SAR* 5 (1989).

——'Building Broad Alliances: The Unity and the Contradictions', *SALB* 13,8 (Feb. 1989).

Bozzoli, Belinda, *Women of Phokeng: Consciousness, Life Strategy, and Migrancy in South Africa 1900–1983* (Johannesburg: Ravan, 1991).

Bradford, Helen, *A Taste of Freedom: The ICU in Rural South Africa, 1924–1930* (Johannesburg: Ravan, 1987).

Bratton, Michael and Nicholas van der Walle, *Democratic Experiments in Africa: Regime Transitions in Comparative Perspective* (Cambridge: Cambridge University Press, 1997).

Brewer, John, 'The Membership of Inkatha in KwaMashu', *African Affairs*, 84,334 (Jan. 1985).

——*After Soweto: An Unfinished Journey* (Oxford: Clarendon Press, 1986).

——'Black Protest in South Africa's Crisis: A Comment on Legassick', *African Affairs* 85,339 (April 1986).

——'Internal Black Protest', in John Brewer (ed.), *Can South Africa Survive? Five Minutes to Midnight* (Basingstoke: Macmillan, 1989).

Bundy, Colin, 'Street Sociology and Pavement Politics: Some Aspects of Student/Youth Consciousness during the 1985 Schools Crisis in Greater Cape Town', *JSAS* 13,3 (April 1987).

——'Around Which Corner? Revolutionary Theory and Contemporary South Africa', *Transformation* 8 (1989).

——'Marxism in South Africa: Context, Themes and Challenges', *Transformation* 16 (1991).

Buntman, Fran, 'Resistance on Robben Island, 1963–1976', in Harriet Deacon (ed.), *A History of Robben Island, 1488–1990* (Cape Town: David Philip and Mayibuye Centre, 1996).

Byerley, Mark, 'The Empangeni/Richard's Bay Bus Boycott', Honours dissertation, University of Natal, Durban (1985).

Caceres, Jorge, 'Violence, National Security and Democratisation in Central America', in Catholic Institute for International Relations (CIIR), *States of Terror: Death Squads or Development?* (London: CIIR, 1989).

Callinicos, Alex, 'Working-Class Politics in South Africa', in Callinicos, *South Africa between Reform and Revolution* (London: Bookmarks, 1988); previously published as 'Marxism and Revolution in South Africa', *International Socialism* 31 (1986).

Carrim, Yunus, 'Trade Unionism in Natal: Shopfloor Relations between Indian and African Workers', *SALB* 11,4 (Feb.–March 1986).

——'COSATU Congress: Interview with Jay Naidoo', *SALB* 14,3 (Aug. 1989).

Carter, Charles, 'Comrades and Community: Politics and the Construction of Hegemony in Alexandra Township, South Africa, 1984–1987', Unpublished D.Phil. thesis, Oxford University (1991).

——'"We are the Progressives": Alexandra Youth Congress Activists and the Freedom Charter, 1983–85', *JSAS* 17,2 (June 1991).

——'Community and Conflict: The Alexandra Rebellion of 1986', *JSAS* 18,1 (March 1992).

Carter, Gwendolen, 'African Concepts of Nationalism in South Africa', in Heribert Adam (ed.), *South Africa: Sociological Perspectives* (London: Oxford University Press, 1971).

Catholic Institute for International Relations (CIIR), *States of Terror: Death Squads or Development?* (London: CIIR, 1989).

Cawthra, Gavin, *Policing South Africa: The South African Police and the Transition from Apartheid* (Cape Town: David Philip and London: Zed, 1993).

Challenor, M., '"Business Built on Stones": A Case-Study of Responses to Service Charge Increases in Port Natal Administration Board Townships', Unpublished B.Soc.Sci. Honours dissertation, University of Natal, Durban (1984).

Charney, Craig, 'Minority Group Politics', *WIP* 75 (1991).

——'Voices of a New Democracy: African Expectations in the New South Africa', *Research Report* No. 38 (Johannesburg: Centre for Policy Studies, 1995).

Chaskalson, Matthew, 'Rural Resistance in the 1940s and 1950s', *Africa Perspective*, n.s. 1,5/6 (Dec. 1987).

——Karen Jochelson and Jeremy Seekings, 'Rent Boycotts and the Urban Political Economy', *SAR* 4 (1987).

Clough, Michael, 'The Superpowers in Southern Africa: From Confrontation to Cooperation', in Robert Jaster, Moeletsi Mbeki, Morley Nkosi and Michael Clough (eds.), *Changing Fortunes: War, Diplomacy and Economics in Southern Africa* (New York: Ford Foundation, 1992).

Cobbett, William and Robin Cohen (eds.), *Popular Struggles in South Africa* (London: James Currey, 1988).

Cole, Josette, *Crossroads: The Politics of Reform and Repression* (Johannesburg: Ravan, 1987)

——'State Urban Policies and Urban Struggles in the Post-1986 Period', Paper presented at the Contemporary South African Research Seminar, University of Stellenbosch (Oct. 1989).

Coleman, Max and David Webster, 'Repression and Detentions in South Africa', *SAR* 3 (1986).

Collinge, Jo-Anne, 'The United Democratic Front', *SAR* 3 (1986).

Corradi, Juan, Patricia Weiss Fagen and Manuel Antonio Garreton (eds.), *Fear at the Edge: State Terror and Resistance in Latin America* (Berkeley: University of California Press, 1992).

Crankshaw, Owen, 'Changes in the Racial Division of Labour during the Apartheid Era', *JSAS* 22,4 (Dec. 1996).

——*Race, Class and the Changing Division of Labour under Apartheid* (London: Routledge, 1997).

Delius, Peter, 'Migrant Organisation, the Communist Party, the ANC and the Sekhukhuneland Revolt, 1940–1958', in Philip Bonner, Peter Delius and Deborah Posel (eds.), *Apartheid's Genesis, 1935–1962* (Johannesburg: Ravan and Witwatersrand University Press, 1993).

——*A Lion amongst the Cattle: Reconstruction and Resistance in the Northern Transvaal* (Johannesburg: Ravan, 1996).

Desai, Ashwin, *Arise Ye Coolies: Apartheid and the Indian, 1960–1995* (Johannesburg: Input Africa Publishing, 1996).

De Villiers, Richard, 'UDF under Attack', *WIP* 39 (Oct. 1985).

——'UDF: Front or Political Party?', *WIP* 40 (Jan. 1986).

Dollie, Na-iem, 'The National Forum', *SAR* 3 (1986).

Edgar, Robert, *Because They Chose the Path of God: The Story of the Bulhoek Massacre* (Johannesburg: Ravan, 1988).

Eldridge, Matt and Jeremy Seekings, 'Mandela's Lost Province: The African National Congress and the Western Cape Electorate in the 1994 South African Elections', *JSAS* 22,4 (Dec. 1996).

Eyerman, Ron and Andrew Jamison, *Social Movements: A Cognitive Approach* (Cambridge: Polity, 1991).

Feit, Edward, *Urban Revolt in South Africa, 1960–1964* (Chicago: Northwestern University Press, 1971).

Filita, Templeton, 'COSATU: Marching Forward', *SALB* 21,1 (Feb. 1997).

Forsyth, Paul, *Pietermaritzburg Conflict Chronology: Political Developments in Pietermaritzburg, 1980–1986* (University of Natal, Pietermaritzburg: Project on Contemporary Political Conflict in Natal, 1991).

——'The Past in the Service of the Present: The Political Uses of History by Chief A.N.M.G. Buthelezi, 1951–91', *South African Historical Journal 26* (May 1992).

Frederickse, Julie, *The Unbreakable Thread: Non-Racialism in South Africa* (London: Zed, 1990).

Friedman, Steven, *Building Tomorrow Today: African Workers in Trade Unions, 1970–1984* (Johannesburg: Ravan, 1987).

Gamson, William, 'The Social Psychology of Collective Action', in Aldon Morris and Carol McClurg Mueller (eds.), *Frontiers in Social Movement Theory* (New Haven: Yale University Press, 1992).

Gerhart, Gail M., *Black Power in South Africa: The Evolution of an Ideology* (Berkeley: University of California Press, 1978).

——and Thomas Karis (eds.), *From Protest to Challenge: A Documentary History of African Politics in South Africa* (Stanford: Hoover Institution Press), Vols. 6 and 7 (forthcoming).

Gilbert, David, *Sandinistas: The Party and the Revolution* (New York: Basil Blackwell, 1988).

Gilbey, Emma, *The Lady: The Life and Times of Winnie Mandela* (London: Vintage, 1994).

Ginwala, Frene, 'Indian South Africans', *Group Report* No. 34 (London: Minority Rights Group, 2nd ed., 1985).

Glaser, Clive, '"When Are They Going to Fight?" Tsotsis, Youth Politics and the PAC', in Philip Bonner, Peter Delius and Deborah Posel (eds.), *Apartheid's Genesis, 1935–1962* (Johannesburg: Ravan and Witwatersrand University Press, 1993).

——'Youth Culture and Politics in Soweto, 1958–1976', Unpublished Ph.D. thesis, Cambridge University (1994).

——'"We Must Infiltrate the Tsotsis": School Politics and Youth Gangs in Soweto, 1968–1976', *JSAS* 24,2 (June 1998).

Glaser, Daryl, 'Discourses of Democracy in the South African Left: A Critical Commentary', in Robin Cohen and Harry Goulbourne (eds.), *Democracy and Socialism in Africa* (Boulder: Westview, 1991).

——'South Africa and the Limits of Civil Society', *JSAS* 23,1 (March 1997).

Goldin, Ian, *Making Race: The Politics and Economics of Coloured Identity in South Africa* (Cape Town: Maskew Miller Longman, 1987).

Green, Pippa, 'Trade Unions and the State of Emergency', *SALB* 11,7 (Aug. 1986).

Gwala, Zilondile, 'Rebellion in the Last Outpost: The Natal Riots', *Indicator SA: Political Monitor* 3,2 (Spring 1985).

Hall, Martin, 'Resistance and Rebellion in Greater Cape Town, 1985', Paper presented at the conference on The Western Cape: Roots and Realities, University of Cape Town (July 1986).

Haysom, Nicholas, 'Vigilantes and the Militarisation of South Africa', in Jacklyn Cock and Laurie Nathan (eds.), *War and Society: The Militarisation of South Africa* (Cape Town: David Philip, 1989).

Helliker, Kirk, André Roux and Roland White, '"Asithengi": Recent Consumer Boycotts', *SAR* 4 (1987).

Hill, Robert A. and Gregory A. Pirio, '"Africa for the Africans": The Garvey Movement in South Africa', in Shula Marks and Stanley Trapido (eds.), *The Politics of Race, Class and Nationalism in Twentieth Century South Africa* (London: Longman, 1987)

Hirson, Baruch, *Year of Fire, Year of Ash: The Soweto Revolt: Roots of a Revolution?* (London: Zed, 1979).

Hughes, Heather, 'Violence in Inanda, August 1985', *JSAS* 13,3 (April 1987).

Hunt, Lynn, *Politics, Culture and Class in the French Revolution* (Berkeley: University of California Press, 1984).

Huntington, Samuel P., *The Third Wave: Democratization in the Late Twentieth Century* (Norman: University of Oklahoma Press, 1991).

Indicator, *Political Conflict in South Africa: Data Trends, 1984–1988* (Durban: Indicator, 1988).

——*Political Violence in South Africa* (Durban: Indicator, 1989).

Jaster, Robert, 'War and Diplomacy', in Robert Jaster, Moeletsi Mbeki, Morley Nkosi and Michael Clough (eds.), *Changing Fortunes: War, Diplomacy and Economics in Southern Africa* (New York: Ford Foundation, 1992).

Jeffreys, John, 'Rocky Road to Peace in Natal', *SALB* 14,5 (Nov. 1989).

Jochelson, Karen, 'Reform, Repression and Resistance in South Africa: A Case-Study of Alexandra Township', *JSAS* 16,1 (March 1990).

Joffe, Avril, 'SAAWU Conference Briefing', *SALB* 9,6 (May 1984).

Johannesburg Democratic Action Committee (JODAC), 'Winning White Support for Democracy', *WIP* 53 (April/May 1988).

Johnson, R.W. and Lawrence Schlemmer (eds.), *Launching Democracy in South Africa: The First Open Elections, April 1994* (New Haven: Yale University Press, 1996).

Jordi, Richard, 'Towards People's Education: The Boycott Experience in Cape Town's Department of Education and Culture High Schools from July 1985 to February 1986', Unpublished Honours dissertation, University of Cape Town (Feb. 1987).

Jung, Courtney, 'Political Identities in Transition: South Africans Then and Now', Unpublished Ph.D. thesis, Yale University (1998).

Kagiso Trust, *From Opposing to Governing: How Ready is the Opposition?* Conference report (Johannesburg: Kagiso Trust, 1990).

Kane-Berman, John, *Political Violence in South Africa* (Johannesburg: SAIRR, 1993).

Kentridge, Matthew, *An Unofficial War: Inside the Conflict in Pietermaritzburg* (Cape Town: David Philip, 1990).

Klandermans, Bert, 'The Social Construction of Protest and Multiorganisational Fields', in Aldon Morris and Carol McClurg Mueller (eds.), *Frontiers in Social Movement Theory* (New Haven: Yale University Press, 1992).

Kuper, Leo, 'African Nationalism in South Africa, 1910–1964', in Monica Wilson and Leonard Thompson (eds.), *The Oxford History of South Africa*, Vol. 2 (Oxford: Clarendon Press, 1971).

Labour Monitoring Group, 'The November Stayaway', *SALB* 10,6 (May 1985).

Lewis, Gavin, *Between the Wire and the Wall: A History of South African Coloured Politics* (Cape Town: David Philip, 1987).

Lodge, Tom, *Black Politics in South Africa since 1945* (London: Longman, 1983).

—— '"*Mayihlome!* Let Us Go to War": From Nkomati to Kabwe, The African National Congress, January 1984–June 1985', *SAR* 3 (1986).

—— 'The African National Congress after the Kabwe Conference', *SAR* 4 (1987).

—— 'Political Mobilisation during the 1950s: An East London Case Study', in Shula Marks and Stanley Trapido (eds.), *The Politics of Race, Class and Nationalism in Twentieth Century South Africa* (London: Longman, 1987).

—— 'State of Exile: The African National Congress of South Africa, 1976–86', in Philip Frankel, Noam Pines and Mark Swilling (eds.), *State, Resistance and Change in South Africa* (London: Croom Helm and Johannesburg: Southern Books, 1988).

—— 'The United Democratic Front: Leadership and Ideology', in John Brewer (ed.), *Can South Africa Survive? Five Minutes to Midnight* (Basingstoke: Macmillan, 1989).

—— 'Rebellion: The Turning of the Tide', in Lodge, Bill Nasson et al., *All, Here, and Now: Black Politics in South Africa in the 1980s* (Cape Town: David Philip, 1991).

—— 'The African National Congress in the 1990s', *SAR* 6 (1992).

—— 'The African National Congress and its Allies', in Andrew Reynolds (ed.), *Election '94 South Africa: The Campaigns, Results and Future Prospects* (Cape Town: David Philip, 1994).

Mandela, Nelson, *Long Walk to Freedom: The Autobiography of Nelson Mandela* (Randburg: Macdonald Purnell, 1994).

Mann, Michael, *Sources of Social Power*, Vol. 2: *The Rise of Classes and Nation-States, 1790–1914* (Cambridge: Cambridge University Press, 1993).

Maré, Gerhard and Georgina Hamilton, *An Appetite for Power: Buthelezi's Inkatha and South Africa* (Bloomington: Indiana University Press and Johannesburg: Ravan, 1987).

Maree, Johann, 'SAAWU in the East London Area, 1979–81', *SALB* 7,4/5 (Feb. 1982).

—— 'The COSATU Participatory Democratic Tradition and South Africa's New Parliament: Are They Reconcilable?', *African Affairs* 97 (1998).

Maritzburg Collective, 'Violence and the "Peace Process" in Pietermaritzburg', *SALB* 13,4/5 (June/July 1988).

Marks, Shula, 'John Dube and the Ambiguities of Nationalism', in *The Ambiguities of Dependence in South Africa: Class, Nationalism and the State in Twentieth Century South Africa* (Johannesburg: Ravan, 1986).

—— and Stanley Trapido (eds.), *The Politics of Race, Class and Nationalism in Twentieth Century South Africa* (London: Longman, 1987).

Marx, Anthony W., *Lessons of Struggle: South African Internal Opposition, 1960–1990* (New York: Oxford University Press, 1992).

Mashinini, Alex, 'Dual Power and the Creation of People's Committees', *Sechaba* (April 1986).

Matisson, John, 'Meeting the ANC in West Africa', *WIP* 49 (Sept. 1987).

Mattes, Robert, *The Election Book: Judgement and Choice in South Africa* (Cape Town: Idasa, 1995).

Mayekiso, Mzwanele, *Township Politics: Civic Struggles for a New South Africa* (New York: Monthly Review Press, 1996).

McCarthy, Jeff, 'Black Local Government Issues in Natal', Unpublished paper (1986).

—— and Mark Swilling, 'Transport and Political Resistance', *SAR* 2 (1984).

McKinley, Dale T., *The ANC and the Liberation Struggle: A Critical Political Biography* (London: Pluto, 1997).

Meer, Fatima (ed.), *South Africa: Treason Trial 1985* (Durban: Institute for Black Research, 1989).

—— (ed.), *Resistance in the Townships* (Durban: Madiba Publications, 1989).

Michels, Robert, *Political Parties: A Sociological Study of the Oligarchical Tendencies of Modern Democracy* (first published 1911; New York: Collier, 1962).

Mlambo, Solomon, 'Popular Front or United Front?', *SALB* 13,8 (Feb. 1989).

Mokoape, Keith, Thenjiwe Mthintso and Welile Nhlapo, 'Towards the Armed Struggle', in N. Barney Pityana, Mamphela Ramphele, Malusi Mpumlwana and Lindy Wilson (eds.), *Bounds of Possibility: The Legacy of Steve Biko and Black Consciousness* (Cape Town: David Philip, 1991).

Molefe, Popo, 'Two Documents, a Single Vision', in Raymond Suttner and Jeremy Cronin (eds.), *Thirty Years of the Freedom Charter* (Johannesburg: Ravan, 1986).

Moodley, Kogila, 'South Africa's Indians: The Wavering Minority', in Leonard Thompson and Jeffrey Butler (eds.), *Change in Contemporary South Africa* (Berkeley: University of California Press, 1975).

—— 'Structural Inequality and Minority Anxiety: Responses of Middle Groups in South Africa', in Robert Price and Carl Rosberg (eds.), *The Apartheid Regime: Political Power and Racial Domination* (Berkeley: University of California Press, 1980).

Morris, Mike, 'Lessons from Mayday: UWUSA, Inkatha and COSATU', *WIP* 43 (August 1986).

Moss, Rose, *Shouting at the Crocodile: Popo Molefe, Patrick Lekota and the Freeing of South Africa* (Boston: Beacon Press, 1990).

Mufson, Steven, *Fighting Years: Black Resistance and the Struggle for a New South Africa* (Boston: Beacon Press, 1990).

Muller, Johan, 'People's Education and the National Education Crisis Committee', *SAR* 4 (1987).

Murray, Martin, *South Africa: Time of Agony, Time of Destiny: The Upsurge of Popular Protest* (London: Verso, 1987).

Mzala, *Gatsha Buthelezi: Chief with a Double Agenda* (London: Zed, 1988).

——'Building People's Power', *Sechaba* (Sept. 1986).

Naidoo, Kumi, 'The Politics of Youth Resistance in the 1980s: The Dilemmas of a Differentiated Durban', *JSAS* 18,1 (March 1992).

Nathan, Laurie, '"Marching to a Different Beat": The History of the End Conscription Campaign', in Jacklyn Cock and Laurie Nathan (eds.), *War and Society: The Militarisation of South Africa* (Cape Town: David Philip, 1989).

Nattrass, Jill, 'The Impact of the Riekert Commission's Recommendations on the "Black States,"' *SALB* 5,4 (Nov. 1979).

Nattrass, Nicoli and Jeremy Seekings, 'Growth, Democracy and Expectations in South Africa', in Iraj Abedian and Michael Biggs (eds.), *Economic Globalization and Fiscal Policy* (Cape Town: Oxford University Press, 1998).

Nekhwevha, Fhulufhuwani, 'The 1985 Schools Crisis in the Western Cape', Unpublished M.A. dissertation, University of Cape Town (Dec. 1991).

Nel, Christo and Rosemary Grealy, 'The Consultative Business Movement', *Indicator SA* 6,1/2 (Summer/Autumn 1989).

Niddrie, David, 'New National Youth Congress Launched', *WIP* 47 (April 1987).

——'SAYCO Eyes of the ANC', *WIP* 65 (April 1990).

Ntsebeza, Lungisile, 'Youth in Urban African Townships, 1945–1992: A Case Study of the East London Townships', Unpublished M.A. dissertation, University of Natal, Durban (Nov. 1993).

NUSAS, *Beyond Reform: The Challenge of Reform* (Cape Town: NUSAS, 1983).

Obery, Ingrid, Karen Jochelson and Yunus Carrim, 'Consumer Boycotts', *WIP* 39 (Oct. 1985).

O'Donnell, Guillermo and Philippe Schmitter, *Transitions from Authoritarian Rule*, Vol. 5, *Tentative Conclusions about Uncertain Democracies* (Baltimore: Johns Hopkins University Press, 1986).

Ohlson, Thomas, 'The Cuito Cuanavale Syndrome: Revealing SADF Vulnerabilities', *SAR* 5 (1989).

O'Meara, Dan, *Forty Lost Years: The Apartheid State and the Politics of Afrikaner Nationalism* (Johannesburg: Ravan, 1996).

Ozinsky, Max and Ebrahim Rasool, 'Developing a Strategic Perspective for the Coloured Areas in the Western Cape', *African Communist* (2nd quarter 1993).

Pillay, Devan, 'Community Organisations and Unions in Conflict', *WIP* 37 (June 1985).

——'Trade Unions and Alliance Politics in Cape Town, 1979–1985', Unpublished D.Phil. thesis, University of Essex (1989).

Price, Robert, *The Apartheid State in Crisis* (New York: Oxford University Press, 1991).

Przeworski, Adam, M. Alvarez, J. Cheibub and F. Limongi, 'What Makes Democracy Endure?', *Journal of Democracy* 7,2 (Jan. 1996).

Reintjes, Claudia, 'Rents and Urban Political Geography: The Case of Lamontville', Unpublished M.Soc.Sci. dissertation, University of Natal, Durban (1986).

Riekert Commission, *Report of the Commission of Inquiry into Legislation Affecting the Utilisation of Manpower* (Pretoria: PR32/1979).

Sapire, Hilary, 'African Political Organisations in Brakpan in the 1950s', in Shula Marks and Stanley Trapido (eds.), *The Politics of Race, Class and Nationalism in Twentieth Century South Africa* (London: Longman, 1987).

Seegers, Annette, *The Military in the Making of Modern South Africa* (London: Tauris, 1996).

Seekings, Jeremy, 'Quiescence and the Transition to Confrontation: South African Townships, 1978–1984', Unpublished D.Phil. thesis, Oxford University (1990).

——'Political Mobilisation in Tumahole, 1984–1985', *Africa Perspective*, n.s. 1, 7&8 (Oct. 1989).

——'Identity, Authority and the Dynamics of Violent Conflict: Duduza Township, 1985', Paper presented at the conference on Political Violence in Southern Africa, Oxford University (June 1991).

——'Township Resistance in the 1980s', in Mark Swilling, Richard Humphries and Khehla Shubane (eds.), *Apartheid City in Transition* (Cape Town: Oxford University Press, 1991).

——'Civic Organisations in South Africa's Townships', *SAR* 6 (1992).

—— 'From "Quiescence" to "People's Power": Township Politics in Kagiso, 1985–1986', *Social Dynamics* 18,1 (June 1992).

——'The Development of Strategic Thought in South Africa's Civic Movements, 1977–1990', in Glenn Adler and Jonny Steinberg (eds.), *From Comrades to Citizens: The South African Civics Movement and the Transition to Democracy* (New York: St. Martin's Press and London: Macmillan, forthcoming).

——*Heroes or Villains? Youth Politics in the 1990s* (Johannesburg: Ravan, 1993).

——'The United Democratic Front and the Media, 1983–1991', in Les Switzer and Mohamed Adhikari (eds.), *South Africa's Resistance Press* (forthcoming).

Seery, Brendan, 'Security Council Resolution 435 and the Namibian Independence Process', *SAR* 5 (1989).

Sibeko, Archie, *Freedom in Our Lifetime* (Durban: Indicator, 1996).

Silver, Isabella and Alexia Sfarnas, 'The UDF: A "Workerist" Response', *SALB* 8,8/9 (Sept./Oct. 1983).

Simkins, Charles, *Four Essays on the Past, Present and Possible Future Distribution of the African Population of South Africa* (Cape Town: University of Cape Town, South African Labour and Development Research Unit, 1983).

Sisulu, Zwelakhe, 'People's Education for People's Power', Keynote address to the conference of the National Education Crisis Committee, Durban, 29 March 1986, published in *Transformation* 1 (1986).

Sitas, Ari, 'Durban, August 1985: "Where Wealth and Power and Blood Reign Worshipped Gods,"' *SALB* 11,4 (Feb./March 1986).

——'Class, Nation and Ethnicity in Natal's Black Working-Class', Paper presented at the Institute of Commonwealth Studies, University of London (1988).

Skocpol, Theda, *States and Social Revolutions* (Cambridge: Cambridge University Press, 1979).

Sparks, Allister, *Tomorrow is Another Country: The Inside Story of South Africa's Negotiated Revolution* (Sandton: Struik, 1994).

Steinberg, Jonny, 'A Place for Civics in a Liberal Democratic Polity? The Fate of Local Institutions of Resistance after Apartheid', in Glenn Adler and Jonny Steinberg (eds.), *From Comrades to Citizens: The South African Civics Movement and the Transition to Democracy* (New York: St. Martin's Press and London: Macmillan, forthcoming).

Suttner, Raymond, 'Popular Justice', Seminar paper presented at the University of the Witwatersrand, (c. May 1986).

——and Jeremy Cronin (eds.), *Thirty Years of the Freedom Charter* (Johannesburg: Ravan, 1986).

Suzman, Helen, *In No Uncertain Terms: Memoirs* (London: Sinclair and Stevenson, 1993).

Swan, Maureen, 'Ideology in Organised Indian Politics, 1891–1948', in Shula Marks and Stanley Trapido (eds.), *The Politics of Race, Class and Nationalism in Twentieth Century South Africa* (London: Longman, 1987).

Swilling, Mark, '"The Buses Smell of Blood": The East London Bus Boycott', *SALB* 9,5 (March 1984).

——'Workers Divided: A Critical Assessment of the Split in MAWU on the East Rand', *SALB* 10,1 (1984).

——'Stayaways, Urban Protest and the State', *SAR* 3 (1986).

——'The Politics of Negotiation', *WIP* 50/51 (Oct./Nov. 1986).

——'Urban Social Movements and Apartheid's Urban and Regional System', in Richard Tomlinson and Mark Addleson (eds.), *Regional Restructuring under Apartheid: Urban and Regional Policies in Contemporary South Africa* (Johannesburg: Ravan, 1987).

——'The United Democratic Front and Township Revolt', in William Cobbett and Robin Cohen (eds.), *Popular Struggles in South Africa* (London: James Currey, 1988).

——and Khehla Shubane, 'Negotiating Urban Transition: The Soweto Experience', in Robin Lee and Lawrence Schlemmer (eds.), *Transition to Democracy* (Cape Town: Oxford University Press, 1991).

Tetelman, Michael, 'We Can: Black Politics in Cradock, South Africa, 1948–85', Unpublished D.Phil. thesis, Northwestern University (Dec. 1997).

Therborn, Goran, 'The Rule of Capital and the Rise of Democracy', *New Left Review*, 103 (1977).

United Democratic Front (UDF), 'Building People's Power', *Isizwe*, 1,2 (March 1986).

——(under the name of Murphy Morobe), 'Towards a People's Democracy: The UDF View', reprinted in *Review of African Political Economy* 40 (1988).

Van der Spuy, Elrena, 'Literature on the Police in South Africa: An Historical Perspective', *Acta Juridica* (1989).

Van Kessel, Ineke, 'Beyond Our Wildest Dreams: The United Democratic Front and the Transformation of South Africa', Unpublished Ph.D. thesis, University of Leiden (1995).

Van Onselen, Charles, 'The Reconstruction of Rural Life from Oral Testimony: Critical Notes on the Methodology Employed in the Study of a Black South African Sharecropper', *Journal of Peasant Studies* 20,3 (April 1993).

Von Holdt, Karl, 'Trade Unions, Community Organisation and Politics: A Local Case-Study on the East Rand, 1980–1986', Unpublished Honours dissertation, Industrial Sociology, University of the Witwatersrand (Oct. 1987).

——'COSATU Special Congress', *SALB* 13,4/5 (June/July 1988).

Waldmeir, Patti, *Anatomy of a Miracle: The End of Apartheid and the Birth of the New South Africa* (London: Viking, 1997).

Walker, Cherryl, *Women and Resistance in South Africa* (2nd ed., Cape Town: David Philip, 1991).

Walshe, Peter, *The Rise of African Nationalism in South Africa* (first published London, 1970; Johannesburg: Donker, 1987).

Webster, David, 'Repression and the State of Emergency', *SAR* 4 (1987).

——and Maggie Friedman, 'Repression and the State of Emergency: June 1987-March 1989', *SAR* 5 (1989).

White, Roland, '"A Tide has Risen, a Breach has Occurred": Towards an Assessment of the Strategic Value of the Consumer Boycotts', *SALB* 11,5 (April/May 1986).

Willan, Brian, *Sol Plaatje: A Biography* (Johannesburg: Ravan, 1984).

Wittenberg, Martin et al., 'The Crisis in Pietermaritzburg', undated paper (*c.* Feb. 1988).

Yembe, J., 'In Defence of the Anti-Apartheid Conference', *SALB* 13,8 (Feb. 1989).

Zald, Mayer and Roberta Ash Garner, 'Social Movement Organisations: Growth, Decay, and Change', *Social Forces* 44,3 (March 1966); republished in Mayer Zald and John McCarthy (eds.), *Social Movements in an Organizational Society* (New Brunswick: Transaction, 1987).

Xayiya, Sobantu, 'Cape of Great Gloom', *Democracy in Action* (Cape Town: Idasa) 8,3 (May 1994).

Zille, Helen 'UDF: Affiliate or Cooperate?' *Black Sash*, Feb. 1994.

Index